ALL·IN·ONE

MCITP Windows Vista® Support Technician

EXAM GUIDE

(Exams 70-620, 70-622, and 70-623)

Darril Gibson

New York • Chicago • San Francisco • Lisbon
London • Madrid • Mexico City • Milan • New Delhi
San Juan • Seoul • Singapore • Sydney • Toronto

The *McGraw-Hill* Companies

Library of Congress Cataloging-in-Publication Data

Gibson, Darril.
  MCITP Windows Vista support technician: exam guide (exams 70-620, 70-622, and 70-623)/Darril Gibson.
     p. cm.—(All-in-one)
  ISBN 978-0-07-154667-6 (alk. paper)
  1. Electronic data processing personnel—Certification. 2. Computer technicians—Certification—Study guides.
  3. Microsoft software—Examinations—Study guides. I. Title.
  QA76.3.G5269 2008
  005.4′46—dc22

008047022

McGraw-Hill books are available at special quantity discounts to use as premiums and sales promotions, or for use in corporate training programs. To contact a special sales representative, please visit the Contact Us page at www.mhprofessional.com.

MCITP Windows Vista® Support Technician All-in-One Exam Guide
(Exams 70-620, 70-622, and 70-623)

1 2 3 4 5 6 7 8 9 0   DOC DOC   0 1 9 8

ISBN: Book P/N 978-0-07-154677-5 and CD P/N 978-0-07-154678-2
of set 978-0-07-154667-6

MHID: Book P/N 0-07-154677-4 and CD P/N 0-07-154678-2
of set 0-07-154667-7

Sponsoring Editor *Timothy Green*	**Technical Editor** *Chris Crayton*	**Production Supervisor** *James Kussow*
Editorial Supervisor *Jody McKenzie*	**Copy Editor** *Bob Campbell*	**Composition** *International Typesetting and Composition*
Project Manager *Vastavikta Sharma, International Typesetting and Composition*	**Proofreader** *Bev Weiler*	**Illustration** *International Typesetting and Composition*
Acquisitions Coordinator *Jennifer Housh*	**Indexer** *WordCo Indexing Services*	**Art Director, Cover** *Jeff Weeks*

I'd like to dedicate this book to my loving wife of 16 years who has supported me in everything I do. I'm grateful to have someone to share my life with, and thankful it is her.

ABOUT THE AUTHOR

Darril Gibson has been working with and teaching Microsoft's products since NT 4.0 days. After retiring from the U.S. Navy, he became a Microsoft Certified Trainer (MCT) over nine years ago, specializing in delivering leading-edge technical training. He has developed several video training courses for Keystone Learning on topics such as A+, MCSE 2003, and Exchange, and written several books on topics such as SQL Server 2005, SQL Server 2008, and Windows Server 2008. He moonlights as adjunct faculty at a local college and is currently working on a key government contract providing extensive training to Air Force personnel in support of a major Network Operations Support Center on a wide array of technologies.

He holds about 20 current certifications, including MCT, several MCTS certifications, several MCITP certifications (including Vista Consumer Support technician and Vista Enterprise Support technician, SQL Server, and Windows Server 2008), MCSE, and MCSD. You can view his Microsoft transcript here:

https://mcp.microsoft.com/authenticate/validate.aspx

Transcript ID: 660310

AccessCode: DarrilGibson

He lives with his wife of 16 years, Nimfa, and two dogs in Virginia Beach. Whenever possible all of them escape to a small cabin in the country on over 20 acres of land where batteries easily recharge and a techno-geek's life finds balance.

About the Technical Editor

Chris Crayton is an author, technical editor, technical consultant, security consultant, and trainer. Formerly, he worked as a networking instructor at Keiser College (2001 Teacher of the Year); as a network administrator for Protocol, an electronic customer relationship management (eCRM) company; and at Eastman Kodak Headquarters as a computer, network, and security specialist. Chris has authored several print and online books, including *The A+ Exams Guide, Second Edition* (Cengage Learning, 2008), *Microsoft Windows Vista 70-620 Exam Guide Short Cut* (O'Reilly, 2007), *CompTIA A+ Essentials 220-601 Exam Guide Short Cut* (O'Reilly, 2007), *The A+ Exams Guide,* (Charles River Media, 2004), *A+ Adaptive Exams* (Charles River Media, 2002), *The A+ Certification and PC Repair Handbook* (Charles River Media, 2005), and *The Security+ Exam Guide* (Charles River Media, 2003). He is also co-author of *How to Cheat at Securing Your Network* (Syngress, 2007). Chris is also a technical editor/reviewer for several publishing companies, including McGraw-Hill, Charles River Media, Cengage Learning, Wiley, Pearson Education, O'Reilly, Syngress, and Apress. He holds MCSE, MCP+I, A+, and Network+ certifications.

CONTENTS AT A GLANCE

CONTENTS

ACKNOWLEDGMENTS

Any technical book takes the efforts of many people. This one is no exception. I'd like to acknowledge a few people that helped me with this project.

First, I'm grateful for my agent, Carole McClendon, who continues to help me find opportunities. It's through her that I've been able to develop a relationship with people like Tim Green and Jenni Housh at McGraw-Hill.

At McGraw-Hill, I'm thankful for the support and encouragement I've received from Tim Green, senior acquisitions editor, and Jenni Housh, acquisitions coordinator. While many more people at McGraw-Hill have been involved in this project, these two have been with me from beginning to end on several projects, including this one.

I also want to thank Chris Crayton for the outstanding work he did as the technical editor. He provided many insightful comments and provided extra help whenever I asked for it. Thanks again, Chris.

INTRODUCTION

Windows Vista is a powerful desktop operating system and is destined to be used in millions of homes and business computers. If you see yourself in an IT role in the foreseeable future, learning Windows Vista is a must. This book is intended to help you gain a solid understanding of Windows Vista. Use it to get certified, and after getting certified use it as a valuable reference on your bookshelf.

Microsoft has several certifications related to Windows Vista, and this book will help you achieve three of them:

- **MCTS: Windows Vista, Configuration**   You can achieve this certification by passing exam 70-620 (TS: Configuring Microsoft Windows Vista Client). See Appendix B for more details on the 70-620 exam.

- **MCITP: Enterprise Support Technician**   You can achieve this certification by passing two exams: 70-620 (TS: Configuring Microsoft Windows Vista Client), and 70-622. See Appendix B for more details on the 70-620 exam, and see Appendix C for more details on the 70-622 exam.

- **MCITP: Consumer Support Technician**   You can achieve this certification by passing two exams: 70-620 (TS: Configuring Microsoft Windows Vista Client) and 70-623 (PRO: Supporting and Troubleshooting Applications on a Windows Vista Client for Consumer Support Technicians). See Appendix B for more details on the 70-620 exam, and see Appendix D for more details on the 70-623 exam.

I've pursued several certifications over the years and know that the process of studying the objectives is an excellent way to guide my studies. It helps me learn the product, and when I'm pursuing Microsoft certifications, the objectives help me understand what Microsoft considers important in the product. I've written this book with this in mind. First and foremost we cover the material to help you pass the tests, but you'll also walk away with knowledge you can use on the job.

One caveat, though. Finish the book and get certified, but don't think you're done learning. Windows Vista is a very deep and robust product. If all you do is work with and manage Windows Vista, I doubt that you'll know it all before the next version comes out. I don't profess to know everything about Windows Vista, and I certainly don't claim this book will cover it all.

Registering for the Exam

To register for any Microsoft exam, visit the following Web site:

www.microsoft.com/learning/mcpexams/register

You can register with Prometric online through this link: www.register.prometric. com/Menu.asp. This link can also be used to find testing locations near you, and the exam fees in your area. The exams currently cost $125 in the United States.

How to Use This Book

You can easily start on the first page of Chapter 1 and continue on until the last page in Chapter 16. If you're not too interested in certification but mostly want to immerse yourself in the product, this will work just grand.

If you're interested in certification, you probably want to take a couple of steps before you dive into the book.

First, you need to know what the objectives are for the test. At the end of this introduction, I've included the objectives in a map that identifies where the objectives are covered. However, test objectives change. I strongly encourage you to check out Microsoft's site to see if the objectives have changed. They are accurate at this writing, but things change. You can find the objectives here:

- 70-620   www.microsoft.com/learning/en/us/exams/70-620.aspx
- 70-622   www.microsoft.com/learning/en/us/exams/70-622.mspx
- 70-623   www.microsoft.com/learning/en/us/exams/70-623.mspx

After you've reviewed the exam objectives, take a look at the appendices that cover the specific exams. There is an appendix for the 70-620 exam, another for 70-622, and a third for 70-623. These appendices include some general notes on the test and a list of concepts you should know and understand. These also include a listing of the chapters that cover material for each test.

As you start each of the chapters, look at the Table of Contents to see if you're familiar with the topics. If you already know the content, feel free to jump to the back of the chapter and try the Test Preparation Questions. If you get them *all* correct, feel free to skip the chapter. If not, go through the chapter.

As a supplement, I've included some short training videos that show how to do some tasks within Windows Vista. A lot of times, a short demonstration can really jump-start your knowledge, and that's the purpose of these videos. Most are under five minutes and cover a simple concept that you can view and then do on your own. These videos are included on the CD, or online if they didn't fit on the CD.

Self-Study Exercises

Toward the end of every chapter, I include self-study exercises you can use to solidify knowledge you've gained in the chapter. Unlike the exercises within the chapter that include step-by-step instructions, these exercises are just task statements telling you what to do.

Summary of What You Need to Know

In the Summary of What You Need to Know section, you'll find a short listing of core topics covered in the chapter for each exam. Most chapters include topics that are covered in all three exams. Some chapters only have topics for one or two exams. When preparing for a specific exam, use the summary section to guide your studying.

Sample Questions

Use the sample exam questions at the end of every chapter to test your knowledge of the material. If you think you have the material in the chapter mastered, go right to these sample questions. If you get them all correct, you may indeed be ready. Additional test questions are included on the test engine on the CD.

Practice Exams on the CD

The CD includes practice exams you can use to help prepare for the exam. There are two practice exams for each of the three exams.

A word of caution: Just doing the questions on the CD-ROM without studying the book to understand why the right answers are right, and why the wrong answers are wrong, is a recipe for failure. For success, both with the exams and on the job, study and understand the material.

Icons

Throughout the book, you'll see a variety of different icons. These include:

 EXAM TIP This book is a preparation book to help you get certified, so exam tips on what to look for in the exam are included in every chapter. These tips include key information you'll need to know to successfully pass the exam.

 TIP Tips are added to provide extra information to save you effort, hassle, pain, or time. Tips often indicate how the material may work on the job.

 NOTE Notes are added to clarify topics. They provide additional information and are also used to clarify what may seem like a contradiction in the text.

 CAUTION Cautions are used to point out potentially harmful or risky situations when working with the technology.

Exam 70-620 Objective Map

Installing and Upgrading Windows Vista	
Identify hardware requirements.	Chapter 1, What to Do Before You Install Windows Vista
Perform a clean installation.	Chapter 1, Installing Windows Vista
Upgrade to Windows Vista from previous versions of Windows.	Chapter 1, Installing Windows Vista
Upgrade from one edition of Windows Vista to another edition.	Chapter 1, Installing Windows Vista
Troubleshoot Windows Vista installation issues.	Chapter 1, Performing Post-Installation Tasks
Install and configure Windows Vista drivers.	Chapter 1, Performing Post-Installation Tasks Chapter 3, Device Manager

Configuring and Troubleshooting Post-Installation System Settings	
Troubleshoot post-installation configuration issues.	Chapter 1, Performing Post-Installation Tasks Chapter 3, Device Manager
Configure and troubleshoot Windows Aero.	Chapter 3, Understanding Vista's Aero
Configure and troubleshoot parental controls.	Chapter 9, Parental Controls
Configure Windows Internet Explorer.	Chapter 13, Internet Explorer 7.0

Configuring Windows Security Features	
Configure and troubleshoot User Account Control.	Chapter 9, User Account Control
Configure Windows Defender.	Chapter 13, Windows Defender
Configure Dynamic Security for Internet Explorer 7.	Chapter 13, Internet Explorer 7.0
Configure security settings in Windows Firewall.	Chapter 7, Configuring Vista's Firewall

Configuring Network Connectivity	
Configuring networking by using the Network and Sharing Center.	Chapter 5, Network and Sharing Center
Troubleshoot connectivity issues.	Chapter 5, Networking Basics, Network and Sharing Center
Configure Remote Access.	Chapter 7, Connecting Remotely

Configuring Applications Included with Windows Vista	
Configure and troubleshoot media applications.	Chapter 15, Windows Media Player, Windows Media Center
Configure Windows Mail.	Chapter 14, Using Windows Mail
Configure Windows Meeting Space.	Chapter 14, Using Windows Meeting Space

Configure Windows Calendar.	Chapter 14, Using Windows Calendar
Configure Windows Fax and Scan.	Chapter 14, Using Windows Fax and Scan
Configure Windows Sidebar.	Chapter 3, Working with the Sidebar

Maintaining and Optimizing Systems That Run Windows Vista

Troubleshoot performance issues.	Chapter 11, Performance and Reliability Monitor, Viewing Events in the Event Viewer Chapter 4, Hard Disks
Troubleshoot reliability issues by using built-in diagnostic tools.	Chapter 11, Performance and Reliability Monitor, Viewing Events in the Event Viewer
Configure Windows Update.	Chapter 11, Keeping Your System Up-to-date with Windows Update
Configure data protection.	Chapter 12, Backing Up and Restoring Data Files. Chapter 4, File Systems, Hard Disks, BitLocker Drive Encryption

Configuring and Troubleshooting Mobile Computing

Configure Mobile Display Settings.	Chapter 16, Windows Mobility Center, Configuring Additional Monitors, Managing Power Consumption
Configure Mobile Devices.	Chapter 16, Windows Mobility Center, Configuring Additional Monitors, Managing Power Consumption
Configure Tablet PC software.	Chapter 16, Using Tablet PCs
Configure power options.	Chapter 16, Managing Power Consumption

Exam 70-622 Objective Map

Deploying Windows Vista

Analyze the business environment and select an appropriate deployment method.	Chapter 1, What to Do Before You Install Windows Vista, Installing Windows Vista
Prepare a system for clean installation or upgrade.	Chapter 1, What to Do Before You Install Windows Vista, Installing Windows Vista
Deploy Windows Vista from a custom image.	Chapter 2, Windows Image-Based Deployment, Using the Windows Automated Installation Kit (WAIK), Preparing Images
Perform post-installation tasks.	Chapter 1, Performing Post-Installation Tasks Chapter 3, Device Manager
Troubleshoot deployment issues.	Chapter 1, Performing Post-Installation Tasks

Supporting and Maintaining Desktop Applications

Support deployed applications.	Chapter 3, Application Compatibility. Chapter 10, Applying Group Policy, Exploring Group Policy Settings
Troubleshoot software restrictions.	Chapter 10, Applying Group Policy, Exploring Group Policy Settings
Maintain desktop applications.	Chapter 3, Application Compatibility. Chapter 10, Applying Group Policy, Exploring Group Policy Settings

Exam 70-623 Objective Map

Install and Upgrade Windows Vista

Evaluate potential upgrade environments.	Chapter 1, Installing Windows Vista
Prepare to install Windows Vista.	Chapter 1, What to Do Before You Install Windows Vista
Troubleshoot and resolve installation issues.	Chapter 1, What to Do Before You Install Windows Vista, Installing Windows Vista, Performing Post-Installation Tasks
Troubleshoot and resolve post-installation issues.	Chapter 1, Performing Post-Installation Tasks

Post-Installation: Customize and Configure Settings

Configure Sidebar.	Chapter 3, Working with the Sidebar
Configure Windows Aero.	Chapter 3, Understanding Vista's Aero
Customize and configure user accounts.	Chapter 9, User Accounts Chapter 9, User Account Control
Evaluate user requirements and recommend, set up, and configure appropriate applications.	Chapter 1, Performing Post-Installation Tasks. Chapter 3, Application Compatibility. Chapter 10, Applying Group Policy, Exploring Group Policy Settings
Evaluate users' systems and recommend appropriate settings to optimize performance.	Chapter 11, Performance and Reliability Monitor, Viewing Events in the Event Viewer, Using the Task Scheduler

Configure Windows Vista Security

Configure Windows Security Center.	Chapter 9, Windows Security Center
Configure Firewalls.	Chapter 7, Configuring Vista's Firewall
Configure Windows updates.	Chapter 11, Keeping Your System Up-to-date with Windows Update
Configure Windows Defender.	Chapter 13, Windows Defender

Configure parental controls.	Chapter 9, Parental Controls
Configure Internet Explorer 7.	Chapter 13, Internet Explorer 7.0
Configure User Account Control.	Chapter 9, User Account Control
Protect data.	Chapter 12, Backing Up and Restoring Data Files. Chapter 4, File Systems, Hard Disks, BitLocker Drive Encryption
Configure, Troubleshoot, and Repair Networking	
Configure and troubleshoot network protocols.	Chapter 5, Networking Basics, Network and Sharing Center
Configure and troubleshoot network services on the client.	Chapter 5, Networking Basics, Network and Sharing Center
Configure and troubleshoot Windows Vista by using the Network and Sharing Center.	Chapter 5, Network and Sharing Center
Configure and troubleshoot wireless networking.	Chapter 6, Wireless Basics, Wireless Network Security, Configuring Vista as a Wireless Client
Troubleshoot file and print sharing.	Chapter 5, Network and Sharing Center. Chapter 8, Accessing and Sharing Resources, Printing
Configure Media Center.	Chapter 15, Windows Media Center
Install, Configure, and Troubleshoot Devices	
Connect peripherals to Windows Vista.	Chapter 8, Accessing and Sharing Resources, Printing. Chapter 5, Network and Sharing Center
Install, configure, and troubleshoot mobile devices.	Chapter 16, Windows Mobility Center, Windows Mobile Device Center
Install, configure, and troubleshoot digital cameras and camcorders.	Chapter 15, Windows Media Player, Window Media Center, Windows Photo Gallery, Windows Movie Maker
Install, configure, and troubleshoot media devices.	Chapter 15, Windows Media Player, Window Media Center, Windows Photo Gallery, Windows Movie Maker
Install, configure, and troubleshoot printers, fax machines, and copy devices.	Chapter 8, Accessing and Sharing Resources, Printing
Troubleshoot and Repair Windows Vista	
Diagnose a specified issue.	Chapter 12, Troubleshooting and Restoring the Operating System, Backing and Restoring Data Files
Repair a corrupted operating system.	Chapter 12, Troubleshooting and Restoring the Operating System, Backing Up and Restoring Data Files
Remove malware from a client system.	Chapter 13, Windows Defender

Installing and Upgrading Windows Vista

In this chapter, you will learn about:

- Windows Vista editions
- What to do before installing Windows Vista
- Installations and Upgrades
- What to do after installing Windows Vista

Whether you're helping end users while working as a consumer technician or as a desktop support technician in a large corporate environment, you need to know the basics of Windows Vista. This includes what to do before the installation, how to perform the installation, and what to do after.

Before starting an installation, you'll need to know what Windows Vista editions are available, the hardware requirements of Vista, and the features. Once you decide on a Windows Vista edition, you'll need to determine if you'll do a clean installation or an upgrade.

While an upgrade will preserve a user's data, applications, and settings, a clean install starts completely clean—without any of those data, applications, or settings. If you're doing a clean install, you should migrate the user's data and settings. Consumer technicians will typically use the Windows Easy Transfer tool, while enterprise technicians will typically use the User State Migration Tool (USMT). You'll learn about both in this chapter.

After the installation is complete, you'll have some final tasks to complete. This includes getting all the current updates with Windows Update, correcting any hardware issues that may exist, and installing any necessary applications.

NOTE Objectives for the 70-620, 70-622, and 70-623 exams are included in this chapter.

What to Do Before You Install Windows Vista

Before installing Windows Vista, you need to decide which edition will meet your needs. To decide this, of course, you'll need to know the capabilities of each edition.

Once you've decided on an edition, check your hardware to ensure it meets the prerequisites. Windows Vista does require more robust hardware than Windows XP. The graphics capabilities of Vista require specific hardware to support all the graphics features, and overall you'll need more memory than with Windows XP.

Before you start an installation, you'll want to protect the user's data. If you're supporting home users or users in a workgroup, you'll use Windows Easy Transfer. In a corporate environment, you'll use the User State Migration Tool, including the LoadState and ScanState command-line tools.

Understanding 32-Bit and 64-Bit Operating Systems

Windows Vista comes in both 32-bit and 64-bit versions. The two significant differences between these two versions are how much memory can be supported by each edition, and the applications they support.

Memory in 32-Bit and 64-Bit Versions

With 32 bits, the maximum addressable memory space is 2^{32}, or 4,294,967,296 bytes. This is commonly called 4GB RAM.

Even this is a little misleading, though. When you load up a Windows Vista system with 4GB RAM, you often have access to only about 3GB to about 3.6GB of RAM. The extra 0.4–1GB is reserved address space, the bulk of it reserved for graphics cards. How much is reserved depends on the hardware.

 NOTE Random Access Memory (RAM) is measured in bytes, with the following progression: kilobytes (KB), megabytes (MB), gigabytes (GB), terabytes (TB), petabytes (PB), and exabytes (EB).

Depending on how much you are doing with Windows Vista, you may often want more than the 3–4GB available on a 32-bit system. This is exactly what has driven the push to 64-bit operating systems. Systems need more RAM to support today's memory-hungry applications and hardware, and the only way to support more RAM is by switching to a 64-bit operating system.

With 64 bits, the maximum addressable memory space is 2^{64}, or 18,446,744,073,709, 551,616 bytes. This is commonly called 18EB RAM. Hopefully an address space of 18EB will last us a while.

Applications in 32-Bit and 64-Bit Versions

Another point to consider when deciding between the two editions is the application support.

64-bit applications will only run on a 64-bit operating system. If an application is written to take advantage of the added memory capabilities of 64 bits, it must run on a 64-bit edition of Vista.

TIP If you need to run a 64-bit application, you must install a 64-bit version of Windows Vista.

However, if you run a 64-bit operating system, you may lose the ability to run some applications. Not all 32-bit applications will run successfully on a 64-bit operating system.

Editions

Windows Vista comes in six editions:

- Windows Vista Starter
- Windows Vista Home Basic
- Windows Vista Home Premium
- Windows Vista Business
- Windows Vista Enterprise
- Windows Vista Ultimate

The majority of support technicians will see only four of these editions. Windows Vista Starter is not available in many countries, and Windows Vista Enterprise is only available to businesses participating in Microsoft's Software Assurance program. Each of the six editions is explored in more depth in the following sections, but Table 1-1 shows some of the main features side-by-side for the four editions you are most likely to see.

TIP When preparing for the exams, make sure you know the capabilities of the various versions and the differences between them. These are illustrated in Table 1-1 and amplified in the following sections.

Microsoft has two web pages you can view to identify the editions and features supported in Windows Vista. They are

www.microsoft.com/windows/products/windowsvista/editions/choose.mspx
www.microsoft.com/windows/products/windowsvista/features/details/backup.mspx

Windows Vista Starter

The Windows Vista Starter Edition is limited to emerging markets. It will not be sold in the U.S., Canada, Europe, Israel, Australia, or New Zealand. When prepping for the Vista MCITP exams, don't expect to see any questions on the Windows Vista Starter Edition.

The Starter Edition includes these limitations:

- Physical memory is limited to 1GB.
- Usable hard disk space is limited to 250GB.

Feature	Home Basic	Home Premium	Business	Ultimate
Windows Defender	✔	✔	✔	✔
Windows Firewall	✔	✔	✔	✔
Parental controls	✔	✔		✔
Automatic Backup[1]	✔[1]	✔	✔	✔
Complete PC Backup[2]			✔	✔
Aero		✔	✔	✔
Windows Meeting Space		✔	✔	✔
Windows Media Center		✔		✔
Movie Maker		✔		✔
DVD Maker		✔		✔
SideShow		✔		✔
Windows Fax and Scan			✔	✔
Remote Desktop			✔	✔
BitLocker Drive Encryption				✔

[1] The Automatic Backup is used to back up files and data. It is available in all versions of Windows Vista except the Starter Edition. However, it has only limited functionality in the Home Basic Edition. Specifically, you cannot schedule backups or store backups to a network in the Home Basic Edition.

[2] The Complete PC Backup can back up everything on your computer. Instead of just backing up files and data, it can also include the operating system and applications.

Table 1-1 Windows Vista Features

- Support exists for only one processor.
- It is only available in 32-bit versions.
- Only three applications can be launched at a time.

Windows Vista Home Basic

The Windows Vista Home Basic Edition is designed for home users that only need the basics. Figure 1-1 shows the features as presented in the Windows Vista Upgrade Advisor.

Supported features include

- Windows Defender
- Windows Firewall
- Instant Search
- Internet Explorer 7
- Capability to view Meeting Space meetings

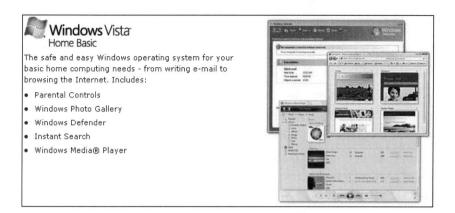

Figure 1-1   Windows Vista Home Basic features

- Parental controls
- Up to five simultaneous connections from other computers

 NOTE   The features mentioned in the available editions are described in different areas of the book. If you want a quick description of any of the features, take a look at the glossary at the back of the book.

Both 32-bit and 64-bit versions are supported. Vista Home Basic supports one physical CPU (multiple cores are supported), and up to 8GB of RAM on 64-bit versions.

A significant item missing from Vista Home Basic is the Windows Aero theme.

Windows Vista Home Premium

The Windows Vista Home Premium Edition is designed for home users but includes many additional features. Figure 1-2 shows the features as presented in the Windows Vista Upgrade Advisor.

Figure 1-2   Windows Vista Home Premium features

All of the features in Vista Home Basic are supported. Additional features include

- Windows Aero
- Windows Media Center
- Windows DVD Maker
- Windows Movie Maker
- Windows Backup and Restore Center
- Support for mobile and tablet PCs
- Windows SideShow
- Windows Meeting Space
- Up to ten simultaneous connections from other computers

The features in Windows Vista Home Premium are similar to the functionality in the Windows XP Media Center Edition.

Both 32-bit and 64-bit versions are supported. Vista Home Premium supports one physical CPU (multiple cores are supported), and up to 16GB of RAM on 64-bit versions.

Windows Vista Business

The Windows Vista Business Edition is comparable to Windows XP Professional. It is designed for business users and includes most of the same features as Windows Home Premium. The exceptions are parental controls, the Windows Media Center, Windows Movie Maker, and its companion the Windows DVD Maker.

Figure 1-3 shows the features as presented in the Windows Vista Upgrade Advisor.

Figure 1-3 Windows Vista Business features

TIP In addition to knowing what the Business Edition can do, you should also know what it can't do. Remember that it does not include parental controls, the Windows Media Center, Windows Movie Maker, and Windows DVD Maker.

Significant additional features included with the Windows Vista Business Edition include

- Windows Complete PC Backup and Restore (with system image backups and restores)
- Previous Versions feature using ShadowCopy
- Windows Fax and Scan
- Full support for Remote Desktop Connection (including incoming connections)
- Internet Information Services (IIS) can be installed on the Business Edition
- Rights Management Services (RMS)
- System image backups and restores
- Windows Media Player

Both 32-bit and 64-bit versions are supported. Vista Business supports up to two physical CPUs (multiple cores are supported in each CPU) and 128GB of RAM on 64-bit versions.

The Windows Vista Business Edition does not support parental controls. This does make sense. It's expected that businesses have employees and employers rather than parents and children. It does not include the Windows Media Center used for watching DVDs and even watching and recording TV (not common business activities). Last, it does not include the Movie Maker or the DVD Maker, which are used to design and create movies.

NOTE While the Windows Vista Business Edition does not support the Windows Media Center, it does include the Windows Media Player.

Windows Vista Enterprise

The Windows Vista Enterprise Edition is similar to Windows Vista Business but includes some additional features. It is only available to businesses participating in Microsoft's Software Assurance program.

Microsoft's Software Assurance program is an additional maintenance offering to businesses that includes software support, partner services, and other tools. Not all businesses take advantage of the program. For more information you can check www.microsoft.com/licensing/sa/default.mspx.

Additional features include

- BitLocker Drive Encryption

NOTE BitLocker Drive Encryption requires special hardware. Specifically, it requires a Trusted Platform Module (TPM) that is used to provide basic security-related functions with encryption keys and a USB flash drive.

- Multilingual User Interface (MUI) packages
- UNIX application support

Both 32-bit and 64-bit versions are supported. Vista Enterprise supports up to two physical CPUs (multiple cores are supported in each CPU) and 128GB of RAM on 64-bit versions.

Windows Vista Ultimate

Windows Vista Ultimate is designed for both home and business users that "want it all." The Ultimate Edition includes all of the features of the Home Premium Edition, the Business Edition, and the Enterprise Edition. Figure 1-4 shows the features as presented in the Windows Vista Upgrade Advisor.

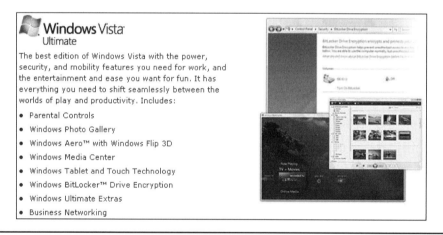

Figure 1-4 Windows Vista Ultimate features

The Vista Ultimate Edition includes additional features such as games, more language packs, and support for Windows DreamScene, all of which aren't available on other editions.

Both 32-bit and 64-bit versions are supported. Vista Ultimate supports up to two physical CPUs (multiple cores are supported in each CPU) and 128GB of RAM on 64-bit versions.

Hardware Requirements

When planning to install or upgrade to Windows Vista, you need to make sure your system has the appropriate hardware.

TIP Make sure you know the minimum hardware requirements when preparing for the exams. The most common shortcomings in existing computers are the RAM (512MB needed), disk space (20GB with at least 15GB free space needed), and support for Aero (DirectX 9, 128MB of graphics RAM, Pixel Shader 2.0, and a WDDM driver).

For any edition of Vista, the following are the minimum system requirements:

- An 800 MHz 32-bit or 64-bit processor
- 512MB of RAM
- A 20GB hard drive with at least 15GB available

To support Aero (which is optional), you need

- DirectX 9 graphics support
- 128MB of graphics RAM
- Pixel Shader 2.0
- Windows Vista Display Driver Model (WDDM) driver

Windows Home Basic does not support Aero, so it only needs VGA graphics with 32MB of graphics RAM.

While the recommended minimum RAM is listed as 512MB, most users will not be satisfied with the experience with this amount of RAM. When it comes to RAM, more is better. If your budget supports it, use at least 3GB or as close to 4GB as your system will recognize.

Both Home Premium and Ultimate Editions have support for media content. You'll need a TV tuner card to take advantage of watching TV on the computer.

The Home Premium, Business, Enterprise, and Ultimate Editions support Windows Tablet and Touch Technology. You'll need a touch screen to enable the technology.

The Ultimate and Enterprise Editions support Windows BitLocker Drive Encryption. This requires a USB flash drive and a system with a Trusted Platform Module (TPM) version 1.2 chip.

Installing Windows Vista

When installing any operating system, you have the choice of doing a clean installation or an upgrade. It's important to know the difference.

- **Clean installation** A clean installation will install the operating system without regard for what else is installed on the computer. It won't include settings or applications from another installed operating system. If other operating systems are installed on the computer, they will remain. However, there are specific guidelines to follow if you're doing a clean install on a system with another operating system. These are covered in the section "Understanding Dual-Boot and Multiboot" later in this chapter.

- **Upgrade** An upgrade will replace the existing operating system with the Vista operating system. A great benefit is that installed applications and settings from the original operating system are available after the upgrade is complete. This can save a great deal of time, since applications don't need to be reinstalled. In order for an upgrade to work successfully, several requirements need to be met. The Windows Vista Upgrade Advisor can be very valuable in helping you identify if you've met the requirements.

Performing a Clean Install

If you want become a professional with Vista (these are MCIT *Professional* certifications after all), you'll need to install it. If you haven't already, the following exercise can lead you through the steps of an installation.

Exercise 1.1: Installing Windows Vista

1. Place the installation DVD into your DVD drive and boot to the DVD. You may have to modify the BIOS to boot to the DVD.

2. After a moment, the Windows Boot Manager will appear. Choose the Windows Setup [EMS Enabled] selection and press ENTER. If you do nothing, it will automatically boot into the Windows Setup.

 TIP You can also access the Windows Memory Diagnostic Tools by pressing the tab key or the Advanced Options menu by pressing F8.

3. At this point, the system will read the files off the installation DVD and load them onto your system in preparation of the installation. After the files load, the AERO background will appear.

4. When the Install Windows screen appears (it may take a few moments), ensure that the correct Language to Install, Time and Currency Format, and Keyboard or Input Method are selected for your location. Click Next.

5. On the next screen, click Install Now.

6. When the Type Your Product Key For Activation window appears, enter your product key and click Next. While you can install the operating system without entering the product key, you will be required to enter it before the 30-day grace period expires. Additionally, the product key identifies what edition you're installing. If you don't enter the product key, you'll have another screen asking you which version to install.

 NOTE The Automatically Activate Windows When I'm Online selection is automatically checked here. This will cause your system to activate when you have Internet connectivity and is really the easiest way to activate the operating system.

7. On the License Terms page, review the license terms and check the box I Accept The License Terms. Click Next.

8. On the Which Type Of Installation Do You Want screen, select Custom (Advanced) to perform a clean installation.

9. On the Where Do You Want To Install Windows screen, the physical disks and partitions on your system will be displayed.

   a. You can click Drive Options (Advanced) here to delete partitions, create partitions, extend partitions, and format partitions. For example, if you have one 320GB hard drive but want to create two 160GB partitions, you can do so here.

   b. Once a partition is created, it needs to be formatted. If you click Format, you will be warned that all data stored on the partition will be permanently deleted. Drives are formatted with the NTFS file system.

   c. If you have drives installed that aren't showing, click the Load Driver link to load the drivers required for the drive.

EXAM TIP   If you have drives that aren't showing because the driver isn't loaded, click the Load Driver link. You will be prompted to browse to the medium where the driver is (such as a CD, DVD, or USB drive) and select the driver. This is common with SCSI drivers.

10. Once you create and/or select the partition where you want to install Windows Vista, click Next. At this point, the system goes through the process of

   • Copying Windows files

   • Expanding files

   • Installing features

   • Installing updates

   • Completing the installation

   This process takes quite a while and will automatically reboot your computer when necessary.

11. Once the installation is complete, the Set Up Windows screen will appear prompting you to choose a User Name, a Password, and a Picture. Enter your name as the user name, and a password. While a password is optional, it is highly recommended to protect your system. If you enter a password, you can also enter a password hint.

TIP   A strong password has at least eight characters, including uppercase and lowercase letters, one or more numbers, and one or more other characters. For example, P@ssword would meet the requirements (though I don't recommend P@ssword for your system at home or work).

12. After entering a User Name and Password, and selecting a Picture, click Next.

13. On the next screen, you are prompted to type in the name of your computer and select a computer background. You can give it any name, such as **MCITPVista**. Select a background and click Next.

14. On the Help Protect Windows Automatically screen, select the option to update Windows. Click the recommended setting of Use Recommended Settings. This will cause important and recommended updates to automatically be downloaded and installed.

15. On the Review Your Time And Date Settings screen, select the correct time zone for your area and set the correct date and time. Click Next.

16. If you are connected to a network, the setup program will automatically detect this. On the Select Your Computer's Current Location page, select Home. You could also select Work if you are installing this in a work environment. Both Work and Home will allow the computer to be discoverable by other computers, and to see other computers and devices. If you were installing Windows Vista in a public location and you didn't want others to see your computer, you would choose Public. Public limits the ability of other computers to find yours and also limits your ability to find other computers.

17. On the Thank You page, click Start. Windows Vista will check your system's performance (a process that may take a few moments) and then launch. The system performance is identified as a score.

18. Once the process is complete, the logon screen will appear with the picture you selected and your user name. Type the password and press ENTER.

Understanding Dual-Boot and Multiboot

A dual-boot system is one that can boot into different operating systems. For example, you may want to install Windows Vista but still keep an existing Windows XP installation. When a dual-boot system is created, a boot menu appears on power-up allowing you to pick and choose which operating system to launch.

It's somewhat of a misnomer calling this a dual-boot system, though. It's possible to have three or more operating systems installed on the system. It'd be more correct to call it a multiboot system, but you'll often hear people call it a dual-boot system.

There are two important rules to remember when creating a dual-boot system:

- *Install the older operating system first.* For example, if you want to support both Windows XP and Windows Vista on the same system, you must first install Windows XP and then install Windows Vista. If you install Windows Vista first, and then install Windows XP, the XP installation will break the Vista installation.

Multiboot Systems and Virtual PC

Regular end users won't typically have dual-boot or multiboot systems. However, it's not uncommon at all for power users to have more than one operating system installed on a single computer. The primary reason for this is testing.

When a new operating system comes out, you may want to install it to learn it but not lose your original operating system that you use for most of your work. You could be using Windows XP and then install Windows Vista or even Linux as a second operating system. You could boot to any of the operating systems, depending on what you wanted to do.

While you can still use multiboot systems for learning, increasingly IT professionals are using Virtual PC (VPC) for this purpose. You can download and install VPC on your current operating system and then run other operating systems within your current operating system.

For example, you could be running Windows Vista but also want to play around with Windows Server 2008. You could install a trial copy of Windows Server 2008 (available as a free download) as a VPC image. While running Vista, you could launch the Server 2008 VPC image and run it as an application within Vista.

One of the great benefits of a Virtual PC image is that you can create a baseline copy after you've done some basic configuration. If the image blows up while you're experimenting, it's no big deal. You just copy your baseline over the working image and start again.

- *Install each operating system on a separate partition.* Each operating system must be installed on a separate partition or drive (such as one on the C: drive and the other on the D: drive). These don't have to be different physical drives, but they must be different partitions. If you don't follow this rule, you can expect both operating systems to become corrupt after booting into each a couple of times (if you can even boot into each of the operating systems).

 EXAM TIP   Know these two rules to create dual-boot systems. Not only will it help you on the exams, but it's useful in real life too.

Boot.ini

In past versions of Windows, the boot.ini file was used to identify where the operating system could be found. After the Power On Self Test (POST), the system ultimately looked for the boot.ini file (commonly located at the root of C:) to identify where any available operating systems were located.

The information in the boot.ini file identified the disk controller, the physical disk, the partition on the disk, and the actual folder on the disk that contained the operating system. Using this information, the system was able to launch the operating system automatically, without user intervention. In a multiboot system, boot.ini would hold the information giving users a choice of which operating system to boot.

However, with Windows Vista, the boot.ini file has been replaced with the Boot Configuration Data (BCD). While boot.ini was a simple text file that could be modified with Notepad, BCD is a little more complex and can only be modified with the bcdedit command-prompt tool.

bcdedit

The bcdedit command-line tool is used to modify the Boot Configuration Data (BCD). The data is actually kept in the Boot Configuration Data (BCD) store, and the only way to modify the data is through the bcdedit command.

 EXAM TIP While you don't have to be an expert on all the switches with the bcdedit tool, you should know that the BCD has replaced the boot.ini file and the only way to modify the BCD store is through the bcdedit tool.

To access the command line, select Start | All Programs | Accessories, right-click Command Prompt, and select Run As Administrator. You could also use the shortcut command of the WINDOWS-R keys to access the Run dialog box and enter **CMD**.

 TIP To successfully run the bcdedit command from the command prompt, you'll need to access the command prompt with administrator credentials. User Account Control (UAC) will query you for verification, and you just need to click Continue.

To view the current settings of bcdedit, you can enter **bcdedit** as shown in Figure 1-5. This shows the actual configuration of the Windows Boot Manager and the Windows Boot Loader.

As with any other command-prompt tool, you can use the /? switch to get help. Enter **bcdedit /?** at the command prompt to get a full listing of available switches or commands. The commands in bcdedit are in several categories as listed next. Each command would be in the format of bcdedit /command:

- Commands that operate on a store, including CreateStore, Export, and Import

- Commands that operate on entries, including Copy, Create, and Delete

- Commands that operating on entry options, including DeleteValue and Set

- Commands that control output, including Enum to list the entries in the store. This is the default switch when entering bcdedit from the command prompt.

- Commands that control the boot manager, including BootSequence, Default, DisplayOrder, TimeOut, and ToolsDisplayOrder

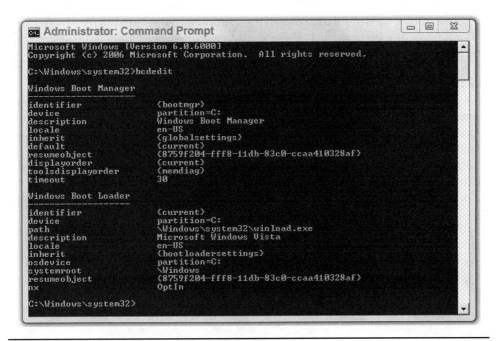

```
Administrator: Command Prompt                                    _  □  ☒

Microsoft Windows [Version 6.0.6000]
Copyright (c) 2006 Microsoft Corporation.  All rights reserved.

C:\Windows\system32>bcdedit

Windows Boot Manager
--------------------
identifier              {bootmgr}
device                  partition=C:
description             Windows Boot Manager
locale                  en-US
inherit                 {globalsettings}
default                 {current}
resumeobject            {8759f204-fff8-11db-83c0-ccaa410328af}
displayorder            {current}
toolsdisplayorder       {memdiag}
timeout                 30

Windows Boot Loader
-------------------
identifier              {current}
device                  partition=C:
path                    \Windows\system32\winload.exe
description             Microsoft Windows Vista
locale                  en-US
inherit                 {bootloadersettings}
osdevice                partition=C:
systemroot              \Windows
resumeobject            {8759f204-fff8-11db-83c0-ccaa410328af}
nx                      OptIn

C:\Windows\system32>
```

Figure 1-5   Running bcdedit from the command prompt

- Commands that control Emergency Management Services (EMS), including BootEMS, EMS, and EMSSettings

- Commands that control debugging, including BootDebug, DbgSettings, and Debug

Preserving User Data

One of the things to consider when doing either a clean installation or an upgrade is the ability to preserve a user's data and settings. You have two primary tools to use, and the tool you use depends on your environment—a home user environment or a corporate environment.

The two tools are

- **Windows Easy Transfer Wizard**   This is intended for home users (or small businesses). It is very simple to use and allows the user some freedom of what data to migrate. It only works with Windows Vista. Windows XP had a similar tool (the Files and Settings Transfer Wizard), but it can't be used with Windows Vista.

- **User State Migration Tool (USMT)**   This is intended to be used within corporate environments. You can use USMT to migrate user files and settings during large deployments of either Windows XP or Windows Vista. USMT is significantly more flexible. It uses XML files to identify what will be captured and restored. The current version of USMT is 3.0.

Neither tool is needed for upgrades. If you are doing an upgrade, the files and settings will automatically be upgraded. These tools are needed only when transferring data from one computer installation to another.

Windows Easy Transfer Wizard

The Windows Easy Transfer Wizard is used to transfer files and settings from one computer to another. It's designed to help users keep their data and settings after they move from one computer to another. It can easily be used by individual users without much assistance.

Remember, if you upgrade to Windows, all of the applications, data, and settings will be transferred automatically. There's no need to use the Windows Easy Transfer Wizard for an upgrade. Instead, you'd use this tool when an older computer (perhaps running Windows XP) is being replaced by a newer computer running Windows Vista.

You can launch the Windows Easy Transfer Wizard from the installation DVD. When launched, it looks like Figure 1-6.

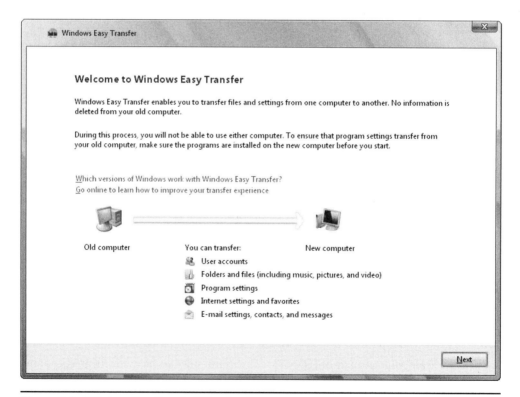

Figure 1-6 Windows Easy Transfer Wizard welcome screen

Using the Windows Easy Transfer Wizard, you can transfer the following types of files and settings:

- User accounts
- Folders and files
- Program settings
- Internet settings and favorites
- E-mail settings, contacts, and messages

The Easy Transfer tool supports transferring files and settings from any normal upgrade paths. In other words, if you're moving from Windows XP, or from one version of Vista to another version of Vista, this tool will help. If you're moving from Windows 2000 to Vista, it will only transfer files, not settings.

Methods of storing and transferring data are shown in Figure 1-7 and described in the following text.

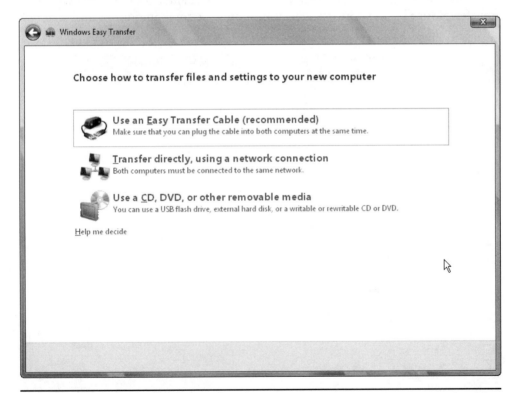

Figure 1-7   Windows Easy Transfer Wizard transfer methods

- **Easy Transfer Cable**   This is the method recommended by Microsoft. It's a specially designed USB cable that will connect two computers and can be used to easily transfer data from the source computer to the target computer.

- **Over the network**   If you have your computers connected to a network, data can be transferred over the network. This includes connections via a hub, a switch, or a router. It's also possible to network two computers directly using a network crossover cable.

- **CDs and DVDs**   You can burn the data onto a CD or DVD on the source computer. You then read from the CD or DVD at the target computer to restore the files and settings. Floppy disks aren't supported.

- **USB flash drives or external hard disk drives**   You can transfer the data and settings to a USB flash drive or external hard disk drive and then retrieve it from the same drive after the new computer is installed.

You have the capability of picking and choosing what to transfer. You can transfer data from all users that have ever logged on to the computer, or only one or two users. You can also pick and choose what data to transfer by selecting the Files in Other Locations. By default all files are selected.

Figure 1-8 shows the screen that allows you to pick and choose what you want to transfer. Notice on the bottom right, it indicates the total amount of data that will

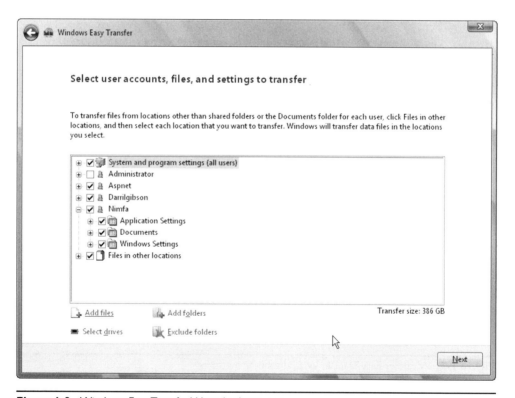

Figure 1-8   Windows Easy Transfer Wizard selection screen

be transferred. On my system that comes to 386GB of data. That's valuable information when you're deciding what method to use. This would take about 78 DVDs! An investment in the Easy Transfer Cable would be worthwhile.

You can deselect the check box for any user if you don't want to transfer that user's data. You can select or deselect any specific group of data for a specific user, and last, you can pick and choose to transfer files from other locations. For example, you may have a folder on your drive named Data (or something else) where you store your data. You can transfer this data also.

User State Migration Tool

The User State Migration Tool (USMT) is similar to the Windows Easy Transfer tool in that it helps to transfer users' data and settings. While the Windows Easy Transfer tool is designed specifically to be used by home users, USMT is designed to be used by corporate support personnel in a network.

USMT has two primary commands that are run: ScanState and LoadState. ScanState collects the information from the source computer, and LoadState restores the information to the destination computer. Both ScanState and LoadState are command-line tools.

Figure 1-9 shows the process of running LoadState and ScanState. Notice that a network server is accessible by both the source computer and the destination computer.

Figure 1-9
USMT process

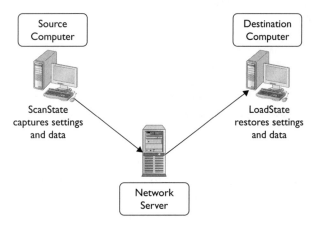

These commands don't have to run right after each other. You could run ScanState on Saturday to capture the data and settings from a computer. Then on Sunday, you could replace the computer and run LoadState to complete the migration.

Additionally, the command don't have to be run on different computers. If a single computer develops significant problems, you can do a wipe and load. Capture the data and settings with ScanState, completely reload the system, and then restore the data and settings with LoadState.

Migration XML files can be used to modify what data to capture and restore. If the XML files are omitted, the default data and settings will be captured and restored.

The most common reason to use these XML files is to exclude specific data or settings, or change the default destination location.

The XML files include

- **MigApp.xml** Migrates application settings.

- **MigUser.xml** Migrates user folders, files, and file types.

- **Custom.xml** Migrates any unique data such as a line of business application, or modifies default migration behavior.

- **MigSys.xml** This file only applies to Windows XP, not Vista.

ScanState ScanState collects files and settings from a source computer. The settings are obtained from the user's profile and the Registry. If a user has a roaming profile, a lot of the user's settings will be stored on a server somewhere, but the profile does not include all of the user's settings.

Once ScanState captures the settings and data, it then compresses and stores them as an image file named usmt3.mig.

The syntax of the ScanState tool is

```
scanstate [StorePath] [/i:[Path\]FileName] [/o] [/v:VerbosityLevel]
[/nocompress] [/localonly]
[/encrypt /key:KeyString|/keyfile:[Path\]FileName] [/l:[Path\]FileName]
[/progress:[Path\]FileName] [/r:TimesToRetry] [/w:SecondsBeforeRetry] [/c]
[/p] [/all]
[/ui:[DomainName\]UserName]|LocalUserName]
[/ue:[DomainName\]UserName]|LocalUserName]
[/uel:NumberOfDays|YYYY/MM/DD|0] [/efs:abort|skip|decryptcopy|copyraw]
[/genconfig:[Path\]FileName] [/targetxp] [/config:[Path\]FileName] [/?|help]
```

 TIP When reading the syntax of command-line tools, note that optional switches or options are placed in brackets.

The following are some of the options used most often with the ScanState tool:

- **StorePath** Indicates where to save the files and settings. If omitted, the settings and data will be stored in the current directory.

- **/o** Overwrites any existing data in the store.

- **/localonly** Specifies that only files that are stored on the local computer will be migrated.

- **/efs:abort | skip | decryptcopy | copyraw** Describes how to handle files encrypted with EFS. For example, if you wanted to skip files encrypted with EFS, you could use the /efs:skip switch.

- **/nocompress** Specifies that the store is not compressed.

- **/c** Causes the program to continue to run even if there are nonfatal errors.

- **/i:*FileName*** Specifies the location and name of an XML file that contains rules that define what state to migrate.

EXAM TIP While you don't always need to know the detailed switches used for different command-line tools off the top of your head when taking exams, ScanState and LoadState are exceptions. Since it can be so valuable within a corporate environment, you should know the switches of both of these commands covered in this section.

LoadState LoadState is used to load the user data and settings onto the target computer. The syntax of the LoadState tool is

```
loadstate StorePath [/i:[Path\]FileName] [/v:VerbosityLevel] [/nocompress]
[/decrypt /key:KeyString|/keyfile:[Path\]FileName] [/l:[Path\]FileName]
[/progress:[Path\]FileName] [/r:TimesToRetry] [/w:SecondsToWait] [/c] [/all]
[/ui:[[DomainName\]UserName]|LocalUserName] [/ue:[[DomainName\
]UserName]|LocalUserName]
[/uel:NumberOfDays|YYYY/MM/DD|0] [/md:OldDomain:NewDomain]
[/mu:OldDomain\OldUserName:[NewDomain\]NewUserName] [/lac:[Password]] [/lae]
[/q]
[/config:[Path\]FileName] [/?|help]
```

Notice that the StorePath is the only required switch.

The following are some of the options used most often with the LoadState tool.

- **StorePath** Identifies where the settings are stored.
- **/q** Allows LoadState to run without administrative credentials.
- **/all** Migrates all the users.
- **/nocompress** Specifies that the store is not compressed.
- **/c** Causes the command to continue to run even if there are non-fatal errors.
- **/i:FileName** Specifies the location and name of an XML file that is used to modify the rules of the migration.

 EXAM TIP To allow users to use LoadState without administrative privileges, you need to use the /q switch. If not, users will see the following error message: "You must be an administrator to migrate one or more of the files or settings that are in the store. Log on as an administrator and try again. Please see the log file for more details."

Exercise 1.2: Installing and Using USMT

1. Use your favorite search engine and enter **Download USMT 3** to find the link to download it. Both 32-bit (x86) and 64-bit (x64) versions are available. You can also go directly to www.microsoft.com/downloads/ and enter **USMT 3** in the search box.

2. After downloading the installation msi file, run it. If a Security Warning dialog appears asking if you want to run the User State Migration Tool, click Run. If a User Account Control dialog appears asking for authorization, click Continue.

3. On the Welcome screen, click Next.

4. Review the License Agreement, select I Agree, and click Next.

5. On the Confirm Installation screen, click Next. When the installation completes, click Close.

6. Open a Command Prompt with administrator privileges. Click Start | All Programs | Accessories, right-click Command Prompt, and select Run As Administrator. If the User Account Control dialog box appears, click Continue.

7. Make a directory to store the user state data with the following command:

```
md c:\usmtdata
```

8. Change the directory to the USMT folder with the following command:

```
cd \Program Files\USMT301
```

9. Enter the following command to view help on the ScanState command:

```
scanstate /?
```

10. Use the following command to create a ScanState data store. You'll use the /c switch to ignore non-fatal errors, and the /cfs:skip switch to ignore any encrypted files.

```
Scanstate c:\usmtdata /c /efs:skip
```

This will take several minutes, so be patient.

11. Use the following command to change to the directory where the data store was created.

```
cd \usmtdata\usmt3
```

Notice that the usmt3 directory was created as part of the ScanState command.

12. Use the following command to view the data.

```
dir
```

You'll see a file named usmt3.mig, which is the data store from running the ScanState command. You can copy this data store to network drive, a USB drive, a CD, or somewhere else for temporary storage. When you have your new computer, you can then run the LoadState command to apply the data store to the new computer.

Upgrades

When considering upgrading to Windows Vista, you need to consider several issues:

- Is the upgrade path supported?
- Does the existing hardware support Windows Vista?
- Will Windows Vista support the existing software?

Upgrade Paths

The upgrade paths are dependent on which operating system you start with. What is particularly noteworthy about these upgrade paths is that you can only upgrade to Windows Vista from either an XP version or a Vista version.

If starting from Windows XP Home, you can upgrade to Windows Vista Home Basic, Windows Vista Home Premium, Windows Vista Ultimate, or Windows Vista Business. This is shown in Figure 1-10.

Figure 1-10
Upgrade paths
from XP Home

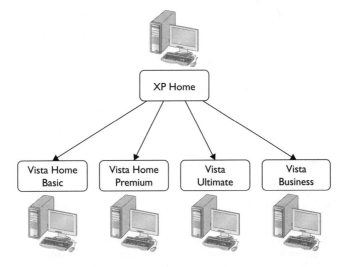

If starting from Windows XP Media Center, you can upgrade to Windows Vista Home Premium Edition, which is the comparable version to the XP Media Center. You can also upgrade to Ultimate, which gives you everything. From XP Professional, you can upgrade to Windows Vista Business or Windows Vista Ultimate.

Paths from both Windows XP Media Center and XP Professional are shown in Figure 1-11.

Figure 1-11
Upgrade paths
from XP Media
Center and XP
Professional

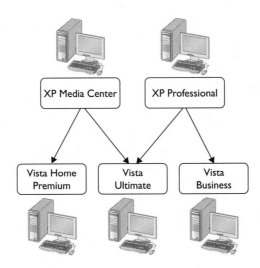

Within any version of Windows Vista, you always have a path to Windows Vista Ultimate. Figure 1-12 shows the upgrade paths from different versions of Windows Vista.

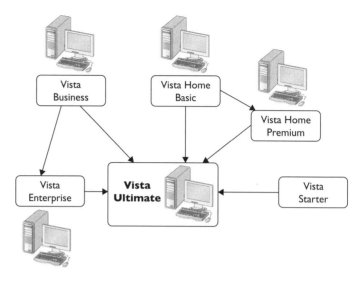

Figure 1-12
Upgrade paths
from Vista
versions to Vista
Ultimate

It's also possible to upgrade the XP Tablet PC edition to either Windows Vista Business or Windows Vista Ultimate.

Notice that you can't upgrade from Windows 2000 or previous editions of Windows. However, there is always more than one path to a destination. If you're running Windows 2000 Professional, you can't do a direct upgrade, but you can do an indirect upgrade.

NOTE To upgrade from Windows 2000 Professional systems to Windows Vista, you can first upgrade the system to Windows XP Professional, and then to Windows Vista.

For example, say you're running Windows 2000 Professional and you don't want to repeat the installation of all the applications installed on your system. You can first upgrade Windows 2000 Professional to Windows XP Professional. Once you successfully upgrade to Windows XP Professional, you can then upgrade to Windows Vista.

Upgrade Advisor

The Windows Vista Upgrade Advisor is a special tool developed by Microsoft to check your system and verify the compatibility of hardware and software. Before doing an upgrade, it makes sense to run the Upgrade Advisor to identify any possible issues.

Before running the Upgrade Advisor, you should plug in and turn on any devices you plan on using regularly. This includes

- USB devices
- Printers

- Hard drives
- Scanners

Since upgrade paths are only available from Windows XP versions and Windows Vista versions, the upgrade advisor will only work on these operating systems. Additionally, it only works on 32-bit versions of the operating systems.

Requirements to run the Upgrade Advisor include

- Administrator privileges
- 20MB of free hard disk space
- An Internet connection
- .NET 2.0
- MSXML6

The following exercise will lead you through steps required to install and run the Windows Vista Upgrade Advisor.

Exercise 1.3: Installing and Running the Windows Vista Upgrade Advisor

1. Download the Windows Vista Upgrade Advisor. At this writing, it can be found here: http://go.microsoft.com/fwlink/?linkid=65926. However, if it has moved, search on "download Windows Vista Upgrade Advisor" with your favorite search engine.

2. Double-click the WindowsVistaUpgradeAdvisor.msi file.

3. On the Welcome page, review the information and click Next.

4. On the License Agreement page, review the license agreement and select I Agree. Click Next.

5. On the Select Installation Folder page, accept the default location and click Next.

6. On the Confirm Installation page, click Next. The installation will start and should finish within a minute.

7. On the Installation Complete page, leave the check box checked to Launch Windows Vista Upgrade Advisor. Click Close.

8. The Windows Vista Upgrade Advisor page will appear. Click Start Scan.

9. While the Upgrade Advisor scans your system, you are presented with a screen showing the capabilities of different editions. Use this screen to answer these questions:
   - Which version(s) include Aero?
   - Which version(s) include the Windows Media Center?
   - Which version(s) include BitLocker Drive Encryption?

NOTE The Windows Vista Upgrade Advisor requires connectivity to the Internet. If you don't have connectivity, it will end with an error saying that either the Web service was busy or you are disconnected from the Internet.

10. When the Vista Upgrade Advisor completes, click the See Details button.

11. The Details report will appear as shown in Figure 1-13. This report makes a recommendation on which version appears to be the best edition for you and also lists potential issues.

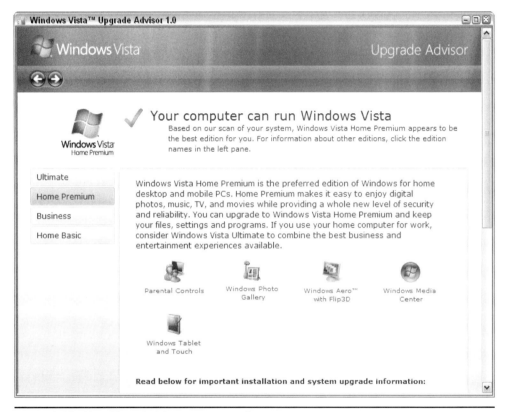

Figure 1-13 Vista Upgrade Advisor recommendation

12. Scroll down to the System Requirements area. Note that issues are listed in the areas of System Requirements, Devices, and Programs. Click any of these buttons.

13. The Vista Upgrade Advisor report will appear, as shown in Figure 1-14. On my system, I have less than 13GB of free space on the C: drive, so it's informing me I need at least 15GB of disk space. On your system, you may see something different.

14. Scroll through the report details on the System tab to review the information.

15. Select the Devices tab and scroll through the report.

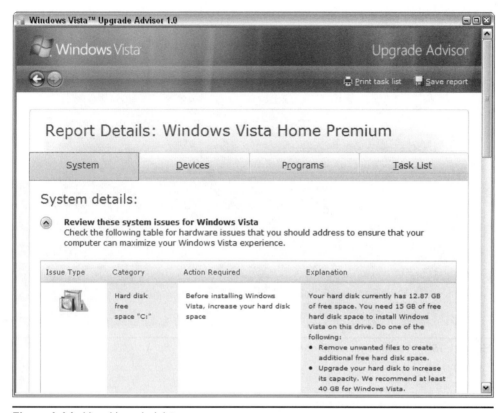

Figure 1-14 Vista Upgrade Advisor report

16. Select the Programs tab and scroll through the report.
17. Select the Task List tab and scroll through the report. Notice how the task list informs you specifically what you need to do before and after the installation.
18. Click the Save report icon to save the report.

Upgrade Procedure

The actual upgrade procedure is rather straightforward. With one of the supported operating systems (such as Windows XP) booted, place the installation DVD into the DVD drive.

If Autoplay isn't enabled, browse to the DVD with Windows Explorer and double-click the Setup file. You'll see the upgrade window appear as shown in Figure 1-15.

Several links are available from this window:

- **Check Compatibility Online** Clicking this link will take you to the Web site that allows you to download the Windows Vista Upgrade Advisor described earlier in this section.
- **Install Now** Clicking this link will launch the Installation Wizard.

Figure 1-15   Windows Vista installation screen

- **What to Know Before Installing Windows**   This link opens a Help And Support window that provides detailed installation instructions.

- **Transfer Files and Settings From Another Computer**   Clicking this link will launch the Windows Easy Transfer Wizard. This tool was presented earlier in this chapter.

After clicking the Install Now link, you will be asked to get the latest updates. This is recommended and will help ensure your computer has the most up-to-date information, including security updates and hardware drivers. Your computer remains online throughout the entire process. It's also possible to do the upgrade without getting the updates.

After entering your product key (or skipping this step), you'll be presented with the license terms, and after agreeing, you can choose from the following options:

- **Upgrade**   The upgrade option allows you to keep your files, settings, and programs. It's still recommended that you back up your data before starting.

- **Custom (Advanced)**   This will install a clean copy of Windows. If you choose to install it on the same partition where an existing Windows folder is located, the existing folder will be renamed as Windows.old and you'll no longer be able to access the previous operating system.

TIP In addition to the older Windows folder, the Windows.old folder also includes the Documents and Settings folder and the Program Files folder. To access the folder, click Start and enter %systemdrive%\Windows.old. For more details, check the Knowledge Base article KB 933209 by entering KB 933209 into your favorite search engine.

From this point on, the installation is automated and doesn't require any more user interaction.

Performing Post-Installation Tasks

After completing the installation, you probably still have some work left to do. Hopefully, you've minimize the remaining work by making sure that your hardware meets the minimum requirements and by running the Windows Vista Upgrade Advisor.

When the install is finished, you should complete the following tasks:

- Visit the Windows Update site to download the latest critical updates.
- Identify any hardware compatibility issues.
- Identify any software compatibility issues.

Visiting Windows Update

You can visit the Windows Update site to download the latest critical updates for your system. This includes both software updates and hardware drivers. With Windows Update, you can solve a lot of problems in a single task.

Windows Update can be accessed from the computer system menu. Select Start, right-click Computer, and select Properties. This will bring up the Computer System properties window as shown in Figure 1-16.

Notice the Windows Update link is at the bottom left of the window. By clicking this, you can access the Windows Update window. Just as with most things in Vista, you can get to the Windows Update window in other ways. For example, you could click Start | All Programs and access the Windows Update program. You could also go to the Control Panel and click Check For Updates under System.

TIP You can get to the Vista System properties with a keyboard shortcut by pressing the windows logo key and the break key at the same time. Getting to know the available shortcuts can often save a lot of time while impressing your customers ("His fingers danced on that keyboard and he made the computer do things quicker than anyone I've ever seen"). From the desktop press FI to access help and search for Keyboard shortcuts. The Microsoft keyboard shortcuts show what you can do with the windows logo key.

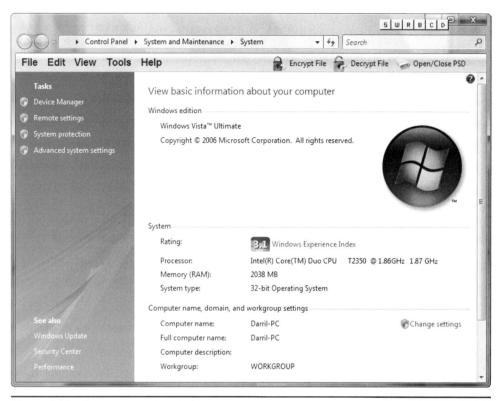

Figure 1-16   System properties window

Figure 1-17 shows the Windows Update window as you'd see it in a Windows Vista Ultimate installation.

Before downloading the updates, you can click View Available Updates to review them. Updates are listed as Optional, Recommended, and Important. You can configure Windows Vista to automatically download and install both Important and Recommended updates. Previously you could only do this with updates classified as High Priority.

Chapter 11 will cover Windows Update in more depth, including the ability to automate updates in both the home and corporate environments.

If you click the Install Updates button on this page, your system will connect to the Windows Update server and download the updates. Before installing them, it will automatically create a restore point. If things go wrong, you can always return to just where you started.

Depending on the number of updates and the speed of your connection, this process may be fairly quick, or quite slow.

Identifying Hardware Compatibility Issues

The easiest way to determine if you have any hardware issues after the upgrade is to check the Device Manager. The Device Manager allows you to view device properties, disable and enable devices, install drivers, and more.

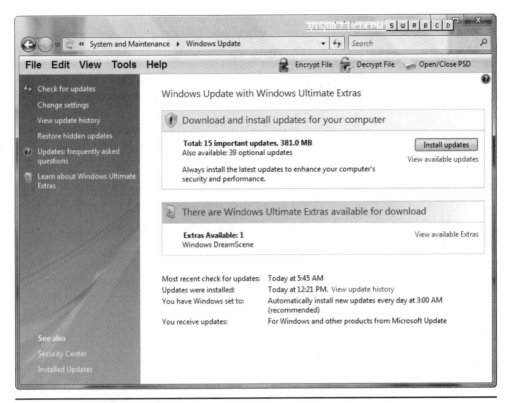

Figure 1-17   Windows Update window

You can access the Device Manager from the System properties window. Click the Device Manager task link at the upper left of the System properties window to launch the Device Manager. Click Continue if the User Account Control prompts you to continue.

Two common problems you may see are

- **Yellow circle with an exclamation mark**   This indicates the hardware is not working properly. Vista will typically display an error message with an accompanying error code. This usually indicates you need to locate and install an updated driver.

- **Down arrow on the device**   This indicates the hardware has been disabled.

Figure 1-18 shows the Device Manager with a modem device disabled. The down arrow isn't so easy to see; however, the Device Manager node will be open as shown in the figure. To enable it, right-click the device and select Enable.

Notice that the Modems node is expanded with the modem device showing; this indicates a problem in itself. None of the other nodes are open, indicating there is no problem with them.

Figure 1-18
Device Manager

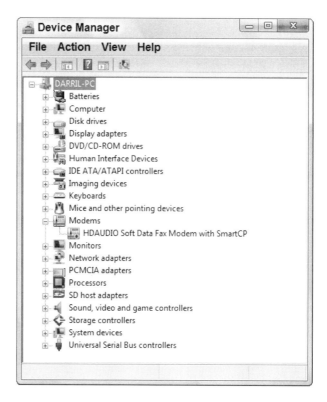

The Device Manager will be covered in more depth in Chapter 3. For now, you may want to update a driver. It's assumed you've used Windows Update already but that didn't work. What you need to do now is locate the correct driver, download it, and then install it using the Device Manager.

Locating the correct driver can sometimes be a challenge, but a good place to start is the manufacturer's Web site. Once you've located it, right-click the device in the Device Manager and select Update Driver Software. Select Browse My Computer For Driver Software and browse to the location where you downloaded it.

Identifying Software Compatibility Issues

Your tasks here depend on whether you've done an upgrade or a clean installation. If you're doing a clean installation, you won't have any applications installed and you'll have to install each application one by one.

If you've done an upgrade, all the applications that were installed prior to the upgrade should still work after the upgrade. Hopefully, you ran the Windows Vista Upgrade Advisor and anything that doesn't work isn't a surprise.

However, occasionally an application you think should work doesn't work after the upgrade. Don't give up right away, though. You can uninstall the application and then reinstall it and it may work. Give that a try. If it doesn't work, check the developer's Web site for compatibility issues.

Chapter Review

Completing a successful installation of Windows Vista doesn't happen by accident. Instead, you need to plan before you begin, follow the right procedures, and take some steps once you're done.

MCITP: Consumer Support Technician will be more focused on Vista Home Editions, and MCITP: Enterprise Support Technician will be more focused on the Business and Enterprise Editions. You learned about the hardware requirements and features of each edition, including the edition that has it all: Ultimate. Knowing the differences between the editions will help you on the job and when approaching these exams.

Migrating a user's data and settings is also important to both groups of technicians. Consumer technicians will typically use the Windows Easy Transfer tool to help users migrate their information. Enterprise technicians will use the ScanState and LoadState commands as part of the User State Migration Tool. These tools are highly useful and highly testable, but at this point you should have a solid understanding of both.

Of course, if you're doing an upgrade, neither of the migration tools are needed, since all of the user's data, applications, and settings should be migrated automatically. You learned how to use the Windows Vista Upgrade Advisor before an upgrade to identify any potential issues.

You also learned what to do after the installation is complete. Downloading updates is one of the most important tasks. Not only will you ensure your computer is protected from any new security risks, it will also download any new device drivers which may be needed in your computer. You learned a little about the Device Manager that can be used to resolve problems with devices not fixed with Windows Update.

Additional Study

Self Study Exercises

Use these additional exercises to challenge yourself.

- Download, run, and install the Windows Vista Upgrade Advisor.
- Install Windows Vista on a computer from the DVD.
- Upgrade a computer from Windows XP.
- Launch the command line and view the bcdedit command, including the help available.
- Use the Windows Easy Transfer tool to save data on a computer.
- Install USMT and view the help for both the ScanState and LoadState commands.
- Perform a manual Windows Update.
- Launch the Device Manager and investigate any issues on your system.

Summary of What You Need to Know

70-620

When preparing for the 70-620 exam, make sure you understand the following concepts:

- **Editions and features**. Ensure you know the Windows Vista editions and features (including the differences).
- **Hardware requirements**. Make sure you know the minimum Windows Vista hardware requirements.
- **Upgrades**. Know the upgrade paths to Windows Vista, upgrade procedures, and use of the Windows Vista Upgrade Advisor.
- **Migration tools**. Know the tools available to migrate user data and settings (such as the Windows Easy Transfer tool and USMT).
- **Dual-boot systems**. You should understand dual-boot and multiboot configurations, and requirements, and how to modify these configurations

70-622

When preparing for the 70-622 exam, make sure you understand the following concepts:

- **Editions and features**. Ensure you know the Windows Vista editions and features used in the corporate environment.
- **Hardware requirements**. Make sure you know the minimum Windows Vista hardware requirements.
- **Migration tools**. Know the tools available to migrate user data and settings in a corporate environment (USMT), including the details on ScanState and LoadState.
- **Dual-boot systems**. You should understand dual-boot and multiboot configurations, and requirements, and how to modify these configurations.

70-623

When preparing for the 70-623 exam, make sure you understand the following concepts:

- **Editions and features**. Ensure you know the Windows Vista editions and features commonly used by home users (including the differences).
- **Hardware requirements**. Make sure you know the minimum Windows Vista hardware requirements.
- **Installation**. Know the procedures for a clean installation.
- **Upgrades**. Know the upgrade paths to Windows Vista, upgrade procedures, and use of the Windows Vista Upgrade Advisor.
- **Migration tools**. Know the tools available to migrate user data and settings in a home environment (Windows Easy Transfer tool).
- **Dual-boot systems**. You should understand dual-boot and multiboot configurations, and requirements, and how to modify these configurations.

Questions

70-620

1. Sally is running a Windows XP Professional computer with the following hardware configuration:

   - 512MB RAM

   - 1.2 GHz Processor

   - 80GB hard disk with 15GB free

   - 64MB video adapter

   She wants to perform a clean installation of Windows Vista Home Premium Edition and wants to ensure that the Windows Aero is supported. What should she do?

   A. Add a new hard disk with at least 30GB free space.

   B. Upgrade the memory to at least 1GB.

   C. Install a graphics card with at least 128MB of RAM and support for DirectX 9.

   D. Upgrade the processor.

2. You need to configure a computer to dual-boot to both Windows XP Professional and Windows Vista Business Edition. How can you accomplish this?

   A. Create two partitions. Install Windows Vista on the first partition and then install Windows XP on the second partition.

   B. Create two partitions. Install Windows XP on the first partition and then install Windows Vista on the second partition.

   C. Create one partition. Install Windows XP first and then install Windows Vista.

   D. Create one partition. Install Windows Vista first and then install Windows XP.

3. You are running Windows XP Professional and are considering upgrading to Windows Vista. You have several applications installed and want to know if these applications are supported by Windows Vista. What should you do?

   A. Look through the Windows Hardware Compatibility List (HCL).

   B. Run the Windows XP Upgrade Advisor.

   C. Run the Windows Vista Upgrade Advisor.

   D. Run the `bcdedit /checkupgradeonly` command from the Vista installation DVD.

4. Harry is running the Windows Vista Home Basic Edition. He is trying to use it to record television programs by using the Microsoft Windows Media Center. He was told that the Media Center won't appear until he installs a TV tuner card. After purchasing and installing the card, he still can't find the Windows Media Center. What should you do?

   A. Ensure the card is registered at the Microsoft Media Center Web site.

   B. Upgrade to the Starter Edition.

    C. Upgrade to the Home Premium Edition.

    D. Upgrade to the Business Edition.

5. You have purchased a new computer running Windows Vista. You have been using a computer running Windows XP Professional. You want the settings and data available on the Windows XP computer available to you on the Windows Vista computer. What should you do?

    A. Run the Files and Settings Transfer Wizard.

    B. Run the Windows Easy Transfer Wizard.

    C. Run the Windows Vista Upgrade Advisor.

    D. Run the `bcdedit` tool.

70-622

1. You are a desktop support technician for MCITPSuccess.com, and you're planning on upgrading a user's computer from Windows XP Professional to Windows Vista Business Edition. You verify the computer has the following hardware configuration:

- 933 MHz CPU

- 768MB memory

- Video card using 128MB shared memory

- 40GB hard drive with 10GB free space

You need to ensure the system meets the minimum requirements. What should you do?

    A. Upgrade the RAM to at least 1GB.

    B. Upgrade the graphics card to at least 256MB RAM.

    C. Clean the hard drive to free up at least 15GB free space.

    D. Upgrade the processor to a speed of at least 1 GHz.

2. Maria is using her computer in a dual-boot configuration. She can boot into both Windows XP and Windows Vista. Most of her work is done in Windows XP, and she wants it to boot into Windows XP by default. How can you accomplish this for her?

    A. Modify the boot.ini file on her computer.

    B. Reinstall Windows XP so that it is the last operating system installed.

    C. Reinstall Windows Vista and uncheck the Default box in the dual-boot window.

    D. Use the `bcdedit` tool.

3. You are replacing several Windows XP computers with Windows Vista computers at your company. You are using USMT to collect user state data

with the ScanState command. You want to ensure that ScanState continues to run even if it encounters non-fatal errors. What option would you use?

A. /Ignore

B. /ErrorOverride

C. /c

D. /p

4. You have replaced several Windows XP computers with Windows Vista computers at your company. You used USMT to collect user state data with the ScanState command. You updated the user-state information using the LoadState tool with a logon script for the users. Unfortunately, they receive the following error:

"You must be an administrator to migrate one or more of the files or settings that are in the store. Log on as an administrator and try again. Please see the log file for more details."

You want to ensure LoadState works without users logging on as an administrator. What option would you use?

A. /q

B. /c

C. /a

D. /x

5. You are a desktop support technician in a medium-sized domain. Users regularly encrypt proprietary data with the Encrypting File System (EFS). You are swapping out several Windows XP computers and replacing them with Windows Vista computers. You've informed the users to move their EFS files to a server. You want to migrate the users' settings, but you want to ensure that encrypted files are ignored. What should you do?

A. Use the /efs:abort switch with ScanState.

B. Use the /efs:skip switch with ScanState.

C. Use the /efs:abort switch with LoadState.

D. Use the /efs:skip switch with LoadState.

70-623

1. You are a consumer support technician working at Best Computers. A customer is considering upgrading her Windows XP computer to Windows Vista. She wants the following features:

- Windows Media Center

- Parental controls

- Ability to do scheduled backups

What version(s) will meet the customer's needs?

A. Vista Home Basic and Vista Home Premium

B. Vista Home Premium and Vista Ultimate

C. Vista Ultimate and Vista Business

D. Vista Home Premium and Vista Business

2. You are a consumer support technician at MCITPSuccess. A user is planning on upgrading his computer to Windows Vista. It has a TV tuner card installed, and he asks you if it is supported. How can he verify the compatibility of the card?

A. From the Vista installation DVD, run the setup program with the /checkupgradeonly switch.

B. From the XP installation DVD, run the setup program with the /checkupgradeonly switch.

C. Download, install, and run the Windows Vista Upgrade Advisor.

D. There's no way to know until Vista is installed.

3. You are helping a customer clean up her computer after it became infected with a virus. You notice that the boot menu has an additional entry in it as if it's a dual-boot system, but only Windows Vista is installed. How can you remove the entry?

A. Use Notepad to modify the boot.ini file.

B. Use the Windows Vista Upgrade Advisor to modify the entry.

C. Boot into Safe mode and run the msconfig command.

D. Run bcdedit.

4. During the installation of Windows Vista, you notice that the Installation Wizard fails to detect any hard disks. You verify the disks have been installed correctly. What else can you do?

A. During the installation process, select the Load Driver option and load the drivers for the installed disks.

B. During the installation process, select the Load Driver option. Select Refresh to detect the disks.

C. Run the bcdedit command using the Load Driver option.

D. Enter Safe mode and run the Load Driver option.

5. A user has installed the 32-bit version of Windows Vista on his computer. He wants to replace the operating system with a 64-bit version, but he doesn't want to lose any of his data. What tool should he use?

A. Windows Vista Upgrade Advisor

B. Windows Easy Transfer tool

C. Files and Settings Transfer tool

D. Application Compatibility Toolkit (ACT)

Answers

70-620

1. **C.** To support Aero, the system must support DirectX 9. This requires at least 128MB of graphics RAM, the WDDM driver, and Pixel Shader 2.0. The install requires at least 15GB of available disk space, at least 512MB of RAM, and a processor running at a speed of at least 800 MHz.

2. **B.** When configuring a dual-boot system, there are two important rules to remember: install each operating system on a separate partition, and install the older operating system first. If you install Vista first and then XP, the XP installation will break the Vista installation. If you install both on a single partition, both operating systems will become corrupt after a few reboots.

3. **C.** The Windows Vista Upgrade Advisor is a downloadable program you can use to determine the compatibility of hardware and software on your system. The HCL will only check compatibility of hardware. The XP Upgrade Advisor was used when you wanted to upgrade to XP. The `bcdedit` command is used to modify the Boot Configuration Data store and does not have a `/checkupgradeonly` switch.

4. **C.** The Microsoft Windows Media Center is supported in the Home Premium and Ultimate Editions. It is not supported in the Home Basic, Starter, or Business Editions. The Microsoft Windows Media Center does not require TV tuner cards to be registered at any Web site.

5. **B.** The Windows Easy Transfer Wizard can be used to transfer files and settings from a one computer to another computer that is running Windows Vista. Windows XP used the Files and Settings Transfer Wizard, but this is not compatible with Windows Vista. The Windows Vista Upgrade Advisor checks hardware and software compatibility but doesn't transfer data. The `bcdedit` tool is used to modify the Boot Configuration Data store but wouldn't help here.

70-622

1. **C.** The install requires at least 15GB of available disk space. The hard drive is big enough at 40GB, but you need more than 10GB free space. Additionally, you need at least 512MB of RAM and a processor running at a speed of at least 800 MHz. The installed processor meets the needs. Even with the graphics card taking 256MB of RAM from the 1GB installed, you still have enough RAM.

2. **D.** The `bcdedit` tool can be used to modify the Boot Configuration Data (BCD) store in Windows Vista. The boot.ini file is replaced by the BCD store. There is no need to reinstall any operating systems, since they both boot and work. Additionally, there isn't a dual-boot window in the installation of Windows Vista.

3. **C.** The /c option will cause ScanState to ignore non-fatal errors. There is no /Ignore or /ErrorOverride switch. The /p switch generates a space estimate text file called usmtsize.txt.

4. **A.** The /q switch will allow LoadState to run without administrative credentials. The /c switch is used to allow the command to run even if it encounters nonfatal errors. There is no /a or /x switch.

5. **B.** The /efs:skip switch can be used with ScanState to ensure that files encrypted with EFS are not included. The /efs:abort switch will cause ScanState to abort if encrypted files are found. LoadState is done last, so it wouldn't help in this scenario.

70-623

1. **B.** Only Windows Vista Home Premium and Vista Ultimate Editions include all of the requirements. The Vista Home Basic Edition does not include Windows Media Center or the ability to do scheduled backups with the Windows Backup and Restore Center. The Vista Business Edition does not include Windows Media Center or parental controls.

2. **C.** The Windows Vista Upgrade Advisor can verify the compatibility of software and hardware of an existing operating system prior to an upgrade. It is a free download. The Vista setup program does not have a /checkupgradeonly switch. Using the /checkupgradeonly switch from the XP setup program will cause the setup program to see if the system is compatible with Windows XP, but the goal is to check compatibility with Vista.

3. **D.** The bcdedit tool can be used to modify the Boot Configuration Data (BCD) store, which includes the boot menu. The boot.ini file is not used with Windows Vista. Neither the Upgrade Advisor nor the msconfig command can modify the BCD store.

4. **B.** A. You can select the Load Driver option to load drivers for unrecognized hard drives. You will then be prompted to load the media that contains the drivers. Just selecting Refresh will not cause the unrecognized drives to suddenly become recognized. The bcdedit command is used to modify the BCD store, but that isn't installed until the operating system is installed. Safe mode is good for troubleshooting an operating system once it's installed, but is not useful until the operating system is installed.

5. **B.** The Windows Easy Transfer tool is used to transfer files and settings from one computer to another. While this scenario concerns the same computer, the tool will still allow the user to save the data from the 32-bit instance and restore it on the 64-bit instance. The Upgrade Advisor will check hardware and software compatibility but won't transfer data and settings. The Files and Settings Transfer tool was used in Windows XP but isn't used in Windows Vista. The Application Compatibility Toolkit is an enterprise tool used to analyze applications and computers within a company.

Automating the Installation of Windows Vista

In this chapter, you will learn about:
- Images and image-based deployment
- The Windows Automated Installation Kit (WAIK)
- Deployment tools such as ImageX, CopyPE, and OSCDimg
- Windows Deployment tools

When deploying multiple systems, you can't afford to sit and wait on each computer as the installation proceeds. Neither can you afford the time necessary to install the same applications over and over onto new systems. Instead, you must find ways to automate the deployment.

The Windows Vista installation can be automated using a variety of different methods. You can use the Windows Automated Installation Kit (WAIK), third-party tools, or Windows Deployment Services (WDS).

Knowing the methods available can help you both on the job and when studying to pass an MCITP exam.

 EXAM TIP Objectives for only the 70-622 exam are included in this chapter.

Windows Image-Based Deployment

One of the challenges larger organizations face is deploying operating systems to many computers. If each operating system were deployed manually, it would simply take too much time.

Consider an installation of a Windows Vista system. It could easily take several hours to manually install the operating system, download current updates, configure security, and install all the needed applications for a single computer. If you need to install 100 systems, it would take 300 man-hours (3 * 100), or 37.5 man-days. And this doesn't include troubleshooting when things go wrong.

A common goal in IT is to reduce the total cost of ownership (TCO). Total cost of ownership (TCO) is the total cost that it takes to deploy, manage, and maintain a system. The system may cost $1000, but when you add the other costs (such as your salary), it is much more than just $1000 per box. In order for your company to be able to afford the raise you deserve, they need to reduce costs elsewhere.

One way to reduce the TCO is by utilizing automated methods of deployment. By using images, you have the capability to quickly and easily deploy a fully functional computer. These are the basic steps of imaging:

- Create a reference computer.
- Capture the image.
- Deploy the image.

Take a look at Figure 2-1 for a better understanding of the overall process.

Figure 2-1

Imaging from a reference computer

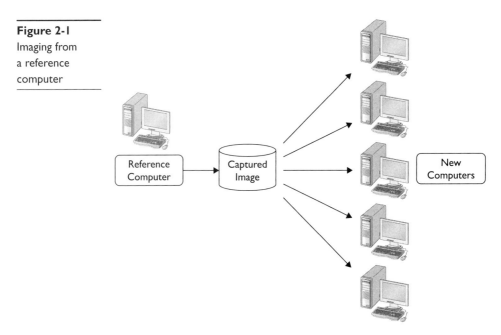

The reference computer would include the operating system, applications, and any desired settings. After creating the image on your reference computer, you then capture the image. The captured image could be stored on a networked computer, a CD or DVD, or even a USB flash drive. Once you have the captured image, you can then deploy the same image to multiple computers.

While this figure does show the basic steps, each step has more detailed tasks that must be completed. These tasks will be covered in more depth throughout the chapter. Before we can really cover how to accomplish these tasks, you'll need to understand a little about the Windows Automated Installation Kit.

Using the Windows Automated Installation Kit (WAIK)

The Windows Automated Installation Kit (WAIK) has a wealth of information and tools used to automate deployment of Windows Vista. You should be very familiar with the contents of the WAIK if you're working in a corporate environment that deploys Windows Vista. Of course, if you plan on taking the 70-622 exam, you should know it too.

You can use the tools within the WAIK to automate deployments of Windows Vista. The available methods to achieve this using the WAIK are

- Windows image-based deployment using the WinPE deployment environment

- Over-the-network installation of images using the WinPE deployment environment

- Windows image-based deployment using Windows Deployment Services (WDS)

- Third-party image-based deployment using tools such as Norton Ghost

Deployed images require very little extra work. Instead, once an image is deployed, the computer is turned on and after a little configuration you have a fully functional computer with all the applications and required settings.

The amount of time to deploy a fully configured computer could be as little as 30 minutes, where most of the time is spent waiting for the image to be copied. Moreover, you can easily do multiple computers at the same time. In other words, ten computers wouldn't take 300 minutes (10 * 30 minutes), but instead maybe as little as an hour—30 minutes of waiting and about 30 minutes to start and complete the process on each of the computers.

When working with the Windows Automated Installation Kit (WAIK), you should understand some basic terminology:

- **Technician computer**   This is the computer where you, as the technician, do the majority of your work. In exercises in this chapter, you will install the WAIK on this computer.

- **Reference computer**   This is also referred to as a master computer. If you want to create a custom image (sometimes called a cloned image), you would install the operating system and applications on this computer. You would then configure it for your environment by, for instance, locking it down with local group policy. Next, you'd test it. After testing, you'd run sysprep to prepare the computer. Last, you'd capture an image of the reference computer using ImageX. You can deploy this image (using ImageX) to multiple computers in your environment as desired.

- **Network Share or other storage location**   After an image is captured, you can store it on a network share so that is available anywhere in the network. It's also possible to store the image on a CD/DVD or even a USB drive, depending on the size. You can boot a bare-metal (no operating system) destination computer using WinPE, connect to the network share with Net Use, and then use ImageX to deploy the image to the destination computer.

- **Destination computers**   These are the computers that will receive the deployed image. They are sometimes referred to as target computers. A single cloned image created on a reference computer can be deployed to as many destination computers as desired. This saves a significant amount of time.

- **Windows System Image Manager (Windows SIM)**   Windows SIM is used to create answer files and network shares. Answer files are created on the technician computer and then transferred to the reference computer before the image is created.

- **Windows Imaging format (WIM)**   A .wim file is a collection of image files. Each image within the windows imaging file is a complete operating system installation. Custom images can be included that also include applications and settings. The Windows Vista installation DVD includes a Boot.wim (WinPE) file, as well as an install.wim file that includes different versions of Vista.

- **OSCDimg**   OSCDimg is a command-line tool that can be used to create an .iso image file of WinPE. This .iso image can then be burned to a CD or DVD to create a bootable CD/DVD with WinPE. If you think of it as **O**perating **S**ystem **CD Image**, the name makes a little more sense.

- **PEImg**   This is a command-line tool that can be used to modify a WinPE image offline. ImageX is used to create the base image. PEImg is used to add packages to the WinPE image such as for HTML application support, or the Windows recovery environment.

- **ImageX**   This is a command-line tool used to capture, modify, and apply images. For example, you could create a reference computer and prepare it with sysprep. You'd then boot using WinPE bootable media with ImageX installed. At this point, you can capture the image on the reference computer with ImageX. Additionally, you could boot to a bare-metal system with WinPE, and then use ImageX to deploy an image onto the computer.

- **Answer file**   This is a text file that provides answers for the installation from an image. Win SIM creates an answer file called unattend.xml. After the image is deployed and started the first time, settings will be retrieved from this answer file instead of asking users for the information.

- **Windows Preinstallation Environment (WinPE)**   A minimal 32-bit operating system. The WinPE environment for Vista (and Windows Server 2008) was built on the Windows Vista kernel. WinPE is used during the preinstallation and deployment phases, and it can also be used for system recovery.

- **System Preparation Tool (Sysprep)**   Sysprep is used to remove unique information (such as the computer name and SID) from a computer prior to cloning. You'd first prepare a reference computer and then run sysprep on it to prepare the reference computer for cloning. This image can then be deployed to multiple computers.

This is the overall process of capturing images using the WAIK:

- Prepare your technician computer by installing WAIK.
- Build a WinPE bootable disc.
- Create an answer file with Windows System Image Manager (Windows SIM).
- Build and test the reference computer (also known as a master computer).
- Prepare the reference computer by running sysprep.
- Capture the image by booting to WinPE and running ImageX.

Once you have created an image, the overall process of deploying the image using the WAIK is to

- Boot the target computer using WinPE bootable media.
- Run ImageX to deploy the image.

WinPE

The Windows Preinstallation Environment (Windows PE, sometimes called WinPE) is a mini–operating system with specific purposes. It is an integral component of both setup and recovery technologies.

If you installed Windows Vista from the DVD, you've already seen the WinPE environment. WinPE is launched as the first phase of the installation process. It's not apparent, but Windows PE is part of the boot.img file in the sources directory of the installation DVD. (The install.wim file holds the full installation files of Windows Vista editions.)

WinPE is used for Windows Vista deployments and is also used in Windows Deployment Services (WDS).

WDS is a Windows Server 2008 role that can be used to automate the deployment of images to Preboot Execution (PXE)–enabled clients. WDS will be covered in more depth later in this chapter.

WinPE can be used to

- Boot a system using only a bootable CD or bootable USB disk.
- Partition and format hard drives using the command-line tool DiskPart.
- Capture or deploy disk images using ImageX.

ImageX is not automatically added to WinPE, but it can easily be added, as you'll see in the exercises in this chapter. ImageX can be used to deploy images from a CD/DVD, a USB disk, or a network share for an over-the-network installation.

 EXAM TIP A bootable WinPE image (CD or USB disk) is needed to do an installation from a CD/DVD or for an over-the-network installation. For an installation with a CD/DVD, you would first boot to the WinPE image and then load the image using ImageX. For an over-the-network installation, you would first boot to the WinPE image, connect to the network share with Net Use, and then deploy the image with ImageX.

Later in this chapter, you can go through an exercise to create a WinPE USB bootable disk. This is a bootable tool used for installation, troubleshooting, and recovery. Our focus in this chapter will be on using WinPE for Windows Vista installation. WinPE runs every time you install Windows Vista during the setup phase.

ImageX

ImageX is the program used to capture and deploy images. It can actually do quite a bit more, but for the purposes of this chapter (and the exam), the focus is only on these two tasks. To capture an image, you can use the /capture switch. To deploy an image, you can use the /apply switch.

The /capture switch will capture an image from a reference computer. The basic format of the ImageX command to capture an image is

```
ImageX /capture imagePath imageFile "imageName" ["description"]
```

ImagePath is the path to the volume image to be captured. ImageFile is the path and filename of the .wim file where the image will be stored. Remember, multiple images can be stored in a single WIM. ImageName is the name of the image being captured. Description is optional (as noted by the brackets) but can include a free text description of the image.

As an example, you may need to capture an image of the C: drive and store it in a .wim file named myImages.wim stored on the D: drive. You could call the image "Sales" with a description of "Includes applications for Sales personnel." The command would be

```
ImageX /capture c: d:\myImages.wim "Sales" "Includes applications for Sales personnel"
```

The /apply switch will deploy an image. Images are contained in .wim files, and it's possible for multiple images to be contained in a single .wim file. So you must specify which image to deploy. Even if there's only one image in the .wim file, you still need to identify the image number (it would be 1).

When using the /apply switch, you need to include three parameters. The basic format of the ImageX command to deploy an image is

```
ImageX /apply pathOfImage imageNumber targetDrive
```

The pathOfImage is the path of the .wim image file. This can be a local drive such as a DVD drive assigned the letter D:, or it could be a mapped drive assigned a different letter such as X:. The imageNumber identifies which image you want to deploy from within the .wim file. Last, the targetDrive identifies which drive on the local system you want the image installed on.

As an example, you could have an image named Sales contained as the first image within an image file named myImages on a DVD drive assigned the letter D:. If you wanted to deploy this image on the C: drive of the local system, you would use the following command:

```
ImageX /apply d:\myImages.wim 1 c:
```

Using WinPE for an Over-the-Network Installation

You can install Windows Vista over the network on a bare-metal system. A bare-metal system is a system with the hardware, but no operating system. Of course, in order to access a share over the network, you need an operating system running on the hardware.

Figure 2-2 shows how you can accomplish an over-the-network install. In Step 1 you'd use WinPE to boot the bare-metal system. In Step 2, you'd use the Net use command to connect to the server. Last, you'd use the ImageX tool from the WinPE command line to download the image from the server.

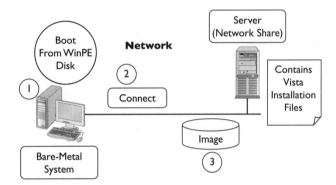

Figure 2-2
Over-the-network
installation

This assumes that an image has been placed onto a folder on a server, and the folder has been shared. The basic command to connect to a share using Net use is

```
Net use driveLetter: \\servername\sharename
```

The \\servername\sharename is known as a Universal Naming Convention (UNC) path.

As an example, if you created a share named VistaInstall on a server named MCITP1, you could map the X: drive to the share using the following command:

```
Net use X: \\MCITP1\VistaInstall
```

EXAM TIP To perform an over-the-network installation without WDS, you'd first install the installation files on a network share. Boot the client to WinPE. Use Net use to connect to the share and then use ImageX to apply an image from the share to the computer.

Remember, the /apply switch is used with the ImageX command to deploy an image. The basic format of the ImageX command with the /apply switch is

```
ImageX /apply pathOfImage ImageNumber targetDrive
```

For example, the following command would deploy an image to the C: drive from the first image held in a file named CustomVistaImages.win held on a network share mapped to the X: drive.

```
ImageX /apply x:\CustomVistaImages.wim 1 c:
```

Using WinPE for a Bare-Metal Installation

There's not much difference between doing an installation on a computer from a network share or from an image available on a DVD or flash drive. The only difference is the path of the image.

For example, you could boot to WinPE from a DVD that also includes a custom image. Imagine the image is the second image in an image file named Custom.wim in a folder named Images. If the assigned drive letter of your bootable DVD is F:, then you would use the following command:

```
ImageX /apply F:\Custom.wim 2 C:\
```

Create Bootable Media

You can create bootable media (a USB disk or a CD/DVD) that can be used to install Windows Vista. The bootable drive will boot you into a WinPE environment. You can then install custom images either from the drive or over the network.

In this section, the focus is on creating a bootable USB drive with WinPE. The overall steps needed to create a bootable drive are

- **Install the Windows Automated Installation Kit (WAIK)** This is a free download from Microsoft and relatively easy to install.

- **Prepare the WinPE environment** The CopyPE command is used to copy all of the files needed for the WinPE bootable disk to a directory. You can also add additional files such as ImageX to this directory structure so that they are added to your bootable disk.

- **Prepare the USB drive with DiskPart** DiskPart is a command-line program that can be used to clean, partition, and format your USB drive before making it a WinPE bootable disk. DVDs don't need to be prepared.

- **Copy the data onto the drive using XCopy** XCopy is used to copy the directory structure (including subdirectories) to your USB. The included files allow the USB to be bootable. If making a bootable CD, you must use the command OSCDimg to convert the directory structure to an .iso image. This .iso image can then be burned to a CD.

EXAM TIP The two programs used to create a bootable CD/DVD are CopyPE and OSCDimg. The CopyPE program will copy all of the required files into a directory. The OSCDimg (Operating System CD Image) program converts the data in your directory to an .iso image file that can then burned to CD.

The following three exercises will lead you through each of the tasks to create a bootable USB disk drive. The fourth exercise shows you how to create the .iso image using OSCDimg.

In Exercise 2.1, you will download and install the WAIK.

Exercise 2.1: Downloading and Installing the Windows Automated Installation Kit

1. Launch a Web browser and go to your favorite search engine. Enter **Download Vista Windows Automated Installation Kit**. If you like, you could use the following link, but I think a search engine would be easier. You decide.

    www.microsoft.com/downloads/details.aspx?familyID=C7D4BC6D-15F3-4284-9123-679830D629F2&displaylang=en

2. You should come to a page named Windows Automated Installation Kit (AIK). It will allow you to download the following image file:

    ```
    vista_6000.16386.061101-2205-LRMAIK_en.img
    ```

3. After downloading the image file, use a DVD image creation tool that will allow you to create a DVD from this image. Burn the image file to a DVD and you're ready to continue.

4. Place the DVD into your DVD drive on a Vista system and launch it. If Autoplay doesn't run automatically, right-click the drive in Windows Explorer and select Open AutoPlay.

5. On the AutoPlay dialog box, select Run StartCD.exe. If the User Account Control dialog box appears, click Continue. Your display will look similar to Figure 2-3.

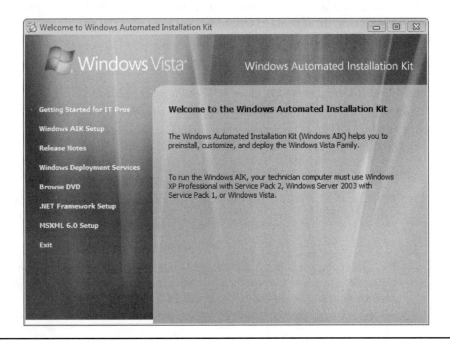

Figure 2-3   Running the Windows AIK startup program

6. Click the Windows AIK Setup link in the menu on the left. The Windows Installer will launch.

 TIP The Windows AIK requires MSXML 6.0 and the .NET Framework 2.0. The install program will prompt you to install these if they aren't installed, and both can be installed from the WAIK menu.

7. On the Welcome To The Windows Automated Installation Kit Setup Wizard screen, click Next.

8. On the License Agreement page, review the license agreement, select I Agree, and click Next.

9. On the Select Installation Folder page, accept the default installation folder of C:\Program Files\Windows AIK\. To allow this to be available for anyone that logs on to your system, accept the default choice of Everyone. Click Next.

10. On the Confirm Installation page, click Next. The WAIK will install.

11. On the Installation Complete page, click Close.

With the WAIK installed on your computer, you will have the tools needed to automate the deployment of Windows Vista.

In Exercise 2.2, you will set up your Windows PE build folders. When you installed the WAIK, it installed a lot of data and tools in the C:\Program Files\Windows AIK folder. You will now use these tools to create the data structure you will ultimately copy onto your USB drive.

Exercise 2.2: Preparing the Windows PE Folders

1. Click Start | All Programs | Windows AIK | Windows PE Tools Command Prompt. This will launch the command prompt in the C:\Program Files\Windows AIK\Tools\PETools directory.

2. At the command prompt, enter the following command:

```
Copype.cmd x86 c:\winpe_x86
```

This will create the C:\WinPE_x86 directory (including data and subdirectories) and modify the path to include the path to the peimg, OSCDimg, and imagex commands.

 TIP The commands in this lab assume you will be working with a 32-bit system. It is possible to create a 64-bit bootable drive, but the steps would need to be slightly modified to reach the 64-bit files.

3. Use the following command to add the ImageX program to your directory. This is a valuable tool to have on your bootable drive that will allow you to capture and apply images.

```
Copy "C:\Program Files\Windows AIK\Tools\x86\imagex.exe" c:\winpe_x86\iso
```

If you entered the command correctly, it will respond with "1 file(s) copied."

 TIP   When typing in these long command-line commands, it's very likely you'll have a typo. Expect them and you won't be disappointed. Common problems are missing spaces or missing quotes. In the preceding command, there is a space between Program and Files, and between Windows and AIK. Quotes are used to identify the entire path and must be included if the path has any spaces.

4. You may also want to modify Windows image (.wim) files from your bootable disk. You can do this with the Package Manager. The Package Manager can be added to your directory with the following two commands. Note that the xcopy command spans two lines but should be entered completely on one line.

```
xcopy "C:\Program Files\Windows AIK\Tools\x86\Servicing"
        c:\winpe_x86\iso\Servicing\ /s


Copy %windir%\System32\msxml6*.dll c:\winpe_x86\iso\servicing
```

The xcopy command will copy over 40 files. The copy command will copy two files.

5. Since you included ImageX in Step 3, you'll want to include an exclusion list. This list will prevent ImageX from failing due to some files being locked.

   a. At the command prompt, enter the following command:

   ```
   Notepad
   ```

   b. Notepad will launch. Enter the following exclusion and compression exclusion lists.

   ```
   [ExclusionList]
   tfs.log
   hiberfil.sys
   pagefile.sys
   "System Volume Information"
   RECYCLER
   Windows\CSC
   [CompressionExclusionList]
   *.mp3
   *.zip
   *.cab
   \WINDOWS\inf\*.pnf
   ```

    c. Click File | Save As. In the Save As dialog box, click Browse Folders and browse to the C:\winpe_x86\iso\ folder.

    d. In the File Name text box, enter **wimscript.ini**. Ensure you include .ini or your file will be saved as a .txt file and won't be interpreted as an initialization file.

In Exercise 2.3, you will prepare your USB flash drive to accept the bootable image. You'll then copy the data and create the bootable USB disk. This procedure will store about 200MB of data, so you need to ensure your USB is at least 256MB. If you want to add a Vista installation image, you'll need extra space, depending on the size of the image. However, the cost of USB flash drives has become quite affordable.

Exercise 2.3: Preparing and Creating Your Bootable USB Disk

1. Insert your USB disk into your system. Use Windows Explorer to identify which drive letter your USB is using. Write the drive letter here: _____.

CAUTION Warning! You will destroy all the data on your USB disk in this exercise. Make sure you don't have anything you can't afford to lose stored on your USB disk before starting. Additionally, make sure you follow the procedure to accurately identify which disk is the USB disk that you want to use. If you use the wrong disk when accessing the drive in DiskPart, you may erase all the data on the wrong disk. It could ruin your day!

2. Launch a command prompt with administrative privileges. Click Start | All Programs | Accessories, right-click Command Prompt, and select Run As Administrator.

3. From the command prompt, launch the DiskPart tool and enter the following commands:

```
DiskPart
List disk
```

Your display will look similar to Figure 2-4. Notice that one disk is 149GB and the other disk is 1968MB (close to 2GB). Can you guess which one is the USB drive? Hopefully, you can identify which drive is your USB drive.

TIP Some USB drives are recognized by the operating system but not by DiskPart. Make sure you are running DiskPart in Vista instead of Windows XP. I've seen several instances where DiskPart in Windows XP will not see a USB disk but DiskPart in Windows Vista will.

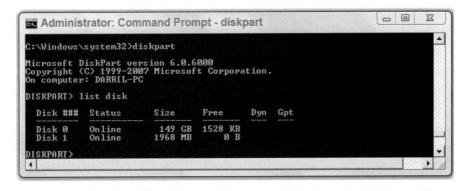

Figure 2-4   Listing disks in DiskPart

4. Assuming that Disk 1 is your USB disk, use the following commands to prepare your USB. If your disk is a different disk, substitute your number in the Select statement.

```
Select disk 1              ` This will select your USB disk
Clean                      ` This will erase all data
create partition primary   ` Creates one partition using all disk space
Select partition 1         ` Selects the created partition
active                     ` Makes the partition active
Format fs=fat32            ` Formats the partition as Fat32 (takes time)
assign                     ` Assigns a drive letter to the USB drive
exit                       ` Exits DiskPart
```

5. Launch Windows Explorer with the WINDOWS-E key. Identify what drive letter has been assigned to your USB disk.

6. Enter the following command to copy all of the data from your prepared iso directory to the USB disk. Substitute the actual letter of your USB disk for the letter x.

```
xcopy c:\winpe_x86\iso\*.* /s /e /f x:\
```

At this point, you have a fully bootable USB drive. Yell Wooo Hooo!

In Exercise 2.4, you will create an .iso image. This image can then be burned to a CD or DVD. Since the image created in this exercise is only about 200MB, a CD is all that's needed. This exercise assumes that Exercises 2.1 and 2.2 have been completed.

Exercise 2.4: Preparing and Creating Your Bootable CD

1. Click Start | All Programs | Windows AIK | Windows PE Tools Command Prompt. This will launch the command prompt in the C:\Program Files\ Windows AIK\Tools\PETools directory.

2. At the command prompt, enter the following command. While the command spans two lines in the book, enter the text all on a single line with just a single space after …etfsboot.com.

```
OSCDimg -n -bc:\winpe_x86\etfsboot.com
       c:\winpe_x86\ISO c:\winpe_x86\winpe_x86.iso
```

3. The command will complete rather quickly. It will create an iso file named winpe_x86.iso in the C:\winpe_x86 directory.

4. Use an image burning program to burn the .iso image to a CD or DVD. Note that burning an .iso image is different than copying the .iso image file to the CD.

TIP To burn an .iso image, you can use commercial software or freeware such as ImgBurn (available at www.imgburn.com). ImgBurn is an easy-to-use program and well worth an optional donation. Once it is installed, you can just double-click the .iso file and it'll launch. If you have a CD in the drive ready to burn, all you have to do is click a single button.

5. Once you burn the .iso file to the CD, you have a bootable WinPE CD.

If you want to automate the installation, you'll also need to create an answer file. If an answer file exists, instead of querying the user (or you, the installer) for a setting, the installation program will retrieve the answer from the answer file. If the answer file includes all the answers, there is almost no user interaction required.

Answer files are XML based and can be quite complex to create if you're using a text editor like Notepad. While you can use Notepad to create the answer file, I consider that similar to repeatedly banging my head against the wall.

The WAIK includes the Windows System Image Manager (Windows SIM), which can automate the process of creating an answer file. Figure 2-5 shows Windows SIM in the middle of building an answer file.

Different editions of Vista ask different questions. In other words, you don't have the same choices when installing Vista Basic as you do when installing Vista Enterprise. One of the first things you'll do when creating an answer file with Windows SIM is identify the image you'll use.

The Vista installation DVD includes two Windows Image (.wim) files.

- **Boot.wim** This file includes the WinPE image used to boot the system from the Windows installation DVD.

- **Install.wim** This file includes all the different Vista images that shipped with the DVD.

Once you select an image, you can then begin creating an answer file. You add components that you want your answer file to complete, and then you add the answers for each property within the component.

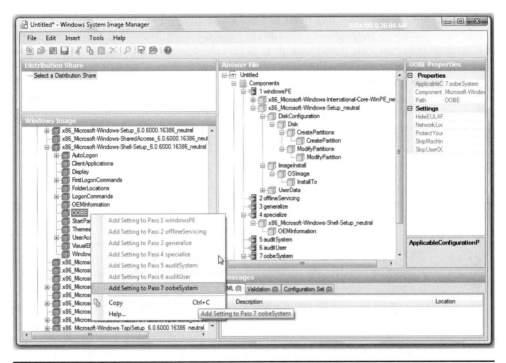

Figure 2-5   Using Windows SIM to create an answer file

The answer file can be as simple or as complex as you desire. Settings are available for virtually hundreds of responses.

Preparing Images

There are only two primary steps required when preparing an image. First you install and configure the computer. Second, you prepare the computer for imaging by running sysprep. Both methods are required whether you are creating and deploying the image using a third-party imaging tool, or using Windows Deployment Services (WDS).

Installation and Configuration

Anytime you want to create an image, you should always start with a clean installation of the operating system on a master computer. After installing the operating system, you would then install all the required applications.

For example, you may want all the users to have the most recent version of Microsoft Office. You would install Microsoft Office on your reference computer, including all of the components you want the end users to have.

When configuring the computer, you would ensure the computer has the most recent updates and service packs installed. You can lock down the computer by adding additional security settings within local group policy.

On the other hand, you may need to weaken security to ensure some applications work. For example, a corporate environment would have a firewall at the boundary to the Internet that everyone goes through to access the Internet. Understanding this, you may choose to either disable the firewall on end-user computers or open up specific ports to ensure these applications work.

Once the computer is configured, you need to do three additional tasks before running sysprep: test, test, and test. It's a whole lot easier to fix problems before you create the image than it is after.

Sysprep

Before cloning a reference computer, you need to remove many of the settings that are intended to be unique. For example, the Security Identifier (SID) is used to uniquely identify a computer within a network.

 EXAM TIP Sysprep is used to remove all unique information on a computer. It must be run on reference computers (sometimes called master computers) before an image is captured. If sysprep is not run prior to capturing the image, you won't be able to join the cloned computers to the domain.

The SID is similar to the name, but it used by the underlying system. Think of a computer named MCITP1. If you make ten copies of the computer image, you'd have ten computers named MCITP1. That simply won't work. While it is relatively easy to change the computer name, it isn't as easy to change the SID. Enter sysprep.

Sysprep has been around since Windows 2000, though there are many versions. You should only use the version for your operating system when running sysprep. You can run sysprep via the command line or using the graphical user interface (GUI). The GUI can be found here:

```
C:\windows\system32\sysprep\sysprep.exe
```

Figure 2-6 shows the sysprep GUI. As you can see, it's a rather simple interface. The GUI allows you to choose the System Cleanup Action, whether to Generalize, and the Shutdown Options.

Figure 2-6

Running sysprep

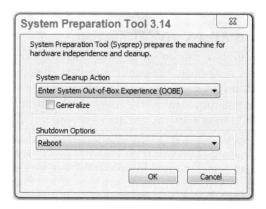

CAUTION   Make sure you can find your installation key before you run sysprep. If you run sysprep on a system just to see how it runs, you won't be able to use that system again until information (such as the installation key) has been added.

The following switches can be used when using sysprep.

- **/oobe**   This switch mimics the GUI choice Enter System Out-of-Box Experience (OOBE). It restarts the computer as if it is the first time the computer has started. Windows Welcome mode prompts users to enter information such as the computer name.

- **/audit**   Audit mode is the second choice in the System Cleanup Action (Enter System Audit Mode) when running the GUI. It is used to test an installation of Windows before an image is finalized. After testing, you would run sysprep with the /oobe switch.

- **/generalize**   Generalize is an important option in sysprep. This switch removes all the unique information (such as the SID) from the installation. It also deletes system restore points and event logs. A SID is created the next time the computer is booted. You can select Generalize by selecting the Generalize check box.

- **/reboot**   Selecting reboot causes the system to restart after sysprep runs. You would use /reboot with the /audit switch so that you could test your system.

- **/quit**   The /quit switch will close sysprep after it runs. This would allow you to view what has been done, but would rarely be used in a production environment.

- **/shutdown**   The /shutdown switch shuts down the computer after sysprep runs. This would commonly be used when you want to capture an image. You would then either boot using a third-party tool or boot with WinPE and then capture the image with ImageX.

When preparing a system to be imaged, you would us the /oobe, /generalize, and /shutdown switches. Your command would look similar to

```
Sysprep /oobe /generalize /shutdown
```

If you wanted the system to apply an answer file when rebooting, you could specify the answer file path and name with the /unattend switch.

Third-Party Imaging

Third-party imaging refers to an entity other than you or Microsoft. Today, this most commonly refers to Symantec's Ghost imaging software. Ghost enjoys a lot of respect with IT professionals and is a common theme in almost every environment I've worked in. Using Ghost, you can easily capture and deploy images.

Using Images in a Large Environment In the environment where I work, we have over 100,000 computers. Deploying these manually would take too much time and also would be difficult to manage. If several different people set up different computers, it would be extremely difficult to ensure all the operating systems were configured exactly the same.

Instead, an image has been created that include the operating system, relatively current updates, all the basic applications, and basic configuration. Additionally local group policy is utilized to deploy security for the computers. This image was then captured, and after extensive testing and tweaking had a standard image for all new computers.

The IT folks talked to some computer companies like Dell and HP. "We want to purchase a few thousand computers from you. Will you install this image onto them before they are shipped?" Of course, the answer was a resounding "Yes," since it represents guaranteed hardware sales.

Now, whenever new computers are received, they already have a complete image as soon as they are taken out of the box. IT support personnel turn the computer on, they do some basic configuration such as naming the computer and joining the domain, and the computer is ready for the end user within 30 minutes. An entire office of ten or more computers can be set up simultaneously in about an hour.

Microsoft has been trying to break into the imaging market for several years now. In Windows Server 2000, Remote Installation Services (RIS) was introduced and continued in Windows Server 2003. Where I saw RIS tried, I saw it abandoned. Mostly RIS was abandoned because Ghost was easier to use.

In Windows Server 2008, Microsoft has introduced Windows Deployment Services (WDS) as the replacement of RIS. WDS is much more versatile than RIS and has the potential to be as popular as Ghost. Of course one of the benefits of WDS is that it is included free with Windows Server 2008. WDS is covered in more depth later in this chapter.

The process of creating an image using Ghost is similar to the process of creating an image with WAIK tools. The basic tasks are

- Create a master, or reference computer.
- Run sysprep.
- Capture the image.
- Deploy the image.

EXAM TIP Microsoft won't test you on the specifics of how third-party (non-Microsoft) tools work. Instead you should focus on the generics of how third-party tools work and the specifics of how Microsoft tools work.

A comparison of using a third-party tool or using WAIK is shown in Table 2-1.

Action	WAIK	Third-Party
Create reference computer	Install OS, install applications, and configure computer.	Install OS, install applications, and configure computer.
Sysprep	Run before imaging.	Run before imaging.
Capture the image	Use WinPE, ImageX	Use third-party tools.
Deploy the image	Use WinPE, ImageX.	Use third-party tools.

Table 2-1 Comparing WAIK with Third-Party Imaging Tools

Notice in Table 2-1 that the creation of the reference computer and running sysprep are identical for both WAIK and third-party tools. The details of capturing and deploying the image work differently in a third-party tool than they do in the WAIK.

32-Bit and 64-Bit Images

When capturing and deploying images, it's important to realize that the 32-bit and 64-bit versions of Vista are significantly different, since they must be deployed to different architectures. If you are deploying to both 32-bit and 64-bit architectures, you will need two images.

Windows Vista images are Hardware Abstraction Layer (HAL) independent. In other words, you can deploy a single 32-bit image to all of your 32-bit computers. It doesn't matter if some have different graphics cards or different sound cards, or even if some are desktops and some are laptops. You can use a single 32-bit image for all of your 32-bit computers.

Similarly, you can use a single 64-bit image for all of your 64-bit computers.

 EXAM TIP If deploying images to both 32-bit and 64-bit platforms, you'll need at least two images of Windows Vista. The other hardware doesn't matter, so you can use a single 32-bit image for all of your 32-bit computers, even if some are desktops and some are laptops, and a second 64-bit image for all of your 64-bit computers. Of course, you can have as many custom images of either platform as your environment needs.

WinPE is a 32-bit application and takes advantage of a 64-bit system to boot into 32-bit mode before switching to 64-bit mode. With this in mind, you can use a single WinPE image to boot into any computer—32-bit or 64-bit.

Using Windows Deployment Services (WDS)

Windows Deployment Services (WDS) is a Windows Server 2008 role that can be used to automate the deployment of images. WDS really doesn't care what the images are— they can be Windows XP, Windows Vista, or even Windows Server 2008.

If you were studying for a Windows Server 2008 MCTS or MCITP exam, you would need to know the details of WDS. However, since this book is instead focused on Windows Vista MCTS and MCITP exams, you really only need to understand the big picture of WDS and the details as it applies to Windows Vista.

Take a look at Figure 2-7 for an overall picture of how WDS works. You would create a reference computer just as you would if using WAIK tools. Once prepared, you would connect to the WDS server to capture the image. You can then use WDS to deploy any captured images.

Figure 2-7
WDS used to
capture and
deploy images

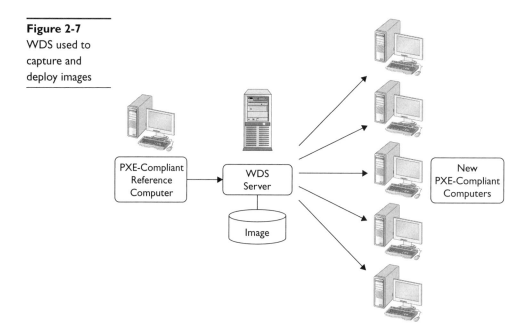

WDS can also use the images available in the boot.wim (WinPE image) and install. wim files. These files are available on the installation DVDs of Windows Vista, Windows Server 2003, and Windows Server 2008.

In other words, you can use WDS to deploy custom images or plain vanilla images that haven't been modified.

The overall tasks involved with using WDS are

- Prepare a PXE-compliant reference computer (including using sysprep).
- Store or capture the image to the WDS server.
- Deploy the image to PXE-compliant computers.

Of course, you may be wondering, "What the heck is PXE?"

PXE-Compliant

A Preboot Execution (PXE, commonly pronounced pixie)–compliant computer is a computer that has the components necessary to allow it to boot using the NIC. Normally, a computer would boot to the hard drive, but it can also boot to a floppy, a CD or DVD, or even a USB drive.

In order to boot using the NIC, the BIOS must be aware of the capability and the NIC must have ROM that knows how to locate the required network components. A PXE boot sequence is initiated by pressing the F12 key on bootup.

WDS NETWORK Requirements

In order for WDS to work properly, your network requires a Dynamic Host Configuration Protocol (DHCP) server, a domain controller (a server hosting Active Directory), and a Domain Name Services (DNS) server.

EXAM TIP The requirements of WDS are: a PXE-compliant computer, a DHCP server, and a WDS server. When you press F12 on the compliant computer, the client connects to DHCP to receive an IP address (and other TCP/IP configuration information) and then connects to the WDS server to download the WinPE image and begin the installation.

A DHCP server is used to give a client an IP address and other TCP/IP configuration information such as a subnet mask, a default gateway, and more.

Active Directory is used to authenticate users in a domain and will identify what images a user should be able to access based on permissions. In order to find servers hosting Active Directory, you must have a DNS server. DNS is used primarily for name resolution of host names (resolving a computer name to an IP address), but within a domain, it is also used to locate domain controllers.

WDS Capture and Deployment Process

There are a lot of similarities between using the Windows Automated Installation Kit (WAIK) and using WDS. Both are image-based. A comparison of using WDS with using WAIK is shown in Table 2-2.

Action	WAIK	WDS
Create reference computer	Install OS, install applications, and configure computer.	Install OS, install applications, and configure computer.
Sysprep	Run before imaging.	Run before imaging.
Capture the image	Use WinPE and ImageX.	Press F12 to start the PXE client and connect to WDS. Follow the wizards.
Deploy the image	Use WinPE and ImageX.	Press F12 to start the PXE client and connect to WDS. Follow the wizards.

Table 2-2   Comparing WAIK with Windows Deployment Services (WDS)

As you can see in Table 2-2, both WDS and WAIK create a reference computer with sysprep the same way. A significant difference with WDS is that you can provide a lot more automation.

For example, you may have ten bare-metal systems that you need to configure. If you have an image captured and stored on the WDS server, you can configure WDS to deploy it to the computers. Once it is configured, you can go to each of the ten computers, connect to the WDS server, and choose the image.

WDS can multicast the image to all ten computers simultaneously. You aren't limited to only ten computers. You can multicast to as many systems as you desire.

WDS Deployment Process

The F12 key is used to start the boot process for a PXE-compliant computer. The NIC will connect to a DHCP server to receive TCP/IP configuration information including an IP address. Next, the PXE-compliant computer will locate the WDS server and download the WinPE image.

Once WinPE is downloaded, it runs and begins the installation process. The user may have a choice of multiple images. Once the user picks an image, it will download and install on the compliant computer.

If you need to multicast a single image to multiple computers, you can set up the WDS server to cast an image. You press F12 on each of the clients, and once they connect, the image will be cast to all of them.

 TIP Multicasting refers to sending from one host to multiple hosts that have joined the multicast group. You could have 100 computers in your network, but only 10 that need to be reimaged. Multicasting an image allows the image to be sent over the network, but only installed on the ten computers that have joined the multicast group.

In a corporate environment, it's very possible you would have multiple custom images. For example, you could have one generic custom image for most end users, another custom image for sales people that includes specific sales applications, and another custom image for IT people with specific settings for personnel in the IT department.

Of course, it's also possible to use just a single custom image for all users. There's a lot be said for standardization. A single standard image is easier to maintain and easier to troubleshoot.

WDS Capture Process

After you have configured your reference computer and run sysprep on it to remove unique settings, you can then capture the image. Remember, you would choose the /shutdown option when running sysprep prior to capturing an image so your system would now be turned off.

Before starting the capture process, WDS has to be set up to accept a captured image. Specifically you would create a capture image that would be selectable from the client.

When WDS is ready, you'd start the reference computer with the F12 key. The PXE client would connect to DHCP, then WDS. The capture image configured on WDS will ultimately be available as a choice. After choosing this capture image, the image on the PXE client would be captured and sent over the network to be stored on the WDS server.

Chapter Review

In this chapter you learned several different methods to automate the deployment of Windows Vista using images.

The Windows Automated Installation Kit (WAIK) is one of the primary resources for automating Vista installations as a desktop support technician. It includes tools such as ImageX that can be used to capture and deploy images. CopyPE and OSCDimg can be used to create a bootable WinPE disk (USB or CD/DVD).

WinPE is a thin operating system used to boot a computer in preparation for installing Windows Vista. After booting, you can use Diskpart to prepare the disk. You can install Windows Vista from a local DVD or over the network from a share on a server. ImageX is the tool you use to deploy Vista from over the network or from a local drive.

Basic images are available on the installation DVD in the sources directory (in the install.wim file). Custom images can also be created that include applications and settings. When creating images, you must have at least one image for 32-bit systems and one image for 64-bit systems.

Before capturing an image, it needs to be prepared. A key tool used to prepare a computer is sysprep. It removes unique information such as the SID. If it is not run, you are sure to experience problems on your network with duplicate SIDs.

Vista can be deployed via third-party tools such as Symantec's Ghost. Just as with images captured with ImageX, images captured with Ghost must be prepared with sysprep.

Windows Deployment Services (WDS) is a Windows Server 2008 role that you may see in networks today. It works very similar to Symantec's Ghost. It needs DHCP and Active Directory on the network, and the clients must be PXE-compliant.

Additional Study

Self Study Exercises

Use these additional exercises to challenge yourself.

CAUTION Make sure you perform these tasks on computers that don't have data you want to save. If you have your own test lab, you can install Vista on a test computer, run sysprep, capture the image, and then redeploy the image onto the test computer. You don't want to run sysprep or deploy an image to the computer you use on a daily basis. You have the capability of losing data, or requiring a complete rebuild.

- Prepare a computer to be imaged by using sysprep.
- Capture an image using ImageX.
- Deploy an image using ImageX.

Summary of What You Need to Know

70-620
This chapter does not include any topics for the 70-620 exam.

70-622
All of the topics in this chapter apply to the 70-622 exam. When preparing, pay particular attention to the following topics:

- **Windows Automated Installation Kit (WAIK) tools** You should understand what tools are available in this kit and how to use them.

- **ImageX** You should be familiar with the ImageX command-line tool and know that it's used to capture, modify and apply images. You would normally add ImageX to your bootable WinPE media.

- **WinPE** You should know that the Windows Preinstallation Environment (WinPE) is a minimal operating system used for preinstallation and deployment. You should also be familiar with how to create and use it.

- **Sysprep** Know that sysprep is used to remove unique information from a computer and must be run prior to creating an image of a computer.

70-623
This chapter does not include any topics for the 70-623 exam.

Questions

70-622

1. You are a desktop support technician for MCITPSuccess.com. The company is planning on deploying Windows Vista to existing computers. The computers meet the hardware requirements for Vista, and they have combined CD/DVD drives and PXE-compliant NICs. You have a WinPE CD and the Windows installation DVD. From the following list of items, which should you do, and in what order?

   1) Start the computer using the PXE NIC.

   2) Create a network boot floppy and start the computer with this disk.

3) Start the computer from the WinPE CD.

4) Use ImageX to partition and format the hard disk.

5) Use Diskpart to partition and format the hard disk.

6) Use ImageX to deploy the image to the computer.

7) Use WALK to deploy the image to the computer.

   A. 1, 5, 6

   B. 2, 4, 7

   C. 3, 5, 6

   D. 3, 4, 5

   E. 1, 4, 6

2. You decide to deploy Windows Vista over the network to several computers. The computers meet the hardware requirements for Vista, and they have combined CD/DVD drives and PXE-compliant NICs. You create a share named VistaInstall on a server named MCITP1 and copy all of the installation files from the Vista installation DVD to the share. You have created a custom answer file and placed it in the share. What else would be needed to do an over-the-network installation from \\MCITP1\VistaInstall?

   A. RIS

   B. WinPE

   C. The Vista installation DVD

   D. A network boot floppy disk

3. You want to automate the installation of Windows Vista to 50 clients in your domain. Each client meets the minimum hardware requirements of Windows Vista and includes a CD/DVD drive and PXE-compliant NICs. What network resources are required?

   A. RIS and DHCP

   B. WDS and DHCP

   C. WinPE, WDS, and RIS

   D. WinPE and DHCP

4. You are planning on deploying a custom Windows Vista image to 50 computers within your domain. You have created a reference computer and want to capture the image. The Windows Automated Installation Kit (WAIK) is installed on your computer, and you want to create a WinPE CD to assist with the capture. What programs should you run? Choose all that apply.

   A. ImageX

   B. Copype.cmd

   C. OSCDimg

   D. Sysprep

5. You are planning on deploying a custom Windows Vista image to 50 computers within your domain. You have created a reference computer and tested it. What should you do to the reference computer before creating an image?

   A. Run OSCDimg

   B. Run sysprep

   C. Run CopyPE

   D. Run ImageX

6. You are the desktop support technician for MCITPSuccess.com. You have created a 32-bit image that you've been successfully using for 32-bit-based desktops. Your company has recently purchased 20 32-bit laptops, 50 64-bit desktops, and 20 64-bit laptops. You want to use images to deploy Vista to all of these computers. How many images will you need?

   A. One

   B. Two

   C. Three

   D. Four

Answers

70-622

1. **C.** You should start the computer using the WinPE CD. You should then use Diskpart to partition and format the hard disk. Last, you'd use ImageX to deploy the image. You'd use the PXE NIC when connecting to a WDS server, but it's not needed to install a disk from DVD. A network boot floppy can be used instead of a PXE NIC, but it wouldn't be useful to install from a DVD. ImageX cannot partition and format hard disks. The WAIK is a kit of different deployment tools, but there is no such thing as WALK. While not a given choice, it'd be easiest to boot from the Windows DVD and use the GUI tools to do all the tasks.

2. **B.** A WinPE bootable disk is all that's needed. You can then connect to the server with the `Net use` command and begin the installation with the `ImageX` command using the `/apply` switch. Remote Installation Services (RIS) has been replaced with Windows Deployment Services (WDS) to deploy Vista. The appropriate contents of the Vista installation DVD have been copied to the share, so it is not needed. The client is Preboot Execution (PXE)–compliant, meaning it can boot from the NIC and connect to a WDS server. A network boot floppy disk would be used with RIS if you didn't have a PXE-compliant NIC.

3. **B.** With Windows Deployment Services (WDS) you can automate the deployment. Users on the PXE-compliant systems can press F12 to start the process of connecting to DHCP and then the WDS server. The three primary requirements are a PXE-compliant computer, DHCP, and WDS. WDS would include the Vista installation files. Remote Installation Services (RIS) has been replaced with WDS and generally would not be a valid answer for any Vista exam. WinPE and DHCP do not include the Windows Vista installation files, so this is an incomplete solution.

4. **B, C.** The question states that " . . . you want to create a WinPE CD . . . ." The programs necessary to do so are CopyPE and OSCDimg. CopyPE can be used to copy all the necessary files to a directory that will be used to create a WinPE disc. Once these files are copied, you'd use the OSCDimg program to create an .iso image from the directory. While you'd want to copy the ImageX program to the directory before you created the image, you wouldn't run the ImageX command until you were ready to capture the image (after booting from a WinPE disc). Sysprep would be used to prepare the image on the reference computer before capturing it but isn't needed to create a WinPE CD.

5. **B.** The only program that needs to be run on the reference computer is sysprep. This will prepare the reference computer before an image is created from it. Sysprep will remove all the unique information (such as the computer name and SID). OSCDimg can create an .iso file from a directory structure and is used to create a WinPE disc. CopyPE copies the appropriate information to a directory for a WinPE disc. ImageX is used to capture and deploy an image.

6. B. You must use a separate image for both 32-bit and 64-bit platforms. Vista images are otherwise hardware independent.

Configuring the Vista Environment

In this chapter, you will learn about:
- Device Manager
- Windows Vista Aero
- Vista's Sidebar
- Application compatibility

Once you have either installed or upgraded Windows Vista, you'll need to configure the Vista environment. The biggest things to configure right off the bat are the devices in your system. Device Manager is the primary tool you'll use to install, configure, and troubleshoot device drivers.

The Windows Vista Aero is the new graphical user interface in Vista. While it provides some great graphical features, it's also sure to cause some problems for users. You'll learn about the requirements to run Aero, how to enable and disable it, and how to troubleshoot some basic issues with Aero.

Additional features you'll need to understand in Vista are the Sidebar and gadgets, ReadyBoost, and Indexing.

Last, you may need to address some application issues. In this chapter, you'll learn about several application compatibility tools you can use to help users continue to use their applications after Vista is installed.

 EXAM TIP Objectives for the 70-620, 70-622, and 70-623 exams are included in this chapter.

Device Manager

When configuring Windows Vista, one of the first things you'll want to do is make sure all your hardware is working. The primary tool you'll use when working with hardware is the Device Manager. Using the Device Manager, you can

- Verify hardware is working.
- Troubleshoot hardware that is not working.

- Enable, disable, and uninstall devices.

- Identify device driver properties, install new device drivers, and roll back drivers to a previous version.

If you've worked with the Device Manager in previous editions of Windows (such as Windows XP), you'll be happy to know that much of the functionality is the same.

Starting the Device Manager

The Device Manager requires administrative permissions to make any changes. If you are logged in as an administrator, then the User Account Control dialog will appear prompting you to continue. If you are logged in with a standard user account, you will access Device Manager in Read-only mode.

You can access the Device Manager in a few different ways.

- Click Start and then click Control Panel. Click System and Maintenance. Click System. In the Tasks pane on the left, click Device Manager.

- Click Start, right-click Computer, and select Properties. This is the same System window that you can access from the Control Panel. In the Tasks pane on the left, click Device Manager.

- Click Start, right-click Computer, and select Manage. If the User Account Control dialog box appears, click Continue. In the left pane under System Tools, click Device Manager.

- Click Start. In the Start Search box, enter **mmc devmgmt.msc**.

Enabling and Disabling Devices

Once launched, the Device Manager looks similar to Figure 3-1.

One of the great things about the Device Manager is that when things are wrong, they jump out at you. For example, in Figure 3-1, the Sound, Video, and Game Controllers node is opened and the Realtek High Definition Audio device has a down arrow icon. This indicates the device is disabled.

Any device can be enabled or disabled within the Device Manager, by simply right-clicking the device and selecting Enable (when it is disabled) or Disable (when it is enabled).

Additionally, you may see a device with a black question mark or a black exclamation mark in a yellow circle. These icons often indicate a problem with the driver.

 EXAM TIP If a device has a down arrow on the icon, it is disabled. Before you can use the device, you must enable it. If the device has a yellow circle with a black question mark or black exclamation mark, there is likely a problem with the driver.

Figure 3-1

Device Manager
with a device
disabled

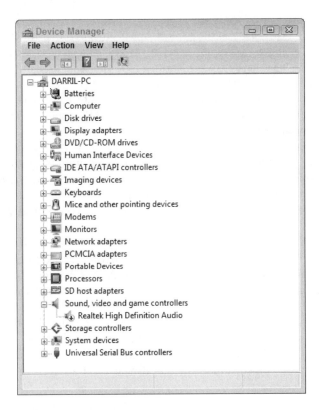

Working with Drivers

Drivers are the files that an operating system uses to communicate with devices. Without the proper driver, even the best hardware is nothing more than a useless mass of silicon.

Thankfully, Plug and Play technology automatically installs and configures drivers for many pieces of hardware you may install. When Plug and Play doesn't work is when you need to get involved.

Understanding Plug and Play and the Driver Store

When a device is detected, the Plug and Play service is notified. The Plug and Play service queries the device to retrieve an identifier. Using this identifier, Plug and Play attempts to locate a driver. The following locations are searched:

- Folders specified in the DevicePath Registry entry. This is known as the driver store.

- The Windows Update Web site. All drivers available through the Windows Update site have been tested and signed.

TIP Early in the deployment of any operating system, hardware support is limited. Obviously every hardware manufacturer would want to have all of their hardware work with a new operating system, but the process of writing new drivers and then having them tested internally, submitted to Microsoft for testing, and deployed to the Windows Update site simply takes time. As time passes, more and more hardware will work with Plug and Play, but in the interim you may have to manually install many drivers.

If a driver is located matching the device identifier, then the driver will be installed. If a driver isn't found, then you need to go on a driver hunt and install the driver manually. Manual installation of drivers will be discussed in the next section. However, only administrators can install drivers manually, and you typically don't want users to be logged on as administrators.

Remember, Plug and Play searches the driver store, and if the driver is found there, Plug and Play works. The driver store is a trusted cache of drivers stored on the hard drive of each system. By default, it contains drivers included from the installation DVD, but you can also add third-party drivers. This is referred to as staging drivers in the driver store.

You can stage drivers in the driver store either by injecting them into images used for deployment, or by dynamically updating them to clients over the network. The actual process is more in the hands of server and enterprise administrators, but as the Vista administrator, you should know that drivers can be staged in the driver store.

EXAM TIP To ensure that device drivers are automatically installed for new hardware, stage the driver in the driver store. If the driver is in the driver store, non-administrative users will be able to use new devices, since Plug and Play will install the correct driver from the driver store.

For example you could purchase a biometric USB drive, which would only work when a user authenticates with a thumbprint or fingerprint (they exist today). However, since the USB drive is so new, the driver wouldn't be in the driver store. You may not know exactly who will get the new USB drive and which systems they may use. You can stage the driver into the driver store of all the systems in your network, and now users will be able to plug in the USB drive and Plug and Play will automatically locate them.

Manually Installing Drivers

There are a couple of instances where you may need to manually install a driver. One is when you want to get a newer driver, and you don't have any driver installed at all.

For example, you may have an older driver, but a new version has been released. This is very common with video drivers. Video cards are very competitive, and they often get products to market quickly and improve the drivers as more testing is done. An easy way to see if your drive is up-to-date or out-of-date is by checking the version.

Figure 3-2 shows the property page of a device from Device Manager. If you learn that a newer driver is available, you can check the driver version of the newer driver against the Driver Version and Driver Date fields on this page.

Figure 3-2
Checking the
driver version
and date

The best place to locate a driver is the manufacturer's Web site. Often a device manufacturer will have created a driver that is compatible with Microsoft Vista, but the process of getting the driver tested and put onto the Windows Update site just hasn't completed.

 EXAM TIP   If device drivers aren't located automatically, the best place to check is the manufacturer's Web site. If the network card driver isn't installed, you won't have Internet access. You'll need to manually locate the driver from another computer, and then install the driver for the NIC.

Once you locate a driver, you can download it to your hard drive. You can then use the Device Manager to manually install the driver by specifying the exact path where the driver is located.

The steps involved in manually installing a driver are

1. Launch the Device Manager.

2. Right-click the device in the Device Manager and select Update Driver Software, as shown in Figure 3-3. You could also double-click the device to access the property page, select the Driver tab, and click the Update Driver button.

Figure 3-3
Updating driver
software from the
Device Manager

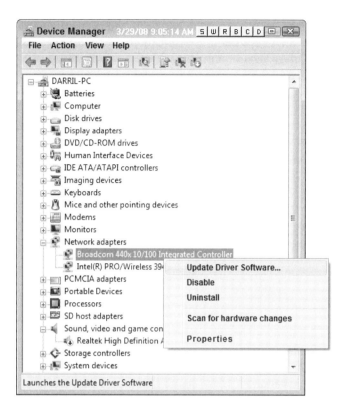

3. Click Browse My Computer For Driver Software to locate and install the driver software manually.

4. On the Browse For Driver Software On Your Computer page, click Browse, and browse to the location where you downloaded the drivers. For example, if you saved the downloaded drivers in a folder named DownloadedDrivers, on your C:\ drive, you'd specify the path of C:\DownloadedDrivers. Click Next.

Windows Vista will then search this folder for the driver and install it.

EXAM TIP When manually installing drivers, you select the Update Driver Software option and then specify the path where the driver is located. You must be logged in as an administrator to do this.

Rolling Back Drivers

The purpose of installing new drivers is to either allow a device to work or allow it to work better. Occasionally, though, you may get the opposite effect. Instead of a device performing better, it performs worse, or perhaps not at all.

Thankfully, Windows Vista includes the same feature available in Windows XP for rolling back drivers.

Imagine that you purchased a video card and installed the driver that came with the video card. It's been working fine, but a friend lets you know that a new driver is available. If you install the new driver, you'll be able to see brighter colors and quicker animations, and it may even improve your gaming abilities. He brought the driver on a USB drive and quick as a flash, you upgrade the driver on your system.

Suddenly, you find that your system has been reduced to a resolution of 800 × 600 with only 16-bit color. Not exactly the Windows Vista experience you've been enjoying up to this point.

However, you can easily undo the damage using the Roll Back Driver feature. Use the following steps to roll back a driver.

1. Launch Device Manager.

2. Right-click your device and select Properties.

3. Click the Driver tab. On the Driver tab, click the Roll Back Driver button. (You can see this button in Figure 3-2 in the Manually Installing Drivers section).

Here are two important points to know concerning rolling back drivers:

- *You can only roll back a driver after a second driver has been installed.* In other words, if you've only installed one driver, there is nothing to roll back to and the Roll Back Driver button is unavailable (grayed out or dimmed).

- *You can only roll back to the last driver.* Multiple driver versions aren't maintained, only the very last driver that was installed. Consider this scenario: You have driver A installed but you decide to update it and install driver B. Driver B doesn't work; at this point you could roll back to driver A. Instead, you install driver C. Driver C doesn't work either. You can only roll back to driver B at this point, not back to driver A.

Disabling Driver Installation Messages

Each time Vista boots, all of the hardware in the system is scanned and the appropriate drivers are installed. If a device is located that hasn't been installed previously, Plug and Play will attempt to locate the driver. If the driver isn't located, a dialog box will appear prompting you about the unknown device.

However, you may not want to install the device and may not want to be harassed by the message every time you reboot.

For example, you may have separate card readers plugged into the system that are used for authentication. A user puts his smart card into the smart card reader, enters his PIN, and logs on. Everything works fine. However, several systems also have a smart card reader embedded in the keyboard that requires a separate driver. You don't want to install the second driver simply because it's unnecessary. The smart card reader won't be used.

 EXAM TIP You can stop warning messages from appearing about unknown devices by disabling the device or selecting the option to not show the warning message anymore for the device.

There are two methods you can use to disable the warning message every time you reboot.

- Disable the device.
- Select Don't Show This Message Again For This Device on the warning message.

Once you select this option, the system will no longer warn you about the device. You can still go into Device Manager and install the driver for the device if you change your mind later.

In Exercise 3.1, you will disable a device on your system, and then re-enable the device.

Exercise 3.1: Manipulating Devices in Device Manager

1. Launch Device Manager. Select Control Panel | System and Maintenance and click Device Manager. If the User Account Control dialog box appears, click Continue.

2. Locate a device within Device Manager that you can do without for a moment. For example, if you have a modem but aren't connected with the modem, locate the modem device in the Modems node. Or, if you have a sound card installed, locate the sound card in the Sound, Video, and Game Controllers node.

3. Right-click the device and select Disable. In the warning dialog box, review the information and click Yes to indicate that you really want to disable it. After a moment, note that Device Manager has refreshed the display and the device is now shown with a down arrow to indicate it is disabled.

4. Right-click the device and select Enable. After a moment, note that Device Manager has refreshed the display and the device is now shown as enabled.

5. Double-click the device to access the properties page.

6. Click the Driver tab. Notice that you can view the information on the driver such as the date it was released and the driver version.

7. Click Driver Details. On the Driver File Details page, you can view all of the files associated with this driver. Click OK.

8. View the Roll Back Driver button. This button could be dimmed and can't be clicked. This indicates that only one driver has been installed for this driver. In other words, there has only been one driver installed, so you can't roll back to a previous driver.

Windows Error Reporting (WER)

Although stop errors are rare in Windows Vista, they can occur. A stop error is when your entire system crashes and you're presented with a blue screen (often called a BSOD or blue screen of death). More often, an application or process hangs, and you have the ability to end it with Task Manager.

Windows Error Reporting The application that handles Windows Error Reporting (WER) in Windows Vista is wermgr.exe. Wermgr.exe occasionally gets a little rambunctious and can take close to 100 percent of processing power.

If your system slows down and Task Manager shows that wermgr.exe is the culprit by hogging all the processing power, use Task Manager to end the process. Stopping this process won't cause any problems, other than stopping automatic reporting for awhile. The next time you restart the computer, wermgr.exe will start again.

Windows Error Reporting (WER) captures information related to any types of crashes and hung applications, including problems related to drivers. When a program stops working or responding, WER can automatically report the problem and check for a solution.

The Problem Reports and Solutions applet is the primary tool used for error reporting within Vista. By using the Problem Reports and Solutions applet, you can check for solutions to common problems and also set how problems are reported. To access the Problem Reports and Solutions applet, follow these steps:

1. Click Start, right-click Computer, and select Properties.

2. Select the Performance link at the bottom left of the screen under See Also.

3. From here, you can select the Problem Reports And Solutions link at the bottom left of the screen under See Also. Figure 3-4 shows the Problem Reports and Solutions screen.

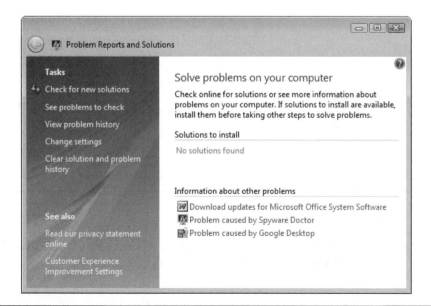

Figure 3-4 Problem Reports and Solutions

Notice that the tasks links on the left pane allow you to

- Check For New Solutions
- See Problems To Check
- View Problem History
- Change Settings
- Clear Solution And Problem History

If you click Change Settings, you'll be able to change how the reporting is done. There are basic choices, but you can also set advanced settings.

- Check for solutions automatically (recommended). Notify me if I can take steps to solve a problem.
- Ask me to check if a problem occurs.

Figure 3-5 shows the advanced settings of the problem reporting page. The administrator has the capability to set problem reporting for all users, or to allow error reporting to be checked on a per-user basis.

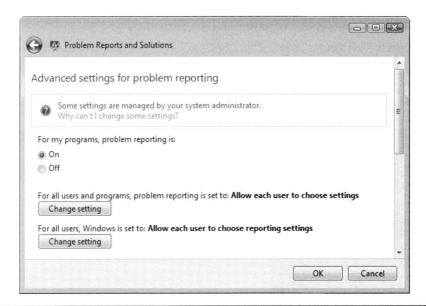

Figure 3-5   Advanced error reporting settings

 EXAM TIP   To enable or disable automatic reporting for all users, use the advanced settings for problem reporting page.

Understanding Vista's Aero

A significant graphics feature of Windows Vista is the Windows Aero experience. Aero provides several graphic enhancements, including

- **Translucent glass** Windows have a translucent effect. You can actually see through some of the Windows border regions.
- **Windows Flip 3D** By pressing the WINDOWS-TAB keys, you can view all of your windows in a 3D display. You can tab through these to select the one you want. Figure 3-6 shows the Flip 3D display.

Figure 3-6 Windows Aero and Flip 3D

NOTE Checking for Windows Flip 3D is an easy way to check to see if Aero is enabled or not. Press the WINDOWS-TAB keys; if Windows Flip 3D works, Aero is enabled. If Windows Flip 3D does not work, Aero is not enabled.

- **Windows Flip** By pressing the ALT-TAB keys, you can see all of your open windows in a horizontal display and tab through them. This is similar to the ALT-TAB feature in previous editions of Windows, but it includes the translucent glass effect.
- **Thumbnails on the taskbar** When you hover over an item on the taskbar, a thumbnail of the window appears. This thumbnail shows the live content of the window.

Aero Requirements

It's possible to have Windows Vista installed without Aero. If Aero is not enabled, your system will use the Vista Basic display. In order for Aero to be enabled, the following requirements must be met:

- **Minimum operating system** Windows Vista Home Basic and Starter Editions do not support Aero. All other editions do support Aero.

- **128MB of graphics RAM** The graphics card must have at least 128MB RAM for monitors up to 20 inches. For larger monitors such as 30-inch flat-panel monitor with a 2560 × 1600 resolution, you'll need at least 256MB of graphics RAM. No matter how much graphics RAM you have, it's also recommended (though not required) that your operating system have at least 1GB of RAM.

- **DirectX 9 graphics support** This includes support for the Windows Display Driver Model (WDDM) and Pixel Shader 2.0 in the hardware.

 EXAM TIP You should be very familiar with the minimum requirements for Aero. This includes 128MB of RAM, support for the WDDM and Pixel Shader 2.0. While Vista will support Aero if the system has the minimum of 512MB RAM, Aero won't start automatically with only 512MB RAM.

The Windows Display Driver Model (WDDM) is a graphics driver model created specifically for Windows Vista. WDDM provides the added rendering functionality needed for the Aero experience. Pixel Shader (PS) is a program executed on graphics chips that can manipulate graphics on a per-pixel basis. PS effects are very common in gaming and include bump mapping, shadows, and explosion effects.

The basic hardware requirements for Windows Vista were covered in Chapter 1, but as a reminder they are

- 800 MHz 32-bit or 64-bit processor
- 512MB of RAM
- 15GB available hard drive space

Notice that the basic requirements for Windows Vista do not include the requirements for supporting the Vista Aero feature. If the hardware requirements are not met, Aero won't be enabled, but otherwise Vista will work fine.

It's also worth noting that while 512MB RAM meets the minimum hardware requirements, Aero won't start automatically with only 512MB RAM. It can be enabled, but you may not be satisfied with the experience. It's recommended to have at least 1GB of RAM when enabling Windows Aero.

Viewing Your Windows Experience Index

One of the ways you can tell if your system supports Windows Aero is by checking the Windows Experience Index. The Windows Experience Index is a new feature built into Windows Vista designed to let you know how well your system is performing.

The Windows Experience Index is expressed as a number between 1.0 and 5.9. Figure 3-7 shows the Windows Experience on a laptop.

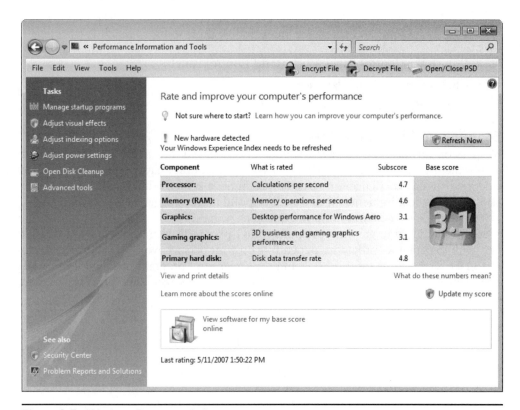

Figure 3-7   Windows Experience Index

Notice that the score is derived from several different components of the system:

- Processor
- Memory (RAM)
- Graphics
- Gaming graphics
- Primary hard disk

The weakest components shown in Figure 3-7 are the graphics and gaming graphics components. This is valuable information when you're considering upgrading a computer. The best performance gains will be achieved by upgrading the graphics card for this system.

A computer with a base score of 2.0 or less is not able to run Aero, though it does have enough processing power to do most computing tasks.

EXAM TIP To view your system's component ratings, check the Control Panel | System and Maintenance | Performance Information and Tools.

To access the Windows Experience Index, follow these steps:

- Launch the Control Panel. Click Start | Control Panel.
- Click System and Maintenance.
- Click Performance Information and Tools.

Enabling and Disabling Aero

It's possible to disable Aero even if your system meets the hardware and software requirements. This is sometimes done on systems that don't have enough RAM to provide a satisfying experience for users. For example, a system with 512MB of RAM that also meets the requirements for Aero will respond rather sluggishly. By disabling Aero, you will enable the system to respond quicker.

Additionally, some graphics programs don't play well with Aero (or Aero doesn't play with the graphics programs, depending on your perspective). For example, I needed to take screen shots for this book and the screen shot program simply doesn't work well with Aero turned on. After I turned Aero off, the screen shot program worked perfectly.

To disable Windows Vista Aero,

- Right-click the desktop and click Personalize.
- Select the Windows Color and Appearance link.
- Click the Open Classic Appearance Properties for More Color Options link at the bottom of the Windows Color and Appearance page.
- Select a different color scheme (not Windows Aero) and click Apply. Figure 3-8 shows this window.

To enable Aero, you can repeat the steps, but instead of selecting a non-Aero color scheme, you would select Windows Aero.

For systems that don't meet the requirements for Aero, Windows Vista Aero will not be available as a choice in the color scheme. This could be due to not enough graphics RAM, not having a WDDM-compatible driver, not having Pixel Shader 2.0, or not supporting DirectX 9.

If your system meets the requirements and you've selected the Aero color scheme but all of the Aero features are not being displayed, check the following settings:

- **Ensure the theme is set to Windows Vista** Right-click the desktop and select Personalize. On the Personalize Appearance and Sounds page, click Theme. Ensure the Windows Vista theme (or a saved theme that started as the Windows Vista theme) is selected.

Figure 3-8
Selecting a
non-Aero color
scheme to disable
Aero

- **Ensure performance options are set to enable Aero features**   From the Control Panel, click System and Maintenance | Performance Information and Tools, and select the Adjust Visual Effects task link in the left pane. Your display should look similar to Figure 3-9. By selecting Adjust for Best Appearance, you will ensure that the Aero features are enabled. By selecting Adjust for Best Performance, some features may be deselected, such as Show Thumbnails Instead of Icons, and Show Translucent Selection Rectangle.

 EXAM TIP   The two most common things to check are the Windows Aero color scheme and the Windows Vista Theme. If Aero features aren't enabled, check these two settings. Next, you should ensure that the performance settings are set to Adjust for Best Performance.

- **Ensure color is set to 32 bit**   Right-click the desktop and select Personalize. On the Personalize Appearance and Sounds page, click Display Settings. Check the Colors setting.

- **Ensure the refresh rate is set to greater than 10 Hz**   From the Display Settings page, click Advanced Settings. The refresh rate setting is available on the Monitor tab.

- **Ensure window frame transparency is turned on**   From the Personalize Appearance and Sounds page, select the Windows Color and Appearance page. The Enable Transparency check box should be checked.

Figure 3-9

Adjusting perfor-
mance options
for best appear-
ance to enable
Aero features

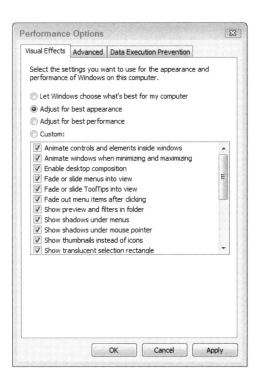

In Exercise 3.2, you will disable Windows Aero and see the effects, and then enable Windows Aero. Before starting this exercise, you should be logged on to a Windows Vista system.

Exercise 3.2: Disabling and Enabling Aero

1. Right-click the desktop and select Personalize.

2. With the Personalize Appearance and Sounds page open, verify that Windows Aero is enabled. Press the WINDOWS-TAB key. You should see the Windows Flip 3D effect; your windows should be shown in 3D in the middle of the screen.

3. On the Personalize Appearance and Sounds page, select Window Color and Appearance.

4. On the Window Color and Appearance page, click the Open Classic Appearance Properties for More Color Options link at the bottom of the page.

5. On the Appearance Settings dialog box that appears, select Windows Vista Basic (or some color scheme other than Windows Aero). Your display will look similar to Figure 3-10.

6. Click OK. After a moment, the screen will normalize with a non-Aero display.

Figure 3-10

Disabling Aero
by selecting the
Windows Vista
Basic theme

7. Click the Windows Color and Appearance link.

8. On the Appearance Settings page, select the Windows Aero color scheme. Click OK. After a moment the Aero settings will be returned. Press the WINDOWS-TAB key to verify Windows Flip 3D works.

9. Launch the Control Panel by selecting Start | Control Panel.

10. Click the System and Maintenance link in Control Panel. On the System and Maintenance page, click System.

11. On the Verify Basic Information About Your Computer page, select the Advanced System Settings task in the Tasks pane. If the User Account Control page appears, click Continue. Your display will look similar to Figure 3-11.

12. On the System Properties page, click Settings in the Performance area to access the Visual Effects.

13. On the Performance Options page, with the Visual Effects tab selected, select Adjust for Best Performance. Click Apply. Notice that the Aero affects are no longer displayed.

14. Change the setting to Adjust for Best Appearance. Notice that all the visual effects are selected. Click Apply. Click OK and close all windows.

Figure 3-11
Accessing Visual
Effects through
the Performance
Settings

Working with the Sidebar

The Windows Sidebar is a vertical bar displayed on your desktop that includes gadgets. Gadgets are mini-programs that provide a specific functionality, such as a clock or calendar.

Normally, the Sidebar launches automatically, but if it has been configured to not start automatically, you can access the properties to change the behavior.

Sidebar Properties

You can access the Sidebar properties by right-clicking the Sidebar and selecting Properties. If the Sidebar is not displayed, you can access the Sidebar by launching Control Panel | Appearance and Personalization and selecting Windows Sidebar Properties.

Figure 3-12 shows the Sidebar property page.

You have the following capabilities with the Sidebar properties page.

- You can set the Sidebar to automatically start when Windows starts, or not, by manipulating the check box for Start Sidebar When Windows Starts.

- You can set the Sidebar so that it's always visible by selecting the check box to have the Sidebar always on top.

- You can move the Sidebar to the right or left side of the screen.

- If you have multiple monitors connected, you can specify which monitor to display the Sidebar on.

Figure 3-12
Sidebar property
page

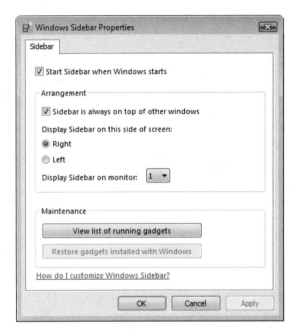

Be careful when moving the Sidebar from one side of the desktop to the other. If you have items on the desktop under the Sidebar, you won't be able to access them unless you either move the Sidebar to the other side or close the Sidebar. Also, if you have items on your desktop that are under the Sidebar and you've configured the properties so that the Sidebar is always on top, you need to either move the Sidebar to the other side or close it to access the items on the desktop.

Gadgets

For some people, gadgets are just eye candy they would just as soon do without. For others, a key gadget can be a reliable tool.

As an example of a reliable tool, I have a battery monitor gadget on my laptop. It helps me realize when my power is getting low and plan accordingly. Other people value the Calendar, the RSS headlines, and the Contacts list just as much.

The Gadget Gallery is shown in Figure 3-13. You can access the gallery by right-clicking within the Sidebar and selecting Add Gadgets.

The default Gadget Gallery includes

- **Calendar**   Displays a calendar as the current date, or in monthly format.

- **Clock**   An analog clock that has multiple display faces.

- **Contacts**   Allows you to list, search, and select Windows contacts and view e-mail address and phone number information.

- **CPU Meter**   Gives information on current CPU and memory utilization.

Figure 3-13 Gadget Gallery

- **Currency**   Converts from one currency to another.
- **Feed Headlines**   Displays headlines from RSS feeds, syndicated content, or Web feeds. You can change content by subscribing to different feeds in Internet Explorer.
- **Notes**   A small notepad you can use to write yourself notes and reminders.
- **Picture Puzzle**   A small game where pictures are scrambled and you move the pieces of the puzzle to put the picture back together.
- **Slide Show**   A picture slide show that displays different pictures on your computer.
- **Stocks**   Allows you to monitor stock prices.
- **Weather**   View the weather in the location of your choice.

Developers and hobbyists are constantly creating new gadgets. You can click the Get More Gadgets Online link within the Gadget Gallery to view, download, and install the available gadgets.

Gadget installer programs have a .gadget extension. If you download and save a gadget, you can double-click the .gadget file to install it. For example, if you download a clock gadget, it may be named clock.gadget. Double-click the clock.gadget file to install it.

Sidebar vs. SideShow

The Sidebar is different than SideShow. In Chapter 16, the SideShow will be covered in more depth.

In short, a SideShow-compatible device allows you to view information from your computer on a secondary display. The secondary display can be a part of your computer (such as a small display embedded in the lid of a laptop), or separate from your computer (such as a mobile phone).

If you have a SideShow-compatible device, you can configure it to display content by configuring the SideShow.

Optimizing Vista's Performance

When considering optimizing Vista's performance, one of the primary steps you can take is to ensure that you have enough hardware resources. The primary resource you need is memory—random access memory (RAM).

While the book has covered some of this material, here's a short summary of RAM requirements.

- 512MB is the minimum amount of RAM needed to run Vista, but more is better.

- 128MB of graphics RAM is needed to support Aero.

- If you have only 512MB of RAM but meet other hardware requirements for Aero, it still won't start by default but must be started manually.

- 1GB is the minimum recommended RAM. With 1GB RAM, Aero will start automatically (if other hardware requirements are met).

 TIP You won't see this on an exam, but many computer enthusiasts consider 4GB as optimal for running Windows Vista. Remember, though, even with 4GB installed, you'll only see about 3–3.5GB, since some address space is used for internal devices.

ReadyBoost

ReadyBoost is a new feature in Windows Vista. It allows you to plug in a USB drive and use the memory space on the USB drive as memory. This can provide increased performance in Windows Vista.

 EXAM TIP By adding a USB flash drive to your system and enabling ReadyBoost, you can increase Windows Vista's performance. Vista uses the additional memory on the USB drive as a fast cache. The recommended amount of ReadyBoost RAM is one to three times the amount of physical RAM.

It helps to understand how Vista uses ReadyBoost to appreciate the performance gains. It doesn't use it as actual memory but instead uses it a disk cache. However, the cache on a flash drive is much quicker than the cache on a hard disk.

Data that the operating system predicts it will use is placed in the cache. When it needs it, it pulls it out of the cache and doesn't need to locate in on the hard disk, which is much slower.

It's possible for you to pull out the USB drive at any time. If the operating system was using the USB as actual memory, Vista would crash in a heartbeat. However, it's only using it as cache. If you pull out the USB, the system recognizes it has to fetch the data from the hard disk. No harm, no foul.

Not all USB drives will work for ReadyBoost. If the USB drive is not quick enough, Vista recognizes that there won't be any performance gains and it won't be used. Additionally, the drive must have at least 256MB of free space. If it meets the performance requirements and there is enough free space, you are prompted to use it as a Ready-Boost drive. You can see this prompt in Figure 3-14.

Figure 3-14
Vista prompt
to speed up the
system with
ReadyBoost

If you click the Speed Up My System selection, you will be prompted to enable ReadyBoost on the drive. Figure 3-15 shows the ReadyBoost configuration page. For the best performance gains from ReadyBoost, it's recommended to use one to three times the amount of physical RAM. In other words, if you have 512MB of physical RAM, you'd reserve between 512MB and 1536MB (1.5GB) of ReadyBoost RAM.

Notice in the figure that the system recommends using 570MB of space on the USB disk for optimal performance. That's the maximum amount of space available on that USB device.

If you declined to enable ReadyBoost when you were first prompted, you can change your mind later. First, access Windows Explorer by pressing the WINDOWS-E keys. Then, select the USB drive and click Properties. You can then select the ReadyBoost tab as shown in Figure 3-15.

You can only configure ReadyBoost on a single USB disk. If you have one disk configured with ReadyBoost, and you access the ReadyBoost tab on a second disk, a message is displayed indicating "A cache already exists on G:. Please remove the cache from that device before creating a cache on this device."

Indexing

Windows Vista includes a search feature that allows you to search all the content on your system. You can improve search capabilities by turning the Windows Search index on.

Figure 3-15

Configuring
ReadyBoost
properties

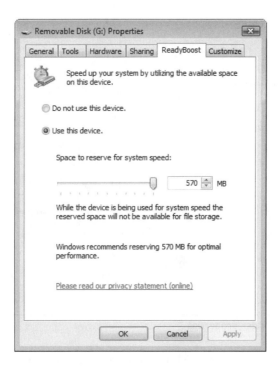

An index on Windows Vista works just like an index in any book. For example, if you were interested in finding information on Windows gadgets in this book, you could do it with two methods:

- Start at page 1 of the book, and look at every page until you reached the last page.
- Look at the index in the back of the book and identify specifically which pages have information on gadgets and turn to those pages.

Obviously, using the index would be much quicker. Of course, the index has to exist in order for you to use it.

Similarly, Windows has the ability to create an index, and then when you do a search for information on your system, instead of reading each and every file in every directory on every disk, Windows Search can just search the index.

You can pick and choose which locations you want to index and the specific file types you want to index.

Figure 3-16 shows the File Types page of the Advanced Options. You can access the Indexing Options page by clicking Control Panel | System and Maintenance | Indexing Options. Click Advanced to access the Index Settings and File Types.

File properties include items such as the name of the file, title, subject, tags (keywords that can be added to describe the file), comments, and more. Only file properties are indexed by default, but you can modify the index to index the file properties and the file contents.

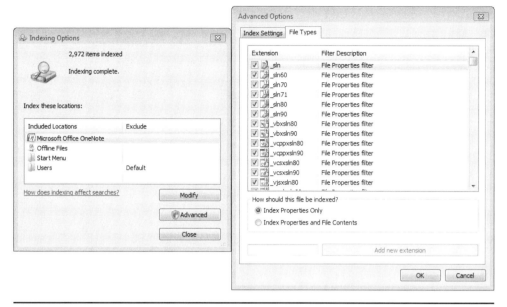

Figure 3-16   Index properties

You can also modify which locations are indexed by clicking Modify. For example, if you want to include or exclude certain locations, you can specify your preferences here.

 EXAM TIP   Indexing can be very resource-intensive, depending on how many locations are being indexed and what file types are included. If the index includes a location that is dynamic (where data is constantly changing), the computer may slow down with frequent disk access. You can either turn the index off or choose not to index dynamic locations.

Application Compatibility

One of the last issues you'll need to address for end users after an upgrade to Windows Vista is to ensure that their applications run in the new environment. You have three tools you can use to help with compatibility issues:

- Application Compatibility Toolkit
- Virtual PC
- Office Compatibility Pack

Application Compatibility Toolkit

The Application Compatibility Toolkit (ACT) is a suite of tools that an enterprise IT professional can use to determine if deployed applications are compatible with a new version of Windows before deploying it. ACT can also be used to determine how Windows security updates will impact their applications.

ACT is a free download from Microsoft. Once you download and install it, you'll have access to all of the ACT tools. At this writing, the current version is ACT 5.0.

The strength of ACT is its ability to analyze and identify potential compatibility issues on a large volume of computers in large enterprises. Once issues are identified, compatibility solutions can be created and deployed to systems in the form of a customized database. The sdbinst.exe command-line tool is used to register the database files so that the solutions are applied.

 EXAM TIP You should know that the Application Compatibility Toolkit can be used to identify application compatibility issues on a large number of systems. Solutions can be deployed to individual systems and the sdbinst command-line tool can be used to apply the solutions.

If you're upgrading one computer, or only a few computers, you can use tools such as the Windows Vista Upgrade Advisor. However, the Vista Upgrade Advisor runs on a single system at a time. It would just take too much time to run the Vista Upgrade Advisor on thousands of computers individually.

ACT can be used to identify issues with thousands of systems. You can use ACT to minimize the amount of administrative time needed to identify issues prior to an upgrade.

Compatibility information for ACT comes from a variety of sources, including

- Microsoft
- Independent software vendors (ISVs)
- The ACT community

You can synchronize your data to download new information, and you can upload your compatibility issues to Microsoft, which can be regularly synchronized using ACT tools.

ACT Tools

ACT includes the following tools:

- **Application Compatibility Manager (ACM)** The ACM is used to collect and analyze data on existing systems, providing reports on possible application issues. Data is stored in a SQL Server database.

- **Compatibility Administrator** This tool can be used to resolve specific compatibility issues, or to configure compatibility modes of operation (such as a specific operating system or service pack) to allow certain software to run.

- **Microsoft Compatibility Exchange** You use this to synchronize your compatibility data with data available from the other sources (Microsoft, ISVs, and the ACT community).

- **Setup Analysis Tool (SAT)** The SAT is used to detect potential issues related to the installation of 16-bit components, the Graphical Identification and Authentication DLLs, and the modification of files or Registry keys protected by Windows Resource Protection in Vista.

- **Standard User Analyzer (SUA)**   The SUA is used to test applications and detect issues related to the User Account Control in Vista.

- **Internet Explorer Test Tool**   This tool collects Web-based issues related to Internet Explorer 7 and uploads the data to the ACT Log Processing Service.

- **Sdbinst.exe**   A command-line tool that is used to register customized databases on end-user computers. The customized database contains the compatibility solution (such as a fix, a compatibility mode, or an AppHelp message) that will allow an application to run.

Application Solutions

You can use the Compatibility Administrator to create application solutions. Solutions can be

- Compatibility fixes that bits of code use to ensure the application will run in Vista

- Compatibility modes of operation (such as Windows 98/Me or Windows XP SP2)

- AppHelp messages used to provide informative messages to users

Once created, the ACT solutions come in the form of customized database files with an .sdb extension.

The core database within the Compatibility Administrator includes many different applications that already have available solutions. It also includes a full range of compatibility fixes and compatibility modes that can be applied to any solution you create.

To create a solution, you'd launch the Compatibility Administrator. From there, you'd right-click the database and select Create New, and then select an Application Fix, an AppHelp message, or a Compatibility Mode.

If you create an Application Fix, you'll be presented with the following screens:

Program Information   Figure 3-17 shows the basic information you need to enter to identify the program you want to fix. You'd enter the name of the application, the vendor, and the file location where it is located.

Compatibility Modes   Figure 3-18 shows the Compatibility Modes selections you can use. Notice you can choose specific Operating System modes (including service packs) or specific selections such as limited color, limited resolution, disabling themes, and much more.

Compatibility Fixes   Figure 3-19 shows the Compatibility Fixes applied based on the Compatibility Mode selected. Only the fixes applied are being shown, but you can select Show All to view and select any of the more than 300 individual fixes that can be applied.

Matching Information   You can specify several different parameters to ensure you are applying the fix to the right application file as shown in Figure 3-20. For example, if a different version of an application is released with the same name, you can specify parameters such as Size and Checksum to ensure only the file you specify is identified.

Figure 3-17
Entering Program
Information for
the Application Fix

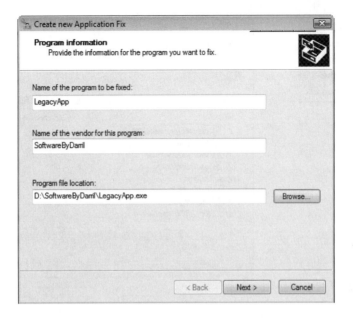

NOTE The checksum of a file is calculated based on a specific algorithm. The
checksum method is commonly used to determine if anything is different in
a file. As an example, a checksum is commonly used when downloading files.
The checksum is calculated at the source and is recalculated after the file is
downloaded. If the source and destination checksums are different, you know the file
is different (perhaps because a bit or two has been lost in the download). Similarly, the
checksum can be used to ensure the application fix is applied to the correct file.

Figure 3-18
Configuring Com-
patibility Modes in
the Application Fix

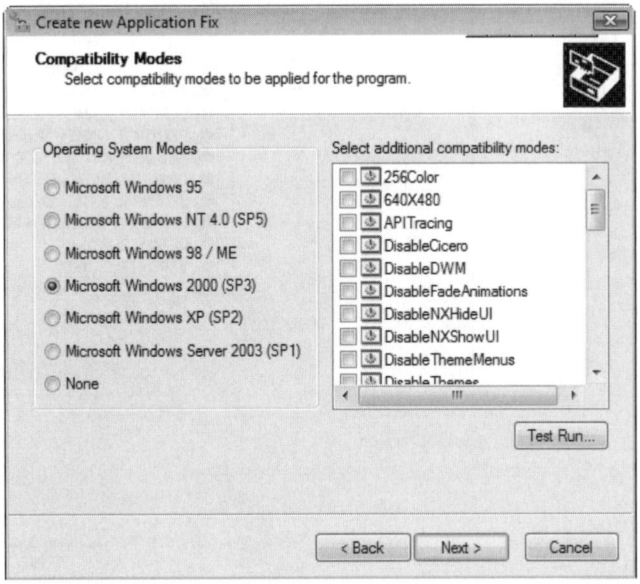

Figure 3-19
Configuring
Compatibility
Fixes in the
Application Fix

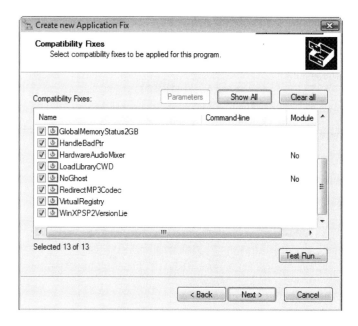

Figure 3-20
Configuring
Matching Infor-
mation for the
Application Fix

Figure 3-21 shows the Compatibility Administrator open with a compatibility fix that was created for an application named LegacyApp. Notice that the compatibility mode of Windows XP SP2 was selected and the file was further identified using specific attributes of Size, Checksum, Product_Version, and PE_Checksum.

Applying Solutions with sdbinst

After using ACT to identify issues and creating solutions, you need to apply these solutions to the computers running Windows Vista.

The solution is in the form of a customized database file. You can either make the database file available on a share on a centralized server, or copy it to each individual computer. Once the customized database file is available to the systems, you need to register the database on the systems using the sdbinst command-line tool.

The customized database files can be deployed to end-user computers using a variety of methods, including

- Group Policy
- Logon scripts
- File copy operations

Once the database files are deployed, you can then run the sdbinst command-line tool. The easiest way to run sdbinst on multiple systems is to use a scripting technique. Since sdbinst is a command-line tool, you'd use a simple batch file (.bat) to store the required commands and then run the batch file on end-user computers.

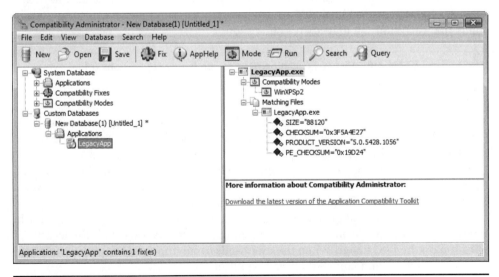

Figure 3-21   Compatibility Administrator open with a new application fix

NOTE   You can create a batch file using Notepad. As a simple exercise, create a Notepad document and enter Dir as the only text. Save the file with the name of myBat.bat in the root of C:\. Notice the extension has .bat instead of .txt. Launch the command line (click Start and enter **cmd** in the Start Search menu). Change the directory to the root of C:\ (**cd**). Run your batch file by entering mybat. bat. You'll see the dir command run and complete.

Depending on whether you want the batch file script to run on specific user systems or for specific computers, you can choose to run the scripts in response to different events. For example, if you want the scripts to be associated with a user you would use the user logon or logoff events.

Group Policy allows you to run scripts at the following events:

- User logon
- User logoff
- Computer startup
- Computer shutdown

Virtual PC

Sometimes the simple solution is the best approach. If an application isn't compatible in Windows Vista, you can simply run it in a different operating system. Of course, you may not want to purchase another computer to do so.

Virtual PC (VPC) is a free download from Microsoft that has been available for many years. It's frequently used in classroom environments to simulate several computers in a network, each running in its own VPC session.

EXAM TIP   Virtual PC can be used to run legacy applications (older applications) that don't run in Vista.

A VPC session runs as an application within the host operating system. Consider Figure 3-22. Vista is the host. It is running several applications (Internet Explorer, Windows Mail, and VPC).

You can think of VPC as its own sandbox. For an application that won't play well with others, you put it alone it its own sandbox. The application can do whatever it wants there, but won't affect anything else running on the system.

If you have a legacy application that won't run in Windows Vista but will run in Windows XP, you can create a VPC image running Windows XP. Install the legacy application on the VPC image. When the user needs to run the legacy application, he can run the VPC image and launch the legacy application.

Figure 3-22
VPC running as
an application on
Vista

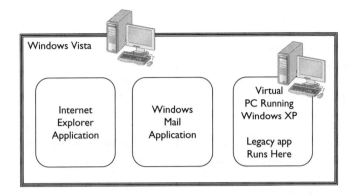

Windows Vista

Internet
Explorer
Application

Windows
Mail
Application

Virtual
PC Running
Windows XP

Legacy app
Runs Here

Office Compatibility Pack

The Office Compatibility Pack is a free download that will allow users to open Office 2007 documents in Office 2003 or Office XP applications.

With the release of Office 2007, Microsoft has switched to a different file format known as Open XML. The file extension of a file saved in the Open XML format has an *x* in the file extension.

For example, a Word document named Project saved in previous versions of Word would be saved as Project.doc. However, if the file were saved in Word 2007, it would be saved as Project.docx.

However, as with any change, there are some growing pains. If you try to open a Office 2007 Word document in Word XP (Office 2002) or Office 2003, it won't work. At least it won't work until you install the compatibility pack.

After you install the compatibility pack, users running Office XP or Office 2003 will be able to open, edit, save, and create files using the Open XML Formats.

Chapter Review

In this chapter you learned about several different steps you can take to configure Windows Vista after the installation.

The Device Manager is the primary tool you'll use to view the status of devices. Icons (such as a down arrow, or a yellow circle with an exclamation mark or question mark) indicate an issue with the device. You can use the Device Manager to enable/disable devices, and install and roll back drivers.

Aero is a graphical feature that gives Vista its unique look and feel. You learned about the requirements for Aero, and how to enable and disable it.

You learned about the Sidebar and gadgets and how to access shortcuts on the desktop if they are trapped under the Sidebar.

To increase performance on a system, you can add a USB flash drive and enable ReadyBoost. Vista will use the USB drive for cache. It's recommended to create Ready-Boost cache sizes between one and three times the size of your physical RAM.

Indexing can be used to increase the speed of searches but can be very resource intensive. You learned how to limit the locations that are indexed if the indexing feature is causing performance problems.

The Application Compatibility Toolkit (ACT) includes several tools that can be used to identify compatibility issues with programs, create solutions for the issues, and deploy the solutions to computers with the sbdinst command-line tool.

You learned how the Office Compatibility Pack can be deployed to systems running older Office products (such as Office 2000 or Office XP) so that they can work with the same file types as Office 2007. For an application that you just can't get to run within Windows Vista, you can run it within its own sandbox using Virtual PC.

Additional Study

Self Study Exercises
Use these additional exercises to challenge yourself.

- Find a driver you can manually update for your system from a manufacturer's Web site. Update the driver and roll it back.

- Download a gadget, save it to your disk, and install it.

- Boost your system's performance by adding a USB flash drive and enabling ReadyBoost.

- Download and install the Application Compatibility Toolkit. Configure the Application Compatibility Manager. Create a fix using the Compatibility Administrator.

- Download and install VPC on your system. Create an image of an operating system and install an application on this image.

Summary of What You Need to Know

70-620
When preparing for the 70-620 exam, pay particular attention to the following topics covered in this chapter:

- **Device Manager**   You should understand the meaning of different icons displayed in Device Manager. You should also know how to use the Device Manager to enable or disable a device.

- **Windows Error Reporting**   Know the purpose and how to configure WER for different users.

- **Aero**   Make sure you know the requirements for Aero, and how to enable and disable it.

- **ReadyBoost**   You should understand the basic features and purpose of ReadyBoost.

- **Sidebar**   Understand how the Sidebar works and how to access shortcuts trapped under it.

70-622

When preparing for the 70-622 exam, pay particular attention to the following topics covered in this chapter:

- **Device Manager**   You should understand the driver store and how to manually add drivers using Device Manager.
- **Aero**   Make sure you know the specific hardware and software requirements for Aero.
- **Application Compatibility**   Make sure you understand what can be done with ACT and how solutions can be deployed.
- **Office Compatibility Pack**   You should understand the purpose of the Office Compatibility Pack and where it should be installed.
- **Virtual PC**   You should know how you can use VPC to deploy applications onto a Vista system that are not compatible with Vista.

70-623

When preparing for the 70-623 exam, pay particular attention to the following topics covered in this chapter:

- **Device Manager**   You should understand the meaning of different icons displayed in the Device Manager. You should also understand how to upgrade drivers and how to roll back drivers.
- **Aero**   Make sure you know the specific hardware and software requirements for Aero, when it's enabled by default, and when it needs to be manually enabled.
- **ReadyBoost**   You should understand ReadyBoost and the specifics of how it works and how it should be configured.
- **Sidebar and gadgets**   You should be familiar with the default gadgets and how they can be configured, and how to add additional gadgets.

Questions

70-620

1. You are trying to use a modem installed on your computer, but it is not responding. You launch Device Manager and notice the device has a down arrow. What should you do?

   A. Reload the driver.

   B. Roll back the driver.

   C. Reinstall the device.

   D. Enable the device.

2. You've installed Windows Vista in an isolated test network without access to the Internet. When you log on, Vista displays a message indicating an unknown device is found and prompts you to install it. You don't want to install the

driver for this device right now, but you also don't want to see the message again. What should you do?

   A. Disable the device.

   B. Uninstall the device.

   C. Connect to Windows Update to install the driver.

   D. Download the driver and install it.

3. After upgrading a computer's graphics card, the driver locks up and you are prompted to report the error to Microsoft. You want to ensure that failure reports are automatically sent without prompting you or anyone else that uses your computer. What should you do?

   A. Turn on automatic updates.

   B. Enable automatic reporting in Device Manager.

   C. When you are prompted to send the report, check the box to automatically send the reports.

   D. In the Problem Reports and Solutions page, enable the Windows Problem Reporting to automatically send the reports and check for solutions.

4. You are helping a friend with her Windows Vista computer. She doesn't have Windows Aero enabled, but you've verified that her hardware meets the requirements. What should you do to enable Windows Aero? (Choose all that apply.)

   A. Download the Aero update from Microsoft's Update site.

   B. Add additional graphics RAM.

   C. Select the Windows Vista theme.

   D. Select the Windows Aero color scheme.

5. You are working on a computer that is running Windows Vista. You notice that the Thumbnails Windows Aero feature isn't being displayed on the taskbar, but other Windows Aero features such as Windows Flip 3D are working. You want to enable all of the Windows Aero features. What should you do?

   A. Select the Windows Vista theme.

   B. Select the Windows Aero color scheme.

   C. Set visual effects to Adjust for Best Appearance.

   D. Set visual effects to Adjust for Best Performance.

6. Joe is using a laptop computer with 512MB of RAM in two 256MB memory slots. He'd like to improve the speed of his memory but has only two memory slots and can't afford to replace the existing memory. What should he do?

   A. Connect a USB drive to his computer and set the computer to be optimized for background services.

   B. Connect a USB drive to his computer and enable Windows Aero.

    C. Connect a USB drive to his computer and enable the USBMemory feature.

    D. Connect a USB drive to his computer and enable the ReadyBoost feature.

70-622

1. You have purchased biometric USB drives for several users. However, each time a user plugs the USB drive into a different Windows Vista system, it's not recognized until an administrator logs on to the machine and installs the correct drivers for the USB. What can you do to streamline this process?

    A. Grant all users of the biometric USB drives administrator rights.

    B. Add the drivers for the USB drives to the driver store.

    C. Use Group Policy to enable the use of USB drives.

    D. Have the users access the manufacturer Web site and install the USB drive.

2. As a desktop support technician in your company, you have upgraded several computers from Windows XP Professional to Windows Vista Business Edition. All of the computers meet the hardware requirements for Windows Vista. However, the computers don't have the Windows Aero theme available. You suspect the problem is a driver issue. What driver should you verify is installed in order to support the Windows Aero theme?

    A. A Pixel Shader 2.0 driver

    B. A Windows Display Driver Model–compatible graphics driver

    C. A Windows Update driver

    D. None. Aero is not available in the Business Edition

3. Management wants to upgrade all Windows XP systems to Windows Vista. Several users in the sales department run a line of business application. Testing shows the application won't work in Windows Vista. A new version is being developed but won't be available for several months. What should you do?

    A. Delay the upgrade to Windows Vista.

    B. Give users in the sales department two computers: one to run the legacy application and one to run Windows Vista.

    C. Run the legacy application in Virtual PC.

    D. Turn off Aero on the Vista machines until the application is upgraded.

4. Your company has upgraded all the computers running Windows XP to Windows Vista. You are in the middle of migrating Office XP to Office 2007. However, several of the users are complaining that files created in Office 2007 are unreadable by users running Office XP. The migration won't be complete for another two months, but you need a way to ensure compatibility now. What should you do?

    A. Install the Application Compatibility Toolkit for all users running Office 2007.

    B. Install the Application Compatibility Toolkit for all users running Office XP.

    C. Install the Office Compatibility Pack for all users running Office 2007.

    D. Install the Office Compatibility Pack for all users running Office XP.

5. An enterprise IT developer has created a customized database from the Application Compatibility Toolkit (ACT) that will allow a line of business application to run on Windows Vista. They have made the database available on a network share and ask you to deploy it to about 300 computers in the enterprise. What should you do?

   A. Configure a logon script and use it to run the sdbinst command-line tool.

   B. Configure a logon script and use it to install the Office Compatibility Pack.

   C. Configure a logon script and use it to run the ACTDeploy command-line tool.

   D. For each of the computers, run sdbinst from the command line.

6. You have created a customized database from the Application Compatibility Toolkit (ACT) that will allow a specific application to run on Windows Vista using Windows XP compatibility mode. The application has a newer version (with the same program name) that is fully compatible with Windows Vista but hasn't been purchased for all users yet. Users running the new version state that it is also running in Windows XP compatibility mode. You want the new version to run in Windows Vista normally. What should you do?

   A. Recreate the customized database but specify the Name attribute.

   B. Recreate the customized database but specify the Company_Name attribute.

   C. Recreate the customized database but specify the Checksum attribute.

   D. Recreate the customized database but specify the Product_Name attribute.

70-623

1. You are troubleshooting a customer's computer that has Windows Vista installed. The computer has 512MB of RAM and 128MB of graphics RAM. The customer states that Windows Flip 3D doesn't work, and the windows borders are not transparent. You try to change the color scheme to Windows Vista Aero, but the choice isn't available. What should you do?

   A. Upgrade the Graphics RAM to at least 256MB.

   B. Upgrade the RAM to at least 1GB.

   C. Install a video card that supports 3D sound.

   D. Install a video card that supports WDDM.

2. You are troubleshooting a system that seems to have a problem with the video. You download a new driver for the graphics card from the Internet and install it. However, after you reboot the system and log on, the system begins to randomly crash. What should you do?

   A. Use Last Known Good to roll back the driver.

   B. Use ReadyBoost to roll back the driver.

   C. Use the Device Manager to roll back the driver for the graphics card.

   D. Use the Device Manager to roll back the driver for the monitor.

3. A user complains that she is unable to use a modem on her system. You look in the Device Manager and notice that the modem is not listed, but one device is listed as Unknown Device with a yellow circle and a black exclamation mark What should you do?

   A. Enable the device.

   B. Update the driver.

   C. Remove the modem and reinstall it.

   D. Enable WDDM.

4. A user has upgraded a computer from Windows XP to Windows Vista. After the upgrade, the graphics display is very poor. What should the user do to improve the graphics quality?

   A. Roll back the upgrade.

   B. Run the Windows Vista Upgrade Advisor.

   C. Use the Device Manager to scan for hardware changes.

   D. Go to the video card manufacturer's Web site and download Vista drivers.

5. Sally is running a Vista computer with 512MB of RAM. She's been trying to run a graphics-intensive program but keeps having performance problems. What could Sally do to improve the performance of her computer?

   A. Add a USB flash drive. Enable ReadyBoost and reserve 256MB of space.

   B. Add a USB flash drive. Enable ReadyBoost and reserve 1.5GB of space.

   C. Add two USB flash drive and reserve 512MB of space on each disk.

   D. Add an additional hard drive with at least 1.5GB of free space.

6. Maria is running a Vista computer with 512MB of RAM and 128MB of RAM on her video card. She wants to run Aero, but it's not running when she boots her system. What is the problem?

   A. She needs to add additional graphics RAM to enable Aero.

   B. She needs to add additional physical RAM to enable Aero.

   C. She needs to manually enable Aero.

   D. She needs to disable the Sidebar to enable Aero.

7. A user is running Windows Vista, which she uses at home for a home-based business. She frequently downloads a large volume of files from an FTP site to her computer. After the download her computer slows down significantly and her hard drive appears very busy. What should she do?

   A. Change the locations specified for indexing.

   B. Turn off Aero.

   C. Increase her physical RAM.

   D. Add a USB flash disk and enable ReadyBoost.

Answers

70-620

1. **D.** A down-arrow icon indicates the device is disabled. You should right-click the device and enable it. If the device had a yellow circle with a question mark or some other icon, the problem might have been with the driver. However, the down arrow indicates it is disabled. Since the device appears to be installed, it wouldn't need to be reinstalled.

2. **A.** If you disable the device, this message will no longer appear when you log on. You can also select a check box on the message screen that says "Don't Show This Message Again for This Device." If you uninstall the device, it will be found again on the next reboot. The scenario says you don't want to install the driver, so you shouldn't.

3. **D.** You can enable automatic reporting and check for solutions in the Problem Reports and Solutions page accessible from the System properties page. Automatic updates don't allow clients to send error reports. Automatic reporting can't be enabled in the Device Manager or via the prompt to send a single report.

4. **C, D.** Two common settings to check if Aero is not working are the theme and the color scheme. The theme should be set to Windows Vista (or a theme based off of the Windows Vista theme). The color scheme should be set to Windows Aero. Aero is included in Windows Vista, so an update is not required. 128MB of RAM is a recommended minimum, but the question states that the hardware meets the minimum requirements.

5. **C.** Since Windows Flip 3D is working, Aero is enabled. To enable the other features, you should select Adjust for Best Appearance in the Visual Effects dialog box accessible from System Properties. If you select Adjust for Best Performance, all of the Aero features will be disabled. The Windows Vista theme and color scheme must already be set to Windows Aero (or a Windows Aero–based theme), since Windows Flip 3D is working.

6. **D.** The ReadyBoost feature allows you to enhance performance of Windows Vista by adding a USB flash drive to your system; the USB drive is used as additional memory. Setting the computer to be optimized for background services (instead of applications) will make applications run slower. Enabling Windows Aero (if it isn't enabled) will make it run slower and isn't associated with a USB drive. There is no such thing as a USBMemory feature.

70-622

1. **B.** By adding the drivers to the driver store, Plug and Play will automatically find the drivers and install them. If Plug and Play works, users do not need to be logged in as administrators. Following the principle of least privilege, which states that users should be granted only those privileges necessary to carry out their specific job functions and nothing more, you would not want to

grant users administrative rights. The problem is not with all USB drives, just these special biometric drives. Users cannot install devices unless they have administrative rights.

2. **B.** A Windows Display Driver Model (WDDM) driver is one of the requirements to support Windows Aero. Pixel Shader 2.0 is also required, but this is a hardware enhancement to the graphics card, not a software driver. Windows Update is a software technology that allows updates to be downloaded to clients from the Windows Update site; it doesn't require a device driver. Aero is available in the Business Edition.

3. **C.** Virtual PC can be used to run legacy applications on Windows Vista. There is no need to delay the upgrade, nor to give users two computers. Nothing indicates that Aero is what is causing the application not to run.

4. **D.** If you install the Office Compatibility Pack on users running Office XP, they will be able to open, edit, save, and create files compatible with Office 2007. Office 2007 is automatically backward compatible to Office XP. The Application Compatibility Toolkit is a suite of tools used to determine if software is compatible before rolling out an upgrade to Windows Vista.

5. **A.** Customized databases created with ACT must be registered on end-user computers with the sbdinst command-line tool. The easiest way to do this is by running a script with group policy. The Office Compatibility Pack is used to allow Office 2003 or Office XP to manipulate files compatible with Office 2007. Running sbdinst on each of the computers would work, but it would take way too long.

6. **C.** The Checksum attribute can verify the application file is the one you want run in the compatibility mode. While the application names are the same, the two different application files would have two different checksums. It wouldn't be as reliable to specify the Name, Company_Name, or Product_Name attributes, since they could also be the same. While the Size attribute isn't listed in the question or answers, it may also be a good choice as an attribute to identify the correct file, since it's unlikely the older application file and the newer application file would have the same sizes.

70-623

1. **D.** Windows Aero needs a graphics card that supports the Windows Display Driver Model (WDDM), Pixel Shader 2.0, and at least 128MB of RAM. If the requirements aren't met, the Windows Aero color scheme won't be available as a choice. The system meets the minimum amount of system RAM and graphics RAM to support Aero, so additional RAM isn't needed. Aero doesn't need sound, and a video card typically wouldn't include sound anyway.

2. **C.** You should use the Device Manager to roll back the driver for the graphics card. Last Known Good can only be used if you haven't logged in yet. ReadyBoost is used to speed up the computer with a USB drive but can't roll

back drivers. Since you installed a new driver for the graphics card, you need to roll back the driver for it, not the monitor.

3. **B.** A black exclamation mark (or a black question mark) in a yellow circle indicates a problem with the driver. Updating the driver is a logical step. If the device had a down arrow, it would be disabled and need to be enabled, but the down arrow icon isn't indicated. Removing and reinstalling the modem won't change the driver. The Windows Display Driver Model (WDDM) is needed for Aero, but it wouldn't help this modem.

4. **D.** If drivers aren't installed automatically via Plug and Play, you'll need to locate the appropriate drivers, and the best place to find them is the manufacturer's Web site. It's not possible to roll back an upgrade from Windows Vista back to Windows XP. The Windows Vista Upgrade Advisor should be run before the upgrade, not after. The Device Manager scans for hardware changes at each boot. Unless you are adding hot-swappable hardware or have recently made a change in the Device Manager, there is really no need to use the Device Manager to scan for hardware changes.

5. **B.** By adding a USB drive, enabling ReadyBoost, and reserving 1.5GB of space for ReadyBoost, she will get the best performance gains. The recommended ReadyBoost cache size is between one and three times the amount of physical RAM. Since she has 512MB, she should set the size between 512MB and 1.5GB. 256MB wouldn't provide significant performance gains. You can't use two USB drives for ReadyBoost. An additional hard drive does not provide any gains for ReadyBoost.

6. **C.** On systems that have 512MB of RAM, Aero is not enabled automatically, but it can be enabled manually. The minimum graphics RAM to support Aero is 128MB and the minimum physical RAM to support Aero is 512MB. Both minimums are met. The Sidebar does not need to be disabled to enable Aero.

7. **A.** The problem only appears after adding files. The system identifies these files as being added to the index location and immediately begins indexing them (which can be very resource intensive). Changing the locations to index to exclude where the downloaded files are stored will resolve the problem. Since the problem is related to the addition of the files on the system, there is no indication of a problem with Aero or not enough RAM.

Configuring Disks

In this chapter, you will learn about:
- File systems
- Hard disk basics
- Shrinking, extending, and defragmenting volumes
- BitLocker Drive Encryption

In this chapter you'll learn about the different file systems that Windows Vista supports, with a focus on NTFS and its features. New to Windows Vista is the ability to shrink and extend volumes from within the operating system (something previously only available with third-party tools).

You'll also learn about BitLocker Drive Encryption. BitLocker is a significant security feature available with some Vista editions. You can use BitLocker to lock entire volumes on Windows Vista to prevent unauthorized access in the event of a theft or loss of your systems.

 EXAM TIP Objectives for the 70-620, 70-622, and 70-623 exams are included in this chapter.

File Systems

Any operating system has the ability to read and write data on to files. Different operating systems can use different file systems, and different file systems have different capabilities. The three file systems supported in Windows Vista are

- FAT
- FAT32
- NTFS

NTFS is the most robust file system and provides significant security features. It is recommended to use NTFS whenever possible.

FAT and FAT32

The File Allocation Table (FAT, also called FAT16) and the File Allocation Table 32 (FAT32) file systems are supported for backward compatibility and for accessing USB drives.

Almost all USB drives (unpowered flash drives and portable USB hard disks) are formatted as FAT or FAT32. By contrast, almost all Vista system disks are formatted as NTFS.

Take a look at Figure 4-1. This shows the properties of a folder on a FAT32 disk (named NotNTFS) and a folder on a NTFS disk (named NTFS folder). You can always tell a NTFS disk by the Security tab, which can be used to assign permissions. A FAT or FAT32 disk does not have a Security tab or a Previous Versions tab.

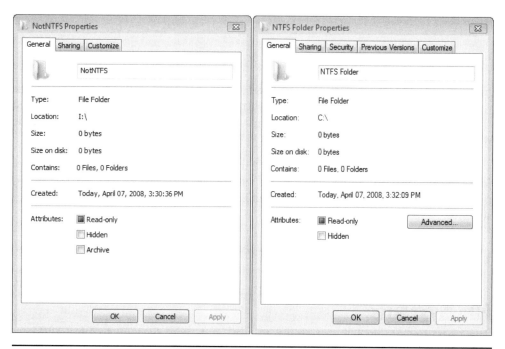

Figure 4-1   FAT32 and NTFS folders

Table 4-1 shows some of the characteristics of FAT and FAT32 disks.

Characteristic	FAT	FAT32
Vista maximum partition size	4GB	32GB (TB)
File size	Max 4GB	Max 4GB
Files per disk	Max 65,536	Max over 4 million

Table 4-1   Characteristics of FAT and FAT32 Disks

Note that while FAT32 supports disks as large as 2TB, the largest partition you can create in Windows Vista is 32GB in size.

 TIP Note the maximum file size allowed on FAT and FAT32 disks is 4GB. Larger files can be stored, but you'll have trouble copying them. As an example, I copied a Virtual PC image onto a portable USB disk that was over 4GB. When I tried to copy it off, I kept getting errors. Once I converted the disk to NTFS, things worked fine.

NTFS

NTFS is an acronym for New Technology File System, though since NTFS was introduced by Microsoft in 1993, it seems a far stretch to still call it New Technology. Still, NTFS has undergone some significant changes over the years. The current version of NTFS is version 5.

Unlike FAT and FAT32, NTFS doesn't have many limitations. Table 4-2 shows the characteristics of NTFS. A maximum partition size of 18EB is theoretical, since current technologies can't support partitions that large.

Table 4-2 Characteristics of NTFS Disks	Characteristic	NTFS
	Maximum partition size	About 18 Exabytes (EB)
	File size	About 16TB
	Files per disk	About 4 billion

 NOTE The terms partition and volume are used interchangeably in much of the documentation for Windows Vista. A single physical disk could be divided into multiple partitions. Each of these partitions would be identified by a drive letter (such as C:, D:, E:, and so on). In past versions of Windows, a partition indicated the disk type was a basic disk, and a volume indicated the disk type was a dynamic disk. However, the lines between partition and volume are blurred. Even within Vista's Help, they present the two terms as synonymous.

Additionally, NTFS brings many more features. The primary feature you have with NTFS is the ability to restrict access with permissions.

Permissions

Permissions can be assigned to any file or folder to control who can access a file or folder, and what they can do once they access it. For example, you may want to allow certain users to be able to read data, but you don't want them to modify the data. By granting read permission and not granting write permission, you can achieve your goals.

Figure 4-2 shows the Security tab of a folder named Project. If a file or folder has a Security tab, you know the drive it is on is NTFS. In the figure, you can see that the ProjectManagers group has been assigned full control permission.

Figure 4-2
NTFS permis-
sions shown on
the Security tab
of a folder's prop-
erty dialog box

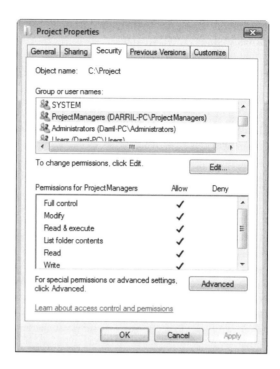

Notice that permissions can be allowed or denied. If a permission is denied, deny takes precedence and the user or group will not have that permission. Similarly, if a user or group is not granted any permission, they will not have access.

You can assign the following permissions to NTFS files and folders:

- **Read**   Read permission grants users the ability to read a file. That's the obvious point. The subtle permission is the ability to read attributes (such as read-only, and hidden), read advanced attributes (such as archiving, indexing, compression, and encryption attributes), and read the permissions assigned to the file.

- **Read & Execute**   The read & execute permission includes the read permission, but also the ability to run executable files.

- **List Folder Contents**   The list folder contents permission allows a user to view the contents of a folder.

- **Write**   Write permission allows a user to make changes to files, create new files, and create new folders within a folder. Additionally, a user is able to make changes to attributes and extended attributes.

- **Modify**   Modify is similar to write permission with a significant difference: A user with the modify permission can delete a file or folder, but users with write permissions cannot delete files or folders.

- **Full Control**   Full control includes all permissions. One significant difference between modify and full control is that full control allows a user to change the permissions, but modify does not.

EXAM TIP In order for a user to change permissions on any file or folder, the user must have full control permissions or be a member of a group (such as the administrators group) that has full control permission.

Shadow Copy and Previous Versions

Shadow Copy is a feature automatically enabled in some Windows Vista Editions. It will automatically create point-in-time backups of files on your hard disk. If you have more than one hard disk, you will need to manually configure the other disks. If you accidentally delete or modify a file or folder, you can restore a previous version of the file or folder.

The Vista editions that support Shadow Copy and Previous Versions are

- Vista Ultimate
- Vista Business
- Vista Enterprise

Previous Versions are created when restore points are created. These are automatically created daily and before significant system events such as installing an application or modifying a device driver.

Figure 4-3 shows the settings for restore points on a system. You can access this dialog box by launching Control Panel | System and Maintenance | System, selecting Advanced System Settings, and selecting the System Protection tab.

Figure 4-3

Viewing system restore points

While the system wasn't configured to create restore points on the D: drive originally, I selected the check box next to D: and clicked the Create button.

To restore any previous version of a file, right-click the file and select Restore Previous Versions. You will see a display similar to Figure 4-4.

Figure 4-4

Accessing the Previous Versions tab

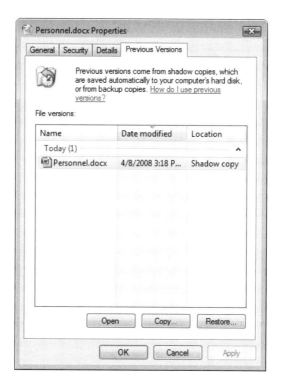

Notice that you have the following choices in the Previous Versions tab:

- **Open**   If you select a previous version and click Open, you will open the file in the appropriate application. If this is the file you want to restore, you can use Save As to restore it.

- **Copy**   By selecting the file and clicking Copy, you can copy the file to a different location.

- **Restore**   If you select the file and click Restore, the previous version of the file will overwrite the current version. Your file will be restored.

The only really tricky thing about Previous Versions is when you need to restore a deleted file. Since the file is deleted, you can't right-click it to access the property dialog box.

However, you can right-click the folder that held the file and restore the file from the previous version of the folder.

Consider this scenario. You have a folder named Data with three documents: Project.docx, Budget.xlsx, and Personnel.docx. You accidentally delete the Personnel document, but before you realize your error, you make changes to the Project and Budget documents. What are your choices?

You can't access the Previous Versions tab of the original file, since it's deleted. If you restore the entire Data folder, you will lose all the changes you made to the Project and Budget documents.

However, you can instead select the previous version of the folder and copy the entire folder to a different location. From here, you can access the Personnel document and copy it into the original folder.

 EXAM TIP You can use Previous Versions to restore files that have been modified or deleted. To restore deleted files without affecting any other files in the original folder, you should copy a previous version of the folder (which will hold all original files) and then copy the deleted file to the original location.

In Exercise 4.1, you will use previous versions to restore a modified file, and then restore a deleted file.

Exercise 4.1: Using Previous Versions

1. Launch Windows Explorer by pressing WINDOWS + E.

2. Browse to the root of C:. Right-click over C: and select New Folder.

3. Rename the folder **Exercise41**.

4. Right-click within the folder and select New Text Document. Rename the text document to **mcitpsuccess.txt**.

5. Repeat the preceding step to create two new documents named **success2.txt** and **success3.txt**.

6. Open the document and type in the text **I will become a MCITP**. Press CTRL-S to save the document. Close the document, but leave Windows Explorer open.

7. Click Control Panel | System and Maintenance | System | Advanced System Properties. If the User Account Control appears, click Continue.

8. On the System Properties dialog box, select the System Protection tab. Ensure that the check box next to the C: drive is selected.

9. Click the Create button to create a restore point. (While restore points will be created automatically on a daily basis, you probably don't want to come back after a day to finish this lab. This step simulates a day passing.)

10. On the Create a Restore Point dialog box, enter Exercise 4.1 as the description. Click Create. After a moment, a dialog box will appear indicating the restore point was created successfully. Click OK.

11. Return to Windows Explorer and open up the mcitpsuccess.txt file you created earlier. Delete all the text and press CTRL-S to save the file. Close the file.

12. Right-click the mcitpsuccess.txt file and select Restore Previous Versions.

13. Select the file and click Open. Notice the original text appears in the file. You could select Save As to save it with a different name. Close the file, but don't save it.

14. In the Previous Versions tab, select the file and click Copy. Notice you are prompted to save the file in the location of your choice. Click Cancel.

15. Select the file and click Restore. On the dialog box that appears asking if you're sure, click Restore. On the dialog box indicating success, click OK.

16. Notice that the Previous Versions tab no longer shows a previous version that can be restored. Click OK.

17. Open the mcitpsuccess.txt file and note that the text is restored. Close the file.

18. Open the success.txt file and type in **I will pass these exams**. Press CTRL-S to save the file. Close it. Open the success2.txt file and type in **Wooo Hoo!** Press CTRL-S to save the file. Close it.

19. Right-click the mcitpsuccess.txt file and select Delete. On the dialog box asking if you're sure, click Yes. Notice that the file is gone.

20. Right-click the Exercise41 folder and select Restore Previous Versions. Note that if you restore this folder at this point, the changes you made to the success.txt and success2.txt files will be lost.

21. Select the previous version and click Copy. In the Copy Items dialog box, select the C: drive and click New Folder. Rename the folder **MyTemp**. Click Copy.

22. In the folder properties dialog box, click OK.

23. Using Windows Explorer, browse to C:\MyTemp\Exercise41 folder. Copy the mcitpsuccess.txt file from the temporary folder and paste it into the C:\ Exercise41 folder. At this point you have restored the deleted file without affecting any other files in the folder.

Encrypting File System (EFS)

NTFS drives include the Encrypting File System (EFS). Using EFS, you can encrypt any files on a hard disk so that prying eyes won't be able to open them.

The first time you encrypt a file, a file encryption certificate and key are created. This certificate and key are used to encrypt and decrypt files. This happens automatically without any additional action required on your part.

When you try to access a file you encrypted, your certificate and key are retrieved to decrypt the file. You can work with it in an unencrypted format, and then when you close the file, it is automatically encrypted again.

If other users attempt to open your encrypted file, they won't be successful, since they don't have access to your certificate and key.

To encrypt a file or folder, follow these steps:

1. Access the properties dialog box of a file or folder. Right-click the file or folder and click Properties.

2. On the General tab, click Advanced.

3. On the Advanced Attributes dialog box, click the check box next to Encrypt Contents to Secure Data. Click OK.

4. On the Properties dialog box, click OK. You will be prompted to confirm the change. If you changed the property on a folder, you will be prompted to either apply the changes to the folder only or to the folder, subfolders, and files.

Figure 4-5 shows a folder being selected to be encrypted.

Figure 4-5
Setting EFS on
a folder

When a folder is configured with EFS, all files placed into the folder will automatically be encrypted.

Encrypted files are easy to spot. They are displayed with green text.

Files can be either encrypted or compressed, but not both.

Converting to NTFS

To convert a FAT or FAT32 volume to NTFS, use the following command:

```
Convert X: /FS:NTFS
```

In the command, the *X*: would be the volume you want to convert. For example, if the C: drive is FAT32 and you wanted to convert it to NTFS, you'd use the following command:

```
Convert C: /FS:NTFS
```

CAUTION Warning! Converting a volume to NTFS is considered a risky operation. While I've done it dozens of times without losing any data, the loss of data is certainly a possibility. Before converting to NTFS, you should ensure you have a backup of any important data.

Converting a FAT or FAT32 volume is a one-way process. You can convert to NTFS without losing any data, but you can't go backward without losing any data. You'll need to completely reformat the partition as a FAT or FAT32 volume.

Boot and System Partitions The boot partition and the system partition are two terms that often confuse people. Both are used to identify where files are located to start a computer and launch the operating system. Usually, the C:\ drive is both the boot partition and the system partition. However, if you have a multi-boot system, the partitions could be on different drives.

The boot partition is the volume that holds the files used to launch the operating system. On a Windows Vista typical installation, these files are typically in the C:\Windows folder.

In a dual-boot configuration, Windows XP could be in the C:\Windows folder and Windows Vista could be in the D:\Windows folder. When booted into Windows XP, C: would be the boot partition. When booted into Windows Vista, D; would be the boot partition.

The system partition is the partition that holds the files needed to start the computer and locate the boot partition. These files are usually on the C:\ drive.

If the partition is the system partition or the boot partition, the Convert command won't be able to take control of the partition to convert it. Instead, you will be prompted to schedule the conversion to happen on the next reboot.

Convert creates an entry in the Registry that causes the system to convert the drive to NTFS on the next reboot. The hive that is modified is

```
HKEY_LOCAL_Machine
```

The Registry key that is modified is

```
\System\CurrentControlSet\Control\Session Manager
```

The BootExecute entry is changed from

```
autocheck autochk *
```

to

```
Auotconv \DosDevices\X: /FS: NTFS
```

Figure 4-6 shows the Registry editor opened to this key. You can view the complete path to the key at the bottom of the window in the figure. You can launch the Registry editor by clicking Start and entering **regedt32** in the search box.

 CAUTION Be careful when modifying the Registry. If the Registry is modified incorrectly, significant damage can occur to the system, including making it completely inoperable.

You can use the knowledge of how the Convert command modifies the Registry to help you understand how to undo a scheduled conversion. For example, if you ran the

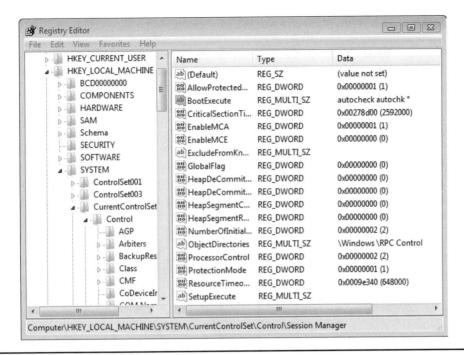

Figure 4-6   Registry editor opened to the BootExecute entry for NTFS

`Convert` command but later realized that the drive still needs to remain as a FAT or FAT32 volume to remain compatible with another operating system, you can modify the Registry.

In other words, you can modify the `BootExecute` entry from

```
Auotconv \DosDevices\X: /FS: NTFS
```

to

```
autocheck auochk *
```

TIP   You should be familiar with the command needed to convert a FAT or FAT32 drive to NTFS (`Convert`). You should also be familiar with the method to cancel a scheduled conversion (modifying the Registry).

For more details on the `BootExecute` entry, check out Knowledge Base article 130913 by entering **KB 130913** in your favorite search engine.

Hard Disks

Hard disks (sometimes called hard drives or hard disk drives) are used for long-term storage and easy access to data. Hard disks can be divided into separate drives (called partitions or volumes).

Partitions can be either primary partitions or extended partitions.

- **Primary partition**   A primary partition would be a single drive letter. You can have as many as four primary partitions on any physical disk. If you have an extended partition, you are limited to only three primary partitions.

- **Extended partition**   An extended partition can contain multiple logical drives. You can only have one extended partition on a disk, but many disks won't have any extended partitions.

For example, consider Figure 4-7. This shows a single disk divided into three primary partitions and one extended partition. The extended partition has three logical drives within it. The drives on the primary partition are identified by the drive letters of C:\, D:\, and E:\.

Figure 4-7
Dividing a hard disk

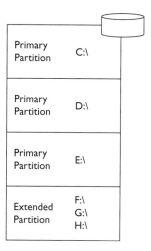

Each drive would be formatted with a specific file system (such as FAT, FAT32, or NTFS). As mentioned earlier, the most common file system would be NTFS because of all the features (including security) that you have with NTFS.

You don't have to divide a disk into separate partitions. It's not uncommon for a single disk to have only a single partition.

One of the primary reasons to divide a disk today is for dual-boot systems. You may remember the two important rules when creating dual-boot systems:

- Install each operating system on a different partition.

- Install the older operating system first and the newer operating system last.

Shrinking and Extending Volumes

A new feature that is available with NTFS disks on Windows Vista (and Windows Server 2008 products) is the ability to shrink and extend volumes. This feature is available only on NTFS volumes. If you have a FAT or FAT32 volume, the commands are dimmed.

You can access the Shrink Volume and Extend Volume commands from Disk Management. You can get to Disk Management from within Computer Management by clicking Start, right-clicking Computer, and selecting Manage.

Figure 4-8 shows the commands dimmed and unavailable on a FAT32 volume. If this were a NTFS volume, both commands would be available.

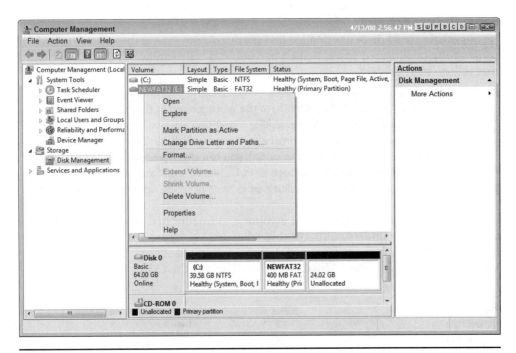

Figure 4-8   Shrink and Extend Volume commands from Disk Management

 NOTE   In the past, if you wanted to resize your partitions (or volumes), you had to purchase a third-party product, such as Norton PartitionMagic for about $70.00. There were UNIX and Linux tools you could download for free, such as the Recovery Is Possible (RIP) bootable CD, and you could run GPart or GParted to resize volumes, but these weren't known by most people running strictly Windows operating systems. But now, for Windows Vista and Windows Server 2008 products, you can resize your partitions for free with tools built right into the operating system.

Shrinking a Volume

If you want to create multiple volumes (or multiple partitions) from a system that has only one volume, you can first shrink the existing volume and then create a new volume from the new unallocated space.

When you choose to shrink a volume, the operating system examines the hard drive to determine how much space is being used, and how small the existing volume can be shrunk to. You are then prompted to choose how small you want the shrunk volume to be.

Once you complete the wizard, the existing volume is shrunk and the remaining space is shown as unallocated space. At this point, you can create additional volumes from the unallocated space.

Extending a Volume

If your existing hard drive has unallocated space, you can extend the volume to include some of the unallocated space. Remember, you can only extend (or shrink) a volume that is formatted as NTFS.

NOTE Although they both have the word extend in them, be aware that an *extended* partition and *extending* a partition are two completely different concepts. In addition to primary partitions (which can be represented with a single drive letter such as C: or D:), you can also have an extended partition (which can have multiple logical drives (such as F:, G:, and so on). Extending a partition is the process of enlarging a partition by combining an existing partition with unallocated space.

Additionally, you can only extend a volume to unallocated space right next to the volume. For a better understanding of this, take a look at Figure 4-9. It shows one physical disk (disk 0), two drives (C: and E:), and unallocated space. Notice that the unallocated space is next to the E: drive, but it is not next to the C: drive.

Figure 4-9

Extending a volume to unallocated space

⌐Disk 0			
Basic	(C:)	Data (E:)	
149.05 GB	144.17 GB NTFS	1000 MB NTF:	3.91 GB
Online	Healthy (System, Boot, Pa	Healthy (Prim	Unallocated

You can extend volume E:, but you would not be able to extend volume C:. If you right-clicked over C:, the Extend Volume command would be dimmed.

System Restore and restore points will be covered in more detail in Chapter 12, but for now you should be aware that the minimum size of a hard drive for System Restore is 1GB. System Restore will not run on disks smaller than 1GB. One of the reasons you may want to extend a volume is to ensure the minimum size is 1GB and system restore points can be created.

In Exercise 4.2, you will shrink a volume, create a new volume, and then extend the new volume.

Exercise 4.2: Shrinking and Extending a Disk

CAUTION Shrinking and extending a disk should be considered a risky operation. I haven't had any problems with it, but you should have in the back of your mind that if things go wrong, you could lose all of your data. To protect against a catastrophe, either back up all your data beforehand or, better yet, do the exercise on a Virtual PC.

1. Launch Computer Management by clicking Start, right-clicking Computer, and selecting Manage.

2. If the User Account Control dialog box appears, click Continue.

3. In Computer Management, select Disk Management.

4. Right-click the disk that you want to shrink and select Shrink Volume. Your display will look similar to Figure 4-10. Notice that the Extend Volume command is dimmed. This is because the volume doesn't have any free space.

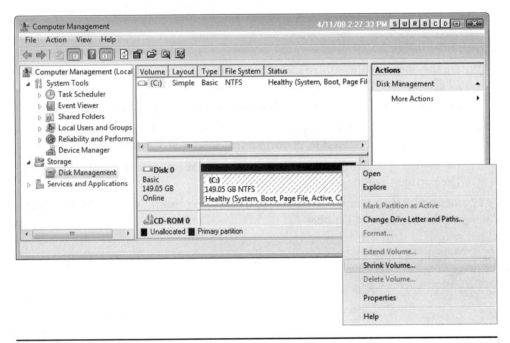

Figure 4-10   Selecting the Shrink Volume command

Later in this exercise, you'll see that the Extend Volume command is enabled.

5. Disk Management will determine how much the volume can be shrunk and will then display the Shrink dialog box. Enter an amount less than or equal to the Size of Available Shrink Space. If possible enter a size at least equal to 200MB. Your display will look similar to Figure 4-11. Click Shrink.

   After a moment, your partition will be resized and you'll see an extra partition identified as unallocated space.

6. At this point, you could create the unallocated space as another partition on your system. Right-click the unallocated space and select New Simple Volume.

7. On the Wizard Welcome screen, click Next.

Figure 4-11

Shrinking your drive space

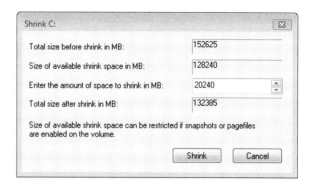

8. On the Specify Volume Size screen, enter **100** in the Simple Volume Size in MB. Click Next.

9. On the Assign Drive Letter or Path screen, accept the defaults and click Next.

10. On the Format Partition screen, ensure NTFS is selected for the File System. Select the check box next to Perform a Quick Format. Click Next.

11. On the Completing the Wizard screen, review the information and click Finish. The partition will be created and formatted.

12. Right-click the volume you just created and select Extend Volume. Your display will look similar to Figure 4-12.

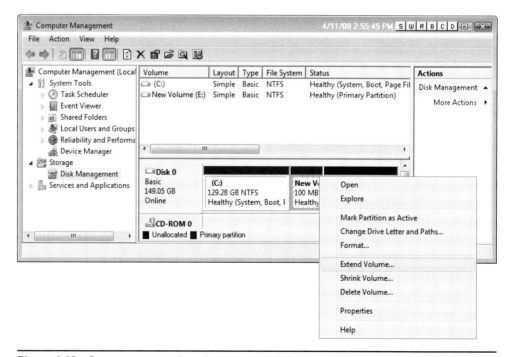

Figure 4-12   Beginning to extend a volume

13. On the Welcome to the Extend Volume Wizard screen, click Next.

14. On the Select Disks screen, ensure the 100MB partition you just created is selected. Enter **100** in the Select The Amount of Space in MB text box. This will change the Total Volume Size In Megabytes (MB) to 200MB. Your display will look similar to Figure 4-13.

Figure 4-13
Extending
a volume

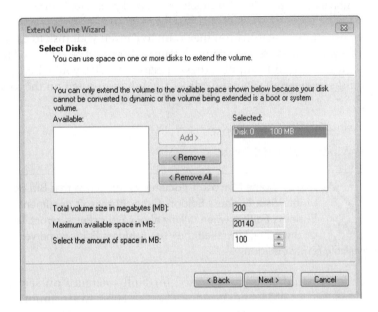

15. On the Completed the Extend Volume Wizard screen, click Finish. Your new volume will now be 200MB in size.

TIP If desired, you can right-click the created volume and select Delete Volume. This will return the created volume to the unallocated disk space. You can then select the original partition and select Extend Volume, and select the defaults to extend your volume to the full size, including all of the unallocated space.

Basic and Dynamic

Windows Vista supports two types of disk configurations: basic and dynamic. When you first install Windows Vista, you will have a basic disk. Later, you can convert your disk to dynamic.

- **Basic** Basic disks use partitions and are limited to only four partitions as described earlier. These are the traditional disk types used with most Microsoft operating systems.

- **Dynamic** Dynamic disks use volumes instead of partitions, and there is no limit to the number of volumes per disk. Additionally, dynamic volumes can contain data from multiple physical disks.

CAUTION You should not use dynamic disks on systems that have more than one operating system (multiboot systems). Moreover, unless you specifically have a reason to upgrade a disk to dynamic, you should avoid doing so. Dynamic disks don't have wide support with third-party tools and aren't even compatible between two operating systems running on the same system. Further, you should consider the conversion a risky operation. You should back up all your data before the conversion.

The two primary reasons you may want to convert your disk to dynamic are to create a striped volume or to create a spanned volume. Both will be explained in the next sections.

If you don't need to support these specific benefits, you're better off not converting your disks to dynamic. Dynamic disks are only supported on the following editions of Windows Vista:

- Windows Vista Enterprise
- Windows Vista Ultimate

NOTE Some Microsoft documentation states that BitLocker is supported on the Vista Business Edition. Other Microsoft documentation omits the Vista Business Edition when talking about BitLocker support. To prove it one way or the other, I installed the Vista Business Edition and verified that BitLocker is *not* available on that edition.

While dynamic disks can be used for fault tolerance on server products such as Windows Server 2003 and Windows Server 2008, you cannot create fault-tolerant volumes on Windows Vista.

Striped Volumes (RAID 0)

A striped volume is also known as RAID-0. Redundant Array of Inexpensive (or Independent, depending on which book you read) Disks (RAID) is a technology that allows you to combine multiple disks into a single logical drive.

Windows Vista supports RAID-0, but it does not support any of the fault-tolerant RAID configurations such as RAID-1 (mirroring) or RAID-5 (striping with parity).

In a striped volume, data is striped across multiple disks to increase the speed of data reads and data writes. You can use two or more disks in a striped volume.

When reading data from a hard disk, you'll use the CPU, memory, and the hard disk itself. The hard disk is the slowest component, and much of the time, the CPU and memory are waiting for the hard disk.

However, by using more than one hard disk, you have the capability to increase performance. Consider Figure 4-14. This shows two disks configured as a striped volume. To the operating system, the two physical disks will be viewed as a single volume (D:\ in the figure).

If you save a file named TestNotes on a striped volume, it will save about half of the file on one physical disk and the remainder of the file on the other physical disk.

Remember, the disk is the slowest subsystem. If it took 100 milliseconds to read the data from one disk, it may take only about 50 milliseconds (maybe a little more) to

Figure 4-14
Reading and
writing from
a striped volume
(RAID-0)

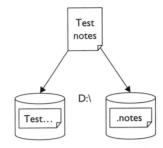

read half of the file. Of course, since you can read from both disks simultaneously, you are able to reduce the read time by about half.

A striped volume increases both read and write performance but provides no fault tolerance.

Other RAIDs

Other RAID configurations do exist, but Windows Vista does not support them. For example, RAID-1 (mirroring) and RAID-5 (striped with parity) can be used for fault tolerance on Windows Server 2008. However, fault-tolerant RAID configurations aren't supported on Windows Vista.

Defragmenting

One of the problems that can occur to hard disks over time is that they can become fragmented. Disk fragmentation occurs when a large quantity of files are written, modified, or deleted.

Normally, a file would be written on contiguous space. When the disk starts reading the file, it is able to continue reading all the way to the end of the file.

As a disk becomes fragmented, files are no longer contiguous. Instead, files can be stored as multiple fragments scattered throughout the disk. The more fragmented a file becomes, the longer it takes for the disk to load all the fragments and put them together.

When too many files are fragmented on a disk, or in other words, the disk itself is fragmented, disk performance slows down considerably. Symptoms of a fragmented disk are known as disk thrashing: you can see the LED for the disk drive constantly flashing, and you can hear the hard drive constantly. Much, much worse, the drive can slow your system down to a crawl. This is often seen when opening files.

To prevent disk fragmentation on Windows Vista, the Disk Defragmenter is automatically scheduled as part of the Task Scheduler. By default it will run weekly, every Wednesday at 1 A.M.

Additionally, there are a couple of ways you can access the Disk Defragmenter to run it manually:

- Click Start and enter **Defrag** in the Start Search box. If the User Account Control dialog box appears, click Continue.
- Click Start and select Computer. Right-click the drive you want to defrag and select Properties. Select the Tools tab and click Defragment Now. If the User Account Control dialog box appears, click Continue.

When launched, the Disk Defragmenter looks like Figure 4-15.

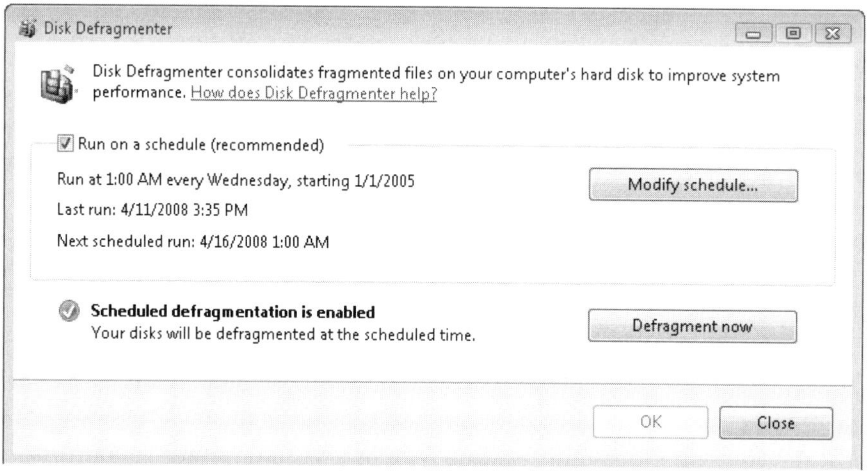

Disk Defragmenter

Disk Defragmenter consolidates fragmented files on your computer's hard disk to improve system performance. How does Disk Defragmenter help?

☑ Run on a schedule (recommended)

Run at 1:00 AM every Wednesday, starting 1/1/2005

Last run: 4/11/2008 3:35 PM

Next scheduled run: 4/16/2008 1:00 AM

[Modify schedule...]

Scheduled defragmentation is enabled
Your disks will be defragmented at the scheduled time.

[Defragment now]

[OK]   [Close]

Figure 4-15   Manually starting the Disk Defragmenter

You can click the Defragment Now button to immediately start the Disk Defragmenter, or modify the schedule by clicking Modify Schedule. When you click Defragment Now, the system will begin defragmenting the hard disks.

However, unlike in previous operating systems (like Windows XP), the Disk Defragmenter doesn't give you any visual indication of its progress. You'll see a status message saying the defragmentation may take from a few minutes to a few hours and you really have no idea which.

EXAM TIP   If your system is running slow after a significant amount of disk writing, it's very possible it is fragmented. You'll notice that files are slow to open, and you may notice disk thrashing. There's a simple solution: defragment the volume.

In Exercise 4.3, you will run the Disk Defragmenter on your system.

Exercise 4.3: Defragmenting Volumes

1. Click the Vista Start icon and select Computer.

2. Right-click the C: drive and select Properties. Select the Tools tab. Your display will look similar to Figure 4-16.

3. Click Defragment Now. If the user Account Control dialog box appears, click Continue.

4. On the Disk Defragmenter dialog box, click Modify Schedule. Notice that the Disk Defragmenter is currently scheduled to run regularly. The defaults are

   • How Often: Weekly

Figure 4-16

Launching the
Disk Defrag-
menter from the
Tools tab

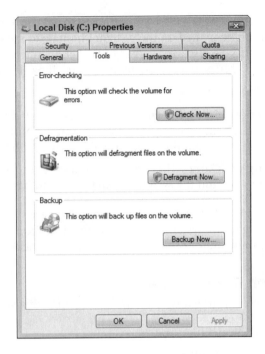

- What Day: Wednesday
- What Time: 1:00 AM

If you want to change the schedule, this is the easiest place to do so. Click Cancel.

5. Click Defragment Now to start a manual defragmentation. You can wait until the defragmentation completes (which could take from a few minutes to a few hours), or click Cancel Defragmentation.

6. When done, click Close.

BitLocker Drive Encryption

Sometimes the most valuable part of a PC is the data. When a PC is lost or stolen, many companies want to ensure that the data is protected and can't be accessed. BitLocker Drive Encryption (often referred to as simply BitLocker) is designed to answer that need.

For systems that have BitLocker installed, thieves are prevented from using some of the common methods used to bypass protection of a system's data.

Without BitLocker, thieves may connect the hard drive to another operating system where they have full administrator permissions. They can then simply take ownership of any of the files and change the permissions as the owner. Additionally, tools are available to change the permission of the administrator account and gain full access to a system.

However, the chance of a thief gaining access to data on a system is significantly reduced if BitLocker is implemented on the system. I hesitate to say that data can't be accessed at all—methods may be discovered—but BitLocker definitely makes it much harder.

BitLocker combines two components to make it harder to access data on a protected system. These components are

- **Drive Encryption**   The entire volume is encrypted to prevent lost or stolen drives from being accessed from other systems. Not only is the data encrypted, but so are all system files including the swap and hibernation files.

- **Integrity Checking**   This process ensures that the drive is located on the original computer and the system doesn't appear to be tampered with.

When BitLocker Drive Encryption is enabled on a system drive, it prevents an attacker from booting to the system or accessing the drive from another operating system. Only an administrator can enable, or disable, BitLocker on a system.

BitLocker Requirements

BitLocker is only available in the following operating systems:

- Windows Vista Enterprise
- Windows Vista Ultimate

BitLocker requires one of the following two hardware components:

- **Trusted Platform Module (TPM) version 1.2 or higher**   This is a special microchip that is embedded in the motherboard. The TPM stores the BitLocker key, which is used to encrypt and decrypt the drive.

- **Removable USB drive**   BitLocker can store the key on this drive to use for encryption and decryption.

 EXAM TIP   You should be familiar with the requirements to implement BitLocker on a system. This includes TPM 1.2, a compatible BIOS, two partitions on the system: the non-Vista partition must be at least 1.5GB and marked as active, and both partitions must be formatted with NTFS.

Additionally, the following requirements must be met:

- **You must have at least two partitions**   One partition is the boot partition (where Windows Vista is installed) and will become encrypted. The second partition will be used by the computer to start the computer and will remain unencrypted.

- **The unencrypted partition must be marked as Active**   You can mark it as active by right-clicking it within Disk Management and selecting Mark Partition as Active.

- **The unencrypted partition must be at least 1.5GB**   If it is less than 1.5GB, BitLocker won't allow the partition to be used. The Windows Preinstallation Environment (WinPE) and other system files will be stored on this drive.

- **NTFS**   Both partitions must be formatted as NTFS partitions.

- **Compatible BIOS**   The BIOS must be compatible with TPM and support USB devices on startup. If your BIOS does not meet these requirements, you can normally contact the BIOS manufacturer and download a program to flash the BIOS.

Once enabled, BitLocker will examine the system for any condition that could represent a security risk (such as changes to startup files, changes to the BIOS, or even disk errors); if it finds one, it will lock the drive. The drive can be unlocked using a special BitLocker recovery password stored on a USB disk. If the recovery password is not available, you could permanently lose access to all the data.

BitLocker and Multifactor Authentication

Multifactor authentication is simply using multiple methods of authenticating. In the world of security, you can be authenticated by something you know (such as a user name and password), something you have (such as a smart card), or something you are (using biometrics to check a fingerprint).

Generally, multifactor authentication combines two or more of these methods.

BitLocker offers multifactor authentication by enabling a second level of authentication beyond what it itself provides. BitLocker authenticates the computer by verifying nothing has changed, and then you can use either of the following two options as the second level of authentication.

- **Requiring a personal identification number (PIN)**   The user is required to enter the PIN on computer startup. If the PIN is not known, the computer will not start. A PIN is optional.

- **Requiring a user to insert a USB flash drive that contains a BitLocker startup key**   On startup, the system looks for a valid BitLocker startup key on the USB device. If the valid key is not found, the computer will not start. A startup key is optional unless the system is not TPM compatible.

 EXAM TIP   You can implement multifactor authentication with BitLocker by requiring the user to know a PIN or have a USB drive with a valid BitLocker startup key.

Enabling BitLocker Drive Encryption Without TPM

If your system doesn't have TPM installed, it is possible to still enable BitLocker on your system. You must first modify the local group policy setting to allow this. The following exercise leads you through the steps to modify the local group policy settings.

Exercise 4.4: Enabling BitLocker Without TPM

1. Click Start | Control Panel. In the Control Panel select Security.

2. Select the BitLocker Drive Encryption link. If the User Account Control dialog box appears, click Continue.

3. You may see a warning message that says "A TPM was not found. A TPM is required to turn on BitLocker. If your computer has a TPM, then contact the computer manufacturer for BitLocker-compatible BIOS." Figure 4-17 shows the warning message.

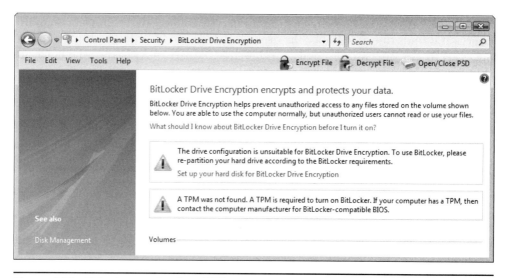

Figure 4-17   BitLocker warning about TPM

If you see this message, you can modify local group policy to enable BitLocker without TPM.

4. Launch the Group Policy Management Console. Click Start and enter **gpedit. msc** in the Start Search box. If the User Account Control dialog box appears, click Continue.

5. Browse to the Computer Configuration | Administrative Templates | Windows Components | BitLocker Drive Encryption area within Local Computer Policy. Your display will look similar to Figure 4-18.

6. Double-click the Control Panel Setup: Enable Advanced Startup Options setting.

7. Click the Enabled radio button. Notice that the check box next to Allow BitLocker Without A Compatible TPM is checked. Your display will look similar to Figure 4-19. Click OK. Close the Local Group Policy Console.

8. If you return to the BitLocker Drive Encryption link from Step 2, you can refresh the display and Bitlocker should be enabled. It may take some time for the local

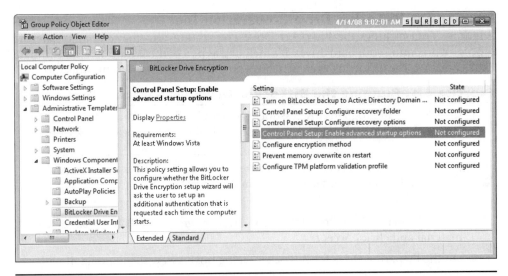

Figure 4-18 Opening the Local Group Policy Console

group policy to apply. If it doesn't appear right away and you don't want to wait, you can launch a command prompt and enter the following command:

```
gpupdate /force
```

Figure 4-19

Allowing Bit-Locker without a compatible TPM

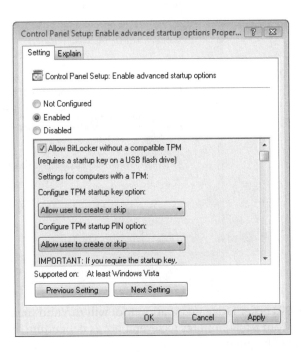

Running the BitLocker Drive Preparation Tool

Windows Vista includes the BitLocker Drive Preparation tool that can automate the process of preparing your hard drives. It's included as part of the Windows Vista Ultimate Extras updates. The following exercise leads you through the steps to run this tool.

Exercise 4.5: Running the BitLocker Drive Preparation Tool

1. Click Start | All Programs | Accessories | System Tools |BitLocker | BitLocker Drive Preparation Tool. If the User Account Control dialog box appears, click Continue.

 TIP If you don't have the BitLocker container within System Tools, you'll need to download the update from Windows Update.

2. In the BitLocker Drive Preparation tool license agreement dialog box, review the material and click I Accept.

3. On the Preparing Drive for BitLocker dialog box, review the material. It will look similar to Figure 4-20. Click Continue.

Figure 4-20
Running the BitLocker Drive Preparation tool

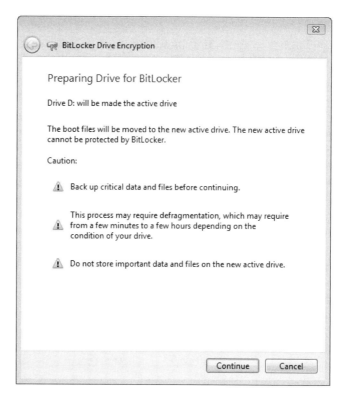

4. The BitLocker Drive Preparation tool will run and prepare your drive. This may take from a few minutes to several hours depending on whether the drive needs to be defragmented.

5. Once the process is complete, click Finish. You will be prompted to restart you system. Click Restart Now.

6. After your system boots, go to Control Panel | Security | BitLocker Drive Encryption. Your display will look similar to Figure 4-21. You can now click the Turn On BitLocker link to enable BitLocker on the C: drive.

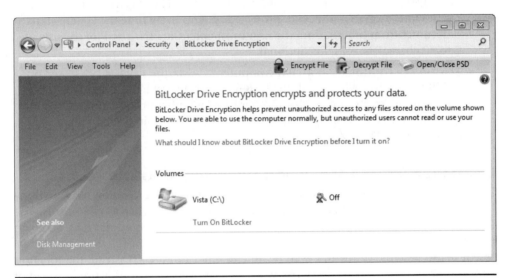

Figure 4-21   Ready to enable BitLocker

BitLocker Keys and Passwords

BitLocker uses multiple keys and passwords. All of them are listed here for clarity.

- **TPM Owner password**   When the TPM is initialized, you are prompted to create a TPM password. This is required if you ever want to change the state of TPM on your system. You are prompted to save the password file as a .tpm file. It's highly recommended you save this password file on removable media.

- **Recovery password**   A recovery password is a numerical password consisting of 48 digits divided into eight groups. If your computer enters a recovery state, you need either the recovery password or the recovery key to unlock the encrypted data. When in the BitLocker Recovery Console, the PIN is entered using the function keys (F1 through F10), since the numeric keys are not usable in the pre–operating system environment on all keyboards.

- **Recovery key**   A recovery key is a file stored on a USB flash drive. If your computer enters a recovery state, you need either the recovery password or the recovery key to unlock the encrypted data. When using the recovery key, you only need to insert the USB device into the computer.

EXAM TIP You must have either the recovery key (a USB drive) or the recovery password to unlock a locked drive. For example, if the TPM module fails, you won't be able to access the drive unless have either the key or the password. You use the key or the password in the BitLocker Recovery Console.

- **PIN (optional)** A personal identification number (PIN) is used to add a layer of authentication to a BitLocker-protected system. Every time the system starts or resumes from hibernation, the user must enter the PIN. The PIN consists of 4 to 20 characters. A PIN is optional.

- **Startup key (optional on a TPM computer)** A startup key is a key stored on a USB flash drive. When used, the USB flash drive must be inserted every time the computer starts. It provides another layer of authentication similar to a PIN. A startup key is optional on a TPM computer but is required on a system that does not have TPM.

BitLocker Drive Encryption Recovery Console

If problems are detected with BitLocker, the partition running Windows Vista will be locked and the system will automatically enter the BitLocker Recovery Console. The Recovery Console is entered very early in the boot process, so you don't have access to many system resources.

For many systems, you won't even be able to enter numbers. Instead, the function keys are used to enter the recovery password (if a recovery password is used instead of a recovery key). Function keys F1 through F9 represent numbers 1–9. F10 represents the number 0.

If using a recovery key, you will be prompted to insert the USB holding the key. Press the esc key and the system will reboot with the BitLocker drive unlocked.

If you are using the recovery password instead, press ENTER when prompted to use the recovery key. You will then be prompted to enter the recovery password. Use the function keys to enter the password. More than likely, you won't remember the 48-digit password but instead will have it saved on a USB drive in a text file. This text file is not the same as the USB recovery key. You can read the text file on another system and then enter the password in the Recovery Console.

Chapter Review

In this chapter you learned about several different elements related to disks.

While Windows Vista supports FAT, FAT32, and NTFS, you will almost always see NTFS enabled on a Windows Vista system. NTFS brings a lot of additional capabilities such as permissions, previous versions, EFS, and shrinking and extending volumes.

You learned about BitLocker Drive Encryption and how it can lock down an entire drive to protect the contents of a drive. You learned about the requirements to enable BitLocker Drive Encryption, and the process of recovering a drive that has become locked.

Additional Study

Self Study Exercises
Use these additional exercises to challenge yourself.

- If you can find a FAT32 drive, convert it to NTFS.
- Create a folder on an NTFS drive and grant a user the minimum permissions required to delete files. Grant another user the required permissions to change permissions.
- Shrink and extend a volume.
- Enable BitLocker on a drive. (Make sure you back up your data first.)

Summary of What You Need to Know

70-620
When preparing for the 70-620 exam, pay particular attention to the following topics covered in this chapter:

- **Previous Versions**   Make sure you understand how Previous Versions can be used to recover data.
- **BitLocker**   You should understand the basic purpose and use of BitLocker.

70-622
When preparing for the 70-622 exam, pay particular attention to the following topics covered in this chapter:

- **NTFS and NTFS permissions**   Make sure you understand what the different NTFS permissions are and what they allow and don't allow.
- **Disk Defragmenter**   You should understand the purpose of the Disk Defragmenter, how and why to launch it, and how to change its automated schedule.
- **BitLocker**   You should have a solid understanding of BitLocker Drive Encryption, including the requirements to enable it and the different methods that can be used to restore a locked BitLocker drive.

70-623
When preparing for the 70-623 exam, pay particular attention to the following topics covered in this chapter:

- **NTFS and NTFS capabilities**   You should have a solid understanding of the different capabilities available with NTFS, including permissions and shrinking and extending drives. You should also know how to convert a drive to NTFS.
- **Disk Defragmenter**   You should understand the purpose of the Disk Defragmenter, how and why to launch it, and how to change its automated schedule.
- **BitLocker**   You should have a solid understanding of BitLocker Drive Encryption, including the requirements to enable it and the different methods that can be used to restore a locked BitLocker drive.

Questions

70-620

1. Sally runs Windows Vista Enterprise on her computer. She is the Research and Development manager and has multiple files in a folder named RnDProjects. For each new project, she creates a spreadsheet from a Microsoft Excel document she uses as a template. Yesterday, she used the template file to create a new project document, but instead of saving it with a new name, she saved it as the template. Now she no longer has the original file to use as a template. What is the easiest method she can use to restore the original file?

   A. From the Previous Versions tab, restore the original template file.

   B. Use the Windows Backup and Restore Center to restore the file.

   C. Use System Restore to restore the file.

   D. Recreate the file from scratch.

2. Sally runs Windows Vista Ultimate. She accidentally deleted a file named Budget.xls last week but didn't notice it until today. The file was in a folder named RnDProjects, where she has modified many other files since she deleted the budget file. How should she restore the Budget.xls file?

   A. From the Previous Versions tab of the file, copy a version of the file and then copy the file to the original folder.

   B. From the Previous Versions tab of the folder, copy a version of the folder that holds the file and copy the file to the original folder.

   C. From the Previous Versions tab of the folder, restore the folder.

   D. From the Previous Versions tab of the file, restore the file.

70-622

1. Sally and you share a Windows Vista system. When Sally logs on, she needs access to a folder named Project held on a NTFS drive. She currently does not have access. You try to change the NTFS permissions, but the system gives an error indicating you don't have permission to change the permissions. Of the following choices, what are the minimum permissions needed to change permissions?

   A. Read and Write

   B. Read and Execute, and Write

   C. Modify

   D. Full Control

2. Sally is running Windows Vista on her computer. She comes in on Wednesday morning and complains that her system is running very slowly. She complained that the same thing occurred last Wednesday. You discover that another maintenance program is being scheduled to run at 1 A.M. on Wednesday morning

and when both run at the same time, neither program completes. You want to have the Disk Defragmenter start at 11 P.M. on Tuesday night. What should you do?

A. Delete the schedule for the Disk Defragmenter and create a new one.

B. Create a new schedule for the maintenance program.

C. Create a new schedule for the Disk Defragmenter.

D. Change the schedule of the Disk Defragmenter to run on Tuesday night.

3. A research scientist within your company uses a laptop that is protected with BitLocker. The TPM chip has failed, and the user can no longer access the system. The password for the BitLocker is stored on a USB drive. How can you restore the system?

A. Enter the BitLocker Drive Encryption Recovery Console and then insert the USB drive when prompted.

B. Open the text file holding the password on another system. Enter the BitLocker Drive Encryption Recovery Console. When prompted, enter the password.

C. Enter the Windows Recovery Console. Insert the USB drive when prompted.

D. Open the text file holding the password on another system. Enter the Windows Recovery Console. When prompted, enter the password.

4. A research scientist within your company uses a laptop that is protected with BitLocker. The TPM chip has failed, and the user can no longer access the system. The recovery key for the BitLocker is stored on a USB drive. How can you restore the system?

A. Enter the BitLocker Drive Encryption Recovery Console and then insert the USB drive when prompted.

B. Open the text file holding the password on another system. Enter the BitLocker Drive Encryption Recovery Console. When prompted, enter the password.

C. Enter the Windows Recovery Console. Insert the USB drive when prompted.

D. Open the text file holding the password on another system. Enter the Windows Recovery Console. When prompted, enter the password.

70-623

1. After reading about NTFS, you realize that your system is still using a FAT32 disk. You run the Convert command to convert the drive from FAT32 to NTFS, and the Convert command indicates the conversion has been scheduled for the next reboot. Shortly afterward, you realize your dual-boot system needs to have the drive as FAT32. How can you stop the conversion from occurring?

A. At the command prompt enter **convert /cancel**.

B. At the command prompt enter **convert /fs:FAT32**.

C. Use the Registry editor to modify the bootexecute key.

D. Use the Registry editor to modify the lastknowngood key.

2. A Windows Vista system has a single 250GB disk, and two NTFS volumes of 200GB and 800MB. You realize that system restore points are not running on both volumes. What should you do to resolve the problem?

   A. Shrink the first volume to 200GB.

   B. Extend the second volume by at least 200MB.

   C. Combine both volumes into a single volume.

   D. Convert the disk to dynamic and then extend the second volume to 1GB.

3. A user has brought in his computer. He says that he recently installed an application that creates and modifies large files. He complains that his system frequently takes a very long time to open the files. What could be done to improve the performance when opening these files?

   A. Purchase another hard drive and install the operating system on the second drive.

   B. Install a USB drive and enable ReadyBoost.

   C. Enable encryption on the same drive where the files are stored.

   D. Defragment the drive.

4. A user has highly valuable data stored on her laptop computer. She wants to protect the data using BitLocker technology and also wants to implement multifactor authentication. Can multifactor authentication be used with BitLocker, and if so, how?

   A. No. Multifactor authentication cannot be implemented with BitLocker.

   B. Yes. Issue her a smart card and have the BitLocker certificate placed on the smart card.

   C. Yes. Configure a USB flash drive to store a startup key.

   D. Yes. Configure a USB flash drive to store a recovery key.

5. A user has a laptop that he will store highly valuable data on. The data must be protected, and he decides to use BitLocker to protect it and asks you for help. You've verified the laptop has TPM 1.2 hardware. Currently the laptop has no operating system on it. How would you proceed?

   A. Install Vista, and then enable BitLocker.

   B. Create two partitions. Enable BitLocker on the first partition and then install Windows Vista on the second partition.

   C. Create two partitions. Install Vista on one partition and make the partition active. Enable BitLocker on the Vista partition.

   D. Create two partitions. Install Vista on one partition. Make the second partition active and enable BitLocker on the second partition.

Answers

70-620

1. **A.** Shadow Copy is enabled automatically on Windows Vista (Business, Enterprise, and Ultimate editions) and creates previous versions of any files that are modified. These can be restored by right-clicking the file, selecting properties, and then accessing the Previous Versions tab. The Windows Backup and Restore Center is used to restore files (or the entire system) from a backup but would be much more time-consuming (assuming a backup exists). System Restore would be used to restore the operating system, not individual files.

2. **B.** She would need to restore the folder to a different location and copy the deleted file from the restored folder location to the original folder. Since the file is deleted, you can't access the properties (or the Previous Versions tab) of the deleted file. If the entire folder was restored without renaming, the changes to the other files would be lost.

70-622

1. **D.** Of the given permissions, only Full Control will give you enough permission to change permissions. The Modify permission will not give you enough permission to change permissions. Read and Write, Read and Execute, or Write permissions are not enough to change permissions.

2. **D.** The easiest way to have the Disk Defragmenter run at a different time is to change the schedule. This can be changed from the Disk Defragmenter page by clicking Modify Schedule, or by going into the Task Scheduler program. There is no need to delete or recreate a new schedule.

3. **B.** If a password was stored on a USB drive, then a password must be entered. The BitLocker Drive Encryption Recovery Console cannot read the password from the USB drive. It can only read a recovery key if stored on a USB drive. The Windows Recovery Console can't be used to recover a BitLocker drive.

4. **A.** The recovery key stored on a USB drive can be used to restore a BitLocker drive from within the Recovery Console. The recovery key is not the same as a recovery password, and a recovery key cannot be entered manually. The Windows Recovery Console can't be used to recover a BitLocker drive.

70-623

1. **C.** If the Convert command can't get control of the drive, it will prompt you to schedule the conversion. It will then modify the bootexecute entry in the

```
HKEY_LOCAL_Machine\System\CurrentControlSet\Control\Session Manager
```

key to

```
autoconv \DosDevices\X: /FS: NTFS.
```

If you change it back to `autocheck autochk *` it will cancel the conversion. You can't cancel the conversion with the `Convert` command. LastKnownGood is used to recover a system to the state it was the last time it had a successful boot (the last time someone successfully logged on) and is not related to converting a drive to NTFS.

2. **B.** The minimum size of a volume to support System Restore is 1GB. You can extend the second volume by 200MB to make it 1GB. There is no need to adjust the size of the first volume or combine both volumes into a single volume. You can extend a volume without making it dynamic, and if given a choice, you should not convert a drive to dynamic.

3. **D.** More than likely the files are becoming fragmented, causing them to take a long time to open. By defragmenting the drives, you can improve the performance. Reinstalling the operating system on another hard disk is way too much work, and the original problem could easily reappear. While a USB can improve the performance of the system, it wouldn't improve the performance while opening these specific files. Encryption would cause files to open even slower, since they would need to be decrypted first.

4. **C.** Multifactor authentication allows more than one method of authentication to be used. The TPM provides the first layer of authentication. A second layer can be provided by the user entering a PIN, or using a USB drive with a stored startup key. It's not possible to use a smart card as a second method of authentication in conjunction with BitLocker. The recovery key stored on a USB flash drive is for recovery purposes, not day-to-day operations.

5. **D.** BitLocker requires two partitions. It requires a non-Vista partition of at least 1.5 GB in size to be marked as active before you can enable BitLocker on the Vista partition. You can't enable BitLocker on a system with only one partition, on a system that isn't running any operating system, or on a partition that isn't marked as active.

Configuring Network Connectivity

In this chapter, you will learn about:
- Networking basics including IPv4 addressing
- IPv6 basics
- The Network and Sharing Center

Networks are everywhere—in homes, in coffee shops, and certainly in work environments. To be an effective Windows Vista professional, you'll need to know how Windows Vista connects to networks. Things don't always go well, so you'll also need some tools to help you troubleshoot when things go wrong.

In this chapter, we'll cover what you'll need for network connectivity in wired networks. In the next chapter, you'll find what you need for wireless networks.

 EXAM TIP Objectives for the 70-620, 70-622, and 70-623 exams are included in this chapter.

Networking Basics

It is rare today to find a computer that doesn't connect to a network. Within businesses, computers are connected via internal networks. Even many homes today have several computers connected together with a network.

One of the primary benefits of a network is the ability to share resources. File and print servers are used on business networks to allow users to share files and print to common printers. A single Internet connection can be shared via a Proxy server providing users within a private network access through a single public connection.

Even networking within homes is becoming quite common. It doesn't take much to buy a wireless router and network several computers within your home. You can share resources and share the single connection providing Internet access.

An integral part of becoming an effective technician or administrator is an understanding of some basics related to networking. In this section, you'll learn some of these basics that you'll build on throughout this chapter and elsewhere in the book.

Network Protocols and Services

The primary protocol suite in use today is TCP/IP. TCP/IP isn't a single protocol, or even just two protocols (TCP and IP), but instead refers to a full suite of protocols such as TCP, UDP, IP, DHCP, HTTP, and much more.

Additionally networks have many services that ensure the functionality of the network. Many of the services and protocols are intertwined. For example, a Dynamic Host Configuration Protocol (DHCP) server uses the DHCP client service and the DHCP server service to support DHCP.

As an example of how different protocols and services work together on the network, take a look at Figure 5-1. It shows the interaction of MAC addresses, IP addresses, and computer names.

Figure 5-1

Interaction of protocols on a computer

You and I work with names much easier than numbers. Instead of us having to remember IP addresses, we assign names to computers (like msn.com or google.com). However, these names need to be resolved to IP addresses. Several different methods of name resolution exist, such as the Domain Name System (DNS). DNS can be queried with a name, and it returns an IP address.

A network interface card (NIC) has a Media Access Control (MAC) address assigned to it. The MAC address is 48 bits long, composed of six pairs of hexadecimal numbers. It's also called a physical address. It looks something like this: 00-16-D4-B1-12-7B.

To get the packet to the computer, the IP address has to be translated or resolved to the MAC address. The Address Resolution Protocol (ARP) is used to resolve the IP address to the MAC address.

You don't need to know all the protocols and services, but there are several pieces of this puzzle that you will need in order to be successful when working with computers on a network (and to pass the Vista exams).

Clients

Take a look at Figure 5-2. It shows all the clients, services, and protocols bound to a network interface card (NIC). The only client in the figure is the Client for Microsoft Networks. It is selected (though it isn't checked, which means that is isn't enabled).

Figure 5-2
Viewing the
clients, services,
and protocols
bound to a NIC

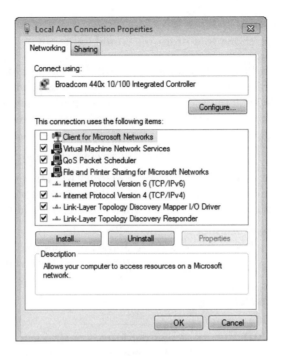

The Client for Microsoft Networks is used to allow your computer to access resources (such as server shares and printers) on your network. With this check box not checked, your computer would not be able to access resources on other computers.

A related component is the File and Printer Sharing for Microsoft Networks service, which allows other computers to access shares on your computer.

EXAM TIP Both the Client for Microsoft Networks and the File and Printer Sharing for Microsoft Networks service should be enabled to fully enable sharing capabilities on a Windows Vista computer.

Services

Figure 5-2 also shows three services that are installed and bound to this NIC.

- **Virtual Machine Network Services** This service provides support for Microsoft virtual machines such as those within the Virtual PC environment.

- **QoS Packet Scheduler** This service provides network traffic control.

- **File and Printer Sharing for Microsoft Networks** This service allows you to share resources on your computer. Without it selected, you won't be able to share resources, or said another way, other users won't be able to access resources on your computer.

Protocols Bound to a NIC

Figure 5-2 also shows four protocols bound to the NIC.

- **Internet Protocol Version 6 (TCP/IPv6)** This protocol is needed to support 128-bit IPv6 addresses, which are being migrated into networks and the Internet. IPv6 will be covered in this chapter. In the figure, the IPv6 protocol is not selected, meaning it wouldn't be running on the computer.

- **Internet Protocol Version 4 (TCP/IPv4)** 32-bit IPv4 addresses are commonly used in networks today. IPv4 will be covered in depth in this chapter.

- **Link-Layer Topology Discovery Mapper I/O Driver** This protocol is used by the Network Discovery protocol to discover and locate other computers on the network. Network Discovery will be covered later in this chapter.

- **Link-Layer Topology Discovery Responder** This protocol is used by the Network Discovery protocol to allow this computer to be discoverable on the network. Network Discovery will be covered later in this chapter.

IP Addressing

NOTE In this section, our focus is on IPv4. Later in this chapter IPv6 specifics will be covered as they relate to the exam objectives.

IP addresses are expressed in dotted decimal format. For example, 192.168.18.1 is an IP address. It's read as "192 dot 168 dot 18 dot 1." Each of the numbers is decimal, and the decimal numbers are separated by dots.

Additionally, each of the numbers is represented by 8 bits. Four sets of 8 bits give an IP address of 32 bits.

In advanced networking topics, you'll need to know how to interpret the bits (also known as subnetting), but for the Vista exams you will only need to know how to interpret the IP address using decimal numbers.

IP addresses are accompanied by a subnet mask. The possible subnet masks without subnetting are

- 255.0.0.0
- 255.255.0.0
- 255.255.255.0

TIP Subnet masks can be more complex when subnetting is used. Instead of the last number being a 0, it can be 128, 192, 224, 240, 248, 252, or 254. Subnetting is an advanced topic that isn't required for Vista exams.

IP addresses can be either public or private. Public addresses are on the Internet, and private IP addresses are internal to a network. Private IP addresses are only in specific ranges as shown in the following bullets. The letters x.y.z can be any numbers between 0 and 255 (as long as all the numbers aren't 0 or all the numbers aren't 255.

- **10.x.y.z**   For example, a valid address in this range would be 10.1.1.5.

- **172.16.y.z through 172.31.y.z**   For example, a valid address in this range would be 172.16.18.1.

- **192.168.y.z**   For example, a valid address in this range would be 192.168.18.1.

IP Address Conflicts

Whether public or private, IP addresses must be unique in their network. On the Internet, no two IP addresses can be the same. Similarly, on any internal network, no two IP addresses can be the same.

If two IP addresses are the same on two computers, you will have an IP address conflict.

For example, suppose Client1 had a manual IP address of 192.168.1.1 and Client2 was then given a manual IP address of 192.168.1.1. The two systems would identify an IP address conflict. If the systems were Windows Vista clients, Client2 would recognize that Client1 had the IP address first and reassign itself an IP address of 0.0.0.0. Client 2 would then not be able to communicate on the network.

As another example, assume Client1 had the same IP address but a printer was then assigned that IP address as well. Printers usually don't have the software to identify the IP address conflict, so it wouldn't assign itself an IP address of 0.0.0.0. Instead, both clients would try to operate with the same IP address, but neither would function on the network.

Two Parts of an IP Address

IP addressing is often compared to street addresses. Within a ZIP code, you have multiple street addresses, all unique. The ZIP code identifies the city and state, and the street address identifies the specific location within the ZIP code.

Similarly, IP addresses have two parts: the network ID and the host ID. The network ID is similar to a ZIP code. It identifies the general location on the network where the computers are located. The host ID identifies the specific computer within that network.

The only way you can determine which portion of an IP address is the network ID and which portion is the host ID is by using the subnet mask. When the subnet mask is maximum, that portion of the IP address is the network ID. In this basic discussion, the subnet masks will only be 255.0.0.0, 255.255.0.0, or 255.255.255.0. Subnet masks can be more complex when using subnetting, but subnetting is beyond the scope of this book.

With this in mind, each octet of the subnet mask could be maximum (255) or minimum (0). By matching each octet in the IP address with each octet in the subnet mask, you can determine the network ID and the host ID.

Consider the following IP address and subnet mask:

- 192.168.18.1

- 255.255.0.0

What is the network ID? The 192 is in the first octet of the IP address, and the first octet of the subnet mask is 255 (maximum). The first octet (192) is part of the network ID. The 168 is in the second octet of the IP address, and the second octet of the subnet mask is 255 (maximum). The second octet (168) is part of the network ID. The 18 is in the third octet of the IP address, but the matching subnet mask in the third octet is a zero (not maximum), so the 18 is not in the network ID.

TIP Subnets follow a rule of contiguous maximums. In other words, you start with a maximum number (255), and once you have a minimum number (0), the rest are minimums. The following subnet masks violate this rule and aren't valid: 255.0.255.0, 255.255.0.255. Valid subnet masks will have only zeros after the first zero is reached.

The network ID is 192.168.0.0. When expressing the network ID, you always express it with trailing zeros.

Of less importance here is the host ID, but for completeness, the host ID is 18.1. The host ID is not expressed with leading zeros.

Consider the following IP address in a different private IP range. Can you tell what the network ID is?

- 10.16.8.1
- 255.0.0.0

Only the first octet in the subnet mask is maximum (255), so only the first octet in the IP address is part of the network ID. The network ID is 10.0.0.0.

EXAM TIP You should be able to look at any IP address and subnet mask combination and easily tell the network ID. This will allow you to easily identify valid and invalid TCP/IP configurations.

Table 5-1 shows several IP address and subnet combinations. Use this table to test your ability to determine the network ID from the IP address and the subnet mask. You can check your answers by comparing them with the answers in Table 5-9 at the end of the chapter.

Table 5-1 Determining the Network ID	IP address	Subnet Mask	Network ID
	10.10.5.2	255.255.255.0	
	192.168.3.7	255.255.255.0	
	172.16.17.1	255.255.0.0	
	192.168.2.5	255.255.255.0	
	10.10.5.2	255.0.0.0	
	192.168.2.5	255.255.0.0	

Once you understand the concept, you should be able to easily glance at an IP address and subnet mask combination and determine the network ID. This is important on the job and for the exams. The following sections explain why.

CIDR Notation

IP addresses are sometimes listed using Classless Inter-Domain Routing (CIDR) notation. CIDR (pronounced as "cider") notation is simply a shortcut method of listing the IP address with the subnet mask.

Instead of listing an IP address and subnet mask of 10.2.3.4 255.0.0.0, it could be listed as 10.2.3.4 /8.

Remember, each octet of the subnet mask is composed of 8 bits. If the subnet mask is 255, then each of the 8 bits is 1. So a subnet mask of 255.0.0.0 would have the first 8 bits as 1 and could be represented as /8.

A subnet mask of 255.255.0.0 could be represented as /16. A subnet mask of 255.255.255.0 could be represented as /24. When subnetting is used, you'll see CIDR notation using numbers other than /8, /16, and /24, but for the scope of this book these are all you'll need.

Table 5-2 shows different IP address and subnet mask combinations with the associated CIDR notation.

Table 5-2	IP Address	Subnet Mask	CIDR Notation
CIDR Notation Examples	10.10.5.1	255.0.0.0	10.0.5.1/8
	10.10.7.3	255.255.0.0	10.10.7.3/16
	192.168.1.5	255.255.255.0	192.168.1.5/24

Routing

TCP/IP traffic is rarely contained within a single subnet. Instead, traffic passes from one subnet to another via routers. Consider Figure 5-3. It shows a relatively simple network configuration with two subnets.

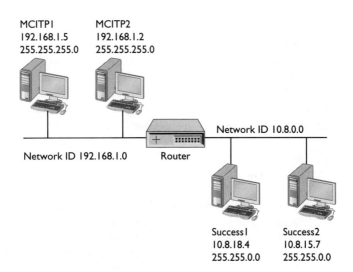

Figure 5-3
Typical network with two subnets separated by a router

MCITP1
192.168.1.5
255.255.255.0

MCITP2
192.168.1.2
255.255.255.0

Network ID 192.168.1.0   Router

Network ID 10.8.0.0

Success1
10.8.18.4
255.255.0.0

Success2
10.8.15.7
255.255.0.0

In the previous topic, you learned about the two parts of an IP address. You should be able to easily determine the network ID of the computers with IP addresses and subnet masks shown. Here's how the network ID is relevant.

When the Internet Protocol (IP) is ready to send data, it takes a look at the source IP and the destination IP. It needs to make an important decision: is the destination local (on the same subnet), or remote (and must go through the router).

Local or remote? The location of the destination is determined by the network ID of each. If they are the same, the destination is local. If they are different, the destination is remote and the data must go through the router.

If MCITP1 wants to send data to MCITP2, the IP protocol looks at both IP addresses and determines the network ID as shown in Table 5-3. Both network IDs are the same, so the destination is local.

Table 5-3	IP Address	Subnet Mask	Network ID
Determining the Network IDs Are Local	192.168.1.5	255.255.255.0	192.168.1.0
	192.168.1.2	255.255.255.0	192.168.1.0

If MCITP1 wants to send data to Success1 instead, the IP protocol looks at both IP addresses and determines the network ID as shown in Table 5-4. The network IDs are different, so the destination is remote.

Table 5-4	IP Address	Subnet Mask	Network ID
Determining the Network IDs Are Remote	192.168.1.5	255.255.255.0	192.168.1.0
	10.8.18.4	255.255.0.0	10.8.0.0

An important concept related to this is that all hosts (computers or any other device with an IP address) on a subnet must have the same network ID. Consider Figure 5-4. It shows MCITP1 with an incorrect IP address for this subnet.

With an IP address of 10.8.1.5 and a subnet mask of 255.255.255.0, the network ID of MCITP1 is 10.8.1.0. If MCITP1 were to try to send data to MCITP2, the two network IDs would be compared to determine if the destination is local or remote.

- MCITP1: 10.8.1.0
- MCITP2: 192.168.1.0

The address looks remote, so MCITP1 would try to send the data through the router instead of directly to the computer on the same subnet. As configured, MCITP1 and MCITP2 would never communicate. Additionally, you'll see in the next section why MCITP1 would also never communicate with any other hosts on the network.

Figure 5-4
MCITP1 host
incorrectly
configured

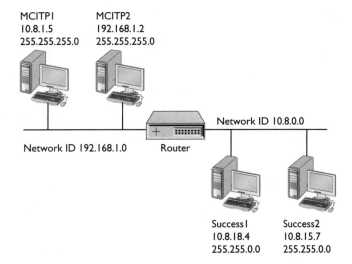

In Figure 5-4, I exaggerated the differences in the IP addresses so that the different network IDs would stand out, but the differences aren't always so dramatic. Often, a simple typo when manually configuring IP addresses causes the problem. For example, consider the TCP/IP configuration in Table 5-5.

Table 5-5
MCITP1 with an
Incorrect Subnet
Mask

Host	IP Address	Subnet Mask	Network ID
MCITP1	192.168.1.5	255.255.0.0	192.168.0.0
MCITP2	192.168.1.2	255.255.255.0	192.168.1.0

In the table, the IP address for MCITP1 is correct but the subnet mask is incorrect. This would also result in an incorrect Network ID. MCIP1 would interpret MCITP2 as remote and never be able to connect to it.

Default Gateway

In order for routing to work correctly, hosts with the subnet mask must have the IP address of the default gateway. The default gateway is the IP address of the NIC on the near side of the router. For example, consider Figure 5-5. In this diagram, the router has two NICs and each NIC is assigned an IP address and subnet mask.

NOTE Occasionally, people refer to the default gateway as the router. This isn't completely accurate. The default gateway refers to the interface (NIC) connected to a subnet; it is only part of a router. A router could have several interfaces connected to several subnets.

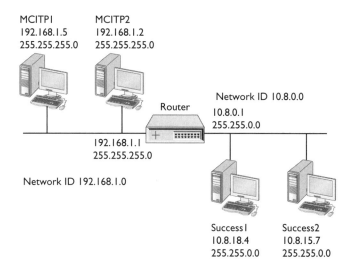

Figure 5-5
Network showing IP addresses of default gateways

If you calculate the network ID of each NIC, you'll notice that each NIC has a network ID that is the same as all other hosts on its subnet. This is a requirement.

When MCITP1 wants to send data to Success1, the source and destination network IDs are determined to be remote. MCITP1 then realizes it must send the data to the default gateway. If the default gateway was configured with an incorrect network ID (or MCITP1 had the default gateway configured with an incorrect network ID), then MCITP1 would never communicate with the default gateway. Traffic would be limited to only the local subnet.

You may realize that the default gateway on both subnets is configured as the very first host on the subnet (192.168.1.**1** and 10.8.**0.1**). This is a common practice, but it is not required.

DHCP

IP addresses can be assigned manually or dynamically. In most networks, desktop systems (such as Windows Vista) have their systems configured to receive IP addresses (and other TCP/IP configuration information) dynamically through a Dynamic Host Configuration Protocol (DHCP) server.

Consider Figure 5-6. MCITP1 is configured to get TCP/IP configuration information from DHCP. A process commonly referred to as DORA begins when MCITP1 turns on.

1. **D - Discover**   The client sends a DHCP discover message. This message is simply looking for a DHCP server to offer a lease.

2. **O - Offer**   The DHCP server responds with a lease offer. A typical lease would include an IP address, a subnet mask, the address of the default gateway, and the IP address of the DNS server.

3. **R - Request**   The client responds with a request. It's possible for a network to have more than one DHCP server. The client will only request the lease from the first DHCP server.

4. **A - Acknowledge**   The DHCP server acknowledges the lease request.

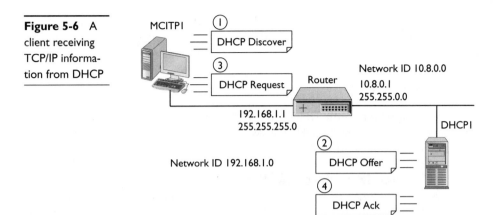

Figure 5-6 A client receiving TCP/IP information from DHCP

Routers don't normally pass broadcasts. However, DHCP broadcasts are special BOOTP broadcasts that pass through routers on UDP ports 67 and 68. RFC 1542 provides the specifics on this process, and routers that can pass the BOOTP broadcasts are referred to as RFC 1542 compliant.

In routers on internal networks, DHCP broadcasts are enabled through the router. DHCP broadcasts are disabled on routers on the Internet, and boundary routers separating the Internet and intranet.

For example, consider Figure 5-7. It shows one DHCP server for the headquarters office, but nothing for the remote office separated by the Internet. The one DHCP server couldn't provide the remote clients with TCP/IP configuration information over the Internet. UDP ports 67 and 68 would be closed on both Router1 and Router2.

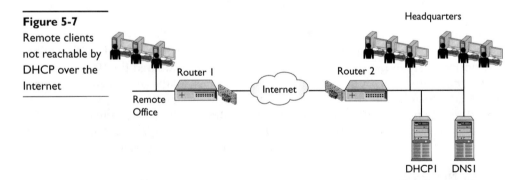

Figure 5-7
Remote clients not reachable by DHCP over the Internet

The clients in the remote office would have to be manually configured. Exercise 5.1 will lead you through the steps to manually configure the clients.

The DORA process is started by the DHCP Client service. You can access the DHCP Client service in the Services applet to verify it is running by clicking Start | Administrative Tools and selecting Services. Also any service in the Services applet can be started or stopped using the command line with the Net start and Net stop commands.

For example, you can stop and start the DHCP Client service with these commands. Since the name of the service (DHCP Client) has a space in it, you need to enclose the entire name in quotes.

```
Net stop "DHCP Client"
Net start "DHCP Client"
```

If something happened to the DHCP server, it wouldn't respond. Likewise, if something happened to the router, the DHCP server response wouldn't be heard. The result is an Automatic Private IP Address.

Automatic Private IP Address (APIPA)

If a client begins the DORA process but never receives a reply from the DHCP server, it will typically assign itself an IP address in the Automatic Private IP Address (APIPA) range. APIPA can be disabled, but is usually enabled on clients. The APIPA range is

- 169.254.y.z
- 255.255.0.0

 EXAM TIP If you see an APIPA address (anything starting with 169.254), you should realize that the DHCP didn't respond. Investigate the DHCP server's functionality and the path to and from the DHCP server.

Seeing an IP address in the APIPA range lets you know you probably have a problem, though the only thing you know for sure is that the DHCP server couldn't be reached. It could be because the DHCP server is down, the router is down, or even that the router is incorrectly configured so that DHCP broadcasts aren't allowed through.

You may be wondering why APIPA was created. It's a valid question. The original purpose was to allow computers to be networked together with minimal configuration.

Consider a small network of five computers. If you configured the IP addresses to be assigned automatically but didn't add a DHCP server, all the computers would have APIPA addresses in the 169.254.0.0/16 range. Since they're all on the same network with the same network ID (169.254.0.0), they could all talk to each other.

A significant drawback today is that APIPA addresses don't have any default gateway. This means that APIPA hosts can't get past a router and can't access the Internet.

Home Networks

Ten years ago, only geeks had a home network. Today, they are quite common. In most urban areas, broadband connections to the Internet are common. Cable companies and phone companies are providing broadband connections to the home that can easily be shared among several computers.

Figure 5-8 shows a typical home network connected through a broadband cable connection. The broadband connection first goes through a cable modem. You could

Figure 5-8
A typical home
network

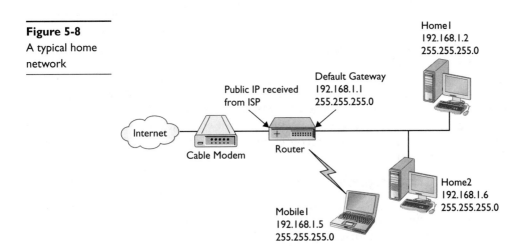

hook up a single computer to the cable modem, but to connect multiple computers in a network, you would hook up a router. You can buy routers (both wired and wireless) at most electronics stores for less than $100.

The router receives a public IP address from your Internet service provider (ISP). While the diagram shows Home1 and Home2 in a typical fishbone type diagram, the cables would be plugged directly into the router. If the router is wireless, wireless clients such as Mobile1 would also be able to connect.

Notice the IP addresses and subnet masks of each component. Each of the clients and the default gateway must be on the same network, and each must have unique host IDs. Incorrectly configuring any of the options will result in the one or more computers not operating.

Home routers often provide several other services built into the router. Some of the common services provided are

- **DHCP** DHCP is used to dynamically assign IP addresses and other TCP/IP configuration information.

- **Firewall** Most routers include firewall capabilities so that your internal network has a layer of protection.

- **NAT** Network Address Translation (NAT) translates private IP addresses to public IP addresses so that internal clients can access the Internet via the router.

Configuring Your NIC
One of the basics of networking is configuring your NIC. You can access the properties of your NIC using the following steps:

- Click Start, right-click Network, and select Properties to launch the Network and Sharing Center.

- Click the Manage Network Connections task from the Network and Sharing Center.

- Right-click your NIC and select Properties. If the User Account Control dialog box appears, click Continue.

By viewing the properties, you can identify the clients, services, and protocols bound to the NIC. Some of these have viewable or configurable properties that you can access.

In Exercise 5.1, you will access the TCP/IP properties of the NIC on your system. You can configure the NIC manually, or configure the NIC to receive a TCP/IP configuration from a DHCP server.

Exercise 5.1: Configuring a NIC

1. Access the Network and Sharing Center by clicking Start, right-clicking Network, and selecting Properties. The Network and Sharing Center will be explored in more depth later in this chapter.

2. Click the Manage Network Connections task in the left pane. Your display will look similar to Figure 5-9. In the figure, two NICs are showing—one for a wired network and one for a wireless network. Wireless networks will be covered in Chapter 6.

Figure 5-9
Accessing the NIC

3. Right-click the NIC and select Properties.

4. On the Local Area Connection Properties page, select Internet Protocol Version 4 (TCP/IPv4) and click Properties. Document the current configuration of your NIC so that you can return it to this state when you are finished.

CAUTION Take note of how your NIC is currently configured. If you don't return your NIC to the current configuration at the end of this exercise, you will lose connectivity with your network.

5. Configure your NIC to automatically receive a TCP/IP configuration through the DHCP server.

   a. Click the radio button next to Obtain an IP Address Automatically.

   b. Click the radio button next to Obtain DNS Server Address Automatically. Your display will look similar to Figure 5-10.

Figure 5-10
Configuring your NIC to obtain TCP/IP information from DHCP

   c. If you wanted this setting to take effect, you could click OK and exit the NIC property page.

6. Configure your NIC manually.

   a. Enter **192.168.1.5** in the IP Address box.

   b. Enter **255.255.255.0** in the Subnet Mask box.

   c. Enter **192.168.1.1** in the Default Gateway box.

TIP The default gateway uses the same subnet mask as the IP address. You don't enter separate subnet masks. Since the default gateway must have the same network ID as the host, the subnet mask must be the same, so there is no need to enter it twice.

   d. Enter **10.5.5.5** as the IP address for the Preferred DNS Server. On a network you would need to know the actual IP address of the DNS server to accurately enter this information. If you have additional DNS servers, you can add the address of a second DNS server in the Alternate DNS Server box to provide fault tolerance. Your display will look similar to Figure 5-11.

Figure 5-11
Manually
configured NIC

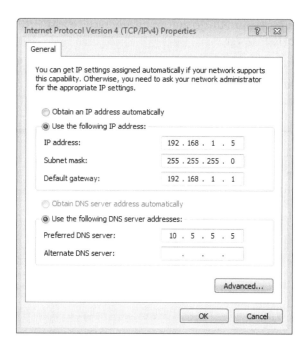

7. Return your NIC to its original configuration.

IPConfig

One of the most common commands you'll use from the command line when troubleshooting networking issues is the IPConfig command. IPConfig can be entered alone, or with one of several switches.

> **TIP** Most command-line commands are not case sensitive. In other words, you can enter the commands in all uppercase, all lowercase, or in any mixture of case you like. The command will work the same. Commands are frequently listed with some letters capitalized, but this is for readability only. As you try the commands in this section, use all uppercase, all lowercase, or a combination of upper- and lowercase letters to prove this yourself.

When entered alone, IPConfig shows the following information for available NICs:

- IPv4 address
- Subnet mask
- Default gateway

Depending on your system's configuration, you may also have a connection-specific DNS suffix and a link-local IPv6 address. For now, our focus is on the basics: IP address, subnet mask, and default gateway.

Several switches are available with IPConfig. Some of the ones most relevant to this topic are listed next. To enter any command, access the command line and enter **IPConfig**, a space, and the switch (including the forward slash).

 EXAM TIP You should be very familiar with the IPConfig command and the available switches. The best way to get a feel for the command and really learn it is to open up a command line with administrative privileges and enter these commands to view how each of them look and behave.

- **/?** This will give you help and show you all of the commands available.

- **/All** The All switch shows a significant amount of information on each of the connections. It includes the basics (such as IP address, subnet mask, and default gateway) but also shows a lot more. For example, it shows the hostname of the computer, and individual settings for each NIC. Figure 5-12 shows the printout for the /all switch for a single NIC (only the part of the printout for this NIC is shown). Note that DHCP Enabled is Yes, Autoconfiguration Enabled (APIPA) is Yes, and the Autoconfiguration IPv4 Address is in the 169.254.y.z range. This indicates that DHCP was unreachable.

```
C:\Windows\system32\cmd.exe                                               _ □ x

Ethernet adapter Local Area Connection:

   Connection-specific DNS Suffix   . :
   Description . . . . . . . . . . . : Broadcom 440x 10/100 Integrated Controlle
r
   Physical Address. . . . . . . . . : 00-16-D4-B1-12-7B
   DHCP Enabled. . . . . . . . . . . : Yes
   Autoconfiguration Enabled . . . . : Yes
   Link-local IPv6 Address . . . . . : fe80::acbc:afbb:4e67:d53c%7(Preferred)
   Autoconfiguration IPv4 Address. . : 169.254.213.60(Preferred)
   Subnet Mask . . . . . . . . . . . : 255.255.0.0
   Default Gateway . . . . . . . . . :
   DNS Servers . . . . . . . . . . . : fec0:0:0:ffff::1%1
                                        fec0:0:0:ffff::2%1
                                        fec0:0:0:ffff::3%1
   Primary WINS Server . . . . . . . : 10.80.1.100
   Secondary WINS Server . . . . . . : 10.80.1.101
   NetBIOS over Tcpip. . . . . . . . : Enabled
```

Figure 5-12 Partial IPConfig /All results

If the system was manually configured, the DHCP Enabled setting would indicate No.

- **/Release** If a DHCP address is automatically assigned, this command will release it. The resulting IP address is 0.0.0.0. This command is often used with the IPConfig /renew command to get a new IP address from the DHCP Server; the /release command is issued first. If the IP address is manually configured, this command won't do anything.

- **/Renew** This will cause the client to send a DHCP discover message looking for a DHCP server to get a lease. If a DHCP server is available and reachable, the client will get an IP address. If a response isn't received from the DHCP server, the client will assign an APIPA address (169.254.y.z). This command is often used with the IPConfig /release command to get a new IP address from the DHCP Server; the /renew command is issued after the /release command. If the IP address is manually configured, this command won't do anything.

- **/RegisterDNS**   This forces the client to register its name and IP address with the DNS server. It creates an A record (also known as a host record) on DNS so that other hosts can locate the client through DNS name resolution queries.

- **/DisplayDNS**   Every time a client does a DNS name resolution query, the result is stored in cache for a time determined by the DNS server. This command will show all the entries stored in cache. It also shows entries stored in the hosts file. The hosts file will be described in the Name Resolution section.

- **/FlushDNS**   If you want to remove items from the DNS cache, you can use the /flushDNS switch. It will remove all items except those in the hosts file. This switch can be useful if servers have new IP addresses assigned but clients still have the old IP address in cache. For example, a client may connect to a server named MCITP1. In the process, MCITP1 was resolved by DNS to a specific IP address. The next time the client wants to connect to MCITP1, it doesn't need to query DNS again, since the address is already in the host cache. This works fine unless MCITP1 is reconfigured with a new IP address. If MCITP1 has a new address, but the old address is still in cache, the client won't be able to connect until the MCITP1 entry is removed from cache. The entry is removed when the Time To Live property expires for the entry (which can be minutes or hours), or by using the /flushDNS switch.

Name Resolution

Name resolution is the process of resolving names to IP addresses. If someone asked you the IP address of msn.com, you probably wouldn't know it. There's really no need to know the address.

Instead, you know the name (msn.com), and if you type that into a Web browser, the site appears. However, what happens under the hood is that DNS is queried for the IP address and then the connection is made.

Within a network, there are two types of names and seven types of name resolution. You should be aware of them all.

Two types of names

The two types of names found on internal networks are host names and NetBIOS names. Host names are much more common, and NetBIOS names are falling into disuse, but you still need to be aware of both.

- **Host names**   A host name can be as long as 255 characters, though it is usually limited to only 15 characters by administrators. Host names are the only type of names you'll find on the Internet, but you will also find them on internal networks with NetBIOS names.

- **NetBIOS names** NetBIOS (short for Network Basic Input/Output System) names are found on internal networks, though their use is declining. The NetBIOS name is limited to only 15 readable characters, with the 16th byte identifying the service running on the computer. Computers will usually have several NetBIOS names registered based on the services running on the computer.

The NetBIOS name is typically the same as the host name. The difference is that the host name can be more than 15 characters. For hosts with host names longer than 15 characters, only the first 15 characters are used. The host name is truncated. You can see this in Table 5-6.

Table 5-6 Long Host Names Truncated as Net-BIOS Names

Host Name	NetBIOS Name
MarketingComputer1	MarketingComput
MarketingComputer2	MarketingCompu

Since the host name is longer than 15 characters, the NetBIOS name truncates the host name. The result is that two computers have identical NetBIOS names, which will cause problems if NetBIOS name resolution is needed. This is why host names are usually limited to 15 characters, even though they can be as long as 255 characters.

Originally NetBIOS names were needed because it was possible to automate the registration of NetBIOS names with a NetBIOS server such as Microsoft's WINS server, but it was not possible to automate the registration of host names with DNS.

When Windows 2000 was released, Microsoft introduced dynamic update or dynamic DNS on internal networks. With dynamic update, clients are able to automatically register a client's host name and IP address with DNS.

Figure 5-13 shows the automated name registration method used with WINS. This method was the primary method used with clients before Windows 2000, but it is still used in some instances today.

Figure 5-13 Name registration with WINS

WINS   DHCP

Registration

Client1
Pre-Windows 2000

When Client1 (a pre–Windows 2000 DHCP client) turns on, it receives TCP/IP configuration information from the DHCP server. The information includes the IP address of the WINS server. Client1 then registers its NetBIOS name (Client1) and new IP address with the WINS server. If any client queried the WINS server for the IP address of Client1, WINS would answer with the correct IP address.

Figure 5-14 shows the automated method of name resolution with DNS. Today (and since Windows 2000 was released) internal DNS servers have been able to accept updates just like the WINS servers. Dynamic update of DNS servers is only done on internal DNS servers. DNS servers on the Internet are updated manually.

Figure 5-14
Name registration with DNS

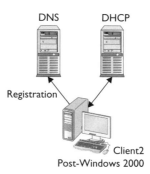

When Client2 turns on, it receives its information from DHCP and then registers its name and IP address with DNS. If any other clients query DNS for the IP address of Client2, DNS answers with the correct address.

While host names and NetBIOS names are treated differently within a network, they often look the same. For example, any name could be both the host name and the NetBIOS name of the client. The difference is in how applications treat the names.

An application will expect the name to be either a host name or a NetBIOS name and will try to resolve it accordingly. This is the reason that WINS servers are still required in networks today. Many applications still expect the name to be a NetBIOS name and still try to resolve the name using NetBIOS methods. With Windows Vista and Windows Server 2008, there are fewer applications using NetBIOS methods, but some applications still exist, so some networks will continue to use WINS.

Seven types of name resolution

It's easy to assume that there are only two types of name resolution (DNS and WINS), but there are actually seven types.

Table 5-7 shows the two types of names and the seven types of name resolution. You can see that host names are primarily resolved using the Hosts file, DNS servers, or the host cache. NetBIOS names are primarily resolved using the LMHosts file, WINS servers, or the NetBIOS cache. Both types of names can be resolved using broadcasts if the client is on the same network.

	Name	File Method	Server Method	Cache Method
Table 5-7 Name Resolution Methods	Host	Hosts	DNS	Host cache
	NetBIOS	LMHosts	WINS	NetBIOS cache
			Broadcast	

Each of these name resolution methods is explained in more depth in the following sections.

Hosts File The hosts file is a simple text file located at %systemroot%\System32\ Drives\etc. It has no extension. You can statically map host names to IP addresses in the hosts file. You'll have an opportunity to see this in action in Exercise 5.2.

 TIP The %systemroot% system variable is used to identify where the Windows files were installed. For example, if you installed the operating system in the default location of C:\Windows, then %systemroot% would have the same value as C:\Windows. You can see this by launching a command line and entering **cd %systemroot%**. This will change the directory to the operating system directory (more than likely C:\Windows).

Comments are added to the hosts file with a # symbol. Any line with a # symbol is ignored when the hosts file is read. Vista includes two lines in the hosts file by default:

```
127.0.0.1     localhost
::1           localhost
```

The first line maps the localhost name to the IPv4 loopback address of 127.0.0.1. The second line maps the localhost name to the IPv6 loopback address of ::1. If you access the command line and enter **ping localhost**, it will resolve it to ::1 and send four packets to the ::1 address. Pinging the localhost is often used to test that TCP/IP is functioning properly on a system.

TIP The ping command can be used at the IP address to check connectivity to a computer. It will send out four packets and return four packets. What often eludes people is the name resolution step that happens within ping. Ping the name of any reachable computer, and the ping response will show its IP address. Try it!

Additional lines can be added to the hosts file. This is not often done in networks today, but the hosts file is sometimes modified for malicious purposes. As soon as the file is modified, the entry appears in the host cache. You can view the host cache with the `ipconfig /displaydns` command.

In Exercise 5.2, you will modify the hosts file and view the impact on the computer. This exercise assumes you have an Internet connection.

Malware and the Hosts File Malware (malicious software such as viruses, worms, and spyware) has been known to modify the hosts file as an attack on systems. The possibilities of damage with this attack are wide.

As an example, one attack adds an entry to the hosts file for Symantec.com and gives the loopback address of 127.0.0.1. This causes all attempts to access Symantec.com to be redirected to your own system. The result is that Symantec anti-virus software that needs to have updated definitions can't reach Symantec and the definitions can't be updated.

Another possible attack may create an entry for a specific banking institution (perhaps the bank that you use for online banking). When you try to access the bank, you are instead redirected to phoneybank.com, which looks exactly like your bank's Web site (except for the Web address). You enter your username and password, which is promptly collected and exploited.

I've also heard of this done as a harmless prank among friends. You can add a host entry to the hosts file of your friend's computer to redirect her to live.com (Microsoft's search site) every time she tries to access Google, or redirect them to Google every time she tries to access live.com.

Your imagination may come up with different sites! Remember what George Harrison said, though—"whatever you do, is going to come right back on you"— so play nice.

Exercise 5.2: Viewing and Modifying the Hosts File

1. Launch the command prompt with administrative privileges. Click Start | All Programs | Accessories and right-click over the Command Prompt. Select Run As Administrator. If the User Account Control dialog box appears, click Continue.

2. At the command prompt, enter **Ping msn.com**. On the very next line you'll see that the name msn.com has been resolved to an IP address. It will look similar to the following line:

```
Pinging msn.com [207.68.172.246] with 32 bytes of data:
```

Whether the ping succeeds or not isn't important. The site could be blocking ICMP traffic, which includes pings, but what you want is the IP address of the site. Write the IP address here: _____

3. Open Internet Explorer and enter **mcitpsuccess.com** in the address line. You'll see the MCITPSuccess.com site appear. Leave Internet Explorer open.

4. At the command prompt, enter **IPConfig /DisplayDNS** to view the host cache. Among the entries, you should see the entries for msn.com and mcitpsuccess.com.

Enter **IPConfig /FlushDNS** to remove all the entries from cache except for what is in the hosts file. Enter **IPConfig /DisplayDNS** again to view the host cache. Leave the command prompt open.

5. Open Notepad with administrative privileges. Click Start | All Programs | Accessories, right-click Notepad, and select Run As Administrator.

6. Within Notepad, click File | Open. Browse to the C:\Windows\System32\ Drivers\etc folder. Right above the OK and Cancel buttons, you'll see a drop-down box set to Text Documents (*.txt). Change this to All Files (*.*) from the drop-down box.

7. Double-click the hosts file to open it.

8. Scroll to the end of the hosts file and add the following line:

```
207.68.172.246    mcitpsuccess.com
```

This maps mcitpsuccess.com to the msn.com address of 207.68.172.246. If you wrote down a different address in Step 2 for msn.com, use that address instead.

9. Press the CTRL-S keys to save the file. Leave the file open.

10. Back at the command prompt enter **ipconfig /displaydns**. You'll see that the hosts file entry for mcitpsuccess.com is immediately displayed in cache.

11. Enter the following command to resolve mcitpsuccess.com.

```
Ping mcitpsuccess.com
```

Notice that mcitpsuccess.com is resolved to the IP address of msn.com.

12. Return to Internet Explorer screen that is viewing the mcitpsuccess.com site. Press F5 to refresh the screen. Notice that instead of showing mcitpsuccess.com, your system is now showing msn.com.

13. Return to the hosts file. Delete the line that sets mcitpsuccess.com to the incorrect address. Press CTRL-S to save your changes.

14. Close all windows.

DNS Server The Domain Name System (DNS) is used to automate the process of resolving host names to IP addresses. The DNS server has A records (also called host records). When a client queries DNS with a host name, DNS responds with an IP address (assuming it either has an A record or can get the IP address from another DNS server). You can query for the existence of A records on a DNS server using the NS-lookup command. For example, to determine if DNS has a record for Client1, you can enter **NSLookup client1** at the command line.

The address of the DNS server is configured either dynamically through DHCP or manually in the properties of the NIC. Figure 5-15 shows the settings for the preferred and alternate DNS servers. The alternate DNS server is used for fault tolerance.

Figure 5-15
Configuring
preferred and
alternate DNS
servers

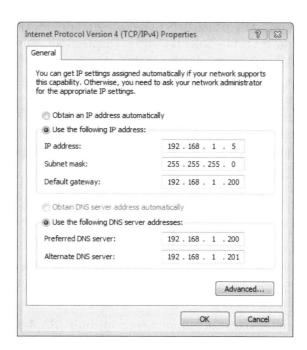

A client will attempt to reach the preferred DNS server first. If unavailable, the client will then attempt to reach the alternate DNS server. When manually configuring the DNS server settings, you would normally configure the closest DNS server as the preferred DNS server.

Host Cache   Any time a client queries DNS and receives a response, the response is stored in the host cache (volatile memory). It stays in the cache for a Time To Live period determined by the DNS server. Additionally, any data saved in the hosts file is automatically stored in the cache.

You can view the contents of the host cache with the `ipconfig /displaydns` command from the command line. If you want to empty the cache, you can use the `ipconfig /flushdns` command. You can't remove hosts file entries from the cache. In other words, any entry in the hosts file is automatically in the host cache; the only way to remove these entries is to remove the entry from the hosts file.

LMHosts File   The LMHosts file can be used to statically map NetBIOS names to IP addresses. It is rarely used any more. The LMHosts file is stored in the same location as the hosts file: %systemroot%\System32\Drives\etc, though it isn't available by default. Instead, a template file named LMHosts.sam is located in this directory; it can be renamed to LMHosts (without an extension).

WINS Server   The Windows Internet Naming Service (WINS) server is Microsoft's NetBIOS server used to register and resolve NetBIOS names. Don't be misled by the name, though. WINS has absolutely nothing to do with the Internet. It is only used on internal networks. When a WINS client turns on, it registers its name with WINS; and when a client wants to resolve a NetBIOS name, it queries WINS with the name. WINS resolves the NetBIOS name to an IP address and sends the IP address back as a response.

NetBIOS Cache   When a name is resolved, it is stored in the NetBIOS cache. You can view the names stored in the NetBIOS cache with the NetBIOS over TCP/IP Statistics command (NBTStat). Specifically, the nbtstat -c command can be entered at the command line to view the cache.

Broadcast   The last method of name resolution is sending a broadcast message (which is processed by every computer on the subnet). If you yell "Joe" into a room, anyone with the name Joe will answer. Similarly, if you broadcast MCITPSuccess1 on a network, any client with the name MCITPSuccess1 will answer.

Remember though, routers don't pass broadcasts, so broadcast name resolution requests are only valid on the same subnet.

Name Resolution and Applications

So with seven types of name resolution, what method is used? It depends on the application. Some applications expect the name to be a host name, so try the different host name resolution methods first (hosts file, DNS, host cache) and then try the other methods. Some applications expect the name to be a NetBIOS name, so they try different NetBIOS name resolution methods first (LMHosts, WINS, NetBIOS cache) and then try the other methods. Some applications try only some of the methods, not all of them.

The biggest thing to take away from this topic is that DNS is not the only name resolution method. DNS certainly the most common name resolution method, but it is not the only one.

IPv6 Introduction

While IPv4 is the prevalent IP addressing protocol today, we are in the midst of a migration to IPv6. As you work with networks, you'll see IPv6 start appearing. In time, IPv6 will be prevalent, as IPv4 usage will dwindle and ultimately disappear.

As a reminder, IPv4 uses 32 bits. The biggest problem with IPv4 was that we were running out of IP addresses on the Internet. If you do the math, 2^{32} is about four billion IP addresses. The original designers of the Internet thought this would be plenty, but Internet growth has been explosive.

IPv5 was designed with 64 bits. It was soon determined that the number of IP addresses available with 64 bits wouldn't be enough for the long term. Ten or so years down the road, the Internet would be running out of addresses. Again.

The solution is IPv6. With 128 bits there should be enough for everyone on the planet to have a few hundred IP addresses in ten years or so. It's not likely we'll run out too soon. 128 bits allows 2^{128} addresses. You can also write this as 340 undecillion or 340,282,366,920,938,463,463,374,607,431,768,211,456 addresses.

IPv6 was designed so that it could coexist with IPv4. Don't be surprised to see both IPv4 and IPv6 addresses in the same network. At this writing, IPv6 has been deployed in Japan and France, DNS root servers support IPv6, and the U.S. government is deploying IPv6 to backbones in the federal agencies.

IPv6 Address Format

Unlike IPv4 addresses, which are displayed in dotted decimal format, IPv6 addresses are displayed in hexadecimal format. Each IPv6 address has eight sets of four hexadecimal characters. Each hexadecimal character is composed of four bits. (4 * 4 * 8 = 128.)

An IPv6 address is looks like this:

FC00:0000:0000:0000:0DB8:CE12:0008:9C5A

Notice each set of four hexadecimal sets is separated by a colon. The first set (FC00) identifies this address as an IPv6 address used within a company that wouldn't be found on the Internet.

With IPv6 you can compress zeros. In other words, instead of writing out all the zeros, you can compress them. This can be done in two ways. Take a look at the following address which is written with the zeros compressed.

FC00::DB8:CE12:8:9C5A

Notice that the three sets of hexadecimal characters that are all zeros in the first address are compressed and expressed as simply two colons (::). Additionally, the zeros in the 0008 set in the first example are compressed and expressed simply as 8.

Table 5-8 shows hexadecimal numbers with the related decimal and binary values. Notice that the values 0 through 9 are the same, but when you reach decimal 10 hexadecimal starts using letters.

Decimal	Hexadecimal	Binary	Decimal	Hexadecimal	Binary
0	0	0000	8	8	1000
1	1	0001	9	9	1001
2	2	0010	10	A	1010
3	3	0011	11	B	1011
4	4	0100	12	C	1100
5	5	0101	13	D	1101
6	6	0110	14	E	1110
7	7	0111	15	F	1111

Table 5-8   Hexadecimal Table

IPv6 Address Categories

IPv6 addresses are categorized according to how they are used.

- **Global unicast addresses**   Used on the Internet with a three-bit prefix of 001. An example of a Global unicast address is 2000::/3.

- **Link-local addresses**   Used automatically when addresses aren't assigned, similar to how APIPA (169.254.y.z) addresses were used. These are identified with FE80::/64 prefixes.

- **Site-local addresses**   These were originally intended to be used internally to companies, similar to how private IP ranges were used. The use of site-local addresses is deprecated (though you may still see them in use). These are identified with FEC0::/10 prefixes. Site-local addresses will be replaced by centrally assigned unique local unicast addresses.

- **Centrally assigned unique local unicast addresses (the new site-local addresses)**   Unique local unicast (ULA) addresses are intended to be the replacement for site-local addresses (which are deprecated). These addresses will be used by companies internally, and are not routable on the Internet. These are identified with FC00::/7 prefixes.

Global Unicast Addresses

IPv6 addresses on the Internet are also known as global unicast addresses. Just as a public IPv4 address can reach any host on the Internet, a global unicast address can also reach any host on the Internet. A global unicast address has four parts. Figure 5-16 shows the four parts.

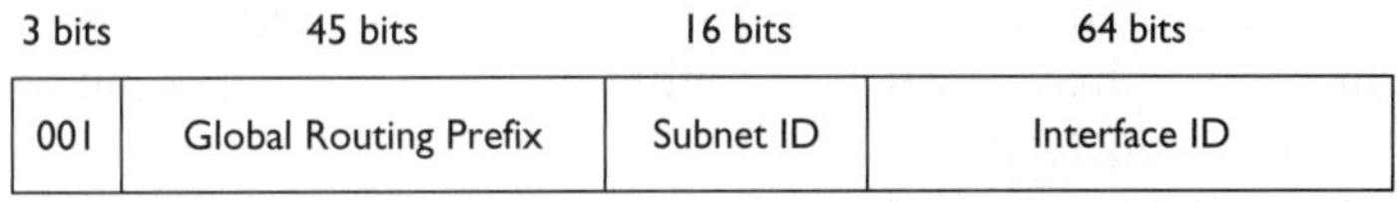

Figure 5-16

The four parts of a global unicast address

3 bits	45 bits	16 bits	64 bits
001	Global Routing Prefix	Subnet ID	Interface ID

- **Fixed portion**   The first three bits of global unicast addresses are 001. Additionally, global unicast addresses are represented as /3. With the /3 you know that this is a global unicast address (an Internet address). These addresses are typically represented as 2000::/3 in documentation.

- **Global Routing Prefix**   This identifies a specific organization's site. In this context, the organizations are Internet service providers (ISPs). IPv6 is designed so that routers can easily route traffic to the organization site based on this prefix combined with the fixed portion of the IPv6 address. The global routing prefix is 45 bits long.

- **Subnet ID**   16 bits are used to identify subnets. This allows an organization to create 65,536 subnets.

- **Interface ID**   The interface ID is used to identify specific hosts within the subnet ID for an organization. The interface ID is 64 bits long.

Link-Local Addresses

Link-local addresses are similar to the Automatic Private IP Addresses (APIPA) in the 169.254.y.z range. If addresses aren't assigned, computers on an IPv6 network can communicate with other computers using link local addresses.

Figure 5-17 shows the parts of a link-local address.

Figure 5-17	10 bits	54 bits		64 bits
A link-local IPv6 address	1111 1110 10			Interface ID

Interface Identifier

The first ten bits of a link-local address are: 1111 1110 10. This equates to FE80. The first ten bits are combined with the next 54 bits to create an interface identifier. The last 64 bits are used as the interface ID. All link-local addresses are expressed as FE80::/64.

Site-Local Unicast Addresses

Site-local unicast addresses were intended to be used within private networks. You may remember that IPv4 addresses have several specifically assigned IP ranges that can be used for private addresses (10.x.y.z/8, 172.16.y.z–172.31.y.z, and 192.168.y.z). The site-local addresses are similar.

However, objections were raised about site-local addresses. If two companies merged, each company would be flooded with significant IP address conflicts. To avoid this problem, site-local unicast addresses have been deprecated (by RFC 3879) in favor of unique local addresses (ULA). In other words, for any new networks you should not use site-local addresses.

However, you may still run across site-local addresses (which is the only reason I'm mentioning them here). They are expressed with FEC0::/10 prefixes.

Centrally Assigned Unique Local Unicast Addresses

Unique local addresses (ULA) are intended to be the replacement for site-local unicast addresses (which have been deprecated). These addresses will be used by companies internally and are not routable on the Internet.

TIP In some documentation, unique local addresses are sometimes referred to as site-local addresses. Since unique local addresses are replacing site-local addresses, this makes sense, but it can also lead to confusion. You need to remember the prefixes to actually know which is which. If "L" stood for local, you could remember it this way: FEC0L (pronounced fecal) is bad, since this is the prefix for the deprecated site local address. FC00L (pronounced F "Cool") is good, since this is the prefix for the unique local addresses that should be used.

These addresses are routable within a company. The company would be set up as a group of cooperating sites that is aware of the unique local addresses in use.

A ULA address has a prefix of FC00::/7, which is combined with the next 40 bits. The 40 bits are intended to be random (or at least pseudorandom) to decrease the possibility that two merging companies can have the same IP addresses.

EXAM TIP You should be able to easily identify an IPv6 address and also know which IPv6 addresses would be found within private networks—those with the FC00::/7 prefix preferably, or possibly with the deprecated FEC0::/10 prefix.

As examples, the following addresses would be valid unique local addresses. The second address is expressed with zero compression.

- FC00:0000:0000:0DB8:0000:CE12:00A8:342A
- FC00::231A:34AC:4:12AB

Scoping

Occasionally, you may come across the % character at the end of an IPv6 address as follows: FE80::1%1. The % symbol is used as a delimiter (a separator) for scopes (or zone identifiers). The use of scopes is known as scoping.

NOTE The use of scoping is more fully explained in RFC 4007 if you're interested. It's only included here so that you'll understand a little about the purpose of the % symbol in an IPv6 address if you see it.

The zone identifier is expressed as a number (such as %1, %2, and so on) on Microsoft networks, but it can also be expressed as a name (such as %zone1, %id2, and so on) on other operating system networks such Unix-based networks.

Scoping can be used on multi-homed computers—computers with multiple NICs. Since the NICs may actually operate on separate networks but have IP addresses that appear to be on the same subnet, zone identifiers are used to indicate which zone the NIC operates on.

Zone identifiers are sometimes expressed with the / character (which identifies the number of bits used in the prefix), and sometimes the / character is omitted. When expressed fully, an IPv6 address with a zone identifier looks like this: FE80::1%1/64.

IPv6 Application Support

The use of IPv6 addresses is expected to grow as time passes. Some applications won't fully support IPv6 right away. Additionally, you can expect other applications to require IPv6.

As an example, the Windows Meeting Space (which will be covered more fully in Chapter 14) requires that clients either have a global IPv6 address or be operating on the same subnet.

Network and Sharing Center

The Network and Sharing Center is your primary point of entry for most of your networking tasks. There are a few ways to get to it, but the easiest way is by clicking Start, right-clicking Network, and selecting Properties.

Figure 5-18 shows the Network and Sharing Center. It shows the typical Vista Tasks list in the left pane and many other features and capabilities in the main window.

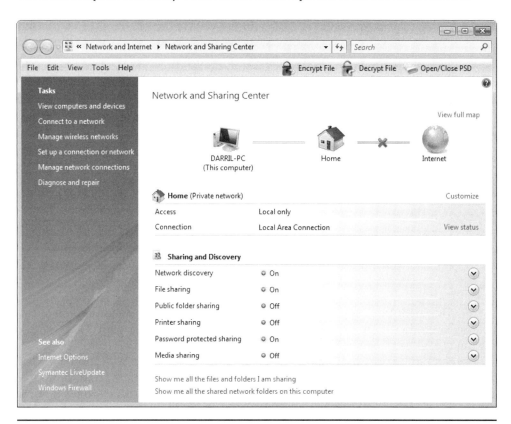

Figure 5-18   Network and Sharing Center

The Tasks list has some tasks you should be very familiar with to be successful with Windows Vista networking:

- **Diagnose And Repair**   Clicking this link will launch the Windows Network Diagnostics tool, which is specifically designed to test and diagnose your Internet connection. This tool goes through a series of tests to test your computer's ability to connect to the Internet. For example, it tries to resolve the www.microsoft.com name to an IP address using your configured DNS server. If it fails, it reports the problem and includes a link in Help that can be used to check the problem further.

EXAM TIP   When troubleshooting Internet connections, you should consider using the Windows Network Diagnostics tool (by selecting Diagnose And Repair) as one of your first steps.

- **Manage Network Connections** Clicking this link provides access to your network interface cards. You had an opportunity to view and manipulate some of the properties of the NICs in Exercise 5.1.

- **Set Up a Connection or Network** This launches a menu you can use to configure connections to the Internet via dial-up, broadband, or wireless connections. You can also configure wireless networks or create remote access connections. You can select any of the options and click Next to access a wizard to lead you through the process.

- **Connect to a Network** This provides a list of dial-up, VPN, and wireless connections that you can access. Remote access and VPN connections will be covered in Chapter 7. Wireless connections will be covered in Chapter 6.

- **Manage Wireless Networks** This menu allows you to add, remove, and manipulate connections to wireless networks; it will be covered in Chapter 6.

Network Discovery

Network discovery is a network setting used to control how easily your computer can view other hosts on the network, and how easily other hosts can find your computer. Network discovery uses broadcasts to detect other computers, so only other devices on the subnet are reachable.

You may remember that routers don't pass broadcasts, so any devices on the other side of a router are not reachable.

Network discovery has three settings:

- **On** When network discovery is set to on, your computer can find other computers and devices, and other computers and devices can find you. The purpose is to make it easier to share resources (such as folders and printers) within a network.

- **Off** When network discovery is set to off, your computer can't easily see other computers and devices on the network, and other devices can't easily see your computer.

- **Custom** This allows a hybrid of network discovery settings and is most often used with a computer within a domain that is affected by group policy.

The Network Discovery settings are directly affected by the network location. When you first configure a network connection in a non-domain environment, you are presented with a choice of a network location. Based on your choice, the network discovery setting is changed.

 EXAM TIP You should have a solid understanding of the meaning of both a Public network connection and a Private network location. You set the network location to Public when in a public location to provide extra protection for your computer. You set it to Private when in a protected location such as in a work or home network that is not directly connected to the Internet, but instead connected to the Internet through a router providing basic firewall and NAT services.

Private

The Private network location is intended to be used when your computer is connected to a private network that you consider protected. Examples of a private network are your work location or a home network. Generally, a private network doesn't have direct access to the Internet, but instead Internet access is via a router providing basic firewall and Network Address Translation (NAT) services.

When the network is designated as private, network discovery is turned on and your computers can easily see and find other computers and devices, and other computers can easily find your computer.

If you ever want to change the setting, you can click the Customize link in the Network and Sharing Center. Figure 5-19 shows the Customize link right next to the network name, and the resulting page that allows you to change a network from Private to Public or from Public to Private.

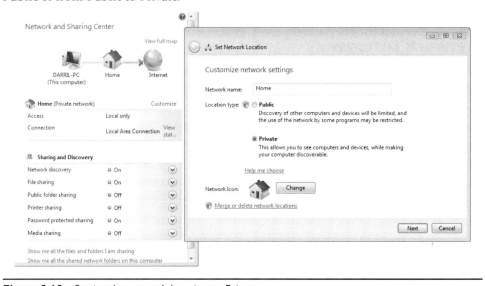

Figure 5-19   Setting the network location to Private

Public

The Public network location is intended to be used when your computer is connected to a public location such as an airport, hotel, or coffee shop.

When your network is designated as public, network discovery is turned off. Your computer can't easily find other computers, and other computers can't easily find you. This provides a layer of protection.

Link Layer Topology Discovery

The Link Layer Topology Discovery (LLTD) protocol was developed by Microsoft to provide the services needed by network discovery. You may remember that two protocols are bound to the NIC in a Windows Vista configuration:

- The Link Layer Topology Discovery Mapper I/O Driver
- Link Layer Topology Discovery Responder

Both protocols must be enabled on Windows Vista in order for network discovery to work. This is the default, so it usually doesn't require any modification.

However, LLTD isn't installed by default on older systems such as Windows XP. If you want the Windows XP clients to be discovered using network discovery in Windows Vista, you need to download and install the LLTD responder. You can download the LLTD responder through Knowledge Base article 922120 at this link: http://support.microsoft.com/?kbid=922120.

 EXAM TIP Windows XP computers in the network aren't automatically found through network discovery. You must install the Link Layer Topology Discovery (LLTD) Responder on Windows XP in order to allow Windows Vista computers to find them using network discovery technologies.

Troubleshooting the NIC

When you lose connectivity, it's possible the problem is with the network interface card (NIC). The Network Connections page provides you with some basic troubleshooting tools you can use to help identify and sometimes resolve the problems.

To access the Network Connections page, click Manage Network Connections from the Network and Sharing Center. Figure 5-20 shows the Network Connections page after the Home NIC has been selected and the Diagnose This Connection link has been selected.

While Figure 5-20 shows that it didn't find a problem, it does provide links to send a report to Microsoft (which may result in a response if this is a common problem) or to reset the connection.

Figure 5-20   Resetting the NIC

Resetting the connection will clear all the cache entries and try to return the NIC to the state it was in just after a reboot. Rebooting the system would perform the same actions on the NIC, but resetting is much quicker.

If the NIC has a DHCP-assigned address, the reset will request a new address from DHCP. This is similar to using IPConfig /release and IPConfig /renew as discussed earlier in the chapter. The biggest difference is that an IPConfig /release results in an address of 0.0.0.0, but if a reset fails to access DHCP, the original IP address will be retained.

Network ID Answers   Earlier in this chapter, Table 5-1 showed several IP address and subnet combinations. You had an opportunity to identify the resulting network ID. Use Table 5-9 to check your answers.

IP Address	Subnet Mask	Network ID
10.10.5.2	255.255.255.0	**10.10.5.0**
192.168.3.7	255.255.255.0	**192.168.3.0**
172.16.17.1	255.255.0.0	**172.16.0.0**
192.168.2.5	255.255.255.0	**192.168.2.0**
10.10.5.2	255.0.0.0	**10.0.0.0**
192.168.2.5	255.255.0.0	**192.168.0.0**

Table 5-9   Network ID Answers (from Table 5-1)

Chapter Review

In this chapter you learned about several basic networking concepts and how they are applied within Windows Vista.

Clients, services, and protocols are automatically bound to a NIC, but they can be deselected, disabling the client service and protocol. IPv4 addresses have two parts—a network ID and a host ID—and it's important that all hosts within a subnet have the same network ID for communication. Clients normally get their addresses from DHCP, but they can be manually assigned. IPConfig is a valuable tool used for troubleshooting problems.

You learned that there are two types of names (host and NetBIOS) and seven types of name resolution. DNS is most commonly used, but simpler methods (such as the hosts file) are important to know about, since they can be manipulated, causing you significant problems.

IPv6 has arrived. You saw what an IPv6 address looked like. Global IPv6 addresses are used on the Internet and have a 2000::/3 prefix. Link-local addresses are automatically assigned in internal networks and have a FE80::/64 prefix. Unique local addresses are manually assigned in internal networks and have a FC00::/7 prefix. Site local addresses are not recommended for use, since they have been deprecated; they have a FEC0::/10 prefix.

Last, you had an introduction to the Network and Sharing Center. You'll see more of the Network and Sharing Center in Chapter 6, but in this chapter you learned about network discovery and setting a network connection to public or private.

Additional Study

Self Study Exercises

Use these additional exercises to challenge yourself.

- Create a home network. Even if you have only one computer hidden behind a router, this is a valuable learning exercise.

- Determine if your computer obtains an IP address automatically, or manually. Change it and observe the results. Change it back.

- Deselect some of the clients, services, and protocols bound to your NIC and observe the results.

- Write out an IPv6 address that may be found on the Internet. Write out an IPv6 address that may be manually assigned within a company. Write out an IPv6 address that may be automatically assigned within a company.

- Use the IPConfig command to determine the IP address of DNS.

- Launch the Network and Sharing Center and select Diagnose and Repair.

- Launch the Network Connections center and diagnose your connection.

Summary of What You Need to Know

70-620

When preparing for the 70-620 exam, pay particular attention to the following topics covered in this chapter:

- **Networking Basics**   You should understand the basics of networking. This includes understanding the network ID, how to calculate it, and why it's important. Additionally much of the section "Networking Basics" will be a foundation for wireless topics covered in Chapter 6.

- **IPv6**   You should be able to identify an IPv6 address and know some basics about it.

- **Public and Private**   You should know the differences between setting a network connection to public or to private and how it affects network discovery.

- **Internet connectivity**   You should have an understanding of how to troubleshoot Internet connectivity issues, including how to use the Diagnose and Repair feature within the Network and Sharing Center.

70-622

This chapter heavily focused on topics for the 70-622 exam. Expect to have several questions directly out of this chapter when you take the exam. When preparing for the 70-622 exam, pay particular attention to the following topics covered in this chapter:

- **Networking Basics**   You should understand the basics of networking, but at a much deeper level than is required for the 70-620 exam. You should understand concepts like routing, DHCP, and name resolution. Additionally, you should be aware of the tools used to troubleshoot problems, including command-line tools (and their switches) such as IPConfig.

- **IPv6**   You should be able to identify an IPv6 address and know which IPv6 addresses are used on the Internet, which are manually assigned internal to a company, and which are automatically assigned internal to a company.

- **Public and Private**   You should know the differences between setting a network connection to public or to private and how it affects network discovery. You should also know about the LLTD protocols that allow network discovery to work on a network.

70-623

When preparing for the 70-623 exam, pay particular attention to the following topics covered in this chapter:

- **Networking Basics**   You should understand the basics of networking, including concepts like routing, DHCP, and name resolution. You should also be aware of the different clients, services, and protocols that can be bound to a NIC.

- **Public and Private**   You should know the differences between setting a network connection to public or to private and how it affects network discovery. You should also know about the LLTD protocols that allow network discovery to work on a network.

Questions

70-620

1. Your Windows Vista computer is configured with the following settings:

   - IP Address: 10.8.1.4
   - Subnet Mask: 255.255.0.0
   - Default Gateway: Blank
   - Preferred DNS Server: 10.64.5.1
   - Alternate DNS Server: Blank

   You need to configure the computer to access computers on different subnets. What should you do?

   A. Provide an IP address for the alternate DNS server.

   B. Provide an IP address for the Default Gateway as 10.64.1.1.

    C. Provide an IP address for the Default Gateway as 10.8.1.1.

    D. Provide an IP address for the Default Gateway as 10.255.1.1.

2. You have started a new job as a help desk professional and are helping a Vista client connect his computer to the network. After requesting help, a supervisor sends you an e-mail and says to configure the client with: 2201:0:0:0:C73E: FA23:601:135A. What should you configure?

    A. The IPv5 address

    B. The IPv6 address

    C. The physical address

    D. The WPA2 key

3. You have a small office network using a wireless router connecting three office computers to the Internet via an ISP. The wireless router fails, but you need to access the Internet to complete some work, including posting and downloading some files via FTP. You connect your primary computer running Windows Vista directly to the Internet. How should you configure your computer to ensure the best protection while connected to the Internet?

    A. Configure the network settings to Protected mode.

    B. Configure the firewall to On With No Exceptions.

    C. Configure the network settings with a location type of Public.

    D. Configure the network settings with a location type of Private.

4. You start using your Windows Vista computer and realize you're unable to access any Internet resources. You were able to access the Internet the last time you used this computer. What can you do to help identify the problem?

    A. Use the Network and Sharing Center and click the Connect to a Network link.

    B. Use the Network and Sharing Center and click the Diagnose and Repair link.

    C. Launch Internet Explorer and select the Tools | Diagnose and Repair option.

    D. Launch Help and Support and click the Diagnose and Repair option.

5. You are unable to access the mcitpsuccess.com Web site from your home computer. You try another computer in your home network and it succeeds. You use the other computer to determine the IP address and try to reach the Web site with the IP address. It succeeds. What can you use to help you troubleshoot the problem further?

    A. Type `IPConfig /RegisterDNS` at the command prompt.

    B. Type `NBTStat -c` at the command prompt.

    C. Disable IPv6 on the NIC.

    D. Use the Diagnose and Repair feature in the Network and Sharing Center.

70-622

1. Your network is configured as shown in the Figure 5-21. All end-user computers are DHCP clients. Users in subnet 2 are complaining that they can't connect to any resources outside subnet 2. There are no problems reported by users in subnet 1 or subnet 3. You use IPConfig to view the IP address of a client in subnet 2 and view the following configuration:

Figure 5-21
Network configuration

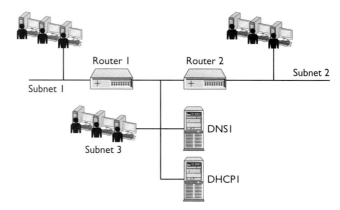

- IP Address: 169.254.45.2
- Subnet Mask: 255.255.0.0
- Default Gateway: Blank
- Preferred DNS Server: Blank

What is the likely problem?

A. Router 1 is faulty.

B. Router 2 is faulty.

C. DHCP is down.

D. The default gateway isn't configured.

2. You are troubleshooting a Windows Vista system that doesn't have connectivity with other clients on the network. You use IPConfig to identify the address and see the following information:

    IP Address: 169.254.37.44

    Subnet Mask: 255.255.0.0

    Default Gateway: Blank

You verify the client is configured to dynamically receive TCP/IP configuration information. You use the IPConfig command to get a new lease from DHCP, but the results are the same. You check other clients, and they can get and renew leases from DHCP. What should you do?

A. Start the DHCP Client service using the Services applet.

B. Start the DHCP Server service using the Services applet.

   C. Start the Default Gateway service using the Services applet.

   D. Set the Default Gateway.

3. Your company is opening a branch office, and you're helping configure the computers. The computers need to be configured with private IPv4 and IPv6 addresses. Which of these would be a valid IPv6 addresses?

   A. 2000::0DB8:0:CE12:A8:342A::/3

   B. FE80::0DB8:0:CE12:A8:342A::/64

   C. FC00::0DB8:0:CE12:A8:342A::/7

   D. FF00::0DB8:0:CE12:A8:342A::/8

4. You are configuring several Windows Vista computers within your company. You want to make sure the computers discover each other and other computers on the network. What should you do?

   A. Install IPv6 and assign a unique local address.

   B. Install IPv6 and assign a global address.

   C. Configure the network settings with a location type of Public.

   D. Configure the network settings with a location type of Private.

5. Computers on your network run Windows Vista and Windows XP. You recently learned about the using the Network and Sharing Center to create a network map. However, none of the Windows XP computers appear on the network map diagram. What should you do to have the Windows XP computers appear on the network map?

   A. Download and install the LLTD Responder for each of the Windows XP computers.

   B. Download and install the LLTD Responder for each of the Windows Vista computers.

   C. Configure the network settings for all the Windows Vista computers with a location type of Public.

   D. Configure the network settings for all the Windows XP computers with a location type of Public.

6. You are configuring 15 clients in a remote office that has connectivity to the Internet. The remote office has its own domain controller and DNS server. The main office has a DHCP server that is used to dynamically assign a TCP/IP configuration. The main office also has its own domain controller and DNS server. How should you configure TCP/IP for the clients in the remote office?

   A. Configure the clients to receive an IP address and DNS server address automatically.

   B. Configure the clients to receive an IP address dynamically and manually assign the remote office DNS server as the preferred DNS server.

C. Manually configure the IP address of the clients. Manually assign the main office DNS server as the preferred DNS server.

D. Manually configure the IP address of the clients. Manually assign the remote office DNS server as the preferred DNS server.

7. You come in Monday morning and find that several users are having problems with connectivity. All users are DHCP clients. You learn that the network had some major problems over the weekend. DNS servers were rebuilt with new IP addresses and DHCP was configured with updated options. What should you do for the users that are having problems with connectivity?

A. Reset their network adapters from Network Connections.

B. Run IPConfig /release from the command line with administrative privileges.

C. Run IPConfig /flushdns from the command line with administrative privileges.

D. Select Diagnose and Repair from the Network and Sharing Center.

70-623

1. You are assisting a user with her Vista computer that is behaving strangely. When accessing the Internet, it is able to go to most sites without any problems. However, attempts to access the Windows Update site fail. You try to enter the IP address of the Windows Update site in the URL (instead of the name) and it succeeds. You try to access Windows Update on another computer normally and it works fine. What is the problem?

A. DNS is down.

B. The hosts file has been modified.

C. The LMHosts file has been modified.

D. WINS is down.

2. You are helping a customer add another computer to a home network. One computer is already connected to the Internet via a router, and you want to add the second computer with the same capabilities. The IP configuration of the first computer is as follows:

- IP Address: 192.168.1.4
- Subnet Mask: 255.255.0.0
- Default Gateway: 192.168.1.1
- Preferred DNS Server: 192.168.1.1

How should you configure the new computer?

A. IP Address: 192.168.1.5
   Subnet Mask: 255.255.255.0
   Default Gateway: 192.168.1.1
   Preferred DNS Server: 192.168.1.1

    B. IP Address: 192.168.1.1
       Subnet Mask: 255.255.0.0
       Default Gateway: 192.168.1.1
       Preferred DNS Server: 192.168.1.1

    C. IP Address: 192.168.1.5
       Subnet Mask: 255.255.255.0
       Default Gateway: 192.168.1.4
       Preferred DNS Server: 192.168.1.1

    D. IP Address: 192.168.1.5
       Subnet Mask: 255.255.0.0
       Default Gateway: 192.168.1.1
       Preferred DNS Server: 192.168.1.1

3. You are assisting a user with her Windows Vista computer connected to a home network. She uses a router that has a firewall enabled and dynamically assigns IP addresses. She is unable to access the Internet or any other resources on her internal network. Her laptop is working fine. You use the IPConfig command to view the output as shown in Figure 5-22:

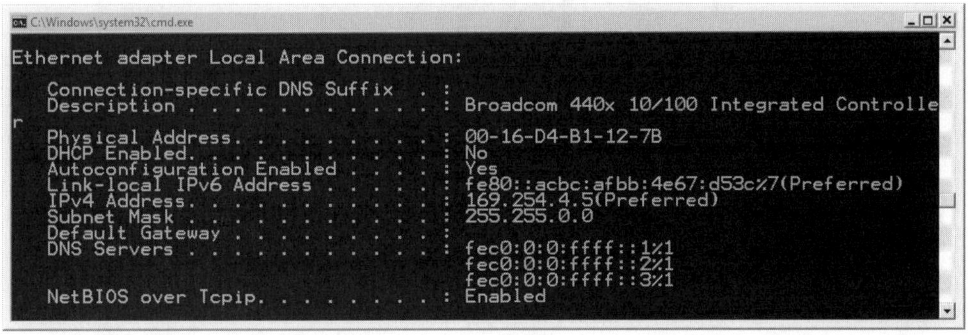

Figure 5-22 Partial IPConfig output

What is the likely problem?

A. The computer is not configured to use DHCP.

B. DHCP is down.

C. The firewall on the router is blocking all traffic.

D. The router is down.

4. You are assisting a small business owner with her Windows Vista computer. She is unable to detect any network resources, but you've verified other computers are on the same subnet and operational. What should be done? Choose all that apply.

A. Turn on the network discovery feature.

B. Enable the LLTD Mapper I/O driver protocol.

    C. Enable the LLTD Responder protocol.

    D. Ensure the network location is set to Public.

5. You are helping a user configure his Windows Vista computer. The computer will be running within a home network using a router for Internet access. He wants to easily be able to find other computers and have them easily find his computer. He also wants to access shares on other computers and allow other computers to access shares on his computer. He will not be using 128-bit addresses. You are looking at his NIC configuration shown in Figure 5-23. What must be enabled to support these requirements? Choose all that apply.

Figure 5-23
NIC configuration

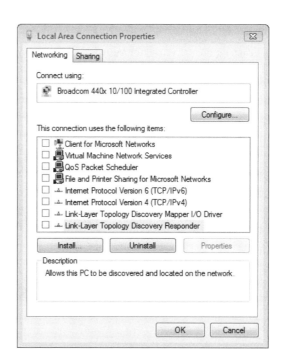

    A. Enable the Client for Microsoft Networks.

    B. Enable the Virtual Machine Network Services.

    C. Enable the QoS Packet Scheduler.

    D. Enable the File and Printer Sharing for Microsoft Networks.

    E. Enable the Internet Protocol Version 6 (TCP/IPv6).

    F. Enable the Internet Protocol Version 4 (TCP/IPv4).

    G. Enable the Link-Layer Topology Discovery Mapper I/O Driver.

    H. Enable the Link-Layer Topology Discovery Responder.

Answers

70-620

1. **C.** The default gateway must be on the same subnet (have the same network ID) as the IP address of the host. The host has an IP address of 10.8.1.4 and a subnet mask of 255.255.0.0, so its network ID is 10.8.0.0. The default gateway shares the same subnet mask as the host, so the first two octets in the default gateway's IP must the same as the host (10.8). An alternate DNS server would only be needed for name resolution if the preferred DNS server failed. An IP address of 10.64.1.1 with a subnet mask of 255.255.0.0 would have a network ID of 10.64.0.0 (not 10.8.0.0 as does the host). If the default gateway was assigned 10.255.1.1, it would have a network ID of 10.255.0.0.

2. **B.** 2201:0:0:0:C73E:FA23:601:135A is an IPv6 address. You should configure the NIC with this IPv6 address. IPv5 addresses are not used. The physical address (also known as the MAC address) is composed of six pairs of hexadecimal numbers, not eight groups of hexadecimal numbers. The WPA2 key is used to encrypt wireless traffic.

3. **C.** Since the computer is directly connected to the Internet, you should configure the location type as Public; this restricts the ability of other computers to find yours. This indicates your network is connected to a public network and provides a layer of protection for your computer. There is no Protected mode for the network settings. Configuring the firewall to On With No Exceptions would prevent any traffic (including the FTP traffic that's needed). When protected by a firewall (such as the wireless router before it failed), it's appropriate to set the location type to Private so that computers can find each other. Setting the location to Private when connected to the Internet makes your computer easier to find and more vulnerable.

4. **B.** The Diagnose and Repair option in the Network and Sharing Center is specifically designed to troubleshoot connectivity problems with the Internet. The Connect to a Network link can help you set up an Internet connection, but since you were able to access the Internet previously, this isn't needed. There is no Diagnose and Repair option from within Internet Explorer or from Help and Support.

5. **D.** The Diagnose and Repair feature can be used to help troubleshoot network connectivity issues on the Internet. Since you can access the Web site with the IP address, but not the name, the problem is name resolution (more than likely with DNS). The Diagnose and Repair feature can zero in on DNS problems and let you know the source of the problem. `IPConfig /RegisterDNS` would register your computer name with an internal DNS server, but this wouldn't be used in a home network. `NBTStat -c` can be used to view the NetBIOS cache, but NetBIOS names aren't used on the Internet. Disabling IPv6 wouldn't affect name resolution with DNS.

70-622

1. **B.** An address of 169.254.y.z indicates that the DHCP server was not reached, so an Automatic Private IP Address (APIPA) was assigned. APIPA addresses always start with 169.254. Since clients in subnets 1 and 3 work, it is a fair assumption that the DHCP server is operating. The path to the DHCP server from subnet 2 is through router 2. Since users in subnet 1 are working, router 1 is working. If the DHCP server were down, all clients would have problems, not only the clients in subnet 2. APIPA addresses don't include a default gateway.

2. **A.** The DHCP Client service is used to start the DHCP discover process to get a lease from the DHCP server. It can be started from the Services applet, or from the command line with the `Net Start "DHCP Client"` command. The 169.254.y.z address is in the APIPA range, indicating the client is not reaching DHCP, yet other clients can reach DHCP, indicating the problem is with the client (more than likely with the DHCP Client service), not the server. The DHCP Server service runs on the DHCP server. There no service named the Default Gateway service. Since the client should receive IP addresses dynamically, you should not manually configure the default gateway.

3. **C.** The FC00::/7 prefix is valid for private networks. This range is known as a centrally assigned unique local address. The FEC0::/10 prefix is also valid but has been deprecated; the FC00::/7 should be used instead. The 2000::/3 prefix is a global address (used on the Internet) identified by having the first three bits 001 and ending in ::/3. The prefix FE80::/64 is used to identify link-local addresses, which can be assigned automatically to clients that don't otherwise have an IPv6 address. The FF00::/8 prefix is used for multicast addresses (which weren't discussed in this chapter).

4. **D.** You can set the network settings to a location type of Private to ensure computers can find each other on the network. IPv6 is not needed for network discovery. If the location type is set to Public, network discovery capabilities will be limited.

5. **A.** If you download and install the Link Layer Topology Discovery (LLTD) Responder to the Windows XP computers, they will be found and appear on the network map. It's not necessary to install the LLTD responder on Windows Vista computers, since the protocol is included by default. Setting the location type to Public limits the ability of computers to be found and to find each other; this setting should be set to Private. Windows XP doesn't have a location type that can be set.

6. **D.** You must manually assign the IP addresses and DNS server addresses. The clients in the remote office should use the DNS server in the remote office. The DHCP server in the main office could not serve the clients in the remote office over the Internet, so it would not be possible to have anything automatically assigned. The local DNS server should be the preferred DNS server, not the DNS server in the main office.

7. **A.** By resetting the network adapters, the clients will get a new lease from DHCP, including the updated options that would have the new IP addresses for the DNS server. Running `IPConfig /release` from the command line will give the users an address of 0.0.0.0, which results in zero connectivity. `IPConfig /flushdns` will remove cached DNS entries but won't give the clients the updated options from DHCP. Diagnose and Repair is designed to troubleshoot problems with Internet connectivity, but connectivity with the DNS server is the core problem.

70-623

1. **B.** Since the computer can't access the Windows Update site normally but can access it with the IP address, the problem is with name resolution. Names on the Internet are hosts names, so the possible problems are DNS or the hosts file (or the hosts cache, which isn't one of the answer choices). Since other Web sites are resolving accurately, DNS is working, so the problem must be the hosts file. The LMHosts file and WINS are used to resolve NetBIOS names, which won't be found on the Internet.

2. **D.** The IP address must be unique but on the same network, and the default gateway and the subnet mask must be the same. Only answer D meets all these requirements. A subnet mask of 255.255.255.0 won't work, because the default gateway is using a subnet mask of 255.255.0.0. An IP address of 192.168.1.1 is the same as the default gateway, so it would cause a conflict. The actual default gateway has an address of 192.168.1.1, so putting 192.168.1.4 in the default gateway box would prevent the computer from accessing the default gateway.

3. **A.** In the figure, DHCP Enabled is set to No, indicating the client is not configured to use DHCP, but the question states that the router is configured to dynamically assign IP addresses. While the manually assigned IP address of 169.254.4.5 is in the Automatic Private IP Address (APIPA) range, it gives a hint that DHCP may be down, but since DHCP Enabled shows No, you know that the address is manually assigned; you can't make any inferences about DHCP from a manually assigned IP address. The firewall typically blocks all traffic from coming in, not out; however, since the laptop is working, the firewall on the router couldn't be the problem. Since the mobile computer is working, the router is working.

4. **A, B, C.** Network discovery isn't working. In order for the network discovery to work, the network discovery feature must be turned on. The Link-Layer Topology Discovery Mapper I/O Driver and the Link-Layer Topology Discovery Responder protocols must also be enabled on the NIC. Setting the network location to Public will turn off the network discovery feature.

5. **A, D, F, G, H.** The Client for Microsoft Networks is needed to allow him to access other resources on the network. The File and Printer Sharing for Microsoft Networks is required for him to share resources from his computer. Internet Protocol Version 4 (TCP/IPv4) is needed for connectivity. The two

Link Layer Topology Discovery protocols are required for network discovery (allowing computers to easily find each other). The Virtual Machine Network Services service isn't needed, since the scenario doesn't say anything about a virtual machine. The QoS Packet Scheduler would make things run better but isn't required. Since 128-bit addresses aren't being used, IPv6 would not be needed.

Configuring Wireless Connectivity

In this chapter, you will learn about:

- Basic wireless networking concepts
- Wireless security
- How to configure Windows Vista as a wireless client

Wireless networking is becoming much more widespread. It's quite easy to purchase a wireless router from an electronics store and create a network in a home or small office, and that's exactly what people are doing.

Early in the life of wireless networking, security was a big issue. It was recognized that wireless networks were highly insecure, and when Wired Equivalent Privacy (WEP) was the only encryption algorithm available, it wasn't even possible to truly lock down a small wireless network. Today, WiFi Protected Access (WPA and WPA2) is available and small networks can now be secured—if you know what to do and how to do it.

In this chapter, you'll learn about wireless networks, including how to configure Windows Vista systems in a wireless network. The topics within this wireless chapter build on the topics within the preceding chapter, on wired networks.

 EXAM TIP Objectives for the 70-620, 70-622, and 70-623 exams are included in this chapter.

Wireless Basics

Wireless networks are becoming more and more common. In home networks, it's a very easy way to share a single Internet connection among several home computers. You don't have to run cable to several different computers. Instead, set up a wireless router or wireless access point (WAP) and you're ready to go.

Wireless Access Point and Wireless Router What's the difference between a wireless access point (WAP) and a wireless router? That's a fair question and the answer isn't obvious.

A WAP is a device that allows wireless devices to connect to it and in turn provides connectivity to a wired network. It includes a receiver and transceiver to communicate with wireless devices. The internal network may have connectivity to the Internet, but required services are only relayed through the WAP instead of being provided by the WAP.

Wireless routers include the capabilities of a WAP. Additionally, they function as DHCP servers providing TCP/IP configuration for clients, and use Network Address Translation (NAT) to allow private clients (with private IP addresses) to access the Internet.

While it's possible to have a WAP with the extra networking capabilities, you can't have a wireless router without WAP capabilities. All that said, don't be surprised if you see the terms WAP and wireless router interchanged. I know I have.

Figure 6-1 shows an example of a wireless network that could easily be set up in your home. Notice the wireless router has a wired connection to the broadband cable connection (connecting to the Internet service provider) on the Internet side. It also has both wired and wireless capabilities on the private network side. This is a common configuration.

Figure 6-1
Typical home-based wireless network

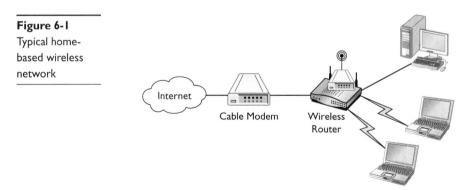

Internet — Cable Modem — Wireless Router

The wireless access point broadcasts using radio frequency (RF) signals. It works similar to a radio. If you want to listen to 99.1 FM, you tune the radio to 99.1 FM and you're in. Wireless networks broadcast on either 2.4 GHz or 5.0 GHz.

Current wireless protocols are 802.11a, 802.11b, and 802.11g. Specifics of each are outlined in Table 6-1. Notice that 802.11b and 802.11g are broadcasting on the same frequency (2.4 GHz). They are compatible with each other on the same network, while 802.11a devices will only be able to communicate with other 802.11a devices.

Table 6-1	Protocol	Top Speed	Frequency Band
Wireless	802.11a	54 Mbps	5 GHz
Specifications	802.11b	11 Mbps	2.4 GHz
	802.11g	54 Mbps	2.4 GHz

TIP Many devices are configured to work with multiple protocols. It's common to find devices rated as 802.11b/g, meaning they can operate using either 802.11b or 802.11g. You might also hear about 802.11n. At this writing this is still a proposed standard.

Since wireless devices transmit and receive radio frequency signals over the air, they are susceptible to radio frequency interference (RFI). If other devices are transmitting on the same frequency bands, it's possible your network won't work optimally, or worse, won't work at all.

RFI will limit the maximum distance between the wireless device and the WAP and limit the bandwidth. While 802.11g is listed with a speed of 54 Mbps, data isn't always transmitted at 54 Mbps. When the WAP and the wireless device connect, they negotiate the fastest speed they can achieve without errors. If your network has a lot of interference, the top speed may be significantly slower.

Network Types

You can create two types of networks when building a wireless network—an ad hoc–mode network or an infrastructure-mode network. The primary difference is the existence, or lack, of a wireless access point (WAP). You can connect to an infrastructure–mode network automatically or manually, depending on how the WAP is configured. An ad hoc network doesn't use a WAP.

Figure 6-2 shows the wizard that will lead you through creating a wireless network. You can access this wizard by selecting Manage Wireless Networks from the Network and Sharing Center and then clicking Add. (To access the Network and Sharing Center, click Start, right-click Network, and select Properties.)

You have three choices when adding a network:

- *Add a network that is in range of this computer.* You can use this wizard to connect to a wireless access point (WAP) if the WAP is broadcasting its Security Set Identifier (SSID). The SSID is also known as the common name of network. This is used for both ad hoc–mode and infrastructure–mode networks.

- *Manually create a network profile.* If the SSID is not broadcasting, you can use this selection to manually enter the SSID to connect to the network. Typically a network that is not broadcasting its SSID would also require a security key (similar to a password or passphrase) to be entered. This choice is also used for both ad hoc–mode and infrastructure–mode networks.

- *Create an ad hoc network.* This choice allows you to set up an ad hoc network between two or more wireless devices without a WAP. The wizard leads you

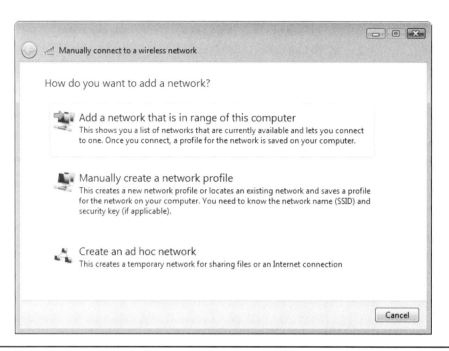

Figure 6-2   Creating a new wireless network connection

through creating the network name, selecting a security type (none, WEP, or WPA2-Personal) and entering a security key or passphrase. This would be used to create the first node in an ad hoc network.

EXAM TIP   You should be aware that you can connect Windows Vista to either an ad hoc–mode network or an infrastructure–mode network. The primary difference between the two is that an infrastructure–mode network uses a wireless access point, while an ad hoc–mode network connects multiple computers together as peers without a wireless access point.

Ad Hoc Network

In an ad hoc network (sometimes called a computer-to-computer or peer-to-peer network) two or more users with wireless devices can create their own wireless network to connect to each other. For example, you may attend a meeting in a conference room. To share data on a wireless network, you could work together to create an ad hoc network.

NOTE   "Ad hoc" is Latin meaning "for this." It indicates something formed to address a specific issue, and when used with IT terminology, ad hoc often indicates "as needed." You may see terms such as ad hoc queries, ad hoc surveys, ad hoc testing and, as indicated in this chapter, an ad hoc network.

Figure 6-3 shows a graphic of an ad hoc network. The biggest distinguishing factor is the absence of a wireless access point. However, in an ad hoc network one computer must first create the network so that other computers can join it. In the figure, the circled computer is highlighted as the computer that creates the network. Any computer can create the ad hoc network, but the point is that one of the computers must create it before other computers can join.

Figure 6-3

Ad hoc–mode
network

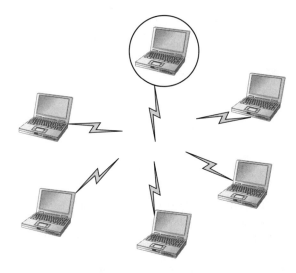

Creating an ad hoc network is a two step process. You must create the ad hoc network on the first device in the network. Other devices can then join the network. Computers and devices in an ad hoc network must be within 30 feet of each other.

Infrastructure Mode Network

Figure 6-4 shows a graphic of an infrastructure-mode network with a WAP used to connect the wireless devices. This is the most common configuration of wireless networks.

The figure also shows a wired client connected to the WAP. Most WAPs have this capability, allowing them to function as a network bridge, bridging wired and wireless devices together.

Network Bridge

Just as a real-life bridge can connect two land masses separated by water, a network bridge can connect two (or more) networks together. A network bridge is either hardware or software (or a combination of both) that connects two dissimilar networks together. In this chapter, the most common network bridge is one that connects a wired network and a wireless network together.

While a WAP is designed to be used as a network bridge, you can also configure an individual Windows Vista computer to bridge two connections.

Figure 6-4
Infrastructure–
mode network

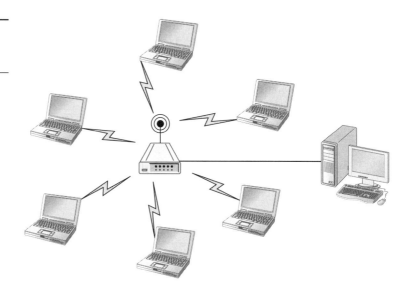

 EXAM TIP Windows Vista can be configured as a bridge if it has two NICs (one to a wired network and one to a wireless network). The bridge will allow computers in one network to access resources in the other network.

As an example, you may have a business using a small network with some wireless devices and another small network with wired devices. If your WAP doesn't support bridging the connections, or you have configured an ad hoc network without a WAP, you can use a Windows Vista system to bridge the two networks together.

In order to bridge two networks together on a Windows Vista system, you need two NICs. You can select NICs from the Network Connections window, right-click, and select Bridge Connections as shown in Figure 6-5.

Once the bridge is connected, you will have a third connection labeled Network Bridge and your Windows Vista system will allow resources to be accessed via the bridge.

TCP/IP Configuration

It's very common for the wireless access point to also include other capabilities such as the Dynamic Host Configuration Protocol (DHCP). DHCP will dynamically configure wireless clients will all of the TCP/IP configuration information that is needed.

This includes:

- IP address
- Subnet mask
- Default gateway
- Address of DNS server

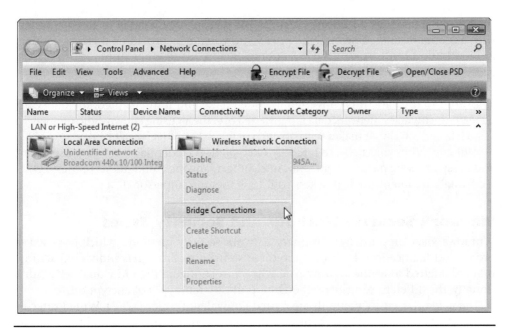

Figure 6-5   Bridging wired and wireless network connections

   TIP   Typically a WAP is connected to the ISP. The ISP provides an address for a DNS server to the WAP, and the DHCP service in the WAP provides this address to the clients. As a reminder, the DNS server provides name resolution service for host names.

A small office or home WAP also includes firewall and network address translation (NAT) features, allowing it to protect internal clients and also provide access to the Internet through a single connection.

Wireless Network Security

If you're running a wireless network at your home, you're probably aware that you can see other wireless networks running in your neighborhood. Some are secure. Some aren't.

Of course, it stands to reason if you can see the other networks, they can see you . . . unless you take steps to protect your network. The single most important wireless protection you can implement is referred to as the network security method, or the security type in Windows Vista.

Authentication and Encryption

When considering wireless security, you should be aware of the differences between authentication and encryption. Both are important parts of the overall security of your wireless devices.

Authentication is used to prove identity. For example, by logging in to your system with a username and password, you prove who you are by providing these credentials. Authentication can be used in wireless networks to ensure only authorized users can access the network.

Encryption is used to encode the data transferred in a session. By applying an encryption algorithm to the data, it is converted to coded data, and if intercepted, the data can't be read. Since wireless network data is transferred over the air using known radio frequencies (2.4 GHz and 5 GHz), it makes sense to encrypt the data so that it can't be read.

Authentication channels are typically encrypted. If credentials such as a user name and password were passed over the air in clear text, anyone could intercept them. Once credentials are intercepted, attackers could use them to impersonate a user.

Network Security Methods and Security Types

Windows Vista supports three primary network security methods, which are used to provide authentication. Each of these three security methods has individual settings that are referred to as the security type when you configure the individual NIC. Additionally, the different security methods support different types of encryption.

The network security methods are, Wired Equivalent Privacy (WEP), Wi-Fi Protected Access (WPA), and 802.1X Authentication. NICs can be configured with individual security types of WPA such as WPA-Personal or WPA-Enterprise. You can also choose not to implement any network security method.

Figure 6-6 shows the manual configuration dialog box with the drop-down box for different security types. You need to configure Windows Vista wireless clients with the same network security method as the WAP in an infrastructure-mode network, or as other clients in an ad hoc–mode network.

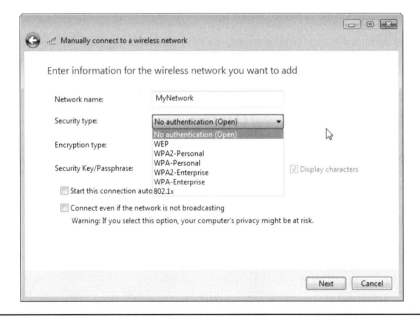

Figure 6-6   Security type choices

No Authentication (Open)

The first security type choice is No Authentication (Open). This is used for networks that are completely open and not requiring any authentication. Public networks use this setting.

It's important to realize that when this setting is chosen, encryption is not used between your computer and the WAP. Data that you send over the network is not encrypted and could be intercepted.

Wired Equivalent Privacy

Wired Equivalent Privacy (WEP) is the oldest security method and has significant security weaknesses. When wireless technologies first emerged, WEP was the only method available, but today there are far better choices. WEP can easily be cracked with off-the-shelf software that anyone can download and use. Whenever possible, you should not use WEP.

 TIP WEP should be avoided completely in wireless networks today due to its security weaknesses. WEP is mildly better than no security, but only mildly. Many devices can be upgraded to use WPA or WPA2, but if you have a legacy device that can't be updated, you may want to consider replacing it instead of using WEP.

Access to the network is granted by knowing the WEP network security key. The key is typically entered as a password or passphrase at the wireless access point and then at each client connecting within the network.

When you select WEP as the security type, it automatically chooses WEP as the encryption type.

Wi-Fi Protected Access

Wi-Fi Protected Access (WPA) has two versions (WPA and WPA2) and two security types (Personal and Enterprise) for each version. When the problems were discovered with WEP, WPA was created and released as an interim fix. Later, WPA2 was released and finalized. WPA2 is more secure than WPA and should be used when your equipment supports it.

Some older equipment doesn't support WPA2. However, any new equipment that has the Wi-Fi certification (from the Wi-Fi Alliance) must support WPA2.

- **WPA-Personal and WPA2-Personal**   Personal is also referred to as preshared key (PSK) mode. You would typically use the Personal choice in small office and home networks. Clients need to be configured with the PSK in order to connect to the network. The PSK provides basic authentication and prevents anyone from accessing your network without knowing the key.

  When you choose either WPA-Personal or WPA2-Personal in Windows Vista, you have the choice of using Advanced Encryption Standard (AES) or Temporal Key Integrity Protocol (TKIP) for encryption.

Figure 6-7 shows the manual configuration dialog box. The Network Name (also known as the SSID) is typed in. WPA2-Personal is selected from a drop-down box. AES is selected as the Encryption Type, and the Security Key/Passphrase is typed in. All of these settings need to match the network's configuration.

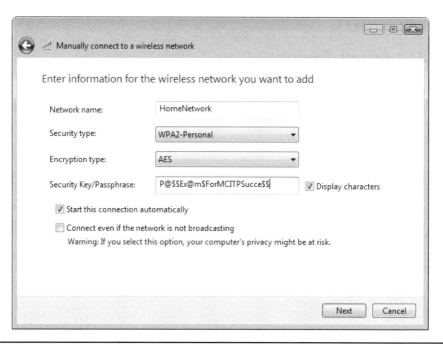

Figure 6-7 Configuring wireless security for a connection

 EXAM TIP You should be aware of the different security methods you can choose. WPA2-Personal is common in small office and home networks and is more secure than WPA-Personal. WPA2-Enterprise is used on larger networks when an authentication server is used and is more secure than WPA-Enterprise.

- **WPA-Enterprise and WPA2-Enterprise** Enterprise is used in larger networks where an authorization server is available. For example, in a Windows Server 2008 environment the user can be required to provide credentials, which are passed to a Remote Authentication Dial-in User Service (RADIUS) server and are compared to an Active Directory account. 802.1X protocols are used to encrypt the authentication process before the user is connected. Since Enterprise requires more resources (such as a RADIUS server), you would only see this in larger enterprise networks.When you choose either WPA-Enterprise or WPA2-Enterprise in Windows Vista, you have the choice of using Advanced Encryption Standard (AES) or Temporal Key Integrity Protocol (TKIP) for encryption.

802.1X

The 802.1X network security method can be used with WEP, WPA, and WPA2. It uses an authentication server (such as a RADIUS server) to validate users and provide network access. It can be used with both wired and wireless networks. You will typically only see this in larger networks.

Configuring the WAP

Most wireless access points can be accessed and configured using a Web browser and entering the address. For example, I'm using a Linksys wireless router (Model WRT54G), and I can access this router using the address of: http://192.168.1.1. I'm then prompted for a username and password (which I changed after purchasing the router).

You won't be tested on how to configure your WAP. After all, the WAP is not a Microsoft product. However, you should be aware of how the WAP is configured, since your wireless NIC must be configured with similar settings.

The significant settings you should know about are:

- Security settings
- SSID
- MAC filtering

Security Settings

Figure 6-8 shows a screenshot of the Wireless Security settings. You can see that the Security Mode is set to the most secure setting for a small office or home network: WPA2-Personal. It's using the WPA algorithm of AES and has a WPA Shared Key (also called a Private Shared Key or PSK) of Not4U2Know.

After configuring the wireless security settings to meet your needs, you can then click the Save Settings button to configure the WAP. Remember, the settings you choose here must also be configured identically in the wireless NIC.

Service Set Identifier

The Service Set Identifier (SSID) is the name of the network. The SSID can be up to 32 characters. Wireless access points are usually configured at the factory with default SSIDS such as: WLAN, Default, Linksys, Netgear, or wireless.

Two best practices with SSIDS are

- *Turn off Secure Set Identifier (SSID) broadcasting.* Normally, the SSID is broadcast, which makes the network easier to find and easier for wireless devices to connect. If the SSID is not being broadcast, it makes it harder for unauthorized wireless devices to find your network.

  Notice I wrote "harder," not "impossible." Since you're broadcasting on 2.4 GHz or 5.0 GHz, someone could tune a receiver to your wireless frequency and capture packets. Embedded in these packets is your SSID.

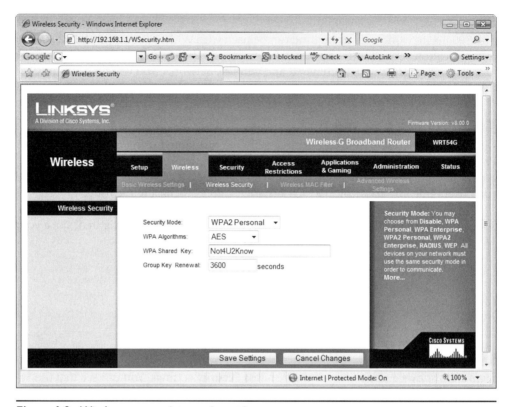

Figure 6-8   Wireless access point security settings

- *Change the default Secure Set Identifier (SSID).* Even if SSID broadcasting is dis-abled, if it's using the default name that came with your wireless router, it can be easy to find. For example, you may have a Linksys router using an SSID name of Linksys. Since it's the factory default, it's well known. It's recommended you change the default SSID to something else.

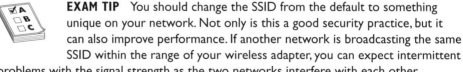

EXAM TIP   You should change the SSID from the default to something unique on your network. Not only is this a good security practice, but it can also improve performance. If another network is broadcasting the same SSID within the range of your wireless adapter, you can expect intermittent problems with the signal strength as the two networks interfere with each other.

Figure 6-9 shows the basic wireless settings for my WAP. The Wireless Network Name (SSID) has been changed from the default to HomeSweetHome. Additionally, you can see that the wireless SSID broadcast has been disabled.

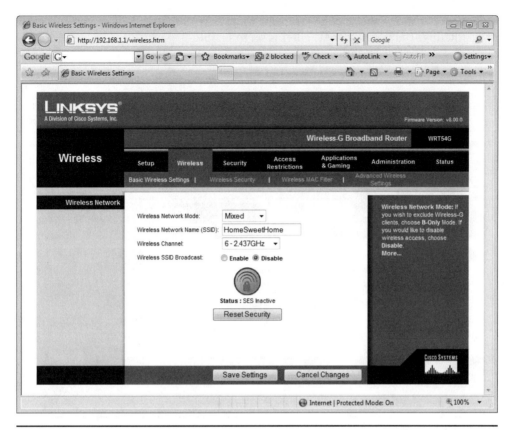

Figure 6-9 WAP basic wireless settings

NOTE The button for SES is for Secure Easy Setup. It's designed for non-networking professionals so that they can easily configure their wireless network with WPA encryption simply by pressing the button on the wireless router and on the screen.

MAC Filtering

Most wireless access points have the ability to restrict connections except for computers with specific media access control (MAC) addresses. Any computers identified with a different MAC address would be denied access.

TIP Each NIC has a MAC assigned to it. It's composed of six sets of hexadecimal pairs (such as 00-16-17-D9-12-C3). You can view the MAC address of your NIC by entering IPConfig /All at the command line. The MAC address is listed as the Physical Address.

Figure 6-10 shows the screen within the Linksys WAP that will allow you to enable MAC filtering. The Wireless MAC Filter is set to Enable.

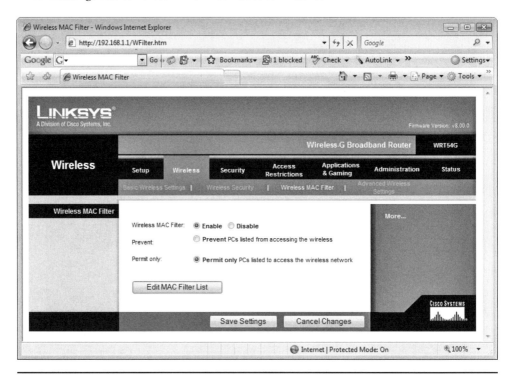

Figure 6-10   Enabling MAC filtering on a WAP

Defense in Depth

When working with security, there is never a single thing that you can do to fully ensure you are protected. Think about a bank. A bank has video cameras, guards, silent alarms, exploding ink packs, vaults, and more to protect itself (and your money). In other words, multiple defenses are enabled. This is also referred to as defense in depth.

When implementing security for a wireless network, many of the methods can be beaten individually. The single most important step today is to implement WPA or WPA2, but additional methods (such as disabling SSID broadcast and using MAC filtering) can be added to lock your network down even more.

If your network is significantly locked down, but your neighbor's is not, which one will an attacker choose? Often the easier target is attacked.

It reminds me of an old logic problem. If you and five other people are being chased by a bear, how quick do you have to run to escape? The answer is that you only have to run quicker than the slowest person.

By clicking the Edit MAC Filter List, you can add the MAC addresses of clients you want to allow to connect. All other clients will be denied.

While using MAC filtering is a good practice, you should be aware that it is also beatable. Packets broadcast over the air can be captured by a wireless receiver. Embedded in the packets are the MAC addresses. Once the acceptable MAC addresses are discovered, software can be used to spoof (impersonate) the accepted MAC addresses.

Network Discovery

Network discovery on a wireless network works the same way as it does on a wired network as presented in Chapter 5. The Link-Layer Topology Discovery (LLTD) protocols allow devices (such as computers) to see other devices on the network.

The primary network discovery settings are

- **On**   Allows this computer to find other computers and allows other computers to find it.

- **Off**   Prevents other computers from finding this computer and prevents this computer from finding other computers using LLTD.

The network discovery setting is directly affected by the network location configured on the Windows Vista computer. The network location can be set as Public or Private.

 EXAM TIP   Network Discovery works the same way on wireless networks as it does on wired networks. You would set it to Public when in a public location and network discovery is turned off, making it harder for your computer to be located. When in a private network, you would set it to Private and network discovery is turned on.

- **Public**   Public indicates the computer is connected to a public network location such as in an airport or a coffee shop. To protect the computer, network discovery is turned off, making the computer harder to find.

- **Private**   Private indicates the computer is operating in a private network such as a home or work network. When first configuring a connection, you are presented with a choice similar to Figure 6-11. Selecting Home or Work is identical to configuring the network as Private. Access to the Internet is via a router.

If your computer is connected directly to the Internet, or connected to the Internet via a publicly accessible network, you should set the network location to Public. Network discovery will be turned off.

On the other hand, if you are not directly connected to the Internet, but instead in a private network, you can set the network location to Private. Network discovery will be turned on and your computer can find other computers on the network, and other computers can find your computer.

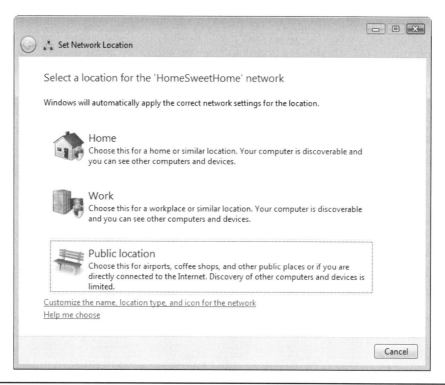

Figure 6-11   Selecting Home, Work, or Public

Configuring Vista as a Wireless Client

One of the tasks you should know how to do (both on the job and when preparing for the exams) is configure Windows Vista as a wireless client. You should be able to configure the connections and connect to a wireless network.

When you are creating and configuring wireless networks on your Windows Vista system, you are actually creating connections that can be used by your wireless network interface card (NIC). Typically you have only one wireless NIC, but you can configure many wireless networks, allowing you to connect to different networks, depending on where you are.

As an example, you could have one wireless network that you connect to at work, another that you connect to at home, and another that you connect to while visiting your favorite coffee shop. All of these connections would use the same wireless NIC.

The majority of configuration with a wireless network can be accessed from the Network and Sharing Center. This is the same Network and Sharing Center covered in Chapter 5. The difference is that Chapter 5 covered wired networks and here you'll learn about configuring wireless networks.

As a reminder, you can access the Network and Sharing Center by clicking Start, right-clicking Network, and selecting Properties. Figure 6-12 shows the Network and Sharing Center on a computer that is connected to a wireless network named Home-SweetHome.

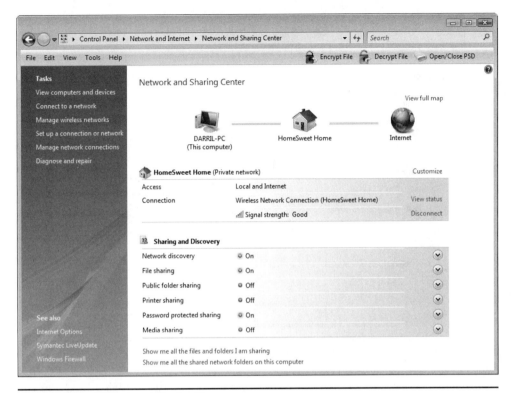

Figure 6-12 Network and Sharing Center

The primary tasks you should understand are

- Connect to a network.
- Manage wireless networks.
- Set up a connection or network.

Connect to a Network

If you want to manually connect to or disconnect from a network, you can select the Connect to a Network task from the Tasks list in the Network and Sharing Center. This will show you a list of wireless networks currently available.

Figure 6-13 shows the Connect to a Network dialog box. In the figure, you can see that this computer is connected to the network named HomeSweetHome. Additionally, the bars to the right of the HomeSweetHome network show the strength of the wireless signal.

Several other connections are also showing. You can hover over any of the connections to get additional information. For example, I hovered the mouse over the network named "rivas" and the information box appeared indicating the SSID, the signal strength, the security type (WEP), and the signal type (802.11g).

Figure 6-13 Connect to a Network dialog box

If your network doesn't appear in the Connect to a Network dialog box, you can connect to it manually. The primary reason it wouldn't appear is because the SSID isn't broadcasting. By clicking the Set Up a Connection or Network link at the bottom of the dialog box, you can manually create a wireless connection.

In Exercise 6.1, you will walk through the steps to manually configure your network interface card (NIC) to connect to a wireless access point. This exercise assumes you have a wireless NIC.

Exercise 6.1: Configuring Your Wireless NIC to Connect to a Wireless Network

1. Access the Network and Sharing Center by clicking Start, right-clicking Network, and selecting Properties.

2. On the Network and Sharing Center screen, click the Connect to a Network task.

3. On the Connect to a Network screen, browse through the available network connections. Assume that the network you want to connect to is not listed.

EXAM TIP The Connect to a Network screen will show all connections that are currently in broadcast range. All connections show right away, but as the computer determines that the network isn't in range, the connections begin to disappear. If the network you're looking for is not listed here but you're sure it's in range, the likely reason is that SSID broadcasting has been disabled. You can connect to the network by manually configuring the settings for the wireless network.

4. Click the Set Up a Connection or Network link at the bottom of the screen. Your display will look similar to Figure 6-14.

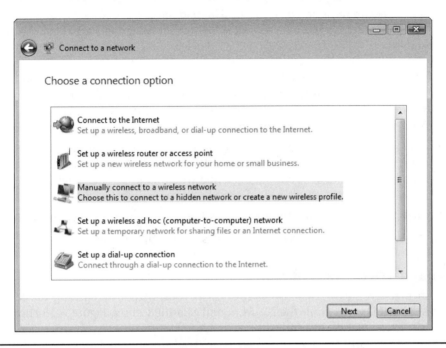

Figure 6-14 Choosing a connection option

5. On the Connect to a Network screen, select Manually Connect to a Wireless Network and click Next.

6. On the Enter Information for the Wireless Network You Want to Add screen, enter the following information:

 TIP If you have a wireless access point configured with different settings, you should modify the following settings to match the configuration of your wireless access point.

- Network Name: **HomeSweetHome**
- Security Type: **WPA2-Personal**
- Encryption Type: **AES**
- Security Key/Passphrase: **Not4U2Know**

7. Ensure the check box for Start This Connection Automatically is selected.

8. Select the check box for Connect Even If The Network Is Not Broadcasting. This allows you to connect to the network when SSID broadcasting is disabled. Click Next.

EXAM TIP It's common for a WAP to have SSID broadcasting disabled. To automatically connect to a WAP when SSID broadcasting is disabled, you need to manually configure the SSID and select the following two settings: Connect Even If The Network Is Not Broadcasting and Start This Connection Automatically.

9. On the Successfully Added screen, click Connect To. The Select a Network To Connect To window appears and your new network is shown at the top. Since the check box for Start This Connection Automatically was checked, the connection should now be connected.

10. After a moment, the Set Network Location dialog box will appear, allowing you to set the network location as Home or Work (Private), or Public. When set to Private, network discovery is enabled and when set to Public, network discovery is disabled.

11. Click Home. If the User Account Control dialog box appears, click Continue.

12. On the Successfully Set Network Settings screen, click Close.

Manage Wireless Networks

You can manage existing wireless networks on your system by clicking the Manage Wireless Networks task from the Network and Sharing Center. Figure 6-15 shows the Manage Wireless Networks window.

All of the networks that you've connected to, you've configured, or are within broadcast range are shown in this window. Above all of the networks are several options that you can select to manipulate and manage your networks.

You can also right-click any network connection and select Properties. The Properties dialog box allows you to reconfigure any of the properties you configured when you originally created the connection.

Add

If you click the Add link, a wizard launches giving you three choices:

- **Add A Network That Is In Range** Clicking this link launches a window showing all the networks that your wireless network adapter can hear. You can then choose the network you want to connect with.

- **Manually Create A Network Profile** This launches the same window used in Exercise 6.1 to manually create a network connection.

- **Create An Ad Hoc Network** Selecting this link will launch a wizard to create an ad hoc network. Exercise 6.2 will show you the steps to complete this.

Remove

You can delete network connections by clicking a network and selecting Remove. Once you confirm the task, the network connection will be deleted. Careful. There's no undo feature. Once it's removed, it's removed for good.

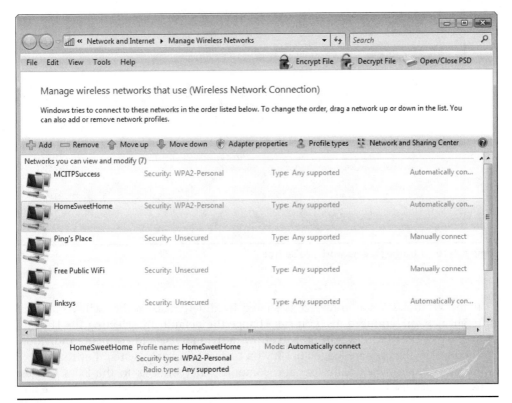

Figure 6-15 Manage Wireless Networks window

Move Up or Move Down

Network connections are listed in priority order. If you want to ensure that you automatically connect to a specific network, you should change the order of the connections so that the desired connection is at the top.

Take a look at Figure 6-15 again. It shows the MCITPSuccess connection at the top and the HomeSweetHome connection second. If you want to ensure you always connect to the HomeSweetHome connection when it is available, you should select the HomeSweetHome connection and click Move Up until it is at the top.

Profile Types

By default, any network connection you create can be used by all users that log on to your Windows Vista computer. If one of the network connections changes (perhaps the shared key is changed), you only have to change the configuration for one user and it affects all users.

If you want to change the default behavior, you can click the Profile Types link in the Manage Wireless Networks dialog box. Figure 6-16 shows the choices available. As shown, anytime a single user changes the network connection properties, it will affect all users.

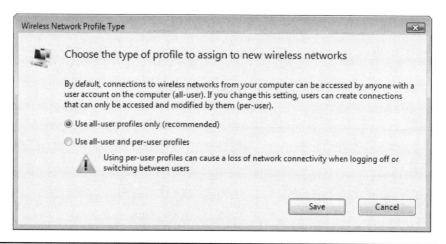

Figure 6-16 Changing the network profile type

If the Windows Vista computer is shared by different users that will connect to different network connections, you can change the default. By selecting the Use All-User and Per-User Profiles setting, you allow individual users to configure individual connections while they are logged on. It won't affect other users when they log on.

As an example, when Sally uses the computer, she connects to the Sales wireless network, which uses WPA2-Enterprise for security. When Joe uses the computer, he tries to connect to the wireless network, but since his account isn't authorized, he isn't able to connect. He's tried to manipulate the settings of the Sales connection. When Sally uses the computer again, the connection to the Sales wireless network has to be configured again.

 EXAM TIP If you want changes to any network connections to affect all users, ensure the profile type is set to Use All-User Profiles Only (Recommended); this is the default. If you have some network connections that need to affect only one user without affecting other users, you can set the Use All-User and Per-User Profiles.

When the Profile Type is set to Use All-User and Per-User Profiles, you have an additional choice when creating a network connection. Figure 6-17 shows the screenshot when the setting has been changed.

The two additional choices are

- **Save This Network For All Users Of This Computer**   When this setting is selected, any changes made by any user will affect all users.

- **Save This Network For Me Only**   When this setting is selected, the network connection is only available to one user and other users are unable to modify the settings.

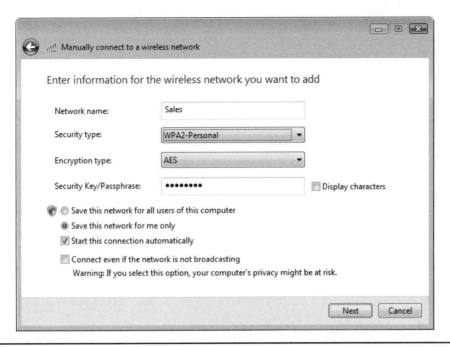

Figure 6-17   Creating a network connection with the profile type changed

Set Up a Connection or Network

You can choose the Set Up a Connection or Network setting from the Network and Sharing Center. Figure 6-18 shows the choices you have.

- **Connect To The Internet**   This launches a wizard you can use to connect to a wireless, broadband, or dial-up connection to the Internet. This choice is not shown in Figure 6-18 but is available if you scroll down.

- **Set Up A Wireless Router Or Access Point**   This wizard helps you detect and configure your wireless access point (WAP). Admittedly, it's easier to use the documentation that came with your WAP, but if it's not available, you can still use this wizard. Additionally, this wizard allows you to save the settings to a USB drive.

- **Manually Connect To A Wireless Network**   You can use this wizard to manually configure a wireless network. This is useful if the wireless access point is not broadcasting the SSID. You had an opportunity to do this in Exercise 6.1.

- **Set Up A Wireless Ad Hoc (Computer-to-Computer) Network**   You can use this wizard to create an ad hoc network. After it is configured, other wireless users can connect to it. Exercise 6.2 will walk you through the steps to do this.

- **Set Up A Dial-up Connection**   You can use this choice to create a simple dial-up connection to an Internet service provider (ISP).

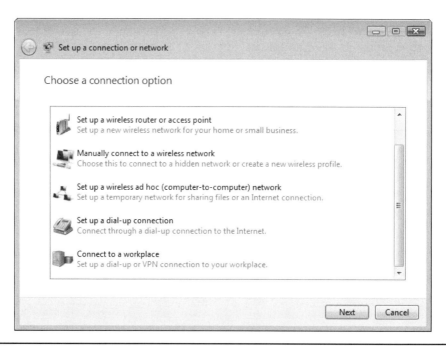

Figure 6-18   Connection options

- **Connect To A Workplace**   If your workplace has a remote access server or a virtual private network (VPN) connection, you can use this wizard to configure the connection. Remote access and VPN connections will be explored more in Chapter 7.

In Exercise 6.2, you will walk through the steps to create an ad hoc connection. Once an ad hoc connection is created, other wireless clients can connect with it using a wireless access point.

Exercise 6.2: Creating an Ad Hoc Network

1. Access the Network and Sharing Center by clicking Start, right-clicking Network, and selecting Properties.

2. Click the Set Up a Connection or Network task.

3. On the Choose a Connection Option window, select Set Up a Wireless Ad Hoc (Computer-to-Computer) Network, and click Next.

4. Review the information on the Set Up a Wireless Ad Hoc Network window, and click Next.

5. On the Give Your Network a Name and Choose Security Options window, enter the following information:

   • Network Name: **MyAdHoc**

   • Security type: **WPA2-Personal**

   • Security key/Passphrase: **MC1TPSucce$$**

   Your display will look similar to Figure 6-19. Click Next.

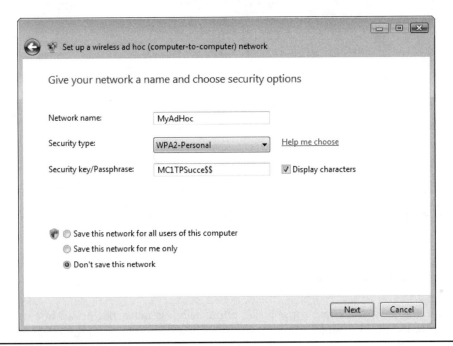

Figure 6-19   Creating an ad hoc network

6. The network will be created, and a display message will indicate the MyAdHoc network is ready to use. Click Close.

7. Back in the Network and Sharing Center, select Connect to a Network. Your display will look similar to Figure 6-20. Notice that your ad hoc network is broadcasting. You can also see that the icon for an ad hoc network is different than a wireless access point connection. Click Cancel.

Figure 6-20   Ready to connect to an ad hoc network

Chapter Review

In this chapter you learned some basics about wireless networks. An ad hoc network is used to connect multiple computers together in a computer-to-computer or peer-to-peer network. You can create an ad hoc network with Windows Vista that other clients can join. An infrastructure network uses a wireless access point (WAP).

You configure WAP security with a Security Set Identifier (SSID), a security type, an encryption algorithm, and either a preshared key (PSK) or an authentication server. The SSID is broadcast by default so that a wired network can easily be located, but SSID broadcasting can be disabled.

Wired Equivalent Privacy (WEP) is the oldest wireless security type and has significant security weaknesses. Instead of WEP, you should use WiFi Protected Access (WPA) or WPA2. In a small network you use WPA-Personal or WPA2-Personal with a preshared key. In a larger network, you use WPA-Enterprise or WPA2-Enterprise with an authentication server.

The primary tool used to configure wireless network connections in Windows Vista is the Network and Sharing Center. You learned how to perform many of the tasks associated with managing wireless networks. This included adding and configuring wireless networks, ensuring Vista automatically connects to specific wireless networks, and modifying profile types.

Additional Study

Self Study Exercises

Use these additional exercises to challenge yourself.

- Create an infrastructure-mode wireless network.
- Modify the WAP configuration (such as with a different SSID, or by disabling SSID broadcast), ensuring you are using WPA2-Personal. Configure all your wireless clients to connect.
- Create an ad hoc–mode network and connect another wireless device.
- Modify the profile type from the default. Create a network connection for one user and then log on as another user to verify it isn't available.

Summary of What You Need to Know

70-620

You will very likely see many questions on wireless topics in the 70-620 exam. Make sure you understand both basic networking and wireless networking. Pay particular attention to the following topics covered in this chapter:

- **SSID and SSID broadcasting**   You should know what the SSID is used for, what's affected if SSID broadcasting is disabled, and how to automatically connect to a network where SSID broadcasting is disabled.
- **Public and private**   You should know the differences between setting a wireless network connection to public or private and how it affects network discovery.
- **Network bridge**   You should understand what a network bridge is and how to configure Windows Vista as a network bridge.
- **Profile types**   You should know how to configure a network connection so that it can be used by all users, or by only a single user.

70-622

Wireless networking topics aren't hit as heavily in the 70-622 exam as other topics, but you should still understand all the concepts covered in this chapter. When preparing for the 70-622 exam, pay particular attention to the following topics:

- **Public and private**   You should know the differences between setting a wireless network connection to public or private and how it affects network discovery.
- **Security types**   You should know that WEP is not be used, WPA-2 Personal uses a preshared key, and WPA-2 Enterprise requires an authentication server.

70-623

When preparing for the 70-623 exam, you need a solid understanding of all of the topics covered in this chapter. Pay particular attention to the following topics:

- **Ad hoc–mode and infrastructure-mode networks**   You should know the differences between ad hoc– and infrastructure-mode networks, and how to create each.

- **SSID and SSID broadcasting** You should know what the SSID is used for, what's affected if SSID broadcasting is disabled, and how to automatically connect to a network where SSID broadcasting is disabled.

Questions

70-620

1. You have configured a wireless network in your home. The wireless router connects to the Internet, and three computers with wireless connections connect to each other via the wireless router. However, you've found that your Windows Vista computer is not able to discover other computers. What should you do?

   A. Set the network category of the wireless router to Public.

   B. Set the network category of the wireless router to Private.

   C. Set the network category of your Vista computer's NIC to Public.

   D. Set the network category of your Vista computer's NIC to Private.

2. Your laptop is running Windows Vista. When on the road, you use the wireless network adapter to connect to wireless networks such as in the airport and at the hotel. While at home, you use the wired network adapter to connect to your home. You want your computer to be able to easily find other computers in your network, and you want maximum security on the road. What should you do?

   A. Set the network location of the wired NIC to Private. Set the network category of the wireless NIC to Public.

   B. Set the network location of the wired NIC to Public. Set the network category of the wireless NIC to Private.

   C. Set the network location of the wired NIC to Public. Set the network category of the wireless NIC to Public.

   D. Set the network location of the wired NIC to Private. Set the network category of the wireless NIC to Private.

3. You are running Windows Vista on your computer, which is connected to a network with a printer that is configured to allow anyone to print. While in a meeting, you create an ad hoc network with several other users. They want to print to the printer. How can this be done?

   A. Have the other clients connect using your wired connection.

   B. Have the users configure their wireless adapters as a network bridge.

   C. Configure the WAP as a network bridge.

   D. Configure the wired and wireless adapters on your system as a network bridge.

4. You are trying to connect to a wireless network that you've recently configured. You find that the wireless network is not listed with other wireless networks on

the Connect to a Network window. What can you do to connect to the wireless network?

A. Manually configure the wireless connection and select the check box to Connect Even If The Network Is Not Broadcasting.

B. Manually configure the WAP and select the check box to Connect Even If The Network Is Not Broadcasting.

C. Manually configure the wireless connection with the IP address of the WAP.

D. Right-click the wireless NIC and select Diagnose and Repair.

5. You are trying to connect to a wireless network that you've recently configured. When you configured the WAP, you disabled SSID broadcasting. What should you do to ensure your computer can connect to the WAP?

A. Select the setting to Connect Even If The Network Is Broadcasting.

B. Select the setting to Connect Even If The Network Is Not Broadcasting.

C. Ensure the wireless NIC is configured to connect an ad hoc network.

D. Ensure the WAP is configured as an ad hoc network.

6. You are running Windows Vista on a laptop computer that has a wireless NIC. You purchased and configured a WAP, but your laptop computer is not connecting to it. What should you do?

A. Configure the NIC with the Public network location.

B. Configure the NIC with the Private network location.

C. Configure the NIC to connect using the Connect to a Network task.

D. Rename the NIC with the name of the SSID.

7. You are running Windows Vista on a laptop computer that has a wireless NIC. You purchased and configured a WAP using security best practices and configured your system to be able to manually connect to the network. However, the network is not currently showing in the Connect to a Network window. You've verified the WAP is operational. What should you do?

A. Weaken security on the WAP to allow the network to be seen.

B. Create a new connection and select the check box to Connect Automatically When This Network Is In Range.

C. On the WAP, disable SSID broadcasting.

D. On the Windows Vista network connection, disable SSID broadcasting.

8. Both Sally and Joe share the same Windows Vista computer. Sally connects to a wireless network when she uses the computer. Often, Sally can't connect to her wireless network because Joe has changed the configuration when he was logged on. What should you do to ensure Sally won't have the same problem?

A. Disable the Network and Sharing Center in Sally's system.

B. Enable SSID broadcasting for the WAP.

C. Set the Profile Type to Use All-Users Profiles Only and recreate the wireless network for Sally only.

D. Set the Profile Type to Use All-Users and Per-User Profiles and recreate the wireless network for Sally only.

9. Your laptop runs Windows Vista and you use it at work and home. You want to automatically connect to your home network (named HomeSweetHome) whenever you're at home. The available network connections are shown in the following figure. What should you do?

A. Change the Adapter Properties to Use All-User Profiles Only (Recommended).

B. Change the Profile Type to Use All-User Profiles Only (Recommended).

C. Add the HomeSweetHome network again so that it is first in the list.

D. Change the order of the networks so that HomeSweetHome is first.

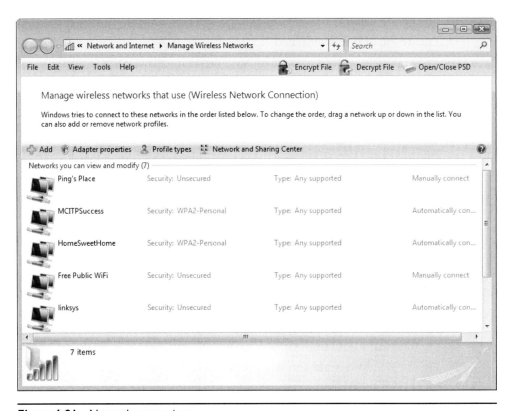

Figure 6-21 Network connections

70-622

1. You are helping the CEO of your company connect her portable laptop computer (running Windows Vista) to the company wireless network. You want to ensure her computer cannot be discovered on the network using LLTD, but you don't want to affect how her computer will function on her home network where she wants her computer to be discovered. What should you do?

   A. Set the location type of her wireless NIC to Private.

   B. Set the location type of her wireless NIC to Public.

   C. Uninstall LLTD.

   D. Set network discovery to on.

2. You are configuring a wireless network within your company. It includes a WAP, but authentication servers are not available. You need to configure the clients with the highest possible level of security with your network. How should you configure the clients?

   A. Configure the WAP and clients to use WEP.

   B. Configure the WAP and clients to use WPA2-Personal.

   C. Configure the WAP and clients to use WPA-Enterprise.

   D. Configure the WAP to use WPA2-Enterprise and the clients to use WPA2-Personal.

3. An administrator has configured a wireless network within your company. It includes a WAP and authentication servers using the highest level of security. How should you configure the Windows Vista clients?

   A. Configure the clients with open authentication.

   B. Configure clients to use WEP.

   C. Configure clients to use WPA2-Personal.

   D. Configure clients to use WPA-Enterprise.

70-623

1. You are assisting a Windows Vista user to configure her two laptops. Both laptops have wireless NICs that are compatible with each other, but she doesn't have any other hardware. She wants the computers to be able to share data with each other. She's properly configured the firewall and enabled file sharing on the computers. What should she do now?

   A. Have both computers connect to the WAP.

   B. Configure an ad hoc–mode network on one computer, and have the other computer join the ad hoc network.

   C. Configure an infrastructure-mode network on one computer, and have the other computer join the ad hoc network.

   D. Configure an ad hoc–mode network on both computers.

2. A user purchased an 802.11g wireless router and installed it in his home using the default settings. He complains that the signal strength varies from Low to Good. What would you recommend to resolve the problem?

   A. Change the default SSID on the WAP and the network connection.

   B. Change the frequency band from 2.4 GHz to 5 GHz.

   C. Change the frequency band from 5 GHz to 2.4 GHz.

   D. Change the security type from WEP to WPA2-Personal.

3. You are assisting a user running Windows Vista on a laptop computer. She has configured a WAP using WPA2-Personal and has a wireless NIC on her laptop. SSID broadcast is disabled on the WAP. She has configured her NIC using WPA2-Personal. However, her computer fails to find and connect to the WAP automatically. What should you do?

   A. Manually configure the IP address and other TCP/IP configuration information.

   B. Configure the network connection to connect to an ad hoc network.

   C. Configure the network connection to connect even if the WAP is not broadcasting.

   D. Configure the WAP to use WEP.

4. A customer has a wireless network at his home. The wireless network is configured with WPA2-Personal, a preshared key, and SSID broadcasting disabled. Each time he wants to connect to the network, he has to manipulate the connection. He wants to know how to have his computer automatically connect. Choose all that apply.

   A. Configure the connection to Recreate Automatically When Network Is In Range.

   B. Configure the connection to Connect Even If The Network Is Not Broadcasting.

   C. Configure the connection to Start This Connection Automatically.

   D. Configure the connection with the Save This Network For Me Only.

5. You are assisting a user who is running Windows Vista on a laptop computer. She is unable to connect to the wireless network in her small office. The WAP is configured with SSID broadcasting disabled. The user is very concerned about security and doesn't want to do anything that will weaken security. What should be done? Choose all that apply.

   A. Enable SSID broadcasting.

   B. Implement WEP as a security type.

   C. Configure the network connection to connect even if the network is not broadcasting.

   D. Manually enter the network name into the connection.

Answers

70-620

1. **D.** By setting the network category of the of the Vista computer's wireless network interface card (NIC) to Private, you will enable network discovery. If it was set to Public, network discovery features will be turned off. The wireless router wouldn't be running Windows Vista, so it wouldn't have network categories associated with Windows Vista.

2. **A.** You will enable network discovery at home (where the wired NIC is used) by setting the network location of the wired network interface card (NIC) to Private. You disable network discovery on the road (where the wireless NIC is used) by setting the network location of the wireless NIC to Public. If you set the wireless NIC to Private, then network discovery would be enabled, allowing the computer to be discovered while in public locations such as the airport (effectively weakening your security). If you set the wired NIC to Public, than network discovery would be disabled in the home network, preventing the computer from being discovered, or discovering other computers.

3. **D.** By configuring your two network interface cards (NICs) as a bridge, you can provide access to the wired network via your Windows Vista system. Having the clients connect using your wired connection (in other words, plugging the wire from your system into their systems) would take a long time and may not be possible, since you don't know if they have wired NICs. An ad hoc network doesn't have a WAP.

4. **A.** If a new wireless network does not appear on the Connect to a Network window, it must not be broadcasting the SSID. You need to manually configure the wireless connection and select Connect Even If The Network Is Not Broadcasting to force it to connect. A wireless access point (WAP) would not have a selection to Connect Even If The Network Is Not Broadcasting; you could disable or enable SSID broadcasting on the WAP. The IP address is only used after the connection is made and wouldn't affect the connection appearing (or not appearing) in the Connect to a Network window. Since some networks are listed, there is no indication there is a problem with the NIC that needs to be diagnosed or repaired.

5. **B.** By configuring the NIC to Connect Even If The Network Is Not Broadcasting, you can connect to a WAP even when SSID broadcasting has been disabled. There is no setting called Connect Even If The Network Is Broadcasting. Since you have a WAP, you would not use ad hoc mode, and a WAP cannot be configured in an ad hoc network.

6. **C.** You need to configure the network interface card (NIC) to connect to the wireless access point (WAP) using the Connect to a Network task from the Network and Sharing Center window. Once the network is added, you can designate it as public or private, but these settings are only done after the NIC

is configured. Renaming the NIC with the name of the network name or Service Set Identifier (SSID) won't have any affect; the NIC's default name is Wireless Network Connection, but this is the name of the NIC, not the name of the SSID.

7. **B.** This question implies that the Security Set Identifier (SSID) broadcasting was disabled on the wireless access point (WAP), which is why it doesn't appear. By selecting the properties of the network connection, you can select Connect Even If The Network Is Not Broadcasting. You could also set the properties to Connect Automatically When This Network Is In Range (instead of manual). Weakening security is never recommended. SSID broadcasting is already disabled on the WAP. The network connection does not broadcast the SSID (unless created as the first ad hoc connection).

8. **D.** You can set the Profile Type to Use All-Users and Per-User Profiles so that you can then create a new profile available to Sally only. It's not possible to disable the Network and Sharing Center. The settings on the wireless access point (WAP) aren't the problem, so they don't need to be modified. When the Profile Type is set to Use All-Users Profiles Only (the default), the changes for one user apply to all users, which is the problem we are trying to resolve.

9. **D.** You can select the HomeSweetHome network and move it to be first in the list so that your system will automatically connect to it when you are at home and the network is available. The Adapter Properties dialog box doesn't have a setting for the profiles, and changing the setting for the profiles won't affect how the networks currently available will behave. You would have to delete the existing HomeSweetHome network to create another one, and it's much easier to just change the order.

70-622

1. **B.** By setting the location type of the wireless network interface card (NIC) to Public, you will turn off network discovery so that her computer is not locatable using Link-Layer Topology Discovery (LLTD). Setting the NIC to Private would enable network discovery, allowing the computer to be reachable. Uninstalling LLTD would disable her ability to connect to her home network with network discovery. Setting network discovery on would allow her computer to be discoverable.

2. **B.** WPA2-Personal is the highest level of security possible without an authentication server. WEP has poor security and should not be used. WPA-Enterprise requires an authentication server. Both the WAP and clients must use the same configuration.

3. **D.** WPA2-Enterprise is the highest level of security possible with an authentication server. Open authentication has no security. WEP has poor security and should not be used. WPA-Personal uses a shared key for authentication.

70-623

1. **B.** You can network two computers with wireless network interface cards (NICs) by first creating an ad hoc network on one computer and then joining the ad hoc network with the other computer. The question stated there wasn't any other hardware, so the computers can't connect to a wireless access point (WAP). An infrastructure-mode network requires a WAP. You should only configure the ad hoc–mode network on one computer and then join the network with the other computer, not create two ad hoc networks.

2. **A.** If the router was installed using default settings, the default SSID was used. If a neighboring network connection is also using the same default SSID, the interference would affect the signal strength. An 802.11g router operates in the frequency band of 2.4 GHz, and this can't be changed. While it's a good practice to use WPA2-Personal instead of WEP, the security type wouldn't cause the problems stated in the question.

3. **C.** You should configure the network connection to connect even if the wireless access point (WAP) is not broadcasting, since the WAP is configured with the Security Set Identifier (SSID) disabled. The TCP/IP configuration is only an issue after you've connected, not before. An ad hoc network doesn't use a WAP. Both the client and the WAP are using WPA2-Personal, which wouldn't stop the client from seeing the WAP. Certainly you wouldn't want to weaken security to Wired Equivalent Privacy (WEP).

4. **B, C.** The connection should be configured to Connect Even If The Network Is Not Broadcasting, since SSID broadcasting is disabled. To connect automatically, you should configure the connection to Start This Connection Automatically. There isn't a setting to Recreate Automatically When Network Is In Range. The profile type could be changed if multiple users were using and changing the connection properties, but this isn't an issue in this question.

5. **C, D.** Since the SSID is not broadcasting, you'll need to configure the connection to automatically connect and manually enter the network name (the SSID) for the connection. Enabling SSID broadcasting would weaken security. WEP is the poorest security method, and using it wouldn't help the scenario.

Configuring Network Access

7

In this chapter, you will learn about:

- Remote Assistance
- Remote Desktop
- Remote Access
- Windows Firewall
- Firewall rules and exceptions

Several remote tools are available within Windows Vista. Remote Assistance allows a helper to assist another user over a network (including over the Internet). Remote Desktop allows an administrator to remotely connect to a network to administer a computer. Remote Access allows users to connect to an internal network via a dial-up or VPN connection.

The Windows Firewall is used to protect a system and a network. This chapter covers some basics about firewalls and then covers the Windows Firewall available in Windows Vista. You can enable or create rules and exceptions to allow or block specific traffic on your system.

 EXAM TIP   Objectives for the 70-620, 70-622, and 70-623 exams are included in this chapter.

Connecting Remotely

You may have heard that "No man is an island." The same goes for a computer. While you can do a lot on Windows Vista by itself, frequently you'll want to connect and interact with other computers.

Windows Vista provides three different methods of connecting to other computers remotely:

- **Remote Assistance**   You can use Remote Assistance to connect to someone else's computer (after being invited) and provide assistance.

- **Remote Desktop Connection**   You can use Remote Desktop Connection to remotely connect to a computer to manage it. This is frequently done to remotely manage servers.

- **Remote Access**   Remote Access allows you to remotely connect to a network via dial-up or a virtual private network (VPN).

Terminal Services is needed to support Remote Assistance and Remote Desktop Connection.

Terminal Services

Terminal Services is a service running on Windows Vista (and other operating systems) used to allow computers to connect to each other. Terminal Services is required to support both Remote Assistance and Remote Desktop.

Figure 7-1 shows the Services applet open with the Terminal Services service selected. As you can see from the Status column, the service is started. If this service was not started, neither Remote Assistance nor Remote Desktop would function.

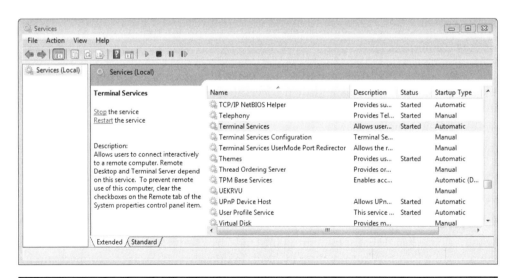

Figure 7-1   Terminal Services service started

 EXAM TIP   The Terminal Services service must be running to support either Remote Desktop or Remote Assistance.

In the figure, you can also see the Terminal Services Configuration service, and the Terminal Services UserMode Port Redirector service. These services have other uses and are not required for Remote Desktop and Remote Assistance.

If this service is not running, you can start it with the following steps:

1. **Launch the Services applet** Click Start and enter **Services.msc** in the search box. You can also access the Services applet through the Control Panel. Select System and Maintenance | Administrative Tools and then double-click Services. If the User Account Control dialog box appears, click Continue.

2. **Select the service** Services are listed alphabetically, so you can browse down to the *T*s to select the Terminal Services service.

3. **Start the service** You can either right-click the service and select Start, or click the Start the Service link in the extended task pane section.

Remote Assistance

Remote Assistance allows a helper to remotely assist another user. You can assist other users (or they can assist you) if both computers are connected via the Internet, or via an internal network. The great benefit of Remote Assistance is the ability to actually take control of a remote desktop and show someone how to complete a task.

As an example, a friend of yours may want to set his home page to a different Web site. You know exactly how to do it but would like to show him. Your friend can send you a Remote Assistance invitation, and then you can request control of his desktop to walk him through the steps.

It's important to realize that you can't take control of someone else's computer without that person's consent. Or said another way, someone else can't take control of your desktop using Remote Assistance without your permission.

In Exercise 7.1, you will verify Remote Assistance is available and go through the steps to create and send a remote assistance invitation.

Exercise 7.1: Creating and Sending a Remote Assistance Invitation

1. Verify Remote Assistance is enabled on your system.

   a. Click Start, right-click Computer, and select Properties.

   b. In the Tasks pane of the System menu, select Remote Settings. If the User Account Control dialog box appears, click Continue.

   c. On the System Properties menu, ensure the Remote tab is selected.

   d. Ensure the check box next to Allow Remote Assistance Connections to This Computer is checked. Your display should look similar to Figure 7-2. Click OK.

 TIP The Windows Firewall also needs to be configured to allow remote desktop connections. You'll see how this is done later in this chapter, in the section "Configuring Vista's Firewall."

2. Click Start | Help and Support.

Figure 7-2
Ensuring Remote
Assistance is
enabled

3. On the Find an Answer page, in the Ask Someone section, click the link for Windows Remote Assistance.

4. On the Do You Want to Ask for or Offer Help page, click the Invite Someone You Trust to Help You link.

5. Click the Save This Invitation as a File link.

6. On the Save the Invitation as a File page, notice the path and name of the file. The default name of the file is Invitation.msrcincident, and it is saved on your desktop. Enter a strong password in the Password and Confirm Password text boxes. If you're in a test environment, you could use P@ssw0rd. Figure 7-3 shows the invitation being saved.

7. Click Finish. The Waiting for Incoming Connection window will appear. However, no one will be able to access your system until you send the invitation to them.

8. Launch your e-mail program (you could use a Web based e-mail program or a dedicated e-mail program such as Outlook or Outlook Express). Send an e-mail to yourself with the invitation as an attachment.

 TIP In practice, you would send the invitation to someone who could help you. If you can trade invitations with someone else to see Remote Assistance in action, it will be much more effective at helping you understand what's going on. You're limited on how much you can do if you just send an invitation to yourself and open it.

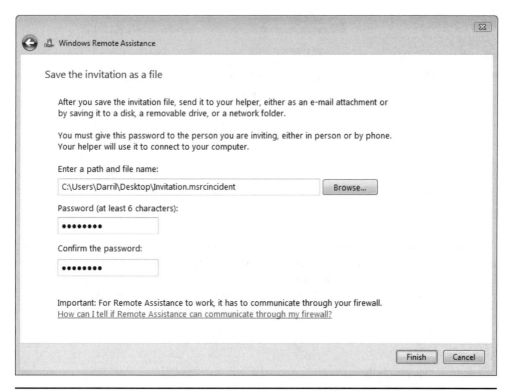

Figure 7-3   Saving the invitation as a file

9. Open the e-mail program and view the attachment. Notice that the invitation is automatically set to expire six hours after its creation. It's possible to cancel an invitation by closing the Waiting for Incoming Connection window that appears after the invitation was created.

Opening an Invitation

If you send an invitation to someone else, he will need to know the password to open it. If you're sending the invitation via e-mail, it's not a good idea to include the password in the same e-mail.

Figure 7-4 shows what the opened invitation looks like. Notice that the invitation is set to expire. The helper would need to know the password that was used when the invitation was sent. After entering the password, the helper would click Yes to connect to your computer.

As soon as a helper clicks to connect to your computer, you would receive a prompt asking if you would like to allow the connection. If you click Yes, then the helper will be able to view all the information on your desktop.

Figure 7-4

Opening a
Remote Assistance invitation

Figure 7-5 shows the new window after the Chat button has been clicked and the two users have started a dialog. In this scenario, Darril has requested help from a helper by sending an invitation. The helper is logged on as Administrator and has opened the request. The two have begun exchanging information via the Chat window.

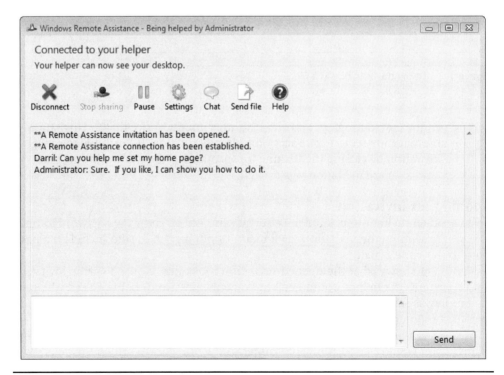

Figure 7-5   Remote Assistance window while connected

Once the connection is created, the helper is able to observe the user's desktop. Figure 7-6 shows what the helper would see on her system. In this figure, the user is researching the objectives for the 70-620 exam, and this can be observed in the Remote Desktop pane.

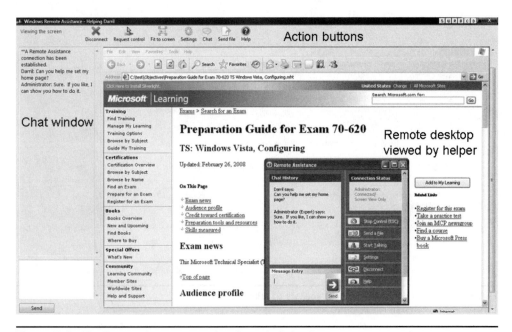

Figure 7-6 The Remote Assistance window from the helper's perspective

In order for a helper to demonstrate how to do something, the person being assisted must grant permission for the helper to take control of the user's desktop. The helper would click the Request Control button to request to take control of the user's desktop. Immediately after the button is clicked, the user is prompted to allow the helper to take control. Figure 7-7 shows the prompt.

Notice the user can click the check box to allow the helper to respond to User Account Control prompts, but this isn't selected by default. Additionally, if the user clicks No, than the helper is unable to take control of the user's desktop.

At any point after control is granted, the user can change his mind. The user can press the ESC key or click the Stop Sharing button to immediately stop sharing his desktop. Additionally, the user can also click the Disconnect button at any time to disconnect from the remote session.

At this point, the helper can start moving the mouse within the remote desktop pane of the Remote Assistance window. All of the mouse movements and keyboard entries can be viewed by the user requesting assistance. If the helper and the user are talking over the phone, the helper can demonstrate the actions while telling the user what she is doing.

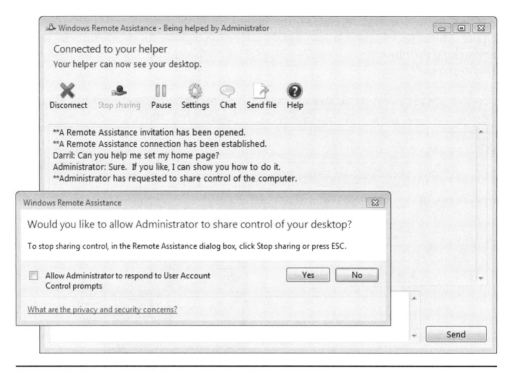

Figure 7-7   Prompt after a helper requests to take control

It's also possible for a helper to send a file to the user requesting assistance. The helper clicks the Send a File button, browses to the file she wants to send, and clicks Send File. The person is then prompted that the helper wants to send a file and asked if he wants to accept it. If the user clicks Yes, he is prompted to save it with the Save As dialog box.

If the user ever wants to hide his desktop from the helper, he can click the Pause button. For example, imagine you were helping me. I receive an e-mail that I need to answer right away but I don't want you to see the contents of the e-mail. I could press the Pause button to hide my screen from you.

 EXAM TIP   The user can hide the screen from the helper by clicking the Pause button. This is useful if the user needs to do something he doesn't want the helper to see, but he also doesn't want to completely close the Remote Assistance connection.

After the Pause button is pressed, the helper only sees a black screen. Even if she is granted control, she can no longer see what is on the screen. By pressing the Continue button (it appears where the Pause button was), the user again enables the helper to see the screen. If the helper previously had control of the desktop, control would immediately be granted again.

Invitation Expiration

Invitations are set to expire after six hours by default. It is possible to change this time by modifying the remote settings of your system.

In Exercise 7.2, you will go through the steps to change the default expiration of a remote assistance invitation.

 EXAM TIP It is possible to modify the expiration of remote assistance invitations, but only before they are created. Exercise 7.2 shows you how to modify the expiration time in Windows Vista.

Exercise 7.2: Modifying the Default Invitation Expiration

1. Click Start, right-click Computer, and select Properties. This will launch the System applet.

2. In the Tasks pane, click Remote Settings. If the User Account Control dialog box appears, click Continue.

3. On the System Properties dialog box, select the Remote tab.

4. Verify that the Allow Remote Assistance Connections to This Computer check box is selected.

5. Click the Advanced button. In the Invitations section, change the number from 6 (the default) to 10. This will modify the expiration of all invitations created in the future. Your display will look similar to Figure 7-8.

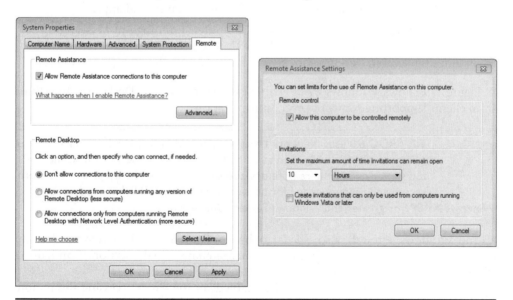

Figure 7-8 Changing the default expiration of Remote Assistance invitations

6. Click OK in the Remote Assistance Settings dialog box. Click OK in the System Properties dialog box.

Remote Desktop

Servers are often locked away in server rooms where the temperature is cool to protect them. You may occasionally see administrators coming out of a server room in the middle of summer wearing a winter parka. It can be downright cold in there.

If you prefer the milder climate of an office setting, you may prefer to manage servers from the comfort of your desk. Remote Desktop Connection (RDC) 6.0 is one of the primary tools used to remotely administer servers from Windows Vista.

 TIP RDC can also be used to remotely administer end-user workstations, though it works significantly different than Remote Assistance. With Remote Assistance, you can access the desktop and the user can observe what you're doing. If you access a user's desktop with RDC, the user's session is preempted and all they can see is a logon screen.

Enabling Remote Desktop

Before RDC can be used to remotely access a system, Remote Desktop must be enabled on the remote computer. You can use the following steps to enable Remote Desktop on Windows Vista:

- Click Start, right-click Computer, and select Properties.
- In the Tasks pane of the System page, click Remote Settings. If the User Account Control dialog box appears, click Continue.
- On the System Properties dialog box, the Remote tab should appear.
- Select either Allow Connections from Computers Running Any Version of Remote Desktop (Less Secure) or Allow Connections Only from Computers Running Remote Desktop with Network Level Authentication (More Secure).

Figure 7-9 shows Windows Vista enabled to accept Remote Desktop connections from clients supporting Network Level Authentication.

 TIP RDC 6.0 uses Network Level Authentication (NLA) when connecting to a remote client. NLA is used to authenticate the user, the client machine, and the server before the remote desktop session begins. The use of NLA is more secure and recommended for use whenever possible. NLA is supported on Windows XP SP2 or greater, and Windows Server 2003 SP1 or greater.

The Windows Firewall also needs to be configured to allow remote desktop connections. You'll see how this is done later in this chapter, in the section "Configuring Vista's Firewall."

Remote Desktop does not need to be enabled on the client accessing the remote computer. In other words, if you're using a Windows Vista system to remotely manage a Windows Server 2008 server, Remote Desktop needs be enabled on the server, but not on the Windows Vista system.

Figure 7-9
Enabling Remote
Desktop access
on Windows Vista

Exploring Remote Desktop Connection

You can access the Remote Desktop Connection on Windows Vista using either of two methods.

- Click Start and select All Programs | Accessories | Remote Desktop Connection.
- Click Start and enter **mstsc** in the Start Search box.

 EXAM TIP You should be very familiar with the available options on Remote Desktop Connection. I strongly encourage you to launch RDC and explore each of the tabs mentioned in the following bullets.

Once launched, the Remote Desktop Connection appears with most of the options hidden. If you click Options, six tabs appear giving you access to several different option pages.

- **General tab** The General tab includes two sections: Login Settings and Connection Settings. You enter the remote computer's name and your user name in the Logon Settings area. You can use the Connection Settings Save and Save As buttons to save your settings in a remote desktop file (.rdp). Once they are saved, you can open the file from here, or simply double-click the .rdp file to launch Remote Desktop Connection.

- **Display tab** You can set the size of the remote desktop displayed on your system. You can make it a specific window size (such as 800 × 600) or have it appear as full screen. You can also select the colors available, such as Highest Quality (32 bit).

- **Local Resources tab** The Local Resources tab allows you to use resources attached to your local computer in your remote session. Sounds played on the remote computer can be played on your computer. You can configure the keyboard to respond to key combinations (such as ALT-TAB) as if you entered them on the remote system. You can also specify which local resources will be available to the remote session.

  As an example, you can specify that printers or specific drives are available to the remote session. When connected to the remote computer, you can then print to your local printer, or save files to your local drives. Figure 7-10 shows the Local Resources tab. By clicking More, you can specify other resources to be available during your remote session. In the figure, the D: drive has been selected to be available.

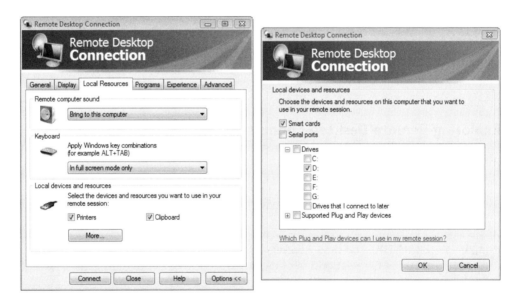

Figure 7-10   Configuring the local D: drive to be available to the remote session

- **Programs tab** You can identify a specific application to start when you connect using the Programs tab.

- **Experience tab** You can specify the connection speed for your connection, and depending on the speed, different elements will be available. Figure 7-11 shows the LAN (10 Mbps or higher) speed selected with all the experience elements available.

Figure 7-11
Setting the
connection speed

The different speeds are

- **Modem (28 Kbps)**   This includes the Bitmap Caching only.

- **Modem (56 Kbps)**   Themes are added to Bitmap Caching.

- **Broadband (128 Kbps – 1.5 Mbps)**   In addition to the features available with a 56 Kbps connection, the following features are added: Desktop Composition, Show Contents of Window While Dragging, and Menu and Window Animation.

- **LAN (10 Mbps or higher)**   All features are available, including the Desktop Background and Font Smoothing.

- **Custom**   You can pick and choose which features you want.

- **Advanced tab**   The advanced tab includes a Server Authentication section and a Connect from Anywhere section. The Server Authentication can be configured to warn you if you are connecting to a remote client that doesn't support Network Level Authentication, or you can disable the warning. If you are connecting to a Terminal Services (TS) Gateway server configured in your enterprise, you can configure the settings from this page.

Remote Access

Remote Access is a group of technologies used to allow a client to access an internal network from an external location. Figure 7-12 shows a possible configuration for

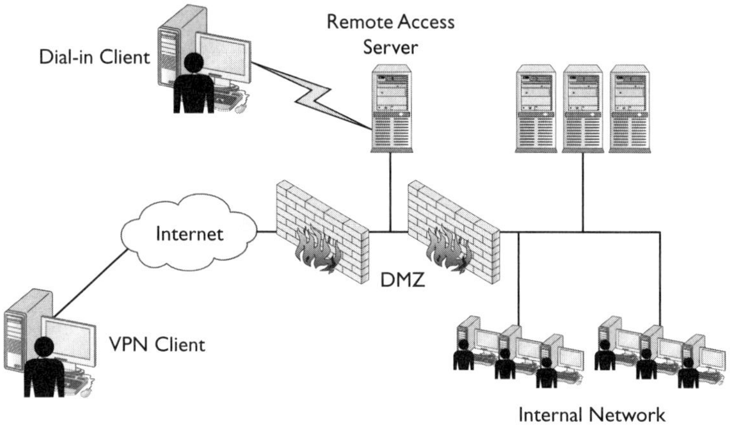

Figure 7-12
Remote Access
server

a Remote Access server. When a user is able to access the Remote Access server, that user is granted access to the internal network.

You can connect to a remote access server in two ways:

- **Dial-in** In a dial-in configuration, both the server and the client must have a modem and access to phone lines. The client initiates the call and dials the number answered by the modem. The client authenticates with the server and can then access the network.

- **Virtual private network (VPN)** With a VPN connection the client connects to the server via a public network (typically the Internet). For example, a client could connect to a local Internet service provider (ISP) and then create a VPN connection to the VPN server. If the VPN server is on the Internet, it would have a public IP address accessible from anywhere in the world. The private connection is often referred to as a tunnel, and several tunneling protocols are available with differing capabilities and levels of security.

Creating the remote access server and properly configuring it is well beyond the scope of this book and the Microsoft Windows Vista exams. Instead, what you need to know is how to configure Windows Vista to connect to the server.

Creating Connections

The Network and Sharing Center was presented in Chapter 5 and Chapter 6. One topic that wasn't covered was connecting to a workplace from the Set Up a Connection or Network page. The following two exercises will lead you through creating a dial-up connection and a VPN connection.

In Exercise 7.3, you will create a dial-up connection. While the phone number in this lab is fictitious, you can use these same steps to create your connection once you know the actual phone number of a dial-up server.

Exercise 7.3: Creating a Dial-up Connection

1. Access the Network and Sharing Center by clicking Start, right-clicking Network, and selecting Properties.

2. In the Network and Sharing Center, click the Set Up a Connection or Network task.

3. On the Choose a Connection Option page, select Connect to a Workplace.

4. On the How Do You Want to Connect page, select Dial Directly.

5. On the Type the Telephone Number to Connect To page, enter 555-777-8888. Change the Destination Name to: Best Company. Click the check box next to Don't Connect Now; Just Set It Up So I Can Connect Later. Your screen should look similar to Figure 7-13. Click Next.

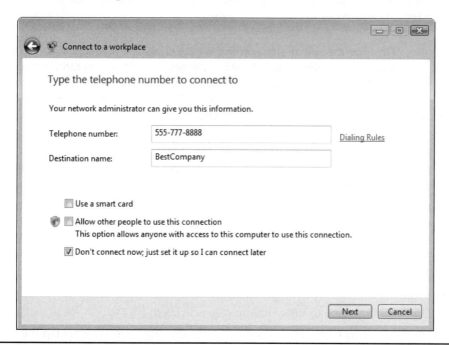

Figure 7-13   Configuring a dial-up connection

6. On the Type Your User Name and Password page, enter your name and use **P@ssword** as the password. Click Create.

7. After a moment, the connection will be created. Click Close.

In Exercise 7.4, you will create a VPN connection. While the IP address in this lab is fictitious, you can use these same steps to create your connection once you know the actual IP address of a VPN server.

Exercise 7.4: Creating a VPN Connection

1. Access the Network and Sharing Center by clicking Start, right-clicking Network, and selecting Properties.

2. In the Network and Sharing Center, click the Set Up a Connection or Network task.

3. On the Choose a Connection Option page, select Connect to a Workplace.

4. On the Do You Want to Use a Connection That You Already Have page, select No, Create a New Connection. Click Next.

5. On the How Do You Want to Connect page, select Use My Internet Connection (VPN).

6. On the Before You Connect page, select Create a New Connection to the Internet. Click Next.

TIP For the sake of this exercise, we are creating a new connection to the Internet, but if you already have an Internet connection, you can use that. A VPN that tunnels through the Internet must first make a connection to the Internet (often through a local ISP). Once an Internet connection is established, you can then create the VPN connection.

7. On the How Do You Want to Connect page, click Dial-up.

8. On the Type the Information from Your Internet Service Provider (ISP) page, enter the following information:

   • Dial-up Phone Number: **555-1234**

   • User Name: *Your ISP username*

   • Password: *Your ISP password*

   • Connection Name: **VPN Dial-up**

9. Click Connect.

10. On the Connecting to VPN Dial-up page, click Skip.

11. On the Internet Connectivity Test Was Unsuccessful page, click Set Up the Connection Anyway.

12. On the Type the Internet Address to Connect to page, enter the following information:

   • Internet address: **10.8.1.1**

   • Destination Name: **VPN BestCompany**

NOTE The address 10.8.1.1 is in the private IP address range, so it would never be found on the Internet and wouldn't work as a VPN server. If your company has a VPN server, it would give you either the host name of the server or the IP address (which would be in the public IP address range).

13. Click Next.

14. On the Type Your User Name and Password page, enter the username and password you would use at your company. Note that this will be different than the username and password you would enter for the ISP dial-up connection. Click Create.

15. On the Connection Is Ready to Use page, click Close.

16. Back in the Network and Sharing Center, click the Connect to a Network task. Figure 7-14 shows the three connections created from Exercise 7.3 and Exercise 7.4. To connect to the remote access server using dial-up, you would select the BestCompany connection. To connect to the VPN server, you would select the VPN BestCompany connection (which is configured to use the VPN Dial-up connection).

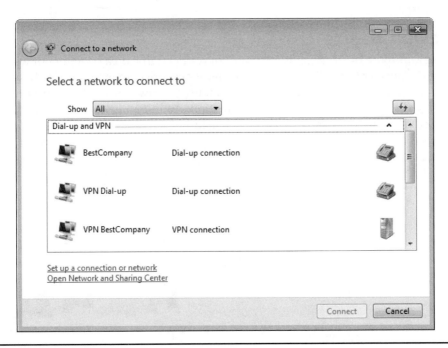

Figure 7-14   Dial-up and VPN connections

Once a VPN connection is created, you can access it via the Network Connections page. You can access this by clicking Manage Network Connections from within the Network and Sharing Center.

By right-clicking the connection, you can manipulate several different properties of the connection. The Properties dialog box includes five tabs: General, Options, Security, Networking, and Sharing. These settings must be configured to match the configuration of the VPN server.

Connection Manager Administration Kit (CMAK)

The Connection Manager Administration Kit (CMAK) is used to create and customize connection profiles for users. The CMAK includes a wizard that you can use to create executable files. You can make the executable files downloadable from a Web site and then users can simply execute the file to configure a connection on their computer.

The primary benefit of using the CMAK is to automate the process for end users. This is much easier than trying to teach them how to create their own connections.

Profiles you create can include information such as the VPN server name, IP address, security choices (such as tunneling and encryption choices), and much more. You can even have a custom phone book, which will list different phone numbers that users can dial, depending on where they are calling from in the world.

While it takes some time to learn the CMAK and create the profiles, if you're supporting multiple users in a large enterprise, this time investment pays off in the long run.

Firewall Basics

The basic purpose of a firewall is to control or restrict traffic on a computer or within a network. Consider Figure 7-15. It shows a typical network configuration. The boundary of the network (between the public Internet and the private network) is protected by two firewalls configured in a DMZ configuration. Additionally, each client and server also includes a firewall configured on the system.

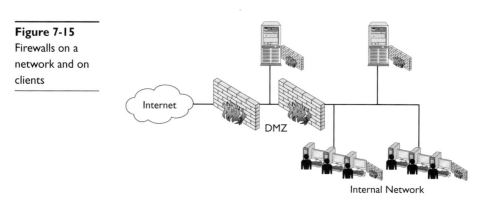

Figure 7-15
Firewalls on a network and on clients

A common question is, if we have a firewall at the boundary of our network, why do we also need firewalls on individual computers? The answer is the standard security principle of Defense in Depth.

Just as a bank can't have just a single security guard at the front door and say "we're protected," most companies also realize they need to use multiple layers of protection. Having boundary firewalls protects against attacks from the Internet, and having firewalls on clients and servers protects against internal attacks.

Internal attacks aren't necessarily from trusted employees. Instead, an internal attack may be from a virus or other malware that passed through the external firewall or was inadvertently brought in via a USB flash drive.

Ports

TCP/IP isn't a single protocol. Instead, it's a suite of protocols that work together to get traffic from one computer to another, and then communicate to the computer what to do with that traffic.

Traffic is transferred via packets. Embedded in the packet is the data, of course, but it also includes the IP addresses of the destination and source computers. This IP address is used to determine where the packet came from and where it is going.

 NOTE Technically a protocol data unit is only called a packet on the Network layer of the Open Systems Interconnect (OSI) model. It would be called a segment on the Transport layer and a frame on the Data Link layer. If you're pursuing CCNA, you absolutely need to know which one is where. For this discussion, I'm generalizing and referring to all the transferred data as packets.

Additionally, the packet includes port information from the source and destination computers. Once the packet reaches its destination, the receiving computer looks at the port information to determine what to do with the data.

As a simple example, consider Figure 7-16. A client clicks a link in Internet Explorer, which sends an HTTP request to an intranet Web server. The packet includes the IP address of the Web server and port 80 (which is the port for HTTP). It also includes a semi-randomly generated port number created specifically for this communication (in this case 45022). The client keeps this port recorded internally so that it knows to send the return packet back to Internet Explorer.

Figure 7-16
Packets from a client to a Web server and back

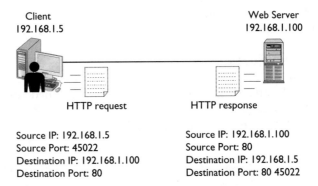

Client
192.168.1.5

Web Server
192.168.1.100

HTTP request   HTTP response

Source IP: 192.168.1.5
Source Port: 45022
Destination IP: 192.168.1.100
Destination Port: 80

Source IP: 192.168.1.100
Source Port: 80
Destination IP: 192.168.1.5
Destination Port: 80 45022

When the Web server receives the packet, it looks at the destination port (port 80) and sends it to the HTTP service. The HTTP service retrieves the Web page, formats it into a packet (or multiple packets), and sends it back to the client.

Notice that the return packet includes the source port of 80, indicating it came from an HTTP server. Additionally, it includes the destination port of 45022 in this example. When the client receives the packet, it sees that the destination port is 45022 and sends the packet to Internet Explorer to display the data.

Why is all of this relevant? In order for the client's HTTP request to get through the firewall, port 80 must be opened on the firewall. Additionally, it's common for a firewall to include a rule that allows return traffic. In other words, since the HTTP request from the client was allowed, the HTTP response would also be allowed.

On the other hand, if port 80 was not open on the firewall, the request would not be forwarded to the server.

TCP and UDP

Port numbers can be either Transmission Control Protocol (TCP) ports or User Datagram Protocol (UDP) ports. The primary difference is in how the traffic is generated with the two protocols.

TCP is known as a connection-oriented protocol and provides guaranteed delivery. Before data is sent between two computers, a TCP handshake process is completed. The sending computer sends out a packet similar to saying "Are you there?" The receiving computer replies to this packet with another packet similar to saying "Yes, what's up?" Then the sending computer sends another packet similar to saying "Glad you're available, I'm going to send you some data."

Once the three-way handshake process is completed, data is transferred between the two computers. If the three-way handshake process failed, the data wouldn't be transferred but instead an error would be generated.

UDP does not have any handshake process but instead just sends the data. UDP is often referred to as connectionless, since it doesn't create the connection as TCP does. UDP is frequently used for data that uses a lot of bandwidth and can afford to lose some packets such as streaming audio or video. Games that transmit data across a network or the Internet often send the audio and video using UDP.

If packets are lost in the audio or video stream, you may see jumpy video or hear blank spots where the data is missing, but the overall majority of the data is received.

Well-Known Ports

There are 64,535 TCP ports and 65,535 UDP ports that can be used or assigned. Of these the first 1024 ports are identified by the Internet Assigned Numbers Authority (IANA) as "well-known ports."

Some well-known ports are listed Table 7-1.

	Protocol	Port	Protocol	Port
Table 7-1 Well-known Ports	HTTP	80	HTTPS	443
	SMTP	25	FTP	20, 21
	Telnet	23	DNS	53

By blocking or allowing specific ports in a firewall, you are able to block or allow specific protocol traffic.

Blocking and Allowing

Firewalls can be used to either block or allow traffic. When traffic is blocked, then it simply isn't forwarded on to the destination. When traffic is allowed, it continues on to the destination just as if the firewall wasn't there. A common type of firewall is a packet-filtering firewall.

Packet-filtering firewalls can be used to block or allow traffic based on

- **IP addresses** You can prevent or allow traffic from specific IP addresses or IP address ranges.

- **Ports** Specific TCP or UDP ports can be blocked or allowed. For example, if you wanted to allow HTTP traffic but block FTP traffic, you could configure a firewall to allow port 80 but block ports 20 and 21.

- **Protocols** Some protocols don't use specific ports. For example, the Internet Control Message Protocol (ICMP) is used for diagnostic tools such as Ping, Pathping, and Tracert. While ICMP can be very useful, it's sometimes used in denial of service (DoS) attacks. Because of this, ICMP protocol traffic is sometimes blocked.

- **Programs** Some firewalls (such as the firewall included with Windows Vista) can be configured to allow or block traffic based on the program. You'll see this in action in Exercise 7.5.

Viewing Open Ports with Netstat

Netstat (network statistics) is a command-line tool you can use to view protocol statistics and TCP/IP connections currently open on your computer.

Just as with most command-line tools, you can modify the behavior of Netstat with the use of switches. Table 7-2 shows several of the switches available with Netstat.

	Switch	Description
Table 7-2 Netstat Switches	a	Displays all connections and listening ports
	b	Displays the name of the program that created the port
	e	Displays Ethernet statistics
	f	Displays Fully Qualified Domain Names (FQDN)
	n	Displays addresses and ports in numerical form
	o	Displays the owning process ID
	p *proto*	Shows connections for a specific protocol
	r	Shows the routing table
	s	Shows statistics on a per-protocol basis
	t	Displays the current connection state

Switches are entered with a dash (-) or a slash (/) and then the letter of the switch. Multiple switches can be entered together. They are entered with only a single dash or slash, and then the letters without any spaces.

For example, if you wanted to view a listing of all connections and listening ports (switch a), with the process ID of each (switch o), you would enter the following command:

```
Netstat -ao
```

Checking ports with Telnet

Telnet is a command-line program that can be used to check for open ports on other computers. For example, if you want to verify if a specific port is open, you use Telnet to try to connect to that port.

You can install Telnet by clicking Start | Control Panel. In the Control Panel, select Programs and click Turn Windows Features On or Off. If the User Account Control dialog box appears, click Continue. Select the Telnet Client feature as shown in Figure 7-17. The Telnet Server feature is not needed unless you want other users to connect to your system using Telnet (which would be rare).

Figure 7-17

Enabling the Telnet Client feature

Once it is installed, you can use the Telnet client to connect to specific ports on remote computers. If you can successfully connect to the port, then the port is open. If you can't connect to the port, the port is not open.

For example, imagine your network had a server named Exch1 running Microsoft Exchange including the Simple Mail Transport Protocol (SMTP). SMTP operates on port 25. You could use the following command to connect to the SMTP service on the server.

```
telnet exch1 25
```

Using Telnet to Impersonate an E-mail Sender   During a vulnerability audit done within a company, the security expert used a Telnet client to
connect to the Simple Mail Transport Protocol (SMTP) service. He then used this
connection to send an e-mail to several employees. He set the sender's address as
the CEO of the company with the subject line as Urgent. He then included in the
body of the e-mail something like this:

> *We have experienced some problems with several employee accounts indicating
> that they have been compromised. We have experts in the building and we need to
> verify these accounts as quickly as possible. Please send me your account name and
> password as soon as possible so we can address this problem.*

Almost half of the employees that received the e-mail sent their account name
and password. This is a sophisticated phishing attack (since it occurred from within the network), but it is a phishing attack nonetheless.

While this shows how Telnet can be used to verify an open port (SMTP in this
case), it also reminds us we need to constantly repeat the message to users to never
give out passwords. Never.

If your connection is successful, you have verified that port 25 is open and the SMTP
service is running. If your connection is not successful, it could be because the server
is not reachable. Often you would first use the `ping` command to check connectivity
as follows:

```
Ping exch1
```

Configuring Vista's Firewall

Any network that you're working in will likely have a firewall configured, but you can
also configure the firewall included with Windows Vista. The firewall included with
Windows Vista applies only to the connections to your system.

There are two tools you can use to configure the firewall:

- **Windows Firewall**   This tool gives you access to basic settings for the firewall.
  You can turn the firewall on or off, and configure some exceptions based on
  ports or programs.

- **Windows Firewall with Advanced Settings**   This tool gives you much greater
  flexibility in configuring the firewall. You can create inbound and outbound
  firewall rules and connection security rules. You also have more sophisticated
  monitoring tools available from this tool.

Windows Firewall

When configuring Windows Vista Firewall, you have three choices as shown in Figure 7-18.

Figure 7-18

Windows Firewall

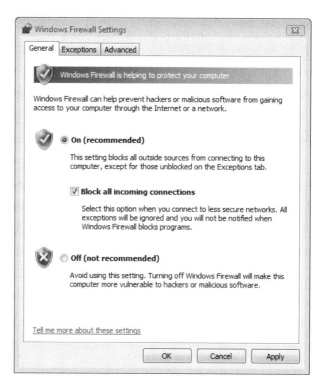

EXAM TIP When configured to Block All Incoming Connections (as shown), you have the highest level of security, preventing other users from connecting to your computer. You would not use this within a network where you wanted to share content on your computer with other users.

The three settings for Windows Firewall are

- **On (Recommended)** This is the default setting. Most programs are blocked at your firewall but some programs can be allowed by configuring exceptions. The Exceptions tab gives you the ability to configure specific exceptions.

- **On (Recommended) with Block All Incoming Connections** This setting turns on the firewall without any exceptions for incoming connections. You would use this when connecting to a public network such as at a coffee shop. You can still make some outbound connections such as browsing Web pages, and still send and receive e-mail, and send and receive instant messages. Any shared content on your computer would be inaccessible to others.

- **Off (Not Recommended)**   This provides no protection to your computer. You could choose this if your computer is within a network protected by other firewalls, but generally it's a good idea to keep it turned on as an extra layer of protection. It may require some extra configuration, but the extra security is worth the extra time required.

Exceptions

You can configure exceptions by using the Exceptions tab available on the Windows Firewall Settings dialog box. Exceptions can be configured by program or by port.

Many common programs are already listed on the Exceptions page. You can simply check, or uncheck, the box next to the program to allow or disallow the program through your firewall. Some of the common programs you'll likely manipulate or allow are

- **Connect to a Network Projector**   Newer projectors can be connected to a network (either wired or wireless). With this setting enabled, you can then connect to it and display your presentation just as if it were connected to your computer. This is not enabled by default.

- **Core Networking**   This allows basic networking capabilities. This is enabled by default.

- **File and Printer Sharing**   This setting allows other computers to connect to your computer and access shared files and shared printers. This is not enabled by default.

- **Network Discovery**   This setting (discussed in greater depth in Chapter 5) allows other computers to easily find you and you to easily find other computers using Network Discovery protocols. This setting is primarily controlled by the network location (Private, Public, or Domain).

- **Remote Assistance**   Allows other users to connect to your computer and provide assistance. You can view what the other user is doing. This setting is primarily controlled by the Remote Settings tab of the System Properties.

- **Remote Desktop**   Allows other users to connect to your computer and remotely administer it. You cannot view what the other user is doing. This setting is primarily controlled by the Remote Settings tab of the System Properties.

 EXAM TIP   You should know what exceptions are in generic terms, what the common exceptions are as listed in the previous bullets, how to manipulate the exceptions, and how to add additional exceptions if needed.

If you want to add a program that's not listed, you can click the Add Program button. One of the benefits of adding an exception by a program is that all the ports that the program uses are automatically included. For example, if you want to allow a program that randomly picks a port above 10,000 each time it connects, you can add the program. It wouldn't matter what port the program picked; it would be allowed.

You can allow access via a single port if desired. For example, if you wanted to play a multiplayer game on a network and wanted to keep the firewalls operational, you could add the port that the game is using. In Figure 7-19 the Add Port button was clicked and an exception is being created. Notice in the exceptions list, a program named Quake III is added. This is not included in the exceptions list by default but was added by me just before creating this screen shot.

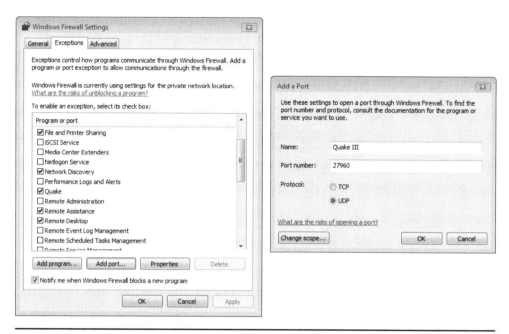

Figure 7-19 Adding a port exception

It's common for games to use UDP ports, but check the documentation to determine if it's a UDP or TCP port that needs to be opened. Remember, TCP port 20000 is not the same thing as UDP port 20000.

In Exercise 7.5, you will view the exceptions automatically created in the Windows Firewall when Remote Desktop and Remote Assistance are enabled.

Exercise 7.5: Viewing Windows Firewall Exceptions

1. Disable Remote Desktop and Remote Assistance on your computer.

   a. Click Start, right-click Computer, and select Properties.

   b. In the Tasks pane, select Remote Settings. If the User Account Control dialog box appears, click Continue.

   c. On the Remote tab of the System Properties dialog box notice your current settings for Remote Assistance and Remote Desktop. At the end of this exercise you'll want to restore your system to their original settings.

   d. If selected, deselect the check box next to Remote Assistance.

    e. In the Remote Desktop section, select Don't Allow Connections to This Computer.

    f. Click Apply. Leave this dialog box open. You will make additional changes later in this exercise.

2. Launch the Windows Firewall. Click Start | Control Panel. In the Control Panel, click Security | Windows Firewall.

3. On the Windows Firewall, click the link to Allow a Program Through Windows Firewall. If the User Account Control dialog box appears, click Continue.

4. The Windows Firewall Settings dialog box will appear with the Exceptions tab open. Your display should look similar to Figure 7-20. Notice that the Remote Assistance and Remote Desktop programs are not checked and are not enabled. Click OK but leave the Windows Firewall program open.

Figure 7-20

Windows Firewall
Exceptions

5. Return to the System Properties dialog box opened in Step 1. Enable Remote Assistance by selecting the check box. Enable Remote Desktop by clicking the Allow Connections Only from Computers Running Remote Desktop with Network Level Authentication (More Secure). Click Apply.

6. Return to the Windows Firewall and click the link to Allow a Program Through Windows Firewall. If the User Account Control dialog box appears, click Continue.

7. Notice that the firewall is now configured to allow Remote Assistance and Remote Desktop programs through. While you configured the system properties, Windows Vista also configured these two exceptions.

8. Return Remote Assistance and Remote Desktop to their original settings as noted in Step 1c. of this exercise.

Advanced Tab

The Advanced tab allows you to select if the firewall settings will apply to all of your network connections or just some of them. Figure 7-21 shows the Advanced tab settings.

Figure 7-21

Windows Firewall Advanced tab

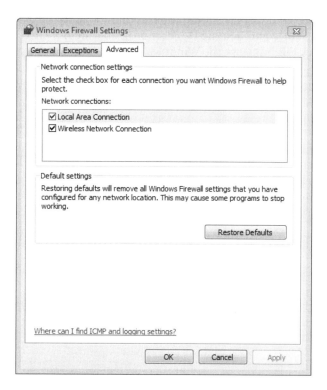

For example, you could use a laptop computer at work (using a wired connection) and on the road (using a wireless connection). While at work, company policy may dictate that the firewall is not needed. On the road, you want as much protection as possible, so you want the firewall to be used.

You could deselect the Local Area Connection check box, which is your wired NIC. The firewall settings won't apply to this NIC. You could keep the check box on the Wireless Network Connection NIC so that all the firewall settings will apply to the wireless NIC.

Windows Firewall with Advanced Security

The Windows Firewall with Advanced Security tool allows you access to more details in your firewall. Don't get confused, though. The rules and settings applied here apply to the same firewall as settings applied with the Windows Firewall discussed just before this section. It's only one firewall, but you have two tools to manipulate it.

You can access the Windows Firewall with Advanced Security console through Administrative Tools. Click Start | Control Panel. In the Control Panel, select System and Maintenance, scroll down to the bottom, and select Administrative Tools. You can then double-click the Windows Firewall with Advanced Security link.

Figure 7-22 shows the Windows Firewall with Advanced Security. In the figure, the Inbound Rules are selected from the tree on the left and you see a listing of Inbound Rules available in the center pane. The Actions pane shows the actions you can take for Inbound Rules.

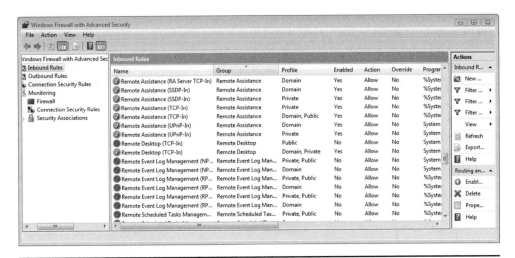

Figure 7-22 Windows Firewall with Advanced Security

Notice in the figure that Remote Assistance has several different rules. Remote Assistance is enabled, so each of the Remote Assistance rules has a white check mark on a green background (as opposed to a grayed-out check mark) and the Enabled column indicates Yes. These rules are associated with different profiles (Private, Public, and Domain), which relate to the Network Locations discussed in Chapters 5 and 6.

TIP A public network location indicates you are in a public place and security is restricted. A private network location indicates you are in a private, protected location (such as at home or work behind a firewall) and security is relaxed. A domain network location indicates you are operating within a domain with domain controllers. Within a domain, group policy is frequently used to configure multiple settings for security.

The Windows Firewall with Advanced Security offers the following capabilities:

- **Inbound Rules**   Inbound rules monitor inbound traffic and can be set to allow or deny traffic.

- **Outbound Rules**   Outbound rules monitor outbound traffic and can be set to allow or deny traffic.

- **Connection Security Rules**   Using Internet Protocol security (IPsec) connection security rules can provide authentication between the connecting computers, data integrity (ensuring the data is not modified), and data encryption.

- **Monitoring**   The monitoring node allows you to view different settings for your firewall and configure detailed logging. For example, you can configure logging to log all dropped packets and log all successful connections.

Rules

You can create a rule to explicitly allow or block traffic. Figure 7-23 shows the properties of one of the preconfigured Remote Desktop rules.

Figure 7-23
Remote Desktop
Rule allowing
Remote Desktop
connections

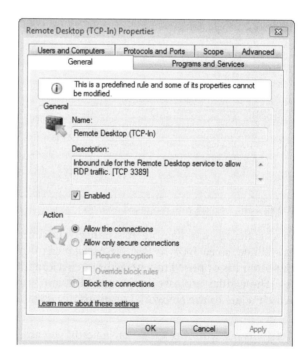

Each rule has multiple tabs that can be used to be very explicit in how the rule functions. You can state specific users or computers that the rule will apply to, specific protocols and ports for the rule, specific IP addresses for the rule, and in which profiles (Public, Private, Domain) the rule will be active.

In addition to the preconfigured rules, you can create your own to meet specific needs.

Logging

There may be times when you want to know what the firewall is doing. For example, when you're troubleshooting an issue you may suspect that the firewall is blocking traffic but you need to confirm it.

By enabling logging, you can see exactly what packets the firewall is allowing through and what packets it is dropping. Logging is enabled on a per-profile basis. You can enable logging on the Private, Public, or Domain profile. By default, logging is not enabled.

To enable logging, follow these steps:

1. Launch the Windows Firewall with Advanced Security (as described earlier in this section).

2. Right-click over Windows Firewall with Advanced Security and select Properties.

3. Select the profile where you want to enable logging.

4. In the Logging area, click the Customize button. You can change the setting for Log Dropped Packets or Log Successful Connections. Your display will be similar to Figure 7-24.

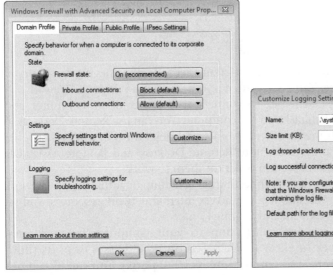

Figure 7-24   Configuring Windows Firewall logging

In the figure, I have changed the Log Dropped Packets from the setting of No (Default), to Yes. You can also modify the location of the firewall and the size limit.

Connection Security Rules

Connection security rules can be used for authentication and encryption. Internet Protocol security (IPsec) is used for either authentication or authentication and encryption.

Authentication is used in a connection security rule to verify that two computers are who they claim to be. This prevents a connection to a computer that may be trying to impersonate another computer to gain information. Encryption is used to protect the data so that unauthorized computers cannot read the data.

Similar connection security rules must be configured on both computers involved in a connection in order for them to communicate. In other words, if one computer has a policy requiring authentication but the other computer doesn't have a compatible policy, the two computers will not be able to communicate.

Within a domain, computers can also be assigned IPsec policies via group policy. A computer assigned a compatible IPsec policy can communicate with computers manually configured with a connection security rule.

 NOTE Group policy is used within a domain to manage multiple users or computers. An administrator can make a single setting and apply it to a domain or organizational unit (OU), and the setting is automatically applied to all users and computers within the scope of the group policy. This is much quicker and more efficient than going to each computer individually and manually configuring the settings.

Chapter Review

In this chapter you learned about several different methods of achieving remote connections with Windows Vista. You also learned about using the Windows Firewall.

Remote Assistance allows a helper to connect to another user's computer and demonstrate how to accomplish tasks on the computer. You can use Remote Desktop to remotely connect to and administer other computers (though the user can't watch what you're doing while you're connected). Both Remote Desktop and Remote Assistance must have firewall exceptions enabled in order for them to work.

You can access internal networks by connecting using dial-up or virtual private network (VPN) connections. Once connected, you can access internal network resources. You set these connections up via the Network and Sharing Center.

The Windows Firewall provides protection to your computer from external sources. Firewalls often block or allow traffic based on IP addresses or ports (both connection-oriented TCP ports and connectionless UDP ports). You can also block or allow traffic based on a program.

The Windows Firewall and the Windows Firewall with Advanced Settings can be used to enable, disable, and create exceptions and rules to allow or block traffic. You can also use the Windows Firewall with Advanced Settings to enable connection security rules to provide both authentication and encryption of traffic.

Additional Study

Self Study Exercises

Use these additional exercises to challenge yourself.

- Work with a friend and create a Remote Assistance connection over the Internet. Do it once with yourself as the helper and once with your friend as the helper.

- Connect to another computer using Remote Desktop. If possible, connect to a computer near you so that can observe what happens to a logged-on user when you connect remotely.

- Create a firewall rule to allow traffic from port 56789. Delete the rule after you create it.

- Enable logging of the Windows Firewall. Connect to the system that has logging enabled and then view the log.

Summary of What You Need to Know

70-620

Topics in this chapter are hit hardest on the 70-620 exam. When preparing, pay particular attention to the following topics:

- **Remote Assistance** Know how to connect and control Remote Assistance sessions. This includes knowing that it must be enabled in the system properties and the firewall, the invitation expiration times can be modified, and the screen can be hidden from the helper by clicking the Pause button.

- **Remote Desktop** Know the purpose and use of Remote Desktop and how to configure it. This includes knowing that it must be enabled in the system properties and the firewall. You should also be familiar with all the options of Remote Desktop, such as how to bring local resources to your remote session and enable all features in the remote session.

- **Windows Firewall** You should be familiar with the basic Windows Firewall, its capabilities and purpose. This includes enabling and configuring it in a public or private area (enabling or disabling Block All Connections), and enabling exceptions based on ports or programs.

70-622

When preparing for the 70-622 exam, pay particular attention to the following topics covered in this chapter:

- **Terminal Services** You should know that the Terminal Services service must be running to support Remote Assistance and Remote Desktop. You should also know the basic purpose of both Remote Assistance and Remote Desktop.

- **Remote Access** You should know the different ways that users can remotely connect to a dial-up or VPN server. You should also be aware that the Connection Manager Administration Kit (CMAK) can be useful in creating connection profiles.

- **Windows Firewall** You should be familiar with the basic Windows Firewall, its capabilities and purpose. This includes manipulating and enabling exceptions. You should also be familiar with some of the tools that can identify open ports (such as Netstat and Telnet).

- **Windows Firewall with Advanced Security** You should be familiar with the advanced capabilities of the Windows Firewall. This includes enabling logging and manipulating inbound rules, outbound rules, and connection security rules (to enforce IPsec).

70-623

The primary topic for the 70-623 exam in this chapter is the Windows Firewall. You should be familiar with all of the firewall topics covered in this chapter.

Questions

70-620

1. You have requested remote assistance and a help desk professional has taken control of your desktop. Your boss comes in and asks you for details on a proprietary project. You want to open up the project file without allowing the help desk professional to see the file. How can you do so with minimal impact?

   A. Click the Pause button in the Remote Assistance window.

   B. Click the Hide Window button in the Remote Assistance window.

   C. Click the Disconnect button in the Remote Assistance window.

   D. Click the Stop Sharing button in the Remote Assistance window.

2. Your friend has sent you a remote assistance request. By the time you responded, the request expired. How can your friend increase the amount of time the invitation will remain valid?

   A. Change the minimum amount of time an invitation will remain open.

   B. Change the maximum amount of time an invitation will remain open.

   C. Modify the properties of the invitation to change the expiration time.

   D. Ensure Remote Desktop is enabled.

3. You need to be able to remotely connect to Sally's computer using the Remote Desktop Connection application. What should be done to support this? (Choose all that apply.)

   A. Enable Remote Desktop in the system properties of your computer.

   B. Enable Remote Desktop in the system properties of Sally's computer.

   C. Enable the Remote Access exception in Microsoft Windows Firewall.

   D. Enable the Remote Desktop exception in Microsoft Windows Firewall.

4. Sally occasionally connects to a remote computer using RDC from her Windows Vista computer. When she connects, she wants to save files to her local C: drive. How can this be done?

   A. Enable sharing of her local C: drive.

   B. Ensure Remote Desktop is configured on her Windows Vista computer.

   C. In the properties of RDC, configure her C: drive as a local resource.

   D. Enable sharing the C: drive on the remote computer.

5. Sally occasionally connects to a remote computer using RDC from her Windows Vista computer. When she connects, the remote computer doesn't display the desktop background. What can she do to display the remote computer's desktop background during her remote session?

   A. Configure her desktop to be available as a local resource.

   B. Change the Display tab of the RDC to indicate Full Screen.

   C. Change the Experience tab of the RDC to indicate a connection speed of LAN (10 Mbps or higher).

   D. Change the Experience tab of the RDC to indicate a connection speed of Modem (28 Mbps).

6. You've installed an application on your Windows Vista system, but you find that it isn't working when it accesses remote systems. You refer to the documentation and learn it randomly picks ports above 10,000. You want to ensure the maximum amount of security, while also allowing this application to work. What would you do?

   A. Disable the firewall.

   B. Enable the firewall with no exceptions.

   C. Open all ports above 10,000.

   D. Create a program exception.

7. A parent is trying to prevent his child from playing a specific online game without restricting access to the Internet. The game uses connectionless traffic over port 28394. How can this game be restricted on the child's Windows Vista computer?

   A. Disable the firewall.

   B. Create a rule in Windows Firewall to block TCP port 28394.

   C. Create a rule in Windows Firewall to block UDP port 28394.

   D. Ensure the child only logs on with a Standard user account.

8. You have created a shared folder on your Windows Vista computer located in your home network. You want other users to be able to access the files you placed in this shared folder, but they can't. What should you do?

   A. Enable the Block All Incoming Connections option on the Windows Firewall.

   B. Disable the Block All Incoming Connections option on the Windows Firewall.

    C. Enable the File and Printer Sharing exception in the Windows Firewall.

    D. Enable the File Sharing exception in the Windows Firewall.

70-622

1. You are trying to help Joe resolve a problem with his computer and decide to use Remote Assistance. After Joe creates an invitation, you realize you can't connect to his system. Joe's computer is within your network and you verify connectivity is good by successfully pinging his computer. You also verify the firewall is not blocking Remote Assistance. What is the likely problem?

    A. The Remote Assistance service is not running.

    B. The Terminal Services service is not running.

    C. The Terminal Services Configuration service is not running.

    D. The Terminal Services UserMode Port Redirector service is not running.

2. Many users in your company will begin using their laptop computers (running Windows Vista) to connect to new VPN servers the company is planning to deploy on Windows Server 2008 servers. What can you use to simplify the setup of the VPN connections?

    A. RDC

    B. CMAK

    C. GPO

    D. Remote Assistance

3. Your system is having some unusual activity, and you want to view a listing of ports that are currently connected on your system. What tool will give you this information?

    A. `Ping`

    B. `IPConfig`

    C. `Telnet`

    D. `Netstat`

4. Sally is running Windows Vista on her computer at work. She's trying to access a server application named MCITPApp, but it always fails with an error message stating the connection has timed out. Other users have been successfully running this application. You want to collect information on the connection from Sally's computer to determine the likely cause. What could you do?

    A. Use `Telnet` to connect to the server.

    B. Run `Netstat`.

    C. Enable logging on the Windows Firewall.

    D. Disable the Windows Firewall.

5. You are configuring two computers to share data via a line of business application created by in-house developers. You need to ensure that both computers are able to authenticate each other prior to establishing a connection and passing data to each other. What can you configure on each computer to support this?

   A. Firewall logging

   B. A firewall outbound rule

   C. A firewall inbound rule

   D. A firewall connection security rule

70-623

1. Your Windows Firewall is configured as shown in Figure 7-25. You want to configure it so that other users cannot access shared data on your system from their computers. What, if anything, should you do?

Figure 7-25

Windows Firewall

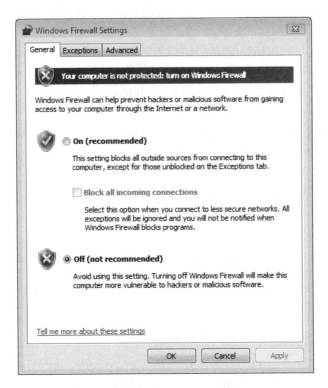

A. Nothing. This setting will support the desired results.

B. Select the On (recommended) setting.

C. Select the On (recommended) setting, with the Block All Incoming Connections.

D. Leave the setting as Off (not recommended), but also select Block All Incoming Connections.

2. You have helped a friend configure her computer by showing her exactly how to perform a task. She asks if you could help again if she has a problem and mentions that it'd be great if you could actually show her how to do something even if the two of you aren't in the same place. You think of Remote Assistance. Of the following choices, what would need to be configured on her computer to enable Remote Assistance?

A. Windows Defender

B. Windows Firewall

C. Windows Update

D. Remote Desktop

3. Sally has a home network with two other computers. She shared a printer from her Windows Vista desktop system and wants other people to be able to print to the computer. Unfortunately, no one can print to it. She suspects a firewall setting is not configured correctly and asks you what she should check. She does not want to needlessly weaken security in her network. What do you tell her?

A. Ensure the firewall is disabled.

B. Enable the exception for Print Sharing.

C. Enable the exception for File and Print Sharing.

D. Enable the exception for Remote Desktop.

4. You need to verify if a remote server is running SMTP. What tool can you use on your Windows Vista system to verify this?

A. Windows Firewall

B. Windows Defender

C. Telnet Client

D. Telnet Server

5. A consultant is preparing to give a PowerPoint presentation in your conference room. She is running Windows Vista but is having trouble connecting to your network projector. She asks you for help. You verify she has successfully connected to the network. What do you suggest she do to enable the connection to the network projector?

A. Enable the Core Networking exception in the Windows Firewall.

B. Enable the Network Discovery exception in the Windows Firewall.

C. Enable the Connect to a Network Projector exception in the Windows Firewall.

D. Enable the Remote Desktop exception in the Windows Firewall.

Answers

70-620

1. **A.** The Pause button will cause the screen to go blank for the helper. It will leave the session open, and when the Continue button is pressed, the session will continue right where it left off. There is no Hide Window button. If you click the Disconnect button, the session will have to be restarted completely again, which isn't "minimal impact." If you click the Stop Sharing button, the helper loses control of the desktop but can still view the contents of the desktop.

2. **B.** The setting for the maximum amount of time invitations can remain open determines the expiration of each invitation. It is six hours by default but can be modified. There is no setting for the minimum amount of time an invitation will remain open. Once an invitation is created, it is encrypted and can't be modified. Remote Desktop doesn't affect Remote Assistance.

3. **B, D.** Sally's computer must have Remote Desktop enabled before remote desktop connections are allowed. Additionally, the firewall must have the Remote Desktop exception enabled. The Remote Desktop exception must also be enabled on the Windows Firewall. It's not necessary to have Remote Desktop enabled on the client connecting to the remote computer; Remote Desktop only needs to be enabled on the remote computer. A Remote Access exception rule does not exist in Windows Firewall.

4. **C.** Local resources (such as drives and printers) can be configured to be available when connected to a remote session. The Remote Desktop Connection (RDC) Local Resources tab includes a More button that can be used to enable the availability of specific drives. She doesn't need to share her C: drive or the remote computer's C: drive, both of which could represent security risks. Remote Desktop does not need to be enabled on her computer to connect to a remote computer, or to enable local resources to be available.

5. **C.** When the Remote Desktop Connection (RDC) Experience tab setting is changed to LAN (10 Mbps or higher), all features are enabled, including the Desktop Background. It's not possible to configure her desktop to be available as a local resource. Setting the display to Full Screen won't enable or disable the Desktop Background feature. With the Modem (28 Mbps) speed selected, only the Bitmap Caching feature is enabled.

6. **D.** If you create an exception for the program, then any ports the program uses will be allowed for the program. Disabling the firewall or opening all ports above 10,000 will significantly weaken security. Enabling the firewall with no exceptions won't allow the program to run.

7. **C.** UDP port 28394 should be blocked by creating a firewall rule. Since the traffic is connectionless, it is a UDP port, which is common for games. If it was connection-oriented, it would be TCP port 28394. Disabling the firewall would not restrict the computer from playing the game. Standard users can still play games.

8. **C.** The File and Printer Sharing exception in the Windows Firewall must be enabled to allow others to access your shared folders. If you enable Block All Incoming Connections, no connections will be allowed at all, and this should be done when you're in a public place. If you disable Block All Incoming Connections, the firewall will work normally, but the File and Printer Sharing exception is not enabled by default. There is no File Sharing exception.

70-622

1 **B.** The Terminal Services service must be running to support Remote Assistance. There is no service named Remote Assistance. Neither the Terminal Services Configuration service nor the Terminal Services UserMode Port Redirector service needs to be running to support Remote Assistance.

2. **B.** The Connection Manager Administration Kit (CMAK) can be used to build connection profiles to automate the creation of the connections on the Windows Vista computers. Remote Desktop Connection (RDC) is generally used by administrators to remotely administer servers; while RDC could be used, it would require you to connect to each of the end user's computers. A Group Policy Object (GPO) is used to manage multiple computers or users, but it doesn't include have an easy method of creating connection profiles for multiple users. If you used Remote Assistance, you would have to manually connect to each computer.

3. **D.** The `netstat -a` command-line tool is the only listed tool that can give you a listing of connections and listening ports on your system. For more details (such as the process ID of each connection and port) you could enter `netstat -ao`. Ping is used to check connectivity between two computers. `IPConfig` shows configuration information. `Telnet` can be used to create a communication channel between two computers.

4. **C.** You can enable logging on the Windows Firewall to collect information on the connection. `Telnet` can be used to check for open ports but doesn't collect information. `Netstat` can be used to check for open connections but doesn't collect information. Disabling the Windows Firewall would probably allow the application to work, but it wouldn't collect any information.

5. **D.** A firewall connection security rule can be used to enforce authentication between two computers before a connection is created. Firewall logging would be used to collect statistics on the firewall but wouldn't provide authentication. Firewall inbound and outbound rules can be used to allow or block traffic but can't provide authentication.

70-623

1. **C.** The On (recommended) setting with the Block All Incoming Connections setting will prevent other users from accessing shared data on your system. With the setting off (as shown), you have no firewall protection. With it On, without the Block All Incoming Connections selection, users can access shared data. It's not possible to select the Block All Incoming Connections setting if the firewall is off.

2. **B.** A Windows Firewall exception or rule would need to be configured to allow Remote Assistance connections. By enabling Remote Assistance, the exception is created automatically. Windows Defender would search for spyware on your system. Windows Update is used to download updates to your system. Remote Desktop would allow you to connect remotely into the system, but the user is unable to observe your activities.

3. **C.** Shared printers can be accessed by other computers when the File and Print Sharing exception is enabled in the Windows Firewall. Disabling the firewall completely would needlessly weaken security. There is no Print Sharing exception. The Remote Desktop exception will allow Remote Desktop connections but won't affect print sharing capabilities.

4. **C.** The Telnet client can be used to check for open ports on remote systems. The Telnet Client is a feature that must be enabled and is then available from the command line. Neither Windows Firewall nor Windows Defender can be used to check ports on remote systems. The Telnet Server feature enables your system as a Telnet server but doesn't enable the Telnet client.

5. **C.** The Connect to a Network Projector exception should be enabled to connect to a network projector. The Core Networking exception must already be enabled, since she has network connectivity. Network Discovery won't be enough to allow her to connect to the projector. Remote Desktop is enabled to allow administrators to remotely connect to your system.

Accessing Resources

8

In this chapter, you will learn about:
- Accessing and sharing data
- Accessing and sharing printers

One of the great benefits of configuring networks is the ability to share resources. When you want data to be available to others, you can place it in a shared folder and then others can access it. You don't have to buy everyone a printer, but can instead share a single printer on a network.

When accessing and sharing resources, you need to make sure the core requirements are met. Additionally, you need to make sure that users have the appropriate permissions to access the resources.

 EXAM TIP Objectives for the 70-622 and 70-623 exams are included in this chapter. The 70-620 exam doesn't have any objectives covered in this chapter.

Accessing and Sharing Resources

Computers are commonly operated in networks today. It's rare to find a business with more than one computer that doesn't have them networked in some manner. Even in homes, users are finding how easy it is to network their computers today and this is becoming more and more common.

It doesn't matter whether the network is wired or wireless (or a combination of both), only that computers are connected. Once networked, you can easily share resources between computers. The primary resources you'll share are

- **Data** This includes any types of files. Data is placed in shares or shared folders. Once shared, the data is accessible over the network.

- **Printers** Printers can be connected to a single computer and then shared by that computer so that they are accessible to other users. A network can also host a network printer (one with a network interface card and its own IP address).

In order to support accessing and sharing resources with a Windows Vista computer, you need to meet some basic requirements. Both the network interface card (NIC) and the Windows Firewall must be configured properly.

Figure 8-1 shows the Windows Firewall and the NIC.

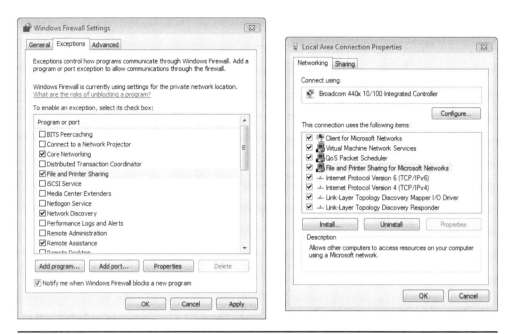

Figure 8-1   Windows Firewall and NIC configured to support File and Printer sharing

In the figure, you can see that the Windows Firewall has the File and Printer Sharing option enabled as an exception. In the NIC, you can see that the File and Printer Sharing for Microsoft Networks service is enabled.

The Windows Firewall was covered in more depth in Chapter 7, and the File and Printer Sharing for Microsoft Networks was covered in more depth in Chapter 5. However, for this chapter I just want to remind you that both options must be enabled to support accessing and sharing resources.

Sharing Data

Very often we want to be able to share data. It could be a project document that a work associate has created and placed on a server share, or something that you created at home and want to be able to share with family members.

With Windows Vista, you can both access and share data.

Accessing Shares on Other Computers

When data is shared and available on your network, you can access it via the Universal Naming Convention (UNC) path. The UNC path is formatted as

`\\ServerName\ShareName`

In this context, a server is any computer that is hosting a share. It doesn't have to be a server such as Windows Server 2008. It could just as easily be another Windows Vista computer.

There are multiple methods of accessing the share. Two popular ways are using the UNC path directly and creating a mapped drive.

Accessing a Share Using the UNC Path

To access a share directly, you can just enter the UNC path. As an example, imagine that your network has a server named MCITP1. Someone has created a share named Projects on this server. To access it, you could use the UNC path name of

```
\\MCITP1\Projects
```

Click Start and enter the UNC path in the Start Search line. This will open Windows Explorer with the connection to the share. You can then access files in the share.

Figure 8-2 shows what the share (named `MCITP1\Projects`) will look like on your computer. While it's hosted on a Windows Server 2008 server, it could just as easily be on another Windows Vista computer. Depending on the permissions, users may be able to read the files, modify or delete the files, or create new files.

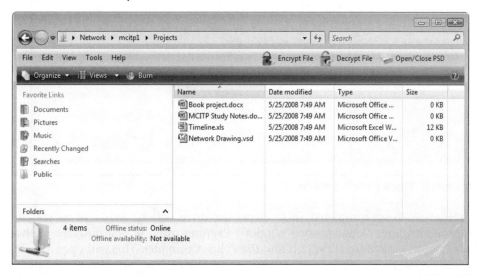

Figure 8-2   Accessing a share

What you can do with the share varies depending on the permissions you are granted.

Access a Share Using a Mapped Drive

You can map a drive letter (such as Z: or any other letter that is available) and then use Windows Explorer to browse to the drive. To map a drive, follow these steps:

1. Launch Windows Explorer by pressing the WINDOWS-E keys.

2. Select the Tools drop-down menu and click Map Network Drive.

3. On the What Network Folder Would You Like to Map page, enter the UNC path name in the Folder text box. You can accept the drive name, or change it to another letter.

4. Select the check box to Reconnect at Logon, if you want this mapped drive to be available to you each time you log on. If this box is not checked, the mapped drive will only be available for this logon session. Your display will look similar to Figure 8-3. Click Finish.

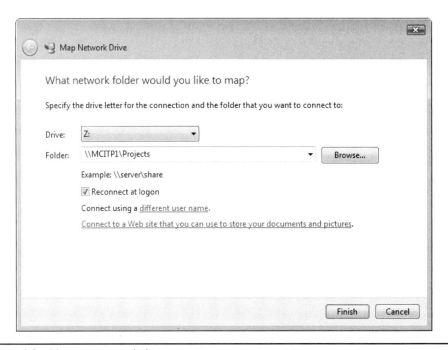

Figure 8-3   Mapping a network drive

Once you have completed these steps, the drive will be available to you from Windows Explorer. You can open Windows Explorer using several different methods. For example, you could click Start and then click Computer. This will open Windows Explorer with the Computer node selected. All available drives from this computer will be shown.

Network and Sharing Center

The primary tool you'll use to share resources on your computer is the Network and Sharing Center. It has several settings in the Sharing and Discovery section that directly relate to file and printer sharing capabilities.

Figure 8-4 shows the Network and Sharing Center with several settings enabled for file and printer sharing.

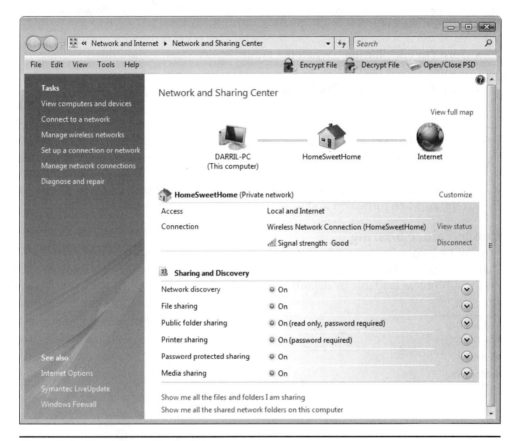

Figure 8-4   Network and Sharing Center

In the figure, you can see that the following sharing capabilities have been enabled:

- File Sharing
- Public Folder Sharing
- Printer Sharing
- Password Protected Sharing
- Media Sharing

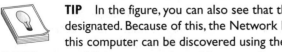

TIP   In the figure, you can also see that the Private network location is designated. Because of this, the Network Discovery is set to On. As configured, this computer can be discovered using the Link Layer Topology Discovery (LLTD) protocol. Private networks, public networks, and the network discovery topic were all covered in Chapters 5 and 6.

File Sharing

When file sharing is enabled, files and printers that you have chosen to share on your computer can be accessed by other computers in your network. There are only two choices for this setting:

- **Turn On File Sharing** When on, Public Folder Sharing and Printer Sharing settings can be enabled.
- **Turn Off File Sharing** When off, all file and printer sharing is disabled.

 EXAM TIP File Sharing must be enabled before you can share files or printers on your computer.

This setting directly affects the firewall exception File and Printer Sharing. It enables the exception when turned on and disables the setting when turned off.

Public Folder Sharing

The Public Folder Sharing setting affects your public folders. Public folders are folders that exist within a default folder named Public. Figure 8-5 shows the Public folder and all the subfolders available by default.

Figure 8-5
Public folder,
including
subfolders

When you enable public folder sharing, you enable users to access any data you place in this folder. Additionally, since the other public folders are within the Public share, they are also accessible by users.

 EXAM TIP Use Public Folder Sharing to easily share multiple folders on your system. When it is enabled, you can allow multiple folders to be accessible. You can also easily control the permissions by configuring it for read-only access, or allow users to add, modify, and delete files.

The three choices when enabling Public Folder Sharing are

- **Turn On Sharing So Anyone With Network Access Can Open Files**   This grants read access to users. Users can open files to read them but cannot modify or delete them, and they cannot create any new files. When this setting is enabled, it will show as On (Read Only). This setting interacts with the Password Protected Sharing setting. Users accessing the Public share may or may not be prompted for credentials, depending on the Password Protected Sharing setting.

- **Turn On Sharing So Anyone Can Open, Change, and Create Files**   This setting grants significantly more control to users accessing the Public folder. Users can read, modify, and delete existing files. Users can also add files in this folder. When this setting is enabled, it will show as On. This setting interacts with the Password Protected Sharing setting. Users accessing the Public share may or may not be prompted for credentials, depending on the Password Protected Sharing setting.

- **Turn Off Sharing (People Logged On To This Computer Can Still Access This Folder)**   The Public folder is not shared, but it can still be accessed locally. When this setting is enabled, it will show as Off.

Printer Sharing
The Printer Sharing feature is used to share printers. This will be discussed in more detail later in this chapter. This setting interacts with the Password Protected Sharing setting. Users accessing shared printers may or may not be prompted for credentials, depending on the Password Protected Sharing setting.

Password Protected Sharing
The Password Protected Sharing setting is used to control access to your computer. You can allow access to anyone on your network, or restrict access to only users that have an account on your computer.

 EXAM TIP   Enable Password Protected Sharing anytime you want to ensure that only users with accounts on your system can access shared resources.

You have two choices when configuring this setting:

- **Turn On Password Protected Sharing**   When on, only users that have an account and password on this computer will be able to access shared resources on your computer. Additionally, when this is set you can assign different access levels for users. In other words, you can allow some users read-only access and other users the ability to add, modify, and delete files. This setting affects both shared folders and shared printers.

- **Turn Off Password Protected Sharing**   When off, anyone that can connect to your computer can access the shares anonymously. This setting affects both shared folders and shared printers.

Media Sharing

Media sharing is used to share music, pictures, and videos. When it is enabled, other users can access these media files on your computer and your computer can find these types of files on the network.

The Windows Media Player (discussed further in Chapter 15) can be used to share media in your library with other people, computers, and devices.

In Exercise 8.1, you will enable File Sharing and Public Folder Sharing. You will then connect to the share and access files. This exercise assumes that these features are currently turned off.

Exercise 8.1: Enabling File and Public Folder Sharing

1. Identify your computer name with the following steps:

   a. Click Start and enter **cmd** in the Start Search area to launch the command line.

   b. At the command line, enter **Hostname**. The name of your computer will appear.

   c. Write down the name of your computer here: _____

2. Launch the Network and Sharing Center by clicking Start, right-clicking Network, and selecting Properties.

3. In the Sharing and Discovery section, locate the File Sharing setting. Click Off.

4. The File Sharing choices will appear. Click Turn On File Sharing and click Apply. If the User Account Control dialog box appears, click Continue. Leave the Network and Sharing Center open.

5. Click Start and enter two backslashes (\\) followed by your computer name in the Start Search box. For example if your computer name is MCITP1, you would enter

   ```
   \\MCITP1
   ```

6. You will see Windows Explorer open with any shares that are available on your computer. Unless you've added shares on your computer, you won't see any folder share here. Leave Windows Explorer open.

NOTE   Accessing your own computer using the \\ComputerName path simulates connecting to your computer over the network. What you are able to see here is what other users can view if they access your computer over the network.

7. Return to the Network and Sharing Center. Locate the Public Folder Sharing setting. Click Off.

8. The Public Sharing choices will appear. Select Turn On Sharing So Anyone With Network Access Can Open, Change, And Create Files. Click Apply. If the User Account Control dialog box appears, click Continue. Leave the Network and Sharing Center open.

9. Return to the Windows Explorer instance connected to \\MCITP1. If the Public shared folder is not present, press F5 to refresh the screen.

10. Double-click the Public folder to open it. Browse through the various folders to show what you can see. When done, browse back to the Public share.

11. Right-click within the Public folder share and click New | Text Document. Double-click the document to open it. Type in **I'm going to be an MCITP.** Press CTRL-S to save the file and close it. This shows you can create and modify files in the share.

12. Right-click within the Public folder share and click New | Text Document again. Select the new document. Right-click and select Delete. On the confirmation screen, click Yes to confirm you want to delete the file. This shows you can delete files in the share.

13. Return to the Network and Sharing Center. Locate the Public Folder Sharing setting. Select Turn On Sharing So Anyone Can Open Files. Click Apply. If the User Account Control dialog box appears, click Continue. Remember, this changes it so that files accessible via the share are read-only.

14. Return to the Windows Explorer instance connected to \\MCITP1. If the Public shared folder is not present, press the F5 key to refresh the screen.

15. Double-click the document you created earlier to open it. Type in **Wooo Hoooo!** Press CTRL-S to save the file. An error message will appear, since you don't have permissions to modify the file. Close the file without saving it.

16. Right-click the document you created earlier and select Delete. On the confirmation screen, click Yes. An error message appears indicating you don't have permission. Click Cancel.

17. Right-click within the Public folder and select New | Text Document. An error message will appear indicating you don't have permission to do this.

Folder Sharing

While you can share the Public folder as demonstrated in the preceding exercise, you may want to share different folders, and you may want to assign different permissions for any folders you share. You can do both on a Windows Vista system.

For example, instead of sharing the Public folder, you may want to share one folder (named ProjectData) and make it accessible to only one other user in your network. You may also want to make another folder (named MCITPStudyNotes) available to everyone that can access your computer. You can achieve this by using the Share Wizard and assigning different permission levels to different users.

Share Permission Levels

You have three permission levels available when you create shares. Depending on what you want users to be able to do, you can assign one of these permission levels. The three levels are

- **Co-owner** Users in this role will be able to read, add, change, and delete files in the share. Additionally, users in the role can modify the permissions.

- **Contributor** Users in this role will be able to read, add, change, and delete files in the share.

- **Reader** Users in this role will be able to read data but not be able to create, modify, or delete files in the share.

Additionally, the Owner permission level is assigned to the user that creates the share. You can't assign the Owner permission level.

The use of permission levels is designed to simplify the process of assigning permissions. In previous editions of Windows you could assign share permissions directly, and you still can by using advanced settings. The three advanced permissions are available as shown in Figure 8-6.

Figure 8-6
Share permissions

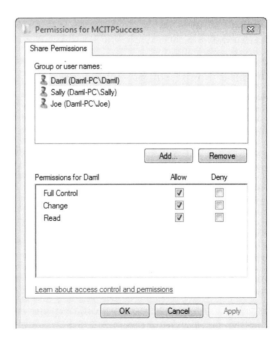

Each of the share permissions directly relates to the permission levels.

- **Full Control** This assigns the same permissions as are assigned to the Owner and Co-owner permission levels. Users can read, add, change, and delete files in the share, and modify share permissions.

- **Change**   This assigns the same permissions as are assigned to the Contributor permission level. Users can read, add, change, and delete files in the share.

- **Read**   This assigns the same permissions as are assigned to the Reader permission level. Users can read files in the share.

In Exercise 8.2, you will create a folder and share it. You can use these steps to share any folders on your system.

Exercise 8.2: Sharing Folders

1. Enable File Sharing and Password Protected Sharing in the Network and Sharing Center.

   a. Launch the Network and Sharing Center. Click Start, right-click Network, and select Properties.

   b. If File Sharing isn't set to On, click Off next to File Sharing and select Turn On File Sharing. Click Apply. If the User Account Control dialog box appears, click Continue.

   c. If Password Protected Sharing is set to On, click the setting next to Password Protected Sharing and select Turn On Password Protected Sharing. Click Apply. If the User Account Control dialog box appears, click Continue.

2. Launch Windows Explorer and create a folder named **MCITPSuccess**.

   a. Launch Windows Explorer by pressing the WINDOWS-E keys.

   b. Browse to the C: drive.

   c. Right-click over the C: drive and select New | Folder. Rename the folder **MCITPSuccess**.

3. Right-click the MCITPSuccess folder and select Share. This will launch the Share Wizard.

4. On the Choose People to Share With page, notice that the account you've logged on with is shown as the Owner.

5. Select the drop-down box next to the Add button and add a user from your system. Click Add. Notice the user is automatically added with the Permission Level of Reader.

 TIP   The Everyone (All Users in This List) group implies that only users in the drop-down list are allowed access. This is a misnomer. In reality users that have logged onto other computers in your network can access the share without having an account on your computer. Users that have accessed your network anonymously are excluded.

6. Add the Everyone (All Users In This List) choice from the drop-down box and click Add. Everyone includes all users that have logged on to your network (not just users in this list). Change the Permission Level to Contributor. Your display will look similar to Figure 8-7. Click Share. If the User Account dialog box appears, click Continue.

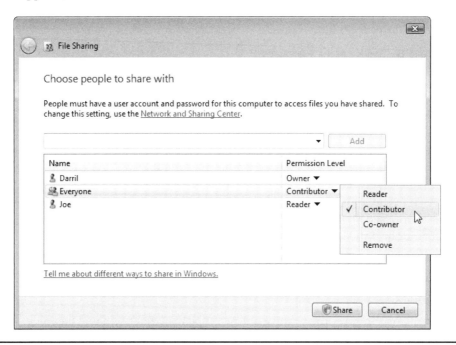

Figure 8-7   Adding users to access a share

 EXAM TIP   The Everyone group includes all users that have logged on in your network. It allows you to easily grant access to everyone for a specific folder while also controlling specific permissions for the folder.

7. On the Your Folder Is Shared page, click Done.

8. Click Start and enter two backslashes (\\) followed by your computer name in the Start Search box. For example if your computer name is MCITP1, you would enter

   \\MCITP1

9. Shares available on your computer will appear. Figure 8-8 shows the shares available (including the MCITPSuccess share) on a computer named Darril-PC.

10. Double-click the MCITPSuccess share. Right-click within the share and select New | Text Document. Notice that as the owner, you have permissions to create documents.

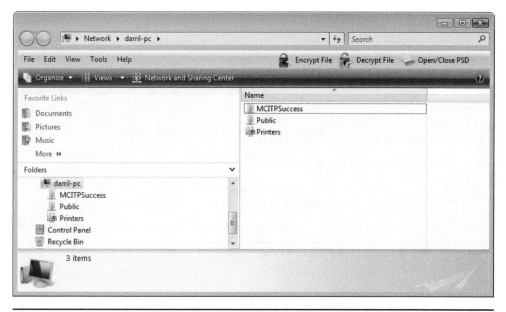

Figure 8-8 Accessing shares available on a Windows Vista computer

Printing

Many people talk about the paperless world where sometime in the future there will no longer be a need to print our important data of the moment on paper. Maybe someday, but that sure isn't today. Today, we need hard copies and we need printers to get those hard copies.

When using a printer, you need to be familiar with the process of installing and sharing a printer. When you share your printer, other people can access it, and if desired, you can control what others can do by manipulating the printer's permissions.

Installing a Local Printer

Most devices are automatically installed using Plug and Play technology. You plug the device in, the driver is automatically installed, and you're ready to play.

Chapter 3 covered the Device Manager and how the Plug and Play technology works. While printers aren't managed in Device Manager, the Plug and Play technology works the same.

When a device is detected, Windows Vista searches in the operating system to determine if it has the driver. If it doesn't, it can connect to the Windows Update site to determine if the driver is there and download it.

Once the driver is found, it is installed and your device will be ready for use. If you look in the Printers applet, you'll be able to see your installed printer. Figure 8-9 shows the Printers applet with my HP OfficeJet 6100 series printer installed and ready to use.

Figure 8-9 Printers applet in the Control Panel

The check mark on the printer indicates that it is set as the default. If you want to set another printer as the default, you can simply right-click any other printer and select Set as Default Printer.

If the driver can't be located, you will receive a message indicating so. Your next choice is to search the manufacturer's Web site looking for the driver. If you can find a driver that is compatible with Windows Vista, you can launch the Add Printer Wizard from the Printers applet. The following steps show you what you can do after downloading the driver.

1. Launch the Printers applet by clicking Start | Control Panel. In the Control Panel, select Hardware and Sound | Printers.

2. In the Printers applet, select Add a Printer to launch the wizard.

3. Select Add a Local Printer.

4. Select the port where you've added your printer.

5. Select your printer from the list of Manufacturers and Printers. Click Have Disk and browse to where you downloaded the printer driver.

Sharing a Printer

Any printer that you have installed on your system can be shared. Once the printer is shared, other users can then print to it. Remember, the Password Protected Sharing feature in the Network and Sharing Center affects who can access your shared printer.

- When Password Protected Sharing is On, only users with a user account and password can access the printer.

- When Password Protected Sharing is Off, any users can access the printer.

Available Printer Drivers   One of the challenges with any new operating system is the availability of drivers. In a perfect world every hardware vendor will write drivers for every piece of hardware they have before the operating system is released. As a user, you could easily plug in your device and it would automatically work.

Alas. It's not a perfect world. One of the common complaints with Windows Vista early in its release was the lack of available drivers—especially the lack of available printer drivers. The problem was twofold.

First, drivers weren't submitted to Microsoft for testing and weren't available from Windows Update. This prevented drivers from being automatically downloaded and installed when you plugged your printer in to your system.

Second, many manufacturers hadn't yet developed printer drivers, so they weren't even available (or were sometimes buggy) when you found them on the manufacturer's Web site.

When I first installed Windows Vista (in the beta stages), I simply wasn't able print directly from my Windows Vista system. I spent a lot of time trying to find and experiment with different drivers but only succeeded in spending a lot of time on the task. No success.

Today, I plugged in my HP OfficeJet 6100 printer into my Windows Vista system and it automatically detected the printer and downloaded and installed the driver. In less than a minute, I had printed a test document to the printer.

In Exercise 8.3, you will share a printer that is installed on your system. You can use these steps to share any printer on your system.

Exercise 8.3: Sharing a Printer

1. Launch the Printers applet by clicking Start | Control Panel. In the Control Panel, select Hardware and Sound | Printers.

2. Select your printer. Right-click your printer and select Sharing. The properties of the printer will appear with the Sharing tab selected.

3. Click Change Sharing Options. If the User Account Control dialog box appears, click Continue.

4. On the Sharing page, select the check box to Share This Printer. Select the check box to Render Print Jobs on Client Computers. Your display will look similar to Figure 8-10.

   - In the figure, you can see from the note at the top of the page that the Password Protected Sharing option is set to Off. It indicates that if you share the printer, any user on the network can print to it. If the Password Protected Sharing were set to On, it would indicate that only users with a username and password on your computer can print to this printer from the network.

Figure 8-10

Sharing a printer

5. Click OK. At this point, your printer will be shared and the Printers applet will look similar to Figure 8-11. Notice the extra icon (two heads) on the HP OfficeJet 6100 Series printer. This icon indicates the printer is shared.

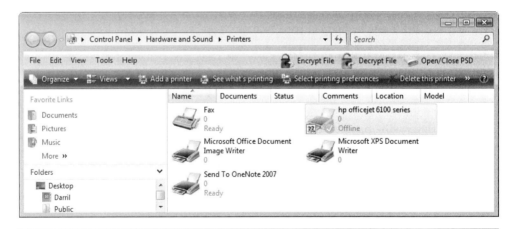

Figure 8-11 The Printers applet with a shared printer

EXAM TIP If a printer has the sharing icon showing in the Printers applet, it is being shared and other users in the network can print to it. If the icon is not showing, the printer is not being shared and other users in the network cannot print to it.

Installing a Shared Printer

If another computer on your network has shared a printer, you can add it as a printer on your system. One thing you'll need to be concerned about is the existence of the printer drivers.

A print server can host the drivers and download them to your system when you connect. In this context, a print server is any computer sharing a printer. For example, a Windows XP or Windows Vista system could be sharing a printer and would be referred to as a print server.

If the print server is running Windows Server 2008, the chances are good that it includes a printer driver for Windows Vista. However, if the print server is running Windows XP, it's very likely that the Windows XP driver doesn't work with Windows Vista. In this situation, you'll need to download and install printer drivers on your Windows Vista system and then add the shared printer.

There's nothing wrong with trying the Windows XP drivers first. The worst that could happen is that you'll waste a few pages of paper when you try to print and get nothing but garbage. Simply delete the shared printer, download and install the Vista drivers, and the share the printer again.

 EXAM TIP When accessing a shared printer from a Windows XP system, you may need to download Windows Vista drivers separately and then add the shared printer. It's not common for Windows XP printer drivers to work with Windows Vista.

Figure 8-12 shows how you can add additional drivers to a shared printer on Windows Vista for Itanium- and X64-based systems. Notice that it doesn't include drivers for older clients (such as Windows XP).

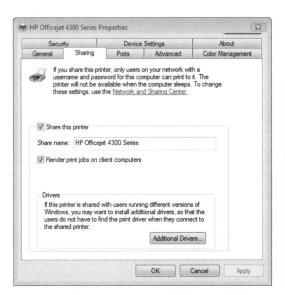

Figure 8-12 Adding additional print drivers

If you need to support Windows XP clients, you can first see if the Windows Vista driver is compatible. If not, you should download and install the Windows XP driver for the printer.

The following steps can be followed to install a shared printer on your system:

1. Launch the Printers applet by clicking Start | Control Panel. Within Control Panel select Printers under Hardware and Sound.

2. In the Printers applet, click Add a Printer. The wizard will search your network for available shared printers.

3. If the shared printer is found, select it and click Next.

4. If the shared printer isn't found on your network, Click the Printer That I Want Isn't Listed. Figure 8-13 shows the screen you'll see allowing you to directly connect to the printer. You can browse for the printer, add the printer using the UNC path, or add a printer using a TCP/IP address or hostname.

Figure 8-13
Finding a network printer manually

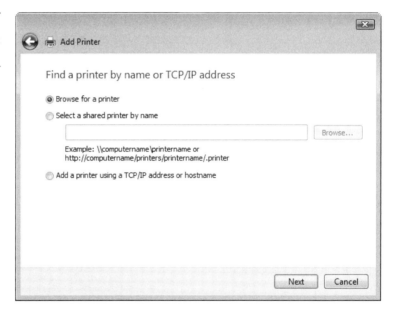

5. Once you add the printer, you have the option of setting it as your default printer. You can also use this wizard to print a test page.

Print Permissions

After sharing your printer, you can assign permissions. Each permission can be assigned as either Allow or Deny.

In general, the use of Deny should be avoided because it makes permissions unnecessarily complex, but there are exceptions. For example you may want everyone to print except Joe. You can add the Everyone group and grant Allow Print, and then add Joe's account and add Deny Print.

TIP If Deny is assigned to an individual or group, Deny takes precedence. In other words if a user is granted Allow Print and Deny Print, then Deny overrides the Allow permission.

Instead of using Deny, you should instead simply not assign permissions to someone. A user that doesn't have any permission on a printer has the same status as a user that has been denied access.

Figure 8-14 shows the permissions you can assign to a printer. You can access the first screen by right-clicking the printer, selecting Properties, and then selecting the Security tab. If you click Advanced, you can then select a user account and click Edit to see all the permissions (including the special permissions).

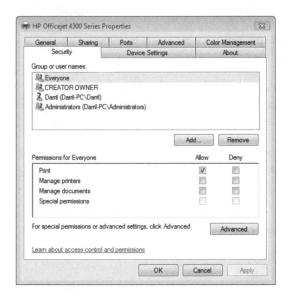

Figure 8-14 Regular and special permissions available for a printer

The print permissions associated with printers are

- **Print** Users with this permission can print to the printer.

 EXAM TIP Grant user's the Print permission to allow them to print documents to the printer.

- **Manage Documents** Users with Manage Documents permission can stop and start other users' print jobs.
- **Manage Printers** The Manage Printers permission allows a user to manipulate the printer properties and do anything except for managing other users' documents.

- **Special Permissions**   Three additional permissions can be assigned through Special Permissions. These are Read Permissions, Change Permissions, and Take Ownership.

Managing Printers with Group Policy

Chapter 10 will cover group policy in a little more depth, but in short, group policy can be used to manage computers and users in a network. By setting group policy once, you can affect multiple users and computers.

 EXAM TIP   The topics in this section only apply to skills needed for the MCITP: Enterprise Support Technician (70-622). An Enterprise Support Technician is expected to have knowledge of group policy in a large environment configured as domains. In contrast, the MCITP: Consumer Support Technician works in a smaller environment in a workgroup and wouldn't be using group policy to affect many clients.

For example, if you have 5000 users in a domain and you want to control which servers that domain's users can access as print servers, you can configure Point and Print Restrictions in a Group Policy Object (GPO). If you link this GPO at the domain level, it will affect all users in the domain.

While you won't be expected to fully administer group policy as a Vista expert, you should be aware of some of the capabilities as they relate to printers. From a big picture perspective, you can do some of the following things with group policy related to printers.

- Allow users to find, add, and delete printers.
- Restrict which print servers are locatable by configuring Point and Print Restrictions.
- Only allow Package Point and Print to ensure only drivers that are signed are downloaded.
- Deploy different printer connections to users in different locations.
- Ensure print jobs are always rendered on the print server.
- Allow printers to be published (so they can be located via an Active Directory Search.

While it's beyond the scope of this book to explain all of the group policy settings, I'll explain two to give you an idea of some of the capabilities of group policy.

Point and Print Restrictions

Point and Print Restrictions is a group policy setting that can restrict which print servers that users can print to within a domain. Figure 8-15 shows a screenshot of a Windows Server 2008 server using the Group Policy Management Console to configure this.

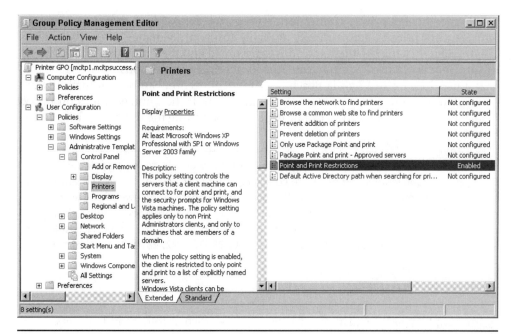

Figure 8-15   Enabling Point and Print Restrictions in a GPO

You can fine-tune this policy by adding another GPO and applying it to users in an Organizational Unit (OU). For example, you may have a special color printer that should only be used by users in the Marketing department.

By adding another GPO with the Point and Print Restrictions setting, you can have users in the Marketing department be able to print to this printer, but no one else will be able to print to it.

Deploying Printer Connections with Group Policy

Group policy can also used to deploy printer connections to users and computers. When deployed to a computer, it will apply to all users that access this printer.

When deployed to a user, printer connections are made available to the user no matter where they are logged on. If a user logs on to a computer in a different physical location, printer connections from the new location will be made available to the user.

This is achieved with multiple steps, but it starts because group policy is site aware. If the domain is configured correctly, a program (such as group policy) can determine where a user logs on and take different actions based on the location.

As an example, if a user logs on at headquarters in Virginia Beach, the Net logon service will locate a domain controller in Virginia Beach to authenticate the user. If the user later tries to log on at a satellite office in San Francisco that also has a domain controller, the Net logon service finds a domain controller in San Francisco to authenticate the user.

When deploying printer connections with group policy, you can ensure that users have network printers automatically available to them no matter where they are located. When they log on, the location is determined and the PushPrinterConnections.exe program is executed, which creates the local printer connections.

If a user logs on in Virginia Beach, a printer connection can be automatically created connecting them to a printer in Virginia Beach. If the same user logs on in San Francisco, a printer connection can be deployed connecting the user to a printer in San Francisco.

 NOTE There are multiple steps involved to enable deploying printer connections, and most are configured on the server. As an MCITP: Enterprise Administrator, you should be aware of the possibilities, even if you aren't the one configuring the server. If you'd like to read more about how to deploy printer connections with group policy, check out this article: http://technet2.microsoft.com/WindowsVista/en/library/ab8d75f8-9b35-4e3e-a344-90d7799927231033.mspx?mfr=true.

Chapter Review

In this chapter you learned about sharing resources such as folders and printers.

The primary tool you'll start with is the Network and Sharing Center. You can configure the File Sharing, Public Folder Sharing, Printer Sharing, and Password Protected Sharing options in the Sharing and Discovery section.

The Public Folder Sharing option allows you to easily share data in the Public folder. You can configure the Password Protected Sharing options to control whether users are required to have a username and password on your system or can connect anonymously.

You can share other folders in addition to the Public folder on your system. When sharing folders, you have the capability of assigning specific permissions based on permission levels. The permission levels are Reader (allows read access), Contributor (allows read, modify, and delete access), and Co-owner and Owner (which both allow full control, including changing permissions).

Printers can also be shared from your system. The Allow Print permission is used to allow users to print to a printer. When a printer is added, the Everyone group is granted Read permission. Other permissions are Manage Documents and Manage Printers.

When managing printers in a domain, you can use group policy to automate many of the processes. For example, Point and Print Restrictions can be used to restrict users to accessing only specific print servers.

Additional Study

Self Study Exercises
Use these additional exercises to challenge yourself.

- Share a folder on a different computer in your network. Connect to the share.

- Manipulate permissions on the share to allow anyone to access your share.

- Manipulate permissions on the share to allow only a single user to access the share.

- Share a printer on your computer in your network. Print to a shared printer.

Summary of What You Need to Know

70-620

Objectives for the 70-620 exam are not covered in this chapter.

70-622

When preparing for the 70-622 exam, pay particular attention to the following topics covered in this chapter:

- **Network and Sharing Center**   Know how to configure the different settings for both folder and printer shares, including: File Sharing, Public Folder Sharing, Printer Sharing, and Password Protected Sharing. Know how to share a folder and share a printer.

- **Shared folders**   Know how to create a share and provide access to the share.

- **Shared printers**   Know how to share a printer. Be aware of some of the group policy settings that can be used to control shared printers.

70-623

When preparing for the 70-623 exam, pay particular attention to the following topics covered in this chapter:

- **Network and Sharing Center**   Know how to configure the different settings for both folder and printer shares, including: File Sharing, Public Folder Sharing, Printer Sharing, and Password Protected Sharing. Know how to share a folder and share a printer.

- **Share Permissions**   Know the different permission levels available with shares, including Reader, Contributor, and Co-owner and what those permissions grant.

- **Printer Permissions**   Know the different printer permissions available, including Print, Manage Printers, and Manage Documents.

Questions

70-622

1. You need to share a file named Project.doc with another user in your network. The project.doc document contains proprietary information and should not be available to any other users. You placed the file in the Public folder and enabled Public Folder Sharing and have also enabled File Sharing. What else (if anything) should you do to make this file available only to one other user?

   A. Nothing.

   B. Enable Network Discovery.

    C. Enable Password Protected Sharing.

    D. Disable Public Folder Sharing.

2. You have installed a printer on your Windows Vista system. You want other users in your network to be able to print to it. What should you do?

    A. Set Password Protected Sharing to On.

    B. Set Password Protected Sharing to Off.

    C. Set the printer as the default printer.

    D. Change the sharing options for your printer to share it.

3. Sally often travels around the country to different corporate offices. She uses a laptop computer running Windows Vista, and the network includes a domain that is available in all corporate offices. You want to ensure that Sally can access network printers no matter which corporate office she is at, without reconfiguring her laptop. What should be done?

    A. Use group policy to deploy a printer configuration for users.

    B. Use group policy to deploy a printer configuration for computers.

    C. Write a script to run when Sally logs on to detect where she logged on, and then use the script to connect to printers in that location.

    D. This is not possible.

4. You are an administrator within a large domain running Windows Server 2008 and hosting several print servers. One print server named MarkPrt1 is used by personnel in the graphics department and creates high-speed, high-quality graphic printouts, but at a high price. Many non-marketing users have been printing to this printer via MarkPrt1. You want to restrict users to only use specific print servers within the network. What can you use?

    A. Use group policy to deploy PushPrinterConnections.

    B. Use group policy to deploy a printer configuration for users.

    C. Use group policy to configure Point and Print Restrictions.

    D. Manually assign the printer permissions for all the printers.

70-623

1. Sally is running Windows Vista in her small business network. She wants to allow some users to access a share she's created with read-only access, and other users to be able to access the same share with permissions to modify the files. The share contains Microsoft Word and Microsoft Excel documents. What should she enable? (Choose all that apply.)

    A. Network Discovery

    B. File Sharing

    C. Public Folder Sharing

    D. Printer Sharing

    E. Password Protected Sharing

    F. Media Sharing

2. Sally is running Windows Vista in her small business network. She wants to allow some users to access her built-in Public folder. However, she doesn't want all the users to be able to access this folder. What should she enable to support this goal? (Choose all that apply.)

    A. Network Discovery

    B. File Sharing

    C. Public Folder Sharing

    D. Printer Sharing

    E. Password Protected Sharing

    F. Media Sharing

3. You want to share files from a folder named MCITPSuccess located on your Windows Vista computer with a user named Joe. Joe should be able to update files in the folder. What should you do?

    A. Assign the user to the Reader permission level or grant the Read share permission.

    B. Assign the user to the Contributor permission level or grant the Change share permission.

    C. Assign the user to the Change permission level or grant the Contributor share permission.

    D. Assign the user to the Full Control permission level or grant the Co-owner share permission.

4. You want to share files from a folder named MCITPSuccess located on your Windows Vista computer. You want any users within your network to be able view and save files to this folder. What should you do?

    A. Configure the Everyone group with the Contributor permission level.

    B. Configure the Everyone group with the Co-owner permission level.

    C. Enable Public Folder Sharing.

    D. Enable Public Folder Sharing with Password Protected Sharing.

5. Sally has shared a LaserJet printer on her Windows XP system, and you are trying to add it as a shared printer on your Windows Vista system. You find that the added printer is not compatible on your system using the Windows XP printer drivers. What should you do?

    A. Add Windows Vista drivers to the shared printer on the Windows XP system.

    B. Have Sally download and install Windows Vista drivers to a share on her computer.

    C. Download and install Windows Vista drivers onto your system and add the shared printer again.

    D. Download Windows Vista drivers onto your system and add them to the Print$ share.

6. Sally has shared her printer on her Windows Vista computer. Joe is trying to print to this printer but is unsuccessful due to a permission error. What should Sally assign to Joe's account to grant him the ability to print but not do anything else on this printer?

    A. Allow Manage Printers.

    B. Allow Manage Documents.

    C. Allow Print.

    D. Allow Print and Deny Manage Printers.

Answers

70-622

1. C. Password Protected Sharing will ensure that only users that have accounts on your system are authorized access to files. You are also able to individually assign permissions. Without enabling Password Protected Sharing, you will allow anyone to have access to the files. Network discovery is used to allow computers to find other computers, and be found on networks. If Public Folder Sharing was disabled, the file placed in the folder will not be accessible.

2. D. You can share your printer to allow users to print to it. Setting the Password Protected Sharing setting to On or Off will determine if users need a user account on your system to be able to access the printer, but this will be meaningful after the printer is shared. Setting the printer as the default printer only affects the local user.

3. A. This is possible by using group policy to deploy a printer configuration for users. Since Sally will be logging on to different locations, you want to deploy it to users, not computers. Part of the process to make this work is executing an application named PushPrinterConnections.exe via a script, but much more is required.

4. C. You can use Point and Print Restrictions in group policy to restrict which print servers users can access. The PushPrinterConnections is used as part of deploying a printer configuration for users to ensure users have print connections no matter where they log on. Using group policy is much more efficient than manually assigning printer permissions to all the printers.

70-623

1. **B, E.** File Sharing should be enabled so that users can access the shares. Password Protected Sharing should be enabled to allow different access levels to the shares. Network Discovery allows computers to be found on a network, but isn't required to share files. Public Folder Sharing is used to share the Public folder, but isn't required to create other shares. Printer Sharing is required to share printers, and Media Sharing is used to share media files (such as music, pictures, and videos).

2. **B, C, E.** File Sharing should be enabled so that users can access the shares. Public Folder Sharing should be enabled to provide access to the Public folder. Password Protected Sharing should be enabled to allow different access levels to the shares. Network Discovery allows computers to be found on a network, but isn't required to share files. Printer Sharing is required to share printers, and Media Sharing is used to share media files (such as music, pictures, and videos).

3. **B.** You can assign the user to the Contributor level or grant change permissions to allow him to update files. The Reader permission level and the Read share permission would only allow him to open and read the files, not update them. There is no Change permission level or Contributor share permission, but instead a Contributor permission level and a Change share permission. Granting Full Control for users that don't need full control runs counter to the basic security principle of least privilege; additionally, there is no Full Control permission level or Co-owner share permission, but instead a Co-owner permission level and Full Control share permission.

4. **A.** By adding the Everyone group with the Contributor permission level, you will grant all users with access to your computer the ability to modify data in the MCITPSuccess folder. Adding the Everyone group to the Co-owner group gives too many permissions and is not the best answer. Enabling Public Folder Sharing only grants access to the Public folder, not the MCITPSuccess folder.

5. **C.** You should download and install the Windows Vista printer drivers onto your system and then add the shared printer again. It's not possible to add Windows Vista drivers to the Windows XP system, and just adding the drivers to a share on her computer won't allow them to be automatically downloaded to your computer. Similarly, just adding them to the Print$ share on your system won't install them.

6. **C.** If you grant Allow Print, the user can print. Granting Manage Printers or Manage Documents grants more than just the ability to print. Explicitly denying Manage Printers is not necessary, since the user wouldn't have permissions unless it was added, and since Joe can't print to start with, he wasn't originally granted Manage Printers permission.

Configuring Local Security

In this chapter, you will learn about:
- Users and groups
- User account control
- Parental controls
- Windows Security Center
- Auditing

There are several steps you can take to ensure your computer is protected. Often, the first step is ensuring that built-in security isn't circumvented. Windows Vista includes many security elements designed to ensure that Windows Vista is protected.

Some users may choose to disable some of the security features without understanding the impact. You need to be able to understand each of the built-in security elements and know how to ensure they are on, or how to turn them back on.

 EXAM TIP Objectives for the 70-620, 70-622, and 70-623 exams are included in this chapter.

User Accounts

To log on to Windows Vista, you need a user account. A user account includes a username and password and other information on a user.

Windows Vista supports three types of user accounts:

- Standard
- Administrator
- Guest

The different types of user accounts grant the user differing permissions and privileges. You need to understand the capabilities and the purpose of each of the user accounts in order to choose which account to use for which purpose.

Standard User Account

A standard user account is intended to be used by most users of Windows Vista. Users logged on with a standard user account can utilize most functions of Windows Vista but won't be able to make changes that affect other users.

 EXAM TIP Users logged on with a standard user account can only make changes to their own user account. Changes made while logged on as a standard user will not affect other users sharing the computer.

For example, a user running Microsoft Word, Microsoft Outlook, and Internet Explorer can log on with a standard user account and use these programs without any trouble. However, the standard user account won't allow a user to make some changes to the options (such as modifying security settings) that could weaken the security.

One of the primary goals of using the standard user account is to protect the computer's security by preventing users from making changes that can weaken security, especially when these changes may affect other users using the computer.

While logged on with a standard user account, you can still perform actions that require the administrator account. However, by default you will be prompted to provide credentials for an administrator account before you can continue. Figure 9-1 shows the prompt.

Figure 9-1
Prompt for
administrative
credentials

 NOTE You can modify the default prompt either by using local security policy (presented later in this chapter) to affect all users on the local computer, or by modifying group policy to affect multiple computers.

I logged on as a standard user and then tried to change the NIC. The User Account Control recognized I wasn't logged on as an administrator, so it prompted me to provide the credentials for an administrator account.

If you have multiple accounts that are members of the administrators group, each account will appear and you can enter the credentials for the account you know.

Administrator User Account

An administrator account is any account that is in the administrators group. The administrators group is granted elevated privileges that allow administrators to change security settings, install software and hardware, access all files on the computer, and make changes to other user accounts.

 EXAM TIP You should be very familiar with the actions that require you to be logged in as an administrator as listed in this section.

Think of membership in the administrators group as keys to the kingdom. You can do anything on the computer. These are some of the common tasks that require an administrator account:

- Install applications.
- Install and configure devices.
- Configure system-wide settings such as Remote settings.
- Configure security settings such as the Windows Firewall.
- Configure parental controls.
- Manipulate user accounts.

Figure 9-2 shows the Control Panel window. Notice that many of the settings have the little security shield icon. Both settings in the User Accounts and Family Safety have this icon and the Allow a Program Through Windows Firewall setting in the Security topic has the icon. Any settings with this icon require a user to have administrative privileges.

When you first install Windows, you're required to create a user account, and this account is an administrator account. Microsoft recommends creating another user account (a standard user account) and using the standard user account for day-to-day work, only logging on with the administrator account when doing administrator work.

 NOTE Throughout this book, I have been logged in with an administrator account, since most of this book shows how to do administrator tasks.

Security is constantly an issue with computers today, and logging on with a standard account provides a layer of protection. As an example, if your system becomes infected by some type of malware and you're logged as an administrator, the malware may be able to elevate its privileges to the administrator level. The User Account Control feature in Windows Vista (discussed later in this chapter) helps to prevent uncontrolled elevation of privileges, but your first line of defense should be the use of a standard account.

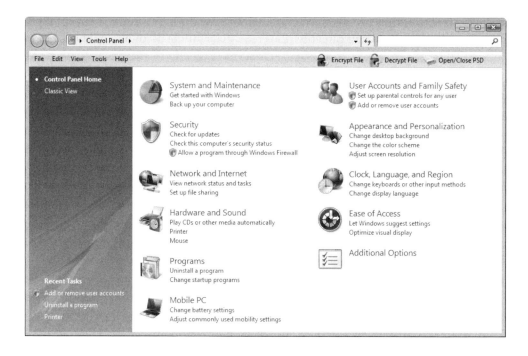

Figure 9-2 Security Shield shows actions requiring administrative privileges.

Using Run As Administrator

A feature that has been available since Windows 2000 days is the Run As feature. This allows users to be logged on as a regular user but occasionally launch applications under the context of a user with administrative privileges.

However, because of the way the User Account Control (UAC) works you will be prompted when administrative privileges are required, so the Run As command is rarely needed today. There are some exceptions.

If you're running a legacy application that specifically needs to be started as an administrator, it may close before UAC has a chance to provide the administrative credentials. In this case, you can right-click the application and select Run As Administrator. This works for most programs accessible via the Start menu and executable files you can access from Windows Explorer.

 TIP It's also possible to open a command prompt with administrative privileges. Click Start and type **cmd** into the Start Search box. Instead of pressing ENTER, press CTRL-SHIFT-ENTER. You'll be prompted with UAC and then have access to the command line with administrative privileges.

Guest Account

A guest account is a built-in account that can be used instead of creating additional accounts for users. It allows people to use your computer without having access to your personal files.

Anyone using the guest account is granted very minimal permissions and privileges. They can't install hardware or software, change any settings, or even create a password for the account.

The guest account is disabled by default.

Account Profile and Data Folders

Every account has its own profile. The profile includes the settings of the user's account (such as desktop background, screen saver settings, installed applications, and so on), and the account's data folders.

The account's data folders are in the C:\Users directory. When a user logs on to the computer for the first time, the profile is created, including the data folders. Figure 9-3 shows the folders for the account named Joe.

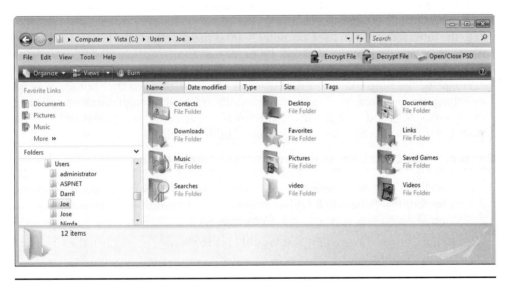

Figure 9-3   Account folders

This data is only available to the user. Other standard users cannot access this data. However, an administrator can override this protection and access the files in the user's profile.

As an example, if Joe stored his data in the folder labeled Documents on this computer, the data would actually be stored under C:\Users\Joe\Documents and only be accessible to Joe.

Password Protection

When creating accounts, you should always use password protection. Password protection simply means that the account has a password. Without a password, anyone can access the account and do whatever they want to do.

 EXAM TIP Use password protection for all your accounts (and especially your administrator accounts) to ensure users are only able to do what you want to allow. If an administrator account is not protected with a password, users can log on to that account and have full administrative access. Non–password protected administrator accounts can be used for many purposes, including circumventing parental controls.

Later in this chapter, we'll cover the Local Security Policy console and how you can use it to enforce the requirement for user accounts to have strong passwords, but you should be aware of a weakness.

If you use the Control Panel to create new user accounts, you can create an account without a password, or said another way, you can create an account with a blank password. This is even possible if the local security policy is set to require strong passwords. Needless to say, blank passwords aren't strong and are certainly easy to guess.

On the other hand, if you use Computer Management or the Local Users and Groups console to create an account, you will be prevented from creating an account with a blank password if your local security policy requires a strong password.

Perhaps by the time you read this, Microsoft will have changed this, but for now be aware that password protection is not automatically enforced through the Control Panel.

In Exercise 9.1, you will create an administrator account, set a password for the account, change it to a standard user account, and then delete the account.

Exercise 9.1: Creating and Manipulating Accounts

1. Launch the Add or Remove User Accounts applet. Click Start | Control Panel. In the Control Panel, click Add or Remove User Accounts. If the User Account Control dialog box appears, click Continue.

2. On the Choose the Account You Would Like to Change page, Click the Create a New Account link.

3. On the Name the Account and Choose an Account Type page, enter **Maria** as the account name. Select Administrator. Your display will look similar to Figure 9-4.

4. Click Create Account.

 CAUTION You have just created an administrator account with a blank password. If you leave this as it is, you have created a significant security vulnerability. Ensure you at least set a password for this account.

5. The Choose the Account You Would Like to Change page reappears and you can see your new user account. Your display will look similar to Figure 9-5. Notice that the Maria account is not password protected.

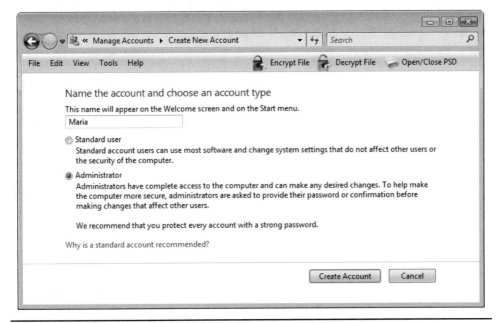

Figure 9-4   Creating a new administrator account

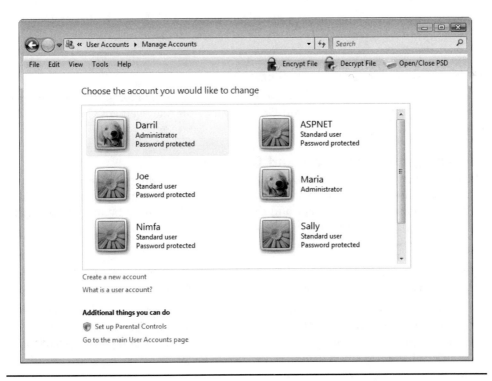

Figure 9-5   New account

TIP If your system has a local security policy that requires a strong password, your display may indicate that the new account is password protected, but it is not.

6. Click the Maria account. On the Make Changes to Maria's Account page, select the link to Create a Password.

7. In the Create a Password for Maria's Account page, enter **P@ssword** in the New Password and Confirm New Password text boxes. You can also type in a password hint here, but it isn't necessary. Click the Create Password button.

8. You will return to the Make Changes to Maria's Account page. Click the Change the Account Type link.

9. In the Choose a New Account Type for Maria page, ensure Standard User is selected. (Maria started as an administrator account, and you are now changing it to a standard user account.) Click the Change Account Type button.

10. You will return to the Make Changes to Maria's Account page. Click the Delete The Account link.

11. On the Do You Want to Keep Maria's Files page, review the information and click Delete Files.

12. On the Are You Sure You Want to Delete Maria's Account page, click Delete Account.

Other Tools to Manage Accounts

There are two other tools you may use to manage accounts and groups in Windows Vista. These are the Local Users and Groups Microsoft Management Console (MMC) snap-in and Computer Management.

Launching the Local Users and Groups MMC

The Local Users and Groups MMC snap-in allows you to manage the users and groups a little more directly than you can via the Control Panel. The Control Panel is intended to be easy to use by regular users, and the snap-ins can be used by more experienced users performing administrative functions.

You can launch the Local Users and Groups console in two ways:

- Click Start and type in **lusrmgr.msc** in the Start Search line. An MMC with the local Users and Groups snap-in will appear as shown in Figure 9-6.

- You can also launch an MMC and add the Local Users and Groups snap-in. Click Start and type **MMC** in the Start Search line. In the Console, select File | Add/Remove Snap-in. Browse to the Local Users and Groups snap-in, select it, and click Add. Click Finish and click OK.

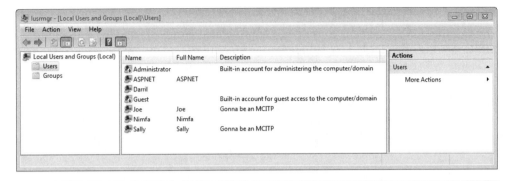

Figure 9-6   Local Users and Groups snap-in

Notice that you can use the Local Users and Groups console to easily browse through the groups. This isn't as easy to do with the tools available through the Control Panel.

Creating a Strong Password   When creating a password, it's important to use a strong password. There are a lot of examples where users have created weak passwords and hackers and attackers are able to easily gain access to an account.

I once worked with a very nice woman who loved angels. In her office, she had pictures of angels, ceramic angels, and hanging angels . . . . Angels were everywhere. Guess what her password was—angel. It was easy to guess and certainly wasn't strong.

A strong password meets several conditions:

- It is at least eight characters in length.
- It includes at least one uppercase and at least one lowercase letter.
- It includes at least one number.
- It includes at least one nonalphanumeric character.
- It does not include your username or real name.
- It is not displayed in your office (okay, I admit, I added this one, but I think it's a good rule to follow just the same).

As an example, I frequently have used the password P@ssw0rd in this book. It has an uppercase letter (P), lowercase letters, a number (0 instead of o), and a symbol (@ instead of a).

Not only should you use strong passwords yourself, but you should also be an advocate to help users create and maintain strong passwords. A strong password is significantly harder to break then a simple password and can make it much more difficult for an attacker to gain access to a system.

Computer Management

The Computer Management console is a consolidated group of snap-ins added into an MMC. Among other tools, you can use it to manage users and groups on your computer.

Figure 9-7 shows the Computer Management console.

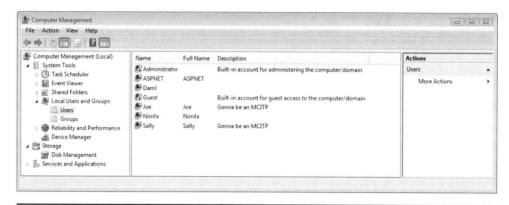

Figure 9-7 Computer Management

You can access the Computer Management console by clicking Start, right-clicking Computer, and selecting Manage. You can also access Computer Management via the Administrative Tools menu.

 TIP If the Administrative Tools menu isn't available from the Start menu, you can put it there by following these steps. Right-click over the Start icon and select Properties. With the Start Menu tab selected, click Customize. Scroll down to the bottom of the frame to locate the System Administrative Tools choices and select Display On the All Programs and the Start Menu. Click OK twice.

User Account Control

User Account Control (UAC) is a feature within Windows Vista designed to provide an extra layer of security to resolve a specific security problem that has existed in previous versions of Windows.

The security problem has occurred when users log in with an account that has administrative permissions. If a computer becomes infected with malicious software (malware) while a user is logged on, the malware can elevate its permissions to the same permissions as the user. If the user has administrative permissions, the malware has administrative permissions.

In the past, the recommendation has been to ensure that users don't have local administrative permissions (meaning they aren't added to the local administrators group). From a security standpoint, this has worked. However, from a usability standpoint it hasn't always worked. Several applications that users need simply don't work without the user's having local administrative permissions.

The solution is UAC. UAC allows a user to be logged on with a non-administrative account, but any time an activity requires administrative permissions, the user is prompted to provide administrative credentials. The obvious benefit is that if malware tries to do something, the user will immediately be notified.

For example, your system may become infected by a new virus. You're working in Microsoft Word or Internet Explorer and suddenly the UAC dialog box pops up asking for approval to do something. This becomes a clear warning to you that something is wrong.

If you are logged on with an administrative account and you try to do a task that requires administrative permissions, by default a dialog box similar to Figure 9-8 will appear. You can modify the local security policy (presented later in this chapter) to change this behavior.

Figure 9-8
UAC dialog box
when logged with
administrative
privileges

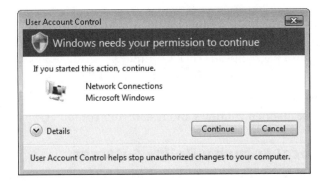

When you are logged on with a standard user account, and you try to do something requiring administrative permissions, you will be prompted with a dialog box that allows you to enter the credentials another account's that has administrative permissions.

Disabling and Enabling UAC

If you do a lot of administrative work on your computer, you may see the UAC dialog box appear quite a bit. Some people get tired of seeing it and simply turn it off. Or, you may come upon a system that has the UAC disabled and you want to enable it.

 CAUTION While it is possible to disable the UAC, it's not recommended. The UAC provides a significant security feature, and disabling it weakens security.

If the UAC setting is changed, you must restart your system before it takes effect. In Exercise 9.2, you will disable and then re-enable the User Account Control settings.

Exercise 9.2: Disabling and Enabling User Account Control

1. Click Start | Control Panel.

2. Click User Accounts and Family Safety.

3. Click User Accounts.

4. On the Make Changes to Your User Account page, click the Turn User Account Control On Or Off link at the bottom of the page. If the User Account Control page appears, click Continue.

5. On the Turn On User Account Control (UAC) page, either check the box for Use User Account Control (UAC) to Help Protect Your Computer to enable UAC, or deselect the check box to disable UAC. Click OK.

6. On the dialog box that states you must restart your computer to apply these changes, choose Restart Later.

 EXAM TIP User Account Control is one of the few settings that require you to restart your computer after it has been changed.

7. Back on the Make Changes to Your User Account page, click the Turn User Account Control On Or Off link at the bottom of the page. If the User Account Control page appears, click Continue.

8. On the Turn On User Account Control (UAC) page, return the setting to what is what it was before you changed it. Click OK.

9. Close all open windows and restart your computer.

UAC Local Security Policy Settings

UAC can be controlled by several local security policy settings. You can access the Local Security Policy console by clicking Start | Administrative Tools | Local Security Policy. If Administrative Tools aren't on your menu, you can access them from the Control Panel System and Maintenance applet.

Admin Approval Mode is a significant part of UAC. It only applies to users logged in as an administrator (not standard users) and affects how UAC behaves.

When an administrator is logged on, Admin Approval mode is enabled by default and the administrator will be prompted to allow any actions requiring administrative privileges. The prompt only requires the administrator to click Continue by default, but this can be modified using the local security policy settings.

Settings applied to the local security policy affect all users that use the computer.

Figure 9-9 shows the Local Security Policy console opened up to the Local Policies, Security Options node. In the figure, I have scrolled down to the settings that affect User Account Control.

 EXAM TIP You can modify the behavior of UAC by modifying the local security policy settings. For example, you can require all administrators to re-enter their username and password any time they want to make a change requiring administrative credentials. Make sure you are familiar with the capabilities of all the settings listed in this section.

- **User Account Control: Admin Approval Mode for the Built-in Administrator Account** This setting only applies to the built-in administrator account, not accounts that are also created as administrators.

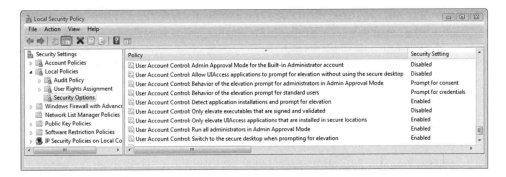

Figure 9-9   UAC Local Security Policy settings

- When this setting is disabled (the default), the built-in administrator account works in XP-compatible mode and will automatically run all applications with full administrative privilege.

- When it is enabled, the built-in administrator account will log on using Admin Approval mode. In Admin Approval mode, actions requiring administrative privileges will prompt for consent or to provide credentials, depending on the User Account Control: Run All Administrators in Admin Approval Mode local security policy setting.

- **User Account Control: Behavior of the Elevation Prompt for Administrators in Admin Approval Mode**   The three possible settings are

  - **Elevate Without Prompting**   Nothing required.

  - **Prompt For Credentials**   Requires users to enter a username and password.

  - **Prompt For Consent**   Requires user to click Continue on the UAC dialog box. This is the default.

- **User Account Control: Behavior of the Elevation Prompt for Standard Users**   The three possible settings are

  - **Automatically Deny Elevation Requests**   Administrative actions are not allowed.

  - **Prompt For Credentials**   Requires users to enter a username and password. This is the default.

    An added benefit of this setting is that you can use it while a regular user is logged on. For example, if a user is logged on and needs to make a change, you can provide your credentials and make the change without requiring the user to log off so that you can log on and make the change.

- **User Account Control: Run All Administrators in Admin Approval Mode**   When this is enabled (the default), UAC works according to the User Account Control: Behavior of the Elevation Prompt for Administrators in Admin Approval Mode setting.

  When disabled, UAC is effectively disabled for any administrative user that logs on with an administrator account. This significantly weakens security.

- **User Account Control: Virtualize File and Registry Write Failures to Per-User Locations** Some legacy applications require access to specific areas of the hard drive (such as the System32 folder) or specific areas of the Registry that are restricted. Instead of having the application fail, this setting redirects the writes to an area the user can access. In the past, these types of legacy applications required the user to be logged on with an administrative account.

  This setting is enabled by default. When it is disabled, these legacy applications will fail.

In Exercise 9.3, you will launch the Local Security Policy console and observe the settings.

Exercise 9.3: Viewing Local Security Policy Settings

1. Launch the Local Security Policy console by clicking Start and selecting Control Panel. Click System and Maintenance and scroll to the bottom to select Administrative Tools. Double-click the Local Security Policy tool. If the UAC dialog box appears, click Continue.

2. In the Local Security Policy console, browse to the Local Policies, Security Options node. Scroll down to the last settings in this section. Your display will look similar to Figure 9-9 shown earlier in the UAC local security policy settings section.

3. Double-click the User Account Control: Admin Approval Mode for the Built-in Administrator Account setting. Click Explain. Notice that a full explanation of this setting is contained here. Review the information and click Cancel.

4. Repeat Step 3 for the following settings:

    A. User Account Control: Behavior of the Elevation Prompt for Administrators in Admin Approval Mode.

    B. User Account Control: Behavior of the Elevation Prompt for Standard Users.

    C. User Account Control: Detect Application Installations and Prompt for Elevation.

    D. User Account Control: Run All Administrators in Admin Approval Mode.

    E. User Account Control: Virtualize File and Registry Write Failures to Per-User Locations.

Parental Controls

It's been said more than once that the toughest job in the world is that of a parent. When I was growing up, parents were very concerned with what children were watching on TV. While that is still a concern, parents now must be concerned with what children can access on the Web.

You can use Parental Controls to control, restrict, and monitor what any standard user can access using four major categories.

- Web restrictions
- Time restrictions

- Games
- Allow or block specific programs

Figure 9-10 shows the Parental Control settings for a user named Little Joe. Parental Controls are turned on and Activity Reporting is also turned on. You can access Parental Controls from the User Accounts and Family Safety section within the Control Panel.

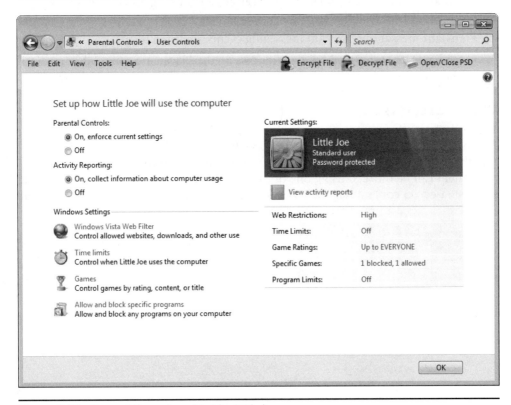

Figure 9-10 Parental Controls enabled for Little Joe

Once parental controls are created, if access is blocked to a Web page or game, a notification is displayed informing the user that the page has been blocked. Additionally, activity is logged.

Activity Reporting

If Activity Reporting is enabled, you can view reports on the activity of all standard users that have Activity Reporting enabled. Activity for a user is organized in the following categories:

- **Web Browsing** Web activity such as the top 10 Web sites visited, the top 10 Web sites blocked, Web overrides, file downloads, and file downloads blocked is listed here.

- **System** Details on logon times, including the duration, is listed here.

- **Applications**   All applications that have been launched when the user is logged on are listed here. Applications are sometimes launched automatically (such as the Windows Sidebar) but are still listed here.

- **Gaming**   A list of games played, when they were played, and the duration are listed here.

- **E-mail**   E-mail events such e-mail received, e-mail sent, and changes to the contact list are included here.

- **Instant messaging**   Instant messaging events are listed here.

- **Media**   Content played by the Windows Media Player and some other media players is listed here.

Web Restrictions

The Web Restrictions page allows you to configure what the user can access via the Internet. It allows a parent to block objectionable content, but it's important to realize that the definition of "objectionable" varies from one parent to another.

Content can be blocked using one of the Web Restriction levels or by choosing categories based on content. Figure 9-11 shows the available choices. If desired a parent

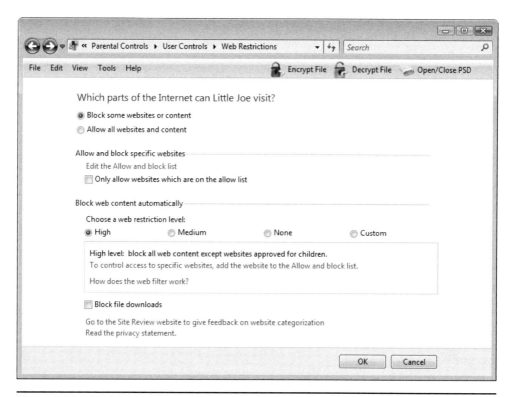

Figure 9-11   Configuring Web Restrictions

can select the Block Some Websites or Content, and then add specific Web sites to the Allow and Block List.

- **High**   All Web sites are blocked except those specifically approved for children.
- **Medium**   Web content in the following categories is blocked: mature content, pornography, drugs, hate speech, and weapons. Additionally, content that isn't rated is also blocked.
- **None**   All content is allowed.
- **Custom**   You pick the specific categories that you want to block, such as pornography, drugs, gambling, and more.

 TIP   Many corporations use a similar technology to block objectionable content at the proxy server. For example, a company may decide they don't want employees gambling with company equipment on company time. The company can subscribe with a third party to get a list of gambling Web sites and apply this list to the company's proxy server. If an employee attempts to access one of the gambling Web sites, the attempt is blocked and logged.

In addition to blocking content by a specific Web restriction level or content category, you can also block or allow specific Web sites using the URL. Figure 9-12 shows how you can specify exactly which Web sites are allowed or blocked.

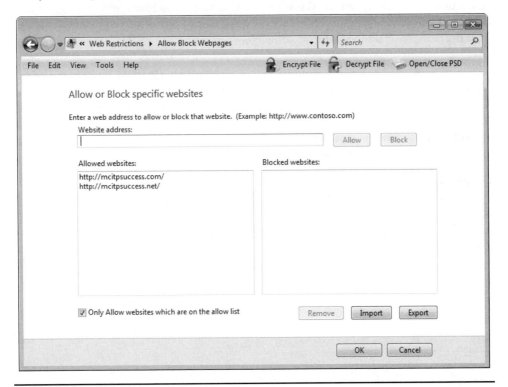

Figure 9-12   Configuring specific allowable Web sites

Time Restrictions

You can use the time restrictions to block or allow specific times when a standard user can use the computer. By default, all days and times are allowed.

To configure time restrictions, click the Time Limits link on the parental controls page for the user. On the time limits page, you can click and drag your mouse within the calendar to change the current setting.

While the time restrictions are a part of parental controls, you can also use them for other purposes. For example, in a small business environment a business owner may need an employee to occasionally check her computer for specific information used for payroll or to place a weekly order. By using parental controls, the employee can be restricted from accessing the computer except at specific times of the day and specific days of the week.

Games

Using the Games parental control, you can control which games a standard user can access. You have the capability to block games by rating, content, or title.

 EXAM TIP   One of the popular features with Parental Controls is the ability to control which games a user can play. Remember that you must enable Parental Controls to configure Game Restrictions and that many games can be unrated, which will bypass the Game Restrictions unless you block all unrated games. Additionally, all administrator accounts should be password protected to prevent a user from bypassing the Parental Controls completely.

Figure 9-13 shows the configuration for a standard user named Little Joe. The settings allow him to play games with a maximum of an Everyone rating. However even if the title has an Everyone rating, but the game includes cartoon violence, it will be blocked.

Additionally, Spider Solitaire is specifically blocked (Little Joe is afraid of spiders) and the Chess Titans game is specifically allowed.

Block by Rating

Game ratings used by parental controls are defined by the Entertainment Software Rating Board (ESRB). Games can be evaluated against these ratings and then assigned a specific rating based on age. The goal is for a parent to be able to easily control what a child can access based on the child's age.

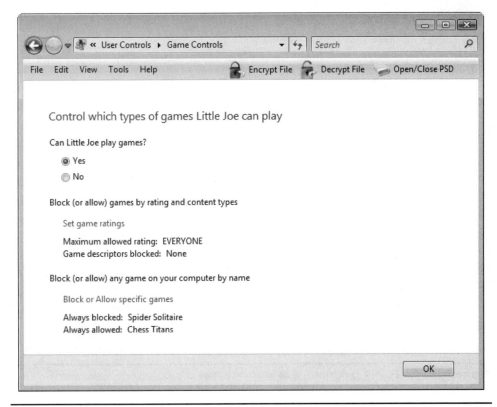

Figure 9-13 Game controls for a standard user

Figure 9-14 shows the screen you can use to configure which games a user is allowed to play based on the ratings. In the figure, Little Joe is restricted to only games rated as E for everyone (which includes those rated EC for early childhood).

Since some games don't have ratings but may be objectionable, you can choose to allow or block all games without a rating. In other words, even if a game is designed for children, but not rated, it will be blocked. Game designers are aware of this, and mainstream games designed for children will be rated, but games designed for adults may not be rated.

Figure 9-14 Configuring game restrictions based on ratings

The listed ratings are

- **Early Childhood (EC)**   Designed for ages 3 and older. No inappropriate material would be found here.

- **Everyone (E)**   Suitable for ages 6 and older. It may contain minimal violence, some comic mischief, and/or some mild language.

- **Everyone 10+ (E10+)**   Suitable for ages 10 and older. These titles may contain cartoon, fantasy, or mild violence, mild language, and/or minimally suggestive themes.

- **Teen (T)**   Suitable for ages 13 and older. Titles may contain violent content, mild language, and/or strong language.

- **Mature (M)**   Suitable for ages 17 and older. Titles may contain mature sexual themes, more intense violence, and/or strong language.

- **Adults Only (AO)**   Only suitable for ages 18 and older. Titles may include graphic depictions of sex and/or violence.

Block by Content

If a game is rated, it will also provide information on the content. You can choose to block based on the content in addition to (or instead of) blocking based on the rating. The list of content is extensive, but Table 9-1 shows many of the content topics that you can choose to block.

Table 9-1 Content Topics	Alcohol, Tobacco, and/or Drugs		Blood	Lyrics
	Mature Humor		Nudity	Language
	Violence		Gambling	Sexual content

Block or Allow by Title

You can also block or allow specific games by their title. When you select the option to Block Or Allow Specific Games, you'll see a menu of all the installed games. You can then select any of the games and choose from one of the following options:

- **User Rating Setting**   The game will blocked or allowed based on what ratings have been set for this user.
- **Always Allow**   The game will be allowed even if it's intended to be blocked by the rating set for this user.
- **Always Block**   The game will be blocked even if it's allowed based on the rating set for this user.

Figure 9-15 shows what happens if a user attempts to launch a program that is blocked from parental controls. You can see that Hold 'Em and Spider Solitaire are being blocked. Hold 'Em is blocked because it is simulated gambling and not suitable for the Everyone rating, and Spider Solitaire was specifically blocked.

Figure 9-15   Parental Controls blocking a game

Allow or Block Specific Programs

By default, a user being restricted by Parental Controls can use all programs. However, you can change the setting to only allow specific programs.

After selecting Parental Controls and selecting the user you want to control, select the Allow and Block Specific Programs link. When you click the radio button to change the setting to only use the programs you allow, the screen changes to what you see in Figure 9-16. In the figure, some of the Office 2007 components have been selected as allowed.

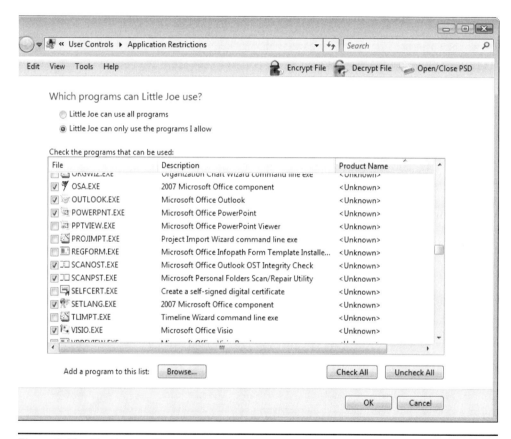

Figure 9-16 Blocking specific programs

Your system will first be scanned to identify all the available programs. You can then select the specific programs you want to allow. If your program is not listed (or you're having trouble finding it in this list), you can also click Browse.

Windows Security Center

The Windows Security Center is designed to enhance security on your computer by ensuring that four essential security features are enabled and operating properly on your computer. If any of the features are not operating, you will be informed with a balloon type notification from the system tray.

For example, if you turn off the Windows Firewall, a notification will appear informing you to check your firewall status. If you click the notification, the Windows Security Center would appear as shown in Figure 9-17.

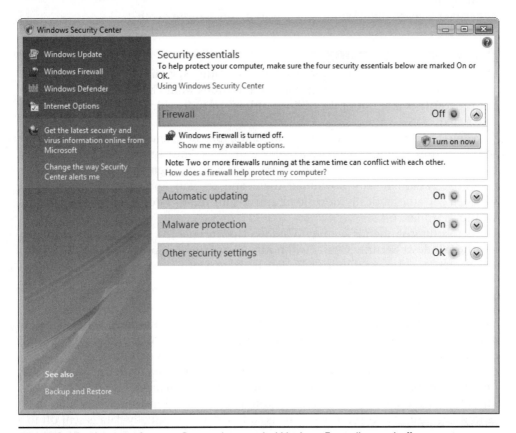

Figure 9-17 Windows Security Center showing the Windows Firewall turned off

The four security essentials monitored by the Windows Security Center are

- Firewall
- Automatic updating
- Malware protection
- Other security settings

Windows Firewall

The Windows Firewall is used to block traffic from accessing your system. When the Windows Firewall is enabled, all but the most essential traffic is blocked and your system is protected. The Windows Firewall is on by default.

You can enable exceptions on the Windows Firewall. For example, if you want others to be able to access your system using Remote Desktop, you can enable an exception so that Remote Desktop connections are allowed.

If the Windows Firewall is turned off, you will receive a notification to check your firewall status.

Chapter 7 covered the Windows Firewall in much more depth.

Automatic Updating

One of the core security principles with any operating system is to keep it up to date. In a perfect world, operating systems and applications would be perfect when released, but the reality is that out of the billions of lines of code, vulnerabilities and flaws are discovered.

When problems are discovered, hot fixes, patches, and updates are released. Microsoft uses Windows Update to release updates. Your system can be configured to automatically check for updates and inform you when they are available for download, automatically download them and let you know they're ready to be installed, or automatically download and install them. Additionally, you can turn Windows Update off.

Microsoft recommends keeping Windows Update enabled. If you turn it completely off, the Windows Security Center will notify you of this as a potential security issue.

Chapter 11 will cover Windows Update in more depth.

Malware Protection

Malicious software (malware) includes viruses and spyware. Malware is simply a part of a computer's life today. It exists and by doing a little bit of surfing or opening up some of your spam e-mail, you're sure to come across some type of malware.

In the past, the goal of malware has been to cause some type of destruction or havoc on your computer. Many malware programs today have changed into data collectors. They don't want to stop you from using your computer, but instead want you to use it as much as possible. As you use it, data is collected and eventually data is sent off to a collection point.

Information is then analyzed to determine what can be used. Perhaps a birth date and social security number can be combined to steal your identity. Perhaps credentials for a banking site can be used to tap into your checking or savings account. Or maybe they can capture the mother lode and capture credentials for your investment account and move all the investment assets into an untraceable offshore account.

The risk is there and it is substantial. Microsoft recognizes the risk and uses the Windows Security Center to check to see if you have both anti-virus software and anti-malware software running on your system. If either protection is not installed, up-to-date, and running, the Windows Security Center provides a notification to inform you of the issue.

Windows includes the Windows Defender as a free anti-spyware product to protect you from spyware threats. Many third-party anti-virus products are available. Symantec and McAfee are popular paid products, and Avast is a popular anti-virus program free for home users. It isn't as important which anti-virus program you use as it is important that you use some anti-virus program.

Chapter 13 covers the Windows Defender in much more depth.

Other Security Settings

The Windows Security Center includes an Other Security Settings category. This category monitors Internet Explorer settings and the User Account Control settings.

Internet Explorer has several security features that are enabled by default and can be manipulated. You can control what features are available for specific Web sites based on zones. You can also implement different privacy settings.

If you weaken the Internet Options settings in Internet Explorer beyond a specific threshold, the Windows Security Center will notify you of the risk.

Chapter 13 covers Internet Explorer in much more depth.

User Account Control was covered earlier in this chapter. If you turn the User Account Control feature off, the Windows Security Center will notify you of the issue.

Enabling Auditing

You can enable security auditing on your computer. When enabled, auditing will log specific events in the security log. You can then periodically view the security log to identify what activity is occurring on your system.

Auditing can be enabled locally on a per-computer basis or with Group Policy affecting multiple computers simultaneously. You use the local security policy to enable auditing on the local computer.

Figure 9-18 shows the Local Security Policy console opened to the Local Policies, Audit Policy node. Notice that several auditing policies can be enabled, but on this system only Audit Object Access is enabled.

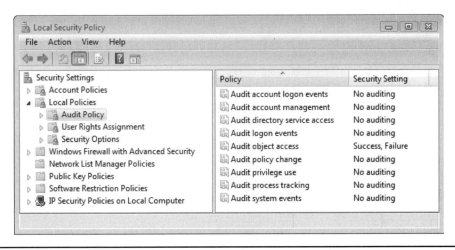

Figure 9-18   Local Security Policy showing audit policies

You can access the Local Security Policy console by clicking Start | Administrative Tools | Local Security Policy. If you don't have Administrative Tools on your Start menu, you can access them via the Control Panel System and Maintenance applet.

Auditing can be enabled on several different elements within your system. Each entry can be enabled for both success and failure events. As an example, you may want to know specifically who deleted a file and when they deleted it; success events for object access will tell you this. You may also want to know who attempted to delete a file even though they weren't successful; failure events for object access will log these events.

- **Object Access.** When a user accesses an object (such as the Registry, a file, a folder, or a printer), this access can be logged. It's important to realize that Object Access must be enabled in two places: in the local security policy and then at the object that you want to monitor.

  If you enable auditing only in the local security policy, it won't automatically enable auditing for every object in your system. You must also access any specific object you want to audit and enabling auditing for that object.

  Figure 9-19 shows auditing being enabled on the HKEY_Current_Config portion of the Registry. You can see these screens by clicking Start and entering regedit in the Start Search line. Right-click the HKEY_Current_Config hive and select Permissions. Click the Advanced button and then click the Auditing tab.

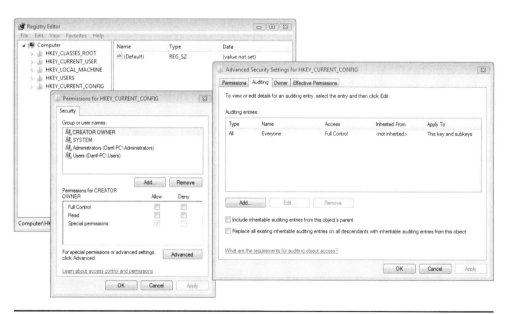

Figure 9-19   Enabling auditing on a Registry hive

EXAM TIP Object Access auditing can be enabled to monitor any attempts to modify any file or folder on your system, including the system Registry.

- **Account Management** This will log entries related to changing an account name, enabling or disabling an account, creating or deleting an account, changing a password, or changing a group.

- **Logon Events** This will log entries if someone logs on or off your computer. Entries will be created if the user logs on locally or logs on to your computer over the network.

- **Policy Change** This will log any attempts to change any settings in the local policies node of the Local Security Policy console. This includes the audit policy, user rights assignment, and security options.

- **Privilege Use** This will log events when a user performs a user right such as changing the time or backing up files.

- **Process Tracking** Program activation and process exits are logged when this is enabled.

- **System Events** This will log when something shuts down, when it is restarted, or when a process or program attempts to do something that it doesn't have permission to do.

- **Directory Service Access** Directory Service Access logs events when someone accesses Active Directory in a domain environment.

- **Account Logon Events** This will log entries if someone logs on or off a computer with a domain account. These entries will only be generated when a user is authenticated with Active Directory.

After you enable auditing, events will be logged in the Security log and can be viewed in the Event Viewer. Figure 9-20 shows the Event Viewer opened up to the Security Log. The event selected shows that the Registry has been accessed and provides details on the access.

The Event Viewer will be covered in more depth in Chapter 11.

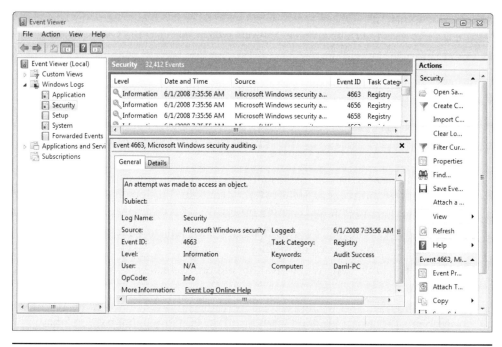

Figure 9-20   Event Viewer showing a Registry object access event

Chapter Review

In this chapter, you learned about several security features that apply to Windows Vista.

Windows Vista supports two types of accounts: standard users and administrators. In order to do many advanced tasks such as installing software and changing security centers, you must use the credentials of an administrator. Accounts can be protected with a password. If an account is password protected, other users won't be able to log on to it.

The User Account Control (UAC) feature prevents unauthorized changes on a system by prompting the user before continuing with any changes that require administrative privileges. If the user is logged on as an administrator, UAC prompts for consent; if the user is logged on as a standard user, UAC prompts for the credentials of an administrator.

You learned how to enable and disable the UAC and how to manipulate the UAC behavior through the Local Security Policy console. The local security policy includes several settings in the Local Policies, Security Options node that directly affect User Account Control.

In the Parental Controls section, you learned how a standard user account's actions can be restricted by an administrator. You can control which Web sites are accessed with the Web Restrictions. A computer account can be restricted with Time Restrictions to control when a user can log on. Game playing can be blocked by rating, blocked by content, or blocked by title. You can also block or allow specific programs.

You also learned how Parental Controls includes reporting capabilities. Activity reports can be accessed for any standard user that has had parental controls enabled.

The Windows Security Center is designed to inform you when your computers security is weakened in four specific areas: Windows Firewall, Windows Update, malware protection, and other security settings (Internet Explorer and User Account Control).

Last, you learned a little about auditing. Several auditing settings are available in Windows Vista. Object Access is often used to identify when anyone accesses objects (such as files, folders, printers, or even the Registry).

Additional Study

Self Study Exercises
Use these additional exercises to challenge yourself.

- Log on with a standard user account and try to install an application. Notice how the UAC prompts you for credentials.
- Create an account without a password and log on to it to verify a password is not needed.
- Disable UAC and open the Windows Security Center to view the results.
- Implement Parental Controls for a standard user account. Restrict the account using each of the different restrictions. Log on to the account and view how the user is restricted.
- Enable auditing on the Registry. Access the Registry and view the Security Log in the Event Viewer.

Summary of What You Need to Know

70-620
When preparing for the 70-620 exam, pay particular attention to the following topics covered in this chapter:

- **User accounts** You should know the difference between a standard user account and an administrator account. Ideally, the standard user account will be used for all normal activity and the administrator account would rarely be used to log on. Instead, the administrator account would only be used when performing administrative actions after providing credentials through UAC.
- **Administrator account** You should be aware of what actions require user privileges (such as installing applications, changing security settings, and creating accounts).
- **Password-protected accounts** Know how to protect accounts by ensuring they have passwords applied. Be able to verify an account is password protected by viewing it in the Manage Accounts applet within Control Panel.

- **User Account Control (UAC)** You should know how to enable and disable UAC and what it does when it is enabled. You should also be familiar with how the behavior can be modified using the local security policy settings.

- **Parental controls** You should know what parental controls are and the different ways they can be used to restrict a standard user's actions. You should also be familiar with the content logged in the Parental Controls Activity Report.

70-622

When preparing for the 70-622 exam, pay particular attention to the following topics covered in this chapter:

- **Administrator account** You should be aware of what actions require user privileges (such as installing applications, changing security settings, and creating accounts).

- **User Account Control (UAC)** UAC is heavily tested in this exam. Make sure you know all the topics covered in the UAC section in this chapter. This includes how to enable and disable UAC, what it does when it is enabled, and how the behavior can be modified using the local security policy settings.

- **Auditing** You should be familiar with the different types of auditing available.

70-623

When preparing for the 70-623 exam, pay particular attention to the following topics covered in this chapter:

- **User accounts** You should know the difference between a standard user account and an administrator account. Ideally, the standard user account will be used for all normal activity and the administrator account would rarely be used to log on. Instead, the administrator account would only be used when performing administrative actions after providing credentials through UAC.

- **Administrator account** You should be aware of what actions require user privileges (such as installing applications, changing security settings, and creating accounts). You should also know the alternative method of running applications as an administrator (by right-clicking and selecting Run As Administrator).

- **User Account Control (UAC)** You should know how to enable and disable UAC and what it does when it is enabled. You should also be familiar with how the behavior can be modified using the local security policy settings.

- **Password-protected accounts** Know how to protect accounts by ensuring they have passwords applied. Know that if an account is not password protected, any users can log on to the account.

- **Parental controls** You should know what parental controls are and the different ways they can be used to restrict a standard user's actions. You should also be familiar with the content logged in the Parental Controls Activity Report.

Questions

70-620

1. You are using the same account you created when you first installed Windows Vista. You decide to share your computer with another user. You don't want the other user to make any changes to system settings. What should you do?

   A. Give the other user your username and password and ask them not to make any changes.

   B. Create an administrator account for the user.

   C. Create a standard user account for the user.

   D. Create a guest user account for the user.

2. Sally has configured parental controls on her child's computer to restrict access during certain days and times. However, her child logs on to the computer using a different account and accesses the computer during these restricted times. What should Sally do to prevent this in the future?

   A. Enable the Task Scheduler service.

   B. Disable the guest account.

   C. Disable the administrator account.

   D. Use password protection for all accounts.

3. You want to modify the local security policy so that any time a user logged on as an administrator tries to make changes requiring administrative privileges, she must enter her username and password. What should you do?

   A. Configure the User Account Control: Behavior of the Elevation Prompt for Administrators in the Admin Approval Mode setting to Prompt for Credentials.

   B. Configure the User Account Control: Behavior of the Elevation Prompt for Standard Users setting to Prompt for Credentials.

   C. Configure the User Account Control: Behavior of the Elevation Prompt for Administrators in Admin Approval Mode setting to Prompt for Consent.

   D. Configure the User Account Control: Behavior of the Elevation Prompt for Standard Users setting to Prompt for Consent.

4. You want to modify the local security policy so that any time a user logged on with a standard user account tries to make changes requiring administrative privileges, they are allowed. Current settings prevent this from occurring. What should you do?

   A. Configure the User Account Control: Behavior of the Elevation Prompt for Administrators in Admin Approval Mode setting to Prompt for Credentials.

   B. Configure the User Account Control: Behavior of the Elevation Prompt for Standard Users setting to Prompt for Credentials.

    C. Configure the User Account Control: Behavior of the Elevation Prompt for Administrators in Admin Approval Mode setting to Prompt for Consent.

    D. Configure the User Account Control: Behavior of the Elevation Prompt for Standard Users setting to Prompt for Consent.

5. Sally is logged on to her computer with a standard user account. She needs to make an authorized change to her firewall to allow a program to work, but she doesn't have administrative privileges. You do have administrative privileges, and Sally asks you for assistance. What should you do?

    A. Have Sally log off. Log on and make the change. Log off and have Sally log back on.

    B. Use the local security policy to configure the Windows Firewall.

    C. Attempt to make the change and when prompted click Continue to make the change.

    D. Attempt to make the change and when prompted provide your credentials to make the change.

6. A user has implemented parental controls for her children. One child has the Everyone rating game restriction enabled for his account but is still able to run some inappropriate games run by his older teenage brother. What should you do?

    A. Configure the Game Restrictions to disallow TEEN games.

    B. Configure the Game Restrictions to disallow games that are not rated.

    C. Configure the Game Restrictions to include EC games.

    D. Configure the Web Restrictions to block unratable content.

70-622

1. You need to disable UAC for local administrators logged on to a Windows Vista system. You want to do this only for administrators, not standard users. How can this be done? (Choose all that apply.)

    A. In local security policy, set User Account Control: Run All Administrators in Admin Approval Mode option to Disabled.

    B. In local security policy, set User Account Control: Run All Administrators in Admin Approval Mode option to Enabled.

    C. In local security policy, set User Account Control: Behavior of the Elevation Prompt for Administrators in Admin Approval Mode to Prompt for Consent.

    D. In local security policy, set User Account Control: Behavior of the Elevation Prompt for Administrators in Admin Approval Mode to Elevate Without Prompting.

    E. In the Control Panel User Accounts applet, select the link to Turn User Account Control On or Off.

2. You are assisting a user with her computer. When you begin installing an application, you realize that you weren't prompted for administrative credentials. You want to ensure that users are prompted for administrative credentials when administrative tasks are accomplished. What should you do?

   A. Enable the Windows Firewall.

   B. Enable UAC.

   C. Have users log on with standard user accounts.

   D. Have users log on with administrative accounts.

3. Joe is successfully running a legacy application on Windows Vista. He says he must be logged on as administrator to run the application and that's why he uses an administrator account to log on all the time. You log on with a standard user account and try to run the application and the application fails. What can you do to allow the legacy application to run using a standard user account?

   A. In local security policy, set User Account Control: Virtualize File and Registry Write Failures to Per-User Locations to Enabled.

   B. In local security policy, set User Account Control: Virtualize File and Registry Write Failures to Per-User Locations to Disabled.

   C. In local security policy, set the User Account Control: Run All Administrators in Admin Approval Mode option to Disabled.

   D. In local security policy, set the User Account Control: Run All Administrators in Admin Approval Mode option to Enabled.

4. When you are logged on as a standard user on your Windows Vista system, you are unable to do any administrative tasks. You must instead log off and then back on with your administrative account to do the tasks. How can you change this behavior in Windows Vista?

   A. In local security policy, set User Account Control: Behavior of the Elevation Prompt for Standard Users to Disabled.

   B. In local security policy, set User Account Control: Behavior of the Elevation Prompt for Standard Users to Enabled.

   C. In local security policy, set User Account Control: Behavior of the Elevation Prompt for Standard Users to Prompt for Credentials.

   D. In local security policy, set User Account Control: Behavior of the Elevation Prompt for Standard Users to Automatically Deny Elevation Requests.

5. Several users are working in a small office in another city. All the users have Windows Vista installed. Occasionally users need to install applications on their systems, but none of the users are able to do so. This office does not have any support staff. What should you do?

   A. Enable UAC.

   B. Disable UAC.

C. Disable the Windows Firewall.

D. Give users access to a local administrator account.

6. You suspect that some users are modifying the Registry, causing you some troubleshooting challenges. You want to ensure that all attempts to modify the Registry are logged. What should you enable?

A. Registry auditing

B. System Events auditing

C. Object Access auditing

D. Privilege Use auditing

70-623

1. Joe is running a Windows Vista computer in his small business. Several users are sharing the computer with different accounts. He's added everyone as an administrator account but is concerned that he granted too much permission. He asks you for help. Users need to be able to do the following tasks:

   • Harry: Install and run applications.

   • Rita: Burn DVDs and run applications.

   • Ron: Connect wireless devices.

   • Hermione: Add and remove user accounts.

   Which users need to remain as administrators?

   • Harry only

   • Harry and Rita

   • Harry and Ron

   • Harry and Hermione

   • All users

2. Joe is configuring accounts on his computer. He's configuring an account for his wife and his daughter. His wife wants to make sure that her account and all the files in her account's profile can't be accessed by her daughter. What should Joe do?

   A. Create an administrator account for his wife.

   B. Password-protect the account for his wife.

   C. Password-protect the account for his daughter.

   D. Create an administrator account for his daughter.

3. You are helping a mother with her Windows Vista computer. The computer is shared between three of her children. The problem is that occasionally when one of her children makes a change, it affects all three children's accounts. She wants to set it up so that each of the children is prevented from making changes to the other children's accounts. What can she do?

   A. Configure Parental Controls.

   B. Create an administrator account for each of the children.

   C. Create a standard user account for each of the children.

   D. Enable the firewall on the account for each of the children.

4. A user running Windows Vista asks you how to ensure that a user logged on with a standard user account is not able to make changes to security settings without logging on as an administrator. What do you recommend?

   A. In local security policy, set User Account Control: Behavior of the Elevation Prompt for Administrators in Admin Approval Mode to Prompt for Consent.

   B. In local security policy, set User Account Control: Behavior of the Elevation Prompt for Administrators in Admin Approval Mode to Elevate Without Prompting.

   C. In local security policy, set User Account Control: Behavior of the Elevation Prompt for Standard Users to Prompt for Credentials.

   D. In local security policy, set User Account Control: Behavior of the Elevation Prompt for Standard Users to Automatically Deny Elevation Requests.

5. You are configuring a computer used in a library environment. You are hardening security for standard users, but when an administrator logs on and attempts to modify any settings requiring administrative privileges, you want the settings to complete without prompting the administrator. What should you do?

   A. In local security policy, set User Account Control: Behavior of the Elevation Prompt for Administrators in Admin Approval Mode to Prompt for Consent.

   B. In local security policy, set User Account Control: Behavior of the Elevation Prompt for Administrators in Admin Approval Mode to Elevate Without Prompting.

   C. In local security policy, set User Account Control: Behavior of the Elevation Prompt for Standard Users to Prompt for Credentials.

   D. In local security policy, set User Account Control: Behavior of the Elevation Prompt for Standard Users to Automatically Deny Elevation Requests.

6. Sally is trying to run a legacy application that requires elevated privileges on her Windows Vista system. Sally does have credentials for an administrator account. When she tries to run the program, it fails. Sally wants to allow the application to run. What should she do?

   A. Right-click the application and select Run with UAC.

   B. Right-click the application and select Run as Administrator.

   C. Disable Windows Firewall and run the application.

   D. Right-click the application, select Properties, and select Previous Versions.

7. Sally wants to control her children's access to Web sites. She has identified 15 Web sites she considers safe for her children to access and wants to restrict all the rest. She has enabled parental controls. What else should she do?

   A. Select All Websites and Content and edit the Allow and Block List.

   B. Set the Web Restriction Level to High.

   C. Select Block Some Websites or Content.

   D. Select Block Some Websites or Content and edit the Allow and Block List.

8. Sally has configured Parental Controls to stop one of her younger children from playing some objectionable games. She suspects the child is somehow circumventing these controls and playing some of these games. What should she do?

   A. Log on with her child's account and check the Parental Controls Activity Reports.

   B. Log on with her account and check the Parental Controls Activity Reports.

   C. Log on with her child's account and check the Event Viewer logs.

   D. Log on with her account and check the Event Viewer logs.

9. Joe owns his own business. One of his employees needs access to his Windows Vista computer every Thursday at 3 P.M. to enter information on weekly jobs. Joe wants to make sure the employee doesn't access his computer at any other times. What could Joe do?

   A. Enable time restrictions for the user account using Windows Defender.

   B. Enable time restrictions for the user account using Computer Management.

   C. Create a standard user account for the employee and configure Parental Controls.

   D. Create an administrative account for the employee and configure Parental Controls.

10. Sally is trying to limit her teenage son from playing some games with more mature content. She sets the game rating to Teen for her son's standard user account. However, she finds that her son is still able to play a game that clearly has objectionable content for the Teen rating. What should she do?

   A. Change the rating to Mature.

   B. Change the rating to Everyone.

   C. Set the Parental Controls to Block All Games with No Rating.

   D. Enable Parental Controls.

Answers

70-620

1 C. You should create a standard user account for the user. The first user account created during the Windows Vista install is an administrator account. You should not give the user access to an administrator account if you don't want the user to make any changes to your system. A guest user account is already created; you can choose to enable it or disable it.

2. D. With password protection enabled for all accounts, the child won't be able to access different accounts without the password. The Task Scheduler doesn't have any control over what accounts a user logs on to. Disabling any specific account would only be meaningful if you knew which account the child is accessing. Protecting all accounts with passwords solves the problem for all accounts.

3. A. By setting the User Account Control: Behavior of the Elevation Prompt for Administrators in Admin Approval Mode setting to Prompt for Credentials, administrators will have to provide a username and password to perform any administrative actions. The default is to Prompt for Consent and only requires the administrator to click Continue. Settings for Standard Users won't affect a user logged on as an administrator.

4. B. By setting the User Account Control: Behavior of the Elevation Prompt for Standard Users setting to Prompt for Credentials, standard users will be able to complete administrative actions after providing credentials. While this is the default, since current settings prevent this behavior, the default must have been changed to Automatically Deny Elevation Requests. There is no Prompt for Consent setting for standard users. Configuring the settings for Administrators won't affect a user logged in as a standard user.

5. D. When a standard user is logged on, UAC will prompt for credentials of an administrator. After entering the credentials, you can make the change. It's not required to have the user log off. Modifying the firewall settings via local security policy still requires more privileges than the standard user. The Continue dialog box only appears when an administrator is logged on and the setting is set to Prompt for Consent.

6. **B.** Not all games are rated, and if unrated games are to be blocked, you must specifically select Block Games with No Rating. The Everyone rating for ages 6 and older includes the Early Childhood (EC) rating for ages 3 and older, but it restricts content rated above Everyone, including the Everyone 10+, Teen, Mature, and Adults Only ratings. Web Restrictions don't impact Game Restrictions.

70-622

1. **A, D.** This can be done for administrators by setting the User Account Control: Run all Administrators in Admin Approval Mode option to Disabled or by setting the User Account Control: Behavior of the Elevation Prompt for Administrators in Admin Approval Mode to Elevate Without Prompting. Setting User Account Control: Run all Administrators in Admin Approval Mode option to Enabled will leave UAC turned on. The default setting of User Account Control: Behavior of the Elevation Prompt for Administrators in Admin Approval Mode is Prompt for Consent, and it will prompt the administrators. If you use the User Accounts page to disable UAC, it will disable it for all users.

2. **B.** When User Account Control (UAC) is enabled, both standard users and administrators are prompted when they try to perform an administrative task. By default, standard users are prompted to provide credentials and administrators are prompted to give their consent. The firewall won't cause prompts. When UAC is enabled with the defaults, both standard users and administrative users will be prompted, and when it is disabled, both types of users will not be prompted.

3. **A.** Legacy applications that need to write to protected file or Registry areas will run if the User Account Control: Virtualize File and Registry Write Failures to Per-User Locations is set to Enabled. Setting this to disabled will cause the application to fail unless the user is logged on as an administrator. Changing the User Account Control: Run All Administrators in Admin Approval Mode setting won't change how the application will behave when run by a standard user.

4. **C.** The User Account Control: Behavior of the Elevation Prompt for Standard Users has only two settings: Automatically Deny Elevation Requests (which is currently set, causing the behavior described in the question), and Prompt for Credentials (which is what you want). This setting cannot be set to Enabled or Disabled.

5. **D.** Administrative privileges are required to install applications. If users can't do this, it's because they don't have administrative privileges and should be given access to an administrator account. UAC won't matter if they don't have an account with administrative privileges. The firewall won't prevent users from installing an application.

6. **C.** You should enable Object Access auditing. Object Access auditing can be used to audit access to any objects including the registry, files, folders, and printers. There is no such thing as Registry auditing. System Events include events such as shutdowns and reboots. Privilege Use auditing will record when a user exercises a privilege such as changing the time.

70-623

1. **D.** Administrator access is needed to install applications and to add and remove user accounts. Administrator access is not needed to burn DVDs, run applications, or connect wireless devices.

2. **B.** If his wife's account is password-protected, his daughter won't be able to access the account; the account and data in the profile will be protected. Creating an administrator account for his wife won't provide additional protection it if is not password-protected. Password-protecting the account for his daughter or creating an administrator account for his daughter won't protect his wife's account.

3. **C.** A user logged in with a standard user account cannot make changes to settings that affect other users. What is apparent (but not stated) is that each of the children has an administrator account allowing each of them to make changes that affect all users. Parental Controls can be used to control activity (such as Web sites visited or games played), and a firewall can control traffic within a session, but neither one can stop an administrator from making changes to the system that affect other users.

4. **D.** To prevent standard user accounts from performing actions as administrators, you can set the User Account Control: Behavior of the Elevation Prompt for Standard Users to Automatically Deny Elevation Requests. Any settings for administrators in Admin Approval mode will affect only administrators, not standard users. Configuring this setting to Prompt for Credentials will allow the users to make the changes (as long as they have administrator credentials).

5. **B.** The User Account Control: Behavior of the Elevation Prompt for Administrators in Admin Approval Mode setting Elevate Without Prompting will allow administrators to make changes without being prompted. If you set this to Prompt for Consent, the administrators will be prompted. Any settings set for standard users will not affect an administrator account.

6. **B.** By right-clicking the application and selecting Run as Administrator, Sally can launch the program with administrative privileges. There is no Run with UAC choice. The Windows Firewall wouldn't prevent a program from launching. Previous Versions is used to restore previous versions of data files but has no meaning for an application file.

7. **D.** After setting the Block Some Websites or Content setting, the Allow and Block Specific Websites selection appears allowing specific Web sites to be added. If the All Websites and Content list appears, the Allow and Block List does not appear. Setting the Web Restriction Level to High blocks all content except Web sites approved for children. Just selecting Block Some Websites or Content isn't enough without adding the Web sites.

8. **B.** The Parental Controls Activity Report can be accessed only by an administrative account and will show activity by any standard user account controlled by Parental Controls. The Activity Report cannot be accessed by non-administrative accounts (such as the child's account). Event Viewer logs do not include parental control activity.

9. **C.** Parental Controls can be configured with time restrictions for any standard user account to restrict logon hours. Windows Defender is used to protect against malware but can't be used to restrict logon times. Computer Management can be used to manage accounts but doesn't have a feature to restrict logon times.

10. **C.** The Block All Games with No Rating setting can be used to block games that don't have a rating. The Teen rating will allow any games rated as suitable for Teens (including EC, Everyone, and Everyone 10+ ratings), but only if the game has been rated. Game rating is optional, and it's possible for objectionable games to not have any rating, allowing the game to be played. Game restrictions can only be set if parental controls are enabled, so Parental Controls are already enabled.

Managing Windows Vista in a Domain

In this chapter, you will learn about:

- Applying group policy
- Group policy settings
- Group policy tools
- Security configuration and analysis
- Certificates

Group policy is a powerful tool used to manage users and computers in a domain, just as local group policy can be used to enforce policy settings on local computers. If you're working as a desktop support technician in an enterprise, you definitely need to have at least a basic understanding of group policy.

You'll learn how group policy is applied, view many of the settings used to manage users and computers, and have an opportunity to access some of the group policy tools in this chapter. Remember, though, the goal of this chapter is just to give you some exposure to group policy, not make you an expert.

Certificates are used for authentication and encryption. You most often come into contact with certificates on the Internet, but they're also used internally.

The topics in this chapter only apply to what you'll see as an Enterprise Support Technician. These topics are a little more advanced than you'll find on the two other Vista exams, so if you're not currently studying for the 70-622 exam, you may want to leave this chapter for later.

 EXAM TIP   Objectives for only the 70-622 exam are included in this chapter.

Applying Group Policy

Group policy is both a magical and mysterious animal to most people. It can do so much, it has a significant amount of power and capabilities, and because of its hundreds of possible settings, it can be quite complex.

The magic of group policy is that you can set a single setting and have it apply to many computers. It doesn't matter if your domain has 50, 500, 5000, or more computers. A single setting of group policy can easily apply to all of the computers.

Group policy is mysterious because it can do so much. There are literally hundreds of possible settings in group policy, such as security, locking down the desktop, and much, much more. While you'll learn some of what group policy can do in this chapter, it's important to realize that we are just scratching the surface. If you continue your studies and become a system engineer or system administrator, you'll learn much more about its capabilities.

When preparing for the 70-622 exam, you need to have a good grasp of how group policy can be used to manage Windows Vista systems in both a domain environment and a workgroup environment.

A domain environment includes a domain controller (running Active Directory). Both computer and user accounts (called objects in Active Directory) are managed centrally on the domain controller. Users have one account that can be used to access any computer in the domain.

Workgroups are used in smaller environments of fewer than 20 computers. User accounts are maintained on each individual computer, and users need a separate account for each computer they access.

Most of the individual group policy settings explored in this chapter can be used in both domain and workgroup environments. The difference is that when you use group policy in the domain, you only need to set it once to have it apply to many computers. When you use it in a workgroup, you must configure it individually on each computer.

Group Policy Nodes

The Group Policy editor allows you to manipulate settings for the user configuration and computer configuration. Figure 10-1 shows the Group Policy editor for the local group policy.

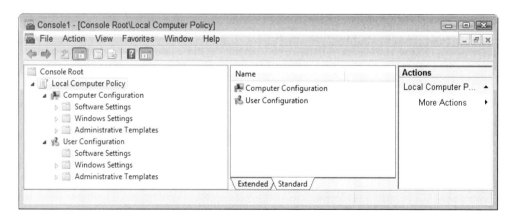

Figure 10-1   Local Group Policy editor

On the surface the computer and user nodes look the same—they both have the same three folders. However, as soon as you start clicking any of the folders and exploring the different settings that apply to users and computers, you'll see that while some settings are the same, many settings are very different.

It is possible to have a single group policy object (GPO) with configuration settings in both the user and computer nodes. If a GPO that includes settings in both nodes is applied to a computer, all of the settings will apply to the computer and to any user that logs on to that computer. Similarly, if a GPO that includes settings in both nodes is applied to a user, all of the settings will apply to the user no matter what computer the user logs on to.

Consider Figure 10-2. It represents a domain named mcitpsuccess.com with three organizational units (OUs) named HR, Sales, and Library. The HR OU doesn't have any GPOs applied, but the Sales OU has a single GPO applied with a single setting in the User Configuration node turning off the Windows Sidebar. The Library OU also has a single GPO applied with a single setting in the Computer Configuration node turning off the Windows Sidebar.

Figure 10-2
Domain and OU
structure with
two GPOs
applied

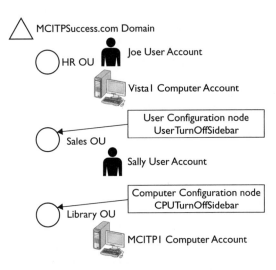

Any computer that Sally logs on to will have the Sidebar turned off. Any user that logs on to the MCITP1 computer will have the Sidebar turned off. You can see how this works in Table 10-1. Notice that even though MCITP1 has a setting in the configuration node, it applies to the user Joe.

User	Computer	GPO	Effect on Sidebar
Joe	Vista1	None	None
Joe	MCITP1	CPUTurnOffSidebar	Off
Sally	Vista1	UserTurnOffSidebar	Off
Sally	Vista1	CPUTurnOffSidebar	Off

Table 10-1 Effects of Group Policy settings

Understanding the Big Picture

As you can see, you can use group policy to manage users and computers by applying group policy settings. The easiest way to fully grasp this is to walk through the process for a single group policy setting. Once you understand how one setting is applied, you can then apply that knowledge to the other hundreds of group policy settings.

Imagine that your company wants to ensure that the Windows Sidebar (covered in Chapter 3) is turned off for all 500 computers in your network. You could visit each computer and modify the settings individually (as shown later in this chapter in Exercise 10.1). However, if you did it individually, you'd have to do this 500 times—once for each computer. This would simply take too long.

Enter group policy. You could create a single domain group policy object and configure the same settings. You would then link the GPO to the domain and it would automatically apply to all 500 computers in the domain.

Figure 10-3 shows the group policy settings to turn off the Windows Sidebar.

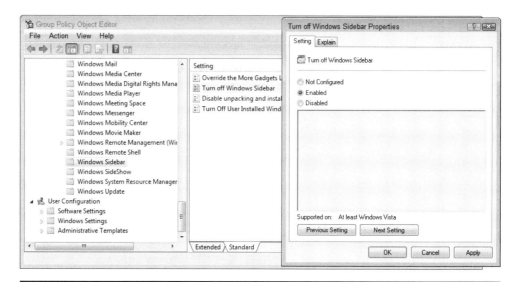

Figure 10-3 Turn Off Windows Sidebar setting

If this setting is set to Enabled in your GPO, then all users affected by the GPO would no longer be able to start the Windows Sidebar. If it is set to Not Configured or Disabled, users would be able to choose whether to run the Sidebar or not.

If you didn't want to apply the group policy setting to everyone in the domain, but instead just everyone in a department, you could apply your GPO to an OU. OUs are used within a domain to organize users and computers.

For example, you could have the following departments in your company: Sales, Marketing, HR, and IT. You could create four OUs to mimic the company's organization: Sales, Marketing, HR, and IT. All user accounts and computer accounts for each department would be placed in their respective OUs.

GPO Inheritance   GPOs are inherited by child objects. In other words, any GPOs applied to a parent are inherited by the children. Of course that begs the questions "What's a parent?" and "What's a child?"

Organizational units (OUs) are created within a domain and are considered child objects of the domain. You use OUs to organize objects such as users and computers to manage them.

Consider Figure 10-4. It shows a domain named MCITPSuccess.com that includes several containers resembling folders. The folders with the extra icon (Domain Controllers, Sales, Virginia Beach, San Francisco, Marketing, HR, and IT) are all OUs and mimic the organization of the company. The Sales OU is selected, showing the two OUs within the Sales OU—Virginia Beach and San Francisco.

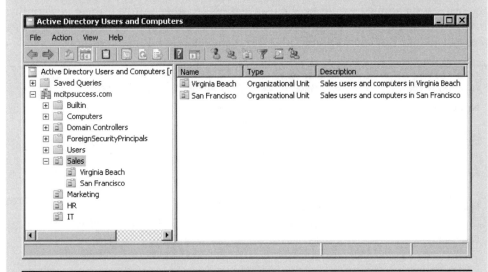

Figure 10-4   Parent-child relationships in a domain

The other containers in the domain (Builtin, Computers, ForeignSecurityPrincipals, and Users) are also children of the domain, and any GPOs applied to the domain will apply to users and computers in these containers.

The Sales OU is also considered a parent of the Virginia Beach and San Francisco OUs. Any GPO applied to the Sales OU would apply to these two child OUs. For example, if you created a GPO and linked it to the Sales OU to turn off the Windows Sidebar, it would also turn off the Windows Sidebar for objects within the Virginia Beach and San Francisco OUs. This would not affect other containers, such as the Marketing, HR, and IT OUs.

If you wanted to ensure that the Windows Sidebar was turned off only for computers in the Sales department, you'd create a GPO to disable the Sidebar and link the GPO to the Sales OU (instead of to the domain). The policy would then apply to all users and computers in the Sales OU, but not to users and computers in other OUs.

Handling GPO Conflicts

In Exercise 10.1 you'll see how to set group policy to turn off the Windows Sidebar setting for either the user configuration or the computer configuration of group policy. If you set both settings to Enabled, there is no conflict. The Windows Sidebar will be turned off.

However, if you set one setting to Enabled and the other setting to Disabled, there is a conflict. The setting that takes precedence is the last one applied (though you'll see later how you can modify this default behavior using loopback processing).

The computer starts first and then the user logs on last (after the computer starts), so the last setting applied would be the user setting. In other words, if there is a conflict between the setting applied to the computer and the setting applied to the user, the user setting will take precedence. Table 10-2 shows the effects of different settings.

GPO Setting Applied to Computer	GPO Setting Applied to User	Conflict?	Effect
Not Configured	Not Configured	No	Sidebar control at user discretion
Enabled	Not Configured	No	Enabled (Sidebar turned off)
Enabled	Enabled	No	Enabled (Sidebar turned off)
Enabled	Disabled	Yes. User setting (Disabled) applies	Disabled (Sidebar can be turned on)
Disabled	Enabled	Yes. User setting (Enabled) applies	Enabled (Sidebar turned off)

Table 10-2 Effects of conflicting settings

Notice that when the computer setting is enabled and the user setting is disabled, the Sidebar isn't necessarily turned off or on. Control passes back to the user. The user can choose whether or not to have the Windows Sidebar running. When a group policy setting is applied, the choice is taken away from the user.

Multiple settings can coexist without any conflicts. For example, a group policy setting applying to a computer may prevent device installations, and another group policy setting applying to a user may turn off the Windows Sidebar. There is no conflict, and both settings will apply.

Loopback Processing

Loopback processing allows you to alter the order of how group policy is applied. Instead of group policies applying to the user taking precedence, loopback processing causes group policies applied to the computer to take precedence.

It's easy to understand loopback processing if you first have a solid grasp of how group policy is applied normally. I'll do a quick review here.

 EXAM TIP To have the group policy settings that apply to a computer take precedence over the group policy settings that apply to a user logged on to that computer, use loopback processing.

When a user logs on to a computer and conflicting policy settings exist that apply to both the user and the computer, the policy applying to the user takes precedence. The easiest way to remember this is the "last policy applied takes precedence."

Consider the following scenario:

- MCITP1 is a computer in the Library OU.

- Sally is in the IT OU.

- The Library OU has a GPO named Turn Off Sidebar. The Turn Off Sidebar setting is set to Enabled, preventing the Sidebar from running on the computer.

- The IT OU has a GPO named Disable Turn Off Sidebar. The Turn Off Sidebar setting is set to Disabled, overriding an Enabled setting.

Figure 10-5 shows a pictorial representation of this scenario.

 Figure 10-5
Two different
GPOs applied to
two different OUs

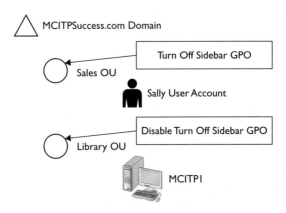

When the MCITP1 computer turns on, the Turn Off Sidebar GPO will be applied, ensuring that the Sidebar doesn't run. When Sally logs on to this computer, the Disable Turn Off Sidebar GPO will apply. We have a conflict, and "the last one applied wins." Sally logs on after the computer starts up, so the policy applying to Sally wins. The Sidebar can run while Sally is logged on.

However, if you want the policy for the computer to take precedence instead of the policy for the user, you enable loopback processing. Figure 10-6 shows the setting for loopback processing.

You can access the loopback processing settings in the following path: Computer Configuration\Administrative Templates\System\Group Policy.

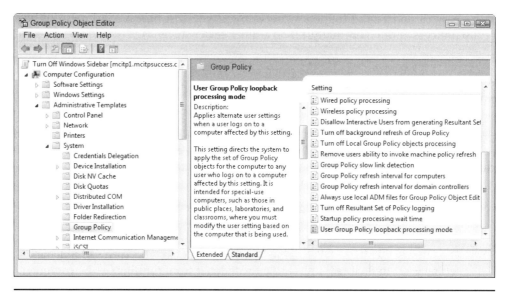

Figure 10-6 Group policy loopback processing setting

If you enable loopback processing for the GPO named Turn Off Sidebar that was linked to the Library OU (where the computer account is located), then this GPO will take precedence.

When Sally (whose account is in the IT OU with a different GPO) logs on to the computer, her GPO settings will be overridden by the computer's GPO.

Group Policy Consoles

The two consoles you use to configure group policy are

- **Local Group Policy**   This is used to apply group policy to a single computer.
- **Group Policy Management Console (GPMC)**   This is used to configure, manage, and deploy GPOs within an enterprise. You can access the GPMC from Windows Vista only when your computer is part of a domain and you are logged on with domain administrator credentials.

Local Group Policy

You can access the Group Policy editor for the local system and apply or modify settings. While this can be effective at locking down the computer; the settings only apply to the local computer.

TIP   Local group policy is sometimes referred to simply as local policy, or local policy settings.

One of the ways this can be useful is if you are creating an image from a source computer. You can configure the local group policy on your source computer, run Sysprep, and then create an image (as described in Chapter 2). You can then deploy this image to multiple computers, and they'll all start with a baseline configuration.

In Exercise 10.1, you will create an MMC console to modify the local group policy for a single computer.

Exercise 10.1: Creating and Manipulating Accounts

1. Click Start, and enter **MMC** in the Start Search dialog box. If the User Account Control dialog box appears, click Continue.

2. Select the File drop-down menu and click Add/Remove Snap-in.

3. In the Add or Remove Snap-ins dialog box, scroll down to the Group Policy Object Editor option. Select Group Policy Object Editor and click Add.

4. On the Welcome to the Group Policy Wizard page, ensure that Local Computer is in the Group Policy Object text box and click Finish. Your display will look similar to Figure 10-7. Click OK.

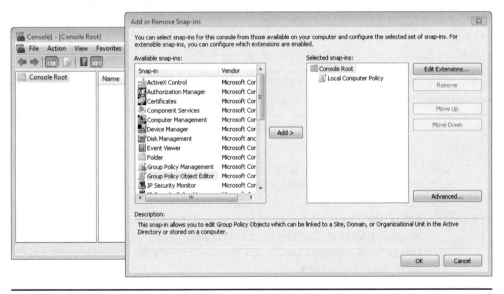

Figure 10-7   Adding the Group Policy snap-in for the Local Computer Policy

  NOTE   While this snap-in only applies to the local computer, it looks very similar to the Group Policy Object editor for a domain group policy.

5. Open the Local Computer Policy by double-clicking it. This will reveal two nodes: Computer Configuration and User Configuration. Double-click each of these nodes to open them. You'll see that each of nodes includes folders for Software Settings, Windows Settings, and Administrative Templates. Note that you can double-click any of the folders to open it, or simply click just to the left of the folder to open it.

6. Browse to the Windows Sidebar settings in the Computer Configuration. You can access it in the Computer Configuration\Administrative Templates\Windows Components folder. Your display will look similar to Figure 10-8.

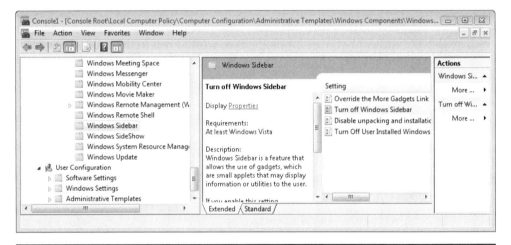

Figure 10-8 Windows Sidebar computer configuration settings

7. Read through the four group policy settings for Windows Sidebar. Notice that you can manipulate several settings for the Sidebar, including simply turning it off.

 EXAM TIP You can use group policy settings to completely disable the Windows Sidebar. This can be done via local group policy for a single computer as demonstrated in this exercise, or via group policy in a domain for multiple computers.

8. Double-click the Turn Off Windows Sidebar setting. Notice that there are three choices: Not Configured (the default), Enabled, and Disabled. You would select Enabled to enable the group policy (and turn off the Windows Sidebar). If you disabled the setting or set it to Not Configured, the net effect is that control of Windows Sidebar is left to the user.

9. Browse to the User Configuration for Windows Sidebar. You can find these settings in the User Configuration\Administrative Templates\Windows Components folder. Notice that you have four settings that you can apply to the user. If you compare the User Configuration Settings with the Computer Configuration settings, you'll see they are identical.

Group Policy Management Console

The Group Policy Management Console (GPMC) is used to manage group policy in a domain environment. As an Enterprise Support Technician, you aren't expected to be an expert in the GPMC, but you should know it exists and its capabilities.

Figure 10-9 shows the GPMC in a domain named MCITPSuccess.com. The Sales OU is selected. A GPO named Turn Off Windows Sidebar has been created and linked to the Sales OU, so it would apply to all users and computers with accounts in the Sales OU and any child OUs within the Sales OU.

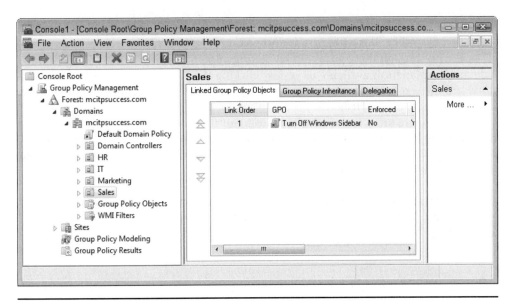

Figure 10-9 GPMC looking at the Sales OU

In order to run the GPMC, you must be logged on to a computer that is joined to a domain and logged on to an account with administrative privileges in the domain.

 EXAM TIP You can't add the GPMC snap-in or run the GPMC unless you are logged on with a domain account with administrative credentials.

The GPMC has a lot more depth and capabilities than you'll see in this chapter. You can create, delete, modify, link, back up, and restore GPOs in the GPMC. The local Group Policy editor only allows you to modify the settings of a single GPO. However, once you access the actual GPO using either the GPMC or the local group policy, the Group Policy editor looks the same.

Throughout this chapter, I strongly encourage you to explore the settings as they're discussed. It doesn't matter if you explore the settings through the GPMC or through the local Group Policy editor as you did in Exercise 10.1, but you should open up the editor and view the settings. Additionally, many of the settings have a tab named Explain. You can click this tab and view additional detail on the group policy.

Group Policy Files

The settings for group policy is actually contained in several different files. Most of the files are static and do not change, but some of the files do change over the lifetime of an operating system. For example, a service pack could be released that gives you access to settings that weren't available before.

Administrative Template settings are the group policy settings that change the most. In past versions of Windows, Administrative Template settings have been deployed in several group policy files with an .adm extension.

As you go through these group policy settings, you'll notice that many of them have a detailed explanation available to you by clicking the Explain button. These explanations and the text for the group policy settings are all in English, which works perfectly as long as you speak English.

However, there are a lot of administrators out there that have another language as their primary language. Windows Vista and Windows Server 2008 group policy files are released in two formats to address the need for administrators to be able to view these settings in their native language.

- **ADMX**   ADMX group policy files have an extension of .admx and are language neutral. These files will be the same in any language.

- **ADML**   ADML group policy files have an extension of .adml and are specific to a language.

If you work in a Spanish-speaking environment and you speak English, your network could have the following group policy files: one .admx file for each group of group policy settings and two .adml files for each group of group policy settings.

Note that the actual settings aren't modified by the addition of any .adml files. The only thing that changes is how they are presented to the administrator.

Exploring Group Policy Settings

In the first part of this chapter, we explored how group policy can be applied, using the Windows Sidebar as an example. However, you can manipulate many more settings for any user or computer than just the Windows Sidebar. At this point, you're probably eager to explore some of the other group policy settings available.

 TIP   One of the challenges with group policy settings is that there are so many of them. Microsoft has two Microsoft Excel files you can download to view and search the different settings. The names of the files are: Windows Server2008andWindowsVistaSP1GroupPolicySettings.xls and VistaGPSettings.xls. Go to Microsoft's download site (www.microsoft.com/downloads) and enter the name of the file to locate it (the actual links are very convoluted with a long string of characters).

Let me state the obvious. The number of group policy settings that can be applied to Windows Vista or users are too numerous to fully explain in a single section of one chapter. If you want to know all the available settings, this isn't the book. My attempt here is only to give you what you're likely to see on the exam.

Some of the settings you should know for the exams are covered elsewhere in this book. I'm listing them here in case you want to browse to the setting and remind yourself of what these settings can do for you.

- **Windows Sidebar**   Covered earlier in this chapter.

- **Point and Print Restriction**   Covered in Chapter 8. The path to the setting is: User Configuration\Administrative Templates\Control Panel\Printers.

- **User Account Control**   Covered in Chapter 9. The path to the several User Account Control settings is: Computer Configuration\Windows Settings\Security Settings\Local Policies\Security Options.

- **Windows Update**   Covered in Chapter 11. The paths to the Windows Update Settings are: Computer Configuration\Administrative Templates\Windows Components\Windows Update and User Configuration\Administrative Templates\Windows Components\Windows Update.

Device Installation Restrictions

The Device Installation Restrictions settings can be used to restrict or control how devices can be installed. As with most group policy settings, these settings are designed to address a specific problem.

USB flash drives are becoming quite common. On the surface that's great, but from a security perspective they can cause problems. It's possible for a user to inadvertently bring in a virus or some other type of malware from their home computer into the network on a USB flash drive. You can configure device installation restrictions to address this risk by preventing users from using USB flash drives on computers within your network.

Figure 10-10 shows the settings for the Device Installation Restrictions. These settings can be used to prevent the installation and updating of device drivers.

 EXAM TIP   You can enable Device Installation Restrictions to stop a user's ability to install any device (including removable devices). If you want administrators to be exempt from this policy, you can configure the Device Installation Restrictions to allow administrators to install devices, but no one else.

Some of the notable settings in this section include

- **Allow Administrators To Override Device Installation Restriction Policies**   This setting will override other settings, but for administrators only.

- **Allow Installation of Devices That Match Any Of These Device IDs**   You can specify specific IDs of devices that you want to allow. For example, your company

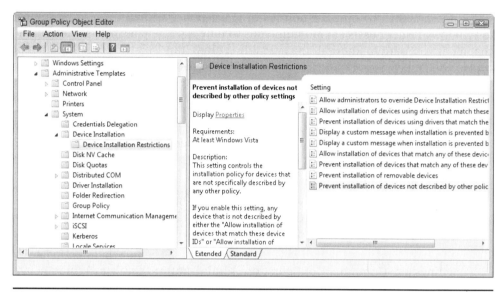

Figure 10-10   Device Installation Restrictions

may have purchased fingerprint-enabled USB flash drives, and you may want to allow these flash drives, but no others. You can add a single device ID, or multiple device IDs.

- **Prevent Installation Of Removable Devices**   This setting prevents the installation of removable devices. If another policy setting allows the user to install a removable device, this setting will take precedence. The only exception is Allow Administrators to Override Device Installation Restriction Policies; if both settings are enabled, administrators will be able to install removable devices but no one else can.

- **Prevent Installation Of Devices Not Described By Other Policy Settings**   This setting prevents the installation of removable devices but will allow exceptions. For example, if you had purchased biometric USB thumb drives and wanted to allow them to be installed based on the device IDs, but disallow the installation of all other devices, you could enable this setting and the setting for the device IDs.

Device Installation Restrictions exist only in the Computer Configuration node of group policy. They don't exist in the User Configuration node. You can see this in Figure 10-11, where both the User and Computer Configuration nodes are opened to the Driver Installation containers, but only the Computer Configuration node has the Driver Installation Restrictions.

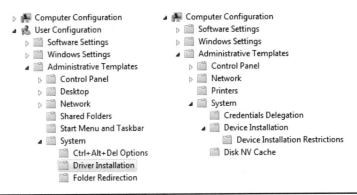

Figure 10-11   Driver Installation nodes in user and computer configuration

Folder Redirection

The Folder Redirection settings allow you to have users' personal folders stored in a different location than their personal computers. This is often done to allow users to have access to their data no matter what computer they log on to, or to store users' data on a central server so that it can be easily backed up.

Many users automatically store their data in their Documents folder on their Windows Vista computer. This folder is accessible from the Start menu, and many applications automatically direct the user to the Documents folder when a file is saved. The actual location of this folder is on the C: drive. For example, if Joe is logged on with an account of Joe, the Documents path is C:\Users\Joe\Documents.

Similarly, Sally could be logged on with an account of Sally and her Documents path would be C:\Users\Sally\Documents.

Other data folders for specific users are Music, Pictures, Favorites, and more. Data stored here is accessible only to the user, though administrators can bypass the restrictions and access the data if necessary.

To modify the location of data in the user's profile, you can access the group policy settings at User Configuration\Windows Settings\Folder Redirection. These settings are shown in Figure 10-12. Note that you can see these settings only by using the GPMC Group Policy editor. These settings aren't available when using the local Group Policy editor.

You can right-click any of the folders in the Group Policy editor and select properties. You can then choose where you want the folder redirected. It's common to create a share on a server and then configure Folder Redirection to access the share.

For example, you could have a server named MCITP1. You could then create a shared folder named Users. This would now be accessible with the UNC path of \\MCITP1 \Users.

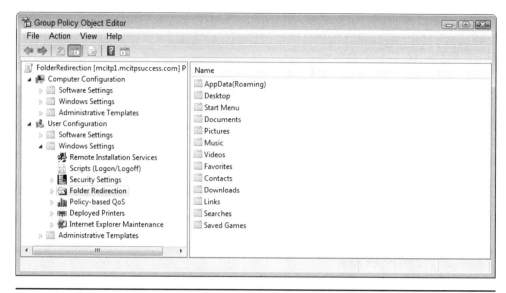

Figure 10-12   Folder Redirection group policy settings

Figure 10-13 shows the properties for the Documents folder. You can have this folder redirected for all users in the scope of the GPO to the \\MCITP1\Users share. Another great feature of redirected folders is that when the user logs on, a folder within the Users share will automatically be created with the correct permissions.

Figure 10-13
Redirecting the
Documents
folder

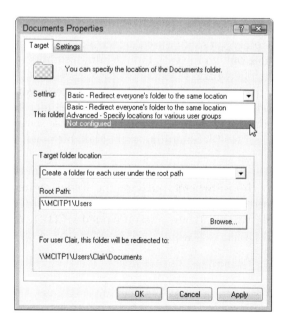

The available choices when redirecting the Documents folder are

- **Basic—Redirect Everyone's Folder To The Same Location**   This will redirect all users folders to the UNC path (as in \\MCITP1\Users), but each user will have his or her own folder within the Users share.

- **Advanced—Specify Locations For Various User Groups**   This setting allows you to have some user groups store their data on one server (based on the UNC path), while other user groups can store their data on another server. This can be useful if a single server can't store all of your users' data.

- **Not Configured**   This is selected when the folders aren't redirected.

Once you have configured the Documents folder, you can easily configure other folders to follow the location of the Documents folder as shown in Figure 10-14. When configured this way, the Pictures folder will be a subfolder of the Documents folder.

Figure 10-14
Having other
folders follow
the Documents
folder

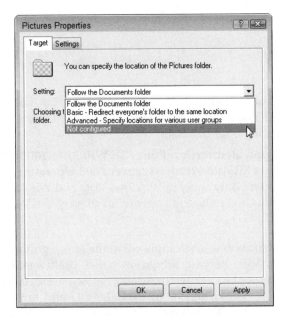

You can select the Follow the Documents folder for the Pictures, Music, and Videos folders.

Redirection Settings

After you configure the target for any folders you've redirected, you can then configure different settings. Figure 10-15 shows the settings for a redirected folder.

- **Grant The User Exclusive Rights To Documents**   This automatically sets the permissions to full control for the user and no one else. However, it is possible for an administrator to gain access to the documents if necessary. This setting is set by default.

Figure 10-15
Configuring
redirection
settings for
the Documents
folder

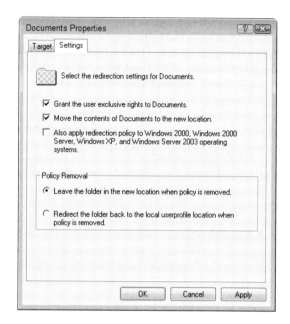

- **Move The Contents Of Documents To The New Location**   This setting causes the folder contents to automatically be moved when the group policy is applied. This setting is set by default.

- **Also Apply Redirection Policy To Windows 2000, Windows 2000 Server, Windows XP, And Windows Server 2003 Operating Systems**   By default, these settings will only apply to Windows Vista and Windows Server 2008, but you can check this box to have it apply to all clients from Windows 2000 to Windows Server 2003.

The following two settings apply when the group policy no longer applies to a user. This could happen because the group policy itself was removed, or because a user account was moved to a different location in Active Directory.

For example, Sally could be in the Sales OU and the Folder Redirection policy is applied to the Sales OU redirecting her Documents folder to the MCITP1\Users share. She transfers to the Marketing department, so her user account is moved to the Marketing OU and the Marketing OU does not have a Folder Redirection policy. What do you want to do with her files?

- **Leave The Folder In The New Location When Policy Is Removed**   The files will stay where they are and remain accessible to the user. This is the default.

- **Redirect The Folder Back To The Local Userprofile Location When Policy Is Removed**   The data is copied back to the C:\Users*Username* location. Careful, though. If the user's hard drive doesn't have enough space, you risk filling up the hard drive and causing significant problems.

Understanding Profiles

A user profile is a set of folders and Registry data used to describe and preserve the user environment from one logon session to another. In Windows Vista, the user's profile is stored in the C:\Users*Username* path by default. This path includes many different folders that are organized to separate user and application data.

In Windows XP and other versions of Windows, profiles existed but were stored separately. First, the following path was used by default: C:\Documents and Settings\ *Username* in Windows XP, but in Windows Vista the path is C:\Users*Username*. Second, the folders available in the profile didn't easily distinguish between user and application data.

Figure 10-16 shows the folders available in Sally's profile folder. The AppData folder is selected, showing the three folders used to hold roaming application data.

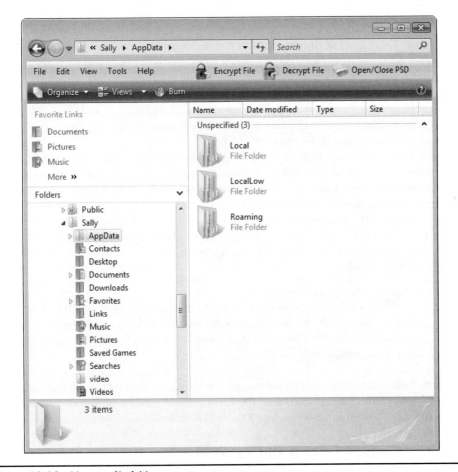

Figure 10-16   User profile folders

You can also see the Public folder right above Sally's folder. The Public folder replaces the All Users folder in Windows XP profiles. If you want to apply profile settings that will apply to all users on a system, you can apply the settings to the Profile folder.

Folder Redirection and Roaming Profiles

It's possible and often beneficial to combine Folder Redirection with Roaming Profiles in Windows Vista.

Roaming Profiles can be used to allow a user's entire profile (all the folders from the C:\Users*Username* path) to be stored on a central server. When the user logs on to any computer in the network, the user's profile is accessed on the central server and then downloaded to the computer.

However, if the user has stored a significant amount of data in her Documents, Music, Pictures, or other folders, it can take a significant amount of time for that data to be downloaded to a computer. If the user is logging in with a slow link (such as a WAN), the amount of time required to download the data can delay a user's logon significantly.

To avoid this problem, Folder Redirection can be combined with Roaming Profiles in Windows Vista. Instead of having all of the user's folders stored as part of the Roaming Profile, some folders (such as the user's Documents, Music, and Pictures folders) can be redirected to another location.

This solution didn't work in Windows XP due to the fact that the profile didn't have a good separation of what was application data and needed to be downloaded, and what was user data and could be left on a server. Because of this, the entire profile was downloaded, including all the application data.

One thing to be aware of with the difference in profiles occurs when you upgrade a Windows XP machine that is using roaming profiles to Windows Vista. Windows Vista can't read roaming user profiles created from Windows XP. This is a problem for upgraded computers and also for users that sometimes log on to Windows XP and other times log on to Windows Vista systems.

The following folders must be redirected to ensure interoperability between Windows Vista and Windows XP: Application Data, Desktop, Documents, Favorites, Music, Pictures, Start Menu, and Videos.

 TIP   To get more detailed information on deploying roaming profiles within a domain, check out the Managing Roaming User Data Deployment Guide in the Windows Vista Technical library. You can access it here: http://go.microsoft.com/fwlink/?Linkid=73760.

All the folders don't have to be redirected. Only folders that have data that you want to share between operating systems, or the folders that had data on Windows XP before it was upgraded to Windows Vista, need to be redirected.

Disabling Local Group Policy Settings

You can use group policy applied through an Active Directory GPO level to turn off local group policy settings. When group policy is applied, the local group policy is applied and then site-, domain-, and OU-level GPOs are applied.

You may remember that if there are any conflicts between GPOs, then the last GPO applied takes precedence. Since the local group policy is applied first, any conflicts will be overwritten by Active Directory GPOs.

However, if there aren't any conflicts, then the local policy will apply. If you want to have the local policy completely ignored, you can enable Turn Off Local Group Policy Objects Processing. Figure 10-17 shows the group policy setting.

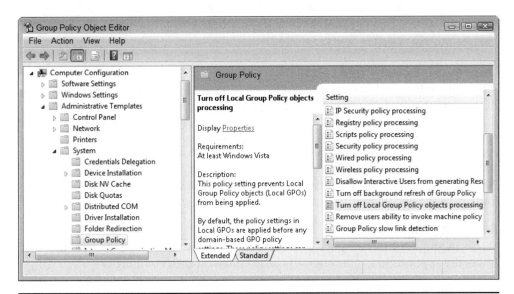

Figure 10-17 Turn Off Local Group Policy Objects Processing

You can find this setting in the following path: Computer Configuration\Administrative Templates\System\Group Policy.

This setting will prevent all settings in the local Group Policy Object from being applied. The local group policy settings can still be configured and manipulated, but they will be meaningless.

Deploying Applications

Group policy can be used to deploy applications to both users and computers within a domain. You can only deploy applications in a GPO deployed with Active Directory, not with the local group policy.

You deploy applications in the Software settings folder. When deploying an application, you either assign it or publish it.

- **Assigning applications**   Applications can be assigned to either users or computers.

- **Publishing applications**   Applications can only be published to users (not to computers).

To deploy applications with group policy, follow these overall steps:

1. Determine if you want to assign or publish it.

2. Open the Software Settings folder in the appropriate node (Computer or User Configuration).

3. Right-click Software Installation and select New | Package.

4. Browse to an installation file (with an .msi extension), select it, and click Open. This should be located on a server share located in your network.

5. Select Published or Assigned.

Document Extension Activation

When an application is assigned or published to a user, it isn't installed by default. One of the ways that it can be installed is through document extension activation.

As an example, imagine that Microsoft Excel 2007 was published or assigned to your computer using the defaults. You could have it installed on your computer, but it hasn't been installed yet. Now, someone sends you a file with an .xlsx extension.

When you double-click the file, your system determines that this is a Microsoft Excel 2007 document and it can be installed. Your system then installs Microsoft Excel 2007 and opens the document.

Assigning Applications

When an application is assigned to a computer, it is installed on the next reboot. This forces the application to automatically be installed on each computer.

However, when you assign an application to a user, it isn't automatically installed. Instead, it is advertised on the Start menu. The first time the user selects the application from the Start menu, it is installed.

You can change default behavior by selecting the Install This Application at Logon setting as shown in Figure 10-18. As an example, you may have mobile users that are

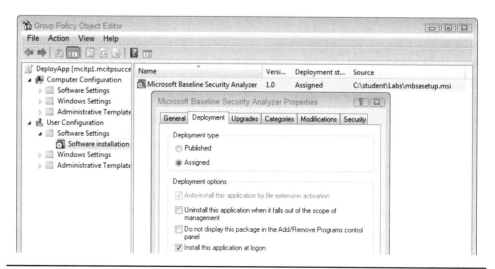

Figure 10-18 Selecting Install This Application at Logon

frequently disconnected from the network. With this set, the first time they are authenticated on the domain, the application will be installed.

All of the deployment options available on this page are

- **Uninstall This Application When It Falls Out Of The Scope Of Management** If the GPO is deleted, or the user or computer is moved to a different OU where the GPO isn't applied, then the application will be uninstalled.

- **Do Not Display This Package In The Add/Remove Programs Control Panel** Published applications can be installed via Add/Remove Programs by default. Selecting this check box changes the behavior.

- **Install This Application At Logon** By default, an assigned application won't be installed until launched via the Start menu or document extension activation, but this check box changes the behavior.

 EXAM TIP Select the check box for Install This Application at Logon for applications that are assigned to users, and that you want to have installed as soon as possible.

Publishing Applications

When an application is published to a user, it is available to be installed from the Control Panel | Programs | Programs and Features | Install a program from the Network link in Windows Vista.

If the user knows to go to the Control Panel to install the program, he can do so. Having it here instead of the Start menu can prevent a user from accidentally installing a program he really doesn't need.

Published applications will also be installed via document activation.

Upgrading Applications

If an application was deployed with group policy, you can also deploy upgrades to the application. For example, you may have deployed version 1 of an application, and then version 2 is released.

Upgrades can be deployed as optional upgrades or mandatory upgrades.

 EXAM TIP If you want users to be able to choose whether or not to upgrade the application, deploy the upgrade as an optional upgrade. If you want to force the upgrade, use a mandatory upgrade.

- **Optional Upgrade** Users will be able to choose whether they want to upgrade or not. This is useful if there are incompatibility issues between the versions.

- **Mandatory Upgrade** Any user with the previous version will automatically be upgraded to the new version. The user doesn't have any choice.

When an upgrade is applied via a GPO, the original application is automatically deinstalled when the newer version is installed. You don't have to take extra steps to desinstall the original application.

Customizing Applications

Some applications can be customized so that different users receive different elements of the same application.

As an example, you may work in an international company where people communicate in several different languages. Some users may need Word installed with English spelling and grammar checkers, but other users may need Word installed with Spanish, French, Chinese, or other languages. This can be done by applying transform files.

A transform file (.mst) can be applied before an application is deployed, and it transforms how it is deployed. Many vendors (Microsoft included) include prebuilt transform files that can be used or modified to suit your needs.

Software Restriction

Software restriction policies can be enabled on a computer to specifically control which applications can run on a system. You can restrict specific applications from running while allowing all other applications to run, or restrict all applications except specifically what you want to allow.

Sometimes, you may want to specifically stop users from running a specific application that may be causing problems on the network. For example, viruses may have been introduced by users using Instant Messenger programs even after a corporate policy was released saying users should not use these programs. By creating a software restriction policy, you can allow anything to run except these Instant Messenger programs.

Other times, you may want to lock down a computer such as one in a library or in a public kiosk. You can use software restrictions to specify which application or applications can be run on the computer, blocking all other applications.

When restricting software, you can restrict by four possible rules.

- **Path rule**   The path rule identifies the software based on its name and path (such as c:\data\app.exe).

- **Hash rule**   The hash rule uses a hash function to uniquely identify the application. Use of a hash rule prevents a user from moving the application to a different location to allow it to run.

- **Certificate rule**   Certificates can be used to uniquely identify an application. When a certificate is created, you can use a certificate rule to allow or disallow the program.

- **Network zone rule**   The network zone rule refers to the zones in Internet Explorer: Internet, local computer, local intranet, restricted sites, and trusted sites. You can use this rule to allow (or disallow) programs to run in certain zones.

In Exercise 10.2, you will create a software restriction policy to prevent a specific application from running on your system.

Exercise 10.2: Implementing a Software Restriction Policy

1. To prepare for this exercise, create a dummy file named MCITPStudyTools.exe.

   A. Launch Windows Explorer by pressing the CTRL-E keys.

   B. Browse to the root of C:.

   C. Right-click and select New | Text Document. Double-click the document to open it.

   D. Click File | Save As. In the Save As dialog box, enter MCITPStudyTools.exe and click Save. Close Notepad.

 NOTE Saving the file with an .exe extension makes it appear as an executable. Of course, you didn't just create an application, but it looks like it to the system.

2. Click Start, and enter **MMC** in the Start Search dialog box. If the User Account Control dialog box appears, click Continue.

3. Click File | Add/Remove Snap-in. On the Add/Remove Snap-in page, select Group Policy Object Editor and click Add.

4. On the Welcome to the Group Policy Wizard page, ensure Local Computer is entered in the Group Policy Object text box, and click Finish. Click OK.

5. Browse to the Computer Configuration\Windows Settings\Security Settings\ Software Restriction Policies folder.

6. Right-click the Software Restriction Policies folder and select New Software Restriction Policy.

7. Right-click the Additional Rules folder and select New Path Rule.

8. On the New Path Rule page, browse to the C:\MCITPStudyTools.exe file you created earlier. Change the Security Level to Disallowed. Your display will look similar to Figure 10-19. Click OK.

9. Select Security Levels. Notice that there are three security levels available and the Unrestricted level has a check box next to it. This setting will allow all software applications to run except those with a security rule (such as the one you just created).

 CAUTION When doing the next step (setting Disallowed as the default policy), do not click Yes when you receive the warning. The purpose of the step is to see the warning.

10. Right-click Disallowed and select Set As Default. Read the warning and click No. If you do not click No for this step, all programs except the MCITPStudyTools program will be prevented from running.

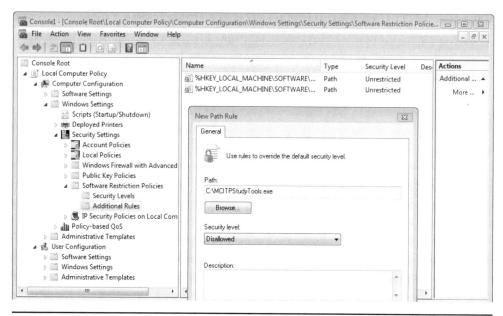

Figure 10-19   Configuring a software restriction policy

TIP   If you'd like to read more about software restriction policies, check out Microsoft's page here: http://technet.microsoft.com/en-us/windowsvista/aa940985.aspx

Implementing Security with IPsec

Internet Protocol Security (IPsec) is commonly used to provide security within a network. Often, you need to be able to ensure that if anyone intercepts data that is sent across the network, the data is unreadable. Additionally, you may want to ensure that when two clients communicate, they are able to authenticate with each to prove who they are. IPsec does both.

- **Encryption**   IPsec uses Encapsulating Security Payload (ESP) to encrypt data sent across the network. If anyone intercepts the packets, they won't be able to decrypt the data to read it without using some very sophisticated and expensive techniques.

- **Authentication**   IPsec uses Authentication Headers (AH) to allow mutual authentication between clients. IPsec can be used with AH alone. When encryption is used, AH is also used.

Three default policies are available for IPsec. You can use them to configure how IPsec will be configured for different purposes.

Figure 10-20 shows group policy with these three default IPsec polices. An important part of understanding how these policies work is based on understanding the settings of allowing communications with other computers that do not support IPsec. In the figure, the Request Security policy has been opened to where this setting is selected.

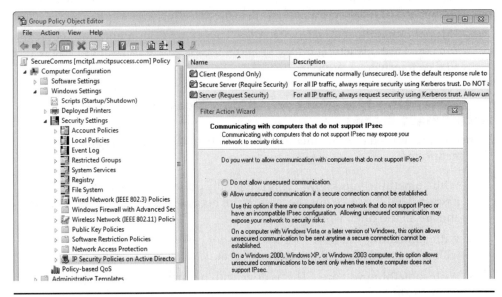

Figure 10-20   IPsec policies

For example, imagine you have some financial servers that you want to ensure are protected with IPsec, and some other file servers that you'd prefer to have protected with IPsec but for which protection isn't critical. Here are the three default policies with details on how you could apply them to meet the needs of this scenario:

- **Client (Respond Only)**   This policy allows a client to negotiate an IPsec secure session, but it will never initiate an IPsec session. You could apply this policy to all computers in your domain so that they can negotiate IPsec sessions with the financial servers and the file servers.

  This policy has the setting Allow Unsecured Communication If a Secure Connection Cannot Be Established selected.

- **Server (Request Security)**   This policy always tries to negotiate an IPsec session with clients. When the client can negotiate, an IPsec session is established and the session is protected. When the client can't negotiate an IPsec session, data is still transferred, but in an unencrypted format.

  This policy has the setting Allow Unsecured Communication If a Secure Connection Cannot Be Established selected.

You could apply this to your file servers. For all clients that communicate with IPsec, the data would be encrypted. For older clients (such as clients that don't have a Client (Respond Only) policy applied, or NT 4.0 clients), an IPsec session couldn't be established, but data would still be transferred.

- **Secure Server (Require Security)**   This policy always tries to negotiate an IPsec session and, if unsuccessful, refuses the connection.

  This policy has the setting Do Not Allow Unsecured Communication selected. You could use this setting for the financial servers where you want to ensure that all data transfers are protected.

Implementing Multifactor Authentication with Smart Cards

Authentication is used to prove identity. There are basically three ways that identity can be authenticated:

- **With something you know**   This is typically done with a user name and password. Of the three it is the least secure because passwords can be cracked and are all too often written down.

- **With something you have**   This is often done with some type of smart card with an embedded certificate to prove identity.

- **With something you are**   This is done with biometrics such as fingerprints or retinal scans.

Kerberos is the network authentication protocol used to authenticate users and computers on a Windows domain (including Windows 2000, 2003, and 2008). It can be used with user names and passwords, smart cards and tokens, and biometrics.

Multifactor Authentication

Multifactor authentication is done by combining at least two of the three methods. It's most commonly done by issuing users smart cards (which they must have), and personal identification numbers or PINs (which they must know).

Another method of multifactor authentication is with tokens. SecureID is a popular company that sells these. Users have a small electronic device with an LED display that shows several numbers. These numbers usually change every 60 seconds but are synchronized with a server. In other words, the server always knows what is displayed on the token.

The user also has a PIN. When he or she needs to authenticate, the user enters a combination of the PIN and the number displayed on the token.

Requiring Smart Cards with Group Policy

Group policy can be used to require users to authenticate using smart cards. Figure 10-21 shows the two settings related to smart cards. You can locate these settings in the Computer Configuration\Windows Settings\Security Settings\Local Policies\Security Options folder.

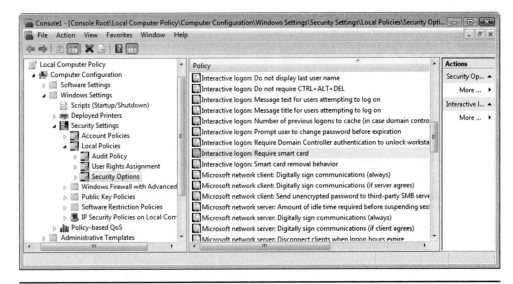

Figure 10-21 Smart card group policy settings

 EXAM TIP Group policy can be used to require users to log on with smart cards. If multifactor authentication is required within a domain, the use of a smart card and a PIN is the most common method.

The two settings are

- **Interactive Logon: Require Smart Card** When this setting is enabled, users can only log on with a Smart Card.

- **Interactive Logon: Smart Card Removal Behavior** If a user is logged on with a smart card and removes the smart card, you can cause one of the following actions to take place:

  - No action
  - Lock Workstation
  - Force Logoff
  - Disconnect if a Remote Terminal Services Session

Group Policy Tools

When managing and troubleshooting group policy, there are a few tools that can help you. Obviously, the local Group Policy editor (for the local system), and the Group Policy Management Console (GPMC) covered in the preceding section are very important. However, you have a few other tools you'll find valuable. These include

- GPUpdate
- GPResult
- RSoP

GPUpdate

GPUpdate is a command-line tool that will cause group policy to be immediately applied to your system. As a reminder, group policy is applied to a computer when the computer starts up, and it is applied to a user when the user logs on.

 EXAM TIP Use the GPUpdate command-line tool to force GPOs to be immediately reapplied to your system.

Additionally, group policy is periodically refreshed typically every 90 minutes. In a domain, the operating system will query Active Directory during this refresh cycle to determine if group policy has changed for the user or computer. If group policy has changed, the new settings will be downloaded and applied.

In a workgroup, the settings are reapplied similarly. However, instead of querying Active Directory, the local group policy settings are read and reapplied.

Group policy is also refreshed once every 16 hours by default. The group policy settings are reapplied whether they've changed or not.

Imagine you've made some changes to group policy and you want them to apply to a computer you're testing. Without GPUpdate, you'd have to wait as long as 90 minutes. That could make for some long days.

Instead, you could go to the computer you're testing, launch the command line, and enter **gpupdate /force**.

GPUpdate with the /force switch will cause group policy to be updated similar the 16 hour refresh cycle.

GPResult

GPResult is a command-line tool that will list all the settings that apply to the computer you've logged on to, with the user account you're logged on with. The resulting report is listed in the command window.

If you want to redirect the output to a file, you can use the greater-than character (>) to redirect it. For example, you can use the following command to redirect the output to a file named gpr.txt in the root of C:.

```
Gpresult > c:\gpr.txt
```

GPResult has many switches you can use to modify the output, but my favorite is the /z switch. I refer to it as the *zuper* verbose switch which certainly helps me remember it. When I'm trying to understand what settings are applied, I use the following commands:

```
Gpresult /z > c:\gpr.txt
Notepad c:\gpr.txt
```

These commands will write all the group policy settings to a text file and then open it so that you can read through it. It provides some detailed information on exactly which settings are being applied.

RSoP

The Resultant Set of Policy (RSoP) console is another program that you can use to view what group policy settings are being applied. This is a snap-in that you can add to the Microsoft Management Console (MMC).

RSoP supports two modes:

- **Logging mode**   The Logging mode shows the settings that apply to a specific user on a specific computer.

- **Planning mode**   Planning mode is used to simulate a policy if you plan to make changes.

In Exercise 10.3, you will create an MMC console to access the RSoP snap-in and view the local group policy settings. This exercise assumes you have completed Exercise 10.2 and added a software restriction rule.

Exercise 10.3: Using RSoP

1. Click Start, and enter **MMC** in the Start Search dialog box. If the User Account Control dialog box appears, click Continue.

2. Select the File drop-down menu and click Add/Remove Snap-in.

3. On the Add or Remove Snap-ins page, select Resultant Set of Policy and click Add. Your display will look similar to Figure 10-22. Click OK.

4. Right-click Resultant Set of Policy and select Generate RSoP Data.

5. On the Resultant Set of Policy Wizard Welcome page, review the information and click Next.

6. On the Mode Selection page, ensure Logging Mode is selected and click Next.

7. Ensure that This Computer is selected on the Computer Selection page. You can also browse to other computers. Click Next.

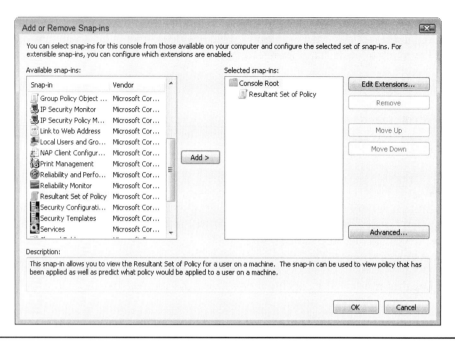

Figure 10-22 Adding the Resultant Set of Policy snap-in

8. The User Selection page allows you to pick which user settings to display. This page only shows users that have actually logged on to the computer you selected in the preceding step. Ensure Current User (the user you are logged on with) is selected and click Next.

9. Review the information on the Summary of Selections page and click Next.

10. On the Completing the Wizard page, click Finish.

11. Back in the MMC console, double-click the report that was just generated. Double-click the Computer Configuration and User Configuration nodes to open them up. You can browse to any settings to determine what is actually being applied.

12. Browse to the Computer Configuration\Windows Settings\Security Settings\ Software Restriction Policies\Security Levels. Your display will look similar to Figure 10-23.

    You can see that the MCITPStudyTools.exe file is being prevented from running with a software restriction rule.

13. Close all open files.

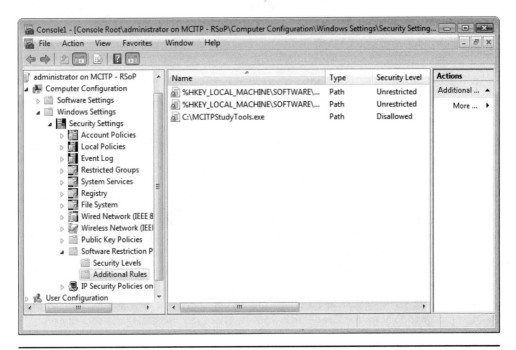

Figure 10-23 Viewing applied group policy in RSoP

Security Configuration and Analysis

The Security Configuration and Analysis snap-in is an advanced tool that you can use to analyze and configure computer security. As a common example, you may be considering applying a more secure security template and be curious what the differences are compared to the current settings.

You can import the security template into Security Configuration and Analysis and run the analysis. The resulting report identifies what is different in a graphical report.

As a reminder, settings in the local computer security policy are part of the overall local group policy. Security Configuration and Analysis doesn't look at all at group policy, but instead only the Security section.

Comparing Policies

Security policy is frequently implemented with the use of templates. You can easily create and modify templates within the Security Configuration and Analysis tool. Once you have a template, you can then compare it to the local computer's settings.

In Exercise 10.4, you will create an MMC console to access the Security Configuration and Analysis and Security Templates snap-ins. You will then create and modify a template and compare your system settings to the template.

Exercise 10.4: Using Security Configuration and Analysis

1. Click Start, and enter **MMC** in the Start Search dialog box. If the User Account Control dialog box appears, click Continue.

2. Select File | Add/Remove Snap-in.

3. Add the Security Configuration and Analysis snap-in and the Security Templates snap-in. Click OK.

4. Browse to the folder under the Security Templates section. It's currently empty. Right-click the folder and select New Template.

5. Name the template **Ch10Exercise** and click OK.

6. Select your template and browse to the Local Policies\Security Options container.

7. Double-click the User Account Control: Behavior of the Elevation Prompt for Administrators in Admin Approval Mode. Select the Define This Policy Setting in the Template check box. Select the Prompt for Credentials choice from the drop-down box. Click OK.

TIP The default selection for this setting is Prompt for Consent. By changing it to Prompt for Credentials, you are effectively increasing the security on your system.

---

8. Right-click Ch10Exercise and select Save. At this point, you have created a template and modified it but it isn't being applied anywhere.

9. Select the Security Configuration and Analysis snap-in. Right-click the snap-in and select Open Database. Type in **Ch10Ex** as the database name. Notice that it is being stored in your ...\Documents\Security\Database folder. Click Open.

10. On the Import Template page, your Ch10Exercise template will be showing. Select it and click Open.

11. Right-click the Security Configuration and Analysis snap-in and select Analyze Computer Now.

12. In the Error Log File Path dialog box, accept the default path and click OK.

13. After a moment the analysis will be complete. Browse to the Local Policies\ Security Options container. Your display will look similar to Figure 10-24. Notice that the Database setting is set to Prompt for Credentials. This is what you set in your template. Since the computer setting is set to Prompt for Consent, there is a conflict and you have a red circle with a white X alerting you to the conflict.

NOTE If the setting isn't modified in the template, Security Configuration and Analysis ignores it and lists it as Not Analyzed.

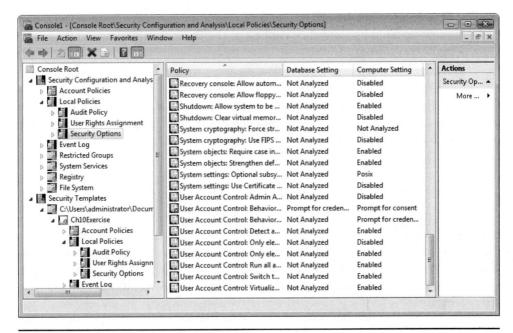

Figure 10-24 Conflict showing in the analysis

Using Secedit

`Secedit` is a command-line tool that can be used similarly to Security Configuration and Analysis. The following high-level steps show you how you can analyze a security template against a computer's settings. This is similar to what you did in Exercise 10.4, but `Secedit` provides different results.

1. Open a command prompt clicking Start and entering **cmd** in the Start Search box. The command prompt will open in your Documents folder, unless you have configured it differently.

2. Change the directory to the ...\Documents\Security\Database folder with the following command:

   ```
   Cd Security\Database
   ```

3. Enter the following command to analyze your database and store the data in a log file named mylog.log:

   ```
   secedit /analyze /db ch10ex.sdb /log mylog.log
   ```

4. Note that this command will only work if you created the ch10ex.sdb database in Exercise 10.4. The log file will be created in the same folder you execute the command in, but you can specify a different path if desired.

5. Enter the following command to open your log file.

   ```
   notepad mylog.log
   ```

6. Within Notepad, press the CTRL-F keys to open the Find menu. Enter **mismatch** in the Find What box and click Find Next. The file will scroll down to the only setting you changed:

```
Mismatch        machine\software\microsoft\windows\currentversion\
policies\system\consentpromptbehavioradmin.
```

7. Note that the Security Options are actually configured by modifying Registry entries, so this is a Registry key. It may take a little time to figure out exactly what was changed, but the clear result is that you know something was changed.

8. Close all windows.

The great strength of any command-line tool is that you're able to script it. In other words, the same commands you enter at the command line, you could instead save in a Notepad text file. Then, instead of saving the file with a .txt file extension, you save it with a .bat extension.

The .bat extension identifies the file as a batch file that can be executed. Taking this a step further, any file that can be executed can be scheduled. The Task Scheduler is covered in Chapter 11, but in short you can use the Task Scheduler to run a program on a repeating basis.

As an example, imagine that a security template has been applied to a Windows Vista computer. You know that the template is applied at this moment in time. However, it's certainly possible for someone to modify the security settings of the computer after the template has been applied. This modification could effectively weaken security.

If you created a batch file and scheduled it to run every Sunday night, you could have the file available to you to do a quick search on Monday morning to see if something has changed. If you want to get fancy, you could also write a script that would search the file for the word "mismatch" and if found send you a notification.

Using Certificates

Certificates are often used with computers to provide both encryption and authentication. A certificate is an electronic file with information that provides the identity of the entity holding the certificate and often holds a key that can be used to encrypt data.

Using a Certificate with Internet Explorer

As a common example, each time you use Internet Explorer in an HTTPS session, a certificate is used. For example, when you purchase something online, an HTTPS session is typically created when you start to check out. HTTPS uses Secure Sockets Layer (SSL) to encrypt the session.

When the session is created, the e-commerce site sends you a certificate. That certificate does two things: it proves the identity of the site, and it also provides the site's public key, which is used to encrypt the session.

Your computer doesn't trust this certificate automatically, but instead it verifies that the certificate was issued from a Certification Authority that your computer trusts.

This is similar to how people trust your driver's license as proof of your identity because it was issued by a trusted authority: the Department of Motor Vehicles (DMV).

Figure 10-25 shows the trusted root certification authority store on my computer. You can access this in Internet Explore by clicking Tools | Options. On the Internet Options page, select the Content tab and then click the Certificates button. Select the Trusted Root Certification Authorities tab.

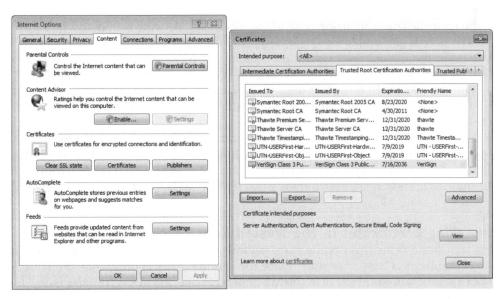

Figure 10-25 Trusted Root Certification Authorities

The Trusted Root Certification Authorities tab shows all of the Certification Authorities (CAs) that your computer trusts. Each of these certificates has been issued by the respective CA. These certificates are loaded into Internet Explorer by Microsoft based on some type of agreement between the CA and Microsoft.

These CA certificates are similar to the DMV. They issue certificates just as the DMV issues licenses. Just as you trust the DMV, your computer trusts the CAs in the Trusted Certification Authority. Since the CA is trusted, any certificates issued by the CA are trusted.

It is very valuable to a CA to have their certificate published in the Trusted Root Certification Authority. If I wanted to stand up my own CA and name it something like Darril's Cheap Certificates, it wouldn't be worth much, since it isn't in the Trusted Root Certification Authority store. If an e-commerce site purchased a certificate from me, when an HTTPS session was started, the user would see a warning letting him know that the certificate is not trusted.

Using Certificates Issued by Your Company

Companies often create their own Certification Authority (CA) to issue certificates for internal uses. This is often cheaper than purchasing a certificate from an external CA that is already in the Trusted Root Certification Authority.

As an example, Outlook Web Access (OWA) is often enabled with Microsoft Exchange and Internet Information Services (IIS). OWA allows employees to access their e-mail using Internet Explorer and an Internet connection anytime they're away from the company's location.

OWA requires a secure connection using HTTPS and SSL, and this requires a certificate. The company creates a CA and issues a certificate to the IIS server hosting the OWA web site.

Imagine the company name is MCITPSuccess. The CA name would also be named MCITPSuccess, and employee's computers wouldn't have a certificate named MCITP-Success in the Trusted Root Certification Authority. When an employee connected to the OWA web site, they would receive an error saying the certificate is not trusted.

While an untrusted certificate used for an e-commerce site is unacceptable, it may be acceptable for a private company. Administrators could simply tell employees, this error is normal and they can ignore it.

However, telling users to ignore security warnings presents its own set of risks. Users may interpret this as a requirement to make judgment calls on what is an acceptable security risk and what isn't an acceptable security risk. Regular users rarely have all the IT knowledge and experience to know when it's okay to ignore a security warning and when it's a valid risk.

Installing Certificates in the Trusted Root Certification Authority

The certificate from the Certification Authority can be imported into the Trusted Root Certification Authority store. Once the certificate is imported into the Trusted Root Certification Authority, it is trusted. This certificate and any certificates issued by this CA are automatically trusted.

 EXAM TIP You can have users import certificates issued by an internal CA to the Trusted Root Certification Authority on their computers. Users must be logged on with administrator credentials to import certificates into this store. Once the certificate is imported, any certificates issued by the CA will automatically be trusted and won't generate security warnings.

Certificates can be imported into the Trusted Root Certification Authority by clicking the Import button from the Certificates page.

The Import button is found in Internet Explorer by accessing the Internet Options page, selecting the Content tab, clicking the Certificates button, and then selecting the Trusted Root Certification Authority tab. After clicking the Import button, the Certificate Import Wizard will guide the user through installing the certificate.

Of course, the users need the certificate from the internal CA. You can e-mail this certificate to them, have it copied to their systems while they are connected internally, or provide access to the certificate via a web site. Once the users have the certificate, it's a simple matter to import it as long as they are logged on with administrator credentials.

Using Certificates with EFS

New Technology File System is commonly known as NTFS, and you can encrypt files with NTFS. NTFS uses the Encrypting File System (EFS) to encrypt files and folders on your hard disk.

On the surface EFS works the same way in any environment. Users can access the properties of a file or folder, access the advanced attributes, and select Encrypt Contents to Secure Data. Figure 10-26 shows a folder being configured with EFS.

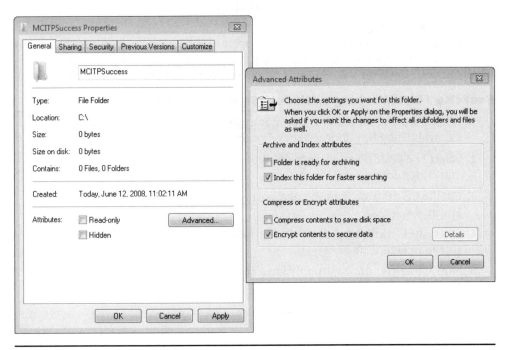

Figure 10-26   Encrypting a folder

EFS requires a certificate to encrypt the data. Users don't have an EFS certificate until they first encrypt a file or folder. The first time the user encrypts the certificate, a certificate is issued. However, the certificate is issued differently in a domain than it is in a workgroup.

EFS in a Domain

Certificates are issued from Active Directory to a domain user account. In other words, the first time a user encrypts a file, Active Directory is queried and an EFS certificate is issued.

Active Directory provides extra protections in a domain. Kerberos is the authentication protocol, and it allows different methods of authentication such as smart cards. Additionally, if a user encrypted files and then left the company, an administrator can access the encrypted files using a designated recovery agent.

EFS in a Workgroup

A workgroup doesn't have Active Directory, so the only way an EFS certificate can be issued is by the local system. A certificate issued to an entity by the same entity is referred to as a self-signed certificate. In other words, if your computer issues a certificate to itself, the certificate is signed by the computer (self-signed).

While a self-signed certificate works well on a single system, if you ever copy encrypted files to another system and want to access them, you won't be able to if your certificate is still on the original system. What you can do is export the certificate from the original system and then import it onto the target system.

Self-signed certificates are stored in the Personal Certificate Store. In Exercise 10.5, you will examine your Personal Certificate Store, create a certificate by encrypting a file, export the certificate, and then simulate importing it onto a different computer. This exercise should be performed on a workgroup computer (not a computer joined to a domain).

Exercise 10.5: Working with Self-Signed Certificates

1. Click Start, and enter **MMC** in the Start Search dialog box. If the User Account Control dialog box appears, click Continue.

2. Select File | Add/Remove Snap-in. Browse to the Certificates snap-in, select it, and click Add.

3. On the Certificates Snap-in page, ensure My User Account is selected and click Finish. Click OK.

4. Open the Certificates snap-in and browse the Personal\Certificates folder as shown in Figure 10-27.

5. Notice that you don't currently have an EFS certificate issued to you. Leave this MMC open.

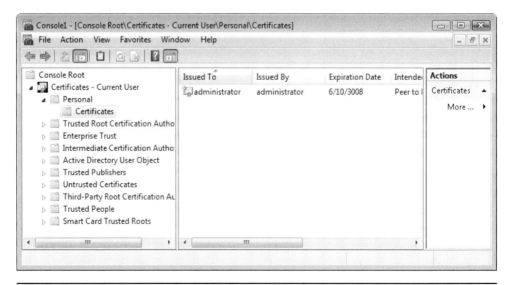

Figure 10-27 Personal Certificates store

NOTE If you do have an EFS certificate, it indicates that you have already encrypted data on your system. You can still walk through this exercise.

6. Encrypt data using Windows Explorer to create an EFS certificate with the following steps:

   a. Launch Windows Explorer by pressing the CTRL-E keys.

   b. Browse to the root of C:. Right-click in the Details pane and select New | Folder. Name the folder **MCITPSuccess**.

   c. Right-click the folder and select Properties.

   d. On the General tab, click Advanced.

   e. On the Advanced Attributes page, select Encrypt Contents To Secure Data and click OK. Click OK.

   f. On the Confirm Attribute Changes page, accept the default and click OK. The folder will be encrypted. Note that it has changed color to green to indicate it is encrypted.

7. Return to the Certificates snap-in. Right-click the Personal\Certificates node and select Refresh. Your EFS certificate will appear as shown in Figure 10-28.

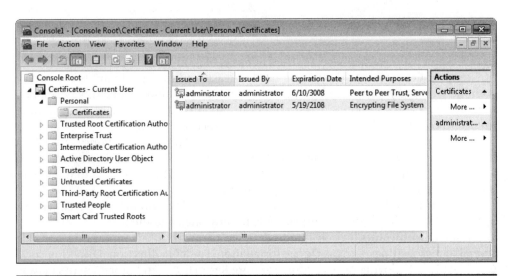

Figure 10-28 Encrypting File System certificate

8. You can use this certificate on another system by exporting it. Right-click the certificate and select All Tasks | Export.

9. On the Welcome to the Certificate Export Wizard page, click Next.

10. On the Export Private Key page, select Yes, Export the Private Key. Click Next.

11. On the Export File Format page, select Export All Extended Properties and click Next.

12. On the Password page, enter a password such as P@ssw0rd in the Password and confirm text boxes. Click Next.

 CAUTION If you are encrypting live data with the certificate, do not use the password of P@ssword. Use a secure password that only you know.

---

13. On the File to Export page, enter **MyEFSCert** as the filename. Click Browse and note where the file is being stored. You can change the default location if desired. Click Next.

14. On the Completing the Certificate Export Wizard page, click Finish.

15. On the Export Was Successful page, click OK.

16. Back in the Certificates console, notice that the certificate is not deleted from your system. You can now copy this certificate to another system and import it into the Personal Certificate store by right-clicking Certificates, selecting All Tasks, and selecting Import.

Chapter Review

In this chapter you learned several different facets of group policy and certificates.

Group policy within a domain is used to easily administer many users and/or computers. You can configure a group policy setting once, and it can easily be applied to many users and computers. Group policy doesn't care if you have 50, 500, or more users and computers in your network. You set it once and it applies.

If you want the setting to apply to all users in the domain, a Group Policy Object can be linked to the domain. If you instead want it to apply to a specific set of users (such as everyone in the Sales department), you can apply the GPO to an OU that includes the users and computers in the Sales department.

You can also configure local group policy for any single computer. However, settings applied using the local policy settings apply to only one computer.

Group policy includes literally hundreds of settings. You had an opportunity to touch several of these settings, such as Device Installation, Folder Redirection, Disabling Local Group Policy, Deploying Applications, Software Restrictions, and more. There's no way to know everything about group policy, but you did have an opportunity to try some of the settings.

Some of the tools used to manage group policy include GPUpdate, GPResult, Resultant Set of Policy (RSoP), Security Configuration and Analysis, and Secedit. You'll need to know what tools are available, and how to use them when you're using group policy on your network.

Last, you learned a little about certificates. Certificates are issued by Certification Authorities, and if your system trusts the root Certification Authority (CA), then your system trusts certificates issued by the CA. In addition to learning how certificates are used on the Internet, you had an opportunity to learn about certificates used internally on a network, and on a single computer.

Additional Study

Self Study Exercises
Use these additional exercises to challenge yourself.

- As an administrator, create policies that will apply to a standard user account. Create a standard user account and log on with this account to see how the policies apply to a standard user. Configure Device Installation Restrictions to apply to the standard user, but not to the administrator.

- Run the command line command that will cause group policy to immediately be refreshed.

- Run the command line command that will show you what group policy settings are being applied to your system.

- Create an MMC and create an RSoP for your computer with the standard user account logged on.

Summary of What You Need to Know

70-620
Objectives for the 70-620 exam were not included in this chapter.

70-622
This entire chapter is required knowledge for the 70-622 exam. Pay particular attention to the following topics:

- **Group policy** You should understand how group policy is applied in a domain. For example, a GPO linked to an OU applies to all the users and computers in that OU, but not other OUs (unless they are children). You should understand the default behavior of how GPOs are applied, and how you can modify the default behavior with loopback processing.

- **Group policy management tools** You should be familiar with both the Group Policy Management Console and the local Group Policy editor.

- **Group policy settings** You should be familiar with some group policy settings. Don't expect to be an expert and know all the settings, but you should be familiar with the settings covered in this chapter.

- **Group policy tools** You should be familiar with the capabilities and purposes of the following tools: GPUpdate, GPResult, RSoP, Security Configuration and Analysis, and Secedit.

- **Certificates**   You should know what certificates are used for and how the Trusted Root Certification Authority is used. You should be familiar with the capability to import and export certificates.

70-623

Objectives for the 70-623 exam were not included in this chapter.

Questions

70-622

1. You are a support technician in a Windows domain environment. Users have installed some gadgets in the Windows Sidebar that aren't fully tested and considered safe. Instead of taking on the responsibility of testing Sidebar gadgets, it's been decided to disable the sidebar. How can this be done?

   A. Modify the Windows Sidebar policy settings in group policy.

   B. Access the Control Panel and uninstall the Windows Sidebar.

   C. Reinstall Windows Vista and disable the Windows Sidebar during the installation.

   D. Run the Sideshow installation program and check the box to Use Windows Sideshow Instead of Windows Sidebar.

2. You have access to the local group policy settings. You want to ensure users aren't able to install or update any devices unless they have administrator credentials. You need to ensure the settings are applied immediately. What should you do? Choose all that apply.

   A. Modify group policy settings for Device Installation Restrictions for users.

   B. Modify group policy settings for Device Installation Restrictions for computers.

   C. Run `GPUpdate /Force`.

   D. Run `GPResult`.

3. You want to prevent users from installing any devices on their computers. However, you want administrators to be allowed to install the devices. What policy settings would you choose? Choose all that apply.

   A. Prevent Installation of Devices Not Described by Other Policy Settings

   B. Allow Installation of Devices That Match Any of These Device IDs.

   C. Prevent Installation of Devices That Match Any of These Device IDs.

   D. Allow Administrators to Override Device Installation Restriction Policies.

4. Several users were upgraded from Windows XP to Windows Vista in your domain. They were using roaming profiles before being upgraded, but the roaming profiles no longer work. What should be done?

   A. Disable roaming user profiles. Run `GPUpdate /force` and re-enable roaming user profiles.

   B. Implement mandatory user profiles.

C. Disable the mandatory user profile group policy setting.

D. Configure Folder Redirection to redirect specific folders in the profile.

5. You are using group policy to redirect the Documents folder for all users in the domain to the MCITP1\Users share. You realize that the Pictures folder isn't being redirected, but it needs to be. What is the easiest way to accomplish this?

A. Create a new GPO and redirect the Pictures folder to the MCITP1\Users share.

B. Create a new folder in the Documents folder on the server for the users and direct them to store their pictures there.

C. Modify the existing GPO and have the Pictures folder follow the Documents folder.

D. Have users move the Pictures folder within the Documents folder on their Windows Vista systems.

6. You are a Windows Vista desktop administrator in a network using an Active Directory domain. You've found that several users have configured local group policy settings that are causing some problems with some applications. You want to ensure these settings are not applied to any of the computers. What should you do?

A. Apply a domain-level GPO and run `GPUpdate`.

B. Apply an OU-level GPO and run `GPUpdate /force`.

C. Use the Security Configuration and Analysis tool to identify the settings and then use GPMC to remove them.

D. Run `Secedit` on each of the computers.

E. Set the Turn Off Local Group Policy Objects Processing setting.

7. An application named MCITPStudyTools has been assigned to users in your domain using group policy. However, several mobile users tried to launch it while on the road and it failed to install. How can you ensure that assigned applications will work for these users in the future?

A. Publish the application to the users.

B. Publish the application to the computers.

C. Select the option to Install This Application at Logon.

D. Deploy the application as a mandatory upgrade.

8. An application named MCITPStudyTools has been deployed to users via group policy. You've just received an upgrade (MCITPStudyTools ver 2), and you want to deploy it to the same users. Users should not be forced to upgrade to the new version. What should you do?

A. Deploy MCITPStudyTools ver 2 as an optional upgrade.

B. Deploy MCITPStudyTools ver 2 as a mandatory upgrade.

       C. Remove MCITPStudyTools and deploy MCITPStudyTools ver 2 as an optional upgrade.

       D. Remove MCITPStudyTools and deploy MCITPStudyTools ver 2 as a mandatory upgrade.

  9. You have deployed a GPO named DisableSidebar that is successfully blocking the Windows Sidebar for users. You have linked it to the Sales OU. While working on a trouble call, you notice that Sally is running the Windows Sidebar on her system. Active Directory is configured as shown in Figure 10-29.

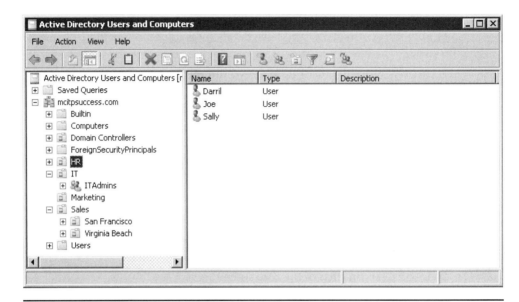

Figure 10-29   Active Directory structure

      What needs to be done so that this GPO applies to Sally?

      A. Add Sally's user account to the IT Admins Group.

      B. Move Sally's user account to the IT OU.

      C. Move Sally's user account to the Sales OU.

      D. Run `GPUpdate /force` at Sally's computer.

 10. You are configuring a public computer that will be used to allow users to check reservation information using a program named Reservations. You don't want any programs other than Reservations to run. What can you configure?

      A. A published application

      B. An assigned application

      C. Software settings

      D. Software restrictions

11. You manage a Windows Vista client where you've created a share and placed some files in the share. You want to ensure that when other users access this data, it is sent across the network in an encrypted format whenever possible. However, if some of the clients can't negotiate the encryption protocol, you still want them to be able to access the data. What should you do?

    A. Enable an IPsec policy using the Do Not Allow Unsecured Communication option.

    B. Enable an IPsec policy using the Allow Unsecured Communication If a Secure Connection Cannot Be Established option.

    C. Enable an EFS policy using the Do Not Allow Unsecured Communication option.

    D. Enable an EFS policy using the Allow Unsecured Communication If a Secure Connection Cannot Be Established option.

12. Maria works as a desktop support technician. Her native language is Spanish. She occasionally works with group policy files, but the explanations are all in English and she has some problems comprehending the explanations. What can be deployed to help her?

    A. The Group Policy translator

    B. The Group Policy interpreter

    C. ADML files

    D. ADMX files

13. You suspect that an application is being restricted from running through group policy on the MCITP1 computer. What tool can you use to view the group policy settings that apply to the MCITP1 computer?

    A. GPUpdate

    B. RSoP

    C. Security Configuration and Analysis

    D. Secedit

14. An administrator gives you a file that contains a security template. She says it will be deployed in 30 days and asks you to identify any differences in the template and the actual settings for the Windows Vista computers that you manage. How can you accomplish this?

    A. Use GPMC.

    B. Use the Security Configuration and Analysis snap-in.

    C. Use RsoP.

    D. Use GPResult.

15. A security template was applied to your computer several weeks ago. You want to verify that none of the settings have been modified. What tool can you use to easily accomplish this task?

   A. GPMC

   B. GPUpdate

   C. RSoP

   D. Secedit

Answers

70-622

1. **A.** You can use group policy to disable the Windows Sidebar. The Sidebar can't be uninstalled through the Control Panel. It's not necessary to reinstall Windows Vista to disable the Sidebar. Windows Sideshow allows an alternate display to be used with portable devices and has nothing to do with Windows Sidebar; there is no Use Windows Sideshow Instead of Windows Sidebar setting.

2. **B, C.** The Device Installation Restrictions policy settings (which are only available in the computers node) for computers can be used to restrict installation of devices. The GPUpdate /Force command can be run from the command line to have group policy settings immediately read and applied. While rebooting the system would also work, it would take much longer than executing a command. GPResult will provide a listing of the group policy settings but won't have them reapplied.

3. **A, D.** You could prevent all users from installing devices with the Prevent Installation of Devices Not Described by Other Policy Settings (or Prevent Installation of Removable Devices, which wasn't listed as a possible answer). The Allow Administrators to Override Device Installation Restriction Policies setting will allow exceptions for administrators. The Allow and Prevent Installation of Devices That Match Any of These Device IDs setting would only be used when you knew specific IDs of devices, but the question isn't that specific.

4. **D.** Due to an incompatibility in profiles between Windows XP and Windows Vista, roaming profiles won't work as needed unless some of the profile folders are redirected to their original profile location. Simply disabling and then enabling roaming profiles won't resolve the problem. Mandatory user profiles are created by first enabling a roaming user profile, renaming the ntuser.dat file to ntuser.man, and then assigning the profile to the users; however, a mandatory user profile won't help the incompatibility issue between XP and Vista.

5. **C.** You can modify the existing GPO to have the Pictures folder follow the Documents folder. While you could create a new GPO, it would take more steps than simply selecting the option to have the Pictures folder follow the

Documents folder. Passing responsibility to the users by telling them to store their pictures on a folder on the server, or by telling them to move the location on their systems, will not achieve consistent results. The GPO can be set once, and it's done accurately for everyone.

6. **E.** You can have turn off local group policy processing for all computers within the domain with the Turn Off Local Group Policy Objects Processing setting at the domain level. Just applying any GPO, at any level, won't be enough unless this specific setting is enabled. The Security Configuration and Analysis tool can be used to compare settings to identify exactly what is different; however, you don't really need to know all the settings that have changed but instead need to just turn them all off. `Secedit` is the command-line equivalent of Security Configuration and Analysis.

7. **C.** If you select the option to Install This Application at Logon, the application will be installed for the users the next time they log on. If this selection is not selected, it won't be installed until they launch the application, and if they try to launch it while disconnected, the install will fail, since the application source file is located on a server within the domain. It won't be installed automatically if published to a user, and it can't be published to a computer. Upgrade options are available only if the application is an upgrade to another application.

8. **A.** To ensure users aren't forced to upgrade to a newer version of an application, you can deploy it as an optional upgrade. A mandatory upgrade will upgrade existing versions without giving users any choice. There is no need to remove the original application.

9. **C.** You need to move Sally's user account to the Sales OU if you want a GPO applied to the Sales OU also apply to her account. GPOs apply to the domain or OUs, not to groups, so adding her account to a group won't change the behavior of any GPOs. Moving her account to the IT OU won't have an effect, since the GPO is linked to the Sales OU. Running `GPUpdate /force` will cause GPOs to be immediately reapplied, but it won't change the GPOs that are applied.

10. **D.** Software restrictions can be configured to allow specific programs to run and block all others. Deploying an application (either published or assigned) won't implement any restrictions. Software settings are used to deploy applications.

11. **B.** An IPsec policy can be configured to have data encrypted before being transferred over the network. The Allow Unsecured Communication If a Secure Connection Cannot Be Established option in IPsec will allow connections that can't communicate with IPsec to still be able to communicate. The Encrypting File System (EFS) is used to encrypt data on the drive, not over the network.

12. **D.** ADML files are language-specific files that can be used to allow administrators to view group policy settings in their native language. There is no such thing as a Group Policy translator or Group Policy interpreter. ADMX files are used for group policy files that are not language-specific.

13. **B.** The Resultant Set of Policy (RSoP) in Logging mode can be used to tell you exactly what policy settings are being applied to a computer with a specific user logged on. GPUpdate can be used to refresh the group policy settings. Security Configuration and Analysis can be used to compare group policy settings but wouldn't easily be able to show you a software restriction policy. Secedit is the command-line version of Security Configuration and Analysis.

14. **B.** The Security Configuration and Analysis snap-in can be used to compare security templates with the existing computer security configuration. The Group Policy Management Console (GPMC) is used to manage Group Policy Objects in a domain. The Resultant Set of Policy (RSoP) snap-in can be used to view the policies that are applied to a computer. The GPResult command-line tool is also used to view the policies that are applied to a computer.

15. **D.** The Secedit command-line tool can be used to check current computer settings against a template. Security Configuration and Analysis could also be used. The Group Policy Management Console (GPMC) is used to manage Group Policy Objects (GPOs) but can't compare them. GPUpdate is used to have a recently changed GPO apply immediately. The Resultant Set of Policy (RSoP) console can be used to view the settings of a computer, but wouldn't be able to compare the current settings against a template.

Using Maintenance and Diagnostic Tools

In this chapter, you will learn about:

- Event Viewer
- Task Scheduler
- Reliability and Performance Monitor
- Windows Update
- DirectX

I was recently researching how to build a pergola for my garden. While nothing looked too challenging, I quickly realized that before I could start the job, I needed the right tools. Without the right tools, I'd be working on the project for weeks or more. With the right tools, I might be able to finish it in a weekend.

The same goes for any job. With the right tools, the job goes smoothly. Part of the challenge is knowing what tools are available and how to use them. You'll learn about several of the available tools within Windows Vista in this chapter.

 EXAM TIP Objectives for the 70-620, 70-622, and 70-623 exams are included in this chapter.

Viewing Events in the Event Viewer

The Event Viewer has been around Windows operating systems for quite a while. Events of interest are logged in one of several logs, and then you can view the logs to determine what's occurred. However, the Event Viewer in Windows Vista is much more robust than the Event Viewer has been in past operating systems.

You can view several different types of logs from the Event Viewer. The standard Windows logs are

- **Application log** Applications (or programs) can log events to the Application log. The application developer chooses to write the events to the log.

- **Security log** The Security log contains any events that have been configured to be audited. This could include any object access such as files being opened or deleted, logon attempts, and much more. Auditing can be configured via local security policy or group policy.

- **Setup log** The Setup log contains events related to application installations or application setup. It is new in Windows Vista.

- **System log** The Windows operating system logs events related to Windows system components to the System log. This includes events related to hardware, such as a driver failing to load, and events related to software, such as a service failing to start. As an example, the Network Diagnostics tool logs its results in the system log.

- **Forwarded Events log** The Forwarded Events log includes events forwarded from remote computers. Before events can be forwarded, an event subscription must be configured as discussed later in this chapter. This log is new in Windows Vista.

In addition to the standard Windows Logs, the Event Viewer includes several more logs in two different categories.

- **Custom Views** This category includes the Administrative Events log by default. The Administrative Events log includes critical, error, and warning events from all administrative logs. You can create custom view logs for anything of interest.

- **Applications and Services logs** Any application can create a log just for application events, and it will be placed in this category. For example, some anti-virus applications create an anti-virus log. Additionally, some Windows components have specific logs in this category.

Figure 11-1 shows the Event Viewer. All of the categories are opened, so you can see all of the logs on my system. You may have different logs in the Application and Services Logs category.

You typically only go into the Event Viewer to view events when something has gone wrong and you're doing some type of troubleshooting. However, you can view the events at any time just to get an idea of the health of your system.

The Event Viewer can be accessed using several different methods.

- **Computer Management** You can click Start, right-click Computer, and select Manage. This will launch the Computer Management console, and the Event Viewer is part of Computer Management.

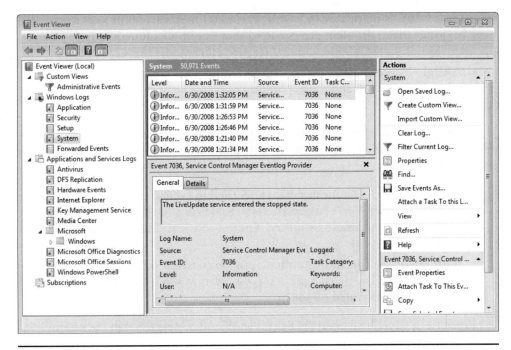

Figure 11-1   Event Viewer

- **Administrative Tools**   You can click Start | Administrative Tools, and then select Event Viewer. This assumes you've configured your Start menu to include Administrative Tools.

- **Control Panel**   You can click Start, and then select Control Panel. From the Control Panel, click System and Maintenance, and select View Event Logs under Administrative Tools.

Viewing the Logs

With the Event Viewer open, you can select any log and view the events within the log simply by pointing and clicking. You'll run across four types of events in non-security event logs.

- **Information**   This is marked with a blue *i* within a white circle. It's normally used to provide information on a change such as a service starting or stopping, or a modification within a component.

- **Warning**   This is marked with a black exclamation mark within a yellow triangle. It indicates that an issue has occurred that can impact a service or result in a more serious problem.

- **Error** This is marked with a white exclamation mark within a red circle. It indicates that a problem has occurred that can impact functionality of the application or the component that triggered the event.

- **Critical** This is marked with a white *X* within a red circle. It indicates that a failure has occurred and the application or component cannot recover from the failure.

The security event logs have two event types. Each of these events would include information such as the actual event, the date and time of the event, and the user that performed the event.

- **Audit Failure** This indicates that a user tried to exercise a right but failed. For example, if a user didn't have permission to delete a file but tried to delete the file, a failure event would be logged if object access auditing was configured on the file.

- **Audit Success** This indicates that a user exercised a right. For example, if a user successfully deleted a file, a success event would be logged if object access auditing was configured on the file.

In Exercise 11.1, you will open the Event Viewer and browse through the various logs.

Exercise 11.1: Opening and Using the Event Viewer

1. Click Start, and select Control Panel. Select System and Maintenance, scroll down to Administrative Tools, and select View Event Logs. If the User Account Control dialog box appears, click Continue.

2. In the Event Viewer, open Custom Views. Click Administrative Events. This view shows all the critical, error, and warning events. Browse through these events. Feel free to double-click any events that interest you.

3. Open Windows Logs. Double-click the System log.
   Notice that the events are sorted by date and time in descending order—most recent events first. You can change this by clicking any of the columns.

4. Click the Filter Current Log link in the Actions pane on the right. Alternatively, you can right-click the System log and select Filter.

5. In the Filter Current Log page, select Critical, Error, and Warning as the Event Levels and click OK. This will effectively remove all events that are information only. Browse through these entries on your computer.

TIP The remaining steps will run the Network Diagnostics and create an event if your NIC has a problem. If you can create a problem in your system by shutting down your wireless access point or disconnecting your NIC, you'll see the events. You can still go through the steps without creating a problem with your NIC, but you just won't see the event. Check out the help article titled "Using Windows Network Diagnostics Event Logs to Solve Network Problems" for more information.

6. If your system has a wireless NIC, you can launch the Windows Network Diagnostics tool to create an event with an event ID of 6100 with the following steps:

   a. Click Start, right-click Network, and select Properties to launch the Network and Sharing Center.

   b. On the Network and Sharing Center, click Diagnose and Repair.

   c. Follow the wizard to complete the diagnostics.

7. Click the Filter Current Log again. In the text box that currently has <All Event IDs> in it, change it to 6100. Clear the Critical, Error, and Warning check boxes selected in the earlier step. Click OK.

8. You should now see the results from the Network Diagnostics tool. Double-click the entry with the 6100 to open it up. Your display should look similar to Figure 11-2. Notice that the text in the opened dialog box is the same as the text in the window below the list of events. You should also notice that the information available in the event is significantly more than displayed by the Network Diagnostics tool.

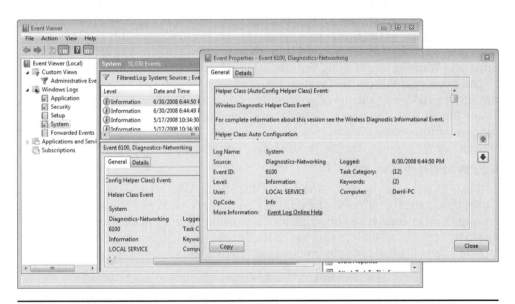

Figure 11-2 Viewing the details of an event

 EXAM TIP The Diagnose and Repair link launches the Windows Network Diagnostics tool. The results of Network Diagnostics are logged in the system log with the Event ID of 6100. The logged events will provide you with significantly more information than the Network Diagnostics tool provides.

9. Click the Clear Filter link in the Actions pane.

10. Right-click the System log and select properties. Note that this page shows the location of the log and some details on the log such as its size and when it was created, modified, and accessed. You can also modify the maximum log size and how events are overwritten from here.

Configuring Custom Views

If you have events of interest to you, you can configure custom views. Custom views can be created to include

- Specific time frames
- Specific event levels (such as Critical, Error, Warning, or Information)
- A Verbose setting to provide the highest level of detail in the logged events
- Specific logs (such as the system log) or specific sources (such as Diagnostics-Networking)

Once you decide on which event logs or which event sources you will include, you can also include specific event IDs, task categories, keywords, users, and computers.

Figure 11-3 shows the Create Custom View page. You can access this page by clicking the Create Custom View link in the Actions pane. In the figure, I've selected Critical, Error, and Warning events using Verbose logging for all of the Windows logs.

Once you click OK on the Create Custom View page, you will be prompted to save the custom view with a name of your choice. Once it is saved, you can select this view at any time just as if it is were a regular log. You won't have to recreate the filter each time you want to view the data.

Forwarding Events

You can forward events to a central computer using Windows Vista. The benefit of this is that instead of monitoring multiple computers, you can monitor just a single computer. You configure subscriptions to forward events from one computer to another.

Computers involved in subscriptions are referred to as a either the collector or the source:

- **Collector** All the events are received by the collector. This computer is also referred to as a subscriber.
- **Source** Events are generated on the source computer and forwarded to the collector.

Event subscriptions have a couple of basic requirements. First, the computers involved in the subscription need to be within a domain. Second, the Windows Event Collector Service must be running. If the Windows Event Collector Service isn't running and you try to work with subscriptions, you will be prompted to start it.

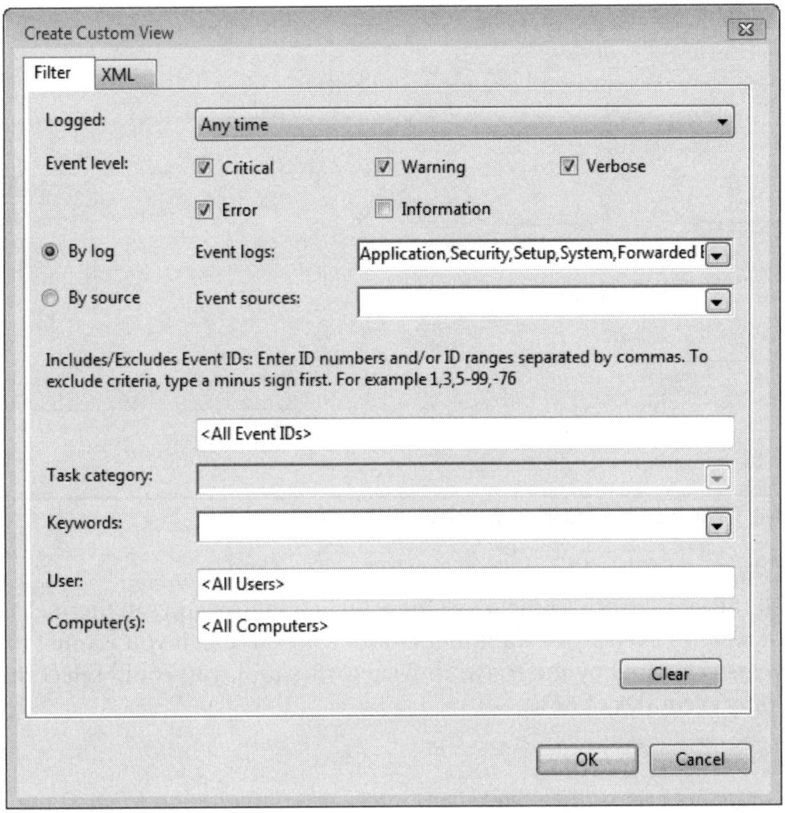

Figure 11-3 Creating a custom view

When configuring event forwarding, you need to determine who will initiate the collection of the events—the source computer or the collector computer. These are referred to as collector initiated or source computer initiated.

Collector-Initiated Events

Collector-initiated events require that all computers exist in the same domain. The collector computer is reaching out and retrieving the events from the computers, and the domain provides an added layer of security.

Figure 11-4 shows the properties of a new subscription being created and computers being added.

You can see in the figure that the subscription type is set to Collector Initiated. You click the Select Computers button, and then you're able to add computers that exist in the domain. In the figure, a computer named mcitp1 in the mcitpsuccess.com domain is being added.

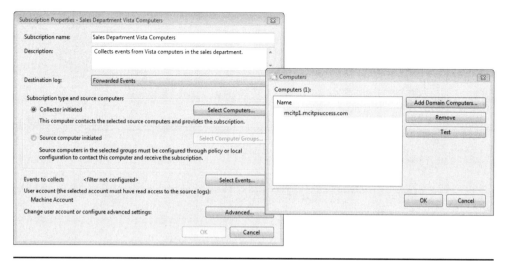

Figure 11-4 Configuring a collector-initiated subscription

The Select Events button launches a Query Filter window. You can then select specifically what types of events you want to forward. For example, if you wanted to forward all the events generated by the Network Diagnostics tool, you could select the System log with only event IDs of 6100.

Source-Initiated Events

In source-initiated events, the source computers are configured to forward the events to the collector. You can add both domain and non-domain computers to a source-initiated event, but non-domain computers must use certificates to authenticate.

Figure 11-5 shows the screens for a source-initiated subscription.

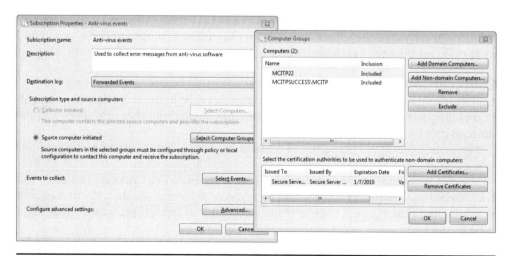

Figure 11-5 Configuring a source-initiated subscription

Notice that both a non-domain computer (MCITP22) and a domain computer (MC-ITPSUCCESS\MCITP) have been added. Additionally, a certificate has been added to provide authentication for MCITP22. Authentication within the domain is handled by Kerberos.

Configuring Advanced Subscription Properties

The advanced subscription properties can be accessed by clicking the Advanced button. Figure 11-6 shows the advanced properties from a collector-initiated subscription. A source-initiated subscription does not have the User Account selections.

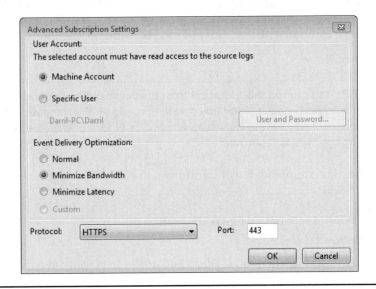

Figure 11-6   Configuring advanced subscription settings

The event delivery optimization choices determine how many events will be included, and how often events will be sent when they are sent to the collector. The Minimize Bandwidth selection sends events less often, the Minimize Latency sends events more often, and the Normal setting is a balance between the two choices.

The protocol determines if the events will be sent in an encrypted format using HTTPS or a plain text format using HTTP. HTTP is selected by default. The "well-known" ports for HTTP and HTTPS are 80 and 443, respectively.

Along the same lines, if firewalls are enabled on either the source or collector computers, you must also open up port 443 when using HTTPS.

Configuring the Source Computer for an Event Subscription

In order for the source computer to forward events to the collector, it must be configured. Consider the following choices when configuring the source computer:

- You will use the `WinRM` command-line tool to configure the basics on the source computer.

- If the computer is not a member of a domain and you want to configure a source computer–initiated subscription, you must include a certificate for authentication.

- If you want to send the events in an encrypted format, you must open port 443 on the firewalls of the source and collector computers.

EXAM TIP Make sure you know what needs to be done on the source computer to configure it for subscriptions.

The Windows Remote Management command-line tool (WinRM) is used to implement the WS-Management protocol, which provides a secure way to communicate with local and remote computers. The command used to configure the source computer is

```
WinRM quickconfig
```

TIP You can run this command from the command line with administrative privileges to view it. If you don't want to configure the computer but instead just want to view the command, simply click N for no when the command prompts you for approval.

After issuing this command, it will inform you that it will perform several actions if you approve. It will

- Set the WinRM service to delayed autostart.
- Start the WinRM service.
- Create a WinRM listener on HTTP://* and accept management requests.
- Enable the WinRM firewall exception.

All you have to do is click Yes to access the changes. Remember, this is done on the source computer so that events can be forwarded to the collector.

Using the wecutil Tool
The Windows Event Collector Utility (wecutil) is used to enable and manage event subscriptions. It is run on the collector computer.

When enabling event subscriptions, you would first run the following command to configure the Windows Event Collector service:

```
Wecutil qc
```

The wecutil command has several other commands that can be used with it. As an example, you can run the following command to view the status of a specific subscription:

```
Wecutil qs "subscription name"
```

Figure 11-7 shows the gs command being used to retrieve information on a subscription named "Anti-virus Events."

```
C:\>wecutil gs "anti-virus events"
Subscription_Id: anti-virus events
SubscriptionType: SourceInitiated
Description: Used to collect error messages from anti-virus software
Enabled: true
Uri: http://schemas.microsoft.com/wbem/wsman/1/windows/EventLog
ConfigurationMode: Normal
DeliveryMode: Push
DeliveryMaxLatencyTime: 900000
HeartbeatInterval: 900000
Query: <QueryList><Query Id="0"><Select Path="Antivirus">*[System[Provi
='avast!'] and (Level=2 or Level=5)]]</Select></Query></QueryList>
ReadExistingEvents: false
TransportName: HTTPS
ContentFormat: RenderedText
Locale: en-US
LogFile: ForwardedEvents
PublisherName: microsoft-windows-eventcollector
AllowedIssuerCAList:
    4463C531D7CCC1006794612BB656D3BF8257846F
AllowedSubjectList:
    MCITP22
DeniedSubjectList:
AllowedSourceDomainComputers: O:NSG:BAD:P(A;;GA;;;S-1-5-21-1670614606-5
2763047394-1106)S:

C:\>
```

Figure 11-7 Viewing subscription configuration information with the wecutil command

EXAM TIP You can view detailed information on event subscriptions using the `wecutil` command-line program. You should be aware of the different commands available using `wecutil`.

Wecutil commands include

- **es**   Enumerate or list subscriptions.
- **gs**   Get subscriptions.
- **gr**   Get subscription runtime status.
- **ss**   Set subscription status.
- **cs**   Create a new subscription.
- **ds**   Delete a subscription.
- **rs**   Retry a subscription.

Creating the Event Subscription on the Collector Computer

You can create the subscription using the `wecutil` command or the GUI within the Event Viewer console. The GUI is the easier of the two tools to use.

The first time you select Subscriptions in the Event Viewer, an Event Viewer dialog box will appear informing you the Windows Event Collector Service must be running and asking if you want to start the service and have it automatically start when the computer is restarted. Click Yes.

You can then select the data for the screens as discussed in the sections on the collector-initiated and source-initiated events presented previously. Remember, the following issues relate to creating the subscriptions:

- You can use the `wecutil` command-line tool to configure the Windows Event Collector service.

- If the source computer is not a member of a domain and you want to configure a source computer–initiated subscription, you must include a certificate for authentication.

- If you want to send the events in an encrypted format, you must open port 443 on the firewalls of the source and collector computers.

Using the Task Scheduler

The Task Scheduler is used to automate tasks. You can configure tasks to run based on a schedule or based on events. The Task Scheduler allows you to perform three types of tasks:

- **Start a Program**   A Program can be compiled executables, script files, or simple batch files.

    As an example, Chapter 10 presented information on how to use `Secedit` to verify a computer's current configuration against an existing baseline. Instead of entering the command every week, you could instead create a batch file and use the Task Scheduler to run it on a weekly basis.

- **Send an e-mail**   E-mails can include attachments.

    For example, the `Secedit` batch file could create an output file. You could create a second scheduled task to e-mail the batch file results to you.

- **Display a message**   This will display a message box on the desktop.

    For example, you can use this to display a reminder such as when a report is due to your boss.

The exercise in the next section will walk you through the process of creating a couple of tasks.

Scheduling Tasks

Tasks are scheduled based on triggers. Triggers can be time based or event based.

Time-based tasks are useful for automating maintenance tasks. For example, if you wanted to automatically run the disk defragmenter on a system once a month, you could create a batch file to launch the `defrag` command-line tool and then schedule the batch file to run on a monthly basis. The following triggers are time based:

- Daily
- Weekly
- Monthly
- One time

Event-based triggers occur based on an event and can be configured based on the following events:

- **When the computer starts** For example, you could run a Visual Basic script each time a computer started to configure the user's environment based on whether the wireless NIC or the wired NIC was active.

- **When a user logs on** For example, if you wanted to be notified if any users logged on outside of normal working hours, you could write a Visual Basic script to run, check the time, and send an e-mail if the logon time was outside the hours of 8:00 A.M. to 5:00 P.M.

- **When a specific event is logged** You could launch a task if a specific event ID within a specific log occurs. For example, if you wanted to take action any time a network diagnostic was run, you could create a task based on Event ID 6100 in the System log. You can specify the log, the source, and the event ID for this trigger.

In Exercise 11.2, you will create a batch file and schedule it to run on a weekly basis.

Exercise 11.2: Scheduling a Task

1. Open a command prompt by clicking Start and entering **cmd** in the Start Search box. The command prompt will open in your Documents folder, unless you have configured it differently.

2. Change the directory to the root of C: with the following command:

   ```
   cd\
   ```

3. Enter **Notepad mybat.bat** to create a file named mybat.bat within Notepad. When the dialog box appears asking if you want to create the new file, click Yes.

4. Enter the following text in the Notepad file.

   ```
   secedit /analyze /db mytemplate.sdb /log mylog.log
   ```

5. Press CTRL-S to save the file.

6. Back on the command line, enter **mybat** to start your batch file. Your batch file will run.

TIP Since a template named mytemplate.sdb doesn't exist in the root of C:, the command within your batch file will fail. However the batch file itself runs, which is the point of this exercise. If you want to ensure that the command within the batch file succeeds, you can do Exercise 10.4, change the name of the database file from Ch10ex.sdb to mytemplate.sdb, and place this file in the root of C:.

7. Launch the Task Scheduler. Click Start, Control Panel | System and Maintenance, scroll to Administrative Tools at the bottom, and select Schedule Tasks. If User Account Control appears, click Continue.

8. Select Task Scheduler Library. You may have one or two tasks already scheduled here, or it may be empty.

9. Select Microsoft and open the Windows container. Select Defrag. Notice it already has a task scheduled to run. Double-click the task to open the properties page. Your display will look similar to Figure 11-8.

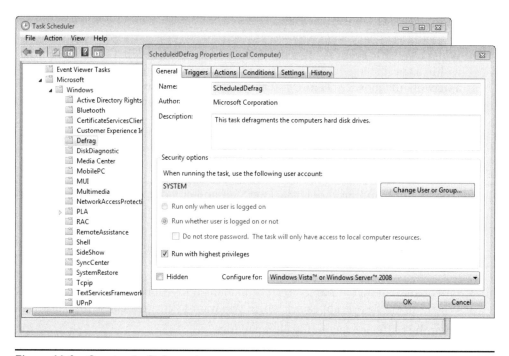

Figure 11-8 Opening the Defrag task

10. Browse through each of the tabs of the Defrag task. Notice that it is scheduled to run every Wednesday at 1 A.M. but is disabled. Several special conditions are set on the Conditions tab. The History tab informs you when the task was run (if at all). Click OK to close the task.

11. In the Actions pane of the Task Scheduler, click Create Basic Task.

12. In the Create a Basic Task page, enter **Run Secedit** as the name of the task. Click Next.

13. On the Task Trigger page, select Weekly. Your display will look similar to Figure 11-9. Click Next.

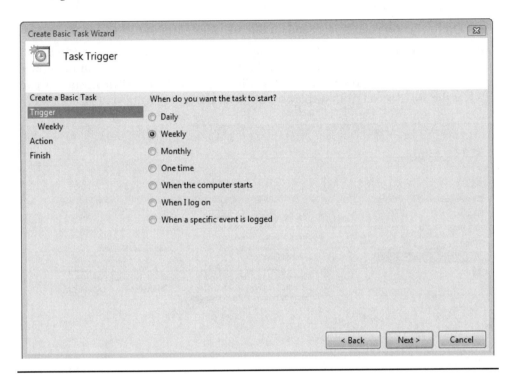

Figure 11-9   Setting the trigger to weekly

14. On the Weekly page, select Monday. Change the time to 1:00:00 AM. Click Next.

15. On the Action page, ensure that Start a Program is selected. Click Next.

16. On the Start a Program page, click the Browse button. Browse to the root of C: and select the mybat.bat file you created. Click Open. Click Next.

NOTE   Some scripts and programs allow you to provide inputs as arguments. These can be added according to the requirements of the program. You can also use the Start In box to specify which path the program should start in (such as c:\data or some other path expected by the program).

17. On the Summary page, review the information and click Finish.

18. With the Task Scheduler selected, click Create Basic Task in the Actions pane.

19. In the Create a Basic Task page, enter **E-mail Secedit Results** in the Name box. Click Next.

20. On the Task Trigger page, select Weekly and click Next.

21. On the Weekly page, select Monday and change the time to 01:30:00 AM. This will give the Run Secedit task 30 minutes to run, which should be more than enough time. Click Next.

22. On the Action page, select Send an E-mail. Click Next.

23. On the Send an E-Mail page, enter your e-mail address in the From and To lines. Enter information in the Subject and Text boxes. Click the Browse button. Browse to the root of C: and select mylog.log. Click Open. Enter **mail1.mcitpsuccess.com** as the SMTP server. Your display should look similar to Figure 11-10. Click Next.

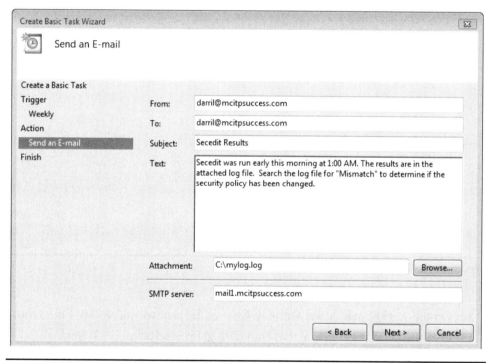

Figure 11-10 Configuring a Send E-Mail task

For an actual e-mail task, you would need to configure this with actual e-mail addresses, and the name of an actual e-mail server in your network.

24. On the Summary page, review your results and click Finish.

25. Select Task Scheduler Library and click Refresh in the Actions pane.

26. Double-click the Run Secedit task. Notice you have the same six tabs as you saw in the Defrag task you explored earlier. Browse through these settings and then click Cancel.

This exercise showed the process to create a basic task. If you right-click the task and select Properties, you'll notice that the task has many more properties that can be configured. Instead of using the Create Basic Task link when creating your task, you can select the Create Task link to access these property pages directly when you first create your task.

Running Scripts at Logon   It's also a simple matter to run scripts to provide some type of notification to the user. In domain environments this is done with group policy, but you can also do it in a workgroup environment by attaching a script to the logon event.

For example, the following script could be created in Notepad and saved as logon.vbs:

```
Msgbox "Help! I'm stuck" & vbcrlf & "inside this computer!", vbCritical, "Success!"
```

Your message can be anything, but by using this script, you can see that the first set of text in quotes is the message and the second set of text in quotes is the title of the message box. Any time you want to start a new line, you can close your text with quotes, use the ampersand (&), add vbcrlf (for a carriage return/line feed), and then add additional text in quotes.

I've seen this method used for welcome messages, warnings that this computer is only to be used by employees, safety messages, and much more.

You can test your script from the command line by just entering the name (such as logon) or double-clicking it from Windows Explorer. Once you're happy with how it appears, configure it as a scheduled task with the When I Log On trigger and the Start a Program action.

Attaching Tasks to Events

An advanced implementation of the Task Scheduler is the ability to attach tasks to events. In a nutshell, you can identify any event and when it occurs, you can specify a task to execute.

In large enterprises this has often been done through third-party applications. The application constantly monitors the different logs available in Event Viewer, and anytime an event is logged, the application checks to see if it is an event of interest, and if so, a task is executed. However, these applications are very expensive and only affordable by large enterprises.

You can now do this yourself. There are two methods of attaching a task to an event.

- Through Event Viewer
- Through Task Scheduler

TIP If you want to monitor for the occurrence of specific events, attach a task to the event. You can then have the task run a program, send an e-mail, or display a message.

Attaching a Task to an Event with Event Viewer

You can select any event in any log in Event Viewer and attach a task to the event. You can also attach tasks to the entire log, but generally, you'll want to narrow down your focus to only specific events.

Figure 11-11 shows the Event Viewer open and several items highlighted.

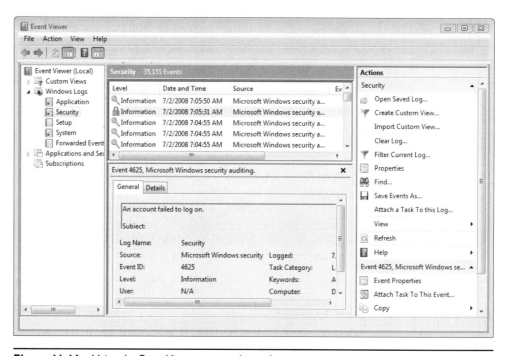

Figure 11-11   Using the Event Viewer to attach a task to an event

In the figure, you can see that the security log is selected. Auditing of failed logon attempts has been enabled, and a failed logon event has occurred and is selected. The Actions pane has a link that can be clicked to attach a task directly to this event.

If you click this link, it will launch the Create a Task Wizard, which will lead you through the steps to attach a task to this event.

Attaching a Task to an Event with Task Scheduler

You can also attach tasks to events using the Create Basic Task Wizard in the Task Scheduler. You simply click Create Basic Task in the wizard and select When a Specific Event Is Logged as the trigger. You are then prompted to select the log from the drop-down box, enter the source, and add the event ID.

Managing Tasks with schtasks

The command-line program `schtasks` is new to Windows Vista. It enables you to perform many of the same functions as the Task Scheduler console from the command line. As with any command-line tool, the strength lies in your ability to script the task and then easily run the script on multiple systems.

For example, if you wanted to attach a task to an event that occured on ten different computers, you could use `schtasks` to create the task, save the text in a batch file, and then run the batch file on each of the ten computers. This would be much quicker than using the GUI to point and click on the ten different systems. Additionally, you'd be assured that the task would be created identically on each of the systems.

 EXAM TIP `Schtasks` can be used to manage scheduled tasks from the command line. This includes creating, deleting, and changing the properties of scheduled tasks.

The `schtasks` command can be used with several different parameters. These are

- **Create**   Create a new scheduled task. The syntax of this command is more complex than using the Task Scheduler console. You would only use this when you wanted to create an identical task on multiple systems via a script.

- **Delete**   Delete a scheduled task.

- **Query**   Display all scheduled tasks.

- **Change**   Change the properties of a scheduled task.

- **Run**   Run a scheduled task immediately.

- **End**   Stop a currently running scheduled task.

- **?**   Display a help message.

You can use the command-line help to get additional information on any of these tasks. For example, if you wanted to get additional information on how to create a task using `schtasks`, you could enter the following command:

```
Schtasks /create /?
```

In Exercise 11.3, you will use `schtasks` to view and manipulate scheduled tasks.

Exercise 11.3: Using the schtasks Command

1. Open a command prompt with administrative privileges by clicking Start | All Programs | Accessories, right-clicking Command Prompt, and selecting Run as Administrator. If the User Account Control dialog box appears, click Continue.

2. View the status of all your scheduled tasks with the following command:

```
Schtasks /query
```

3. Scroll through the results and locate the scheduled task named ScheduledDefrag. Note the Next Run Time and Status of this task. If the Next Run Time is listed as N/A, it indicates the task is not enabled.

4. Enter the following command to disable the task. Notice that you have to include the path of the task (\Microsoft\Windows\) in addition to the task name (ScheduledDefrag).

```
Schtasks /change /tn \Microsoft\Windows\Defrag\ScheduledDefrag /Disable
```

5. View the status of just the ScheduledDefrag task with the following command:

```
Schtasks /query /tn \Microsoft\Windows\Defrag\ScheduledDefrag
```

You can see that the task is disabled and will not execute.

6. If you want the task to run as scheduled, you can use the following task to enable it.

```
Schtasks /change /tn \Microsoft\Windows\Defrag\ScheduledDefrag /Enable
```

7. Verify the status of the ScheduledDefrag task with the following command:

```
Schtasks /query /tn \Microsoft\Windows\Defrag\ScheduledDefrag
```

Performance and Reliability Monitor

The Reliability and Performance Monitor is a group of snap-ins in a Microsoft Management Console. You can use it to get a clear indication of how your system is performing.

Figure 11-12 shows the Performance and Reliability Monitor in the Resource Overview view. As you can see, the system is quite busy. I ran a virus check while working on different files and downloading data from the Internet.

You can launch the Performance and Reliability Monitor by clicking Start and typing in **perfmon** in the Start Search area. In addition to the Resource Overview, you have the following tools:

- **Performance Monitor**   This provides a visual display of built-in counters. You can use this to view performance in real time or view counter logs to study the performance of a system over a period of time.

- **Reliability Monitor**   The Reliability Monitor performs trend analysis and provides a historical look at the performance of your system. It is summarized with a stability index between 1 and 10, with 10 being the most stable.

- **Data collector sets**   Data collector sets identify multiple data collection points that can be used to measure the performance of your system. Several data collector sets are preconfigured to measure specific data points within your system. You can also create your own data collector sets.

- **Reports**   Reports are created when a data collector set is run. The data points from the data collector sets are actually within many different files, and the reports display the data so that it's easy to browse.

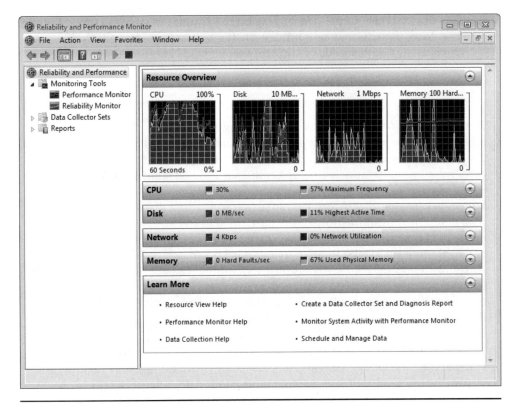

Figure 11-12   Performance and Reliability Monitor

Monitoring Resources

Any computer has four primary resources, and if any of these are overloaded, your entire system will be slow. When measuring data points on your system through the use of data collector sets, you will often see these four resources being measured. The four resources are

- **CPU**   This is your processor. In general, if your CPU is averaging over 80 percent utilization, it's in danger of being a bottleneck. You should consider either reducing the workload on the system or upgrading the processor.

- **Disk**   The disk is usually the slowest subsystem, so if it is heavily used, you will see your system slow down. If it is heavily used, you may be able to increase the performance by moving the paging file off the hard drive holding the operating system, increasing RAM, or replacing the hard drive with a higher performing RAID-0.

- **Memory**   Every operating system I can remember required more memory than the last, and Vista is no exception. The sweet spot is between 3 GB and 4 GB, while the sweet spot for Windows XP is about 2 GB.

- **Network Interface Card**   Depending on the amount of data you upload or download, the NIC may be a bottleneck. It's easy to upgrade a NIC today. Wireless NICs with speeds of 100 Mbps and 1 Gbps are common.

A Busy Disk Often Means Not Enough Memory   If your disk is very busy, it could be because you don't have enough memory. The reason is the way the paging file is used.

When all your memory is already being used and you launch another program, some of what is in the physical memory is stored on your hard drive in a file known as a paging file. If you need to access something that's in the paging file, data is swapped from memory to the hard drive to free some space, and the necessary data is swapped from the hard drive to memory. Memory is swapped back and forth in 64KB blocks; in memory 64KB is known as a page.

Think about this. Your system is busily swapping pages between the hard drive and memory, and what you'll see is the hard drive LED blinking away, and you may even hear the hard drive moving. This is referred to as disk thrashing. Disk thrashing could be due to a fragmented hard drive (and defragging it will resolve the problem), or it could be due to excessive paging.

If memory is the problem, a quick look at the Resource Overview page will show you that both the disk and the memory are overloaded. Adding more memory will resolve the overloaded disk. A System Performance data collector set could also be used to give you an indication of how much memory is being used.

Monitoring Your System with the Monitoring Tools

You can use the two monitoring tools to get an idea of how your system is performing. The Performance Monitor allows you to add counters to view performance of individual components such as memory or the processor. The Reliability Monitor gives you an indication of how well your system is performing with a stability index.

Using the Performance Monitor

The Performance Monitor uses objects and counters as measurement points. An object is a measurable resource within the computer. For example, the four primary resources of CPU, memory, disk, and NIC are all objects. Within each object, there are several measurements that can be taken. Each measurement is referred to as a counter.

For example, the % Processor Time is a counter within the Processor object (CPU).

In Exercise 11.4, you will launch the Performance Monitor and view some basic counters.

Exercise 11.4: Using the Performance Monitor

1. Launch the Reliability and Performance Monitor by clicking Start | Control Panel | System and Maintenance | Administrative Tools and double-clicking Reliability and Performance Monitor.

2. Open the Monitoring Tools folder and select the Performance Monitor.

3. Right-click within the main window and select Add Counters. You could also click the green + symbol on the toolbar above the main window.

4. In the Add Counters dialog box, scroll down to the Processor object. Click the down arrow to access the counters within the Processor object. Scroll down to % Processor Time. Click Add. Your display will look similar to Figure 11-13.

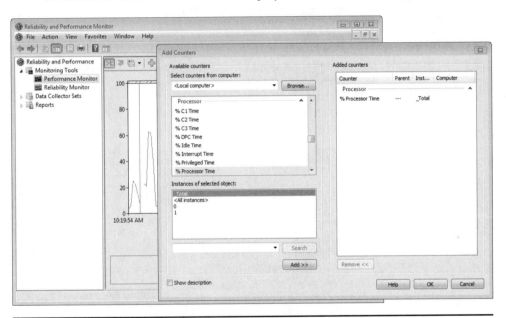

Figure 11-13 Adding counters to the Performance Monitor

 TIP You can click the Show Description check box at the bottom of the Add Counters window to give you more information on each counter.

5. Scroll up to the Memory object. Open the Memory object and select Page Faults/Sec. Click Add.

6. Scroll down to the Network Interface object. Open the Network Interface object and select Bytes Total/Sec. Click Add.

7. Scroll down to the Physical Disk object. Open the Physical Disk object and select % Disk Time. Click Add. Click OK.

8. Press the Highlight button (shaped like a pen) on the toolbar. Notice that the counter that is selected is now highlighted.

You can select a different counter, and it will be highlighted. This tool allows you to view (on a real-time basis) performance of different resources within your system.

Using the Reliability Monitor

The Reliability Monitor constantly monitors your system and records key events. Based on the events and how they impact your system, it creates a reliability index that you can use to determine the health of your system.

Figure 11-14 shows the Reliability Monitor on a very healthy system. Notice the Index is 9.39. You can also see that this system has only been operational for about a month and had some type of critical failure on June 12.

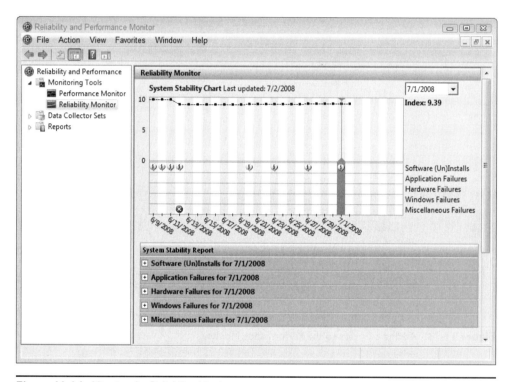

Figure 11-14   Viewing the Reliability Monitor

You can drill into any part of the System Stability Report (below the System Stability Chart) to get more details on events. In the figure, July 1 is selected and there is one information event on the Software (Un)Installs line. If you opened up the report for Software (Un)Installs for 7/1/2008, you could get more details on this event.

Similarly, you can see that the critical event on 6/12 is on the Miscellaneous Failures line. More details on this failure could be viewed by selecting the date and opening the Miscellaneous Failures report.

Measuring Performance with Data Collector Sets

The Reliability and Performance Monitor includes data collector sets. A *data collector set* is a predefined set of measurements. You can start a data collector set, and it will monitor the predefined data points for a predetermined amount of time and then provide you with a report on the results.

Data collector sets fall into two generic categories:

- **System** These have been created and are included within the Reliability and Performance Monitor. You can run these at any time and view the corresponding report to get an idea of your system's performance.

- **User defined** These are defined by you. You can create a data collector set completely from scratch or create it from a template. Three predefined templates exist: Basic, System Diagnostics, and System Performance.

System Data Collector Sets

The System data collector sets allow you to quickly and easily run performance and diagnostics checks on your system. They are predefined, so you don't have to struggle over what measurements to include—they're all there.

Four System Data Collector Sets are included. They are

- **LAN Diagnostics** This data collector set collects LAN service–related data on your local system. It includes wired debug logs, Registry keys, and system hardware information that can help troubleshoot LAN service–related problems. If you run this data collector set, it will run until you stop it.

- **System Diagnostics** This data collector set creates a report detailing the status of local hardware resources, system response times, and processes on the local computer, along with system information and configuration data. The report includes suggestions for ways to maximize performance and streamline system operation.

  If you run this data collector set, it will automatically stop after ten minutes.

- **System Performance** This data collector set generates a report detailing the status of local hardware resources, system response times, and processes on the local computer. You can use this information to identify possible causes of performance issues.

  If you run this data collector set, it will automatically stop after one minute.

 EXAM TIP The System Diagnostics data collector set provides the most information and detail for monitoring systems. It includes details on the core hardware resources, services, and programs.

- **Wireless Diagnostics** This data collector set collects wireless service–related data on your system. It includes wireless debug logs, Registry keys, and system hardware information that can help troubleshoot wireless service–related problems.

  If you run this data collector set, it will run until you stop it.

Data collector sets have several properties that you can view. However, System data collector sets only allow you to view the properties—they can't be changed. User-defined data collector sets can be modified. The properties of the data collector sets will be explored later in this chapter.

In Exercise 11.5, you will run two of the System data collector sets and view the associated reports.

Exercise 11.5: Using the System Data Collector Sets

1. Launch the Reliability and Performance Monitor by clicking Start | Control Panel | System and Maintenance | Administrative Tools and double-clicking Reliability and Performance Monitor. If the User Account Control dialog appears, click Continue.

2. Open the Data Collector Set container, and then open the System container.

3. Right-click the System Performance data collector set and click Start. This will run for one minute and then stop.

4. When the System Performance Data Collector stops, right-click the System Diagnostics data collector set and click Start. It will run for ten minutes and then stop. While it is running, you can view the report from the System Performance data collector set.

5. Scroll down to the Reports section and open the Reports | System | System Performance container. Find the report that was just run and select it. Your display will look similar to Figure 11-15. Notice that this report shows summary data for three of the four primary system resources: CPU, disk, and memory. (Data is also available for the NIC but it isn't included in the Summary section.)

6. Click and view the following sections of the report: Diagnostics Results, CPU, Network, Disk, Memory, and Report Statistics.

   As you can see, the report provides a significant amount of information on your system.

7. When the System Diagnostics data collector set completes, select its report in the Reports | System | System Diagnostics section. Notice that in addition to identifying issues, this report also often provides recommendations labeled as Resolution in the Diagnostic Results section.

8. Scroll through the entire report to view the performance of your system.

User-Defined Data Collector Sets

While the System data collector sets are very handy and convenient, they may not meet your needs. Fear not. You can create your own data collector sets, and even better, you can use existing System data collector sets as templates for starting points.

 EXAM TIP   You should be aware of the different capabilities of user-defined data collector sets.

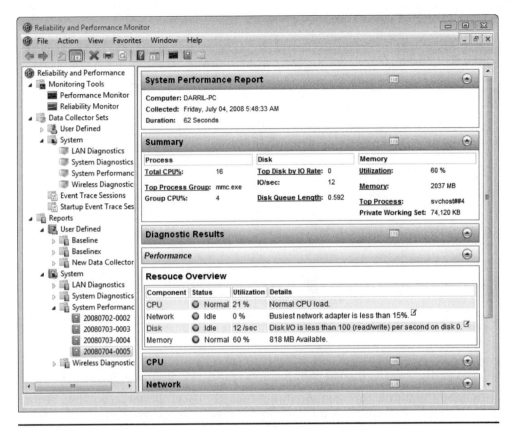

Figure 11-15 Viewing a System Performance report

As an example, you may need to collect performance data on a system over a period of time. You can't modify the schedule properties of a System data collector set, but you can modify the schedule of a user-defined data collector set.

Figure 11-16 shows a new data collector set named "Monitor MCITP1" with the property pages opened. The schedule tab is selected and it shows one schedule has already been created to run this daily at 1 PM and another schedule is being created to run it daily at 8 AM. You can create as many schedules as you want.

The user-defined folder is empty when you first install Windows Vista, but you can add as many user-defined data collector sets as you desire. Other property tabs are

- **General**   This includes the name, a description, and keywords for the data collector set. Additionally, you can modify the user account that it will use when executing.

- **Directory**   You can specify where the resulting data is stored and how the sub-directories will be named. By default subdirectories are named with a date and serial number format.

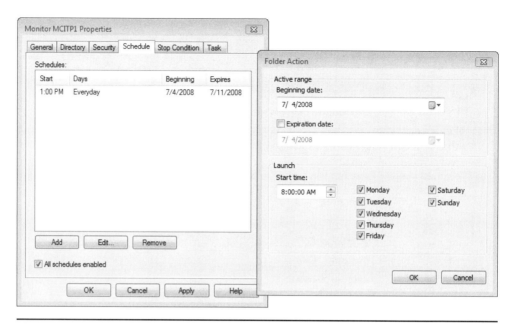

Figure 11-16 Creating schedules for a user-defined data collector set

- **Security**   You can assign permissions to the data collector set from here.

- **Stop Condition**   You can specify how long the data collector set will run. Setting the value to 0 will cause it to run until stopped. The System Performance data collector set has a default value of 1 minute, and the System Diagnostics set has a default value of 10 minutes. You can't modify the System data collector sets, but you can modify them in the user-defined data collector sets. You can also set a time limit or a size limit for the logs.

- **Task**   If you want to run a task when the data collector stops, you can identify it here.

In addition to modifying the properties of the data collector set, you can also modify the properties of the Performance Counter portion of the data collector set.

In Exercise 11.6, you will create a user-defined data collector set from the System Performance template and schedule it to run for seven days. This can be used as a baseline. If performance changes sometime in the future, you can look at baseline readings and compare it to the current readings.

Exercise 11.6: Creating and Scheduling a User-Defined Data Collector Set

1. Launch the Reliability and Performance Monitor by clicking Start | Control Panel | System and Maintenance | Administrative Tools and double-clicking Reliability and Performance Monitor. If the User Account Control dialog appears, click Continue.

2. Open the Data Collector Sets container. Right-click User Defined and select New Data Collector Set.

3. In the Create New Data Collector Set dialog box, enter **Monitor System Performance** as the name. Ensure that Create From a Template (Recommended) is selected. Click Next.

4. On the Which Template Would You Like To Use page, select the System Performance template. Your display will look similar to Figure 11-17. Notice that you can select from a Basic, System Diagnostics, or System Performance template. Click Next.

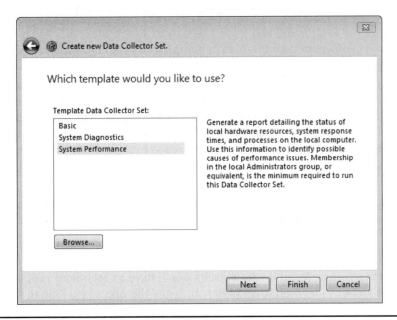

Figure 11-17   Selecting a template for a data collector set

5. Accept the default location on the Where Would You Like The Data To Be Saved page and click Next.

6. On the Create The Data Collector Set page, click Finish. After a moment, your new data collector set will be created and appear.

7. Right-click the Monitor System Performance data collector set and select Properties. Click through each of the tabs to familiarize yourself with the properties that can be manipulated.

8. Click the Stop Condition tab. Change the Overall Duration from 1 minute to 1 week.

9. Click the Schedule tab. Click the Add button.

10. On the Folder Action page, click the Beginning Date and change the date to tomorrow's date. This will cause the data collector set to start running tomorrow. With the duration set to 1 week, it will continue to run for 7 days. Click OK.

11. Click OK to close the Properties page.

12. With the Monitor System Performance data collector set selected, right-click the Performance Counter object and select Properties.

13. Review the Performance Counters that are selected. Notice that each of the objects are using an asterisk (*) in their path. This is a wildcard, and it indicates that all of the counters for each of the objects are being included.

14. Change the Sample Interval from 1 second to 30 minutes. This will cause each of these performance counters to be sampled twice an hour instead of once per second.

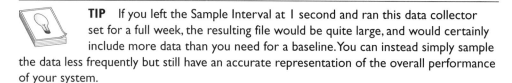

TIP If you left the Sample Interval at 1 second and ran this data collector set for a full week, the resulting file would be quite large, and would certainly include more data than you need for a baseline. You can instead simply sample the data less frequently but still have an accurate representation of the overall performance of your system.

---

15. Click Add. If desired, you can add additional counters to the Performance Counter component of your data collector set. This is the same dialog box you saw in Exercise 11.4.

16. Click Cancel to return to the Performance Counter Properties page. Click OK.

17. After this completes (it'll take a week), you'll have a baseline of your system. These steps can be used to accurately measure the overall performance of any system.

Reading Performance Logs with relog.exe

The Performance Monitor creates log files in binary format (.blg for binary log) by default. Data collector sets include Performance Monitor data, and there may be times when you want to view or analyze only the Performance Monitor data.

Relog.exe is a command-line tool you can use to retrieve information from existing .blg files and output them to different formats. If the existing file is too big and contains more samples than you really need, you can modify it using the `relog` command.

- **Modify which counters are included** Instead of retrieving all the counters, you can narrow the log down to just what you want. The `-c` switch can be used to filter counters.

- **Modify the output format** You can create comma-separated value files (csv), tab-separated value files (tsv), binary files (bin), and SQL Server database files (SQL). The `-f` switch allows you to specify the format.

- **Modify the size of the output** You can choose how many samples to retrieve from the source file with the -t switch. For example, you could choose to only retrieve every second sample (with -t 2), or every fifth sample (with -t 5).

- **Modify the start and end times** If you have a week-long file but want to narrow your focus to between 10 A.M. and 4 P.M. on Wednesday, you can do so. The -b switch specifies the start time, and the -e switch specifies the end time.

 EXAM TIP Relog can be used to convert performance logs to other formats, such as CSV, TSV, and SQL. It can also be used to extract specific information from performance logs.

As with any command-line tools, you can use the /? switch to get a listing of help on the command. From an administrative command-line prompt, enter this command:

```
Relog /?
```

When running the relog command, you must either include the path to your performance log file or change the path when you run the command. For example, the following command could be used to change the path to the location of the files created when the System Performance data collector set was run on July 4, 2008.

```
Cd %systemdrive%\Perflogs\System\Performance\20080704-0001
```

Then the following relog command could be used to retrieve every fifth sample (-t 5) from the performance counter.blg file, format it as a comma-separated value file (-f csv) and send it to a file named output.csv (-o output.csv). Notice that since the performance counter.blg file has spaces in it, it must be enclosed within quotes in the command.

```
Relog "performance counter.blg" -f csv -o output.csv -t 5
```

To open and view the file, you could use the following command:

```
Notepad output.csv
```

You could also use Microsoft Excel or other applications to view the data. However, the key here is that you can use relog to extract information from performance logs into other formats.

Keeping Your System Up-to-Date with Windows Update

Windows Update was mentioned in Chapter 1 as part of the post-installation tasks. However, you'll very likely touch Windows Update settings in the life cycle of any system, so you should have a solid understanding of how updates work.

Microsoft categorizes updates as

- **Important** Important updates on Windows Vista are critical to the security of your computer. They include fixes that protect against security threats and boost its reliability. Important updates are called high-priority updates on Windows XP and earlier operating systems.

- **Recommended** Recommended updates help keep your computer running smoothly or add additional capabilities such as the Windows Media Player or the Windows Movie Maker.

- **Optional** Optional updates include software components or applications from Microsoft or its partners designed to enhance your computing experience. As an example, the Windows Vista DreamScene (a video that plays on your desktop) can be downloaded as an optional update on Windows Vista Ultimate systems.

Windows Updates can be received differently, depending on how the computer is configured. You can receive updates directly from the Windows Update site or via a Windows Server Update Services (WSUS) server. WSUS will be explained in more depth later in this section.

The Windows Update applet is shown in Figure 11-18. You can access this by clicking Start | Control Panel | System and Maintenance and selecting Windows Update.

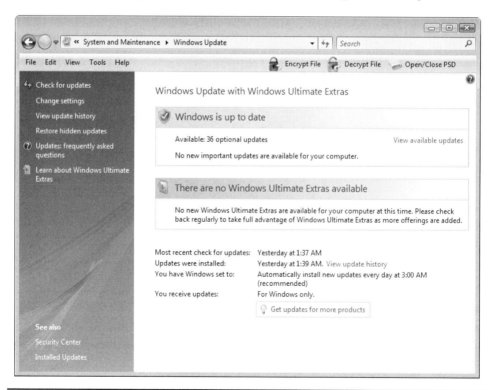

Figure 11-18 Windows Update applet in the Control Panel

This applet offers you many capabilities to manage Windows Update.

- Check for Updates
- Change Settings
- View Update History
- Restore Hidden Updates
- View Available Updates

The link at the bottom of the page with the light bulb icon "Get Updates For More Products" can be used to configure your system to download updates for applications in addition to the Windows operating system. This link enables Microsoft Update, which can be enabled in addition to Windows Update.

Comparing Windows Update with Microsoft Update

Although similarly named and often confused, Windows Update and Microsoft Update are two separate programs.

- **Windows Update**   Windows Update provides updates for the operating system and installed components. Windows Update is automatically available and simply needs to be enabled to work.

- **Microsoft Update**   Microsoft Update provides updates for Windows, Office, and other Microsoft applications. Microsoft Update is optional and must be downloaded and installed. Once downloaded and installed, Microsoft Update will work in tandem with Windows Update.

EXAM TIP   Updates for applications aren't automatically included unless you install Microsoft Update. You can do this through the Get Updates For More Products link on the Windows Update page.

Checking for Updates

You can check for updates manually by clicking the Check For Updates link. If you have an Internet connection, your system will visit the Windows Update site to see if any new updates are available. It will either show the available updates or let you know your system is up-to-date.

Figure 11-19 shows the result after connecting and checking to see if the system is up-to-date. In the figure, one important update has been located that is available to be downloaded and installed.

To install updates immediately, you only need to click the Install Updates button and follow the onscreen instructions.

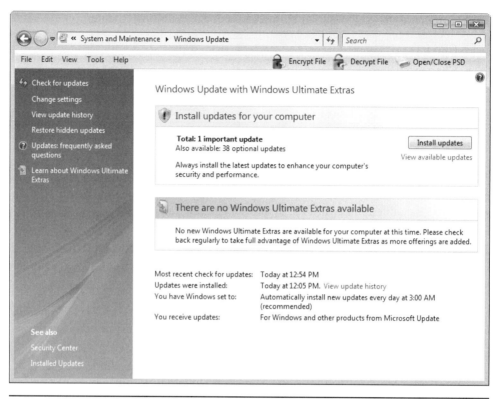

Figure 11-19   Checking for updates

Changing Settings

You can choose how Windows installs the updates and whether or not the updates are automatically downloaded and installed or not. When you click the Change Settings link on the Windows Update page, you can configure how updates are installed.

You can configure your system to only check for important updates, or to check for both important and recommended updates. Figure 11-20 shows the page used to configure how Windows installs updates.

Your choices are

- **Install Updates Automatically (Recommended)**   Your system will periodically check for updates and automatically download new updates when they are available. The updates are then automatically installed based on the schedule set on your system. By default, updates are scheduled to be installed at 3 A.M.

- **Download Updates But Let Me Choose Whether To Install Them**   This choice is useful if you want to know exactly when the updates are installed. Some updates require a reboot. If you tend to leave windows open on your desktop and you don't want to come back to rebooted system, choose this option.

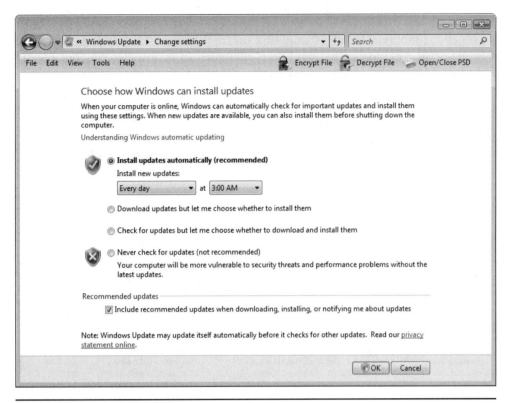

Figure 11-20   Configuring how Windows installs updates

- **Check For Updates But Let Me Choose Whether To Download Them**   This choice is useful if you connect to the Internet with a slow Internet connection. For example, if you connect with a 56K modem to download your e-mail, you wouldn't want your system filling the link with a download of the most recent service pack.

- **Never Check For Updates (Not Recommended)**   The only way updates are downloaded is when you do so manually. This completely removes the automation of updates and can easily result in a system not being updated at all.

- **Include Recommended Updates When Downloading, Installing, Or Notifying Me About Updates**   You can check or uncheck this box, depending on whether you want to include recommended updates.

Optional updates aren't installed automatically. In order to download optional updates, you must visit the Windows Update site.

Viewing Update History

If you click the View Update History link on the Windows Update page, you'll see a listing of all the updates that have been attempted to be installed on your system. Figure 11-21 shows the update history page.

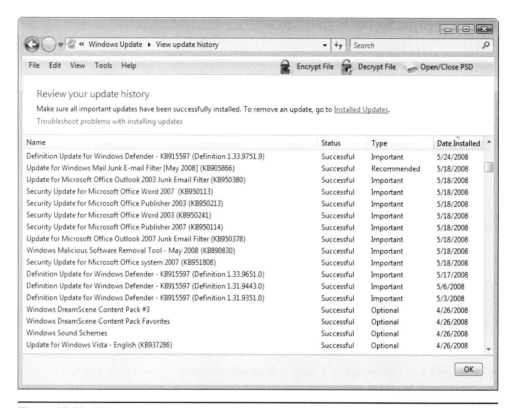

Figure 11-21 Viewing the update history page

Each update in the history page has four columns:

- **Name**   This is the name that Microsoft has given for the update and usually explains what the update is in simple terms.

- **Status**   The status can be either Successful or Failed. Microsoft recommends that you ensure that all Important updates have been successfully installed.

- **Type**   Three types of updates can be installed: Important, Recommended, Optional. Each of these types were defined earlier in this chapter.

- **Date Installed**   When the update was installed.

The display is shown ordered by date, with the most recent updates installed first. If you look back at Figure 11-21, you'll notice a down arrow in the Date Installed column header. If you click the Date Installed header, it will change to an up arrow and the data will be ordered by date but in ascending order (most recent date last). You can also click the header of any other column to order the report by that column for easier searching.

Removing Updates

You can remove, or uninstall, any updates that have been installed on a Windows Vista system. This is done through the Installed Updates page.

Figure 11-22 shows the Installed Updates page. To uninstall an update, you simply select the update and click the Uninstall link on the page.

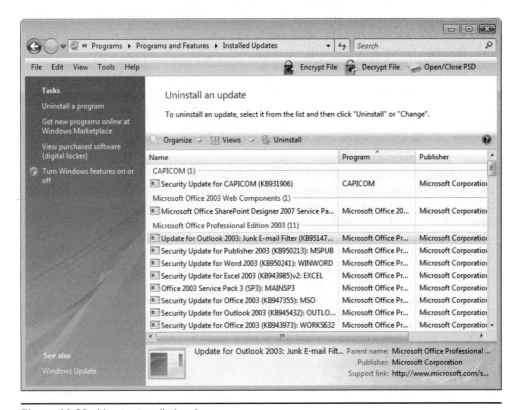

Figure 11-22 Viewing installed updates

You can access the Installed Updates page through two methods.

- Click the Installed Updates link on the View Update history page.
- Click the Installed Updates link from the Control Panel | Programs | Programs and Features page.

Restoring Hidden Updates

Hidden updates are updates that you've chosen not to install and have also configured to be hidden. If an update is available and you choose not to install it, Windows will keep reminding you to install the update. You can choose to hide the update so that Windows no longer keeps reminding you.

If you later decide you want to install the update, you must first restore it. You can access the Restore Hidden Updates screen from the Windows Update page. Select the update you want to install and click Restore.

Viewing the Software Distribution Folder

All downloaded updates are stored in the %windir%\SoftwareDistribution folder. The folder holds update files used by Windows to update your computer. It includes several subfolders and ReportingEvents.log.

 EXAM TIP The environmental variable %windir% is a variable indicating the drive and folder location where Windows was installed. This is C:\Windows on most systems. If Windows was installed in C:\Windows on your system, then the Software Distribution folder is in C:\Windows\SoftwareDistribution.

Recovering from Error 80070002 or 80070003

Two known Windows Update errors are error 80070002 and 80070003. It's possible for files to become corrupt within the temporary update folder and the Windows Update service will be unable to continue.

The DataStore folder is within the SoftwareDistribution folder. It's referred to as a temporary update folder, and if you experience one of these errors, you can delete all the files in the folder. The overall steps to recover from this error are

1. Stop the Windows Update service. You can do this from the Services applet.

2. Browse to the ..\SoftwareDistribution\DataStore folder with Windows Explorer.

3. Delete all the files within this folder.

4. Restart the Windows Update service.

 NOTE For more information on this error, check out Knowledge Base article 910336. You can find this by typing in "KB 910336" in your favorite search engine.

If you try to resolve problems with Windows Update by deleting the contents of the DataStore folder but the problems remain, you can take more drastic steps. Specifically, you can change the name of the SoftwareDistribution folder. When Windows Update starts, it'll see the folder is missing and rebuild it from scratch.

It just may be my paranoia, but I don't recommend deleting this folder entirely, but instead just renaming it. You may want to review the ReportingEvents.log or other folders at some later date. The overall steps to rename this folder are

1. Stop the Windows Update service. You can do this from the Services applet.

2. Browse to the ..\SoftwareDistribution\DataStore folder with Windows Explorer.

3. Rename the folder to SoftwareDisbutionOld.

4. Restart the Windows Update service.

Reviewing reportingevents.log

Earlier in this section you learned about viewing the update history. You can also view reportingevents.log in the %windir%\softwaredistribution folder. This log includes detailed information on all the updates for your system.

Just as the Update History page includes both successful and failed updates, reportingevents.log also includes both. However, this log file includes much more detailed information on the failure. It includes the date, the time, the error number, and a phrase on what the problem was. Of course, it also includes detailed information on all the successful updates.

 EXAM TIP You can check either reportingevents.log or the Update History page to verify if updates have been installed on a Windows Vista system.

Using a WSUS Server

It's very common to create a Windows Server Update Services (WSUS) server to be used to deploy updates to computers within a domain environment. Figure 11-23 shows a typical network configuration for an environment that uses a WSUS server.

Figure 11-23
Using a WSUS
server

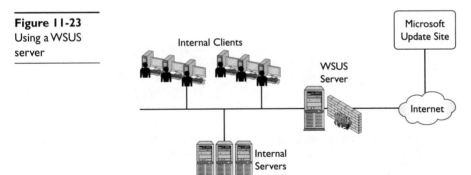

Instead of every individual computer going out to retrieve updates from the Windows Update site, only the WSUS server retrieves the updates. All the internal computers then retrieve their updates from the WSUS server.

Centralizing Windows Updates through a WSUS server provides two benefits:

- **Conserves bandwidth** Since only one computer is retrieving the updates, less bandwidth is used to download the updates.

- **Provides administrative control** WSUS administrators can approve and deploy only the updates they want to deploy. Unwanted or unneeded updates aren't approved and aren't deployed. Additionally, administrators can use the WSUS console to easily determine which computers have received updates and which computers haven't received updates.

When using a WSUS server, individual computers must be configured to retrieve their updates through the WSUS server instead of through the Windows Update site. This is often done through group policy. Group policy was covered in more depth in Chapter 10, but in Figure 11-24 you can see the Group Policy dialog box used to configure systems to use WSUS.

Figure 11-24
Configuring group policy for a WSUS server

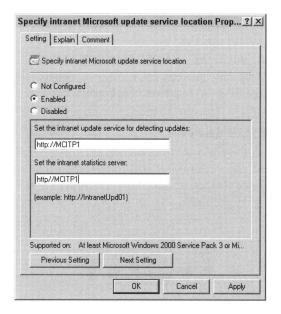

 EXAM TIP After configuring a WSUS to centralize the deployment of Windows Update, you must configure the clients to use WSUS. The easiest way to do this is through group policy.

You can see that you can configure two services from this dialog box:

- **Set The Intranet Update Service for Detecting Updates** This is the WSUS server configured to deploy updates to internal clients.

- **Set The Intranet Statistics Server** This is the server that clients report back on the status of the update installation. This is normally the same as the Intranet Update Service server, but in large environments with multiple WSUS servers, you can centralize statistics onto a central server.

Using DirectX Diagnostics

The DirectX diagnostics tool can be used to troubleshoot multimedia issues such as problems with graphics and sound. DirectX includes DirectDraw, Direct3D, and AGP Texture for graphics.

DirectX is embedded within Windows Vista and allows application developers to create programs with complex graphics and sound. It's very common for games to use DirectX technologies, and if you have problems with DirectX, it can impact many of your games.

The primary tool to use to troubleshoot problems with DirectX is the DirectX diagnostic tool. You can launch it by clicking Start and entering **dxdiag** in the Start Search line. Figure 11-25 shows the DirectX diagnostic tool.

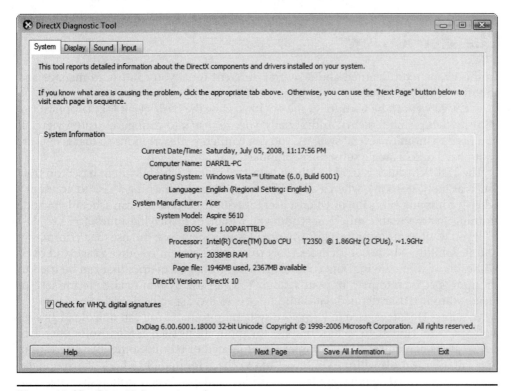

Figure 11-25 DirectX diagnostic tool

As you can see, `dxdiag` has four tabs. They are

- **System tab** The System tab is just informative, allowing you to verify information about your system and which version of DirectX you are running. Windows Vista was released with DirectX 10.

- **Display tab** The Display tab includes information on your graphics devices and drivers. It also lets you know what DirectX features are enabled. When you run `dxdiag`, display diagnostics will run and the results will be displayed in the Notes section. If successful, the notes will indicate "No problems found."

- **Sound tab** The Sound tab includes information on your sound devices and drivers. When you run `dxdiag`, sound diagnostics will run and the results will be displayed in the Notes section. If successful, the notes will indicate "No problems found."

- **Input tab** The Input tab includes information on DirectInput devices. This can be just basic input devices such as the mouse and keyboard, or more elaborate input devices such joysticks used for specific games. When you run `dxdiag`, diagnostics will run on your input devices and the results will be displayed in the Notes section. If successful, the notes will indicate "No problems found."

Chapter Review

In this chapter you learned about several different tools you can use to manage and monitor Windows Vista.

Event Viewer can be used to do the obvious: view the basic event logs (Application, Security, Setup, and System). Additionally, you can use it to configure custom views. If you need to monitor several systems, you can configure subscriptions so that events are centralized onto a single subscriber computer.

The Task Scheduler is used to schedule tasks. You can schedule them based on time (such as daily at noon), when a specific event is logged (attaching a task to an event), when a computer starts up, or when a user logs on. Tasks that you can schedule include running any executable program, sending an e-mail, or displaying a message.

If you want to monitor the performance of your system, you can use the Performance and Reliability Monitor. It includes tools to monitor system resource usage and overall health of your system. Data collector sets are groups of metrics that can be used to monitor specific resources in your system. You can use System data collector sets, or create your own user-defined data collector sets to meet specific needs.

Windows Update is used to keep your system up-to-date. You can download and install Microsoft Update to include updates for applications such as Microsoft Office. Updates can be configured to be completely automated or require some user interaction. You can use the tools within Windows Vista to check for updates, check which updates have been installed, remove updates, and hide updates. When troubleshooting, you can manipulate the contents of the SoftwareDistribution folder. In large environments, you can install a WSUS server and configure clients to retrieve updates from WSUS.

Last, you learned about `dxdiag`. DirectX provides enhanced graphics and sound capabilities to Microsoft applications (especially games), but occasionally things go wrong. The DirectX diagnostics tool (`dxdiag`) can be run to identify problems and issues with DirectX.

Additional Study

Self Study Exercises
Use these additional exercises to challenge yourself.

- Create an event that will fire when a user logs on.
- Attach a task to an event.
- Run the System, System Performance data collector set and view the results.
- Run the System, System Diagnostics data collector set and view the results.
- View the installed updates on your system. Identify if any updates failed.
- Review the reportingevents.log file on your system.
- Run the DirectX diagnostics tool.

Summary of What You Need to Know

70-620
When preparing for the 70-620 exam, pay particular attention to the following topics covered in this chapter:

- **Event Viewer**   You should have a basic understanding of what events are logged and where they are logged. This includes knowing the logs that are available (application, system, setup, and security logs) and how to create custom views.

- **Scheduled Tasks**   You should be familiar with attaching tasks to events.

- **Windows Update**   Know the purpose of Windows Updates, how to configure Windows Updates, how to verify updates are installed, how to remove them, and how to hide them.

70-622
This entire chapter includes a significant amount of material required for the 70-622 exam. When preparing for the 70-622 exam, pay particular attention to the following topics covered in this chapter:

- **Event Viewer**   Make sure you know which logs (such as the application, system, setup, and security logs) are used for which purposes.

- **Event Subscriptions**   Know what event subscriptions are and how to configure them.

- **Scheduled Tasks**   You should know the basics of scheduled tasks, including how to create a scheduled task, the types of tasks that can be created, and the events that can be used to schedule a task.

- **Reliability and Performance Monitor**   You should know the purpose and capabilities of the Reliability and Performance Monitor. This includes understanding the monitoring tools, data collector sets, and reports.

- **Windows Update**. Know the purpose of Windows Updates, how to configure Windows Updates, how to verify updates are installed, how to remove them, and how to hide them.

70-623

When preparing for the 70-623 exam, pay particular attention to the following topics covered in this chapter:

- **Reliability and Performance Monitor**   You should know the purpose and capabilities of the Reliability and Performance Monitor. This includes understanding the monitoring tools, data collector sets, and reports.

- **DirectX diagnostics**   You should be familiar with `dxdiag`, what it does, and how to run it.

Questions

70-620

1. You need to regularly check your Windows Vista system for critical, error, and warning events in the System and Application logs. You also want to ensure you can view the maximum amount of detail in these logs. What should you do?

   A. Create a task schedule and forward critical, error, and warning events to a custom view log.

   B. Create a custom view log. Include critical, error, and warning events for the Windows logs. Select verbose.

   C. Create a custom view log. Include critical, error, and warning events for the System and Application logs. Select verbose.

   D. Create a custom view log. Include critical, error, and warning events for the System and Application logs.

2. Users run an application named Travel on a kiosk computer designed to display information. When they try to save data from the program, it fails by design and generates an event in the Application log. When this error occurs, you want the system to create a display window to tell the users that they can get more information from the travel agent, but the program doesn't allow them to save data. What should you do?

   A. Ask the developer to rewrite the program.

   B. Create a custom view.

    C. Use `schtasks` to run a script.

    D. Attach a task to the event.

3. Vista has installed an update on your system that prevents sounds from playing within an application. You want to remove the update. What should you do?

    A. Remove the application and reinstall it.

    B. Hide the update.

    C. Remove the update.

    D. Reinstall the sound driver.

4. Sally has enabled the Disk Defragment task on her computer. However, she's finding that it's interfering with a backup task running on her computer at the same time and neither task is completing. She would rather have the Disk Defragment task run at 6 P.M. on Tuesday after she's gone for the day but with enough time to complete before the backup. What should she do?

    A. Delete the Disk Defragment task in Task Scheduler and recreate it with the new day and time.

    B. Modify the existing Disk Defragment task in Task Scheduler with the new day and time.

    C. Use the Task Scheduler to schedule the `schtask` program to only run the Task Scheduler if the backup is not running.

    D. Modify the existing Disk Defragment task to run in response to the Backup Complete event in the Application log.

5. The CEO has asked you to develop a method to determine if anyone is logging on to two specific computers after hours. Specifically, he wants to be notified with an e-mail to his mobile phone if someone logs on to one of these computers outside the hours of 7 A.M. to 7 P.M. Monday through Friday. What could you do on each computer?

    A. On each computer create a scheduled task to run at logon. Run a script to check the time and send an e-mail if the time is outside the stated hours.

    B. On each computer create a scheduled task to run at startup. Run a script to check the time and send an e-mail if the time is outside the stated hours.

    C. On each computer create a scheduled task to run hourly. Run a script to check the time and send an e-mail if the time is outside the stated hours and a user is logged on.

    D. On each computer create a scheduled task to run at 7 P.M. Run a script to send an e-mail if a user is logged on.

70-622

1. You are troubleshooting a problem for a user with his wireless NIC. You've configured the connection to connect to the MCITPSuccess wireless NIC, but it is not connecting. What can you do to get more information on the problem?

   A. Run the Network Diagnostics tool and check for Event IDs of 6100 in the System log.

   B. Run the Network Diagnostics tool and check for Event IDs of 6100 in the Application log.

   C. Schedule the Network Diagnostics tool to run when a specific event is logged and use Event ID of 6100.

   D. Schedule the Network Diagnostics tool to run when the computer starts, and check for Event IDs of 6100 in the System log.

2. You've configured event forwarding between two computers. However, events aren't being forwarded as you'd expect. You want to get more detailed information on the status of the subscription. What should you do?

   A. Run WinRM on the source computer.

   B. Run WinRM on the collector computer.

   C. Run wecutil on the source computer.

   D. Run wecutil on the collector computer.

3. A new application named SalesContacts has been installed on a Windows Vista computer. It logs detailed errors in the Application log. Users are having problems with an intermittent error, and you've learned that a specific application event is logged prior to the error occurring. You want to be notified by e-mail when this error occurs. What should you do?

   A. Configure wecutil to send an e-mail when the error occurs.

   B. Configure WinRM to send an e-mail when the error occurs.

   C. Configure Task Scheduler to send an e-mail when the error occurs.

   D. Configure a Custom View in Event Viewer.

4. You are troubleshooting a computer that slows down significantly when users launch an application named SalesTracker from the command line. You discover that a task is launched after the SalesTracker application is started and repeatedly calls itself, causing it to continuously run. You want to stop the task. What should you do?

   A. Use Task Manager to stop SalesTracker.

   B. Use schtasks to run the task.

   C. Use schtasks to delete the task.

   D. Use schtasks to end the task.

5. You want to collect performance data on a Windows Vista system in your network. You need to collect data at least twice a day: in the morning and the afternoon. What is the best way to achieve this?

   A. Ask the user to run the System Performance data collector set twice a day.

   B. Create a System Performance data collector set.

   C. Create a user-defined data collector set.

   D. Use `schtasks`.

6. Your company has decided to centralize the deployment of Windows Updates of internal clients using a single WSUS server. How should you configure the clients?

   A. Configure the clients to automatically download and install updates.

   B. Configure the clients to use Automatic Updates.

   C. Configure the clients to use different servers for intranet statistics and intranet update services.

   D. Configure the clients to use the WSUS server as both the intranet statistics server and the intranet update service server.

7. You need to verify that updates have been successfully installed on a Windows Vista computer. How can this be done?

   A. View the Check for Updates page or the reportinghistory.log file.

   B. View the Update History page or the reportinghistory.log file.

   C. View the Check for Updates page or the reportingevents.log file.

   D. View the Update History page or the reportingevents.log file.

70-623

1. You are assisting a user with his computer. He complains that it runs inconsistently throughout the day. What can you do to narrow down the problem on the computer?

   A. Ask him to bring his computer in when it slows down.

   B. Create and schedule a user-defined data collector set.

   C. Attach a task to an event.

   D. Run `relog.exe`.

2. You are playing a game on your computer. It is very graphics intensive, and it has stopped working several times in the middle of a video playback. You suspect that one of the four core system resources are at fault, but you're not sure which one. What should you do?

   A. Check the Windows Media Center.

   B. Check the Performance and Reliability Monitor.

  C. Check the Windows Experience Index.

  D. Check the Security log in Event Viewer.

3. You are assisting a user with his Windows Vista system. He complains that when he runs a game, the graphics don't display properly. You verify that his graphics card has 512MB of onboard memory and his Windows Vista system has 2GB of onboard RAM. What should you do next?

  A. Run the Performance and Reliability Monitor to check the System Stability Index.

  B. Run the System, System Performance data collector set.

  C. Launch Event Viewer and check the Security log.

  D. Run `dxdiag`.

4. You've discovered that some applications on your system are abnormally stopping after specific services stop. You want to implement a procedure that will regularly monitor services and applications on your system. What would you do?

  A. Create a user-defined data collector set from the System Diagnostics data collector set.

  B. Create a user-defined data collector set from the System Performance data collector set.

  C. Create a System data collector set from the System Diagnostics data collector set.

  D. Create a System data collector set from the System Performance data collector set.

5. Joe is running Windows Vista on his computer. When he runs a specific application, he notices that the response time of his system is significantly reduced. He needs to run this application, and he asks you for help. What can you do to identify the problem and a possible solution?

  A. Run Task Manager and end his application.

  B. Run `schtasks` to run a script when the application starts.

  C. Start a data collector set.

  D. Attach a task to an event.

Answers

70-620

1. **C.** You can create a custom view log and include the specific events of interest (critical, error, and warning events) in the two logs of interest (System and Application logs). By selecting verbose, you will be assured of including the most detail in the logs. A task schedule can be used to create a custom view log.

If you select Windows logs, all the Windows logs will be selected instead of just the System and Application logs. If you don't select verbose, you won't get the maximum amount of detail.

2. **D.** You can use Task Scheduler to attach a task to the event and have the task display a message when the event occurs. It wouldn't be necessary to rewrite the program. A custom view wouldn't display a message. `Schtasks` is used to manage tasks but wouldn't display a message.

3. **C.** If an update causes a problem, you can remove the update. If you want to ensure Windows doesn't keep reminding you of the update, you can hide it, but it first must be removed. The problem is with the update, so you don't need to remove the application or reinstall hardware drivers.

4. **B.** The existing task can be modified with a new day and time; this would be the simplest method. You could delete and recreate the task, but that is much more work than necessary. Associating any task with the completion of the backup doesn't meet the desire to run the task at 6 P.M.

5. **A.** A scheduled task can be scheduled to start at logon and run a script. When the user logs on, the task will launch the script, which can check the time and send the e-mail. Running the script at startup won't capture a user logon, since it's possible a computer is rebooted once a month but users would log on much more frequently. Having the script run hourly is much more often than is needed and wouldn't capture a user logging on at 8:05 P.M. and logging off at 8:15 P.M. Just running the task at 7 P.M. wouldn't capture a user logging on at any other time.

70-622

1. **A.** You can run the Network Diagnostics tool by clicking Diagnose and Repair in the Network and Sharing Center. Event ID 6100 in the System log will provide more detail on the wireless connection. Network Diagnostics will log the results in the System log, not the Application log. There is no need to schedule the Network Diagnostics tool; it should just be run manually.

2. **D.** The Windows Event Collector Utility (`wecutil`) can be run on the collector with the `gr` command to get details on the subscription's runtime status. Since subscriptions are kept on the collector computer, it won't do any good to run `wecutil` on the source computer. WinRM is used to configure the source computer with the WS-Management protocol but does not configure subscriptions.

3. **C.** You can configure Task Scheduler to send an e-mail when a specific error occurs. WinRM and `wecutil` are used to configure event subscriptions and can't be configured to send an e-mail. A custom view can't send an e-mail.

4. **D.** You can use the `schtasks` command-line tool to end the task so that it stops repeatedly running. The problem isn't with the program (SalesTracker) but with the task. You don't want to run the task, but to stop it. You may want to troubleshoot the task, but if you delete it, it's gone and you have to start over. Additionally, the question states that you want to stop the task.

5. **C.** The easiest way to accomplish this is to create a user-defined data collector set and schedule it to run twice a day. You can't create a schedule for a System data collector set. Asking a user to accomplish the task wouldn't be reliable. Using `schtasks` would be much more difficult than is required.

6. **D.** You should configure the clients to use the WSUS server as both the intranet statistics server and the intranet update services server. Simply configuring Automatic Updates or configuring the clients to automatically download and install the updates won't ensure they receive their updates from the WSUS server. Since only a single server is being used, clients should be configured to only use a single server for both updates and statistics.

7. **D.** You can check the Update History page, or the reportingevents.log file located in the %windir%\SoftwareDistribution folder. A history of updates can't be viewed on the Check for Updates page. There is no such thing as a reportinghistory.log file.

70-623

1. **B.** A user-defined data collector set could be created and scheduled to run throughout the day to capture data on what may be causing the problem. It's not reasonable to ask the user to bring the computer in when it slows down; by the time he arrived, the problem will likely have resolved itself, especially if the computer was shut down. Attaching a task won't identify a problem. `Relog` is used to work with existing performance logs by changing the sampling rate or converting the file format.

2. **B.** The Performance and Reliability Monitor can be used to check the performance of individual resources (such as CPU, memory, and disk) on your system. The Windows Media Center is used for media playback but wouldn't identify which system resource is causing a problem. The Windows Experience Index gives you an overall rating of your system's performance but doesn't identify a specific resource as a problem. The Security log would log audited events such as file access.

3. **D.** The DirectX diagnostics tool (`dxdiag`) will run diagnostics on graphics and sound resources that are often used in games. The System Stability Index will give an indication of well the computer has been running, but you already know a problem with the graphics is occurring. The System Performance data collector set will measure your system resources but won't focus on the graphics. You may find some useful information in either the System or the Application log related to the graphics driver, but the Security log will only include information relating to audited events.

4. **A.** You can create a user-defined data collector set from the System Diagnostics data collector set to collect detailed information on services and applications. The System Performance data collector set focuses on hardware (the four core resources) but not services and applications. You can't create a System data collector set, only a user-defined data collector set.

5. **C.** You could run one of the System data collector sets (such as System Performance or System Diagnostics) to identify the problem. It could be related to a bottleneck such as not enough memory, and an upgrade to the system may resolve the problem. Ending the application, running `schtasks`, or attaching a task to an event won't identify the problem or a solution.

Using Disaster Recovery Tools

In this chapter, you will learn about:

- Troubleshooting and restoring the operating system
- Windows Complete PC Backup and Restore
- System Recovery options
- System Restore and restore points
- Advanced Boot options
- Volume Shadow Copy service
- Windows Resource checker
- Backing up and restoring data files

Disasters happen. We all wish it weren't true, but if you work with computers long enough, something will go wrong. Knowing how to be prepared and how to recover from a disaster is valuable information—not only to prepare for exams, but to prepare for the inevitable.

The ability to recover an operating system can often save valuable time. Depending on how many applications are installed, or the configuration of your system, it may take a significant amount of time to rebuild a system. However, if you can instead spend a few minutes performing a system restore, or accessing some of the recovery options or advanced boot options, you can save yourself a lot of time and energy.

In addition to being able to recover your system, it's also important to be able to restore your data. Of course you can only do that if you've spent some time creating backups.

 EXAM TIP Objectives for the 70-620, 70-622, and 70-623 exams are included in this chapter.

Troubleshooting and Restoring the Operating System

Like it or not, occasionally operating systems develop problems that require troubleshooting. One of the most important things you can do to prepare is to understand the tools available to keep your system operational, and to know what tools to use to bring it back when problems occur.

When backing up and restoring the operating system, you'll be working with system files. When backing up and restoring user files, you'll be working with data files. It's important to understand the difference between system files and data files.

- **System files**   These are files used by the operating system, such as dynamic link libraries (DLLs), executables (such as .exe and .com files found in the Windows directory), and the Registry. Users rarely interact with these files directly. System files are backed up using System Restore by creating restore points. You can restore these system files by applying a restore point using System Restore.

- **Data files**   These are the files you use, open, and access directly on an ongoing basis. They can include pictures, e-mail, music, videos, documents, and any other data files you create using applications.

  Data files are backed up using the Backup and Restore Center (choosing Back Up Files on Your Computer), or the Backup Status and Configuration tool. Similarly, you can restore files using the Backup and Restore Center (choosing Restore Files on Your Computer), or the Backup Status and Configuration tool.

Only the Windows Complete PC Backup tool backs up both system and data files. However, if you use the Windows Complete PC Backup tool, it's strongly recommended that you also perform regular backups of your data.

In this section, you'll learn how to back up and restore system files. Later in this chapter you'll learn how to back up and restore data files.

Three of the primary tools you have at your disposal to troubleshoot and restore the operating system are

- **Backup and Restore Center**   You can access System Restore through here to apply restore points. You can also back up and restore data files with this tool.

- **System Recovery Options**   This can be accessed through the repair option after booting from the installation DVD.

- **Windows Complete PC Backup And Restore**   You can back up and restore your entire hard disk (including the operating system, program files, and data) to an image. This tool is only available in Windows Vista Business, Ultimate, and Enterprise Editions.

- **Windows Resource Checker (sfc)**   This command-line tool can be used to check and repair system files.

- **Advanced Boot Options**   Available by pressing the F8 key during bootup, these tools can be used for advanced troubleshooting. They include the safe modes and the Last Known Good Configuration.

- **Backup Status And Configuration**   This tool is primarily used to configure automatic backups of files, but it also includes a path to the Windows Complete PC Backup and Restore tool (in Windows Vista Business, Ultimate, and Enterprise Editions).

Using the Backup and Restore Center

The Backup and Restore Center can be used to back up and restore system files and data files to your system. You can access the tool by going to the Control Panel and clicking the Back Up Your Computer link under System and Maintenance.

Figure 12-1 shows the Backup and Restore Center.

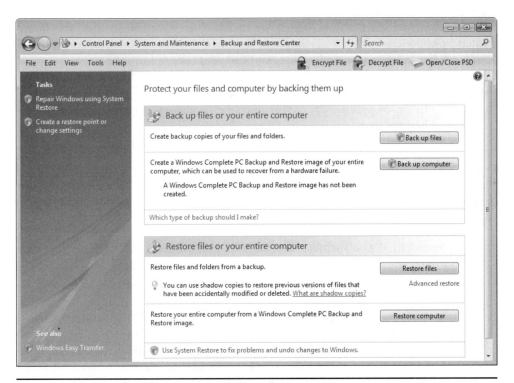

Figure 12-1   The Backup and Restore Center

When using the Backup and Restore Center to back up and restore system files, you work with two different methodologies:

- **Windows Complete PC Backup** The Complete PC Backup creates an image of your entire computer and allows you to restore the entire image. The Back Up Computer and Restore Computer buttons begin this process for you.

- **System Restore** System Restore is used to create system restore points that capture key system settings before changes occur and can be restored to undo those changes. The tasks in the Tasks pane and the link at the bottom of the page lead to the pages to perform System Restore tasks.

Creating a Windows Complete PC Backup and Restore Image

The Windows Complete PC Backup and Restore tool creates a complete image of everything on your computer, including the operating system, applications, and data. In addition to a Windows Complete PC Backup and Restore, you can also regularly back up your data using Automatic backups.

Unlike system restore points, which are installed on your system disk, the image created from the Complete PC Backup and Restore tool is stored on separate media. If your hard disk fails you can replace the hard disk and restore from the image.

EXAM TIP If you need to ensure you can recover from a complete hard disk failure, create an image backup using the Windows Complete PC Backup and Restore tool.

Microsoft recommends creating a Windows Complete PC Backup image when you first set up your computer, and then update the image at least every six months. If you ever have a catastrophic failure of your system, you can restore the image, restore recent data backups, and be back in business.

Image backups can be backed up to

- Separate hard disks (such as a second internal hard disk or an external hard disk connected via a USB connection).

- One or more DVDs.

TIP You cannot back up to tape using Windows Vista native tools. While it is common to back server data up to tape in a corporate environment, Microsoft did not include support for tape drives in the native backup tools. With the low cost and convenience of external USB drives, this makes a lot of sense. End users are much more familiar with disks than they are with tape drives.

The high-level steps to create an image using Windows Complete PC Backup and restore are

1. Launch the Backup and Restore Center.

   Click Start | Control Panel and select the Back Up Your Computer link under System and Maintenance.

2. Click Back Up Computer.

   Your system will scan for suitable backup devices and will look similar to
   Figure 12-2. In the figure, you can see that I have a Kingston USB flash drive
   connected but since it is not formatted with NTFS it can't be used to create
   an image.

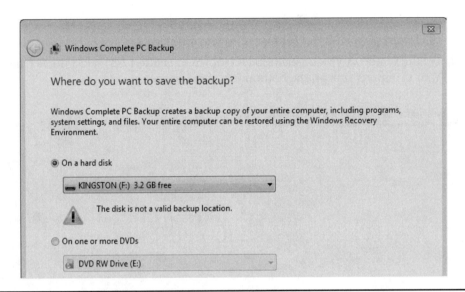

Figure 12-2 Windows Complete PC Backup and Restore

3. Select On a Hard Disk (and select a suitable hard disk), or select On One or
   More DVDs. Click Next.

4. The Confirm Your Backup Settings page appears.

   It identifies both the backup location and the disk or disks that will be backed
   up. Click Start Backup to begin the operation.

 TIP To restore an image created from Windows Complete PC Backup and
Restore, you must boot from the DVD and access the System Recovery
Options menu as discussed in the next section.

You can also access the Windows Complete PC Backup tool through the Backup
Status and Configuration tool. This tool will be explored in more depth later in this
chapter when discussing how to back up and restore files. However, it also includes an
icon and link named Complete PC Backup that can be used to access Windows Complete PC Backup.

Accessing the System Recovery Options Menu

If your system won't boot at all, you can access the System Recovery Options from the installation DVD. The System Recovery Options provide you with a group of tools you can use to recover Windows from serious errors.

You can access the System Recovery Options menu by following these steps:

1. Boot to the installation DVD.

2. Click Next on the Set the Following Preferences page.

3. On the Windows Vista Install Screen (shown in Figure 12-3) select the Repair Your Computer link on the bottom left of the screen.

Figure 12-3 Windows Vista Install screen

4. The program will scan your system for installed operating systems, and you can pick the operating system you want to repair. Select the operating system you want to repair and click Next. It's very likely you'll only have one operating system installed.

5. The System Recovery Options menu will appear as shown in Figure 12-4.

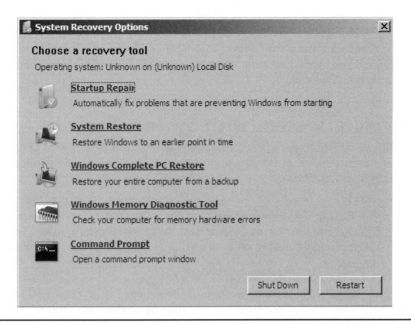

Figure 12-4   System Recovery Options

You have the following choices from the System Recovery Options menu:

- **Startup Repair**   The Startup Repair option will scan your system for missing or damaged system files that prevent Windows from starting. It attempts to repair any problems that if finds. It does not recover data files or repair hardware errors.

- **System Restore**   You can use this option to apply restore points to restore your computer's system files to an earlier time. For example, if an update to the operating system or a driver prevented you from starting your computer, you could use System Restore from this menu to undo the change by applying a restore point from before the update. Remember that System Restore does not restore any data.

- **Windows Complete PC Restore**   If you've created backup images using the Windows Complete PC Backup tool, you can restore the image from here. If possible, you should try to recover all of your data before applying the image. All data on the hard drive will be erased when the previous image is installed. It will restore the operating system, applications, and any data that existed on the hard drive when the image was created.

- **Windows Memory Diagnostic tool**   This will scan your computer for memory errors. Windows often detects memory errors and will give you an indication of a possible error that you can verify with this tool.

- **Command Prompt**   The command prompt allows you to run command-line tools for diagnosing and troubleshooting problems.

NOTE If you've worked with previous editions of Windows, you may be wondering about the Recovery Console. The Recovery Console has been replaced by the Command Prompt within the System Recovery Options menu in Windows Vista.

Restoring a System with System Restore

Occasionally, installing an application or device driver causes your system to misbehave. You can use System Restore to restore your system to a previous state. System restore only affects system files—not data such as documents or e-mail.

EXAM TIP You should be aware of the different ways restore points are created and how to use System Restore to apply restore points. Restore points are only created on drives larger than 1GB and with at least 300 MB of free space.

Restore points are used to save the state of your system files, Registry settings, and program files. A restore point contains information about the Registry and other system files and is created automatically when certain events occur. You can also manually create system restore points as a precaution before performing a risky operation. Restore points are automatically created at the following times:

- Daily
- Before the installation or upgrade of a program
- Before the installation or upgrade of a device driver

System Restore won't run on hard disks smaller than 1GB, and it requires at least 300 MB of free space. It can use as much as 15 percent of the space on each disk that is used to create restore points.

Manually Creating a Restore Point

You can manually create a restore point anytime you desire. As an example, you may be planning on upgrading several different drivers in your system and want to make sure you know exactly where to restore to if things go badly. You could manually create the restore point, give it a name that makes sense to you, and then proceed with your upgrades.

In Exercise 12.1, you will manually create a restore point.

Exercise 12.1: Manually Creating a Restore Point

1. Launch the Backup and Restore Center by clicking Start, and Control Panel. In the Control Panel, select the Back Up Your Computer link under System and Maintenance.

2. In the Tasks pane of the Backup and Restore Center, select Create a Restore Point or Change Settings. If the User Account Control dialog appears, click Continue.

3. Your display will look similar to Figure 12-5. In the display, two drives have been selected. Whenever a system restore point is created, it will be created on both drives.

Figure 12-5
Accessing System
Restore settings

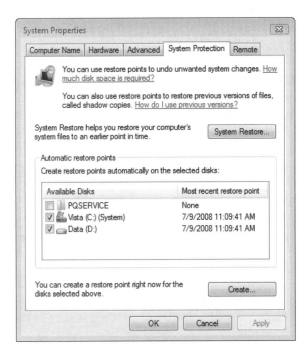

4. Click Create. On the Create a Restore Point page, enter **Chapter 12 Exercise** as the name for the restore point and click Create. After a moment, you will be notified that a restore point was successfully created. Click OK.

Using System Restore to Restore Your System with a Restore Point

If Windows is not operating correctly, one of the easiest troubleshooting steps is to use the System Restore to apply a restore point and return your system files and settings to a previous time. Restore points are most useful if you recognize a problem right after making a change to your system such as installing an application or device driver. If you're not really sure when the problem occurred, it may be difficult to identify which restore point to apply.

For example, if a problem occurred sometime in the past week, applying a restore point from yesterday won't resolve the problem. You'll have to experiment with different restore points. Additionally, when you apply a restore point from some point in the past, you'll also undo any desired system changes that you performed since then, which may require some more troubleshooting.

In Exercise 12.2, you will restore your system to a previous point. This exercise assumes you completed the preceding exercise, in which a restore point was created.

Exercise 12.2: Using System Restore to Apply a Restore Point

1. Launch the Backup and Restore Center by clicking Start, and Control Panel. In the Control Panel, select the Back Up Your Computer link under System and Maintenance.

2. In the Tasks pane of the Backup and Restore Center, select Repair Windows Using System Restore. If the User Account Control dialog appears, click Continue.

3. The Restore System Files and Settings page appears. Notice that the operating system recommends a specific restore point to restore. You can choose this or pick a different restore point. Select Choose a Different Restore Point and click Next.

4. The Choose a Restore Point page appears as shown in Figure 12-6. Notice there are several restore points already created. A System: Scheduled Checkpoint is created daily. A few restore points were created before a Windows Update installation, and two were created manually.

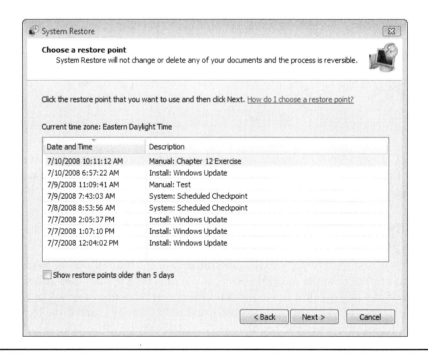

Figure 12-6   Choosing a restore point

5. You should have a restore point named Manual: Chapter 12 Exercise created from the previous exercise. Select the Manual: Chapter 12 Exercise restore point and select Next.

CAUTION Your system will reboot to apply the restore point. Make sure all files are saved before applying the restore point.

6. Click Finish to confirm your selection. Applying a restore point requires a system reboot.

Undoing System Restore

If you apply a system restore point and it doesn't give you the desired results, you can usually undo it. The only exception is when you apply a system restore point in Safe mode.

Prior to applying a restore point, the system creates a restore point. If you want to undo the system restore, you simply repeat the process but select the restore point created immediately prior to the system restore.

However, when you perform a system restore in Safe mode, it doesn't create a restore point, so you can't undo it. You can still repeat the process to select a different restore point from within Safe mode if desired.

Performing System Restore from the Installation DVD

It's also possible to restore your system when you have a system failure preventing you from booting into the operating system. For example, after installing a faulty application, some key files may become corrupt, preventing you from successfully booting.

You can boot into the System Recovery Options menu from the installation DVD. This process was described in more detail earlier in this chapter. Select System Restore from the System Recovery Options menu and select the desired restore point.

The System Restore process will restore your operating system. Once complete, you'll be prompted to restart your system.

Understanding Shadow Copy in Windows Vista

Shadow copy was introduced in Windows to solve a basic problem. The problem was that open files were locked and couldn't be backed up. Shadow copy takes a snapshot of an open file, allowing it to be backed up.

Additionally, in Windows Vista shadow copy uses an incremental-based technology. In other words, when a shadow copy backup is created, the entire file isn't backed up, but instead only the changes are backed up. Consider a 50-page project document that you've been working on, which has already been backed up. You open the document and change a single date in the document and save it. The next backup doesn't back up the entire document but instead only backs up the portion of the document that has changed.

The Volume Shadow Copy service must be enabled in order for shadow copies to work. Figure 12-7 shows the services applet with the Volume Shadow Copy service. Notice it's not running but is instead set to Manual. When the service is needed (such as by System Restore), it will be automatically started and stopped.

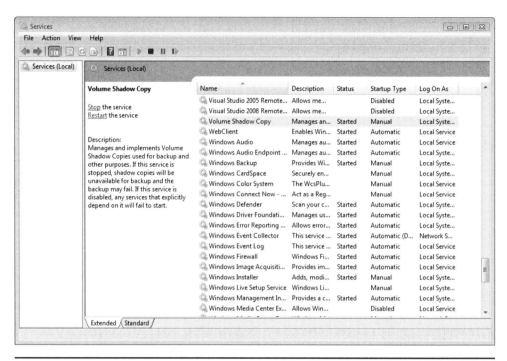

Figure 12-7   Volume Shadow Copy service

If the Volume Shadow Copy service is disabled, you will see a variety of different errors when using System Restore and running backups. Some of the errors point you directly to the Volume Shadow Copy service and let you know that you need to start it. Some of the errors are a little more cryptic.

EXAM TIP   The Volume Shadow Copy service must be enabled to run backups and create restore points in Windows Vista.

For example, Figure 12-8 shows a Catastrophic Failure error message you'll receive if you try to do a Windows PC Complete Backup. Notice it doesn't say anything about Volume Shadow Copy at all.

"Catastrophic Failure" sounds scary, but you can probably just check the Volume Shadow Copy service and ensure it is set to either Manual or Automatic. If it's set to Automatic, it will start when Vista starts. If it's set to Manual, the backup program can start it when it's needed.

While Volume Shadow Copy sounds a lot like Shadow Copy and Previous Versions, they aren't the same thing. Shadow Copy and Previous Versions were explained

Figure 12-8
Catastrophic
failure

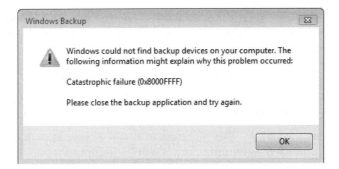

in Chapter 4. As a reminder, Previous Versions is a feature within some Windows Vista editions (Ultimate, Business, and Enterprise) that allows a user to restore any files they have changed to a previous version of the file without any administrative intervention.

Checking System Files with the Windows Resource Checker

The Windows Resource Checker is part of the overall Windows Resource Protection technology used to protect operating system files. As with most solutions, it came into existence due to a specific problem.

In older versions of Windows operating systems, files needed by the operating system could be overwritten by applications. For example, program A needs version 3 of a file named 3DControl.dll, so it installs it. Then program B is installed; it needs version 2 of the 3DControll.dll file. Program B installs version 2, overwriting version 3, so program A no longer works.

Microsoft implemented Windows Resource Protection (WRP) to protect system files. It prevents the files from being overwritten. If they somehow are overwritten, you can use the Windows Resource Checker (sfc) utility to restore them.

When Windows Vista is first booted, it will check certain system files to ensure they haven't been overwritten. If they have, it will try to restore the files from a source folder. If this source folder is overwritten or files within it become corrupt, you can restore the files using the Windows Resource Checker (sfc) utility.

NOTE In previous operating systems, SFC was short for System File Checker. In Windows Vista, you still have access to the SFC tool, but it's now called the Windows Resource Checker. On the surface this might seem confusing, but if you used the SFC tool in other operating systems you can easily find it on Windows Vista. It wouldn't be so easy if they changed the name to WRC.

The `sfc` utility supports several different switches. As a reminder, most command-line tools include switches used to modify how a command functions. The following switches can be used with SFC.

- **/?** The /? switch will provide help on the command.
- **/ScanNow** This will initiate a scan of your system to check the integrity of all protected system files. It will repair problems when possible.
- **/VerifyOnly** This will initiate a scan of your system to check the integrity of all protected system files, but it won't attempt to repair the files.
- **/ScanFile** This will initiate a scan of a specific file. It will check the integrity of the file and attempt repair if necessary.
- **/VerifyFile** This will initiate a scan of a specific file. It will check the integrity of the file but not attempt any repairs.
- **/OffBootDir** This will allow you to repair boot files offline (when Windows is not running). You must specify the location of the boot directory that you want to repair.
- **/OffWinDir** This will allow you to repair files offline (when Windows is not running). You must specify the location of the Windows directory that you want to repair.

In Exercise 12.3, you will run the `sfc` utility and view the results.

Exercise 12.3: Running the SFC Utility

1. Launch a command prompt with elevated permissions by clicking Start | All Programs | Accessories, right-clicking Command Prompt, and selecting Run as Administrator. If the User Account Control dialog box appears, click Continue.

2. At the command prompt enter the following command:

   ```
   sfc /?
   ```

   Review the information on the available switches.

3. Enter the following command to initiate a scan on your system:

   ```
   sfc /ScanNow
   ```

   This will take some time.

4. Once the scan is complete, enter the following command to review the results of the scan contained within the cbs.log file to view the detailed results of the most recent scan.

   ```
   notepad c:\Windows\logs\cbs\cbs.log
   ```

   Scan results are appended to the end of the file, so you'll need to scroll to the end of the file to see the results of the most recent scan.

Accessing the Advanced Boot Options Menu

The Advanced Boot Options menu gives you access to several tools you can use to troubleshoot a Windows Vista system. You press the F8 key while your system is booting to access the menu.

 EXAM TIP   You should know how to access the Advanced Boot Options menu, what the options are, and when to use the different options for troubleshooting scenarios.

Figure 12-9 shows the Advanced Boot Options menu. Once it launches, you can select the different choices using the UP ARROW and DOWN ARROW keys.

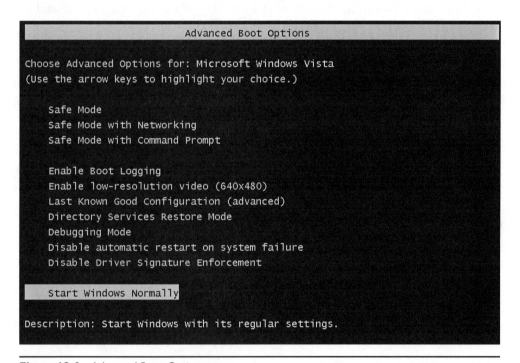

```
                    Advanced Boot Options

Choose Advanced Options for: Microsoft Windows Vista
(Use the arrow keys to highlight your choice.)

    Safe Mode
    Safe Mode with Networking
    Safe Mode with Command Prompt

    Enable Boot Logging
    Enable low-resolution video (640x480)
    Last Known Good Configuration (advanced)
    Directory Services Restore Mode
    Debugging Mode
    Disable automatic restart on system failure
    Disable Driver Signature Enforcement

    Start Windows Normally

Description: Start Windows with its regular settings.
```

Figure 12-9   Advanced Boot Options menu

The choices available from this menu are

- **Safe Mode**   Safe mode will start Windows Vista with only the core drivers and services. You can use this when your system can't boot after installing a new device or driver. A more advanced method of using Safe mode is to boot into it to run System Restore when you can't boot normally because of a system change.

- **Safe Mode With Networking**   This is similar to Safe mode but adds in the capability of a system to access network resources.

- **Safe Mode With Command Prompt** This is similar to Safe mode, but instead of the Windows GUI interface, only the command prompt can be used.

- **Enable Boot Logging** A file named ntbtlog.txt is created that lists all drivers that load during startup. If your system is crashing because of a faulty driver, enable boot logging, and then after the unsuccessful boot, access Safe mode. In Safe mode, you can open the file and determine the last driver that was loaded before the failure.

- **Enable Low-Resolution Video (640 X 480)** If the screen resolution is configured with a setting that prevents the screen from being displayed (but it was displayed long enough for you to confirm the settings), you can select this setting. You can then launch Windows and reconfigure the screen resolution.

- **Last Known Good Configuration (advanced)** When a computer successfully boots (a user logs on), important system settings are saved in the Registry. If system changes (such as a driver installation) prevent the system from successfully booting, Last Known Good configuration can be selected to restore the settings to the last time they were known to be good.

- **Directory Services Restore Mode** This does not apply to Windows Vista systems. It allows a server configured as a domain controller to start in restore mode, but Windows Vista will never be a domain controller.

- **Debugging Mode** This enables the Windows kernel debugger. It is only used in advanced troubleshooting scenarios such as with an original equipment manufacturer (OEM).

- **Disable Automatic Restart on System Failure** Setting this prevents Windows from automatically rebooting after a system crash.

- **Disable Driver Signature Enforcement** This will allow unsigned drivers to be loaded.

- **Start Windows Normally** Exit the Advanced Boot Options menu.

Backing Up and Restoring Data Files

One thing is certain with computers: if you haven't lost any data files in the past, you will in the future. Count on it.

If you have a recent backup of your data, losing a file here or there just means you only need to restore it from a recent backup. If you don't have a backup, you may need to restore the complete file from scratch. Recreating a letter to Mom may not be such a big deal, but if you lose a project file you've been working on for weeks, it could be a significant step backward.

Windows Vista includes two primary tools you can use to back up and restore files on your computer. You can even automate the backup process so that you only have to set it once and then occasionally manage it. The two tools are

- Backup Status and Configuration tool
- Backup and Restore Center

The backup files feature in both of these tools was designed to be easy to use. Comments from members of the Microsoft team mentioned that they designed this for the core audience of Windows Vista. In other words, they didn't design it for techies like you and me but instead regular end users. The goal is to encourage more end users to do backups.

There's a trade-off in keeping things simple, though. You lose some advanced capabilities. One of the capabilities lost that may surprise you is that you can't pick and choose which files are backed up. You choose the type of files (such as pictures, music, and documents), but you can't pick an individual folder.

You must have administrative access to manually perform backups, perform restores, or change backup settings. When configuring or launching backups, you'll be prompted to provide administrative credentials.

 EXAM TIP   Regular users can not perform backups, or restores, or change backup settings. Administrative access is required for security purposes.

Using the Backup Status and Configuration Tool

The Backup Status and Configuration tool is used to create automatic backups of your data. Figure 12-10 shows the Backup Status and Configuration tool. In the figure, you can see that automatic backups haven't been configured yet.

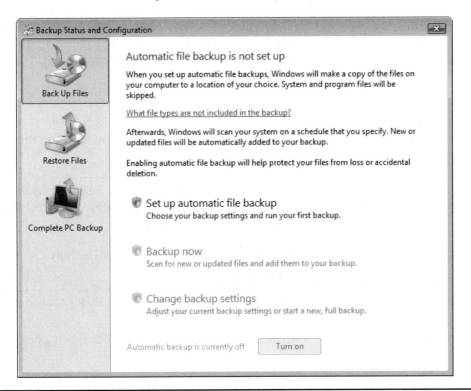

Figure 12-10   Backup Status and Configuration tool

The Backup Status and Configuration tool starts with a full backup and then regularly backs up files that have changed.

Back Up Files

When using this tool, you can choose to back up data to a hard disk, CD, DVD, or network location. When selecting a network location, you use a Universal Naming Convention (UNC) path of \\ServerName\ShareName.

One limitation is that you can't back up files to the same hard drive that you're backing them up from. In other words if you're backing files from the C: drive, you can't back them up to the C: drive.

Instead of picking locations of data that you want to back up, you choose from a list of types of files that you want to back up. The following list is available when configuring backups:

- **Pictures**   This includes graphics files. Some of the extensions of graphics files are: gif, bmp, jpg, and tiff.

- **Music**   This includes Windows Media Audio and MP3 files. Some of the extensions of these files are: wma, mpa, and mp3.

- **Videos**   This includes video files such as those with the wmv extension.

- **E-mail**   This includes e-mail files. Some of the extensions of these files are: eml and pst.

- **Documents**   This includes word processing, spreadsheet, and PowerPoint files. Some of the extensions of these files are: doc, docx, xls, xlsx, ppt, pptx, pdf, and txt.

- **TV shows**   This includes TV shows recorded within the Windows Media Center.

- **Compressed files**   This includes a wide assortment of compressed files. It also includes compressed folders. Some of the extensions of compressed files are: zip, cab, iso, wim, and vhd.

- **Additional Files**   This includes other data files that aren't included in the preceding categories. It does not include system files.

 EXAM TIP   You can pick and choose which types of files are backed up by selecting the categories. For example, if you want to ensure all your MP3 files are included in backups, select the Music category.

Exercise 12.4 leads you through the steps to configure automatic backups.

Exercise 12.4: Configuring Automatic Backups

1. Launch the Backup and Status Configuration tool by clicking Start | Accessories | System Tools and selecting Backup Status and Configuration.

2. Click Set Up Automatic File Backup. If the User Account Control dialog box appears, click Continue.

3. On the Back Up Files page, you choose a target location to back up your files. This must be a different hard disk than where your files are located. You can choose a CD, DVD, USB flash drive, or network location. Figure 12-11 shows an 8GB USB flash drive (with 3.2GB free) available. The On A Network location is selected and I've typed in a path to a network location available on my network.

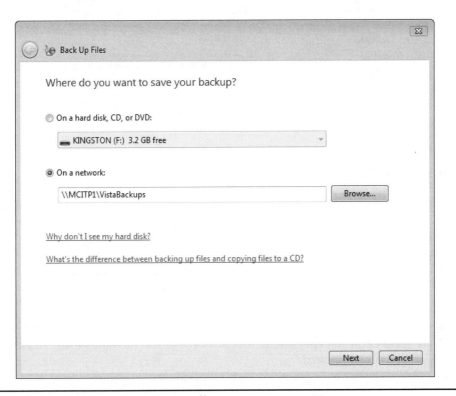

Figure 12-11   Choosing where to back up files

4. On the Which Disks Do You Want to Include in the Backup page, select a disk that holds the data that you want to back up. By default, all the disks are selected. Click Next.

5. On the Which File Types Do You Want to Back Up page, review the file types that are backed up and deselect any files you don't want backed up. Figure 12-12 shows the file types that are selected by default.

6. Hover over each of the file categories and view the text in the category details. This lets you know exactly what files will be included in the backup. Click Next.

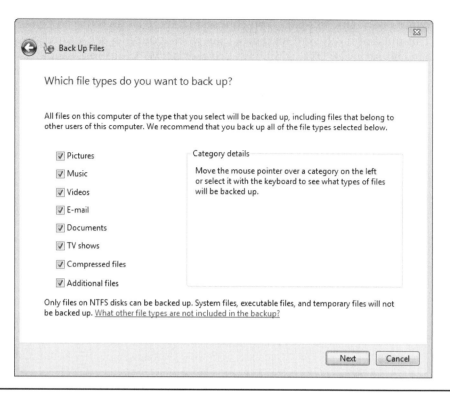

Figure 12-12   Choosing file types for a backup

7. On the How Often Do You Want to Create a Backup page, verify that backups are set to occur weekly, each Sunday at 7:00 P.M. You can change the frequency, day, and time if desired.

8. Click the Save Settings and Start Backup button. The length of time required for the backup is dependent on the amount of data contained on your hard disk.

9. Once the backup completes, the Backup Status and Configuration display will change as shown in Figure 12-13. It now shows that Automatic Backups are enabled and shows the status of the last backup.

While automatic backups will run regularly based on your schedule, if you ever want to run the backup immediately (such as after saving a number of pictures onto your computer from a holiday), you can click Back Up Now.

Additionally, you can change the backup options at any time by clicking Change Backup Settings. This allows you to change the destination of the backup, the file types you want to back up, and the frequency of the backups.

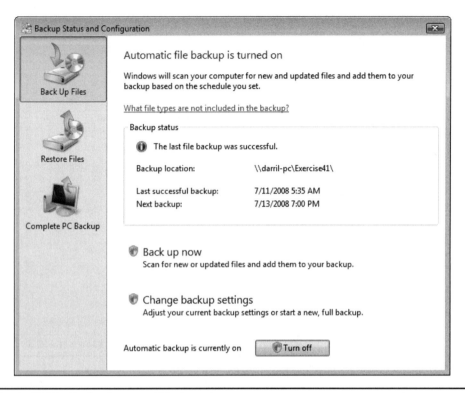

Figure 12-13 Backup Status and Configuration

Restore Files

If you click Restore Files, the menu changes from backup options to restore options. The Restore Files menu gives you two options. Both options allow you to choose the backup and the files you want to restore.

- **Advanced Restore**   The Advanced Restore option allows you to restore files that were created on another computer or restore files for other users. This option requires administrative access.

- **Restore Files**. The Restore Files option allows you to restore files onto the same computer where they were backed up from.

If you click the Restore Files option, you'll get a display similar to Figure 12-14. This option gives you the choice of restoring from the latest backup or an older backup.

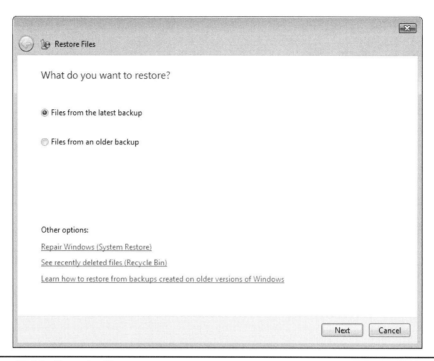

Figure 12-14   Restoring files

Testing Your Backups   Imagine this scenario. You enabled your backups and they've been working for months. One day, you lose some key files. No problem, you think. You've been doing backups for months. You can just restore the files.

However, when you try to restore the files, the restore fails. Ultimately, you discover that the backups you thought were occurring weren't. You don't have any backups and your data is lost.

This might sound far fetched, but the same scenario is repeated daily around the world. I've been asked to help people restore data only to discover that either the most recent backups weren't good, or they didn't even have a single good backup.

The solution is simple. Do a test restore occasionally. This does two things for you:

1. It proves that your backups are valid. If a problem occurs with your backups, you'll know right away—not after you've already lost key data.

2. It gives you practice restoring your data. The first time you restore data shouldn't be during a crisis. If you regularly do practice restores, an actual restore will be easy.

If you've never tested your backups before, now is a good time.

At the bottom of the figure, you can see there are three other links:

- **Repair Windows (System Restore)** This will launch the same System Restore tool covered earlier in the chapter to apply restore points.
- **See Recently Deleted Files (Recycle Bin)** This is an easy link to the recycle bin to recover deleted files.
- **Learn How To Restore From Backups Created On Older Versions of Windows** This will take you to a Web site explaining this process.

You can pick and choose exactly which files you want to restore. In Figure 12-15 you can see that I added a single file (named MCITP Study Notes) that was backed up previously. You can also choose to restore entire folders.

Once you've identified the files you want to restore, you can then choose to restore them to the original location or identify an alternate location. If you restore the files to the original location and a file exists with the same name, it will be overwritten. If you choose an alternate location, you will have both the old and new files.

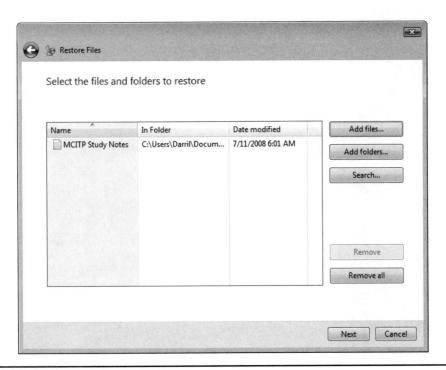

Figure 12-15   Restoring a specific file

Complete PC Backup

The Complete PC Backup button will launch the Windows Complete PC Backup tool as discussed earlier in this chapter. It will create a complete image of your entire system, including the operating system, program files, and data files.

You shouldn't use this to protect your data, but instead to protect your system.

Using the Backup and Restore Center

At first glance, the Backup and Restore Center looks like it's a different program, but it's really just another method to access different backup and restore technologies. At this point in the chapter, you've already learned everything that the Backup and Restore Center can do.

Figure 12-16 shows the Backup and Restore Center.

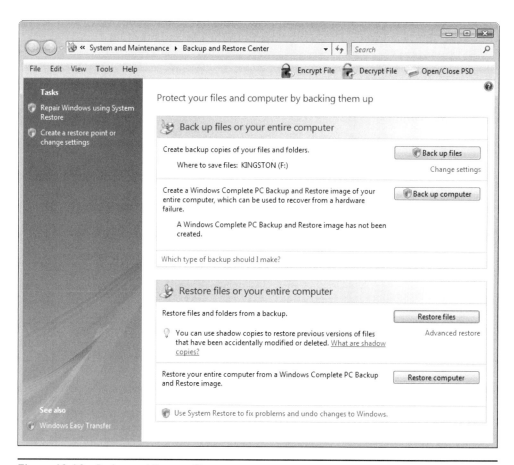

Figure 12-16 Backup and Restore Center

For clarification, each of the tasks and tools accessible through here is listed in the following text:

- **Repair Windows Using System Restore**   This will launch System Restore so that you can apply a previous restore point.

- **Create A Restore Point Or Change Settings**   This will bring you to the System Protection tab of System Properties. You can view recently created restore points or click Create to create a restore point.

- **Back Up Files**   This button will launch an immediate backup (as long as backups have been configured) using the backup settings.

- **Change Settings**   This will launch Backup Status and Configuration, where you can click Change Backup Settings to change the target location, types of files to be backed up, and frequency of the backups.

- **Back Up Computer**   This button launches the Windows Complete PC Backup tool.

- **Restore Files**   This button will launch the Restore Files tool so that you can restore files from the latest backup or older backups. This is the same tool launched from the Backup Status and Configuration tool Restore Files menu.

- **Advanced Restore**   This launches the Backup Status and Configuration tool in the Restore Files menu so that you can select Advanced Restore.

- **Restore Computer**   This opens a dialog box telling you how to go through a restore using the Windows Complete PC Restore tool from the System Recovery options. As a reminder, you must reboot and press the F8 key to access the System Recovery Options menu.

Chapter Review

In this chapter you learned about the different tools within Windows Vista that you can use to troubleshoot and restore problems with the operating system, and also how to back up and restore data.

The two primary tools you can use to back up system and data files are the Backup and Restore Center and the Backup Status and Configuration tool. Some of the tasks are repeated in each of the tools, but generally, you can access all tasks through the Backup and Restore Center.

You can protect your entire computer by creating an image of your computer using the Windows Complete PC Backup and Restore tool. If your hard drive fails, you can restore the entire computer (including the operating system, applications, and data) by restoring the image through the System Recovery Options menu (available by selecting Repair Your Computer after booting with the installation DVD).

System Restore provides the ability to automatically and manually create restore points of your operating system. Restore points do not include data. If the operating system develops problems after an upgrade of an application or a device driver, you can apply a previous restore point to easily get your operating system to a previous state.

If you need to check or repair individual system files, you can use the Windows Resource Checker (`sfc`) command-line tool. This can be used to check and repair all your system files, or check and repair a single file.

The Advanced Boot Options menu can be accessed by pressing F8 when booting. This menu includes all of the Safe modes, the Last Known Good Configuration, and more. Safe modes can be used to boot into the operating system with only the bare essentials, which can be useful if one of the services or drivers that normally start is causing you problems. Last Known Good Configuration can be useful to return your system to the state it was in the last time you had a successful boot (meaning you logged on).

Backing up data files is streamlined within Windows Vista. Once you configure backups using the Backup Status and Configuration tool, backups will automatically be done on a regular basis. You can also restore files using this tool.

Additional Study

Self Study Exercises

Use these additional exercises to challenge yourself.

- Boot using your Windows Vista installation DVD and select the Repair Your Computer option. Explore all the System Recovery Options choices.
- Boot to the Advanced Boot Options menu. Complete the boot cycle by booting to each of the options.
- Enable automatic backups on your computer.
- Perform a test restore of data on your computer.

Summary of What You Need to Know

70-620

When preparing for the 70-620 exam, pay particular attention to the following topics covered in this chapter:

- **System recovery tools**   This includes the Windows Complete PC Backup and Restore, and System Restore tools.
- **Data backup tools**   This includes the Backup and Restore Center and the Backup Status and Configuration tool.

70-622

When preparing for the 70-622 exam, pay particular attention to the following topics covered in this chapter:

- **System recovery tools**   This includes the Windows Complete PC Backup and Restore, and System Restore tools.

- **Windows Resource Checker utility (sfc)**   Know how to check and repair system files with this tool.
- **Advanced Options**   Know how to boot into this menu (press F8 on boot), and the different capabilities such as the Safe modes, and Last Known Good Configuration.

70-623

When preparing for the 70-623 exam, pay particular attention to the following topics covered in this chapter:

- **System recovery tools**   This includes the Windows Complete PC Backup and Restore, System Restore tools, the System Recovery Options tool, and the Advanced Options menu.
- **Data backup tools**   This includes the Backup and Restore Center and the Backup Status and Configuration tool.

Questions

70-620

1. Sally has recently purchased a Windows Vista system. She wants to ensure that she can recover the Windows Vista system in the event of a hard disk failure. What should she do?

   A. Use the System Restore tool.

   B. Use the Backup and Restore Center to create a restore point.

   C. Use the Backup and Restore Center to back up all the files on her computer.

   D. Use the Windows Complete PC Backup and Restore tool.

2. You're getting ready to leave on a business trip, and you want to back up your data on your laptop. The laptop has Windows Vista installed. You want to be able to restore individual files if any of them become corrupt. What should you do?

   A. Perform a Complete PC Backup.

   B. Use System Restore to create a restore point.

   C. Click Back Up Files in the Backup and Restore Center.

   D. Click Back Up Computer in the Backup and Restore Center.

3. Sally is considering disaster protection strategies for her Windows Vista computer. She has stored all her data files in a folder named C:\Sales. She purchased an external USB drive to store the data. She wants to be able to restore individual files to the C:\Sales folder if any files are lost, are accidentally deleted, or become corrupt. What's the easiest way to accomplish this task?

   A. Use the Backup and Restore Center.

   B. Create a Windows Complete PC Backup.

    C. Use System Restore.

    D. Purchase a third-party backup tool.

4. Sally uses her Windows Vista computer to create graphics files and also stores her MP3 files on her system. She wants to ensure that these files are backed up regularly. What should she do?

    A. Use Back Up Computer in the Backup and Restore Center.

    B. Use the Recovery Options tool to perform regular backups.

    C. Use Back Up Files in the Backup and Restore Center. Configure the settings to include Additional Files.

    D. Use Back Up Files in the Backup and Restore Center. Configure the settings to include Music and Pictures.

70-622

1. You've been troubleshooting a Windows Vista system and have discovered that a specific dll file is corrupt. What command and switch can you use to quickly repair this dll file without checking any other files?

    A. `Sfc /scannow`

    B. `Src /scanfile`

    C. `Sfc /scanfile`

    D. `Sfc /verifyfile`

2. Joe has installed a device driver for his system. After rebooting and logging on, he accesses the device, but his Windows Vista system crashes. Each time he tries to restart Windows Vista, an error message appears and the system locks. Joe needs to return his system to operation using the least amount of effort. What should he do to restore his system to a bootable state without the faulty driver?

    A. Insert the Vista installation DVD and reinstall Windows Vista.

    B. Insert the Vista installation DVD and use System Restore to apply a restore point.

    C. Use the Last Known Good Configuration selection from Advanced Boot Options.

    D. Run `sfc /scannow` after booting normally.

3. You are responsible for ensuring that you can restore a Windows Vista system in the event of a system hard disk failure. What should you do?

    A. Access the System Recovery Options and create a Complete PC Backup and Restore image.

    B. Access the Backup and Restore Center and create a Complete PC Backup and Restore image.

   C. Access the Backup Status and Configuration tool and back up all the files on your system.

   D. Create a system image using the Windows Resource Checker utility.

4. A user complains that he is unable to boot into his system after installing an upgrade. It is stuck in a constant reboot cycle. You tried to use the Last Known Good Configuration, but you were unsuccessful. What should you try next?

   A. Perform a Complete PC Restore from the Advanced Options menu.

   B. Perform a Complete PC Restore from the Recovery Options menu.

   C. Reboot the computer into Safe mode.

   D. Use System Restore to apply a previous restore point.

70-623

1. Sally runs an application named SalesTracker on her Windows Vista system. She upgraded it on Monday morning. It worked inconsistently through the week, occasionally crashing her system and occasionally locking up. On Thursday, it simply won't run at all. Backups are completed on her system every evening. Sally wants to restore the SalesTracker application to the state it was in prior to the upgrade. What should she do?

   A. Restore the backup that was completed on her system on Sunday evening.

   B. Boot to the installation DVD and apply a restore point to just before the time the application was upgraded. Restore the backup that was completed on Sunday evening.

   C. Perform a System Restore, applying a restore point to the time before the application was upgraded. Restore the backup that was completed on Sunday evening.

   D. Perform a System Restore, applying a restore point to the time before the application was upgraded.

2. A user is contemplating installing an application named NotGonnaRun. He is a little concerned that the program is not going to run and wants to ensure he can successfully return his system to the state it was in before installing the application. What should he do?

   A. Create a full backup of his data.

   B. Enable shadow copies.

   C. Create a restore point.

   D. Convert his hard drive from basic to dynamic.

3. Joe downloaded and installed an application named SalesTracker onto his Windows Vista system. After shutting down his system, he is no longer able to successfully boot into Windows Vista. He keeps getting a stop error message. What can he do to restore his system?

   A. Boot into the system and use System Restore to apply a restore point.

   B. Insert the Vista installation DVD and use System Restore to apply a restore point.

   C. Insert the Vista installation DVD and select Last Known Good Configuration.

   D. Uninstall the application.

4. Joe was experimenting with some Registry settings on his system. After he reboots his system gives a stop error before he's able to log on. What should Joe try first to return his system to an operational state?

   A. Use Last Known Good Configuration from the Advanced Boot Options screen.

   B. Use Safe mode from the Advanced Boot Options screen.

   C. Use Safe mode with Command Prompt from the Advanced Boot Options screen.

   D. Boot from the installation media and select Last Known Good Configuration.

5. Sally ran Windows Complete PC Backup and Restore to create an image of her system. After surfing the Internet, downloading and installing some applications that turned out to be Trojans, she finds that her system is significantly infected with viruses. Her attempts to clean the system result in stop errors and blue screens and her system no longer starts. What should she do?

   A. Start the Windows Complete PC Backup and Restore tool and restore from the created image.

   B. Start the Windows Backup and Restore Center and restore from the created image.

   C. Start from the installation DVD and restore her system using the Recovery Console.

   D. Start from the installation DVD and restore her system using the System Recovery Options.

6. You are assisting a user that is having problems backing up files onto her computer. She belongs to the Users group on her Windows Vista computer and has a user account. However, each time she tries a manual backup, she receives an error message. What is the likely problem?

   A. A recent restore point hasn't been created.

   B. The user needs to have administrative access.

   C. The Volume Shadow Copy service is set to Manual.

   D. The Volume Shadow Copy service set to Automatic.

Answers

70-620

1. **D.** A complete image of the system can be created with the Windows Complete PC Backup and Restore Tool. This image will include the operating system, the installed applications, and all data on the system at the time and can be restored using the System Recovery Options menu. Restore points (created with the System Restore tool and accessible through the Backup and Restore Center) can be used to restore the operating system to a previous time, but not if the entire hard drive fails, since the restore points are stored on the same disk as Windows Vista.

2. **C.** If you back up files using the Backup and Restore Center, you can restore individual files from the backup. If you perform a Complete PC Backup (which is done when you click the Back Up Computer button in the Backup and Restore Center), you create an image and you can only restore the entire image. Restore points don't include data.

3. **A.** The Backup and Restore Center can be configured to perform automatic backups of data on a system. While it can't be configured to specifically back up only the C:\Sales folder, this folder will be included in the backups and files can be individually restored. Files can't be individually restored from an image created from Windows Complete PC Backup. System Restore only creates restore points to restore system files, not data files. A third-party tool is not required.

4. **D.** You can configure categories to be backed up. Graphics files are included in the Pictures category. MP3 files are music files and are included in the Music category. The Back Up Computer option creates a Windows Complete PC Backup image. The Recovery Options tool is available by booting to the installation DVD and is used for recovery options, not backups. Additional files include other files not included in the other categories but wouldn't include the files in the Music and Pictures category.

70-622

1. **C.** The Windows Resource Checker (`sfc`) command-line utility can be used to check and repair files. When the `/scanfile` switch is used, you can check and repair a single specific file. You must also list the path and name of the file. The `/scannow` switch will check all the protected files. There is no such thing as an `src` command. The `/verifyfile` switch will check files but won't repair them.

2. **B.** You can use System Restore after booting with the installation DVD and apply a system restore point. Reinstalling Windows Vista is not the least amount of effort. The Last Known Good Configuration won't work after the user has logged on. The user can't boot the operating system, so `sfc` can't be run after booting normally.

3. **B.** The Backup and Restore Center can be used to create a Complete PC Backup and Restore image, which can be used to recover a system in the event of a disk failure. The System Recovery Options tool can be used to restore an image but not create one. Backing up files in the Backup Status and Configuration tool only backs up data files, not system files. The Windows Resource Checker (`sfc`) can be used to verify and repair system individual files, but not the entire disk.

4. **C.** The next logical step is to boot into Safe mode and troubleshoot from there. For example, you could apply a restore point in Safe mode (but you can't apply a restore point until you boot into Safe mode first, since the system is stuck in a reboot cycle). A complete PC restore is more drastic than may be necessary; troubleshooting within one of the Safe modes should be tried first.

70-623

1. **D.** System Restore can be used to apply a restore point to return the system to the state it was in just prior to an upgrade. Restore points don't include data, and data restores are not needed when restoring restore points. A full backup would hold data but not system configuration information. Restoring a backup from Sunday evening would overwrite all the changes to her data that she's completed since Sunday.

2. **C.** If a restore point is created prior to the installation of an application, you can use System Restore to return the system to the state it was in prior to the installation. Restore points only include system settings (not data). Backing up the data won't allow the system to be restored. Shadow copies are used to allow users to restore previous versions of their data but don't affect system settings. A dynamic volume allows a system to use more advanced implementations of hard disks but won't preserve system settings prior to an application installation.

3. **B.** After booting with the Vista installation DVD, you can select Repair Your Computer to access system restore points. By selecting a restore point that was created before the application was installed, the system can be restored. Stop error messages are sometimes referred to as blue screens or BSODs (blue screens of death) and indicate the system can't boot. Since the system can't boot, you can't apply a restore point normally; neither can you simply uninstall the application. Last Known Good Configuration is selected from Advanced Boot Options, not from the installation DVD.

4. **A.** The Last Known Good Configuration choice can be selected from the Advanced Boot Options. It will restore key system settings (including important system settings saved in the Registry). Safe modes could also be tried, but they will require additional work after booting into Safe mode, whereas selecting the Last Known Good Configuration will restore the system in a single step.

5. **D.** After booting from the installation DVD, the Repair Your Computer option can be selected to access the System Recovery Options menu and restore the image by selecting the Windows Complete PC Restore choice. Since the system can't boot, the Windows Complete PC Backup and Restore tool and the Windows Backup and Restore Center tool can't be accessed. Windows Vista does not include a Recovery Console.

6. **B.** Administrative access is needed to perform backups. Restore points aren't required to do backups. If the Volume Shadow Copy service is set to Manual, it can be started when needed to perform backups. When set to Automatic, it is already running.

Configuring Internet Applications

In this chapter, you will learn about:

- Internet Explorer
- Windows Defender
- RootkitRevealer

Windows Vista includes three key Internet applications you should be familiar with when supporting Vista users. While Internet Explorer is a product you probably use all the time, you may be surprised at the depth of configuration that is possible within it.

Windows Defender and the RootkitRevealer are two tools used to help protect you from malware—malicious software. Vista systems will typically run Windows Defender all the time, but the RootkitRevealer is a special tool used for special occasions.

 EXAM TIP Objectives for the 70-620, 70-622, and 70-623 exams are included in this chapter.

Internet Explorer 7.0

If you're reading this book, I'm going to take a wild leap and assume you've browsed the Internet once or twice. You may have even used Internet Explorer 7.0 (IE). However, don't underestimate the depth of IE, or Microsoft's ability to test your knowledge of its complexity.

 NOTE You'll be specifically tested on Internet Explorer version 7.0. This is shortened to IE in this chapter.

You may think "I use this every day, so I don't need to study these topics." Perhaps, but you can expect Microsoft to test you on the inner workings of IE, and just regularly using IE won't be enough to pass the exam questions, especially when it comes to the many different security features that are available and configurable.

It's important that you understand many of the different configuration options you have available. Almost all of these are accessible via the Tools drop-down menu.

Using Internet Explorer

Internet Explorer 7.0 uses a tabbed browser. It allows you to open many Web sites within a single browser window.

When you have many Web sites open at a time, the Quick Tabs feature allows you to easily choose the page you want to view from a list of icons showing the page. The Quick Tabs feature can be accessed by pressing CTRL-Q or by selecting the leftmost tab (the one with four small boxes within it) that appears after you've opened several windows.

IE includes a menu bar that is disabled by default. If you press the ALT key, you can bring the menu bar into view and select commands from the drop-down menus.

Figure 13-1 shows the menu bar with the File menu opened. In addition to making this temporarily available using the ALT key, you can also make it persist by selecting the Tools | Menu Bar selection.

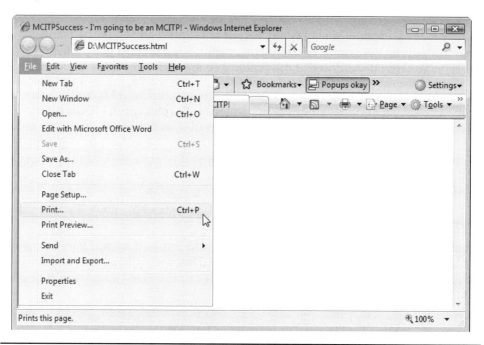

Figure 13-1 Accessing the menu bar by pressing the ALT key

TIP If any of these menu commands don't look familiar to you, I strongly encourage you to try them out and see where they take you.

The menu bar includes the following common menus. Many of these menu commands can be accessed via different means, and the more important ones will be explored more fully in this chapter.

- **File**   This menu includes the New Tab, New Window, Open, Edit With Microsoft Office Word, Save, Save As, Close Tab, Page Setup, Print, Print Preview, Send, Import and Export, Properties, and Exit commands.

- **Edit**   This menu includes the Cut, Copy, Paste, Select All, and Find on This Page commands.

- **View**   The View menu includes the Toolbars, Status Bar, Quick Tabs, Explorer Bar, Go To, Stop, Refresh, Text Size, Encoding, Source, Security Report, International Website Address, Web Page Privacy Policy, and Full Screen commands.

- **Favorites**   You can access the following commands from the Favorites drop-down menu: Add to Favorites, Add Tab Group to Favorites, Organize Favorites; or launch any saved favorites.

- **Tools**   The Tools drop-down menu includes the Delete Browsing History, Diagnose Connection Problems, Pop-Up Blocker, Phishing Filter, Manage Add-ons, Subscribe to This Feed, Feed Discovery, Windows Update, and Internet Options commands.

- **Help**   The Help menu includes the following common Help commands: Contents and Index, Internet Explorer Tour, Online Support, Send Feedback, and About Internet Explorer.

Printing

Internet Explorer includes some new printing features to make it easier to print pages from Web sites.

Pages can be scaled to fit the paper you're using on your printer. In previous versions of IE, when a page was viewed with a wide screen, the printed page would attempt to print it as wide as it was viewed, and a significant portion of the printout would be missing. The print preview feature allows you to manually scale the page to exactly the size you want.

 EXAM TIP   You should be aware of the different methods that can be used to print Web pages, including specifics related to printing graphics.

Additionally, you can print a single picture from a Web page. Simply right-click over the picture and select Print Picture.

You can access the print capabilities via several methods.

- Right-click within the page and select Print.
- Click the Printer button on the command bar.
- Select the drop-down menu next to the Printer icon and select Print.
- Press CTRL-P.

Phishing

Phishing is a form of social engineering where an e-mail or Web site attempts to trick a user into divulging personal information.

For example, a user may receive an e-mail that looks like it comes from BigBank.com (but actually came from a phishing attacker). It informs the user that their account has had some suspicious activity and will be locked unless they log on and verify their information. If the user follows the link and provides information such as their username and password, this information is used for an attack on the user's actual account.

Internet Explorer 7.0 provides a Phishing Filter designed to provide a layer of protection against phishing attacks. The Phishing Filter uses three methods to protect against phishing attacks.

- It compares addresses you visit with a list of Web sites reported to Microsoft as legitimate. (This list is stored on your local computer and regularly updated).

- It analyzes sites to determine if they have some of the common characteristics of phishing Web sites.

- It allows you to report Web site addresses as possible phishing Web sites (or Web sites that you believe are erroneously reported as phishing Web sites).

If you visit a Web site that is on the list of reported phishing Web sites, a warning Web page will appear along with a notification in the address bar. You can continue to the suspected Web site (at your own peril) or close the page.

The Phishing Filter menu is accessible from the Tools drop-down menu as shown in Figure 13-2.

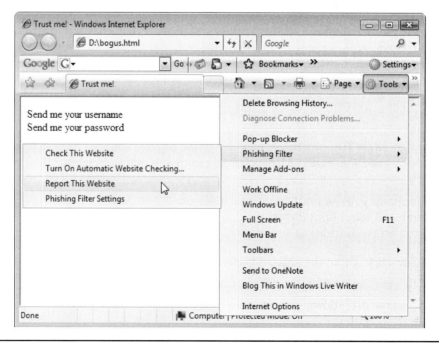

Figure 13-2 Using the Phishing Filter to report a Web site

The choices available from the Phishing Filter are

- **Check This Website**   This selection allows you to manually check the Web site address to determine if it is in a list of reported phishing Web sites.

- **Turn On Automatic Website Checking**   You can turn on or turn off the automatic Phishing Filter from this menu item.

- **Report This Website**   You can use this setting to report a suspected phishing Web site or a Web site that you believe is erroneously being reported as a phishing Web site.

 EXAM TIP   You can report Web sites to Microsoft so that they can be investigated and possibly be included on a list of phishing Web sites. Additionally, if you think a Web site is erroneously listed as a phishing Web site, you can report it to have it removed from the list.

- **Phishing Filter Settings**   This selection launches the Internet Options dialog box with the Advanced tab selected. You can access the Phishing Filter settings in the Security section. Three choices are available:

  - Disable Phishing Filter.

  - Turn off automatic website checking.

  - Turn on automatic website checking.

Secure Sessions and Certificates

Secure sessions are often needed when using Internet Explorer. For example if you ever purchase something with your credit card or enter your user name and password into a Web page, you want to ensure that information is sent over the Internet encrypted. There are two ways you can ensure the session is secure when using IE:

- The address shows that it is an HTTPS address (instead of HTTP).

- Internet Explorer displays a picture of a lock to the right of the address bar.

The way that a secure session is created is through the use of the Secure Sockets Layer (SSL) protocol and certificates. When you connect to a site using an HTTPS session, the site sends you a certificate that includes an encryption key. This certificate and key are used to create a secure session.

Usually companies will purchase a certificate from a trusted root certification authority (such as VeriSign). IE includes several certificates in the Trusted Root Certification Authorities store. If the trusted root certificate is in the IE store, then certificates issued by the trusted root certification authority are also trusted. This is similar to how the clerk at the store trusts your driver's license as identification because it was issued by a trusted authority—the Department of Motor Vehicles for your state.

When a Web site sends your computer a certificate, your computer does a couple of things before a session is created. The certificate is checked to see if was issued from a company in your Trusted Root Certification Authority store, and the root authority is queried to verify the certificate is still valid. If a certificate is compromised, it can be revoked and the root authority will not verify the certificate. The root authority is only queried when the session begins. If you close the browser and start another secure session, the process is repeated.

Occasionally, someone may give you a certificate that wasn't purchased by a public certification authority. You can install this in your Other People certificate store as shown in Figure 13-3. You would only want to import a certificate from a company or person you trust. To start the process, select the Tools drop-down menu, click Internet Options, and select the Content tab. From the page shown in Figure 13-3, click Certificates and then click Import and follow the wizard to import the certificate.

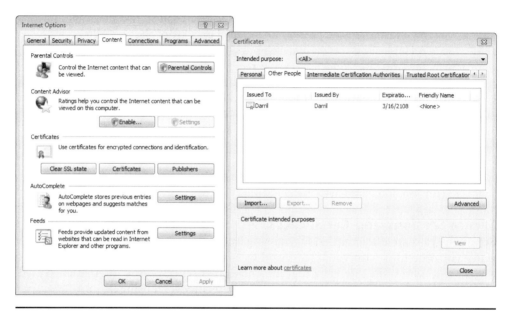

Figure 13-3   Importing a certificate into the Other People store

One of the reasons you may use this feature is for friends or companies you implicitly trust such as your employer. Instead of purchasing a certificate, they can create their own certificates and issue them to users such as you.

 EXAM TIP   You should know how to add and remove certificates in the Other People store. Additionally, you should know that certificates are checked to determine if they are valid when a session starts. To repeat the validation process, all instances of IE need to be terminated.

You can also remove outdated certificates that you have added to this store. To remove a certificate, simply select the certificate and click Remove. The primary reason to remove a certificate is because you've replaced it with a newer one. You wouldn't want to receive the errors from the older certificate, so it should be removed.

Pop-ups and the Pop-up Blocker

Some Web sites use pop-up windows to flood your system with advertising. You go to the Web site or click a link and new browser windows appear. Generally, what the pop-ups mostly do is annoy users. In response, many different versions of pop-up blockers have appeared.

EXAM TIP In past versions of IE, pop-ups were allowed and users frequently used add-ons to block them. For example, by adding the Google Toolbar, you also enjoyed the benefit of the pop-up blocker. With Microsoft in direct competition with Google for Web searches; they really don't want you to add the Google Toolbar; and so they have added pop-up blocker features to eliminate that as a reason to add the Google Toolbar. Microsoft wants you to know about the pop-up blocker features in IE7, and you can expect questions on each of the three exams related to the pop-up blocker.

However, there are times when you want to see pop-ups. For example, many companies use Outlook Web Access (OWA) to allow employees to access e-mail from home or while on the road using Internet Explorer. OWA takes advantage of pop-ups for things like notifying a user with calendar reminders. With pop-ups blocked from the OWA site, the user would lose desired functionality.

Pop-up blockers need to block pop-ups, but also give you the option to pick and choose when you want pop-ups to appear.

Internet Explorer 7 includes a pop-up blocker that is used to block most pop-ups. When a pop-up attempts to open, it is detected but instead of opening, the information bar displays a message saying that the pop-up was blocked. You can click the information bar, and you'll have several choices:

- **Temporarily allow pop-ups** This will allow pop-ups to appear for this session.
- **Always allow pop-ups from this site** A dialog box appears asking if you want to allow pop-ups from this site. If you click Yes, it adds the site to your exceptions list.
- **Settings** Allows you to access the settings page for the pop-up blocker.
- **More information** Launches help.

In addition to selecting the Settings menu item from the information bar when a pop-up appears, you can also access the Pop-up blocker settings by selecting Tools | Pop-up Blocker | Pop-up Blocker Settings from within Internet Explorer. Figure 13-4 shows the Pop-up Blocker Settings window.

You can type in addresses and click Add to add them to the permanent exception list. If you select Always Allow Pop-ups from This Site from the information bar, sites will be added to this exception list of allowed sites.

In the Notifications and Filter Level section, you can select or deselect one of two notifications:

Figure 13-4

Configuring pop-up blocker settings

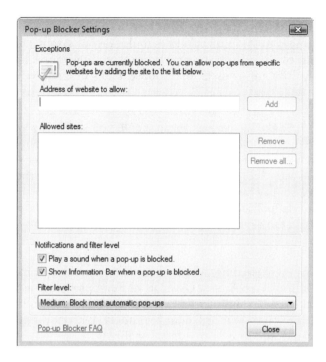

- Play a sound when a pop-is blocked.
- Show Information Bar when a pop-up is blocked.

Additionally, you can set one of three filter levels for the pop-up blocker.

- Low: Allow pop-ups from secure sites.
- Medium: Blocks most automatic pop-ups.
- High: Block all pop-ups (CTRL-ALT to override.)

Really Simple Syndication (RSS)

There's a wide assortment of people creating Web logs, or blogs. A blog is simply an online journal used by companies and individuals to share information in an informal way. If you want to read a blog, you can go directly to a Web site to access it.

You're also able to subscribe to a feed that will publish information from a blog. Really Simple Syndication (RSS) is the term used to describe the technology used to create feeds.

 EXAM TIP When preparing for the exams, you should understand RSS and feeds, what it means to subscribe to a feed, how to subscribe to a feed, and how to adjust the different feed settings.

In addition to text content, you can also subscribe to digital content feeds that include audio and video. For example, audio feeds come in MP3 format and are commonly referred to as podcasts.

If a feed is available from a Web site you visit, the feed button will change color from a grayish color to a shade of orange. If enabled, a sound will also play to indicate a feed is available.

Any feeds you subscribe to are available in the Vista sidebar Feed Headlines gadget. The Feed Headlines gadget is one of the default gadgets available in Windows Vista. Once the gadget is added to the sidebar, you can right-click the gadget and select Options. From there, you can pick the feed (or group of feeds) you want displayed.

Figure 13-5 shows the available options in the Feed Settings dialog box. You can access this box from the Tools menu, Internet options, and selecting the Content tab from within IE.

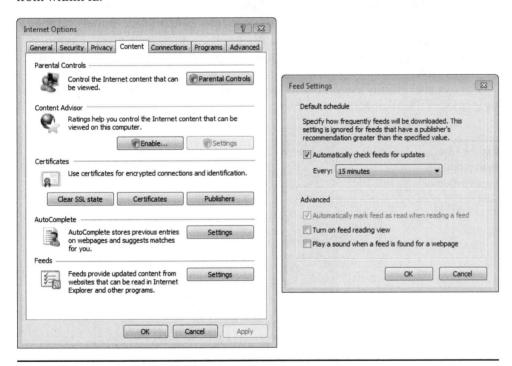

Figure 13-5   Internet Explorer feed settings

The available settings are

- **Default Schedule: Automatically Check Feeds For Updates**   This can be set to check for feeds every 15 minutes, every 30 minutes, every hour, every four hours, every day, or once every week. If you want to ensure you have the most current content (such as from a news service), you'd set the schedule update at the minimum interval—every 15 minutes.

- **Advanced: Automatically Mark Feed As Read When Reading A Feed** When enabled, the feed is marked as read when it's opened. This can help you know what you've read and what you haven't. For high-volume feeds, it's possible to turn this feature off, and mark individual items within the feed as read.

- **Advanced: Turn On Feed Reading View** When this check box is checked, the feed is converted to text from the native XML format. If unchecked, the feed is displayed in XML format.

TIP When first turning this feature on or off, you may not see the display as you expect. You may need to browse away from the page and then return. A typical refresh hitting the F5 key or even a hard refresh (with the CTRL-F5 keys) doesn't cause the display to change.

- **Advanced: Play A Sound When A Feed Is Found For A Webpage** When selected, a sound will play each time you go to a Web page that has a feed available.

You can also modify the properties of any individual feeds. Figure 13-6 shows the properties of the Microsoft at Home feed.

Figure 13-6
Feed properties
for an individual
feed

This setting page allows you to primarily do three things with feeds:

- Modify the schedule on an individual feed basis.
- Set attached files to be automatically downloaded (this can be useful for downloading audio or video files) from a feed.
- Set your archive settings.

In Exercise 13.1, you will access a site that hosts an RSS feed and subscribe to the feed.

Exercise 13.1: Accessing and Subscribing to an RSS Feed

1. Launch Internet Explorer and enter the following address in the address bar:

   ```
   http://msn.com
   ```

   This page includes RSS feeds. You'll know because the RSS feed button just to the right of the home button changes color from grayish to an orange color.

2. Select the RSS drop-down menu and select Games as shown in Figure 13-7.

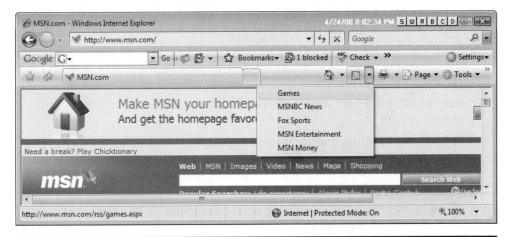

Figure 13-7   Accessing an RSS feed

3. After selecting the RSS feed, you'll see the MSN feed displayed in text format. It includes a header on the MSN games feed, and summaries of several different articles. This page is referred to as the RSS subscription page. You can click the green arrow of any of the articles to view the Web page for the full article.

4. Select the Subscribe to This Feed link in the RSS subscription page. Don't worry, we'll unsubscribe later.

5. In the Subscribe to This Feed dialog box that appears, click Subscribe.

6. Add the feed to your Sidebar Headlines gadget.

   a. If the Feed Headlines gadget isn't in your sidebar, right-click within the sidebar and select Add Gadgets. Double-click the Feed Headlines gadget to add it.

   b. Right-click within the Feed Headlines gadget and select Options.

   c. In the Feed Headlines dialog box, click the drop-down box under Display This Feed. Select the MSN Games feed and click OK. You'll notice the same headlines in the Feed Headlines gadget as you saw in the RSS subscription page.

   d. If desired, put the Feed Headlines back to another feed or remove it from your sidebar.

7. Back in Internet Explorer, click the Tools drop-down menu, and select Internet Options. Select the Content tab and click Settings.

8. In the Feed Settings page, change the interval to automatically check feeds for updates to the minimum interval of 15 minutes.

9. In the Advanced area, deselect the check box next to Turn on Feed Reading View. Click OK. On the Internet Options page, click OK.

10. In Internet Explorer browse away from the Games RSS subscription page and return. You'll see the RSS subscription page displayed in XML.

11. Normalize the Feed Reading view by selecting Tools | Internet Options, selecting the Content tab, and clicking Settings. Click the check box next to Turn on Feed Feeding View and click OK.

12. Edit the RSS subscription properties of the MSN Games subscription with the following steps.

    a. Click the Favorites button (the star icon at the far left of the same toolbar that holds the RSS icon). Select the Feeds link to list the feeds you've added. You'll see a folder labeled Microsoft Feeds, and the MSN Games feed you subscribed to in an earlier step.

    b. Right-click the MSN Games feed and click Properties. You'll see the Feed Properties page for the MSN Games.

    c. Click Settings. Notice you can change the settings for this feed. Click Cancel.

    d. Notice that you can also click the button to Automatically Download Attached Files. This may be useful in some feeds that include audio or video downloads but probably wouldn't do much in the Games feed.

    e. Click Cancel in the Feed Properties page.

13. Unsubscribe to the feed with the following steps.

    a. Click Favorites again. Select the Feeds link to list the feeds you've added.

    b. Right-click the MSN Games feed you subscribed to earlier and select Delete.

    c. On the dialog box that appears asking if you're sure, click Yes.

Configuring Internet Explorer Options

You can configure many options within Internet Explorer. The options can be accessed by selecting the Tools | Internet Options selection from the IE menu. When selected, the Internet Options dialog box appears with seven tabs. Each of the seven tabs is described in the following sections.

General Tab

The General tab is shown in Figure 13-8. It is used to configure many of the basic settings of IE.

Figure 13-8
Internet Options
General tab

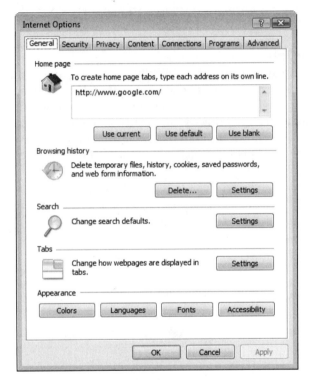

You can use this tab to configure the following options:

- **Home Page**   You can set the Web page that opens when you first launch Internet Explorer. Some malware occasionally changes this. You can come back to this page to restore your original settings.

- **Browsing History**   Internet Explorer stores many temporary files such as Web pages, images, and media to optimize reloading pages. You can configure how much disk space to use for storing these files, where they are stored, and how many days of browsing history to keep. Any of this temporary data can be viewed from the settings page, and all of it can be deleted by clicking Delete.

- **Search**   You can change your default Internet search settings. This changes how searches are done if IE doesn't understand what you've entered in the address bar.

- **Tabs**   Internet Explorer uses tabs for each new page, instead of a completely different instance of Internet Explorer being launched. Clicking Settings gives you a full page of options you can configure to manage the tabs.

- **Appearance**   The appearance section allows you to choose different default colors, languages, fonts, and accessibility features. While most Web pages will be acceptable as presented, some users may want to control how data is displayed. For example, someone with sight problems may want to override how text is normally displayed so that it is displayed in a way that is more visible.

Security Tab

The Security tab allows you to modify the different security zones available in Internet Explorer. You have two primary capabilities within this page. First, you can add specific sites to a specific zone. Second, you can modify the default security settings for the zones to either enhance security or weaken security so that certain applications or add-ons run.

Figure 13-9 shows the different security zones. Notice that the Internet zone is selected and the Enable Protected Mode check box is selected.

Figure 13-9
Security zones on
the Security tab

The Enable Protected Mode check box is designed to make it more difficult for malware to be installed on your computer. Protected mode is enabled by default on all zones except for the Trusted Sites zone. The status bar at the bottom of Internet Explorer indicates what zone you are in and the status of Protected mode (on or off). You can see in Figure 13-10 that the zone is Internet and the status is Protected Mode: On.

Figure 13-10   Internet zone with Protected mode status on

The Protected mode limits the access that Web sites that have to your computer. If a Web page tries to install software or run applications, Protected mode will stop the action and give you a chance to approve or disapprove the action.

When the warning appears, you can click a check box to allow the Web site to run the program.

EXAM TIP   Protected mode is used to protect your system. It prevents malicious Web sites from installing or running malicious software by limiting the access. If you trust a program being launched from a Web site and want to allow it to run, you can select the Always Allow Web Sites to Use This Program to Open Web Content check box on the warning dialog box.

Four zones exist. Each of the zones has default security levels where several settings are configured based on the security risk of the zone. Each zone has a default security level. Except for the restricted sites zone, you can modify the security levels of the zone to meet your needs.

Additionally, Protected mode can be enabled or disabled on each of the zones.

EXAM TIP   Microsoft generalizes the zone settings as High, Medium-High, Medium, Medium-Low, and Low. High provides the strictest environment with the highest security, whereas Low provides the least security. However, you should be aware that you can modify any of the underlying settings of each the zones and configure a custom level.

The four security zones are:

- **Internet zone**   The Internet zone is implemented for any Internet Web sites that aren't in the trusted or restricted sites zones. The default security level for this zone is Medium High.

- **Local intranet zone**   This zone is set for Web sites and content stored on the internal network. The default security level is set to Medium-Low. The intranet can be automatically detected, or you can configure the intranet to include the following sites:

  - **All local Intranet sites not listed in other zones**   Intranet sites are automatically detected by how they are named.

  - **All sites that bypass the proxy server**   Target addresses in the private range (10.0.0.0 networks, 172.16.0.0–172.32.0.0 networks, and 192.168.0.0 networks) will be recognized as internal and will automatically bypass the proxy server.

  - **All network paths (UNCs)**   A Universal Naming Convention (UNC) is composed of \\ServeName\ShareName.

- **Trusted sites zone**   The trusted sites zone is for sites that you intrinsically trust and have specifically added to the zone. The default security level is set to Medium. One of the significant differences in the trusted sites zone is in how ActiveX controls behave.

ActiveX Controls   One of the challenges when managing security within Internet Explorer is with ActiveX controls. ActiveX controls are small programs that can run. They can do great and wonderful things within a Web application, but if programmed by an attacker, they can do significant damage.

ActiveX controls can be signed or unsigned. A signed ActiveX control has a certificate associated with it that identifies the developer or company that created the control. If a company is willing to purchase a certificate so that you know where the ActiveX control came from, it's probably safe. However, an attacker would not purchase a certificate to identify himself as the author of a malicious ActiveX control. Signed ActiveX controls are often trusted, while unsigned ActiveX controls are considered unsafe unless you trust the Web site where it's coming from.

When a Web site tries to install an ActiveX control, you will usually get a warning on the information bar. The information bar appears right below the address bar in Internet Explorer. By clicking on the information bar, you can get a list of actions including the option to install the ActiveX control.

In general, it's a good idea to avoid installing unsigned ActiveX controls. The exception is when you are visiting a Web site that you intrinsically trust. If you trust the Web site, you should consider adding it to the trusted sites zone.

- **Restricted sites zone**   The restricted sites zone is for sites that you recognize as a significant risk and have specifically added to the restricted sites zone. Among other protections, scripting and active content are prevented from running on any sites in the restricted zone. The security level of the restricted sites zone is high, and this can't be changed.

Some of the differences between the zones can be very subtle, as shown in Figure 13-11. The left figure shows some of the ActiveX settings for the Local Intranet Zone, and the right figure shows some of the same ActiveX settings for the Trusted Sites Zone.

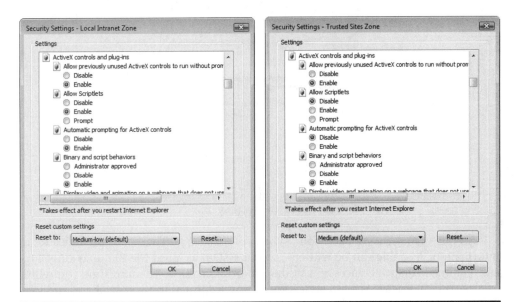

Figure 13-11   A comparison of ActiveX controls and plug-ins settings

You can see that two of the settings are different in the display. The Local Intranet Zone enables Automatic Prompting for ActiveX Controls, but the Trusted Sites Zone disables Automatic Prompting for ActiveX Controls (meaning that prompts won't occur for users in the Trusted Sites Zone). The scriptlets setting is also different.

Privacy Tab

The Privacy tab can be used to modify how cookies are used and how the pop-up blocker behaves. Figure 13-12 shows the options available from the Privacy tab.

In general, cookies are used to provide a personalized experience. Most cookies are used to identify you so that the next time you return to the site, the cookie can be read, and the site is personalized for you.

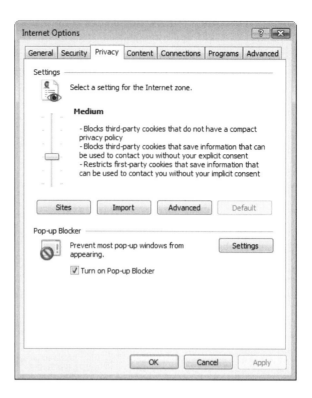

A simple example is Amazon.com. When you make a purchase, you provide a lot of information. A cookie can be written on your system as a text file that may only contain a number that references you in the Amazon database. The next time you return to Amazon, the cookie is read, your information is located in their database, and they display a message saying "Welcome Back, Darril" (but probably with your name instead of mine). They also know what you've purchased and what you've browsed and use that information to display relevant ads.

You have several settings possible for cookies, with the default setting at Medium.

In the Pop-up Blocker section, you can click Settings to access pop-up blocker settings. This will bring you to the settings discussed in the earlier section "Pop-ups and the Pop-up Blocker."

Content Tab

The Content section includes several sections you can manipulate to control different Web content. Figure 13-13 shows the options available in the Content tab.

The available options are

- **Parental Controls** Parents can use this section to control what Internet content can be viewed by users. Parental controls were explored in more detail previously in Chapter 9, Configuring Local Security.

Figure 13-13
The Content tab
of the Internet
Options

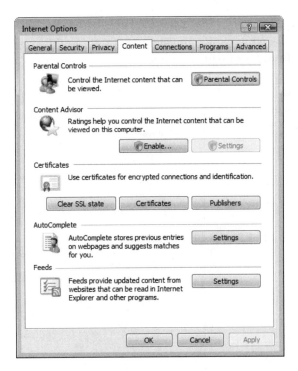

- **Content Advisor** This can be used to control the content that users can view. Web sites are often rated according to the content they contain (such as violence, language, nudity, and so on). An administrator can configure the Content Advisor to restrict access to Web sites based on the content rating for any non-administrative users. It's also possible to restrict access to any Web sites that don't have a content rating.

- **Certificates** The Certificates section is used to monitor and maintain certificates used within the system. The primary reason to use this section is to import, export, or delete certificates as was described earlier, in the section "Secure Sessions and Certificates" of this chapter.

- **AutoComplete** The AutoComplete section can be enabled to automatically complete Web forms. When you fill in data in a Web form, it will be captured and saved, and if a text box is named the same way in another Web page, the data can be automatically filled in for you.

- **Feeds** The Feed Settings page can be accessed from here. RSS feeds were described in more depth in the Really Simple Syndication (RSS) section earlier in this chapter.

Connections Tab

The Connections tab provides access to sections that can be used to create connections for your computer to other networks. This includes wireless, wired, dial-up, and VPN connections. These topics were covered in Chapter 5, "Configuring Network Connectivity"; Chapter 6, "Configuring Wireless Connectivity"; and Chapter 7, "Configuring Network Access."

Programs Tab

The Programs tab is shown in Figure 13-14. From this page, you can designate default programs from four major sections.

Figure 13-14

Internet Options
Programs tab

It has four different sections:

- Default Web browser
- Manage add-ons
- HTML editing
- Internet programs

By default, Internet Explorer is set to tell you if it is not the default Web browser and offer to fix this for you. For example, you may be running Firefox or some other Web browser. Checking the box Tell Me If Internet Explorer Is Not the Default Web Browser will cause a dialog box to appear each time you launch Firefox.

If you tire of the warning, you can uncheck this box. If you ever want IE to be your default Web browser again, you can click Make Default.

The most significant option on this page for Vista specialists (exam takers) is the Manage add-ons section. If you click Manage Add-ons, you can view and manage any Internet Explorer add-ons that have been added to your system.

Figure 13-15

Manage Add-ons

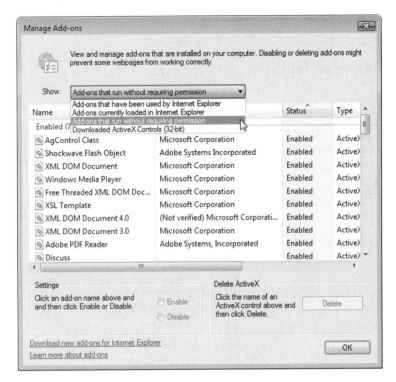

Add-ons are used to add additional functionality to Internet Explorer. Figure 13-15 shows the Manage Add-ons dialog box. Any of the add-ons can be enabled or disabled from this view.

You can also access the Manage Add-ons menu by selecting Tools | Manage Add-ons | Enable or Disable Add-ons. Notice that this dialog box has four views.

- **Add-ons that have been used by Internet Explorer**   This list shows all add-ons that have ever been used by IE.

- **Add-ons currently loaded in Internet Explorer**   This shows add-ons used by the current Web page or recently viewed Web pages.

- **Add-ons that run without requiring permission**   This view shows you the add-ons that are preapproved and won't pop up additional dialog boxes asking for approval to run. These are preapproved by Microsoft, your computer manu-facturer, or a service provider (such as your Internet service provider, or ISP).

- **Downloaded ActiveX Controls (32-bit)**   This shows additional ActiveX controls that have been downloaded and installed.

EXAM TIP   To view a list of add-ons that are preapproved by Microsoft, your computer's manufacturer, or your ISP, view the list of add-ons that run without requiring permission.

Any of the add-ons can be enabled or disabled.

You can also choose the program you use for HTML editing, and for other Internet services such as e-mail from this page.

Advanced Tab

The Advanced tab allows you to set several specific options. Figure 13-16 shows the Advanced options page open with some of the security settings showing.

Figure 13-16
Advanced tab with Security settings showing

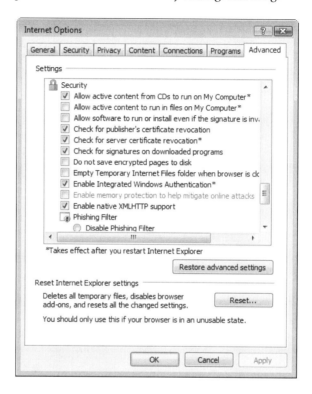

Settings are grouped into the following categories:

- **Accessibility**   These options can be optimized for individuals that have accessibility issues such as vision problems.

- **Browsing**   You can configure many of the browser properties via this page. For example, you may have Web developers that want to enable script debugging so that they can test and debug their Web pages and actually see the script errors. This can be done by deselecting either the Disable Script Debugging (Internet Explorer) or Disable Script Debugging (Other) for non-Microsoft web browsers.

- **HTTP 1.1 Settings**   These two settings specify if the additions of HTTP 1.1 (over HTTP 1.0) are to be used. HTTP 1.1 has been used since 1990 and is considered the standard today. For backward compatibility, these settings can be deselected, but it would be rare to do so.

- **International**   The International section can be used to specify how some information is formatted for ease of use by clients outside the country.

- **Multimedia**   Several settings are available to specify how multimedia documents (such as pictures, animations, and sound) are handled within a Web page.

- **Printing**   You can enable or disable the printing of backgrounds here. By default backgrounds are not printed.

- **Search from the address bar**   You can manipulate how the address bar can be used for searches. For example, you can enter the search command directly into the address bar. If you enter just "Google," the Google Web site appears. If you enter "trika," several choices come up, including the blog for Trika—a great source of information on Microsoft certifications.

- **Security**   You have a wealth of settings you can access and manipulate in the Security section. This includes things like checking for revoked certificates, emptying the Temporary Internet Files folder, and manipulating the Phishing Filter settings.

You may notice the little asterisk (*) under the scrolling settings window marked Takes Effect After You Restart Internet Explorer. Several settings have the asterisk, but you should pay close attention to the security settings that include the asterisk:

- Allow Active Content from CDs to Run on My Computer

- Allow Active Content to Run in Files on My Computer

- Check For Server Certificate Revocation

- Enable Integrated Windows Authentication

- Warn about Certificate Address Mismatch

For example, one of the security settings is to Check for Publisher's Certificate Revocation. This is set by default and causes IE to query the trusted root certification authority to determine if the certificate has been revoked. If you change this setting, you must close and restart Internet Explorer for the new setting to take effect.

Windows Defender

Windows Vista includes the Windows Defender, an anti-spyware tool. Spyware is a form of malicious software (malware) that can be used to display advertisements, collect information about you, send the information to outside sources, and change settings on your computer.

Spyware is similar to a virus or worm in that it installs itself on your computer without your consent. While viruses and worms often have an intended goal of destroying data or affecting the operability of your computer, spyware instead just wants information on you.

Some of the more malicious spyware will capture keystrokes and send them to the attacker. This can be especially damaging if you use your computer for things like banking. Your usernames and passwords can be captured and used.

Less damaging (but no less annoying), spyware can add additional toolbars to Internet Explorer and randomly cause pop-up advertisements to appear.

Windows Defender is intended to protect you from spyware using three different methods:

- **Real-time protection**   Any time spyware (or potentially unwanted software) attempts to install or run on your computer, Windows Defender will intercept the action and bring up an alert. If you didn't initiate the action, you can force it to abort.

- **Scheduled scans**   Windows Defender can be scheduled to run on a periodic basis. It can check all the files on your computer that are recognized as spyware and automatically remove threats.

- **Microsoft SpyNet**   When spyware is first written and released, it isn't known or classified as spyware. However, based on actions it takes, Windows Defender can alert on the action and provide information to you on what others have done. When you participate, information on how you responded to the alert is also submitted to Microsoft.

Launching Windows Defender

You can launch Windows Defender by clicking Start | All Programs and then selecting Windows Defender. Figure 13-17 shows the home page of Windows Defender after a quick scan was completed.

The top of the page gives you a status message on the existence of Spyware as "No Unwanted or Harmful Software Detected." The center of the page shows the statistics of a recently completed quick scan. The bottom of the page includes valuable status information such as when the last scan was completed, the scan schedule, whether real-time protection is on or off, and the version and date of the installed definitions.

If you want to initiate a manual scan, you can click the Scan button at the top of the window. This will start a quick scan. Once the scan completes, scan statistics will be displayed as shown in Figure 13-17.

You can also click the arrow to the right of the Scan button and select one of the following:

- **Quick Scan**   The quick scan checks the locations that spyware is most likely located, such as the Registry and Temporary Internet files.

- **Full Scan**   A full scan will scan all the locations on all your installed hard drives.

- **Custom Scan**   In a custom scan, you can select specific drives and folders to scan.

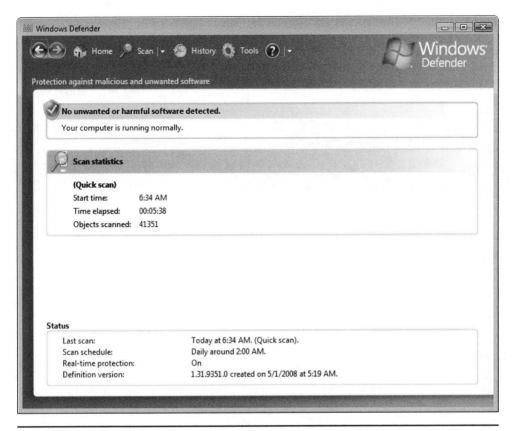

Figure 13-17 The Windows Defender home page

 TIP If you suspect your system is infected with spyware, you should initiate a full scan. This can be done at any time. A quick scan will usually complete in just a few minutes (though it can take longer depending on resources on your system), but a full scan can take significantly longer.

Updating Windows Defender

Just as anti-virus software needs to be regularly updated, Windows Defender needs to be regularly updated. Windows Defender identifies spyware by definitions.

In order to keep Windows Defender up-to-date, you must regularly download definition files. Definition files are downloaded via two methods:

- Automatically as part of Windows Update
- Automatically prior to a scheduled scan

While both these methods are automatic, they can both be disabled. If your system is not configured to download and install Windows Update (and you aren't doing so manually), then the definition files won't be downloaded.

Figure 13-18 shows the Windows Defender Options page. This page has several options, but the definition update can be configured in the Automatic Scanning section.

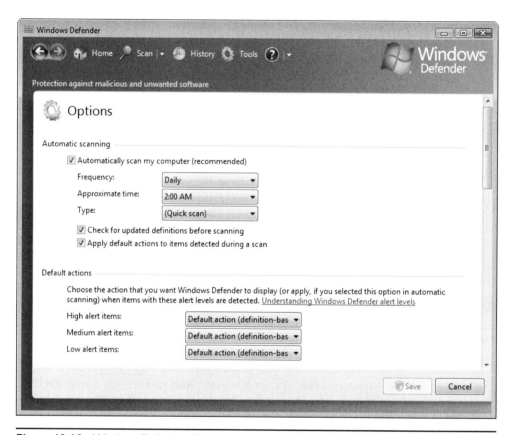

Figure 13-18   Windows Defender Options

Notice the check box for Check for Updated Definitions before Scanning is checked. This is the default setting.

If definitions are not updated, Windows Defender will display a message indicating "Windows Defender Definitions haven't been updated."

EXAM TIP   You should know how the Windows Defender definition files are updated (Windows Update or automatically prior to a scan), and what the symptoms are if the definitions aren't updated (a warning message).

If you receive a warning message indicating definitions aren't being updated, you should complete a Windows Update as soon as possible.

Microsoft SpyNet

The Microsoft SpyNet is an online community of individuals (like you) that Microsoft is bringing together to help identify and stop spyware infections. Information on potential spyware is sent to Microsoft for any computers that have this authorized. When a potential spyware event occurs, an alert appears (for any computers that have authorized the alert) and Windows Defender will provide you with information on how other users have handled the alert.

NOTE Any program that has been identified as spyware is included in the Windows Defender definitions. The difference between the definitions and the SpyNet data is that data in the definitions is known to be spyware, while what is reported in SpyNet is only potentially spyware. The configuration of the SpyNet settings does not affect how Windows Defender responds to known risks documented in the definitions.

You can configure how your computer uses the Microsoft SpyNet with three possible choices. Two of the choices refer to a membership, which implies a charge, but there is no charge for membership.

These settings can be viewed and modified by launching Windows Defender (click Start | All Programs | Windows Defender), click the Tools link, and select Microsoft SpyNet.

The three choices you have are:

- **Join with a Basic Membership** With a basic membership, your system reports possible spyware events to the Microsoft SpyNet community along with actions taken by you or Windows Defender, and whether these actions were successful. The basic membership does not provide any alerts to you on unclassified risks. Windows Defender will still alert on risks known and documented in the definition files.

- **Join with an Advanced Membership** With an advanced membership, Windows Defender will provide alerts for potential spyware issues (beyond what is known in the definitions), and also provide you with information on how other users handled the issue. Additionally, your system will provide more detailed data to Microsoft.

- **I don't want to join Microsoft SpyNet as this time** Your system doesn't send data and doesn't receive any alerts on unclassified risks.

Windows Defender Options

The Windows Defender tool has several options that can be used to control how it behaves. To access the options, launch Windows Defender (click Start | All Programs | Windows Defender), click Tools, and select Options.

Options are grouped into five separate areas as described in the following sections.

Automatic Scanning

You can enable and schedule Automatic Scanning of your computer for spyware. In this section, you can configure the following items:

- **Frequency** You can schedule an automatic scan to occur daily, or on any specific day.

- **Approximate time** You can schedule the hour (such as 2:00 A.M.) when you want the scan to start.

- **Type** You can schedule the scan as a quick scan or a full system scan.

As mentioned earlier in this chapter, you can also choose to check for updated definitions before a scan. If an item is detected during a scheduled scan, you can choose to apply the default actions described in the next section.

Default Actions

Some spyware is exceptionally malicious and can significantly affect your privacy and the security of your computer. Other spyware is relatively benign and its actions are often agreed to via licensing terms.

Windows Defender classifies spyware based on several alert levels:

- **Severe** These programs are known to be exceptionally malicious and could significantly affect your privacy and the security of your computer.

- **High** These programs might collect information that could negatively affect your privacy. These programs could also damage your computer by changing your system settings without your consent.

- **Medium** These programs might negatively affect your computing experience by collecting information about you or your computer and make changes without your consent.

- **Low** These programs might collect information on you or your computer, or change your system settings, but are doing so in accordance with a licensing agreement.

When spyware is detected, Windows Defender takes different actions depending on the classification of the spyware. Figure 13-19 shows the different alerts and the possible choices for each alert (Default Action, Ignore, or Remove).

Each of the three alert levels allow you to choose the Default Action, Ignore, or Remove. Ignore will ignore the alert, and remove will Remove the spyware.

The default action is based on the definition. If the definition says to remove it, the spyware will be removed. If the definition says to ignore it, the spyware will be ignored.

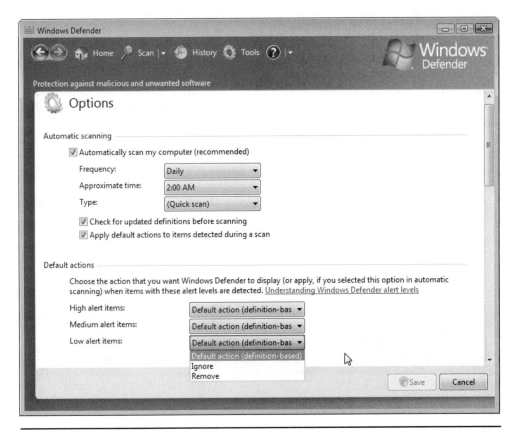

Figure 13-19 Default Actions for alerts

The three alert levels are

- **High Alert Items** This level includes both the Severe and the High categories. Spyware in this category will typically be directed to be removed in the definition file.

- **Medium Alert Items** This level includes the Medium category.

- **Low Alert Items** This level includes the Low category.

If doing a manual scan and the Automatic Scanning option Apply Default Actions to Items Detected During a Scan is checked (the default), the action associated with the alert will automatically be applied.

For alerts that occur as part of the real-time protection, the defaults specified here will appear as the recommended action. The user is able to review the choices and make a different decision if desired.

Real-Time Protection Options

Figure 13-20 shows the real-time protection options available in Windows Defender.

The real-time protection options define how Windows monitors your system on a real-time basis. Spyware can use a variety of different methods to gather information on your computer and, based on that information, discover vulnerabilities. Once vulnerabilities are discovered, the spyware can then try to exploit the vulnerability to gather personal information or modify computer settings.

When real-time protection is enabled, attempts to gather information on your system are intercepted and blocked. Windows Defender includes several security agents that can intercept spyware attempts to gather information on your computer. These are all enabled by default.

 TIP Microsoft recommends enabling all of the real-time protection agents for best protection. This is done by accepting the default of having all the check boxes checked.

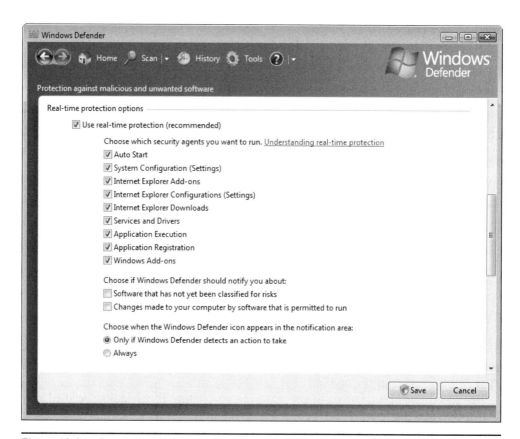

Figure 13-20   Real-time protection options

This section allows you to choose how Windows Defender notifies you of different events. Both choices are disabled by default. The two choices are

- **Software That Has Not Been Classified For Risks**   If checked, Windows Defender will notify you when an unclassified application is launched.

- **Changes Made To Your Computer By Software That Is Permitted To Run**   If checked, Windows Defender will notify you changes are being made even by authorized programs. The notification is: "An application request change was made for a known application file" and then the file and path of the approved application making the change is listed. This can get annoying, so it is left unchecked by default.

You can also choose when the Windows Defender icon appears in the notification area.

When real-time protection is enabled, you will be alerted when spyware is detected. The alert will provide you with four choices:

- **Ignore**   Allows the program to be installed or run at this time. If the program attempts to install or run again later, Windows Defender will alert on it again.

- **Quarantine**   Moves the software to a safe place on your computer where it will be prevented from running. Quarantined items can be restored if you later discover that this program is needed or desired.

- **Remove**   Deletes the software from your computer.

- **Always Allow**   This adds the program to the Windows Defender allowed list.

 EXAM TIP   You should know what each of the real-time protection choices does for any Windows Defender alerts.

Advanced Options
The Advanced Options section is shown in Figure 13-21. All three options are selected by default.

Notice that the Create a Restore Point Before Applying Actions to Detected Items is checked. If you find that the actions that Windows Defender took are unacceptable, you can always return to the state before Windows Defender modified your system.

You can also specify files or locations that you don't want Windows Defender to scan.

Administrator Options
Only two options are listed here. You can choose to enable or disable Windows Defender by selected or deselecting the check box next to Use Windows Defender.

Additionally, you can specify whether non-administrative users can scan the computer, choose responses to alerts, and review Windows Defender activities.

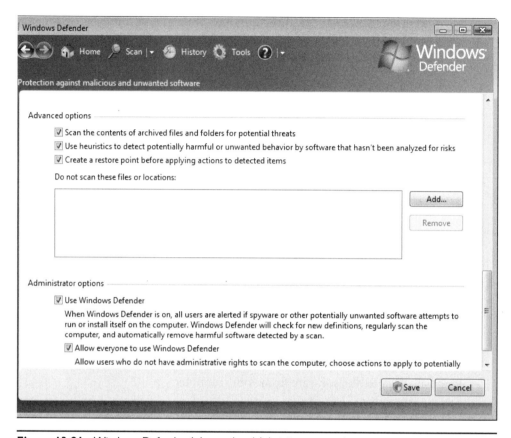

Figure 13-21 Windows Defender Advanced and Administrator options

Windows Defender Tools

The Tools section of the Tools and Settings page shows the different tools available within Windows Defender. You can use the tools to manage how Windows Defender treats different software.

Quarantined Items

Instead of permanently removing spyware items, you can choose to move them to a quarantined area. Quarantined items will not run and don't present any risk to your computer.

The primary reason to quarantine an item instead of deleting it is because you think you may want to restore it later. In addition to the list of items that have been quarantined, you also have three buttons available in the quarantined items list.

- **Restore** By selecting any item in the quarantined items list and selecting Restore, you will remove the item from the quarantined list and allow it to run.

- **Remove**   By selecting any item in the quarantined items list and selecting Remove, you will permanently remove the item from your computer.

- **Remove All**   By clicking Remove All, you will permanently remove all items from your computer.

Allowed Items

The Allowed Items list shows software that you have marked as safe and will no longer be monitored by Windows Defender. If Windows Defender is alerting on an item that you do not consider spyware, or you don't want Windows Defender to alert on, you can add it to the list of allowed items.

You can remove an item from the allowed items list by selecting it and then clicking Remove.

TIP   If an item is in the Allowed Items list and also in the Quarantined Items list, it will be treated as quarantined. You must restore it from the quarantined list in order to allow it to run.

Software Explorer

The Software Explorer within Windows Defender is used to view detailed information on software running on your computer. Figure 13-22 shows the Software Explorer

Figure 13-22   Windows Defender Software Explorer

opened with the Startup programs shown and the Google Toolbar Notifier program selected.

Notice in the right pane, you can view a significant amount of information on the selected programs. You can monitor programs in four categories from within the Software Explorer.

- **Startup programs**   These are programs that are configured to run automatically when Windows starts. Some programs will have the Remove, Disable, and/or Enable buttons available. If you click Remove, the program will be removed from the startup list. Enable allows the program to run, and Disable prevents the program from starting (though doesn't terminate a program that is currently running). You can also manipulate startup programs using the MSConfig utility covered later in this chapter.

 EXAM TIP   Disable may sound like you are disabling an application, but you are only disabling the auto-start capability of the program. It won't start when the computer starts, but it can be started manually later. If you change a program to disabled and you want to ensure it is not running, you can reboot your system. On reboot, the program will be recognized as disabled and won't start.

- **Currently running programs**   These are programs that are currently running (including programs that are running in the background). The two buttons available in this view are Task Manager (which launches the Task Manager) and End Process, which works the same as the End Process function within Task Manager.

- **Network-connected programs**   These are programs that connect to the Internet. For some processes two buttons are available: End Process and Block Incoming Connections. Spyware may be using incoming connections to gather information on your computer, and you can block these connections by clicking the button.

- **Winsock service providers**   These are low-level networking and communication services used within Windows. They are granted access to several important areas of the operating system. All you're able to do with these programs is view the details.

Enabling and Using Windows Defender

The Windows Defender runs by default, so it is probably running on your system. Exercise 13.2 you will lead you through many of the actions and activities you can take with Windows Defender.

Exercise 13.2: Enable and use Windows Defender

1. Launch the Control Panel by selecting Start | Control Panel. Click the Security section.

2. In the Security section, click the Security Center. The Security Center will tell you if you have any security issues. The Malware protection is used to inform you if anti-virus and anti-spyware programs are running on your computer. At this point, you probably have all four settings green, indicating they are all running. Keep the Security Center window open.

3. Stop Windows Defender with the following steps:

   a. Click Start | All Programs and select Windows Defender.

   b. Click Tools and select Options.

   c. Scroll to the bottom of the Options page and select Administrator Options. Uncheck the Use Windows Defender check box and click Save. If the User Account Control dialog box appears, click Continue.

   d. On the Windows Defender warning dialog box, review the information and click Close.

4. Return to the Security Center window. Your display will look similar to Figure 13-23. Notice that when Windows Defender is turned off, the Malware Protection item turns red and the Check Settings warning also appears. Leave this window open.

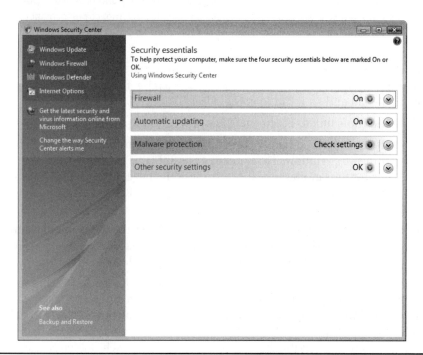

Figure 13-23   Security Essentials page indicating Windows Defender is not running

5. Turn on Windows Defender with the following steps.

  a. Click Start | All Programs and then select Windows Defender.

  b. On the Windows Defender dialog box, review the information and click the link to Turn On and Open Windows Defender. If the User Account Control dialog box appears, click Continue.

  c. Click Tools and select Options. Scroll to the bottom of the Options page and notice that the selection to Use Windows Defender is selected.

  d. Scroll to the bottom of the Options page and select Administrator Options. Uncheck the Use Windows Defender check box and click Save. If the User Account Control dialog box appears, click Continue.

6. Return to the Security Center window. Notice that when Windows Defender is turned back on, the Malware protection item is green again. Close this window by clicking the X at the top right of the window.

7. Back in Windows Defender, click the Home link. Notice at the bottom of the page, Status information is listed. You can tell when the last scan was performed, the scan schedule, whether or not real-time protection is enabled, and which definition version you have.

8. To initiate a scan immediately, click the Scan link at the top of the Windows Defender window. This will initiate a scan of your computer for spyware.

 TIP Depending on the resources (such as memory and processing power) you have available for your system, this may significantly impact performance. It is best to schedule the scans to occur at a time when you're not using the computer.

9. Click Stop Scan to stop the scan. This will allow you to move on to the next step in the exercise. When you're done with the exercise, feel free to begin another manual scan and let it run to completion.

10. Click the Tools link to access the Tools and Settings page.

11. Click the Quarantined Items. This will show the items that have been quarantined by Windows Defender. It's possible this list is blank. Notice the three buttons available at the bottom of the page. If you want to allow a quarantined item to run, you can select it and click Restore. If you click Remove, the program will be deleted from your computer.

12. Click Tools and click Allowed Items. This list shows the items that have been allowed by your overriding Windows Defender alerts. You can remove an item from the list so that Windows Defender will again alert on it if it runs.

13. Click Tools and then click Software Explorer. Select the Startup Programs category. This lists all the programs that are configured to start automatically when the computer starts. Notice that some programs can be modified by selecting the program and clicking Disable, but other programs are required by Windows and the Disable button is dimmed and not selectable.

MSConfig

When troubleshooting malware there are times when you want to ensure a specific program is not started. While you learned how to configure this in Windows Defender Software Explorer, you can also perform the same task with the MSConfig utility.

To launch MSConfig, click Start and enter **MSConfig** in the Start Search box. If the User Account Control dialog appears, click Continue. Figure 13-24 shows the Startup tab of the MSConfig utility.

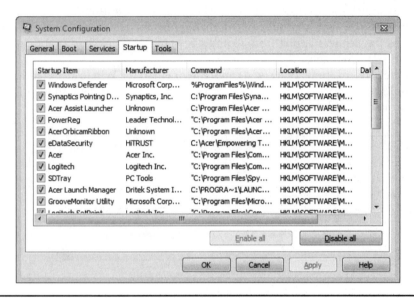

Figure 13-24   Configuring startup items in the MSConfig utility

You can deselect the check box in the Startup Item column for any item that you don't want to start on bootup. As soon as you apply a change, the General tab changes from Normal Startup to Selective Startup.

Similarly, you can select the Services tab and deselect the check box in the Service column for any services you don't want to start on bootup.

If you select the Boot tab, you can manipulate different options for advanced troubleshooting.

Windows Defender and the Services Applet

In naval warfare someone discovered that submarines could very effectively sneak up on large ships undetected, surface, and sink the ship. In response, anti-submarine warfare was begun to detect and attack submarines. This launched the anti-anti-submarine warfare technologies where the submarines attempt to either attack or fool the detection mechanisms.

The same scenario is played out in many different arenas. Malware is launched to attack systems. Anti-malware is created and updated to attack and circumvent malware. Malware is then modified to attack the anti-malware programs (anti-anti-malware if you will).

In other words, it's possible for malware to attack Windows Defender and prevent it from running so that the malware can run undetected. One of the ways you can protect yourself against attacks on Windows Defender is to configure what happens if Windows Defender fails to start with the Services applet.

You can launch the Services applet by clicking Start | Administrative Tools and selecting Services. If the User Account Control dialog box appears, click Continue. You can also access the Services applet from Computer Manager (click Start, right-click Computer, and select Manage).

With the Services applet open, you can scroll down to the Windows Defender service and double-click it to access the properties. Figure 13-25 shows the Windows Defender service properties with the Recovery options showing.

Figure 13-25
Windows
Defender
service properties

Notice that Windows Defender is configured to restart if it fails to start. If it fails a second time, it will attempt to restart again. For any subsequent failures, Windows Defender is configured to Take No Action.

In other words, if malware successfully attacks Windows Defender, Windows Defender will just roll over and die.

You can actually choose one of four actions:

- **Take No Action**   This is the default.
- **Restart The Service**   When this is selected, the service will continually attempt to restart.
- **Run A Program**   A program of your choosing can be started. For example, you could run another anti-virus or anti-spyware program.
- **Restart The Computer**   If the computer is restarted, then the start counts will be restarted. On the reboot, Windows Defender will try to restart once, twice, and then on the third time the computer will reboot again.

TIP   Setting the computer to restart on subsequent failures (after the first and second failures) will put your computer into a reboot loop if Windows Defender is prevented from starting. While this sounds like a real problem, it's better than allowing the malware to attack unabated. If your computer is caught in a reboot loop, you can enter Safe mode and troubleshoot it from there.

Running in Safe Mode

It's not uncommon for malware to protect itself from being deleted or stopped. Occasionally when Windows Defender attempts to remove or quarantine malware, it fails. For example, the spyware could be running, and as soon as Windows Defender stops it (or you stop it using Task Manager), the spyware could immediately restart itself.

One way to circumvent malware that protects itself in this way is to restart your computer in Safe mode. Safe mode was covered in more depth in Chapter 12, but you may remember that it starts using only minimal hardware and processes. Extra applications and processes (such as malware) would not be running.

Within Safe mode, you can run Windows Defender, which can successfully remove the malware.

Using Programs and Features to Uninstall Spyware

Occasionally a user may be tricked into installing spyware. For example, a Web site could advertise an add-on and present it as something that a user may want.

A common example is an add-on that adds an additional toolbar to Internet Explorer. The directions on the Web site show the user exactly how to bypass the warnings so that the add-on is installed.

The Programs and Features applet within Control Panel can be used to uninstall this add-on if the user later changes their mind. To access the Programs and Features applet, click Start, and select Control Panel. In Control Panel, select Programs and then click Programs and Features. Figure 13-26 shows the Programs and Features applet open.

You can browse to the unwanted application or add-on and select Uninstall. Some applications also give the option to Change and/or Repair. The availability of the extra choices will be different with different applications.

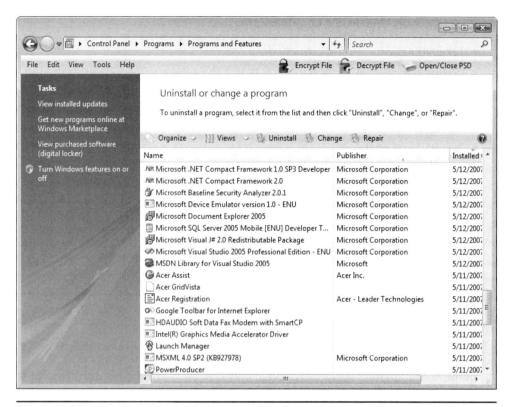

Figure 13-26   Using Programs and Features to uninstall an application

RootkitRevealer

A rootkit is a program (or group of programs) designed to take control of a computer at the root level. Once installed, all commands go through the rootkit. The rootkit can then decide what programs it wants to allow, and what parts of your computer it wants the program to be able to see.

From a malware perspective, rootkits can be very damaging. Once installed, they can allow other malware to run unabated. If you run Windows Defender or anti-virus software on the computer, the rootkit can prevent access to any malware. Windows Defender scans show everything is normal, but your system is infected with malware—the rootkit just hides it.

Rootkits come in different categories. The first two just identify if the rootkit will survive a reboot.

- **Persistent rootkit**   A persistent rootkit will survive reboots. The program is stored on the hard drive and will typically be configured to start on computer bootup.

- **Memory-based rootkit**   A memory-based rootkit is stored in memory. Once the computer is rebooted, the rootkit is gone.

The next two categories identify how the rootkit operates and how it evades detection.

- **User-mode rootkit**   A user-mode rootkit intercepts calls to the file system to control what the user can see and do. It can hide the existence of files on your system.

- **Kernel-mode rootkit**   A kernel-mode rootkit intercepts calls to the operating system. In addition to being able to control calls to the file system, it can also control calls to the operating system. It can hide the existence of processes running on your system.

Microsoft has released a tool called the RootkitRevealer written by two individuals at Sysinternals. The RootkitRevealer is designed to detect persistent rootkits. Figure 13-27 shows RootkitRevealer after being run on a system that does not have a rootkit installed. Notice that some entries are normal.

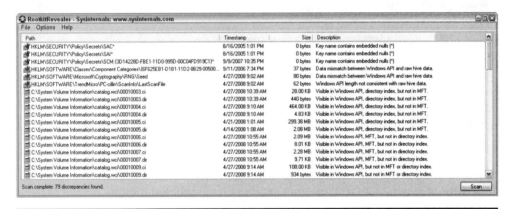

Figure 13-27   RootkitRevealer after a scan on a clean system

 EXAM TIP   You should know that the RootkitRevealer tool is available for advanced troubleshooting and it can be used to accurately detect rootkits.

If you suspect your system is infected by malware but all your malware scans are showing your system as clean, then you should download and run the RootkitRevealer.

You can get more information on the RootkitRevealer, including a link to download it, at this address: http://technet.microsoft.com/en-us/sysinternals/bb897445.aspx.

 TIP   Before running RootkitRevealer, you should save all your work and shut down all applications. This application will take quite a long time to run and may run outside the Windows desktop.

After some Internet surfing recently, I suspected I may have picked up a rootkit. I ran the RootkitRevealer which showed a lot more entries than normal as shown in Figure 13-28. Of particular note, several entries had the description "Hidden from Windows API" which indicates a rootkit may be installed.

Figure 13-28   RootkitRevealer showing a likely rootkit installed

Some entries are normal, but the volume of entries in the figure is definitely not normal. Compare Figure 13-28 to Figure 13-27 to show the differences between an infected system and a clean system.

If you suspect that your system is infected by a rootkit, take the following steps.

- Download and run the RootkitRevealer to detect any possible persistent rootkits.

- Reboot your system to flush any possible memory-based rootkits.

- Delete all Temporary Internet files and Cookies (select Tools and Internet Options from within Internet Explorer). In the Browsing History Section, click Delete and delete the files from within this menu.

- Download and run the RootkitRevealer again to see if you notice differences.

- Run all your malware scans again.

NOTE   When troubleshooting malware, one of the things that can often solve many of your problems is to delete all the Temporary Internet files. You can access the menu by selecting Tools | Internet Options from the Internet Explorer menu. On the general tab, select Delete from the Browsing History menu. Delete all the Temporary Internet Files and all the Cookies. If some files aren't deleted, you can perform the same actions from Safe mode to delete them.

Chapter Review

In this chapter you learned the details about different Internet applications you can use within Windows Vista.

Internet Explorer 7 is the default Web browser in Windows Vista. It includes many new features. Some security features include the Phishing Filter and the Pop-up Blocker, in addition to many different Internet Options that allow you to specifically configure many security settings.

Windows Defender is included in Windows Vista and is designed to protect you and your system from spyware. It will normally run by default providing real-time protection. You can also launch manual scans at any time.

Last, you learned about RootkitRevealer, a tool that can be used to detect rootkits. You also learned some basics about rootkits.

Additional Study

Self Study Exercises
Use these additional exercises to challenge yourself.

- Launch Internet Explorer and add a site to your list of Trusted Sites.

- Access the Internet Options from Internet Explorer and access each of tabs.

- Start your system in Safe mode and run the Windows Defender.

- Launch the MSConfig utility and stop the Windows Defender.

- Download the RootkitRevealer and run it on your system.

Summary of What You Need to Know

70-620
When preparing for the 70-620 exam, pay particular attention to the following topics covered in this chapter:

- **Internet Explorer features and capabilities**   These include: how to use IE, how to print, managing add-ons, Pop-up Blocker, Protected mode, and RSS feeds.

- **Windows Defender features and capabilities**   These include: how to run a scan, how to update Windows Defender definitions, how to restore applications from the quarantined list, and how to handle Windows Defender alerts.

- **Using the MSConfig utility**   You should be familiar with the capabilities and uses of MSConfig For example, it can be used to identify malware that is running at startup and, when launched in Safe Mode, can be used to prevent applications and services from starting.

70-622

When preparing for the 70-622 exam, pay particular attention to the following topics covered in this chapter:

- **Internet Explorer features and capabilities**   These include: the different zones and how they can be used, handling pop-ups, and modifying Internet Options settings.

- **Windows Defender features and capabilities**   These include: handling notifications, configuring options, and configuring real-time protection.

70-623

When preparing for the 70-623 exam, pay particular attention to the following topics covered in this chapter:

- **Internet Explorer features and capabilities**   These include: the Phishing Filter, working with certificates, RSS feeds, and configuring advanced options.

- **Windows Defender features and capabilities**   These include: performing scans, handling notifications, configuring real-time protection, configuring service failures using the Services applet, and running Windows Defender in Safe mode.

- **Using the MSConfig utility**   You should be familiar with the capabilities and uses of MSConfig For example, it can be used to identify malware that is running at startup and, when launched in Safe Mode, can be used to prevent applications and services from starting.

- **Rootkits and the RootkitRevealer**   You should know what a rootkit is and how it can mask activity on your system preventing typical anti-virus tools from identifying it. Additionally, you should be familiar with the RootkitRevealer including how it can be used to help detect rootkits.

Questions

70-620

1. You are doing some research on the Internet and suspect you may visit some sites that have malicious software installed. You want to prevent these sites from installing malware on your system. What should you do?

   A. Run an anti-virus scan before and after visiting the sites.

   B. Run Windows Defender before and after visiting the sites.

   C. Run the RootkitRevealer before and after visiting the sites.

   D. Ensure that Enable Protected Mode is enabled for the Internet zone.

2. You frequently visit a fantasy football Web site that uses pop-ups to provide relevant information. You want pop-ups from this site to always be enabled, but you don't want to change the behavior for other Web sites. How can you achieve your goals? Choose all that apply.

   A. From the information bar, select the option to Temporarily Allow Pop-ups.

   B. Turn off the pop-up blocker.

    C. Add the site to your pop-up blocker exception list.

    D. Add the site your Phishing filter exception list.

    E. From the information bar, select the option to Always Allow Pop-ups from This Site.

3. You have configured several RSS subscription feeds on your computer, including one for a stock notification service. You notice that the content for the stock notification service is not the same as displayed on the actual source page for the feed. What should you do?

    A. Configure the RSS feed properties with a minimum interval for updates.

    B. Configure the RSS feed properties with a maximum interval for updates.

    C. Unsubscribe and re-subscribe to the feed.

    D. Close Internet Explorer and open it again to update the feed.

4. You have subscribed to an RSS feed that frequently includes video files. The videos take a long time to download and view when you access the feed, and you want to minimize the delay while watching them. What should you do?

    A. Configure the Feed Settings page to Automatically Download Attached Files.

    B. Configure the Feed Settings page to keep the maximum number of items in the archive.

    C. Configure the properties of the individual feed to keep the maximum number of items in the archive.

    D. Configure the properties of the individual feed to Automatically Download Attached Files.

5. You suspect that malware is running on your Windows Vista system. What should you do? (Choose two.)

    A. Run an anti-virus scan.

    B. Run a Windows Defender scan.

    C. Run a Phishing Filter scan.

    D. Perform a System Restore.

6. You have started the Windows Defender application but receive a warning saying that the Windows Defender definition files are not up-to-date. How can you update the Windows Defender definition files?

    A. Use Windows Update.

    B. Launch Windows Defender, select the Tools menu, and click Download Definition Files.

    C. Launch Windows Defender, select the Options menu, and click Download Definition Files.

    D. Perform a System Restore.

70-622

1. In-house users are accessing an intranet Web site. They are being prompted to install an ActiveX control when they access that site. You would like the ActiveX control to be installed without prompting users. What should you have the users do?

   A. Add the intranet Web site to the Internet zone.

   B. Add the intranet Web site to the local intranet zone.

   C. Add the intranet Web site to the trusted sites zone.

   D. Add the intranet to the restricted sites zone.

2. Currently, Windows Vista systems provide notifications when Internet Explorer 7 blocks a pop-up. You want to disable pop-up notifications without affecting security. How can you do so? Choose all that apply.

   A. Turn off the pop-up blocker.

   B. Clear the check box for Play A Sound When A Pop-up Is Blocked in the Pop-up Blocker Settings window.

   C. Clear the check box for Show Information Bar When A Pop-up Is Blocked in the Pop-up Blocker Settings window.

   D. Clear the check box for Enable Notifications When A Pop-up Is Blocked in the Pop-up Blocker Settings window.

3. Sally is a Web developer and is creating an intranet Web site. She's included scripts that occasionally don't work, but when she tests pages using Internet Explorer 7, she doesn't see any of the script errors. What should she do to see the script errors?

   A. She needs to test the pages using a previous version of Internet Explorer to view the scripting errors.

   B. She needs to modify the Browsing settings in the Advanced tab of Internet Options.

   C. She needs to modify the Security settings in the Advanced tab of Internet Options.

   D. She needs to modify the Browsing settings in the Content tab of Internet Options.

4. Maria complains that every time she starts her computer, her system gives an error message stating that an application request change was made for a known application. She dismisses the error message but would like to get rid of it completely. What should she do?

   A. Use the Services applet to stop the application from starting automatically.

   B. Use MSConfig to prevent the application from starting on bootup.

   C. In Windows Defender, clear the check box to notify for Changes Made to Your Computer by Software That Is Permitted to Run.

   D. In Windows Defender, change the alert response to Ignore.

5. All the computers in your company run Windows Vista. Joe's computer becomes infected with a known spyware program after visiting a Web site. Sally mentioned that she visited the same Web site but didn't get infected. You look at Joe's Windows Security Center as shown in the Figure 13-29. What, if anything, should be done?

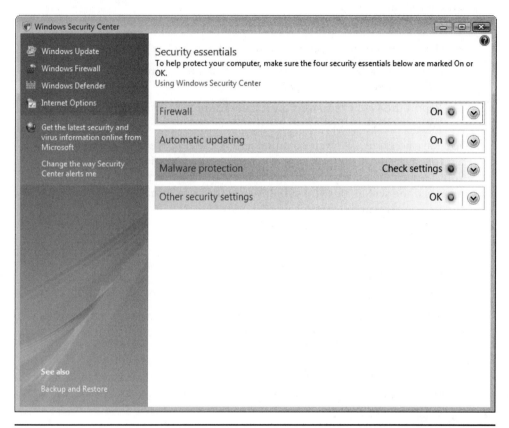

Figure 13-29 Windows Security Center

    A. Nothing. These settings are the recommended settings.

    B. Enable both the check boxes in the Choose If Windows Defender Should Notify You About section.

    C. Enable all the check boxes in the Choose Which Security Agents You Want to Run section.

    D. Enable the check box for the System Configuration (Settings).

70-623

1. Your mother has launched her own business. You visit the Web site, but the Phishing Filter displays a warning Web page that indicates your mother's business page is a phishing Web site. You know your mother's business site is legitimate and you want to help her remove it from the list of phishing Web sites. What can you do?

   A. Disable the Phishing Filter on your computer.

   B. Have your mother disable the Phishing Filter on her Web site.

   C. Report the Web site to Microsoft and ensure the I Think This Is a Phishing Website check box is checked.

   D. Report the Web site to Microsoft and ensure the I Think This Is a Phishing Website check box is not checked.

2. You have accessed a Web site maintained by a friend. He told you the site has a revoked certificate, but when you access it, it doesn't give you any warning. You changed the advanced setting to check for server certificate revocation and refreshed the screen, but you still don't get the error. What needs to be done to ensure you are warned about a revoked certificate?

   A. Add the site to the Trusted Sites zone.

   B. Add the site to the Restricted Sites zone.

   C. Reboot Vista.

   D. Close all instances of IE and connect again with IE.

3. A customer is running Windows Vista and is concerned that his computer may become infected with malware. What should he enable on his computer?

   A. Windows Update

   B. Vista Anti-Virus protector

   C. Windows Firewall

   D. Windows Defender

4. A user installed a certificate on his system from a gaming site he regularly visits. However, IE now reports a problem with the certificate. He learned a new certificate is available, so he downloaded and installed it. However, IE still reports the problem. What should he do?

   A. Remove the older certificate from the Other People store.

   B. Remove the older certificate from the Trusted Root Certification Authority store.

   C. Reboot Vista and try again.

   D. Close all IE sessions and try again.

5. You've learned about an emerging threat that attacks Windows Defender, preventing it from starting, and then infects your computer. You want to ensure that Windows Vista fails to start if Windows Defender fails. What should you do?

   A. Configure the Services applet to try to restart Windows Defender if it fails the first and second times, and restart the computer after subsequent failures.

   B. Configure the Windows Defender Advanced Options to restart the computer if it fails.

   C. Configure the Windows Defender real-time protection Options to restart the computer if it fails.

   D. Configure MSConfig to restart the computer if it fails.

6. Joe has installed many different applications on his system that he downloaded from the Internet. He notices that his computer seems to be acting as though it's infected by malware. However, full scans by Windows Defender and anti-virus software don't show any problems. He suspects the malware is hiding from the scans. What should he do?

   A. Check for spyware by using Windows Defender.

   B. Check for a virus by using anti-virus software.

   C. Check for a phishing Web site by using the Phishing Filter.

   D. Check for a rootkit by using the RootkitRevealer.

Answers

70-620

1. **D.** By ensuring that Enable Protected Mode is enabled for the Internet zone, you can reduce the level of access Web site programs have to your system. It will prevent programs from running or installing without your permission. While running tools such as anti-virus software, Windows Defender, and the RootkitRevealer before and after visiting the sites are good steps to take to detect malware that has been installed, these steps wouldn't prevent the site from running or installing the program. The Enable Protected Mode is preventive in nature.

2. **C, E.** You can either add the site to your pop-up blocker exception list or select the option to Always Allow Pop-ups from This site from the information bar. If you select the option to Temporarily Allow Pop-ups, pop-ups will be allowed for this session, but not the next time you visit the site. If you turn off the pop-up blocker, pop-ups will appear from other Web sites. The Phishing Filter does not affect pop-ups.

3. **A.** If you configure the Feed Settings page to Automatically Check Feeds For Updates every 15 minutes (the minimum interval), the RSS subscription page will show the updated content. If you set it at the maximum value (1 week), the content will only be updated once a week. Subscribing and re-subscribing is taking too many steps and won't set the feed to a minimum interval; neither will restarting Internet Explorer.

4. **D.** You can set the properties of an individual feed to Automatically Download Attached Files. You can't set this from the Feed Settings page to apply to all feeds. The Archive is only set at the individual feed property page, but it wouldn't cause attachments to be automatically downloaded.

5. **A, B.** To detect malware (malicious software) on your system, you should run an anti-virus scan and an anti-spyware scan. Windows Vista includes Windows Defender, which can perform an anti-spyware scan. You can't perform a Phishing Filter scan; you can only enable or disable the Phishing Filter and configure some properties. A System Restore would be done to recover your system if it has suffered damage, but it wouldn't detect malware.

6. **A.** Windows Defender definition files are updated through Windows Update (or automatically before a scan if configured to do so). There is no link to download the definition files in either the Tools menu or the Options menu. A System Restore would be done to recover your system if it has suffered damage, but it wouldn't update definition files.

70-622

1. **C.** The default setting for the Automatic Prompting for ActiveX controls is enabled for the local intranet zone, and disabled for the trusted sites zone. By adding the site to the trusted sites zone, the prompting will stop. It's already in the local intranet zone. Adding the site to the Internet zone or the restricted sites zone will increase security and the prompting will continue.

2. **B, C.** The Pop-up Blocker Settings window has two notification settings that can each be enabled or disabled with a check box: Play a Sound When a Pop-up Is Blocked and Show Information Bar When a Pop-up Is Blocked. Disabling the pop-up blocker will enable all pop-ups, which could affect security. There is no Enable Notifications check box.

3. **B.** The Disable Script Debugging selections can be manipulated to allow script errors to be viewed. These settings can be accessed by selecting Tools, Internet Options, Advanced Tab and they are in the Browsing section. Internet Explorer 7 can be used to view the errors, so this isn't a reason to use an older version. The Security Settings section does not include a setting to view script errors. The Content tab does not include a way to access Browsing settings.

4. **C.** On the Windows Defender Options page, the real-time protection option of Changes Made to Your Computer by Software That Is Permitted to Run setting would normally be cleared, preventing notification of changes made by approved applications. If this box is checked, the warning message would appear each time the application is launched. The Services applet is used to modify services, not applications. MSConfig could be used to modify when an application starts, but it couldn't be used to modify how Windows Defender responds to the application.

5. **C.** Microsoft recommends enabling all the security agents listed under real-time protection. All of check boxes in the Security Agents section should be checked. By default, the check boxes under the notification section are not checked, and even if they were checked, they wouldn't catch the new infection of a known spyware program. Enabling the System Configuration (Settings) agent is a good start, but all the security agents should be enabled.

70-623

1. **D.** If you suspect a Web site is erroneously being reported as a phishing Web site, you can report it. Disabling the Phishing Filter on your computer won't stop it from being reported as a phishing Web site to other users. It's not possible to disable the Phishing Filter from a Web site. If you suspect a Web site is a phishing Web site, you can report it and check the appropriate box.

2. **D.** The reason the certificate wasn't being reported as revoked is because the Check for Server Certificate Revocation setting wasn't checked. This is one of the settings that won't take effect until you restart Internet Explorer (marked with an asterisk on the Advanced tab of the Internet Options page). Adding the Web site to a zone won't change how the certificate is checked. Rebooting Vista would work, since it would close IE, but it's overkill.

3. **D.** Windows Defender can protect against spyware, which is a category of malicious software (malware). Windows Update installs patches and fixes, which is a good step to prevent exploits against known vulnerabilities, but it isn't targeted at malicious software (malware).

4. **A.** While you've added the newer certificate, the system is still using the older certificate. You need to remove the older certificate by clicking Tools | Internet Options, selecting the Content tab, clicking Certificates, selecting the certificate, and clicking Remove. You wouldn't want to remove certificates from the Trusted Root Certification Authority. Rebooting or restarting a session won't solve the problem.

5. **A.** You can configure the Services applet to restart the computer on subsequent failures (after the first and second failures). There aren't any Windows Defender options that can be configured to automatically restart the Windows Defender service or cause Windows Vista to fail if Windows Defender fails. MSConfig can be configured to not start services, but it can't be configured to cause Windows Vista to fail if a service fails.

6. **D.** The RootkitRevealer can check for rootkits. A rootkit can hide the existence of malware running on a system. The question stated that full scans were already done, so checking again with Windows Defender or anti-virus software won't do any good. The Phishing Filter does not check for malware.

Using Vista Applications

In this chapter, you will learn about:
- Windows Mail
- Windows Meeting Space
- Windows Calendar
- Windows Fax and Scan

Microsoft has included several additional applications within Windows Vista that can be used for personal productivity and professional tasks. Some of these applications replace similar applications that were available in previous versions of Windows.

Windows Mail replaces Outlook Express as a tool to access e-mail and newsgroups. Windows Meeting Space replaces NetMeeting. Windows Fax and Scan replaces the fax console. Windows Calendar is new but provides capabilities very similar the calendar in Microsoft Outlook.

 EXAM TIP Objectives for the 70-620, 70-622, and 70-623 exams are included in this chapter.

Using Windows Mail

Windows Mail takes the place of Outlook Express on Windows Vista. It's a free application that you can use to send and receive e-mail and participate in newsgroups. Windows Mail includes several built-in features.

- **E-mail search** You can search saved e-mail messages by looking for the occurrence of a word in the subject line or body of the message. For example, if you wanted to search for all messages with exam number 70-620 in them, you could search with "70-620".

- **Junk mail filters** If you're not interested in sharing the wealth with the deposed dictator's brother, refinancing your mortgage, or taking advantage of the newest get rich quick scheme, then you'll value the junk mail filter. The Microsoft SmartScreen technology attempts to filter unwanted junk e-mail (often called spam) and move it to the Junk E-Mail folder.

- **Phishing Filters**   The Phishing Filter detects possible phishing messages and blocks any suspected links or dangerous content.

- **Newsgroup Communities**   You can easily access Microsoft public newsgroups using the Communities feature. You can use the Communities feature even without signing in, but you have access to more capabilities when signed in using a Windows Live ID account.

 NOTE   You can create a Windows Live ID account for free. You can access various Microsoft online services with this Windows Live ID account. Windows Live ID was previously known as Microsoft Passport.

Setting Up E-mail

The core use of the Windows Mail application is to allow you to easily send and receive e-mail. Before you can use Windows Mail, you need to configure it with your Internet service provider (ISP).

As an example, the following steps are used to configure Windows Mail to use my ISP (cox.net).

1. Launch Windows Mail. Click Start | All Programs | Windows Mail.

2. From the Tools drop-down menu, select Accounts.

3. On the Internet Accounts page, click Add.

4. On the Select Account Type page, select E-Mail Account and click Next.

5. On the Your Name page, enter your name. Click Next.

6. On the Internet E-Mail Address page, enter the e-mail address that you have with your ISP. Click Next.

7. On the Set Up E-Mail Server Type page, select POP3 from the drop-down box. Enter, for example, **pop.east.cox.net** as the Incoming E-Mail Server and enter **smtp.east.cox.net** as the Outgoing E-Mail Server. Your display will look similar to Figure 14-1. Click Next.

8. On the Internet Mail Logon page, enter your username and password (provided by your ISP). If you leave the Remember Password box checked, you won't have to provide your password each time you send and receive mail. Click Next.

9. On the Congratulations page, click Finish.

Managing Junk E-Mail

You have several options to help you manage junk e-mail from within Windows Mail. One of the easiest ways to manage your junk e-mail is to select an e-mail message and select Junk E-Mail from the Message drop-down box as shown in Figure 14-2.

- **Add Sender To Safe Senders List**   This selection will prevent e-mail from this specific sender from being put into the Junk E-Mail folder.

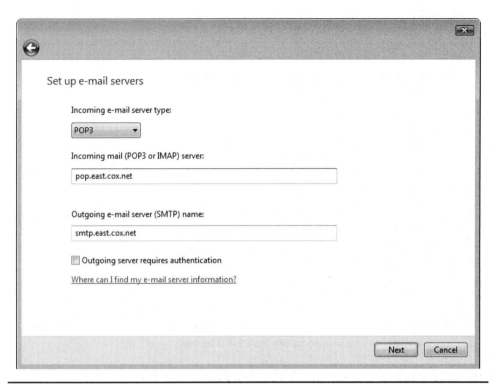

Figure 14-1 Configuring the POP3 and SMTP servers

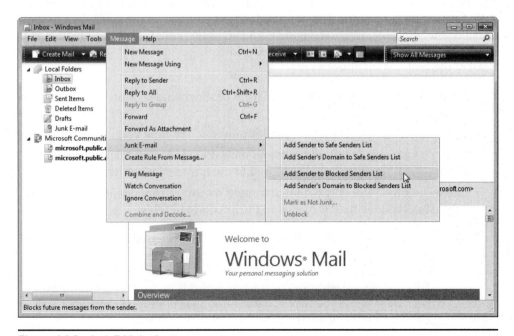

Figure 14-2 Junk E-Mail selections

- **Add Sender's Domain To Safe Senders List**   This selection will prevent e-mail from any sender in this domain (after the @ symbol in the e-mail address) from being put into the Junk E-Mail folder.

- **Add Sender To Blocked Senders List**   This selection will automatically move e-mail from this specific sender into the Junk E-Mail folder.

- **Add Sender's Domain To Blocked Senders List**   This selection will automatically move e-mail from any sender in this domain (after the @ sign in the e-mail address) into the Junk E-Mail folder.

- **Mark As Not Junk**   If you have an e-mail in the Junk E-Mail folder that is valid, you can move it into your Inbox with this selection.

It is possible to add a sender to both the safe senders list and the blocked senders list. Obviously, this is a conflict. Windows Mail resolves this conflict by giving the safe senders list priority. In other words, if both settings are selected, the e-mail will be considered safe.

 EXAM TIP   If you've added an e-mail address to the blocked senders list but are still receiving e-mail from this address, it's because the address is in the safe senders list. Remove the e-mail address from the safe senders list and e-mails will be moved to the Junk E-Mail folder.

The blocked senders list allows you to block e-mail from specific e-mail addresses or specific domains. For example, you can block all e-mail from the e-mail address of spammer@spammer.com, or block all e-mail from the entire domain of spammer.com.

By default, the Junk E-Mail filter is set to Low so that it moves the most obvious junk e-mail to the Junk E-Mail folder. Figure 14-3 shows the Junk E-Mail options that you can access by selecting Tools | Junk E-Mail Options.

All of the Junk E-Mail options are

- **No Automatic Filtering**   Only mail from blocked senders is moved to the Junk E-Mail folder.

- **Low**   The most obvious junk e-mail is moved to the Junk E-Mail folder.

- **High**   Most junk e-mail is caught and moved to the Junk E-Mail folder. Some regular e-mail mail may also be moved to the Junk E-Mail folder.

- **Safe List Only**   The only e-mail that you'll receive is from people listed in your safe list. All other e-mail is moved to the Junk E-Mail folder.

This page includes a selection to Permanently Delete Suspected Junk E-Mail instead of moving it to the Junk E-Mail folder.

 TIP   The danger when setting the Junk E-Mail filter too high is that it may filter some e-mail you want to receive. You should regularly check your Junk E-Mail box to see if wanted e-mail was misdirected here.

Figure 14-3
Junk E-Mail
options

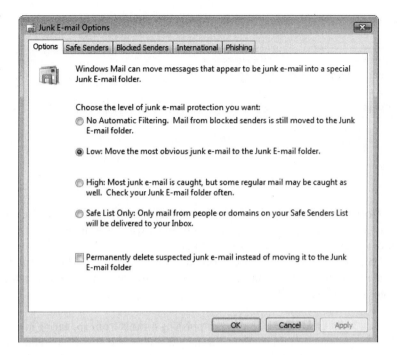

Protecting Your Privacy with the Phishing Filter

The Phishing Filter is a built-in feature designed to warn you about possible phishing attempts. The Phishing Filter in Windows Mail is integrated with Internet Explorer and will warn you about Web sites suspected of being involved in phishing scams.

Phishing is a social engineering tactic where an e-mail is sent trying to trick you into revealing personal or financial information.

A common ploy goes like this:

> We have detected suspicious activity on your account. In your best interest, we will suspend any further transactions on your account unless you can verify your account information. Please access our company website and verify your account information as soon as possible.

The e-mail often uses the actual images of the company they are trying to impersonate. It includes a link that also looks very similar to the actual Web site. However, any information you enter is captured with the intent of using it against you.

For example, if you're tricked into giving your banking account numbers and access codes, your money may be transferred to an offshore account. If you give up your social security number, your identity may be stolen.

 TIP Most companies have a stated policy that they will never use these tactics to have you verify information online. If you suspect that the e-mail is bogus, you should either ignore it or identify the contact information from another source and contact the company asking for confirmation that the request is valid.

Figure 14-4 shows the default settings for the Phishing Filter.

Figure 14-4
Windows Mail
Phishing Filter
settings

Notice that the Phishing Filter is turned on by default. If you click any links that are suspected of being phishing sites, Internet Explorer will display a warning Web page and a notification on the Address bar.

You can also select the check box to Move Phishing E-Mail to the Junk Mail Folder. This will prevent the e-mail from appearing in your Inbox but doesn't delete the messages completely.

EXAM TIP To prevent phishing e-mails from appearing in your Inbox, select the option to Move Phishing E-Mail to the Junk Mail Folder option from the Junk E-Mail Options page. This will move suspected phishing e-mails to the Junk E-Mail folder.

Sending Secure E-Mail

You can use Windows Mail to encrypt your e-mail and use digital signatures. When your e-mail is encrypted, no one except the recipient will be able to read it. When it is digitally signed, the recipient will know it came from you and no on else.

The two primary protocols used to encrypt e-mail are S/MIME and PGP.

- **S/MIME** Secure Multipurpose Internet Mail Extensions. S/MIME is commonly used in a corporate environment, and certificates are often deployed to users automatically.

- **PGP** Pretty Good Privacy. PGP can be used between two private parties. Certificates are first shared with each other, and then both parties can then encrypt and digitally sign their e-mails.

EXAM TIP If you need to ensure that e-mail is sent over the Internet in an encrypted format, use either S/MIME or PGP. S/MIME is the most common solution used within a corporate environment, and PGP is commonly used between private individuals.

Accessing Newsgroups

Newsgroups are discussion forums on the Internet. If you can think of a topic, there's probably a newsgroup already created where people around the world are sharing their knowledge and passions. Sending a message to a newsgroup is referred to as posting a message.

Some newsgroups are free and open to anyone to read and post. Others are restricted to a certain audience, and you have to either pay or subscribe in some other way.

As an example of a free newsgroup, Microsoft hosts the microsoft.public.cert.itpro .mcitp newsgroup, and people regularly post with questions and comments about the MCITP certifications.

For example, you may be studying for the 70-620 exam and have a question about a topic you're not completely clear about. You can post your question to the newsgroup, and very often you'll get a response.

> **TIP** When posting to newsgroups, read a little first. It will give you an idea of what types of posts generate responses, and it's possible your question was already answered in a recent post.

As a Microsoft Certified Trainer (MCT), I frequently have questions and issues related to Microsoft technologies and courseware. Microsoft hosts several MCT newsgroups (though you have to be a current MCT to access them).

With over 12,000 MCTs in the world and many of them active in these newsgroups, I've found that answers to highly technical questions are just a few clicks away. By just browsing through the topics, I often find answers to questions I have (and even some answers to questions I didn't have but still find valuable).

Visiting Microsoft Communities

In Exercise 14.1, you will launch Windows Mail and use it to access the Microsoft Communities. This exercise assumes you have connectivity to the Internet.

Exercise 14.1: Launching and Using Windows Mail for Newsgroups

1. Launch Windows Mail by clicking Start | All Programs | Windows Mail.

> **TIP** If this is the first time you've launched Windows Mail, you'll be prompted to configure it. You can just click Cancel for this exercise. When using it with your Internet service provider, you should follow their instructions for configuration.

2. Launch the Newsgroups menu by clicking Tools | Newsgroups. Your display will look similar to Figure 14-5.

> **TIP** Windows Mail includes connectivity to Microsoft Communities. You don't have to configure anything else to access the Microsoft Communities newsgroups. If your ISP provides NNTP connectivity, you can configure Windows Mail to connect to other newsgroups.

3. In the text box under Display Newsgroups That Contain, enter **mcitp**. Only newsgroups with "mcitp" in their title will appear. Find the microsoft.public. cert.itpro.mcitp newsgroup. At this writing, this is the only newsgroup with mcitp in the title, but this may change. Select this newsgroup and click OK.

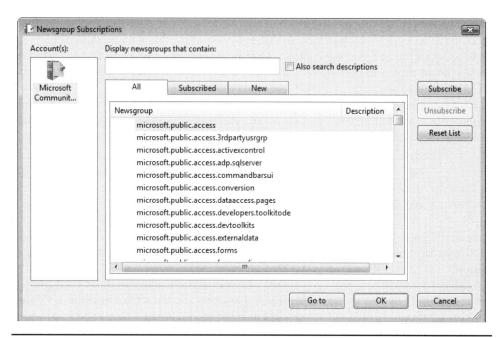

Figure 14-5 Viewing the Newsgroup Subscriptions page

NOTE Searches aren't case-sensitive, so uppercase MCITP will return the same results as lowercase mcitp.

4. In the Windows Mail page, double-click the microsoft.public.cert.itpro.mcitp newsgroup to open it. Scroll through and read some of the messages. Your display will look similar to Figure 14-6.

TIP If you want to be able to have the full features available when sending messages with Windows Mail, you will need to sign in with a Windows Live account. MSN Hotmail, MSN Messenger, or Passport accounts are also Windows Live ID accounts. You can create a Windows Live ID account here: https://accountservices.passport.net.

Configuring NNTP

It's also possible to configure Windows Mail to access other newsgroups available on the Internet. Newsgroups use the Network News Transfer Protocol (NNTP).

If your ISP supports newsgroups, you can configure Windows Mail to access public newsgroups. The following steps can be used (just use the information for your ISP instead of mine unless you're lucky enough to live in Hampton Roads).

1. Launch Windows Mail. Click Start | All Programs | Windows Mail.

2. From the Tools drop-down menu, select Accounts.

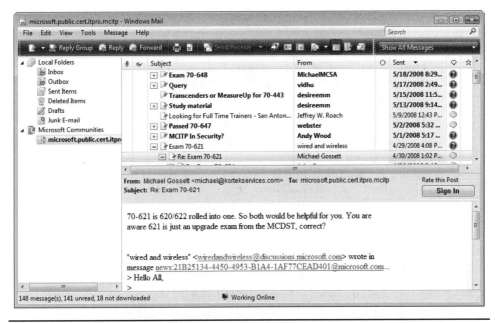

Figure 14-6 Viewing MCITP newsgroup messages in Windows Mail

Netiquette in Newsgroups When participating in newsgroups, you'll get more out of the experience by following some general practices known as netiquette. The word netiquette was created by combining etiquette and the Internet (net).

Etiquette refers to what most people consider socially acceptable behavior. Netiquette is a group of commonly followed behaviors that people use on the Web. Etiquette and being kind and courteous to others is a choice. So is netiquette. Often, those that don't follow rules of netiquette are simply ignored.

Some of the common repeated rules are

- **The golden rule** Do unto others as you would have them do unto you—even when you can be anonymous on the Internet. Some people have said the greatest judge of character is what people do when no one else knows what you're doing.

- **Read the newsgroup messages before posting** Just as you can learn a lot just by listening, you can learn a lot just by reading the conversations that have already been posted. Often, a question you have has already been posted and answered. All you have to do is read it.

(Continued)

- **Don't yell**   WORDS IN ALL CAPS LOOK LIKE YOU'RE YELLING.
- **Be kind**   Don't send heated messages ("flames") even when provoked. Some people get a kick out of sending a provoking message and then watching the flame war.
- **Use subject lines**   Let people know what your message is about.
- **Share knowledge**   If someone else posts a question that you can answer, then do so. Often when you answer a question that is asked, you are answering it for more than just the person that asked the question, but also for others that will read the post.

3. On the Internet Accounts page, click Add.

4. On the Select Account Type page, select Newsgroup Account and click Next.

5. On the Your Name page, enter your name. Click Next.

6. On the Internet E-Mail Address page, enter the e-mail address that you have with your ISP. Click Next.

7. On the Set Up E-Mail Server Type page, select POP3 from the drop-down box. Enter **news.east.cox.net** (or your ISP's news server name) as the News (NNTP) Server. Your display will look similar to Figure 14-7. Click Next.

8. On the Congratulations page, click Finish.

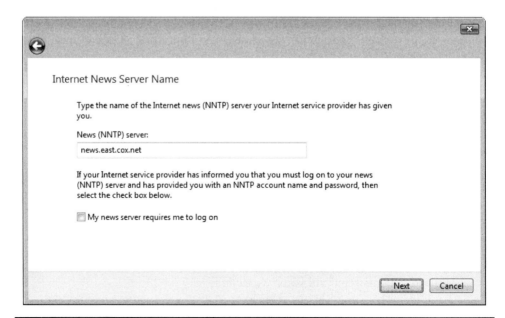

Figure 14-7   Configuring the NNTP server

9. On the Internet Accounts page, click Close.

10. The Subscribe to Newsgroups page will appear. Click Show Available Newsgroups. A list of newsgroups will be downloaded onto your system. Be patient. There are many newsgroups, and this may take a minute or two depending on the speed of your connection.

At this point you can type anything that interests in you in the Display Newsgroups That Contain box and you'll see there is probably already a newsgroup that exists on the topic.

Using Windows Meeting Space

Windows Meeting Space is a Windows Vista built-in application that allows you to easily share documents, programs, and your desktop with other users running Windows Vista. A meeting can be created with as many as ten participants.

NOTE Windows Meeting Space is not available in previous editions of Windows (such as Windows XP). Previous editions of Windows included NetMeeting. NetMeeting is not included in Windows Vista.

Figure 14-8 shows Windows Meeting Space. I have shared my desktop and clicked the view that shows what meeting attendees can see. As you can see, it shows my entire desktop (including my Calvin and Hobbes gadget). You can also limit the view of meeting attendees, allowing them to see only a single application, such as a PowerPoint presentation.

In the classroom, Windows Meeting Space has been a backup solution for me. Occasionally projector bulbs go out and a replacement bulb isn't handy. Instead, I've used it as a learning experience to teach Windows Meeting Space. The PowerPoint presentations and any demonstrations I do are completely visible on everyone's desktop computer. The only limitation is that only nine other participants can join the meeting.

NOTE Windows Meeting Space allows a maximum of only ten participants.

You can launch Windows Meeting Space by clicking Start | All Programs and selecting Windows Meeting Space. The first time you launch Windows Meeting Space, you'll be led through a short wizard to set things up. You'll then be able to create a meeting. Exercise 14.2 will lead you through these steps.

Windows Meeting Space supports only one meeting at a time. In other words, if you have one meeting open, you can't also open another meeting. You must first leave the first meeting before you can join another meeting.

EXAM TIP You must leave an existing meeting in Windows Meeting Space before you can join another meeting.

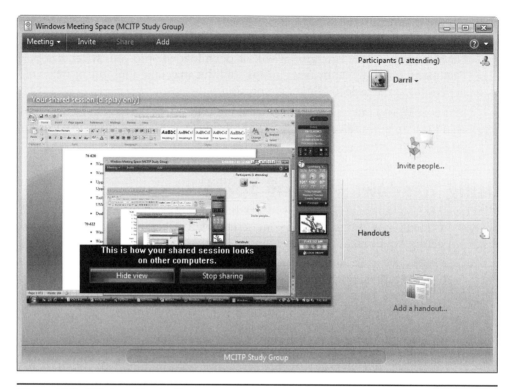

Figure 14-8 Windows Meeting Space

Windows Meeting Space and IPv6

Windows Meeting Space uses several of the features of IPv6 to create the peer-to-peer framework used in the meeting. It has the ability to automatically detect an existing network and create an ad hoc wireless network if an existing network is not available.

The requirement to use IPv6 may seem like a limitation. However, Windows Vista uses IPv6 by default, and Windows Meeting Space only works with other Windows Vista operating systems, so it shouldn't be an issue unless IPv6 has been disabled. If IPv6 is disabled on any of the Windows Vista systems, it will need to enabled on any of the systems that want to join the meeting.

 EXAM TIP Windows Meeting Space requires IPv6, and the Windows Meeting Space exception must be configured in the firewall.

The Windows Firewall also needs to be configured to support Windows Meeting Space. The Windows Firewall was covered in more depth in Chapter 7, but you can see the Windows Meeting Space exception enabled in Figure 14-9.

Figure 14-9
Windows Firewall with the Windows Meeting Space exception

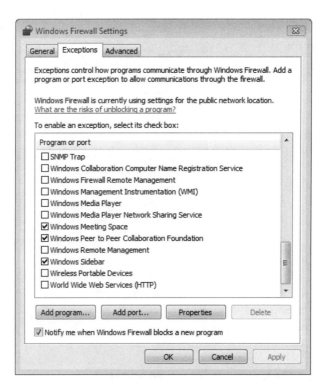

One of the great strengths of Windows Meeting Space is its ability to automatically create a wireless ad hoc network if a network doesn't already exist. In Chapter 6, we covered wireless ad hoc networks in greater detail, but in short an ad hoc network is a network created for a specific purpose. The only requirement is that all participants must have a wireless NIC.

Configuring People Near Me

The People Near Me feature is an important part of Windows Meeting Space. It identifies people near you that you can invite to your meeting. Similarly, it allows others to invite you to their meeting.

Figure 14-10 shows the Set Up People Near Me configuration page. If the Sign Me In Automatically When Windows Starts selection is checked, then others will be able to send you invitations by simply selecting your Display Name in the invitation window. If this selection is not selected, invitations have to be sent via e-mail or a file.

You configure the People Near Me option when you first run and set up Windows Meeting Space (as you'll see in Exercise 14.2). You can later change the setting by modifying the People Near Me applet in the Control Panel.

The People Near Me applet can be accessed by clicking Start | Control Panel. In the Control Panel, select Network and Internet, and click the People Near Me applet. You can use this applet to change the options used to automatically sign in, and to sign in or sign out.

Figure 14-10
People Near Me

Inviting Others to Your Meeting

After you've created a meeting, you'll want to invite others to join it. There are three ways you can invite others. First you'd click the Invite People link in the Windows Meeting Space page, and then you'd use one of the following options:

- Select a check box for anyone that is listed on the Invite People page and send an invitation. Figure 14-11 shows how the Invite People page appears. In the figure, only one person (Sally) was located. (Sally is running Windows Vista with IPv6 enabled and is automatically signed in to People Near Me.)

 EXAM TIP If other users aren't signed into the People Near Me option (or aren't running Windows Vista), you won't be able to see them from the Invite People page. If their system isn't configured to be signed in automatically, they can sign in manually using the People Near Me applet within the Network and Internet section of the Control Panel.

- Send an invitation via e-mail.
- Send an invitation by creating an invitation file that others can access. The invitation can be placed on a share available to others.

When you configure Windows Meeting Space, you can limit who your computer will accept invitations from. Your choices are

- Allow invitations from anyone.

Figure 14-11
Inviting a
participant to
your meeting

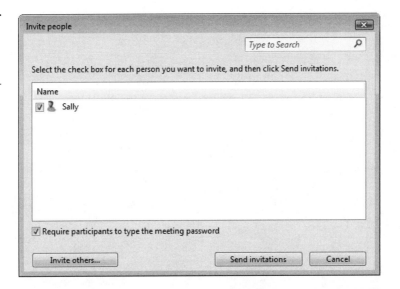

- Allow invitations from trusted contacts.
- Allow invitations from no one.

In Exercise 14.2, you will launch and configure Windows Meeting Space.

Exercise 14.2: Launching and Configuring Windows Meeting Space

1. Launch Windows Meeting Space by clicking Start | All Programs and selecting Windows Meeting Space.

2. If this is the first time you've launched Windows Meeting Space, the Ready To Set Up Windows Meeting Space dialog box appears. If you've already set up Windows Meeting Space, continue to Step 3; otherwise, follow steps a and b.

   a. Click Yes, Continue Setting Up Windows Meeting Space. If the User Account Control dialog box appears, click Continue.

   b. After a moment, the People Near Me dialog box will appear. You can modify your display name. Notice that the check box is selected by default to sign you in automatically when Windows starts, and it's configured to allow invitations from anyone. Click OK.

3. The Windows Meeting Space page will appear. Click Start a New Meeting.

4. Enter **MCITP Study** as the meeting name and enter a password of **P@ssw0rd**. Your display will look similar to Figure 14-12.

   Press ENTER. Notice you have links to share a program or your desktop, invite people, and add a handout.

5. Click the Share a Program or Your Desktop link. On the Do You Want Other People to See Your Desktop link, review the information and click OK.

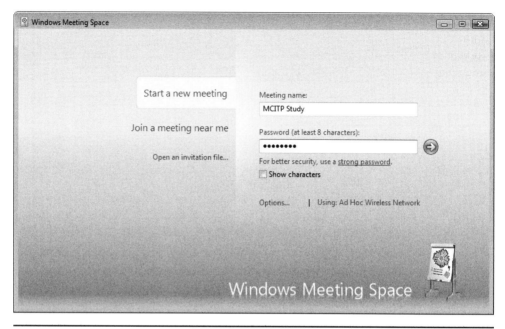

Figure 14- 12   Starting a meeting with Windows Meeting Space

6. On the Start a Shared Session page, browse to the bottom of the list and select the Desktop link. Clicking this link will allow users to view your entire desktop. Alternately, you could choose to share just a single program. Click OK.

7. After a moment, Windows Meeting Space will appear and indicate you are sharing your desktop. Click Show Me How My Shared Session Looks on Other Computers.

8. Click Invite People. If other Windows Vista systems are available on your network, running IPv6 and signed in to Windows Meeting Space, they will appear here. Click Cancel.

9. Click Add a Handout. On the dialog box informing you that handouts will be copied to each participant's computer, click OK.

10. Browse to a document on your system and select it. Once it is selected, a copy of this document will be copied to each participant's system.

11. Select the Meeting drop-down menu and select Leave Meeting.

12. Close all open Windows.

Using Windows Calendar

You can use the Windows Calendar to keep track of appointments, remind you of appointments, and track tasks. The capabilities in Windows Calendar are very similar to those of the calendar in Microsoft Outlook.

Figure 14-13 shows the month view (July 2008) of Windows Calendar. In the left pane is the currently selected month (which can be changed by clicking the right or left arrows). Only one calendar is available in this view, though it's possible to subscribe to other calendars.

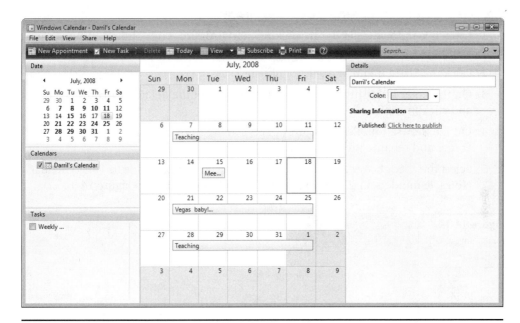

Figure 14-13   Windows Calendar

You can launch the Calendar by clicking Start | All Programs, and selecting Windows Calendar.

Publishing a Calendar

You can publish your calendar so that it's accessible to others. Calendars can be published to the following locations:

- **Internet**   You must have access to an Internet location that will allow you to publish to it, such as a Webdav Web site.

- **Network location**   You can post your calendar to a share on a computer within your network. Network locations use the universal network connection (UNC) path of *servername**sharename*. For example, if a share named Calendars exists on a server named MCITP1, you could publish your calendar to \\MCITP1\ Calendars.

- **Elsewhere on your computer**   You can publish it to any location on your computer so that other users of the same computer will have access to it.

You can also configure a published calendar to publish the changes you make to it. This way, as you modify, add, and delete appointments and tasks, anyone that has access to your calendar can see them.

In Exercise 14.3, you will publish your calendar to location on your computer.

Exercise 14.3: Publishing Your Calendar

1. Launch Windows Calendar by clicking Start | All Programs and selecting Windows Calendar.

2. Click the Share menu and select Publish.

3. On the Enter Publishing Information page, accept the default Calendar Name, and click Browse.

4. On the Browse for Files or Folders page, browse to the C: drive. Click Make New Folder and rename the folder **Calendars**. Click OK.

5. Select the check boxes for Automatically Publish Changes Made to This Calendar, Notes, Reminders, and Tasks. Your display will look similar to Figure 14-14.

Figure 14-14
Publishing
a calendar

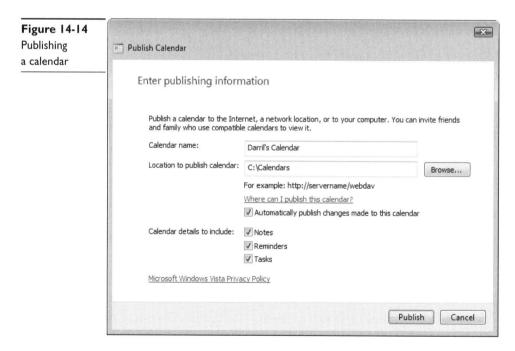

EXAM TIP If you want to ensure that other people can see all the changes to your shared calendar, select the check box for Automatically Publish Changes Made to This Calendar.

6. Click Publish.

7. After a moment, the calendar will be successfully published. If you want to send an e-mail to others announcing that the calendar is available, click Announce. It will open up a Windows Mail message similar to Figure 14-15. You can address it to whomever you want.

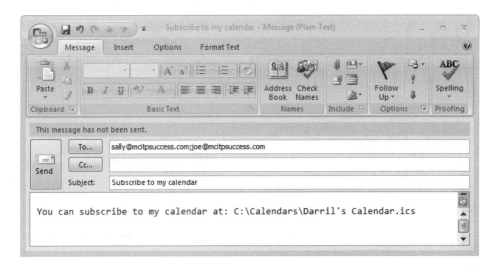

Figure 14-15   Sending an e-mail announcing your calendar

   TIP   You need to have a mail profile created before you can announce your calendar.

8. Click Finish.

Subscribing to a Calendar

You can subscribe to any calendar that has been published. The process is straightforward after you select Subscribe from the Share menu. You simply specify the location of the shared calendar.

Once you subscribe to another calendar, events from each of the calendars will be displayed within Windows Calendar. Figure 14-16 shows two calendars (Darril's and Sally's) displayed in Windows Calendar.

While you can't see it in the black and white figure, each of the calendars has events displayed in a different color. If you want to show only a single calendar, you can deselect the check box for the other calendar.

On the right pane, you have access to options for subscribed calendars that can be manipulated. You can specify how often the calendar will be updated. The choices are

- No update
- Every 15 minutes
- Every hour

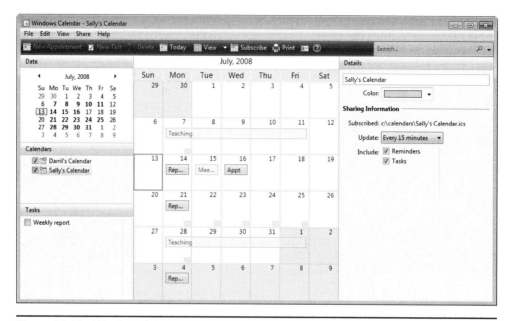

Figure 14-16 Windows Calendar displaying two calendars

- Every day
- Every week

 EXAM TIP If you want to ensure that the subscribed calendar is as up-to-date as possible, select Every 15 Minutes as the Update Interval.

It's also possible to force a synchronization of calendars by selecting Sync or Sync All from the Share menu.

Using Windows Fax and Scan

The Windows Fax and Scan program replaces the Fax Console that was available in previous versions of Windows. You can use Windows Fax and Scan to fax and scan documents and pictures. This tool has two built-in capabilities:

- **Faxing** Allows you to send electronic documents over phone lines to a fax machine. You must have a modem and phone line, or access to a fax server.

- **Scanning** You can scan documents and pictures into electronic files, which can then be e-mailed or copied. You must have a scanner to accept the documents.

You can launch the Windows Fax and Scan program by clicking Start | All Programs and selecting Windows Fax and Scan.

Configuring Fax and Scan

In order to use Windows Fax and Scan, you must have either a modem and a phone line or access to a fax server to send and receive faxes. You'll need a scanner to scan documents and pictures. Once you have the hardware installed and configured, you'll need to create a fax account before you can send a fax. Accounts are not needed to scan documents and pictures.

A fax server accepts faxes electronically over the network and can then send them. The process from the user's point of view is similar to sending a print job to a printer. The difference is that instead of the server sending the job to a print device, it sends it as a fax to the specified destination.

You also must have a Windows Fax and Scan account. You won't be able to create any faxes until you create an account. Figure 14-17 shows Windows Fax and Scan with the Fax Accounts dialog box open. A new account named Fax Modem has been created.

Figure 14-17   Windows Fax and Scan with an account created

EXAM TIP   You will not be able to use Windows Fax and Scan to send and receive faxes until you create a fax account.

In Exercise 14.4, you will create a Windows Fax and Scan account. This lab assumes you have a modem installed on your computer.

Exercise 14.4: Creating a Windows Fax and Scan account

1. Launch Windows Fax and Scan by clicking Start | All Programs and selecting Windows Fax and Scan.

2. Click the Tools menu and select Fax Accounts.

3. On the Fax Accounts page, click Add.

4. On the Choose a Fax Modem or Server page, select Connect to a Fax Modem.

5. On the Choose a Modem Name page, accept the default name of Fax Modem and click Next.

6. On the Choose How to Receive Faxes page, select Answer Automatically (Recommended). If the User Account Control page appears, click Continue.

7. Your account will be created and the Fax Accounts page will appear. Click Close.

Sending Faxes

Once you've created a fax account, you can click the New Fax button to start the creation of your fax. Figure 14-18 shows a fax being created.

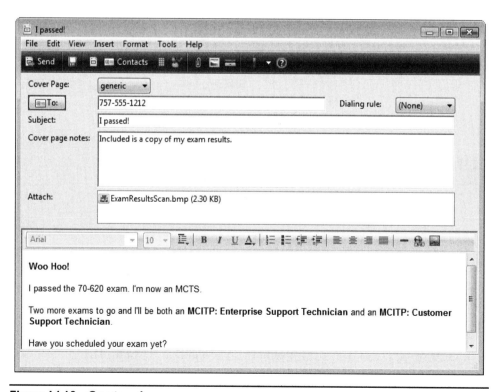

Figure 14-18   Creating a fax

Notice that it has a cover page selected. You can configure multiple cover pages and select the one you want when you create any fax. This fax also has an attachment of a scanned document, which will be sent as another page in your fax.

Once the fax is created, you simply click Send.

Chapter Review

In this chapter you learned about several different free applications available within Windows Vista. Many of the applications were available in previous versions of Windows (albeit in a slightly different form), so they were probably familiar to you.

Windows Mail is used to send and receive e-mail and can also be used to access Microsoft Communities and newsgroups. You need access to a Network News Transport Protocol (NNTP) server to access newsgroups beyond the newsgroups offered through Microsoft Communities.

You can use Windows Meeting Space to host and join meetings. When you host a meeting, you can share a specific application or your entire desktop with meeting participants, and you can also share documents. Windows Meeting Space requires IPv6; and others must be signed in to People Near Me to be invited to a meeting.

The Windows Calendar can be used as a personal planner to track appointments and tasks. However, the real value of Windows Calendar is its ability to share calendars with others. Calendars are shared by publishing them and others can access a shared calendar by subscribing. To ensure changes to a shared calendar are available to others, calendars should be shared with the option to automatically publish changes. Subscribers can choose the update interval (such as every 15 minutes) to specify how often the original calendar can be checked for changes.

Windows Fax and Scan replaces the Fax console. It can be used to send and receive faxes and to scan documents. You'll need a modem and phone line or a fax server to support sending and receiving faxes. A scanner is needed to scan documents and pictures. Before you can send and receive faxes, you'll need to create a fax account.

Additional Study

Self Study Exercises
Use these additional exercises to challenge yourself.

- Add a friend's e-mail address to both the Blocked Senders list and Safe Senders list and ask them to send you an e-mail. What is the result?

- Research newsgroups and respond to one newsgroup message.

- Create a Windows Meeting Space meeting with a friend and share a file.

- Log on as a different user on your system. Share a calendar with an update interval of 15 minutes. Log on with your user account and subscribe to the calendar.

Summary of What You Need to Know

70-620

The 70-620 exam includes objectives for all topics in this chapter. Expect questions from each section: Windows Mail, Windows Meeting Space, Windows Calendar, and Windows Fax and Scan.

70-622

When preparing for the 70-622 exam, pay particular attention to the Windows Mail topic. You should have a basic understanding of the e-mail capabilities with Windows Mail. Additionally, you should know that e-mail can be secured using S/MIME or PGP.

70-623

When preparing for the 70-623 exam, pay particular attention to the following topics covered in this chapter:

- **Windows Mail** You should have a basic understanding of the e-mail and newsgroup capabilities with Windows Mail. Newsgroups require access to a NNTP server.

- **Windows Meeting Space** You should know the requirements to configure Windows Meeting Space, including that it requires IPv6 and people must be signed into People Near Me to be invited.

Questions

70-620

1. You've added the spammer@spammer.com address to your Blocked Senders list in Windows Mail, but you're still receiving messages from this address. What needs to be done to ensure you don't receive any e-mail from this address?

   A. You need to move the e-mail to the Junk E-Mail folder.

   B. You need to block the spammer.com domain.

   C. You need to remove the e-mail address from the Safe Senders list.

   D. You need to configure the firewall to block this domain.

2. You've received some e-mail messages that try to encourage you to go to bogus Web sites and enter your private and financial information when using Windows Mail. You want to prevent these messages from appearing in your Inbox. What can you do?

   A. Change the Junk E-Mail filter to High.

   B. Add the sender's to the Blocked Sender's list.

   C. Remove the sender's from the Safe Sender's list.

   D. Enable the Phishing Filter to move e-mail to the Junk Mail folder.

3. You are running Windows Vista on your laptop and are collaborating with two other users. One user is running Windows XP and the other is running Windows Vista. All three of you have wireless NICs. You decide to start a Windows Meeting Space, but neither of the other two users are available in the Invite People list. What's a possible problem? Choose all that apply?

   A. Windows Meeting Space is not supported on Windows XP.

   B. Users aren't signed in to People Near Me.

   C. IPv6 is not enabled.

   D. Net Meeting is not enabled.

4. You are using Windows Meeting Space to attend a meeting hosted by Joe. Sally hosts another meeting and you want to join it, but Windows Meeting won't respond to your attempts to join the second meeting. What should you do?

   A. Launch Net Meeting and join the second meeting with Net Meeting.

   B. Leave the first meeting and join the second meeting.

   C. Enable the Windows Firewall to allow Windows Meeting Space.

   D. Host your own meeting and use it to join Sally's meeting.

5. You have published a calendar showing all your appointments and tasks. Sally has subscribed to your calendar but complains that she doesn't see any changes you make. What should you do?

   A. Publish your calendar with the synchronize option.

   B. Have Sally select the synchronize option.

   C. Have Sally select the option to automatically subscribe to changes.

   D. Select the option to automatically publish changes.

6. You are leading a team of ten technicians on an IT project. You've created a calendar listing all of the tasks and milestones of the project, and you've published the calendar. You want the technicians on your team to be able access the calendar, including the most recent updates. What should be done?

   A. Have the technicians regularly log on to your system to check the calendar.

   B. Have the technicians configure a calendar subscription with an update interval of 15 minutes.

   C. Have the technicians publish their calendars with an update interval of 15 minutes.

   D. Configure Windows Calendar to send e-mail messages to all the technicians each time an event is modified.

7. Joe wants to use Windows Fax and Scan to send and receive faxes. What must be done?

   A. A fax server must be configured.

   B. A fax account must be created.

C. An external modem must be added.

D. Joe must be logged on with an administrative account.

70-622

1. Users in your company send e-mail that contains proprietary information. You're asked how this information can be protected when it's sent so that only the recipient can read it. What can be used to protect the e-mail?

    A. Use S/MIME.

    B. Use NNTP.

    C. Use POP3

    D. Use SMTP.

70-623

1. You are helping a customer configure her Windows Vista computer. She wants to subscribe to several newsgroups on photography using her computer. What needs to be done to provide access to public newsgroups?

    A. Configure the Phishing Filter in Windows Mail.

    B. Enable NNTP in Internet Explorer.

    C. Configure the e-mail account information in Windows Mail.

    D. Configure the NNTP information in Windows Mail.

2. Sally is running Windows Vista but is unable to use the Windows Meeting Space feature. She asks you for help. You suspect the firewall and see the current configuration as shown in Figure 14-19.

    Is the problem with the firewall, or elsewhere?

    A. The problem is elsewhere.

    B. Yes, the Windows Meeting Space exception should be checked.

    C. Yes, the Windows Media Player exception should be checked.

    D. Yes, the Windows Remote Management exception should be checked.

3. You are working with Windows Meeting Space, but one computer just won't work. You suspect a problem with the network interface card (NIC) properties and view it as shown in Figure 14-20.

    Is the problem with the NIC's properties, or elsewhere?

    A. The problem is elsewhere.

    B. Yes the Internet Protocol Version 6 (TCP/IPv6) should be checked.

    C. Yes the Link-Layer Topology Discovery Mapper I/O Driver should be checked.

    D. Yes the Link-Layer Topology Discovery Responder should be checked.

Figure 14-19
Firewall
configuration
for question 2

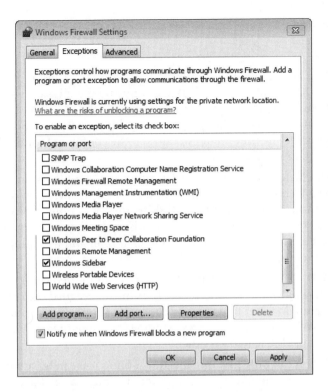

Figure 14-20
NIC properties
for question 3

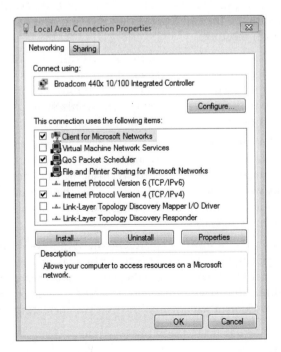

Answers

70-620

1. **C.** If an e-mail address is in the Blocked Senders list and the Safe Senders list, the Safe Senders list will take priority and the message will be put into your Inbox. You don't need to manually move the e-mail to the Junk E-Mail folder. Even if you block the spammer.com domain, the Safe Senders list will take priority. The firewall doesn't need to be configured for the Junk E-Mail filter to work in Windows Mail.

2. **D.** Phishing is the process of sending an e-mail to try and trick you into going to a Web site and entering your username, password, and/or other account information. To help stop phishing messages from appearing in your Inbox, you can ensure the Phishing Filter is enabled and configure it to move e-mail to the Junk Mail folder. The junk mail filter and its settings aren't dedicated to preventing phishing e-mails.

3. **A, B, C.** Windows Meeting Space is not supported on Windows XP. Windows Meeting Space requires IPv6. Users must be signed into the People Near Me feature in order to be seen in the Invite People list. Windows Meeting Space on Windows Vista replaces Windows Net Meeting on Windows XP. They aren't compatible with each other.

4. **B.** You can only join one meeting a time. You can leave the first meeting and then join the second meeting. Net Meeting is available on Windows XP but is not available on Windows Vista. If one meeting is working, nothing needs to be done with the firewall for a second meeting. You can't join a meeting by hosting your own meeting.

5. **D.** You can select the option to automatically publish changes when publishing your calendar so that others are able to see changes you make. This option must be selected when the calendar is published, not when the subscription is created. While a calendar can be synchronized, this must be done manually and can only be done if the calendar has been set to automatically publish changes.

6. **B.** Technicians can configure a calendar subscription with an update interval of 15 minutes to have changes automatically updated. If ten other people had to log on to your system regularly to check the calendar, you wouldn't be able to get any work done. You don't need to see the technician's calendars; they need to see the one you have published. Windows Calendar can't be configured to send e-mail messages.

7. **B.** A fax account must be created before Windows Fax and Scan can send and receive faxes. You can use a fax server or a fax modem (internal or external); it's not required that you specifically have a fax server or an external modem. An administrative account is not required to send or receive faxes, though User Account Control will prompt the user when creating a fax account.

70-622

1. **A.** Secure/Multipurpose Internet Mail Extensions (S/MIME) can be used to encrypt and digitally sign e-mail. Network News Transfer Protocol (NNTP) is used for newsgroups. POP3 and SMTP are mail protocols but do not encrypt the contents.

70-623

1. **D.** The Network News Transfer Protocol (NNTP) account information needs to be configured in order to allow Windows Mail to access public newsgroups. The Phishing Filter is used to block phishing e-mails. NNTP can't be enabled in Internet Explorer. Configuring the e-mail account information will not connect you with an NNTP server.

2. **B.** The Windows Meeting Space exception needs to be checked to support Windows Meeting Space. Neither the Windows Media Player nor Windows Remote Management exceptions need to be checked for Windows Meeting Space.

3. **B.** Windows Meeting Space requires IPv6 to support invitations. Link-Layer topology protocols are used to allow computers to easily find each other, but aren't required for Windows Meeting Space.

Using Vista Multimedia Applications

In this chapter, you will learn about:
- Windows Media Player
- Windows Media Center
- Windows Photo Gallery
- Windows Movie Maker
- Network projectors

Windows Vista includes several tools you can use to access and manipulate your media files. This includes audio, video, and pictures. If you enjoying being creative every now and then, you'll enjoy the capabilities of many of these tools.

Windows Media Player is used primarily to manipulate audio files. You can rip music to many different formats, create your own music mixes, and burn your own CDs. Windows Media Center can be used as an entertainment hub to record and play back TV shows, DVDs, and more. The Windows Photo Gallery can be used to easily import pictures from devices such as digital cameras. With the Windows Movie Maker you can create some movie shorts that may be shown at the next Cannes Film Festival (well, maybe not, but you may be surprised at the sophisticated tools this application provides).

If you do presentations in public places, you may come across network projectors. You'll learn how to connect to network projectors in this chapter.

 EXAM TIP Objectives for the 70-620 and 70-623 exams are included in this chapter.

Windows Media Player

The Windows Media Player is a built-in tool that allows you to play audio and video and view images. You can rip music (copy music) from CDs, burn music to CDs, sync files with a portable music player, and shop for digital media online.

You can play DVD movies and recorded TV shows with Windows Media Player. DVD movies are played by simply popping the movie DVD into your DVD player and selecting play. TV shows can be recorded with Windows Media Center, which is explained later in this chapter.

Figure 15-1 shows the Windows Media Player as it is playing music from the library. The display provides eye candy; it constantly changes in sync with the music, and you have a lot of different views you can choose.

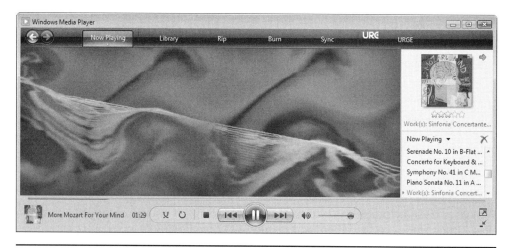

Figure 15-1   Windows Media Player

Notice across the top, you have a menu to access the different elements of the Media Player. These choices are explained in the following sections.

Viewing the Now Playing Menu

The Now Playing menu shows the information on the CD currently in the CD player and any visualization you may have picked. The Now Playing menu has a full list of options you can select to modify the quality of the sounds and the visualization. In Figure 15-2 I've selected SRS WOW effects.

SRS is short for Sound Retrieval System, and WOW is for WOW! There really is a difference when listening to the music with SRS WOW enabled. You can choose small speakers, large speakers, or headphones. I wouldn't call myself a true audiophile, but I was impressed at the improved quality of sound by enabling some of these settings. (Of course, listening on Bose headphones certainly helps the sound a lot too).

Viewing Your Library

Your library is a database that contains information about all of your digital media files on the computer or accessible to the computer. Any music CDs you've ripped to your computer are easily accessible here.

Figure 15-2 Now Playing menu

The library has several views you can choose from. You can choose to view the files based on what was recently added, the artist, the album, individual songs, the genre, the year, or even ratings that you define.

You can simply double-click any album within your library to play it. Or, if you only want to play a single song, you can double-click the song. You can also create your own playlists to pick and choose the music you want as shown in Figure 15-3. You can drag

Figure 15-3 Creating a playlist

and drop entire albums to the playlist, or double-click any album and drag and drop individual tracks.

The high-level steps to create a playlist are

1. Open the Playlists menu in the left pane.

2. Select Create Playlist and give it a name.

3. Select songs or albums from your library and drag them to the playlist in the far-right pane.

4. Click Save Playlist.

Ripping CDs

You can rip music (copy music) using Windows Media Player in Windows Vista. Once the ripped music is added to your library, you can then play it without the CD in your system.

If you put a music CD into your CD or DVD player, an AutoPlay dialog box similar to Figure 15-4 appears. You can play the audio CD or rip music from the CD using Windows Media Player. You can also choose to play the audio CD from the Windows Media Center or simply open the folder in Windows Explorer.

Figure 15-4
Audio CD
AutoPlay

Ripping a CD is surprisingly easy with the Windows Media Player. Interestingly, you can't copy the files using Windows Explorer. It will only copy the shortcuts, and it certainly doesn't convert the files to WMA format.

Figure 15-5 shows a music CD in the process of being ripped. This process copies the contents to your user's music folder as Windows Media Audio (WMA) files (or other formats if you modify the defaults). WMA is an audio data compression technology created by Microsoft. The files have an extension of .wma.

Figure 15-5 Ripping a music CD

If you choose Rip Music from CD, Windows Media Player launches and begins ripping the CD to your music folder. The compression retains the music quality while significantly reducing the size. The CD ripped in Figure 15-5 was reduced to 64MB on the hard drive. This is close to about 10 percent of the size on the CD.

Stop the Automatic Ripping If you select Rip Music from CD with the Always Do This for Audio CDs check box checked, every music CD you put into your system will be ripped. This may be what you want, or you may have just not noticed it was checked the first time you inserted a CD.

Since the check box is checked by default and people often want to try out the ability to rip music, this is often a cause of frustration by users. You can't reverse this setting using options within Windows Media Player but must instead modify it in the Control Panel.

You can modify the setting with the following steps:

- Launch the Control Panel. Select Classic View.
- Select Hardware and Sound.
- Change the Audio CD setting from Rip Music from CD Using Windows Media Player to something else such as Ask Me Every Time.
- Click Save.

Choosing a Format for Ripped Music

When ripping a music CD, you can choose from various formats. These are

- **Windows Media Audio**   This is the default setting and creates the .wma files native to the Windows Media Player.

- **Windows Media Audio Pro**   This can be selected for some low storage capacity portable devices such as mobile phones. You should only choose this format when you're trying to save space and you're sure your device supports it.

- **Windows Media Audio (Variable Bit Rate)**   This can be used to reduce the file size while retaining the quality. It takes longer to rip files in this format.

- **Windows Media Audio Lossless**   This format provides the best audio quality but increases the files size. Use this when you want to ensure the best audio quality.

- **MP3**   Can be used to create MP3 files. Use when your device plays MP3 files.

- **WAV (Lossless)**   Can be used to create WAV files.

 EXAM TIP   Windows Media Player can rip music in different formats. The Windows Media Audio is the default setting, and the Windows Media Audio (lossless) ensures the best quality.

Configuring Options for Ripping Music

You can access the options to use when you rip music by selecting More Options from the Rip menu. This is the same properties page that you can access from most menus by selecting More Options, but when selected from the Rip menu it will appear with the Rip Music tab selected as shown in Figure 15-6.

Notice in the figure that you have the option to change many of the settings for the ripped music. The format settings are the same as those you can access via the Format menu described previously—this just gives you another way to choose them.

You can also select the Copy Protect Music option from here.

Copy-Protecting Your Music

You can choose to copy-protect any music you rip. This will attach media usage rights to the files and can be used to limit their ability to be played, burned, or synced.

Media usage rights files are often used by online music stores to grant you to the right to play a song, burn a song, or sync a song. The rights are used to limit the number of times that the song can be played, burned, or synced. For example, you can purchase a song that can be played an unlimited number of times on your computer and can be burned once, and synced twice.

If you have recorded your own music and want to earn money for what you've created, you can choose to copy-protect it. This will prevent unrestricted copying of your music. This is referred to as "personal" copy protection, which is similar to copy protection as used by an online music store (which is referred to as "Standard" copy protection). Both methods use Digital Rights Management (DRM) technologies.

Figure 15-6

Rip Music options

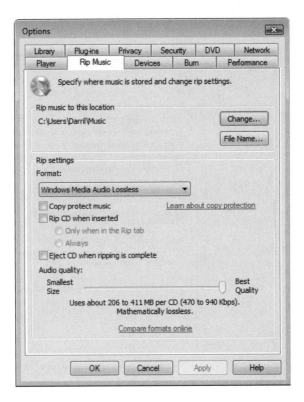

If you copy-protect music, you can't remove the copy protection. If you later decide you want copies of the files without copy protection, you must rip the music again, and then burn it again without copy protection.

NOTE DRM is a controversial technology. Some believe that it interferes with the lawful use of music, movies, and other copyrighted media and does nothing to actually stop piracy. Publishers and copyright holders believe that without protection, copyrighted works are shared freely, preventing artists and others in the industry from receiving fair market value for the efforts.

If you copy-protect music, you can't remove the copy protection. If you later decide you want copies of the files without copy protection, you must rip the music again, and then burn it again without copy protection.

Downloading Usage Rights Automatically

The Privacy tab of the Advanced options page in Windows Media Player contains a couple of important settings related to Digital Rights Management (DRM). The settings are Download Usage Rights Automatically When I Play or Sync a File and Automatically Check If Protected Files Need to Be Refreshed. Both are shown in Figure 15-7.

The first setting (Download Usage Rights Automatically . . .) causes the Windows Media Player to automatically download media usage rights if the existing rights are missing or out-of-date. This allows the Windows Media Player to obtain the rights automatically without prompting you to do so. If this setting is not enabled, usage rights

Figure 15-7
Privacy tab of
Windows Media
Player Advanced
Options

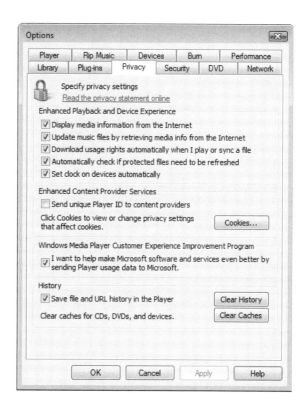

will still need to be checked if the existing rights are missing or out-of-date. The only difference is that you'll be prompted before the check.

Automatically Check If Protected Files Need to Be Refreshed is checked by default. This will cause the system to be a little more proactive in checking media usage rights. It will periodically scan your library for purchased and subscription files that have missing media usage rights, files that have expired rights, and files that have rights that are about to expire. This can be useful for a computer that isn't always connected to the Internet. When connected the Internet, the Windows Media Player will attempt to automatically download rights files. Later, when you're no longer connected, the rights will already be downloaded and you won't be required to make another Internet connection.

Configuring AutoPlay

AutoPlay can be configured to choose what happens when you insert media or a device. It can be enabled or disabled by accessing the Control Panel | Hardware and Sound and selecting AutoPlay. Figure 15-8 shows the AutoPlay configuration page.

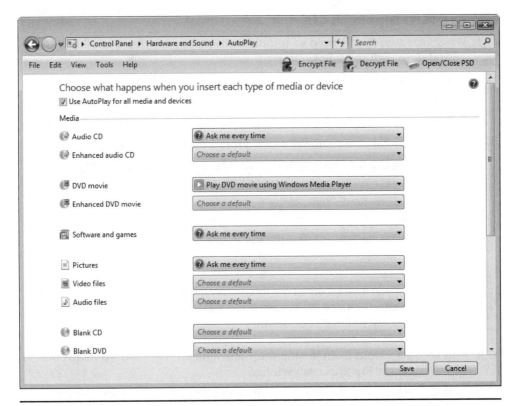

Figure 15-8 Configuring AutoPlay

To enable AutoPlay, ensure the check box next to Use AutoPlay for All Media and Devices is selected. You can then choose the specific AutoPlay response for each media type and device from this list. For example, The Audio CD has the following choices:

• Play Audio CD Using Windows Media Player

• Rip Music From CD Using Windows Media Player

• Play Audio CD Using Windows Media Center

• Open Folder To View Files Using Windows Explorer

• Take No Action

• Ask Me Every Time

The following exercise will lead you through the process of ripping a CD using the Windows Media Player.

Exercise 15.1: Ripping a CD

1. Verify CDs aren't configured to automatically be ripped when placed in the optical drive with the following steps.

   a. Launch the Control Panel by clicking Start | Control Panel.

   b. Select Hardware and Sound and click AutoPlay.

   c. Ensure the check box for Use AutoPlay For All Media and Devices is checked.

   d. Ensure Ask Me Every Time is selected for Audio CD. Click Save.

2. Place a music CD into your optical drive. After a moment the AutoPlay dialog box will appear asking what you want to do. Close this box.

3. Launch Windows Media by clicking Start | All Programs and selecting Windows Media Player.

4. In Windows Media Player, select the Rip menu. Your audio CD will be shown with all the tracks.

 TIP If you have access to the Internet, Windows Media Player will retrieve information on the CD and display it. If you don't have access to the Internet, the CD will be listed as unknown.

---

5. Select More Options from the Rip drop-down menu. The Options dialog box appears with the Rip Music tab selected.

   a. Note the location of where the audio will be ripped. Notice you can change this location if desired.

   b. In the Rip Settings area, click the drop-down box for the Format. Change the format to Windows Media Audio Lossless (for the best quality).

 TIP While you can't use the Windows Media Player to convert .wma files to .mp3 files, you can rip CDs directly to the popular MP3 format using the Player.

---

   c. Ensure Copy Protect Music is not selected. Click OK.

6. Ensure each of the tracks are selected and click Start Rip. The Rip Status of all the tracks will change to Pending, and the first track will change to Ripping with a percentage indicating how much has completed.

7. Once all tracks have been ripped, you can remove your CD and play the tracks from the library.

Burn a CD or DVD

If you select the Burn display, you can then create your own music mix and then burn it onto CD or DVD. It's as simple as dragging the songs you want on your CD to the Burn List in the right pane. Put a burnable CD or DVD into the drive and click Start Burn.

The following exercise will lead you through the process of burning a CD using the Windows Media Player. This exercise assumes you have already ripped a CD in Exercise 15.1 and that you have an optical drive that will burn CDs or DVDs.

Exercise 15.2: Burning a CD

1. Launch Windows Media Player by clicking Start | All Programs and selecting Windows Media Player.

2. Click Burn on the top menu bar.

3. Insert a blank CD or DVD into your drive. If the AutoPlay dialog box appears, close it. You'll see the disk listed with its capacity (such as 702MB for a CD, or 4.3GB for a DVD).

4. Click the Recently Added selection in your library. Browse to the CD you ripped in the preceding exercise.

5. Select Track 1 and drag it to the Burn List in the right pane.

6. Drag Tracks 3, 5, and 7 to the Burn List. Notice how much space remains on your music disc.

 TIP While this exercise is only using the odd tracks from a recently ripped CD, you can create your own music mix by picking and choosing which tracks you want to burn.

---

7. Once you have added all the tracks you want, click Start Burn. Depending on how many tracks you added to the mix, this may take a while.

8. Once complete, remove your CD or DVD, label it, and test it in the Windows Media Player.

Synchronizing Your Media Files

You can synchronize (or sync) your media devices. This means that files stored on your computer are compared with files stored on your media device, and differences are reconciled between the two.

After you connect and configure a device, the Windows Media Player selects either automatic sync or manual sync depending on the storage capacity of the device and the size of your library. You can configure a device by selecting Set Up Sync as shown in Figure 15-9. This page allows you to rename the device and then click Finish.

The Sync page will show your device synchronizing until the items between your computer and the device match.

Modifying Synchronization Options

If you ever want to change the sync options, you can select the Advanced Options selection from the device. This page includes two tabs, the Sync tab and the Quality tab.

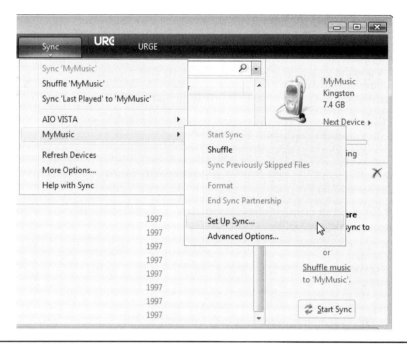

Figure 15-9 Setting up sync for a device

The Sync tab gives you the following options:

- **Device Name**   You can change the name of your device.
- **Create Folder Hierarchy On Device**   This causes folders to be set up on your device so that it's easier to find the music and playlists. This setting is set by default.
- **Start Sync When Device Connects**   When selected it will enable automatic synchronization allowing new music added to or changed in one place to be added to or changed in the other.
- **Reserve Space On The Device For Use By Other Programs**   You can ensure that the entire device is not used for music by adjusting this slide bar.

The Quality tab allows you to adjust the conversion and qualify settings for devices. It's recommended to leave the check box checked for Convert Music, Pictures, Videos, and TV Shows as Required by This Device (Recommended). This is the default setting, but if you're using a device that needs something else, you can modify it.

Starting Synchronization

If synchronization is not configured to start when the device connects, you need to initiate synchronization manually. You can do this by clicking the Start Sync button in the Sync List pane on the right. Alternately, you can select Sync *name of device* from the Sync drop-down menu.

Sharing Media on a Network

When you enable media sharing, people and devices on the network can share music, pictures, and videos with each other. This makes a lot of sense for a home network. You enable media sharing in the Network and Sharing Center.

The Network and Sharing Center was covered in much more depth in Chapter 5. However, the last option (Media Sharing) was barely mentioned. Figure 15-10 shows the Network and Sharing Center and the resulting screen when you try to change media sharing from Off to On.

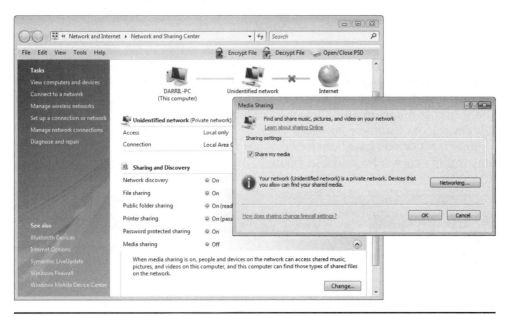

Figure 15-10   Enabling media sharing

As a reminder, you can access the Network and Sharing Center by clicking Start, right-clicking Network, and selecting Properties. If Media Sharing is turned off, you can click Change to turn it on; however, media sharing can be enabled only if your computer is connected to a private network. Select the check box to share your media and click OK.

Next, the Media Sharing dialog box will appear and you have the choice of allowing or denying access to your media to other users on the same PC. Figure 15-11 shows that Other Users of This PC have been allowed access (note the check in the icon).

If you click Settings, you can further specify the files types you want to share and restrict shared files based on ratings. Additionally, you can check the box to allow new devices and computers to automatically be able to share media (though this setting is not recommended).

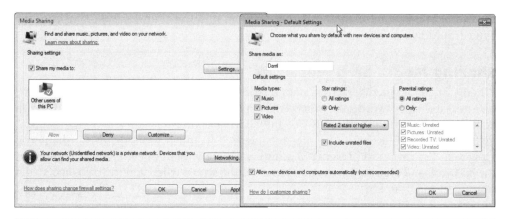

Figure 15-11   Enabling media sharing for users and on the network

If the Allow New Devices and Computers Automatically check box is not checked, then you individually allow or deny devices in the Media Settings dialog box. As a new device is found, it will appear next to the Other Users of This PC icon. You can select it and then click Allow (to fully allow media sharing), Deny (to prevent media sharing to this device), or Customize (to selectively allow and deny different file types).

Once other devices have been found on the network and approved, the media on the other computers will be available. Figure 15-12 shows Windows Media Player running

Figure 15-12   Using Windows Media Player to access media on another PC

on one computer, but accessing the media from the Darril user account on the computer named darril-pc.

Buying Media Online

The last menu on the Windows Media Player is Urge. It allows you to connect to an online music store to purchase music. While it's certainly convenient to purchase and download music files via the Windows Media Player, there are many different online music stores out there.

Windows Media Center

The Windows Media Center is available in the Windows Vista Premium and Ultimate Editions. It's intended to be used a core console for digital entertainment.

You can launch the Windows Media Center by clicking Start | All Programs and selecting Windows Media Center. The first time you launch it, you will be prompted to go through a setup process with a wizard. It's best to start this process with an Internet connection.

If you want to launch the setup wizard again later, you can access it using the Tasks menu and selecting Settings | General and Windows Media Center Setup, and then selecting the Run Setup Again menu item.

Figure 15-13 shows the Windows Media Center accessing music files in the music library. This is the same content you can access via the Windows Media Player, but imagine accessing this via a remote control on a large-screen HDTV. It's quite a different experience.

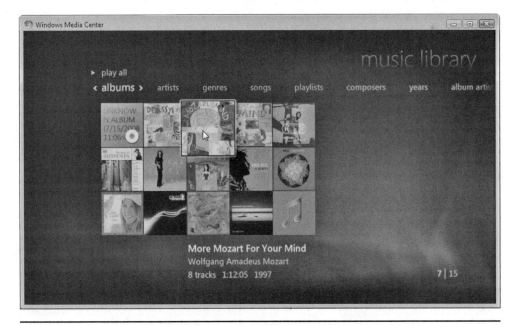

Figure 15-13 Windows Media Center accessing music files

Of course, the Windows Media Center can do much more than just play music. You can

- **View what's on TV**   You can access a free electronic programming guide that shows what's on for the next two weeks.

- **Record and play TV**   An additional digital video recorder (DVR) isn't needed, and there's no monthly fee. As when using the popular Tivo DVRs, you can even pause for breaks while watching a program, and fast-forward through the commercials.

- **Record one channel while watching another**   If you have more than one tuner, you can record two channels at a time, or watch one channel while recording another. In the U.S., you can have as many as four tuners (such as two regular TV tuners and two HDTV tuners).

 EXAM TIP   You can add additional tuners to your Windows Vista system to record and watch channels simultaneously. Similar to how some TVs have two tuners to show a primary channel and a second picture-in-picture channel, a second tuner allows you to view one channel while recording another.

- **Play movies**   Pop your DVDs into your computer's DVD player and you can view the movie on your display.

- **Play music**   You can play any music in your library.

- **View photos**   You can view your photos in a slide show format.

The video output of the Windows Media Center is optimized for large-screen TVs. You can plug your Windows Vista computer into a 50-inch 1080i video display (or even smaller ones if that's what you have) and browse through your TV shows, DVDs, music, and photos.

By adding a Windows Media Extender Device, you can access all the content from your computer running Windows Media Center from another device located in another room in your house.

 NOTE   For more details on the Windows Media Center (including some demos), check out Microsoft's Windows Media Center home page here: www.microsoft.com/windows/products/winfamily/mediacenter/default.mspx.

Windows Media Center Extender Device

Windows Media Center Extenders are devices such as a TV, a DVD player, or an Xbox 360 console that can be connected to a home network. Extender devices are used to allow you to access digital media in the Windows Media Center from a variety of places.

For example, you may record TV shows on a Windows Vista computer using the Windows Media Center. If you want to watch the TV shows on a TV in another room (and the TV is a Media Center Extender device), you can add the TV to your network, and then configure the Windows Media Center on the Windows Vista computer to recognize the device. The device can now play the TV shows that have been recorded on the Windows Vista computer.

Requirements for a Windows Media Center Extender

You need to meet some basic requirements in order to use a Windows Media Center Extender. These include

- **A network**   This can be either a wired or wireless network. The Windows Media Center Extender device and the computer running Windows Media Center must both be on the same subnet. Because some of the communication is done via broadcasts, and routers don't pass broadcasts, both devices must be on the same side of the router (same subnet). Check out Chapter 5 for a complete description of what a subnet is and how to verify both are on the same subnet.

- **A Media Center Extender device**   This can be any device that has Windows Media Center Extender functionality built in. This device has a setup key that will uniquely identify it in your network.

- **A Media Center computer**   You need a computer running Windows Vista Home, Premium, or Ultimate Editions. You configure this with the setup key of the extender device.

 EXAM TIP   The Windows Media Center and the Windows Media Center Extender device must be on the same subnet. Initial communication is done through broadcasts, and if they aren't on the same subnet, they won't be able to establish the initial communication. This is generally not a problem in a home network, but if the setup key has been entered correctly and the extender device is still not working, check the subnet.

Setting Up a Windows Media Center Extender

After you've met the requirements to use a Windows Media Center extender, you next need to add the device to your home network. If you're running a wired network with DHCP, simply plug the device into the network with an Ethernet cable. For more information on creating and configuring wired networks, check out Chapter 5.

For wireless networks, you'll need to configure the wireless information such as the SSID and the WPA password. Hopefully you're not using WEP anymore, but if so, you'll need to configure the WEP key. See Chapter 6 for more information on configuring wireless networks and devices in a wireless network.

Next, you need to identify the setup key for your extender device. This setup key is used by the Windows Media Center to authenticate the extender device. Most Windows Media Center Extender devices include a remote with a special button known as the Windows Media Center Green Start button. When you press this, you'll be able to access the setup key.

You then need to enter the setup key into the Windows Media Center. Launch the Windows Media Center by clicking Start | All Programs and selecting Windows Media Center. Select Tasks | Add Extender. On the Extender Setup screen, click Next.

The Extender Setup screen will appear as shown in Figure 15-14. Enter the setup key here. Click Next and follow the remaining steps in the Extender Setup Wizard.

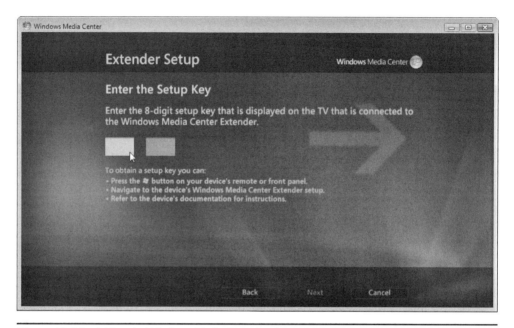

Figure 15-14   Adding the Windows Media Extender device setup key

Once you complete the configuration, you can then use the extender device to play content that is on the Windows Media Center computer.

Playing Media Only

It's possible to configure the Windows Media Center in Media Only mode. This can be used on public computers used to play media content in full-screen mode. It hides the Windows Minimize and Close buttons so that users are less likely to accidentally stop the display.

Figure 15-15 shows the menu choice to select Media Only. This choice is found on the Tasks menu, scrolled all the way to the right. Once selected, the Windows Media Center will be displayed in full-screen mode.

You can exit the full screen mode by pressing the CTRL-ESC keys simultaneously to access other windows. You can also select Tasks | Exit Media Only mode to return to normal.

Figure 15-15   Selecting Media Only

Windows Photo Gallery

Windows Vista includes several tools you can use with your digital cameras or camcorders. Windows Photo Gallery is a core tool used to work with cameras, but you can also use the Windows Media Player and the Windows Media Center to work with pictures and videos.

Most digital cameras and camcorders include USB connections, and when you connect either the camera itself or the media from the camera, it's automatically recognized. Depending on how you have AutoPlay configured, it can automatically launch one of these tools for you. For digital cameras that hold snapshots, your system will normally launch the Windows Photo Gallery.

Using the Windows Photo Gallery

The primary built-in tool used to work with pictures and videos is the Windows Photo Gallery. Figure 15-16 shows the Windows Photo Gallery.

The Windows Photo Gallery can be used to locate and view pictures on your computer. It will automatically show all the photos and videos that are located in your pictures folder, and you can also add other folders to the gallery. Windows Photo Gallery supports a wide range of file formats for pictures (bmp, jpeg, jfif, tiff, png, and wdp) and videos (asf, avi, mpeg, and wmv). The video formats are only supported when Windows Movie Maker is installed, which is only on the Vista Home Premium and Vista Ultimate Editions.

Figure 15-16 Viewing pictures with the Windows Photo Gallery

Notice the menu across the top of the Windows Photo Gallery. This menu includes the following tools:

- **File** The file menu includes the following functions: Delete, Rename, Make a Copy, Revert to Original (if the original has been modified), Copy; and the ability to view the properties.

- **Fix** This launches a different view, where you can make some basic modifications to the picture, including Auto Adjust (to automatically adjust color), Adjust Exposure (to change brightness and contrast), Adjust Color (to change the temperature, tint, and saturation), crop the picture, and fix red eye.

- **Info** Information is shown in the right pane. If this has been closed, you can make it appear again by clicking Info. You can view basic file info from here and also add tags (keywords) and captions.

- **Print** You can either print directly to a printer or order prints of your photograph online.

- **E-Mail** This creates an e-mail message with the picture as an attachment using your native e-mail application. You can pick the picture size of the attachment by adjusting the resolution.

- **Burn** You can choose to burn the picture (or pictures) to a data disc or a video DVD.

- **Make a movie**   This will launch the Windows Movie Maker (discussed later in this chapter) with the image added.

- **Open**   This allows you to access other programs installed on your system. The programs accessible aren't only Microsoft programs, but any other graphics programs installed on your system. For example, on my system JASC Paint Shop Photo Album and Macromedia Fireworks MX were among the choices.

Viewing Pictures from a Digital Camera

If you plug in a digital camera (or plug in the flash memory from your camera using a USB reader) and AutoPlay is enabled, you will be prompted for what to do with the images. Figure 15-17 shows the AutoPlay screen for pictures.

Figure 15-17
AutoPlay for a
digital camera

TIP   Remember, if AutoPlay isn't working, you can configure this in the Control Panel. Select Hardware and Sound, and then select AutoPlay. Ensure that Use AutoPlay for All Media and Devices is checked and then configure the associated media. For a digital camera, you would configure either pictures or video files, depending on the type of camera.

The following choices are always available:

- **Import Pictures Using Windows**   This will copy all of the pictures from the device to your hard drive in the Pictures folder. The Windows Photo Gallery is then launched, allowing you to browse the pictures one at a time.

- **View Pictures Using Windows**   This option will launch the Windows Photo Gallery and allow you to browse the pictures while still on the camera.

- **View Pictures Using Windows Media Center**   If you select this option, a slide show of all the pictures begins. The Windows Media Center uses a neat feature of automatically slowly changing the view of the picture. It gives the impression of a moving image, by slowly zooming in, zooming out, or changing the view from the one edge to another.

Changing Windows Photo Gallery Import Options

One of the biggest uses of the Windows Photo Gallery is its ability to easily import pictures just by plugging in the device and answering a prompt or two. This is a whole lot easier than having to copy the files by hand.

Additionally, Windows Photo Gallery uses tags to identify your pictures. Tags are words or phrases you use to describe your pictures and videos and can also be used to name them. When you import pictures and video, you are prompted to enter a tag as shown in Figure 15-18.

Figure 15-18
Windows Photo
Gallery prompt
for a tag

For example, if I have just taken pictures of several flowers and want to import them, I can use a tag of Flowers. Windows Photo Gallery will import them and name them Flowers 001, Flowers 002, and so on. Additionally, all the pictures will be organized in a folder and the folder will be named using the tag also.

You can manipulate how these options function by accessing the Import tab of the Windows Photo Gallery Options. This tab is shown in Figure 15-19 and can be accessed by selecting the Options menu choice in the File drop-down menu of Windows Photo Gallery. These options will be used if you select the Import Pictures selection in the AutoPlay screen.

 EXAM TIP   You can automate how pictures are imported by first enabling AutoPlay via the Control Panel and then configuring the options within Windows Photo Gallery.

Figure 15-19 Manipulating the Import Tab options

The Windows Photo Gallery import options are

- **Settings For** You can configure different settings for cameras, CDs and DVDs, and scanners.

- **Import To** You can specify the target folder for the imported pictures. This defaults to the user's Pictures folder.

- **Folder Name** You can specify the name of the folder where the pictures are to be imported (within the Pictures folder). You have several choices for how to combine the tag with either the date the pictures were taken or the date the pictures were imported.

- **File Name** You can specify the tag to be used to identify the name of the pictures (such as Flowers 001, Flowers 002, where Flowers is the tag), or use the original filename and even the original filename and folder structure.

- **Example** As you change the options, the example shows you an example of how the folder and filenames will appear.

- **Prompt For A Tag On Import** When checked, the user will be prompted to enter a tag. When not checked, a tag will not be used.

- **Always Erase From Camera After Import** This will clear the pictures from the camera after the pictures have been copied.

- **Rotate Pictures On Import** Some cameras can automatically detect when a picture should be rotated (by sensing the position of the camera when the picture was taken). If the camera has this capability and you check this box, the pictures will automatically be rotated.

- **Open Windows Photo Gallery After Import** This will launch Windows Photo Gallery so that you can browse and manipulate your files.

Windows Movie Maker

You can use the Windows Movie Maker to create and edit your own videos and slide shows. If you have a little bit of creativity in you, you can have a lot of fun with this. I've seen videos created by middle-school students using the Movie Maker that are quite amazing. You can add your own video clips, text and titles, transitions, special effects, music, and voice over narration.

The Windows Movie Maker is launched by clicking Start | All Programs | Windows Movie Maker. Figure 15-20 shows the Movie Maker.

Figure 15-20   Windows Movie Maker

On the left is the Task pane. Here you work on importing, editing, and publishing tasks. The center pane shows all the media that you've imported into your movie; this pane changes when different tasks are selected. The storyboard is at the bottom. You can drag and drop media from the imported documents into the storyboard and manipulate the order. The right pane shows any individual element you can select from the storyboard.

Importing Media into Windows Movie Maker

If you're going to create a movie, you need some content. This includes movies from a camcorder, other videos, pictures, and sound. You can import these documents using the Import tasks from the Tasks pane. Tasks include

- **From Digital Video Camera**   You can hook up your digital video camera (or camcorder) to your Windows Vista PC, set the digital video camera to playback mode, and select this option.

- **Videos**   The following video formats are supported: asf, avi, dvr-ms, m1v, mp2, mp2v, mpe, mpeg, mpt, mpv2, wm, and wmv.

- **Pictures**   The following picture formats are supported: bmp, dib, emf, gif, jfif, jpeg, jpg, png, tif, tiff, and wmf.

- **Audio Or Music**   The following audio formats are supported: aif, aifc, aiff, asf, au, mp2, mp3, mpa, snd, wav, and wma.

To import videos, pictures, and audio or music, you click the one you want in the Import task and an import media items dialog box appears. You can browse to the files you want and click Import; the items will be in your project.

If you want to view the items you've added, you can always select Imported Media in the Edit tasks.

You add the media items to your movie by dragging and dropping them onto your storyboard at the bottom of the Windows Movie Maker screen. You can easily move items around in your storyboard by dragging and dropping them.

Editing a Movie

Once you've imported the files and added them to your storyboard, you can then edit them by adding effects, transitions, titles, and credits.

Effects are applied to the pictures or video to change the way they appear. For example, you can use pan effects (such as pan right or zoom) to give still pictures the effect of movement; or use Sepia Tone or Film Age effects to give your movie a historical or antique appearance.

Transitions are used to control how one video clip or picture closes and how the next one appears. There are many different types of built-in transitions that you can choose from.

Titles and credits can be used to add a beginning title screen, a closing credit screen, and titles before or on individual clips.

Adding Audio to a Movie

You can add audio to your movie, but you have to change the view from the storyboard to the timeline view. Click View and select Timeline (or you can press the CTRL-T keys to toggle between the views).

While in the Timeline view, you can drag and drop audio onto the Audio/Music area of the timeline. You'll have an opportunity to do this in Exercise 15.3, where you'll create a movie from scratch, edit it, and publish it.

Once audio is added to the timeline, you can do a lot to manipulate it. You can easily resize the audio just as if it were a picture that you were cropping. Figure 15-21 shows the movie with pictures, titles, video, and audio added. The audio has been cropped so that it ends when the graphics end.

Figure 15-21   Creating a movie in Windows Movie Maker

Publishing a Movie

Last, you're able to publish your completed movies to several different targets. These include

- **This Computer**   This option gives you the most flexibility. You can choose where to publish it (which drive and folder) and the output format. The output formats include several different formats, such as Windows Media Portable Device, DVD Quality, DVD Widescreen quality, HD 720p, HD for XBox 360, HD 1080p, Low Bandwidth, and VHS quality. You could publish the same movie in Low Bandwidth to make it available on your Web site or in HD 1080p to show on your 50-inch HD TV.

- **DVD**   If your computer has a DVD burner, you can insert a blank DVD into the burner and select this option. It will then launch the Windows DVD Maker.

 TIP   You can use the Windows DVD Maker to create DVDs of your movies, and also to create a DVD containing other video, pictures, audio, and even slide shows. It's surprisingly easy to create a slideshow. Launch it and give it a try.

- **Recordable CD**   If your computer has a CD burner, you can insert a blank CD into the burner and select this option. A CD can typically hold about 700MB of storage.

- **E-Mail**   The E-Mail option will make the video into a relatively small size. You can then play the movie to check the quality, save a copy of the movie on your computer, or choose to attach the movie to an e-mail. If you choose to attach it, it will launch your e-mail application and open a new e-mail with the movie as an attachment.

- **Digital Video Camera**   If you have a digital video camera attached to your system, you can choose to send the movie to the camera. This is useful for some cameras that allow you to create video tapes.

The following exercise will lead you through the process of creating, editing, and publishing a movie using the Windows Movie Maker.

Exercise 15.3: Creating a Movie with Windows Movie Maker

1. Launch Windows Movie Maker by clicking Start | All Programs and selecting Windows Movie Maker.

2. Locate the Import tasks in the Tasks pane. Click Videos. Browse to the Public, Public Videos, Sample Videos folder and select Butterfly. Click Import.

3. Click Pictures. Browse to the Public, Public Pictures, Sample Pictures folder. Hold down the CTRL key and select Garden and Toco Toucan. Click Import. This will import both pictures.

4. Click Audio or Music. Browse to the Public, Public Music, Sample Music folder. Select I Guess You're Right and click Import.

5. Drag the Garden picture to the first block of the storyboard.

6. Drag the Toco Toucan picture to the second block of the storyboard.

7. Drag the Butterfly video to the third block of the storyboard. This video also includes sound.

8. Select Effects in the Edit task area. Scroll down to the Ease In effect. Drag and drop this to the Garden picture.

9. Scroll down to the Pan Down and Zoom Out effect. Drag and drop this to the Toco Toucan picture.

10. Locate the Film Age, old effect and drag and drop this onto the Butterfly video.

11. Right-click the Butterfly video and select Effects. Select the Spin 360 effect and click Add (this causes both effects to be used for the video). Click OK.

12. Click Transitions. Drag and drop the Bow Tie, Vertical effect to the area between the Garden and the Toco Toucan picture. Drag and drop the Dissolve, Rough Transition to between the Toco Toucan picture and the Butterfly video.

13. Click View and select Timeline. This will change from the Storyboard view to the Timeline view so that you can add audio.

14. Drag and drop the I Guess You're Right audio to the Audio/Music area of the timeline. Notice that this audio clip is quite a bit longer than your movie. You can adjust what is played by hovering over the start or end and dragging. In my movie, I cut the slow intro and ended the audio when the butterfly video ends.

15. Click Titles and Credits. Click Title at the Beginning and type in a name for your movie. Click Add Title. Your video should look similar to Figure 15-22. Click Play to play your movie.

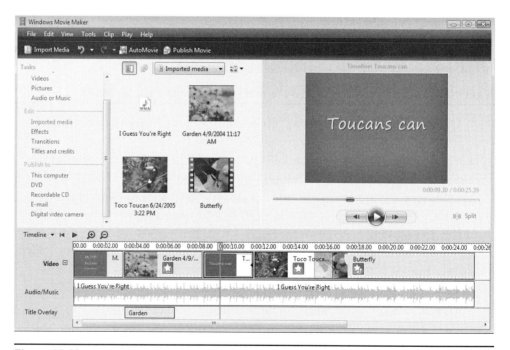

Figure 15-22   Adding elements to your movie

16. Feel free to adjust the movie by adding additional media and additional titles or credits, and by adjusting the transitions and effects.

17. Once you're satisfied with your movie, select E-Mail in the Publish To task area. This will take about a minute to complete. Click Attach Movie. Your native e-mail program will launch, and an e-mail message will be created with your movie as an attachment. You can send this or close it.

18. In the Publish To tasks, click This Computer. Accept the defaults and click Next.

19. On Choose the Settings for Your Movie, click More Settings. Notice that you can publish your movie in a lot of different formats, ranging from a compact Windows Media Portable Device format all the way to Windows Media HD 1080p. Select Best Quality for Playback on My Computer (Recommended). Click Publish.

20. Once the movie has completed, click Finish. The movie will play in the Windows Media Player. Close all the open windows.

Using Network Projectors

A network projector is a projector used for presentations (such as PowerPoint presentations) that is connected to a network instead of directly connected to a computer. Network projectors can be connected to either a wired or wireless network. When you connect to the projector, your desktop can be displayed by the projector. This works well for presentations and also for any type of demos you do as part of the presentation.

If the network projector is connected to a network, it must have basic networking capabilities (such as a NIC and an IP address). You can then use a Windows Vista computer to connect to the network projector and display your presentation on it.

Windows Vista includes a wizard used to connect to a network projector. Click Start | All Programs | Accessories and select Connect to a Network Projector to launch the wizard. Figure 15-23 shows the wizard.

If the network projector is located on the same subnet, then the wizard is able to locate it once you click Search for a Projector (Recommended). This method uses broadcasts, which don't pass through routers. In other words, the network projector must be on the same subnet in order for the wizard to locate it.

 EXAM TIP The network projector must be on the same subnet in order for the Connect to a Network Projector Wizard to be able to successfully locate it. If it's not on the same subnet, you need to enter its address.

You can also enter the projector's address and the wizard will be able to locate it even if it's on a different subnet. The projector address can be entered as

- An HTTP address if configured as a HTTP network projector
- A UNC address if shared from a server
- An IP address

Some network projectors are security-enabled, requiring you to enter a password before access is granted. Obviously, if a password is required, you need to enter it.

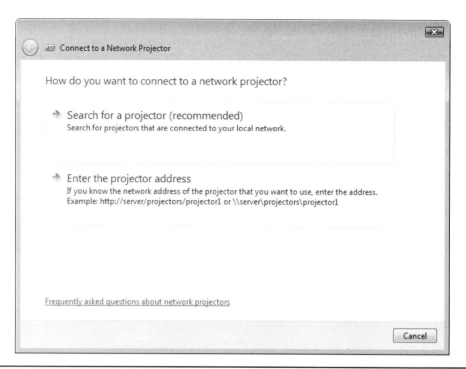

Figure 15-23   Connect to a Network Projector Wizard

Chapter Review

In this chapter you learned about several different applications available within Windows Vista that you can use to work with media.

The Windows Media Player can be used to play music, rip your music CDs, create your own music mixes, and burn music CDs. Two exercises in this chapter gave you an opportunity to rip a CD and burn a CD. The Windows Media Player gives you a lot of flexibility with an assortment of options. You can modify the format of the ripped music and easily configure synchronization with mobile devices.

You can use the Windows Media Center as a central entertainment center where you can easily set up slide shows of your pictures, record TV, play back TV, and play DVDs. You can add a Windows Media Center Extender device (such as an Xbox 360 or a compatible TV) so that you can access content in any room in your house. You learned that the Media Center Extender devices must be on the same subnet in order for them to work with the Windows Media Center, and that you need a setup key to authenticate the device.

The Windows Photo Gallery can be used to manipulate your photos, but its great strength is the ability to easily import photos from your digital camera. You can also add tags that will be used to rename the pictures and the folder where they're stored.

You can combine it all with the Windows Movie Maker, which can be used to create movies from your pictures, songs, and video clips. Once you're done, you can publish your movies to DVD (using the Windows DVD Maker) or to your computer, in a wide variety of formats including a compressed version for e-mail, or high-definition versions for your HDTV.

Last, you learned a little about network projectors. A network projector is on your network (with an IP address). If it's located on the same subnet, the Connect to a Network Projector Wizard can easily find it and connect. If it's on a different subnet, you can connect to it using its address in a name format, or with an IP address.

Additional Study

Self Study Exercises
Use these additional exercises to challenge yourself.

- Rip some of your music CDs to different formats.
- Create your own music mix and burn it to a music CD.
- Open and review each of the tabs in the Options page of Windows Media Player.
- Launch and configure the Windows Media Center. Review all the options and settings in the Tasks menu.
- Create and publish a movie using your own pictures.
- Create a slide show using the Windows DVD Maker.

Summary of What You Need to Know

70-620
When preparing for the 70-620 exam, pay particular attention to the following topics covered in this chapter:

- **Windows Media Player**   You should be very familiar with this tool, including how to rip music and burn CDs, and how music can be protected.
- **Windows Media Center**   You should be familiar with the capabilities of Windows Media Center. You should also be aware of the requirements to watch and record TV (such as TV tuner cards) and what's needed to add a Windows Media Extender device (such as being on the same subnet and having the setup key).
- **Network Projector**   You should know how to connect to a network projector: either it needs to be on the same subnet to automatically connect with the wizard, or you need the network address or the IP address.

70-622

There are not any 70-622 objectives covered in this chapter.

70-623

When preparing for the 70-623 exam, pay particular attention to the following topics covered in this chapter:

- **Windows Media Player**   You should be very familiar with this tool, including how to rip music and burn CDs, and how music can be protected. You should also know how media can be shared on a network.

- **AutoPlay**   You should know how to configure AutoPlay for various media that you can connect to your Windows Vista system.

- **Windows Media Center**   You should be familiar with the capabilities of Windows Media Center. You should also be aware of the requirements to watch and record TV (such as TV tuner cards) and what's needed to add a Windows Media Extender device (such as being on the same subnet and having the setup key).

- **Network Projector**   You should know how to connect to a network projector: either it needs to be on the same subnet to automatically connect with the wizard, or you need the network address or the IP address.

- **Windows Movie Maker**   Know the capabilities of Windows Movie Maker, such as how to import and add media. You should also know how to publish a movie and the different formats available for publishing.

Questions

70-620

1. You have downloaded a song from an online music store. You've successfully played the file several times and even synced it to a portable media device. Later, when you try to sync it again, you get an error stating that you don't have rights to sync the file. You know you have purchased the right to sync it an unlimited number of times. What should you do to ensure you can sync this protected file? Choose all that apply.

   A. Select the check box to Automatically Check If Protected Files Need to Be Refreshed.

   B. Select the check box to Display Media Information from the Internet.

   C. Select the check box to Update Music Files by Retrieving Media Info from the Internet.

   D. Select the check box to Download Usage Rights Automatically When I Play or Sync a File.

2. You have purchased a TV that is advertised as being a Windows Media Center Extender device. You want to use it to play TV shows that are recorded on a Windows Vista computer in another room. What do you need to do to configure the Windows Media Center Extender device? (Choose all that apply.)

   A. Input the Setup Key from Windows Media Center into the Windows Media Center Extender device.

   B. Input the Setup Key from the Windows Media Center Extender device into Windows Media Center.

   C. Ensure the Windows Vista computer and the Windows Media Center Extender device are on different subnets.

   D. Ensure the Windows Vista computer and the Windows Media Center Extender device are on the same subnet.

3. You are preparing to give a presentation on a project you're working on. You have created a PowerPoint presentation on your laptop computer running Windows Vista, and the conference room where you're doing the presentation has a network projector. How can you connect to the projector?

   A. Use the Windows Media Center and connect using either an IP address or a MAC address.

   B. Use the Windows Media Center and either connect using an IP address or ensure your computer is on the same subnet.

   C. Use the Connect to a Network Projector Wizard and use either an IP address or a MAC address.

   D. Use the Connect to a Network Projector Wizard and either use the projector's IP address or ensure your computer is on the same subnet.

4. You are hosting a party and want your guests to be able to browse through your music selections and make their own choices using the Windows Media Center. However, you want to minimize the chances that users may accidentally close the Windows Media Center. What should you do?

   A. Use Group Policy to configure Software Restrictions.

   B. Use Media Only mode.

   C. Configure the Windows Media Center in user mode.

   D. Add a Windows Media Center Extender device.

70-623

1. A user has an 8GB mobile Windows Media Player device used to play music files. Her music library on her Windows Vista computer is about 4GB. When she adds music to her library, the files aren't automatically added to her device when she plugs it in. She wants the music to automatically be added to the device. What should she do?

    A. Configure the properties of the device in Windows Media Player to Start Sync When Device Connects.

    B. Change the Media Player settings to Add Media Files to Library When Played.

    C. Enable AutoPlay via Group Policy.

    D. Enable Media Sharing.

2. A user has an extensive collection of CD files and wants to store the music on her Windows Vista computer. She wants to ensure the files are stored at the highest possible quality. What should she do?

    A. Use Windows Media Player and choose the Windows Media Player Audio Pro format option.

    B. Use Windows Media Player and choose the Windows Media Player Audio Lossless format option.

    C. Use Windows Media Center and choose the Audio Pro format option.

    D. Use Windows Media Center and choose the MP3 format option.

3. Joe has ripped three CDs to his Windows Vista computer. He's configured the format as Windows Media Audio Lossless files with Copy Protect Music enabled. He then transfers a playlist from the Windows Vista computer to a laptop running Windows Vista. However, when he attempts to play the files on his laptop, he receives an error message. What can he do to ensure that playlists he creates on his computer will run on the laptop?

    A. Delete all the files. Rip the CDs again using Windows Media Player and the format of Windows Media Audio Pro.

    B. Delete all the files. Rip the CDs again using Windows Media Player with Copy Protect Music not enabled.

    C. Use Windows Media Player to remove copy protection on the laptop running Windows Vista.

    D. Use Windows Media Player to remove copy protection on the original Windows Vista computer.

4. You have a Windows Vista PC in your home network. You've ripped about 50 CDs from your music collection and are storing them on this PC. You want to be able to play the music from other PCs in your home. What should you do?

    A. Burn the music DVDs and copy it to the other PCs.

    B. Use a network connection to rip the music to each PC.

   C. Enable Media Sharing in the Network and Sharing Center.

   D. Enable Media Sharing in the Windows Media Center.

5. Sally uses her Windows Vista Ultimate computer to watch and record TV shows. She finds that she often wants to view two TV shows that are on at the same time, but her system doesn't currently allow her to record one and watch the other. What does she need?

   A. A Windows Media Center Extender device

   B. An additional tuner

   C. Two additional tuners

   D. A third-party DVR

6. Sally uses her Windows Vista Ultimate computer to watch and record TV shows. She wants to be able to watch the TV shows in another room. What does she need?

   A. An additional tuner

   B. Two additional tuners

   C. A Windows Media Center Extender device

   D. A third-party DVR

7. You have added a Windows Media Center Extender device on your home network. You've verified the network connectivity is configured correctly, but the device is unable to access any content from the Windows Media Center. What is the likely problem?

   A. The Setup Key hasn't been entered into the Windows Media Center Extender device.

   B. The Setup Key hasn't been entered into Windows Media Center.

   C. The Windows Media Center Extender device isn't configured with the default gateway.

   D. Windows Media Center hasn't been configured with the IP address of the Windows Media Center Extender device.

8. Sally recently purchased a digital camera and took several pictures with it. She connects the camera to her Windows Vista computer, but it does not prompt her to do anything with the pictures. She ultimately uses Windows Explorer to copy the files from her camera to her system. She wants to be prompted to copy the images when she plugs in her camera. What should she do?

   A. Enable AutoPlay within the Windows Media Player.

   B. Enable AutoPlay within the Windows Photo Gallery.

   C. Enable AutoPlay within the Control Panel.

   D. Use the Device Manager to configure her digital camera.

9. Joe has created several videos with his digital video camera. He wants to create a movie with the Windows Movie Maker using these videos. How can he get the videos from the camera into the Windows Movie Maker?

    A. Copy the videos to a DVD using Windows DVD Maker and then add the videos from the DVD.

    B. Select Import From Digital Video Camera in the Windows Movie Maker.

    C. Use the Windows Media Center to import the movies.

    D. Use the Windows Media Player to rip the videos to the computer and then import them into Windows Movie Maker.

10. Joe has created several videos with his high-definition digital video camera. He's created a movie with the Windows Movie Maker using these videos. He wants to publish the movie so that he can play it on his new HD TV without losing any quality. What should he do?

    A. Publish the movie to the computer and choose the Windows Media HD 1080p format.

    B. Publish the movie to DVD and choose the Windows Media HD 1080p format.

    C. Use Windows DVD Maker to publish it to the Windows Media HD 1080p format.

    D. Publish the movie to e-mail.

Answers

70-620

1. **A, D.** Both correct selections are available on the Privacy tab of the Windows Media Player Advanced Options. The Automatically Check If Protected Files Need to Be Refreshed option causes files to be checked periodically to ensure media usage rights are up-to-date. The Download Usage Rights Automatically When I Play or Sync a File selection will cause the file to be checked when it is played or synced. The Display Media Information from the Internet option and the Update Music Files by Retrieving Media Info from the Internet option both only relate to information about the media but are not related to rights.

2. **B, D.** The Windows Media Center Extender device has a character key that must be identified and entered into Windows Media Center before the extender device can communicate. Additionally, both devices must be on the same subnet. The Setup Key is obtained from the extender device and entered into Windows Media Center, not vice versa. If the devices are on different subnets, broadcast communications will not occur.

3. **D.** The Connect to a Network Projector Wizard is used to connect to network projectors. If the projector and the Vista computer are both on the same subnet, the wizard can find the projector. If not, you must either enter the HTTP address

or an IP address. The Media Access Control (MAC) address cannot be used to connect to a network projector. You can't use the Windows Media Center to connect to a network projector.

4. **B.** Windows Media Center can be configured to use Media Only mode, which will display the program in full screen and remove the minimize, maximize, and close buttons. Using Group Policy is much more work than is necessary. There's no such thing as user mode in the Windows Media Center. An extender device is not required to use Media Only mode.

70-623

1. **A.** The Start Sync When Device Connects option is selected from the Advanced Options page of devices in the Sync menu; this is also referred to as automatic synchronization. Adding media files to the library won't cause them to automatically be synchronized with mobile devices. AutoPlay is used to enable connected devices such as CDs or cameras to automatically be recognized when they are inserted into the drive. Media Sharing is used to share files over the network.

2. **B.** Windows Media Player can be used to rip the files. The Windows Media Player Audio Lossless format option ensures the music is captured in the best possible audio quality. The Windows Media Player Audio Pro option is used for low storage capacity devices and uses lower bit rates; it can achieve good quality on smaller devices but isn't the best quality possible. While the Windows Media Center can be used to burn music, it doesn't have the capability to rip music.

3. **B.** The error is likely being caused by copy protection (and most of the answers deal with how to remove copy protection). Copy protection can't be removed, but the files can be ripped again with the Copy Protect Music check box not checked. The Copy Protect Music check box causes Digital Rights Management (DRM) to be used when the files are created. Files created in the Windows Media Audio Lossless format (the best quality) can work on other systems.

4. **C.** You can enable media sharing in the Network and Sharing Center to enable other PCs or devices on your network to access media on different computers or devices. Burning all the music to DVDs and copying it would take significantly more time. You can't rip music from a network connection. You can't enable media sharing in the Windows Media Center.

5. **B.** With two tuners, you can watch one channel while viewing another. Since Sally is already able to watch and record one channel, she must have a tuner. An extender device allows you to access digital content from one computer on the extender device in a different room in your home. Two additional tuners would give a total of three tuners, but only one additional tuner is needed. The Windows Media Center allows your system to work like a digital video recorder (DVR), and a third-party DVR is not required.

6. **C.** A Windows Media Center Extender device can be used to view content that is located on a Windows Vista system running Windows Media Center. Since the information is already being recorded on one TV, additional tuners are not needed. A digital video recorder (DVR), is not needed, since the Windows Media Center is already functioning as the DVR.

7. **B.** You must add the Setup Key of the Windows Media Center Extender device to Windows Media Center. This key is used by Windows Media Center to authenticate the extender device. The extender device doesn't need to be configured with a default gateway, since it must be on the same network as the computer running Windows Media Center. Windows Media Center doesn't need to be configured with the IP address of the Windows Media Center Extender device.

8. **C.** AutoPlay can be configured within the Control Panel (by clicking Start | Control Panel | Hardware and Sound and selecting AutoPlay). The Windows Photo Gallery is configured to prompt you for a tag by default, and the files and folders will be named using this tag as part of the name. AutoPlay cannot be enabled in the Windows Media Player or the Windows Photo Gallery. Since the pictures can be copied using Windows Explorer, Device Manager is already configured correctly.

9. **B.** You can import videos directly from digital video cameras with the Windows Movie Maker using the From Digital Video Camera choice in the Import Task menu. It's not necessary to copy the videos to a DVD first. The Windows Media Center doesn't have the ability to import a movie. You can use the Windows Media Player to rip music, but not videos.

10. **A.** You can choose different formats when publishing the movie to your computer. The Windows Media HD 1080p format would provide the highest quality for a high-definition (HD) TV. If you publish a movie to DVD, it launches the Windows DVD Maker, and you can't choose the format in the Windows DVD Maker. The Publish the Movie to e-Mail option creates a relatively small file (at the expense of quality).

Using Vista on Mobile Devices

In this chapter, you will learn about:

- Power consumption
- Windows Mobility Device Center
- Windows Mobile Device Center
- Windows SideShow
- Configuring additional monitors
- Tablet PCs

Windows Vista isn't only installed on desktop computers. It can run on different mobile devices such as laptop computers and Tablet PCs. When running Windows Vista on a mobile computer, you have some different settings and concerns, such as how to handle power.

Additionally, you can have a variety of different mobile devices that connect to your Windows Vista computer. These include personal digital assistant (PDA) devices, and mobile phones that run one of the current versions of Windows Mobile. The built-in Windows Mobility Device Center and the free download of the Windows Mobile Device Center can both be used to manage your mobile devices.

While the following sections are focused on laptops and other mobile computers, many of the settings are also available on desktop PCs. For example, conserving power on desktop computers can save valuable energy dollars and many of the features used to preserve battery life on a mobile PC can be used to conserve energy on desktop PCs.

 EXAM TIP   Objectives for the 70-620, 70-622, and 70-623 exams are included in this chapter.

Managing Power Consumption

One of the great things about mobile computers is that you're able to use them even when they're not plugged in. However, there is a limit to how long they can operate on battery power. If you used a 50-pound battery, your computer would probably last quite a while, though your arms might get tired lugging it around.

The balance that laptop manufacturers seek is having a battery powerful enough to power your computer for a long time, but that is light enough that it doesn't require a crane to move around. There is a constant effort to increase the power of a battery while decreasing its weight.

You also have the ability to modify the power consumption of your mobile computer with a few settings. You can use the Power Options applet in the Control Panel to select and modify power plans. You can access this applet by launching the Control Panel, selecting Mobile PC, and clicking Power Options.

Figure 16-1 shows the Power Options applet. It includes three power plans. For any of these power plans, the system can automatically sense when it is using battery power and when it is plugged in.

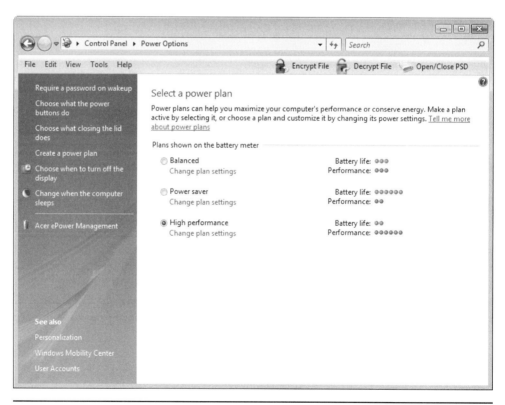

Figure 16-1   Power Options applet

- **Balanced** The goal of this plan is to provide a balance between solid performance and conservation of the battery's power. The following table shows the default settings for the Balanced power plan.

Setting	On battery	While plugged in
Turn off the display after	15 mins	30 mins
Put the computer to sleep after	30 mins	1 hour

- **Power Saver** This plan saves power by reducing system performance. It will allow you to work longer using only battery power. The following table shows the default settings for the Power Saver power plan.

Setting	On Battery	While Plugged In
Turn off the display after	3 mins	15 mins
Put the computer to sleep after	10 mins	20 mins

- **High Performance** This plan will give you maximum performance and responsiveness without trying to conserve power. Battery power doesn't last as long with this plan. The following table shows the default settings for the High Performance power plan.

Setting	On battery	While plugged in
Turn off the display after	30 mins	Never
Put the computer to sleep after	3 hours	5 hours

Turning off the display is simple enough to understand; the display can be turned off via a software signal. However, you can also use the sleep, hibernate, and hybrid power saving modes. The high-level explanations of these modes are

- **Sleep** Puts the computer into a low power state. Can wake up rather quickly.
- **Hibernate** Saves the entire computer environment to hard disk and completely powers down. Takes time to restart, but it is quicker than a cold start and the original environment is completely restored.
- **Hybrid sleep** Saves the computer environment to hard disk and puts the computer into a low power state (does not shut down completely). Consumes less power than sleep mode, but is restored more quickly than hibernate.

 EXAM TIP If you want your systems to be completely powered off when not being used, configure them to hibernate after an idle period.

These modes will be explored in further depth in the following sections.

Put Your Computer to Sleep

Sleep mode is a low-power state where your computer uses very little power. It's enough power to keep the memory refreshed, and have the CPU occasionally check for activity but little else. Once activity is detected (such as a key pressed on the keyboard or mouse movement), the computer wakes up. It will return to full power quickly, and your desktop will appear just as you left it.

 TIP Sleep mode replaces standby mode, which was available in previous versions of Windows. You won't find standby mode on Windows Vista.

You can put your computer to sleep by pressing the sleep button on your system (if it exists). You can also put your computer to sleep by selecting Start and clicking the Power button. Figure 16-2 shows the Power button just to the right of the Start Search text box.

Figure 16-2
Sleep button

Putting your computer to sleep will cause all open files to be saved and put your system in the low-power status. The sleep setting requires video card support. If the sleep option isn't available, upgrading your video card driver may resolve the problem.

Figure 16-3 shows the default settings for the power button, the sleep button, and when you close the lid. You can access this page from the Choose What the Power Buttons Do link on the Power Options applet.

Additionally, the link Choose What Closing the Lid Does from the same Power Options applet launches the same page. Each option includes three choices:

- Do nothing
- Sleep
- Hibernate
- Shut down

Using Hibernate

The hibernate mode allows your computer to save the current computer environment and completely shut down. Unlike in sleep mode, the computer does not use any power at all while hibernated. When the computer is powered back up, the existing environment is completely restored.

For example, a computer could be configured to go into hibernate mode if it is left on for over 60 minutes without any activity. The user may be working on a Microsoft Word document with Word still open. Just prior to hibernating, all the data in RAM is stored on the hard drive. The system then powers completely off.

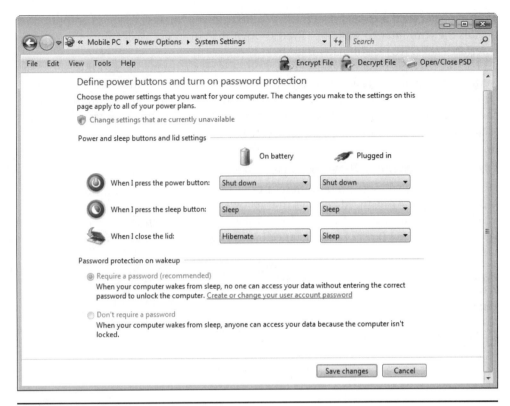

Figure 16-3   Defining power button actions

When the system is turned back on, it recognizes that it was hibernated and the data is read from the hard drive and put back into memory, completely restoring the environment. Microsoft Word would be launched with the document opened.

Using the Hybrid Sleep Mode

Hybrid sleep is a combination of the sleep and hibernate modes. It will save your work to your hard disk and put your PC into a low-power state. Your computer will awaken quicker from hybrid sleep than it will awaken from hibernate mode.

However, hybrid sleep is slower than sleep because data that has been saved to the hard drive needs to be restored to RAM.

Waking a Computer Up

Once your computer is asleep, you can wake it up by moving the mouse, pressing a mouse button, or pressing a key on your keyboard.

Additionally, if your computer has a wake-on-LAN-compliant network card, it can be awakened remotely. Wake-on-LAN is sometimes called remote wake-up. A remote computer can send a special data packet (called a magic packet) to your computer that signals the computer to wake up. Even though the computer is sleeping, the network interface card (NIC) is still listening.

The primary purpose of wake-on-LAN NICs is so that network administrators can perform maintenance tasks remotely. In other words, administrators may have scripts or servers running in the middle of the night that will perform administrative tasks on these computers. The computers can go to sleep, and then when the tasks begin, the wake-on-LAN NIC will wake up the computer.

Using Advanced Power Options

Windows Vista includes several different power options that you can configure individually using the Advanced Settings in the Power Options.

Figure 16-4 shows the Advanced Settings page. Each of the options can be configured individually for the Power Saver, Balanced, and High Performance power plans.

Figure 16-4
Advanced
Settings page
of the Power
Options applet

 EXAM TIP You should be familiar with the capabilities of the advanced settings, such as changing the amount of inactive time to turn off the display or to turn off the hard disks, or even requiring the user to enter a password when waking up the system. Configuring one advanced setting does not affect other advanced settings.

The settings available are listed in the following bullets and a few of the more commonly adjusted settings are explained further in the following sections:

- **Require A Password On Wakeup**   This is enabled by default. This setting is explained in more depth later in this section.

- **Hard Disk**   This can be configured to turn off the hard disk after a period of inactivity. This setting is explained in more depth later in this section.

- **Wireless Adapter Settings**   You can adjust transmitter and receiver power here.

- **Sleep**   This includes Sleep After, Allow Hybrid Sleep, and Hibernate After settings. These settings are explained in more depth later in this section.

- **USB Settings**   This can be used to enable or disable power settings for USB devices.

- **Power Buttons And Lid**   You can manipulate what happens when the lid is closed, the power button is pressed, the sleep button is pressed, and the Start menu power button is clicked with these settings.

- **PCI Express**   You can configure link state power management settings for PCI express cards.

- **Processor Power Management**   Minimum and maximum processor states can be configured for when the system is plugged in or using battery power.

- **Search And Indexing**   You can configure how much time and resources the system will use for searching and indexing when the system is plugged in or using battery power.

- **Display**   You can configure how long the system waits before turning off the display. This setting is explained in more depth later in this section.

- **Windows DreamScene Settings**   If your system is running Windows Vista Ultimate and you have the Windows DreamScene installed, you can specify what the DreamScene will do when the system changes power modes.

- **Multimedia Settings**   You can specify what a system does if the power state changes and it is playing or sharing media.

- **Battery**   You can configure alarm and notification settings when your battery is at low or critical power levels.

Enabling Hibernate and Hybrid Modes

Hibernate and hybrid sleep modes are only available by manipulating the advanced power settings. Figure 16-5 shows the advanced power settings under the Sleep settings.
   In Exercise 16.1, you will enable hybrid sleep and hibernate modes.

Figure 16-5
Configuring
hibernate with
the advanced
power settings

Exercise 16.1: Enabling Hybrid Sleep and Hibernate Modes

1. Click Start | Control Panel. In the Control Panel, click Mobile PC and select Power Options.

2. Select the Change Plan Settings for the Balanced power plan.

3. Click the link to Change Advanced Power Settings.

4. On the Advanced Settings page, scroll down to Sleep and click the + symbol next to Sleep to open it up.

5. Click the + symbol next to Sleep After and view the settings for On Battery and Plugged In. By default this is 30 minutes while on battery, and 60 minutes while plugged in, for the Balanced power plan.

6. Click the + symbol next to Allow Hybrid Sleep and view the settings for On Battery and Plugged In. By default this is off for both the On Battery and Plugged In settings in each of the power plans.

7. Click the + symbol next to Hibernate After and view the settings for On Battery and Plugged In. By default this is set for 1080 minutes for both the On Battery and Plugged In settings in each of the power plans.

8. Click Cancel.

You can access the advanced power settings by clicking the link Change Advanced Power Settings from any of the power plan pages: Power Saver power plan, Balanced power plan, and High Performance power plan.

Requiring a Password on Wakeup

You can configure the system to require a password on wakeup. Figure 16-6 shows the Power Options Advanced Settings that can be configured.

Figure 16-6
Require a password on wakeup

A password is required by default for both On Battery and Plugged In. If you are using the computer at home, you may wish to change it so that a password isn't required. In a work environment, it would be common to have these settings enabled for security purposes.

Turning Off the Display

The display can consume a lot of power, and you can conserve energy by turning it off. Almost all displays in use today (for both desktops and mobile PCs) support the ability to remotely turn them off.

The following table shows the default settings for the display. These settings are available in the Advanced Settings of the Power Options applet and can be changed individually without affecting any other settings.

	On battery	Plugged in
Power Saver	3 mins	15 mins
Balanced	15 mins	30 mins
High Performance	30 mins	Never

The Adaptive Display setting in this section allows your system to be a little more intelligent. If the system senses that you are continuously turning the display back on (by pressing a key at jiggling the mouse) as soon as it's turned off, it adapts and waits longer before turning it off again. This setting can be either On or Off.

Turning Off the Hard Disk

The hard disk takes a lot of power and is automatically configured to be turned off. If you look back at Figure 16-6 in the preceding section ("Requiring a Password on Wakeup"), you'll see where you can access the advanced settings for the hard disk. The default settings are shown in the following table.

	On battery	Plugged in
Power Saver	5 mins	15 mins
Balanced	15 mins	30 mins
High Performance	30 mins	Never

Depending on which power plan you are using, you can see that the hard disk is always turned off after a period of non-use while on battery power. If plugged in and set to high performance, the hard drive is never turned off.

Windows Mobility Center

The Windows Mobility Center is a Vista built-in application you can access to adjust many of your mobile PC settings. It's designed so that you can use it to adjust settings for your system when used in different settings.

For example, you may use the same laptop computer at the office, on the road (or waiting for your flight at the airport), and to give presentations. You can use the Windows Mobility Center to easily adjust settings.

Figure 16-7 shows the Windows Mobility Center on my laptop computer.

 TIP The settings available to you are based on the hardware on your system. You may not see all of the available settings on your computer.

The available settings are

- **Brightness** This can be used to temporarily adjust your display's brightness.
- **Volume** This can be used to adjust the speaker volume (or select Mute).
- **Battery status** You can view the current charge of your battery.
- **External Display** This can be used to connect an additional monitor or use a secondary display with Windows SideShow.
- **Sync Center** You can configure sync partnerships and view synchronization progress here.

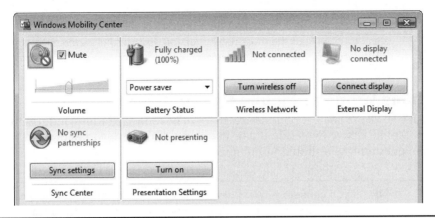

Figure 16-7 Windows Mobility Center

 TIP The Windows Mobile Device Center can be downloaded and installed on Windows Vista to get the most out of synchronization. The Windows Mobile Device Center will be explored further in its own section in this chapter.

- **Presentation Settings** You can adjust different settings used when you give a presentation from your computer.

- **Screen Rotation** You change the orientation from landscape to portrait and back on a Tablet PC screen.

Windows Mobile Device Center

Microsoft has created a new version of the Windows Mobile Device Center (version 6.1) exclusively for Windows Vista that replaces Microsoft ActiveSync, available in previous editions of Windows. Microsoft ActiveSync will not install on Windows Vista, and the Windows Mobile Device Center v6.1 is only supported on Windows Vista.

The Windows Mobile Device Center is used to synchronize mobile devices with Windows Vista. You can use it to connect to mobile devices such as PDAs, MP3 players, and cameras.

For example, you can synchronize

- **Data files** This includes e-mail, calendars, contacts, tasks, favorites, and files.

- **Photo files** Picture management within the Mobile Device Center can detect new photos on your mobile device and import them to the Windows Vista Photo Gallery.

- **Media files** The Windows Media Player can synchronize and shuffle music files on your mobile device.

TIP For more information on the Windows Mobile Device Center, including a link to download the most recent version, visit this link: www.microsoft.com/windowsmobile/devicecenter.mspx.

Installing Windows Mobile Device Center

If you (or your clients) have mobile devices that will be connected with Windows Vista, the Window Mobile Device Center should be installed. Of course, if you want to understand the exam questions, you should install it too.

TIP If you connect wireless devices to your system running Windows Vista, it's possible that the Windows Mobile Device Center has already been downloaded via Windows Update and installed on your system.

In Exercise 16.2, you will install the Windows Mobile Device Center. You must first download the Windows Mobile Device Center before beginning this lab.

Exercise 16.2: Installing the Windows Mobile Device Center

1. Press the WINDOWS-E keys to launch Windows Explorer.

2. Browse to the location where you downloaded the Windows Mobile Device Center. Double-click the downloaded file. If the User Account Control dialog box appears, click Continue. After a couple minutes, the installation will complete.

3. Launch the Windows Mobile Device Center by clicking Start | All Programs and selecting Windows Mobile Device Center.

4. On the Microsoft License Terms page, review the information and click Accept. The Windows Mobile Device Center will launch. Hover over Mobile Device Settings to access Connection Settings as shown in Figure 16-8.

TIP Note that a device isn't currently connected, as shown with the Not Connected message in the lower-left corner. If you connected a mobile device such as a PDA, it would connect and this would be displayed in this window.

5. Click Connection Settings. The Connection settings dialog box will appear as shown in Figure 16-9. These settings will be explored in the next section.

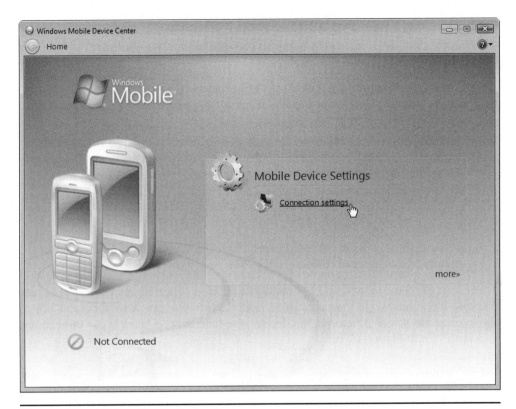

Figure 16-8 Windows Mobile Device Center

Figure 16-9
Windows Mobile
Device Center
Connection
Settings

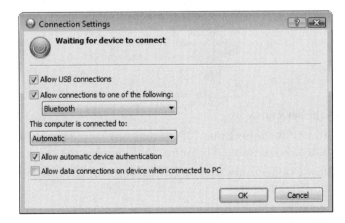

Connecting Your Mobile Device to Vista

The Windows Mobile Device Center supports connecting your mobile devices to Windows Vista using multiple methods, including

- **Bluetooth** Bluetooth is a wireless technology used to connect devices without cables. If your PC and your mobile device are both Bluetooth enabled, you can use Bluetooth as your connection.

- **USB cables** Many devices come with USB cables that connect to the device and the PC. The PC connection is a standard USB connection, but the device side of the USB cable may be specific to the device.

- **Infrared** Infrared (IR) signals use beams of light to transfer data between the device and your PC. IR signals require a clear line of sight between the infrared ports to make the connection.

- **Device-specific cradle** Some devices have cradles with either USB cables or other types of cables to connect to the PC.

You can pick and choose which connections are supported on your system. For example, if you only want to support Bluetooth devices, you can select the check box to allow connections with Bluetooth, but deselect the check box to Allow USB Connections. This is shown in Figure 16-10.

Figure 16-10
Configuring
Windows Mobile
Device Center
to only allow
Bluetooth
connections

All of the selections are

- **Allow USB connections** If selected, any device using a USB connection can connect. To prevent USB connections, deselect the check box.

- **Allow Connections To One Of The Following** This section gives you the following choices:

  - **COM3** COM3 is a serial port typically using a DB9 connector. Many older mobile devices used this serial port, though it has largely been replaced with the USB connection. If the device needs to connect to the serial port, you can select it here.

  - **Bluetooth** Bluetooth is a common wireless protocol that can be used to connect Bluetooth-enabled devices with your computer.

- **Infrared (IR) port**   If your PC has an IR port, you can select it.
- **DMA**   The DMA transport was used by applications developed with Visual Studio 2005 to connect to mobile devices and is included for backward compatibility.

 TIP   Your system may not show all the choices if it doesn't have the supporting hardware. For example, if you don't have an IR port, you won't see an infrared (IR) port connection choice.

- **This Computer Is Connected To**   This allows you to choose the type of network that the PC is connected to. The choices are
  - **Automatic**   The system will automatically determine the connection.
  - **Work Network**   Indicates that the computer is connected within a LAN.
  - **Internet**   Indicates that the computer has a direct connection to the Internet.
- **Use Automatic Device Authentication**   This can be enabled to require a user to authenticate when the device is connected. Authentication can be done via a PIN or a certificate.
- **Allow Data Connections On Device When Connected To PC**   When selected, this allows the device to connect to the network through the PC, effectively giving it multiple connections. It is only supported on Windows Mobile 6 devices.

Windows Mobile   Windows Mobile is a compact operating system designed for mobile devices such as Smartphones, Pocket PCs, and other personal digital assistant (PDA) devices.

Windows Mobile originally appeared as Pocket PC 2000 and has been upgraded several times:

- Pocket PC 2002
- Windows Mobile 2003
- Windows Mobile 2003 SE
- Windows Mobile 5.0
- Windows Mobile 6
- Windows Mobile 6.1

Windows Mobile allows a mobile device to run compact customized versions of many desktop applications. This allows mobile users to access e-mail and many different file types while on the road. Office Mobil is a suite of mobile versions of Microsoft Office (including Word, Excel, and PowerPoint).

Windows Mobile 7.0 is expected to be released in 2009.

Synchronizing Devices

Data is synchronized between the PC and the mobile device by creating partnerships. When you first connect your device, you will be prompted to create a synchronization partnership. After setting up the partnership, you can synchronize data between the device and your PC.

 TIP It is possible to connect a device without creating a partnership. You would do this if you don't plan on connecting the device on a regular basis and don't plan on synchronizing with the computer. This connection will allow you to browse files on the device, as well as import files from the device.

When setting up partnerships, you can pick and choose what types of data you want to synchronize. For example, you may choose to synchronize e-mail files, or music files, or both.

After setting up the partnership, you are able to change the content you want to synchronize at any time from the Windows Mobile Device Center.

Let me state the obvious here. In addition to configuring the computer to accept and transfer files, you must also configure the mobile device to accept and transfer files. This process is largely automated when the device is connected. However, if the device isn't connected, you can't just start sending data to it.

 EXAM TIP You must configure the mobile device to accept file transfers before you can begin sending data to the device.

Using Windows SideShow

Windows SideShow is cool new technology available in Windows Vista that enables data to be displayed on auxiliary devices. For example, you could have a display embedded on the outside of a laptop lid, or a mobile phone. Data can be viewed on the auxiliary device even when Vista is on, off, or in sleep mode.

SideShow devices are designed so that they use very little power, and many can run for hundreds of hours on battery power. You can use SideShow displays to view e-mail, a calendar, and other Outlook data for common productivity purposes. You can also display gadgets on SideShow, to display things like top news stories, or RSS feeds.

 EXAM TIP You can configure the Windows SideShow to show e-mail, a calendar, contacts, and other types of gadgets. When configured, the data will be displayed on the SideShow device even when the Vista computer is asleep.

Figure 16-11 shows the Windows SideShow applet. You can access this by clicking Start | Control Panel | Hardware and Sound and selecting Windows SideShow.

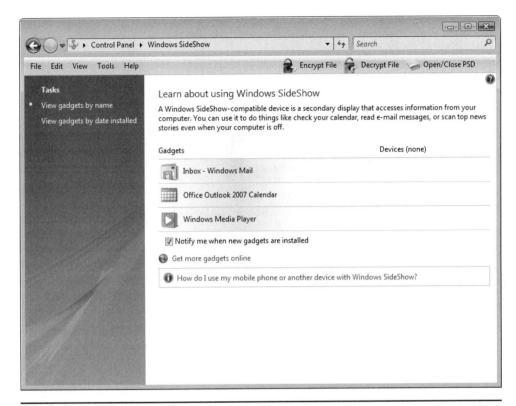

Figure 16-11 Windows SideShow

Notice in the figure that there are no devices connected. Windows SideShow–compatible devices will have a Windows SideShow logo and will come with information on how to connect and configure the device for Windows Vista.

Configuring Additional Monitors

One of the challenges of laptops is that the display is very frequently smaller than a regular desktop display. While this works great while on the road, in the office you may want to have the use of a larger display.

Docking ports are often used. A docking port may include connections to a larger monitor, a larger keyboard, and a faster NIC. When you plug your laptop into the docking port, your computer will automatically take advantage of these additional devices (after some initial configuration).

You can also simply connect an additional monitor to your system as long as your laptop has the connector. When you connect the additional monitor, a display similar to Figure 16-12 will appear.

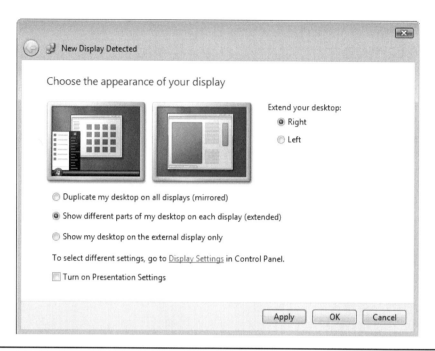

Figure 16-12   Choosing an additional monitor

This choice gives you the following choices:

- **Duplicate My Desktop On All Displays (Mirrored)**   This is commonly used when doing presentations. You can show PowerPoint presentations and do demonstrations, and the audience will see everything you do.
- **Show Different Parts Of my Desktop On Each Display (extended)**   When you extend the display, you can have different data shown on the different displays.

 EXAM TIP   If you want to be able to use both monitors (the laptop display and an external monitor), configure the display to be extended. This allows you to drag windows from one display to another.

- **Show My Desktop On The External Display Only**   Only the external display will be used. The laptop display will not be used. This would be commonly used with docking ports.

You can also change the configuration of your monitor later. Figure 16-13 shows the display settings. You can access this page by right-clicking the desktop, selecting Properties, and then clicking Display Settings.

Figure 16-13
Extending
the desktop

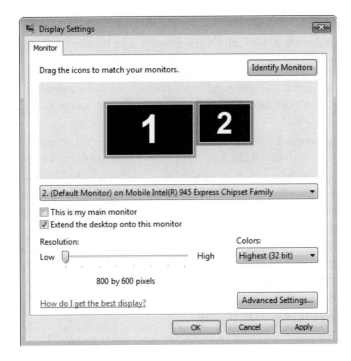

You have two main selections on this page that are important:

- **This Is My Main Monitor**   Dialog boxes and pop-up windows will appear on this monitor.
- **Extend The Desktop Onto This Monitor**   Selecting this will allow you to drag windows from one display to another.

Using Tablet PC

A Tablet PC is a cross between a PDA and a laptop computer. Similar to PDAs, Tablet PCs have handwriting capabilities where users can use a stylus pen to actually write notes.

The Tablet PC has a full screen, but instead of a keyboard and a mouse, input is normally done through the use of the stylus pen. Some Tablet PCs either include a keyboard or can use an additional keyboard, but they all support the stylus for direct input.

NOTE   Tablet PCs were supported by Microsoft's Windows XP Tablet PC edition (and are currently supported by Windows Vista Tablet PC editions), but they've been around a lot longer. The first Tablet PC (called the GRiDPad) was introduced in 1989.

Tablet PC Models

Tablet PCs come in basically three models. The primary difference in each is related to the keyboard.

- **Slate**   A slate Tablet PC is a Tablet PC without a dedicated keyboard. Slates often support a keyboard connection via wireless or USB, but they come without a keyboard.

   The primary purpose of the slate is to be carried around. Taking away the weight and bulkiness of the keyboard adds to the mobility of the slate.

- **Convertible**   A convertible includes an attached keyboard and looks very similar to a conventional laptop computer. The screen can be rotated and lay flat over the keyboard to support data entry with just the stylus. Convertibles are usually larger and heavier than slates.

- **Hybrid**   A hybrid includes an attached keyboard just as a convertible does. The screen can be rotated and lay flat over the keyboard. Additionally, the keyboard can be completely detached.

Handwriting Analysis

One of the most challenging aspects of successfully using the Tablet PC is handwriting analysis. Handwriting analysis allows the system to understand the words when you write them. If you're like me, you don't write in a Times Roman font. Instead, each of us writes a little bit differently.

When you first get a Tablet PC, you can teach it how to interpret your handwriting by providing handwriting samples. You can provide samples using the handwriting personalization tool. Figure 16-14 shows the handwriting personalization tool.

Notice that you can use the handwriting personalization tool in two ways:

- **Target Specific Recognition Errors**   If you find that the Tablet PC is frequently not recognizing specific words or characters, you can use this selection to provide specific handwriting samples.

- **Teach The Recognizer Your Handwriting Style**   This option will allow you to provide a more extensive set of handwriting samples.

 EXAM TIP   You can use the handwriting personalization tool to improve the accuracy of handwriting analysis. You can target specific recognition errors, or provide a large volume of samples to teach the recognizer your handwriting style.

You can also opt in to use the automatic learning for personalization. The recognizer gathers information about the words you use and how you write them to improve its ability to interpret your writing. This is not enabled by default and is governed by a privacy statement.

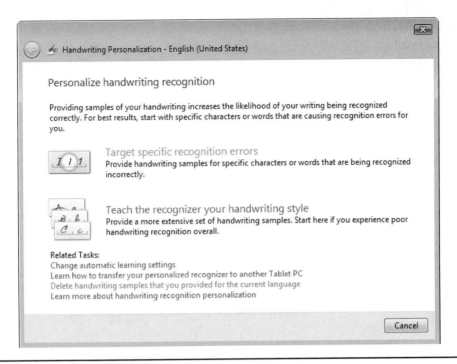

Figure 16-14 Handwriting personalization tool

Calibrating Your Tablet PC

It's possible for the Tablet stylus and screen to become misaligned. In other words, your stylus writes a little off where it hits the screen. This can be a little frustrating when you're trying do things like cross a *t* or dot an *i*. The cross and the dot are a little off.

In addition to your handwriting being a little off, you may find that the stylus doesn't seem to cause the screen to respond where you tap. You may try to tap a button, but instead, the screen interprets the tap as a little away from the button.

The simple solution is to calibrate the Tablet PC. Figure 16-15 shows the Calibrate button. Using your Tablet PC, you can select this button to begin the calibration process.

 EXAM TIP Calibrate your Tablet PC if the display doesn't respond to the specific areas where you tap the screen.

You can access this screen through the Control Panel. Select Mobile PC and click Tablet PC Settings. Once your system is calibrated, your screen will respond to where the stylus is tapped on it.

Figure 16-15
Calibrate button
on the Tablet PC

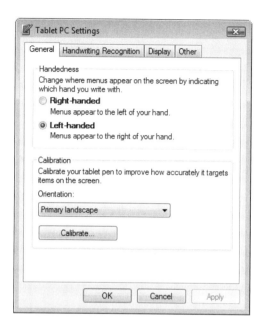

Chapter Review

In this chapter you learned about using mobile devices with Windows Vista. One of the primary concerns with mobile devices such as laptops is conserving power, and you learned about using the different sleep modes (including sleep, hibernate, and hybrid sleep). You also learned about several of the advanced settings, such as turning off the display and the disk, and forcing the use of the password when the system wakes up.

The Windows Mobility Center is built into Windows Vista and enables you to interact with many mobile devices. The Windows Mobile Device Center is an upgrade only available in Windows Vista and provides a lot more capabilities associated with Windows Mobile devices. Once it is configured, you can transfer data between your computer and your mobile device.

Windows SideShow is a technology that allows you to connect smaller displays (including mobile phones) and display data from gadgets such as e-mail, calendars, and contact information, even if the computer is asleep.

If you have multiple displays attached to your laptop, you can configure them to be a mirror display (such as when you're doing a presentation), or to extend your desktop. When multiple monitors are configured to extend your desktop, you can drag windows from one display to another.

Tablet PCs are devices that will accept input just as if you were writing with a pen. They use a stylus to write on the screen. If your Tablet PC is not recognizing your handwriting, you can teach it to with the handwriting personalization tool. If the stylus begins writing off the mark of where it's touching the screen, you can calibrate the Tablet PC.

Additional Study

Self Study Exercises

Use these additional exercises to challenge yourself.

- Put your system to sleep.

- Configure your system to use a password when it wakes up.

- Access the Windows Mobile Device Center page and review the different devices supported: www.microsoft.com/windowsmobile/devicecenter.mspx.

- Read about mobile devices supported by Windows products by accessing the Windows Mobility page here: www.microsoft.com/windows/products/winfamily /mobility/default.mspx.

- Read about Tablet PC support on Windows Vista from this page: www.microsoft .com/windows/products/windowsvista/features/details/tabletpc.mspx.

Summary of What You Need to Know

70-620

When preparing for the 70-620 exam, pay particular attention to the following topics covered in this chapter:

- **Power Management**   You should know how to manipulate power settings for a laptop. This includes the basic plans (Balanced, Power Saver, and High Performance), and the advanced settings.

- **Windows Mobile Device Center**   You should be familiar with the basic settings of this. Of course, this means you must download and install it.

- **Windows SideShow**   You should understand what SideShow is and how it differs from Windows Sidebar.

- **External displays**   You should know the capabilities available when an external display is added.

- **Tablet PCs**   You should understand the basic capabilities and purpose of Tablet PCs, including how users can teach them how to understand their handwriting, as well as how to calibrate the Tablet PC.

70-622

- When preparing for the 70-622 exam, pay particular attention to the Power Management topic. You should know how to manipulate power settings for a laptop. This includes the basic plans (Balanced, Power Saver, and High Performance).

70-623

When preparing for the 70-623 exam, pay particular attention to the following topics covered in this chapter:

- **Windows Mobile Device Center** You should be familiar with the basic settings of this. Of course, this means you must download and install it.

- **Mobile devices** You should be familiar with basic capabilities of mobile devices, including how they connect and the kind of data that can be transferred.

Questions

70-620

1. You want to configure the power settings of a Windows Vista computer so that the display turns off after 15 minutes of idle activity. What should you configure?

    A. The Power Saver power plan

    B. The Balanced power plan

    C. The High Performance power plan

    D. The advanced settings of the active power plan

2. Sally's laptop computer is configured to enter the hibernate mode after being inactive for 60 minutes. When Sally wakes the computer, it allows her access to her desktop without requiring her to log on. She wants to ensure her computer prompts her for a password. What should she do?

    A. Disable hibernate mode.

    B. Configure the computer to require a password when recovering from sleep mode.

    C. Configure the computer to require a password when recovering from hibernate mode.

    D. Configure the computer to use the Balanced power plan.

3. You have installed the Windows Mobile Device Center on your system, and you want to configure it to connect with your Bluetooth-enabled device. You want to ensure that only Bluetooth connections are enabled. What should you do? Choose all that apply.

    A. Clear the check box to Allow USB Connections.

    B. Set the check box to Allow USB Connections.

    C. Clear the check box to Allow Bluetooth Connections.

    D. Set the check box to Allow Bluetooth Connections.

    E. Select the Allow Bluetooth Connections option.

    F. Set the check box to Allow Connections to One of the Following.

    G. Clear the check box to Allow Connections to One of the Following.

4. You've purchased a mobile computer that has a secondary display built into the lid. You want to display gadgets on this display. What should you do?

 A. Boot the secondary display and install the gadgets.

 B. Configure the gadgets to be displayed on the Windows Sidebar.

 C. Configure the gadgets to be displayed on Windows SideShow.

 D. Extend the desktop to the secondary display.

5. Sally has connected an external monitor to her computer. She can see the same thing on the external monitor as she can see on her laptop display. She wants to be able to drag windows from one display to another. What should she do?

 A. Configure the display to be mirrored.

 B. Change the display to be extended.

 C. Enable the Sidebar.

 D. Enable Windows SideShow.

6. Joe is using a Tablet PC with Windows Vista installed. He finds that it regularly interprets his *a* as an *e*, and several words are also interpreted incorrectly. He wants better performance from the Tablet PC. What should he do?

 A. Calibrate the Tablet PC.

 B. Use the handwriting recognition personalization tool.

 C. Enable the Times Roman font interpreter.

 D. Use the keyboard instead of the stylus.

7. Joe is using a Tablet PC with Windows Vista installed. He finds that when he taps the display with his stylus, the tap is frequently recognized in a different place than where he tapped. He wants to ensure that the Tablet PC responds where he taps. What should he do?

 A. Calibrate the Tablet PC.

 B. Use the handwriting recognition personalization tool.

 C. Use his finger instead of the stylus.

 D. Replace the stylus with a mouse.

70-622

1. Users in your network are issued laptops that they use at work and on the road. While using these laptops at work, you want to ensure they are powered off if they are idle for a period of more than 60 minutes. What should be enabled?

 A. Standby mode

 B. Sleep mode

 C. Hibernate mode

 D. Screen savers

2. You are asked to research a purchase of several computers. The administrators want to ensure that the computers purchased can be awakened remotely from a low power state. What should be included in the computer?

   A. NICs that can hibernate

   B. NICs with wake-on-LAN capability

   C. NICs that can sleep

   D. CPUs with wake-on-LAN capability

70-623

1. Sally is running Windows Vista on her computer. She recently purchased a Windows-compatible PDA, but she is unable to use her Windows Vista computer to synchronize her e-mail. What should she do?

   A. Download and install Windows Mobile Device Center.

   B. Download and install ActiveSync.

   C. Enable Bluetooth on her Windows Vista system.

   D. Enable the IR connection on her Windows Vista system.

2. Joe is running Windows Vista on his system and has recently purchased a new PocketPC mobile device. He tried to send some data to the device using his system's IR port, but was unsuccessful. What should be done?

   A. Configure the device to accept the file transfer.

   B. Configure the USB port to send the data.

   C. Configure Bluetooth on the device.

   D. Move the device closer to the IR port.

Answers

70-620

1. **D.** You can configure advanced settings of any power plan to manipulate settings such as the display, the hard drive, and whether or not a password is required on wake-up. The basic settings of the individual power plans don't allow you to configure the display settings without accessing the advanced settings, and you must manipulate the advanced settings of the plan that is currently active.

2. **B.** The Require a Password When Recovering from Sleep Mode advanced setting in the Power Options applet can be used to require a password when awakening from any sleep (including hibernate) . It's not necessary to disable hibernate mode. There isn't a setting to require a password when recovering from hibernate mode. Just configuring the computer to use the Balanced power

plan doesn't guarantee that the advanced setting is configured to require the use of passwords when the system wakes up.

3. **A, E, F.** You should clear the check box to Allow USB Connections, set the check box to Allow Connections to One of the Following, and select Allow Bluetooth Connections. If the check box to Allow USB Connections is set, USB connections will be allowed. There is no check box for Allow Bluetooth Connections. The check box to Allow Connections to One of the Following must be checked; if cleared, Allow Bluetooth Connections can't be selected.

4. **C.** You can configure many gadgets to be displayed on Windows SideShow; for example, you can configure e-mail, calendar, and contact gadgets to be displayed on Windows SideShow. A secondary display can't be booted but can only be configured to display gadgets. The Windows Sidebar is displayed on the side of the desktop, not on secondary displays. You can extend your desktop to second monitors, but a secondary display built into the lid wouldn't be a full monitor but instead is designed specifically for Windows SideShow.

5. **B.** If the display is extended, you can drag windows from one display to another. If it is mirrored, the same thing appears on both displays. The Sidebar displays gadgets on the side of the desktop but doesn't allow you to drag Windows from one display to another. The Windows SideShow is a small external display used to display things such as e-mail and the calendar in a gadget on the external display.

6. **B.** The handwriting recognition personalization tool can be used to increase the likelihood of writing being correctly recognized by the Tablet PC. You would calibrate the Tablet PC if the display doesn't respond where the stylus is used. There's no such thing as a Times Roman font interpreter. The primary benefit of the Tablet PC is the ability to use the stylus to write; giving up the stylus for the keyboard isn't a good option.

7. **A.** You can calibrate the Tablet PC to ensure that the display responds where it is tapped. The handwriting recognition personalization tool can be used to improve recognition of your handwriting. A Tablet PC will not respond to touches with a finger, and Tablet PCs aren't configured to use a mouse.

70-622

1. **C.** Computers that are put into hibernate mode will store all their data from memory onto the hard disk and will then be completely powered off. Standby mode is replaced with sleep mode in Windows Vista. Sleep mode puts the system into a low power state. Screen savers will not power a system off.

2. **B.** The computers should have network interface cards (NICs) that are wake-on-LAN compliant so that they can be awakened when the system is sleeping or hibernating. NICs themselves can't hibernate or sleep, only systems. CPUs don't have a wake-on-LAN capability.

70-623

1. **A.** The Windows Mobile Device Center can be used to synchronize e-mail, contacts, and other data on Windows Vista. ActiveSync does not work on Windows Vista and is replaced by the Windows Mobile Device Center. The question doesn't specify what type of connection the mobile device uses, so simply enabling Bluetooth or Infrared (IR) wouldn't necessarily resolve the problem.

2. **A.** The mobile device must be configured to accept the file transfer before the data will be accepted. If the transfer is using infrared (IR), there is no need to configure the USB port or Bluetooth. Moving the device closer to the IR port won't cause the data to be accepted if the device hasn't been configured to accept the data.

About the CD

The CD-ROM included with this book comes complete with MasterExam, the electronic version of the book, and Session #1 of LearnKey's on-line training. The software is easy to install on any Windows 2000/XP/Vista computer and must be installed to access the MasterExam feature. You may, however, browse the electronic book directly from the CD without installation. To register for LearnKey's online training and a second bonus MasterExam, simply click the Online Training link on the Main Page and follow the directions to the free online registration.

System Requirements

Software requires Windows 2000 or higher, and Internet Explorer 6.0 or above, and 20MB of hard disk space for full installation. The Electronic book requires Adobe Reader. To access the Online Training from LearnKey you must have Windows Media Player 9 or higher and Adobe Flash Player 9 or higher.

LearnKey Online Training

The **LearnKey Online Training** link will allow you to access online training from Osborne.Onlineexpert.com. The first session of this course is provided at no charge. Additional sessions for this course and other courses may be purchased directly from www.LearnKey.com or by calling 800-865-0165.

The first time that you run the training, you will be required to register with the online product. Follow the instructions for a first-time user. Please make sure to use a valid e-mail address.

Installing and Running MasterExam

If your computer CD-ROM drive is configured to auto run, the CD-ROM will automatically start up upon inserting the disk. From the opening screen you may install MasterExam by pressing the MasterExam button. This will begin the installation process and create a program group named "LearnKey." To run MasterExam use Start | All Programs | LearnKey | MasterExam. If the auto run feature did not launch your CD, browse to the CD and click on the LaunchTraining.exe icon.

MasterExam

MasterExam provides you with a simulation of the actual exam. The number of questions, the type of questions, and the time allowed are intended to be an accurate representation of the exam environment. You have the option to take an open book exam, including hints, references, and answers; a closed book exam; or the timed MasterExam simulation.

When you launch MasterExam, a digital clock display will appear in the bottom right-hand corner of your screen. The clock will continue to count down to zero unless you choose to end the exam before the time expires.

Electronic Book

The entire contents of the Study Guide are provided in PDF. Adobe Reader has been included on the CD.

Help

A help file is provided through the help button on the main page in the lower left hand corner. Individual help features are also available through MasterExam and LearnKey's Online Training.

Removing Installation(s)

MasterExam is installed to your hard drive. For best results removing programs use the Start | All Programs | LearnKey | Uninstall option to remove MasterExam.

Technical Support

For questions regarding the technical content of the electronic book or MasterExam, please visit www.mhprofessional.com or email customer.service@mcgraw-hill.com. For customers outside the 50 United States, email international_cs@mcgraw-hill.com.

LearnKey Technical Support

For technical problems with the software (installation, operation, removing installations), and for questions regarding LearnKey Online Training content, please visit www.learnkey .com, email techsupport@learnkey.com, or call toll free at 800-482-8244.

Exam 70-620: What You Need to Know to Pass

70-620 TS: Windows Vista, Configuring

Introduction

The 70-620 exam covers the basics of installing and configuring Windows Vista. As a Technical Specialist (TS) exam it is a little easier than the IT Professional (Pro) exams.

You're expected to have at least one year of experience in the IT field (though that isn't a requirement), and it's expected that you provide support to end users in a wide range of environments, including retail stores and midsize or enterprise environments. Your experience should include resolving issues related to network connectivity, desktop operating systems (especially Windows Vista), security, and applications.

It's expected that you would take the 70-620 exam first (before the 70-622 or 70-623), but that isn't a requirement.

Pick a Date

I suggest you pick a date 60 to 90 days from now as your target to take the 70-620 exam. You may be ready sooner, and you can adjust your date, or you may not be ready in time and you can change it, but pick a date. Picking a date can be a great motivator in helping you get ready.

Consider actually registering for the test. If you're registered, it adds a layer of commitment. You can always reschedule the test later if a significant life event comes up.

When teaching some certification courses in the college classroom, I've had students register for a test on the first night of a class. They pick a date about a week after the course ends, and we walk down to the test center en masse as everyone registers. The percentage of students taking and passing these tests has been over 70 percent.

In contrast, I've taught the same course to other students and provided encouragement to take and pass the test, but didn't have them register on the first night of class. Following up three months later (at the end of a six-month track), I've found that only 10–20 percent of the students had taken and passed the test.

This concept isn't unique to test taking. For any goal you are pursuing, you are much more likely to achieve it by writing it down. Goals not written down become forgotten daydreams.

Pick a date to take the 70-620 exam. Write it down here: _____.

What You Can Expect

The types of test questions you can expect on the 70-620 exam are primarily multiple-choice questions. You may also see a mix of simulation exams (where you need to accomplish a task), and one or two "point-and-click" or "drag-and-drop" questions, which are really just testing whether you're familiar with the interfaces.

For the multiple-choice questions, pay attention to the wording. Sometimes you're required to pick more than one choice, such as "Select two" or "Select all that apply."

Simulation exam questions are a great new addition to certification exams. They prevent someone from just memorizing test questions and answers. If you want to prepare for these types of questions, do all the exercises in the book. These exercises are designed to convert your "book knowledge" into the ability to actually do tasks.

One good thing about simulations is that it takes a lot of programming to make the simulation complex. Because of this, expect simulations on the exams to be straightforward, with a limited number of steps.

The 70-620 exam is designed for professionals who are either working in or pursuing careers in the IT field providing end-user support for Windows Vista. It can be used as one of the exams for the following certifications:

- **MCITP: Enterprise Support Technician**   After the 70-620, take the 70-622 exam to earn this certification. See Appendix C for more details on the 70-622 exam.

- **MCITP: Consumer Support Technician**   After the 70-620, take the 70-623 exam to earn this certification. See Appendix D for more details on the 70-623 exam.

- **MCITP: Enterprise Administrator**   This requires passing several exams in addition to the 70-620 exam. The other exams for the MCITP: Enterprise Administrator are not covered in this book.

The number of questions on the test is not published by Microsoft and sometimes changes from one test taker to another. A score of 700 is required to pass. You typically have about two hours to complete about 50 questions.

Some tests include beta test questions. The test developers are testing the question before it goes live. Beta test questions don't count for or against you, and you are given extra time to answer them. You could leave them blank, and it wouldn't impact your score at all. Unfortunately, you never know if a question is live or beta, so you have to answer them all.

What's Expected of You

Someone who has successfully passed this test is expected to be able to accomplish tasks in the following categories:

- Installing and upgrading Windows Vista
- Configuring and troubleshooting post-installation system settings
- Configuring Windows security features
- Configuring network connectivity
- Configuring applications included with Windows Vista
- Maintaining and optimizing systems that run Windows Vista
- Configuring and troubleshooting mobile computing

 EXAM TIP As a reminder, test objectives are listed at the beginning of the book with an objectives map showing which chapter contains the appropriate information. However, remember that these objectives might change. The legalese on Microsoft's site says, "This preparation guide is subject to change at any time without prior notice and at Microsoft's sole discretion." Before taking the test, take a look on Microsoft's web site for the current objectives.

Chapters Covering 70-620 Topics

The following list identifies chapters within this book that include objectives for the 70-620 exam with a list of specific topics where you should focus your studies. Notice that several chapters (Chapter 2, Chapter 8, and Chapter 10) do not have any topics for the 70-620 exam. You can skip these chapters when focusing on this exam.

Chapter 1: Installing and Upgrading Windows Vista
Make sure you understand the following concepts:

- Windows Vista Editions and features (ensure you know the differences)
- Windows Vista hardware requirements
- Upgrade paths to Windows Vista, upgrade procedures, and use of the Windows Vista Upgrade Advisor
- Tools available to migrate user data and settings (Windows Easy Transfer Tool and USMT)
- Dual-boot and multiboot configurations and requirements

Chapter 2: Automating the Installation of Windows Vista
This chapter does not include any topics for the 70-620 exam.

Chapter 3: Configuring the Vista Environment

Pay particular attention to the following topics covered in this chapter:

- **Device Manager**   You should understand the meaning of different icons displayed in the Device Manager. You should also know how to use the Device Manager to enable or disable a device.

- **Windows Error Reporting**   Know the purpose of and how to configure WER for different users.

- **Aero**   Make sure you know the requirements for Aero, and how to enable and disable it.

- **ReadyBoost**   You should understand the basic features and purpose of ReadyBoost.

- **Sidebar**   Understand how the Sidebar works and how to access shortcuts trapped under it.

Chapter 4: Configuring Disks

Pay particular attention to the following topics covered in this chapter:

- **Previous Versions**   Make sure you understand how Previous Versions can be used to protect data.

- **BitLocker**   You should understand the basic purpose and use of BitLocker.

Chapter 5: Configuring Network Connectivity

Pay particular attention to the following topics covered in this chapter:

- **Networking Basics**   You should understand the basics of networking. This includes understanding the network ID, how to calculate it, and why it's important. Additionally, much of the section "Networking Basics" will be a foundation for wireless topics covered in Chapter 6.

- **IPv6**   You should be able to identify an IPv6 address and know some basics about it.

- **Public and Private**   You should know the differences between setting a network connection to public or private and how it affects network discovery.

- **Internet connectivity**   You should have an understanding of how to troubleshoot Internet connectivity issues, including how to use the Diagnose and Repair feature within the Network and Sharing Center.

Chapter 6: Configuring Wireless Connectivity

Make sure you understand both basic networking and wireless networking. Pay particular attention to the following topics covered in this chapter:

- **SSID and SSID broadcasting**   You should know what the SSID is used for, what's affected if SSID broadcasting is disabled, and how to automatically connect to a network where SSID broadcasting is disabled.

- **Public and Private**   You should know the difference between setting a wireless network connection to public or private and how it affects network discovery.

- **Network Bridge**   You should understand what a network bridge is and how to configure Windows Vista as a network bridge.

- **Profile Types**   You should know how to configure a network connection so that it can be used by all users, or by only a single user.

Chapter 7: Configuring Network Access

Pay particular attention to the following topics:

- **Remote Assistance**   Know how to connect and control Remote Assistance sessions. This includes knowing that it must be enabled in the system properties and the firewall, the invitation expiration times can be modified, and the screen can be hidden from the helper by clicking the Pause button.

- **Remote Desktop**   Know the purpose and use of Remote Desktop and how to configure it. This includes knowing that it must be enabled in the system properties and the firewall. You should also be familiar with all the options of Remote Desktop, such as how to bring local resources to your remote session and enable all features in the remote session.

- **Windows Firewall**   You should be familiar with the basic Windows Firewall, its capabilities and purpose. This includes enabling and configuring it in a public or private area (enabling or disabling Block All Connections), and enabling exceptions based on ports or programs.

Chapter 8: Accessing Resources

This chapter does not include any topics for the 70-620 exam.

Chapter 9: Configuring Local Security

Pay particular attention to the following topics covered in this chapter:

- **User accounts**   You should know the difference between a standard user and an administrator account. Ideally, the standard user account will be used for all normal activity and the administrator account would rarely be used to log on. Instead, the administrator account would only be used when performing administrative actions after providing credentials through UAC.

- **Administrator account**   You should be aware of what actions require user privileges (such as installing applications, changing security settings, and creating accounts).

- **Password-Protected accounts**   Know how to protect accounts by ensuring they have passwords applied. Be able to verify an account is password protected by viewing it in the Manage Accounts applet within Control Panel.

- **User Account Control (UAC)**   You should know how to enable and disable UAC and what it does when it is enabled. You should also be familiar with how the behavior can be modified using the local security policy settings.

- **Parental Controls**   You should know what parental controls are and the different ways they can be used to restrict a standard user's actions. You should also be familiar with the content logged in the Parental Controls Activity Report.

Chapter 10: Managing Windows Vista in a Domain

This chapter does not include any topics for the 70-620 exam.

Chapter 11: Using Maintenance and Diagnostic Tools

Pay particular attention to the following topics covered in this chapter:

- **Event Viewer**   You should have a basic understanding of what events are logged and where they are logged. This includes knowing the logs that are available (application, system, setup, and security logs) and how to create custom views.

- **Scheduled Tasks**   You should be familiar with attaching tasks to events.

- **Windows Update**   Know the purpose of Windows Updates, how to configure Windows Updates, how to verify updates are installed, how to remove them, and how to hide them.

Chapter 12: Using Disaster Recovery Tools

Pay particular attention to the following topics covered in this chapter:

- **System recovery tools**   This includes the Windows Complete PC Backup and Restore, and System Restore tools.

- **Data backup tools**   This includes the Backup and Restore Center and the Backup Status and Configuration tool.

Chapter 13: Configuring Internet Applications

Pay particular attention to the following topics covered in this chapter:

- **Internet Explorer**   Features and capabilities such as: how to use it, how to print, managing add-ons, Pop-up Blocker, Protected Mode, and RSS feeds.

- **Windows Defender**   Features and capabilities such as: how to run a scan, how to update Windows Defender definitions, how to restore applications from the quarantined list, and how to handle Windows Defender alerts.

- **MSConfig**   How this utility is used.

Chapter 14: Using Vista Applications

The 70-620 exam includes objectives for all topics in this chapter. Expect questions from each section:

- Windows Mail

- Windows Meeting Space

- Windows Calendar

- Windows Fax and Scan

Chapter 15: Using Vista Multimedia Applications

Pay particular attention to the following topics covered in this chapter:

- **Windows Media Player**   You should be very familiar with this tool, including how to rip music, how to burn CDs, and how music can be protected.

- **Windows Media Center**   You should be familiar with the capabilities of Windows Media Center. You should also be aware of the requirements to watch and record TV (such as TV tuner cards) and what's needed to add a Windows Media Extender device (such as being on the same subnet and having the setup key).

- **Network Projector**   You should know how to connect to a network projector: either it needs to be on the same subnet to automatically connect with the wizard, or you need the network address or the IP address.

Chapter 16: Using Vista on Mobile Devices

Pay particular attention to the following topics covered in this chapter:

- **Power Management**   You should know how to manipulate power settings for a laptop. This includes the basic plans (Balanced, Power Saver, and High Performance), and the advanced settings.

- **Windows Mobile Device Center**   You should be familiar with the basic settings of this. Of course, this means you must download and install it.

- **Windows SideShow**   You should understand what SideShow is and how it differs from Windows Sidebar.

- **External displays**   You should know the capabilities available when an external display is added.

- **Tablet PCs**   You should understand the basic capabilities and purpose of Tablet PCs, including how users can teach one how to understand their handwriting and how to calibrate the Tablet PC.

Exam 70-622: What You Need to Know to Pass

70-622 PRO: Supporting and Troubleshooting Applications on a Windows Vista Client for Enterprise Support Technicians

Introduction

The 70-622 exam covers the knowledge you'd be expected to have to support end-users running Windows Vista in a corporate environment. As an IT Professional (Pro) exam, it is a little more in-depth and can be more difficult than the Technical Specialist (TS) exams (such as 70-620).

You're expected to have at least three to five years of experience in the IT field (though that isn't a requirement), and it's expected that you provide support to end users in midsize or enterprise environments. Your experience should include deploying Windows Vista, managing security, and troubleshooting network-related issues with Windows Vista.

When preparing for this exam, imagine that you are a desktop support technician in a company. In other words, regular users are using their computers for their day-to-day jobs, and when they have problems and need assistance, they call you. You are the expert on how Windows Vista operates in the corporate environment.

It's expected that you would take the 70-620 exam first (before the 70-622), but that isn't a requirement.

Pick a Date

I suggest you pick a date 60 to 90 days from now as your target to take the 70-622 exam. You may be ready sooner, and you can adjust your date, or you may not be ready in time and you can change it, but pick a date. Picking a date can be a great motivator in helping you get ready.

Consider actually registering for the test. If you're registered, it adds a layer of commitment. You can always reschedule the test later if a significant life event comes up.

When teaching some certification courses in the college classroom, I've had students register for a test on the first night of a class. They pick a date about a week after the course ends, and we walk down to the test center en masse as everyone registers. The percentage of students taking and passing these tests has been over 70 percent.

In contrast, I've taught the same course to other students and provided encouragement to take and pass the test, but didn't have them register on the first night of class. Following up three months later (at the end of a six-month track), I've found that only 10–20 percent of the students had taken and passed the test.

This concept isn't unique to test taking. For any goal you are pursuing, you are much more likely to achieve it by writing it down. Goals not written down become forgotten daydreams.

Pick a date to take the 70-622 exam. Write it down here: _____.

What You Can Expect

The types of test questions you can expect on the 70-622 exam are primarily multiple-choice questions. You may also see a mix of simulation exams (where you need to accomplish a task), and one or two "point-and-click" or "drag-and-drop" questions, which are really just testing whether you're familiar with the interfaces.

For the multiple-choice questions, pay attention to the wording. Sometimes you're required to pick more than one choice, such as "Select two" or "Select all that apply."

Simulation exam questions are a great new addition to certification exams. They prevent someone from just memorizing test questions and answers. If you want to prepare for these types of questions, do all the exercises in the book. These exercises are designed to convert your "book knowledge" into the ability to actually do tasks.

One good thing about simulations is that it takes a lot of programming to make the simulation complex. Because of this, expect simulations on the exams to be straightforward, with a limited number of steps.

The 70-622 exam is designed for professionals who are either working in or pursuing careers in the IT field providing end-user support for Windows Vista in a corporate environment. Combined with the 70-620 exam, it will earn you the MCITP: Enterprise Support Technician certification. In other words, you need to pass both the 70-620 and the 70-622 exams to earn this certification. See Appendix B for more details on the 70-620 exam. You can read more about the MCITP: Enterprise Support Technician certification at www.microsoft.com/learning/mcp/mcitp/entsupport/default.mspx.

The number of questions on the test is not published by Microsoft and sometimes changes from one test taker to another. A score of 700 is required to pass. You typically have about two hours to complete about 50 questions.

Some tests include beta test questions. The test developers are testing the question before it goes live. Beta test questions don't count for or against you, and you are given extra time to answer them. You could leave them blank, and it wouldn't impact your score at all. Unfortunately, you never know if a question is live or beta, so you have to answer them all.

What's Expected of You

Someone who has successfully passed this exam is expected to be able to accomplish tasks in the following categories:

- Deploying Windows Vista

- Managing Windows Vista security
- Managing and maintaining systems that run Windows Vista
- Configuring and troubleshooting networking
- Supporting and maintaining desktop applications

 EXAM TIP As a reminder, test objectives are listed at the beginning of the book with an objectives map showing which chapter contains the appropriate information. However, remember that these objectives might change. The legalese on Microsoft's site says, "This preparation guide is subject to change at any time without prior notice and at Microsoft's sole discretion." Before taking the test, take a look on Microsoft's web site for the current objectives.

Chapters Covering 70-622 Topics

The following list identifies chapters within this book that include objectives for the 70-622 exam with a list of specific topics where you should focus your studies. Notice that Chapter 15 does not have any topics for the 70-622 exam. You can skip this chapter when focusing on this exam.

Chapter 1: Installing and Upgrading Windows Vista

Make sure you understand the following concepts:

- **Windows Vista Editions** Know the features used in the corporate environment and which editions support them.
- **Hardware requirements** Know the Windows Vista hardware requirements such as memory and hard drive requirements.
- **Migration Tools** Know the tools available to migrate user data and settings in a corporate environment (USMT), including the details on ScanState and LoadState.
- **Dual-boot configurations** Understand what dual-boot and multiboot configurations are, their requirements, and how to modify the configuration using bcdedit.

Chapter 2: Automating the Installation of Windows Vista

This entire chapter is devoted to only 70-622 objectives. You need to understand all the topics in this chapter, but pay particular attention to the following topics:

- **Windows Automated Installation Kit (WAIK) tools** Know what the WAIK is and what it's used for.
- **ImageX** Know the purpose and usage of ImageX.
- **WinPE** Know what the WinPE environment is, and how it is used.
- **Sysprep** Know the requirements to run Sysprep.

Chapter 3: Configuring the Vista Environment

Pay particular attention to the following topics covered in this chapter:

- **Device Manager**   You should understand the driver store and how to manually add drivers using the Device Manager.

- **Aero**   Make sure you know the specific hardware and software requirements for Aero.

- **Application Compatibility**   Make sure you understand what can be done with ACT and how solutions can be deployed.

- **Office Compatibility Pack**   You should understand the purpose of the Office Compatibility Pack and where it should be installed.

- **Virtual PC**   You should know how you can use VPC to deploy applications onto a Vista system that are not compatible with Vista.

Chapter 4: Configuring Disks

Pay particular attention to the following topics covered in this chapter:

- **NTFS and NTFS Permissions**   Make sure you understand what the different NTFS permissions are and what they allow and don't allow.

- **Disk Defragmenter**   You should understand the purpose of the disk defragmenter, how and why to launch it, and how to change its automated schedule.

- **BitLocker**   You should have a solid understanding of BitLocker Drive Encryption, including the requirements to enable it and the different methods that can be used to restore a locked BitLocker drive.

Chapter 5: Configuring Network Connectivity

You'll need to know this entire chapter for the 70-622 exam. Expect this material to be heavily tested. Pay particular attention to the following topics covered in this chapter:

- **Networking Basics**   You should understand the basics of networking, but this exam will go much deeper than the 70-620 exam. You should understand concepts like routing, DHCP, and name resolution. Additionally, you should be aware of the tools used to troubleshoot problems, including command-line tools (and their switches) such as IPConfig.

- **IPv6**   You should be able to identify an IPv6 address and know which IPv6 addresses are used on the Internet, which are manually assigned internal to a company, and which are automatically assigned internal to a company.

- **Public and Private**   You should know the difference between setting a network connection to public or private and how it affects network discovery. You should also know about the LLTD protocols that allow network discovery to work on a network.

Chapter 6: Configuring Wireless Connectivity

Wireless topics are light in the 70-622 exam; however, make sure you understand both basic networking and wireless networking. Pay particular attention to the following topics covered in this chapter:

- **Public and Private**   You should know the difference between setting a wireless network connection to public or private and how it affects network discovery.

- **Security types**   You should know that WEP is not be used, WPA2–Personal uses a preshared key, and WPA2–Enterprise requires an authentication server.

Chapter 7: Configuring Network Access

Pay particular attention to the following topics:

- **Terminal Services**   You should know that the Terminal Services service must be running to support Remote Assistance and Remote Desktop   You should also know the basic purpose of both Remote Assistance and Remote Desktop.

- **Remote Access**   You should know the different ways that users can remotely connect to a dial-up or VPN server. You should also be aware that the Connection Manager Administration Kit (CMAK) can be useful in creating connection profiles.

- **Windows Firewall**   You should be familiar with the basic Windows Firewall, its capabilities and purpose   This includes manipulating and enabling exceptions. You should also be familiar with some of the tools that can identify open ports (such as Netstat and Telnet).

- **Windows Firewall with Advanced Security**   You should be familiar with the advanced capabilities of the Windows Firewall. This includes enabling logging as well as manipulating inbound rules, outbound rules, and connection security rules (to enforce IPsec).

Chapter 8: Accessing Resources

Pay particular attention to the following topics covered in this chapter:

- **Network and Sharing Center**   Know how to configure the different settings for both folder and printer shares, including: File Sharing, Public Folder Sharing, Printer Sharing, and Password Protected Sharing. Know how to share a folder and share a printer.

- **Shared folders**   Know how to create a share and provide access to the share.

- **Shared printers**   Know how to share a printer. Be aware of some of the group policy settings that can be used to control shared printers.

Chapter 9: Configuring Local Security

Pay particular attention to the following topics covered in this chapter:

- **Administrator account** You should be aware of what actions require administrator privileges (such as installing applications, changing security settings, and creating accounts).

- **User Account Control (UAC)** UAC is heavily tested in this exam. Make sure you know all the topics covered in the section "User Account Control" in this chapter. This includes how to enable and disable UAC, what it does when it is enabled, and how the behavior can be modified using the local security policy settings.

- **Auditing** You should be familiar with the different types of auditing available.

Chapter 10: Managing Windows Vista in a Domain

This entire chapter is devoted to only 70-622 objectives. You need to understand all the topics in this chapter, but pay particular attention to the following topics:

- **Group Policy** You should understand how Group Policy is applied in a domain. For example, a GPO linked to an OU applies to all the users and computers in that OU, but not other OUs (unless they are children). You should understand the default behavior of how GPOs are applied, and how you can modify the default behavior with loopback processing.

- **Group Policy management tools** You should be familiar with both the Group Policy Management Console and the local Group Policy editor.

- **Group Policy settings** You should be familiar with some Group Policy settings. Don't expect to be an expert and know all the settings, but you should be familiar with the settings covered in this chapter.

- **Group Policy tools** You should be familiar with the capabilities and purposes of the following tools: GPUpdate, GPResult, RSoP, Security Configuration and Analysis, and Secedit.

- **Certificates** You should know what certificates are used for and how the Trusted Root Certification Authority is used. You should be familiar with the capability to import and export certificates.

Chapter 11: Using Maintenance and Diagnostic Tools

This entire chapter includes material needed for the 70-622 exam. Pay particular attention to the following topics covered in this chapter:

- **Event Viewer** Make sure you know which logs (such as the application, system, setup, and security logs) are used for which purposes.

- **Event Subscriptions** Know what event subscriptions are and how to configure them.

- **Scheduled Tasks** You should know the basics of scheduled tasks, including how to create a scheduled task, the types of tasks that can be created, and the events that can be used to schedule a task.

- **Reliability and Performance Monitor** You should know the purpose and capabilities of the Reliability and Performance Monitor. This includes understanding the monitoring tools, data collector sets, and reports.

- **Windows Update** Know the purpose of Windows Updates, how to configure Windows Updates, how to verify updates are installed, how to remove them, and how to hide them.

Chapter 12: Using Disaster Recovery Tools

Pay particular attention to the following topics covered in this chapter:

- **System recovery tools** This includes the Windows Complete PC Backup and Restore, and System Restore tools.

- **System Resource Checker utility (sfc)** Know how to check and repair system files with this tool.

- **Advanced Options** Know how to boot into this menu (press F8 on boot), and the different capabilities such as the safe modes, and Last Known Good Configuration.

Chapter 13: Configuring Internet Applications

Pay particular attention to the following topics covered in this chapter:

- **Internet Explorer** Know the features and capabilities, such as the different zones and how they can be used, handling pop-ups, and modifying Internet Options settings.

- **Windows Defender** Know the features and capabilities such as handling notifications, configuring options, and configuring real-time protection.

Chapter 14: Using Vista Applications

Pay particular attention to the following topics covered in this chapter:

- **Windows Mail** You should have a basic understanding of the e-mail capabilities with Windows Mail. Additionally, you should know that mail can be secured using S/MIME or PGP.

Chapter 15: Using Vista Multimedia Applications

This chapter does not include any topics for the 70-622 exam.

Chapter 16: Using Vista on Mobile Devices

Pay particular attention to the following topics covered in this chapter:

- **Power Management** You should know how to manipulate power settings for a laptop. This includes the basic plans (Balanced, Power Saver, and High Performance).

Exam 70-623: What You Need to Know to Pass

70-623 PRO: Supporting and Troubleshooting Applications on a Windows Vista Client for Consumer Support Technicians

Introduction

The 70-623 exam covers the knowledge you'd be expected to have to support end users running Windows Vista in homes or small businesses. As a Technical Specialist (TS) exam, it is a little more knowledge based than the IT Professional (Pro) exams.

You're expected to have experience with a wide range of desktop operating systems (though the focus of the exam is Windows Vista). You should also be familiar with issues related to desktop applications, mobile devices, other hardware typically used with a desktop system, and viruses and other malicious software.

When preparing for this exam, imagine that you are a desktop support technician supporting consumers. In other words, regular users are using their computers at home or in small businesses, and when they have problems and need assistance, they call you. You could be working as a consumer support technician in a retail store, a small consulting business, or independently. You are the expert on how Windows Vista operates in home and small business environments.

It's expected that you would take the 70-620 exam first (before 70-623), but that isn't a requirement.

Pick a Date

I suggest you pick a date 60 to 90 days from now as your target to take the 70-623 exam. You may be ready sooner, and you can adjust your date, or you may not be ready in time and you can change it, but pick a date. Picking a date can be a great motivator in helping you get ready.

Consider actually registering for the test. If you're registered, it adds a layer of commitment. You can always reschedule the test later if a significant life event comes up.

When teaching some certification courses in the college classroom, I've had students register for a test on the first night of a class. They pick a date about a week after the course ends, and we walk down to the test center en masse as everyone registers. The percentage of students taking and passing these tests has been over 70 percent.

In contrast, I've taught the same course to other students and provided encouragement to take and pass the test, but didn't have them register on the first night of class. Following up three months later (at the end of a six-month track), I've found that only 10–20 percent of the students had taken and passed the test.

This concept isn't unique to test taking. For any goal you are pursuing, you are much more likely to achieve it by writing it down. Goals not written down become forgotten daydreams.

Pick a date to take the 70-623 exam. Write it down here: _____.

What You Can Expect

The types of test questions you can expect on the 70-623 exam are primarily multiple-choice questions. You may also see a mix of simulation exams (where you need to accomplish a task), and one or two "point-and-click" or "drag-and-drop" questions, which are really just testing whether you're familiar with the interfaces.

For the multiple-choice questions, pay attention to the wording. Sometimes you're required to pick more than one choice, such as "Select two" or "Select all that apply."

Simulation exam questions are a great new addition to certification exams. They prevent someone from just memorizing test questions and answers. If you want to prepare for these types of questions, do all the exercises in the book. These exercises are designed to convert your "book knowledge" into the ability to actually do tasks.

One good thing about simulations is that it takes a lot of programming to make the simulation complex. Because of this, expect simulations on the exams to be straightforward, with a limited number of steps.

The 70-623 exam is designed for professionals who are either working in or pursuing careers in the IT field providing end-user support for Windows Vista in small environments such as at home or small businesses. Combined with the 70-620 exam, 70-623 will earn you the MCITP: Consumer Support Technician certification. In other words, you need to pass both the 70-620 and the 70-623 exams to earn this certification. See Appendix B for more details on the 70-620 exam. You can read more about the MCITP: Consumer Support Technician certification at www.microsoft.com/learning/mcp/mcitp/vista/consumer/default.mspx.

The number of questions on the test is not published by Microsoft and sometimes changes from one test taker to another. A score of 700 is required to pass. You typically have about two hours to complete about 50 questions.

Some tests include beta test questions. The test developers are testing the question before it goes live. Beta test questions don't count for or against you, and you are given extra time to answer them. You could leave them blank, and it wouldn't impact your score at all. Unfortunately, you never know if a question is live or beta, so you have to answer them all.

What's Expected of You

Someone who has successfully passed this exam is expected to be able to accomplish tasks in the following categories:

- Installing and upgrading Windows Vista
- Post-installation: customizing and configuring settings
- Configuring Windows Vista security
- Configuring, troubleshooting, and repairing networking
- Installing, configuring, and troubleshooting devices
- Troubleshooting and repairing Windows Vista

 EXAM TIP As a reminder, test objectives are listed at the beginning of the book with an objectives map showing which chapter contains the appropriate information. However, remember that these objectives might change. The legalese on Microsoft's site says, "This preparation guide is subject to change at any time without prior notice and at Microsoft's sole discretion." Before taking the test, take a look on Microsoft's Web site for the current objectives.

Chapters Covering 70-623 Topics

The following list identifies chapters within this book that include objectives for the 70-623 exam with a list of specific topics where you should focus your studies. Notice that two chapters (Chapter 2 and Chapter 10) do not have any topics for the 70-623 exam. You can skip these chapters when focusing on this exam.

Chapter 1: Installing and Upgrading Windows Vista

Make sure you understand the following concepts:

- **Windows Vista editions** Know the features commonly used by home users and the editions that support these features.
- **Hardware requirements** Know the Windows Vista hardware requirements, such as memory and hard drive requirements.
- **Installation** Know the procedures for a clean installation.
- **Upgrades** Know the upgrade paths to Windows Vista, upgrade procedures, and use of the Windows Vista Upgrade Advisor.
- **Migration tools** Know the tools available to migrate user data and settings in a home environment (Windows Easy Transfer Tool).
- **Dual-boot configurations** Understand what dual-boot and multiboot configurations are, their requirements, and how to modify the configuration using bcdedit.

Chapter 2: Automating the Installation of Windows Vista

This chapter does not include any topics for the 70-623 exam.

Chapter 3: Configuring the Vista Environment

Pay particular attention to the following topics covered in this chapter:

- **Device Manager**   You should understand the meaning of different icons displayed in the Device Manager. You should also understand how to upgrade drivers and how to roll back drivers.

- **Aero**   Make sure you know the specific hardware and software requirements for Aero, when it's enabled by default, and when it needs to be manually enabled.

- **ReadyBoost**   You should understand ReadyBoost and the specifics of how it works and how it should be configured.

- **Sidebar and gadgets**   You should be familiar with the default gadgets and how they can be configured, as well as how to add additional gadgets.

Chapter 4: Configuring Disks

Pay particular attention to the following topics covered in this chapter:

- **NTFS and NTFS capabilities**   You should have a solid understanding of the different capabilities available with NTFS, including permissions, as well as shrinking and extending drives. You should also know how to convert a drive to NTFS.

- **Disk Defragmenter**   You should understand the purpose of the disk defragmenter, how and why to launch it, and how to change its automated schedule.

- **BitLocker**   You should have a solid understanding of BitLocker Drive Encryption, including the requirements to enable it and the different methods that can be used to restore a locked BitLocker drive.

Chapter 5: Configuring Network Connectivity

Pay particular attention to the following topics covered in this chapter:

- **Networking Basics**   You should understand the basics of networking, including concepts like routing, DHCP, and name resolution. You should also be aware of the different clients, services, and protocols that can be bound to a NIC.

- **Public and Private**   You should know the difference between setting a network connection to public or private and how it affects network discovery. You should also know about the LLTD protocols that allow network discovery to work on a network.

Chapter 6: Configuring Wireless Connectivity

Make sure you understand both basic networking and wireless networking. You'll need an understanding of all the topics in this chapter, but pay particular attention to the following topics:

- **Ad hoc and infrastructure mode networks**   You should know the differences between ad hoc– and infrastructure-mode networks, and how to create each.

- **SSID and SSID broadcasting**   You should know what the SSID is used for, what's affected if SSID broadcasting is disabled, and how to automatically connect to a network where SSID broadcasting is disabled.

Chapter 7: Configuring Network Access

The primary topic for the 70-623 exam in this chapter is the Windows Firewall. You should be familiar with all of the firewall topics covered in this chapter.

Chapter 8: Accessing Resources

Pay particular attention to the following topics covered in this chapter:

- **Network and Sharing Center**   Know how to configure the different settings for both folder and printer shares, including: File Sharing, Public Folder Sharing, Printer Sharing, and Password Protected Sharing. Know how to share a folder and share a printer.

- **Share Permissions**   Know the different permission levels available with shares and what those permissions grant, including Reader, Contributor, and Co-owner.

- **Printer Permissions**   Know the different printer permissions available, including Print, Manage Printers, and Manage Documents.

Chapter 9: Configuring Local Security

Pay particular attention to the following topics covered in this chapter:

- **User accounts**   You should know the difference between a standard user and an administrator account. Ideally, the standard user account will be used for all normal activity, and the administrator account would rarely be used to log on. Instead, the administrator account would only be used when performing administrative actions after providing credentials through UAC.

- **Administrator account**   You should be aware of what actions require administrator privileges (such as installing applications, changing security settings, and creating accounts). You should also know the alternative method of running applications as an administrator (by right-clicking and selecting Run As Administrator).

- **User Account Control (UAC)**   You should know how to enable and disable UAC and what it does when it is enabled. You should also be familiar with how the behavior can be modified using the local security policy settings.

- **Password-Protected accounts** Know how to protect accounts by ensuring they have passwords applied. Know that if an account is not password protected, any users can log on to the account.

- **Parental Controls** You should know what parental controls are and the different ways they can be used to restrict a standard user's actions. You should also be familiar with the content logged in the Parental Controls Activity Report.

Chapter 10: Managing Windows Vista in a Domain

This chapter does not include any topics for the 70-623 exam.

Chapter 11: Using Maintenance and Diagnostic Tools

Pay particular attention to the following topics covered in this chapter:

- **Reliability and Performance Monitor** You should know the purpose and capabilities of the Reliability and Performance Monitor. This includes understanding the monitoring tools, data collector sets, and reports.

- **DirectX diagnostics** You should be familiar with dxdiag, what it does, and how to run it.

Chapter 12: Using Disaster Recovery Tools

Pay particular attention to the following topics covered in this chapter:

- **System recovery tools** This includes the Windows Complete PC Backup and Restore, System Restore tools, the System Recovery Options tool, and the Advanced Options menu.

- **Data backup tools** This includes the Backup and Restore Center and the Backup Status and Configuration tool.

Chapter 13: Configuring Internet Applications

Pay particular attention to the following topics covered in this chapter:

- **Internet Explorer** Know the features and capabilities such as the Phishing Filter, working with certificates, RSS Feeds, and configuring advanced options.

- **Windows Defender** Know the features and capabilities such as: performing scans, handling notifications, configuring real-time protection, configuring service failures using the Services applet, and running Windows Defender in Safe mode.

- **MSConfig** Know what this utility is and how to use it.

- **Rootkits and the RootkitRevealer** Understand what rootkits are and how the RootkitRevealer can be used to detect them.

Chapter 14: Using Vista Applications

The 70-623 exam includes objectives for all topics in this chapter. Expect questions from each section:

- **Windows Mail**   You should have a basic understanding of the e-mail and newsgroup capabilities with Windows Mail. Newsgroups require access to a NNTP server.
- **Windows Meeting Space**   You should know the requirements to configure Windows Meeting Space, including that it requires IPv6 and people must be signed into People Near Me to be invited.

Chapter 15: Using Vista Multimedia Applications

Pay particular attention to the following topics covered in this chapter:

- **Windows Media Player**   You should be very familiar with this tool, including how to rip music, how to burn CDs, and how music can be protected. You should also know how media can be shared on a network.
- **AutoPlay**   You should know how to configure AutoPlay for various media that you can connect to your Windows Vista system.
- **Windows Media Center**   You should be familiar with the capabilities of Windows Media Center. You should also be aware of the requirements to watch and record TV (such as TV tuner cards) and what's needed to add a Windows Media Extender device (such as being on the same subnet and having the setup key).
- **Network Projector**   You should know how to connect to a network projector: either it needs to be on the same subnet to automatically connect with the wizard, or you need the network address or the IP address.
- **Windows Movie Maker**   Know the capabilities of Windows Movie Maker, such as how to import and add media. You should also know how to publish a movie and the different formats available for publishing.

Chapter 16: Using Vista on Mobile Devices

Pay particular attention to the following topics covered in this chapter:

- **Windows Mobile Device Center**   You should be familiar with the basic settings of this. Of course, this means you must download and install it.
- **Mobile devices**   You should be familiar with basic capabilities of mobile devices, including how they connect and data that can be transferred.

ad hoc-mode wireless network A wireless computer-to-computer or peer-to-peer network where two or more users with wireless devices can create their own wireless network to connect to each other. One computer creates the ad hoc network, and the other computer joins it. Compare this to an infrastructure wireless network that uses a wireless access point (WAP).

administrator account An administrator account is any account added to the administrators group, which includes elevated permissions. Users with an administrator account can do anything on the computer, such as install applications, install and configure devices, configure system-wide settings, configure the Windows Firewall, configure parental controls, and manipulate user accounts.

Advanced Boot options A troubleshooting menu available by pressing the F8 key on boot up. This menu includes the safe modes and the Last Known Good Configuration.

answer file A text file that provides answers for an installation from an image. Windows SIM creates an answer file called unattend.xml. After the image is deployed and started the first time, settings are read from the answer file instead of asking users for the information.

Application Compatibility Toolkit A suite of tools used to determine if deployed applications are compatible with a new version of Windows before it is deployed.

auditing Auditing monitors system events and logs those events in the security log. You can then use the Event Viewer to view the security log. Auditing can be enabled for many different events, such as object access (which can log when any files such as the Registry file are read, written to, or deleted).

Automatic Private IP Address (APIPA) An IP address in the range of 169.254.y.z with a subnet mask of 255.255.0.0. An APIPA address is given to DHCP clients when the DHCP server isn't reachable.

AutoPlay A feature within Windows that allows you to choose which program to start for different types of media. For example, you can cause Windows Media Player to automatically rip CDs when they're placed in the CD player.

Backup and Restore Center   A tool you can use to back up and restore data files for your computer. You can also launch System Restore (to create or apply restore points) and the Windows Complete PC Backup and Restore tool to create an image of your computer from this tool.

Backup Status and Configuration   This tool is used to configure and monitor backups, and begin restores of your data. You can also launch the Windows Complete PC Backup tool from here.

BCDEdit   A command-line tool used to modify the Boot Configuration Data (BCD). For example, you use the /Create switch to create new entries for a multiboot system. Boot configuration data is used to identify how an operating system boots. The Boot Configuration Data replaces the boot.ini file available in previous editions of Windows.

BitLocker Drive Encryption   A security feature within Windows Vista that allows you to lock an entire volume. This prevents unauthorized access to the Windows Vista operating system in the event of a theft or loss of your system. Others won't be able to move the hard drive into a different system to access the contents of the hard drive.

burn   The term used to identify how data is copied onto optical drives (such as CDs or DVDs).

certificate   A digital document used to verify the identity of a person, application, or Web site. Public certificates are issued by trusted companies known as Certification Authorities.

command line   A window that mimics the old MS-DOS display and can be used to enter command-line instructions such as ping and sfc. One of the strengths of the command line is that commands can be saved in batch files (simple text files with the .bat extension) and the batch file can then be executed later (either manually or on a schedule).

data collector set   A collection of multiple data collection points used to measure the performance of your system from the Performance and Reliability Monitor console. Built-in system data collector sets are included, and you can create your own user-defined data collector sets.

default gateway   A router's NIC on the same subnet as other hosts in the network. Routers have multiple NICs, but only the NIC on the same subnet is referred to as the default gateway. The default gateway must have the same subnet mask as the IP address of the local computer.

Device Manager   The primary tool used to configure and troubleshoot hardware devices (such as sound cards, graphics cards, and USB hubs). The Device Manager is also used to update device drivers.

Digital Rights Management (DRM)   A technology used to control how digital music and video files are used and distributed. DRM is commonly used by online stores that sell and rent songs and movies to prevent unauthorized sharing of the media.

DirectX   A technology designed to help create the special visual and audio effects common with games. It includes Direct3D (for three-dimensional animation), Direct-Draw (for two-dimensional visual effects), and DirectSound (to boost the performance of audio effects).

disk defragmenter   A built-in tool that allows you to rearrange the data on your system so that fragmented files are recreated as contiguous files.

disk fragmentation   A condition of a disk where a significant number of files are no longer contiguous but are instead fragmented. A fragmented file is one where the data is not all contained in the same space on the hard drive, but instead has pieces stored in multiple locations. When the file is opened, all the pieces must be read and put back together.

Domain Name System (DNS)   A system of servers used to resolve host names to IP addresses. DNS is used on the Internet as the primary name resolution method, and it is used within private networks as one of several name resolution methods.

driver store   A trusted cache of drivers stored on the hard drive. If a driver is stored in the driver store, Plug and Play will find it and automatically install the driver. Third-party drivers can be added to the driver store.

dual-boot   Said of a system that can boot to more than one operating system. For example, if your system can boot to both Windows XP and Windows Vista, it's known as a dual-boot system.

Dxdiag   A diagnostic tool specifically designed to test DirectX. You can also use it to identify which version of DirectX is installed on your system.

Dynamic Host Configuration Protocol (DHCP)   A server service that dynamically provides IP addresses and other TCP/IP information (such as the address of the default gateway and the address of DNS servers) to clients. If DHCP is unreachable, clients receive an Automatic Private IP Address (APIPA) address in the range of 169.254.y.z.

Easy Transfer Cable   This specially designed USB cable is recommended by Microsoft to connect two computers and can be used to transfer data between two computers while using the Windows Easy Transfer Wizard.

event subscription   A process where Event Viewer events are configured to be collected on a target computer. Subscriptions can be initiated by the target computer (where the events are collected and viewed) or the source computer (where the events occur).

Event Viewer   A tool used to view event logs. Event logs that are commonly viewed in the Event Viewer are the system, security, and application logs, but other logs can also be viewed here.

firewall   A method used to block traffic from accessing your system. A firewall can be a combination of both hardware and software (such as is often done with routers), or strictly software (such as the Windows Firewall). A firewall is used to specifically allow traffic and/or specifically block traffic.

firewall exception   An instruction that tells the firewall to let traffic through. A firewall typically starts by blocking all traffic, and exceptions are added to identify what traffic to allow. For example, if Remote Assistance connections are to be allowed, a Remote Assistance exception is created on the firewall.

Gadgets   Add-in programs designed to run in either Windows Sidebar or Windows SideShow. Gadgets are mini-programs that can provide information (such as e-mail messages or status of the battery), offer entertainment (such as Calvin and Hobbes cartoons), or perform simple tasks such as shut down your computer.

GPResult   A command-line tool that can be used to view most of the Group Policy settings that apply to the currently logged-on user on the computer where the command is executed. For example, gpresult /z will give a super-verbose view of the policies.

GPUpdate   A command-line tool that can be used to update Group Policy settings. For example, gpupdate /force will cause the system to read and reapply all Group Policy settings that apply to the currently logged-on user on the computer where the command is executed.

Group Policy   An administrative tool that can be used to manage user and computer settings in a network. Group Policy has the most power within a domain, where it can be set once and apply to a group of users or computers such as all the users or computers in the domain, or all the users or computers within individual organizational units.

hosts file   A text file used to map host names to IP addresses. Mappings in the hosts file are automatically stored in the host cache and will be used before DNS is queried. Viruses have been known to change the hosts file to control access to different Web sites.

ImageX   A command-line tool used to capture, modify, and apply images. For example, you could create a reference computer and prepare it with sysprep. You'd then boot using a WinPE bootable disk with ImageX installed. At this point, you can capture the image on the reference computer with ImageX. Additionally, you could boot to a bare-metal system with WinPE, and then use ImageX to deploy an image onto the computer.

infrastructure-mode wireless network   A wireless network that uses a wireless access point (WAP). Compare this to an ad hoc network that is used by clients to connect to each other in peer-to-peer networks without the use of a WAP.

Internet Information Server (IIS)   A service used to serve Web pages (also known as a Web server). Typically IIS is installed on a server product (such as Windows Server 2008), but it can also be installed on Windows Vista.

IPConfig   A command-line tool that can be used to view TCP/IP configuration. For example, ipconfig /all will show all the current settings applied to the computer.

IPv4   IPv4 indicates an IP address (and the supporting protocols) of 32 bits. IPv4 addresses are typically displayed in dotted decimal format, such as 192.168.1.1./24 or 192.168.1.1 with a subnet mask of 255.255.255.0. The Internet is running out of IPv4 addresses, so IPv6 has been introduced.

IPv6 IPv6 indicates an IP address (and the supporting protocols) of 128 bits. Some applications (such as Windows Meeting Space) require IPv6 to function properly. IPv6 addresses are displayed in hexadecimal format, such as FC00:0000:0000:0000:0DB8: CE12:0008:9C5A.

Last Known Good Configuration An option in the Advanced Boot Options menu (press F8 when booting to access this menu). This will allow you to return your system to the state it was in the last time you successfully booted your system. A successful boot is identified by a successful logon. In other words, Last Known Good returns your system to the state it was in the last time you logged on.

Link Layer Topology Discovery (LLTD) A protocol used by Windows to map computers and devices on a network. It's used in conjunction with network discovery. A network connection needs both the Link Layer Topology Discovery Mapper I/O Driver and the Link Layer Topology Discovery Responder protocols enabled to fully support Link Layer Topology Discovery.

LoadState LoadState is part of USMT and is used during a migration in a large enterprise. ScanState is run on the source computer to collect files and settings. Later LoadState is run on the destination computer to load the saved files and settings onto the destination computer.

Media Extender device A device such as a TV, DVD, or an Xbox 360 console that can be connected to a home network and used to access digital media stored on with Windows Media Center. Media Extender devices must be on the same subnet as the Windows Media Center and they are identified with a setup key.

Microsoft Update A Web site hosted by Microsoft that helps you update Microsoft Windows and other installed Microsoft programs such as Microsoft Office. When Microsoft Windows Update is installed, it will include the features of Windows Update.

MSConfig A system configuration tool used to identify problems that might prevent Windows from starting correctly.

multifactor authentication Authentication using multiple methods. Authentication is proving who you are and what you can do by what you know (such as a password), what you have (such as a smart card), and who you are (such as through biometrics). Multifactor authentication combines at least two of these methods.

name resolution The process of resolving names to an IP address. For example, DNS and the hosts file are used to resolve host names to an IP address, and WINS and the LMHosts file are used to resolve NetBIOS names to an IP address.

Netstat A command-line tool that can be used to display protocol statistics and current TCP/IP network connections. For example, `netstat -a` displays all connections and listening ports and is sometimes useful when troubleshooting malware that is generating network activity.

Network and Sharing Center A Control Panel applet you can use to configure and monitor network activity. It includes configuration pages for both wired and wireless pages.

Network Discovery A network setting that affects whether your computer can see and find other computers on the network, and whether other computers on the network can discover your computer. It can be accessed and manipulated in the Network and Sharing Center.

Network News Transfer Protocol (NNTP) A protocol used to read and post newsgroup messages to a newsgroup. Windows Mail supports NNTP and can connect to Microsoft Communities once you launch it. If your Internet service provider (ISP) supports NNTP, you can configure Windows Mail to access other newsgroups.

network projector A projector on the network (meaning that it has an IP address). The Connect to a Network Projector Wizard can be used find network projectors as long as they are on the same subnet.

newsgroup A forum on the Internet where people can participate in discussions.

Office Compatibility Pack A free download you can use to open Office 2007 documents from within Office 2003 or Office XP applications.

organizational unit (OU) A container within Active Directory in a domain. Objects (such as users, computers, and groups) are placed in OUs and can then be managed with Group Policy.

OSCDimg A command-line tool that can be used to create an .iso image file of WinPE. This .iso image can then be burned to a CD or DVD to create a bootable CD/DVD with WinPE. If you think of it as Operating System CD Image, the name makes a little more sense.

Parental Controls A tool used to allow parents to control and monitor their children's activity on the computer. Many different elements of the computer can be controlled and monitored, such as access to Web sites, games that can be played, specific applications that can be launched, and even specific times when the child can use the computer.

password-protected account An account using a password. Passwords aren't required but are strongly recommended and provide a layer of security protection.

password-protected sharing A setting within the Network and Sharing Center that can be used to specify that only people with a user account and password can access the Public folder over the network.

PEImg A command-line tool that can be used to modify a WinPE image offline. ImageX is used to create the base image. PEImg is used to add packages to the WinPE image such as for HTML application support, or the Windows recovery environment.

People Near Me   A service that identifies people nearby who are using computers. It allows invitations to be sent to these people from Windows Meeting Space.

PGP   Pretty Good Privacy. A method of security used with e-mail for users in a workgroup (such as home and small business users). Business users typically use S/MIME for e-mail security within a domain environment.

phishing   A form of social engineering where an e-mail or Web site attempts to trick a user into divulging personal information.

Phishing Filter   A filter within Windows Mail and Internet Explorer designed to identify links and e-mail that are likely phishing e-mails or phishing sites.

Ping   A command-line tool that can be used to check connectivity with another computer. For example, you could enter `ping mcitpsuccess.com` to check to see if the site is operational.

pop-up   A window that pops up when you are accessing a Web site using a Web browser. Some pop-ups are desirable; for example, a pop-up that appears when you click a link on a page giving you additional information is desirable. Some pop-ups are not desirable; for example when you access a Web site, multiple pop-ups may appear with advertising links.

pop-up blocker   A tool used with a Web browser designed to stop pop-ups. Internet Explorer 7 includes a pop-up blocker.

Power Management Plans   Plans you can implement to save energy on mobile computers, especially when the computer is running on battery power. The three plans are High Performance, Balanced, and Power Saver.

Previous Versions   A feature of Shadow Copies available with the NTFS file system in Windows Vista. It allows a user to restore a file to the state it was in previously without requiring administrator intervention.

printer permissions   Permissions assigned to a printer that identify what users can do. Printer permissions include: Print, Manage printers, and Manage documents.

Private   A term used to describe a network location. When set to Private, network discovery is turned on so that other computers can see your computer.

Protected mode   A mode used within Internet Explorer 7 designed to prevent malicious Web sites from installing or running malicious software on your system.

Public   A term used to describe a network location. When set to Public, network discovery is turned off so other computers cannot see yours.

Public folder sharing   A setting within the Network and Sharing Center that can be used to specify that the Public folder is accessible to people over the network.

PXE-compliant Said of a computer that can be booted using a pre-boot execution (PXE) environment. A PXE-compliant computer can be booted from the NIC, connect to a server (such as a Windows Deployment Services server), and download and install an operating system.

RAID Redundant Array of Inexpensive (or Independent) Disks. RAID disk configurations such as RAID-1 (mirroring) and RAID-5 (striping with parity) are often used to provide fault tolerant capabilities. Windows Vista supports only RAID-0 in a software configuration.

RAID-0 A striped array. RAID-0 is used to increase the read and write performance of disks on a computer. RAID-0 is supported on Windows Vista.

ReadyBoost A feature within Windows Vista that allows you to use the memory of a USB flash drive as a fast cache. The recommended size is 1–3 times the amount of physical RAM in your system.

Reliability and Performance Monitor A console used to monitor the performance of your computer. It includes many tools such as the Performance Monitor, the Reliability Monitor, data collector sets, and a report viewer.

Remote Access A group of technologies that allow an external computer to remotely connect to an internal network via dial-up or a virtual private network (VPN).

Remote Assistance A technology that allows one computer user to provide assistance to another computer user over a network (including the Internet). If the person being helped grants permission, the helper can take control of the desktop and demonstrate how to perform a task. A Windows Firewall exception must be enabled to allow Remote Assistance sessions through. Remote Assistance uses the Terminal Services service.

Remote Desktop A technology that allows a user to connect to another computer remotely. This differs from Remote Assistance in that a user sitting at the remote computer won't be able to view what the remote user is doing. A Windows Firewall exception must be enabled to allow Remote Desktop sessions through. Remote Desktop uses the Terminal Services service.

Remote Desktop Connection A tool used to connect to remote computers using Remote Desktop technologies. It can be accessed from the Accessories menu. Remote Desktop Connection uses the Terminal Services service.

restore points A set of key system settings such as system files and Registry settings. User data is never included in a restore point. Restore points are captured with System Restore and can be applied with System Restore. Restore points are captured automatically but can also be captured manually.

restricted sites zone A zone within Internet Explorer designed for sites that you recognize as a significant risk. Among other protections, scripting and active content is prevented from running on any sites in a restricted zone.

Resultant Set of Policy (RSoP)   A snap-in used to identify what Group Policy settings are being applied within a domain.

rip (as in rip music)   Copy music. When music is copied from a CD to your system, it is referred to as ripping music.

rootkit   A program (or group of programs) designed to take control of a computer at the root level. Once installed, all commands go through the rootkit and the rootkit can then decide what programs it wants to allow, and what parts of your computer it wants the program to be able to access.

RootkitRevealer   A program designed to discover rootkits, or rootkit activity. It's a free download from Microsoft.

routing   The process of sending data packets in a network from one subnet to another. Routers are used to route packets. The NIC on the same subnet as other computer hosts is configured as the default gateway and packets with a destination on a different subnet are sent to the default gateway.

RSS   Really Simple Syndication. A family of Web feed formats used to publish frequently updated content such as blog entries. This is also known as feeds, or RSS feeds.

S/MIME   Secure/Multipurpose Internet Mail Extensions. A method of security used with e-mail for users in a domain environment. Users in a workgroup (such as home and small business users) use PGP for e-mail security.

Safe mode   Safe mode starts Windows Vista with only the core drivers and services. It allows you to start your system when one or more of the non-core drivers or services are causing a problem. You can troubleshoot faulty drivers and services, apply restore points, and troubleshoot malicious software problems.

ScanState   ScanState is part of USMT and is used during a migration in a large enterprise. ScanState is run on the source computer to collect files and settings. Later LoadState is run on the destination computer to load the saved files and settings onto the destination computer.

scheduled task   A task scheduled to run within the Task Scheduler.

schtask   A command-line tool that allows you to do many of the same functions as the Task Scheduler. For example, you can use the /query switch to check the status of a task, and use the /change switch to modify the status (such as disabling or enabling the task).

Secedit   A command-line tool that allows you to do many of the same functions as the Security Configuration and Analysis tool. For example, you can use secedit with the /analyze switch to compare the current configuration of a system against a security template.

Security Configuration and Analysis A snap-in used to analyze and configure computer security. It can be used to import and configure security templates. It can also be used to compare existing computer configurations against a template to identify any differences.

share A folder on a computer made available to others in the network. A share is accessed using the Universal Naming Convention (UNC) of \\ServerName\ShareName. In this context, Windows Vista can be referred to as a server, since it will serve the resources in the share. The Public folder can easily be shared, but other folders on a Windows Vista can also be shared.

share permissions Permissions that can be granted to users when they access the share. Permissions can be granted to users or groups using three primary permission levels. A co-owner is granted permissions to do anything in the share. A Contributor is able to read and modify data in a share. A Reader can read data in the share.

SSID Service Set Identifier. An SSID is used by a wireless access point (WAP) to identify it. SSIDs are a combination of as many as 32 letters and numbers and are sometimes referred to as network names.

SSID broadcasting A process where a wireless access point (WAP) broadcasts its SSID so that other computers and devices can easily locate it. A common security practice with WAPs is to disable SSID broadcasting so that the wireless network isn't easily locatable. Wireless devices can connect to WAPs if the SSID is known, even if SSID broadcasting is disabled.

standard user account A user account intended for regular users. A standard user account allows a user to use Windows Vista but does not give elevated permissions. Elevated permissions are granted to administrators.

subnet A part of an IP address that identifies a group of computers that can communicate with each other without going through a router. All computers in the same subnet must have the same subnet mask (such as 255.255.0.0 or 255.255.255.0).

System Preparation Tool (Sysprep) A tool used to remove unique information (such as the computer name and SID) from a computer prior to cloning. You'd first prepare a reference computer and then run sysprep on it to prepare the reference computer for cloning. This image can then be deployed to multiple computers.

System Recovery Options A set of menus you can access from the installation DVD. It includes startup repair, system restore, and Windows Complete PC restore options.

System Restore A tool used to create and apply restore points. Restore points are created to capture system settings. If things go wrong, System Restore can be used to apply older restore points to return a system to a previous state.

Tablet PC A cross between a personal digital assistant (PDA) and a laptop computer. A Tablet PC has a full screen, but instead of a keyboard and a mouse, it uses a stylus pen for input.

Task Scheduler A built-in tool used to schedule automated tasks. Tasks can be scheduled to start a program, send an e-mail, or display a message. Tasks can be configured to start based on a schedule, or trigger events such as when the computer starts, a user logs on, or the computer is idle.

Telnet A command-line program that can be used to connect to another computer. The `telnet` command is often used to check if services are running on another computer.

Terminal Services A service used to connect interactively to a remote computer. Remote Desktop Connection and Remote Assistance both use Terminal Services.

Trusted Platform Module (TPM) A special microchip embedded in the motherboard. The TPM stores the BitLocker key, which is used to encrypt and decrypt a hard drive.

trusted root certification authority A certification authority (CA) issues certificates. A trusted root CA is one that has its root certificate in the trusted root certification authorities store. Any certificates issued by a CA in the trusted root certification authorities store are automatically trusted.

trusted site zone A zone within Internet Explorer designed for sites that you intrinsically trust. You can add sites to the trusted sites zone and they will have more freedom, such as the ability to run ActiveX controls.

TV tuner card A hardware card added to a computer that allows it to receive television broadcasts. If you have two TV tuner cards, you can watch one broadcast while recording a broadcast on another channel.

User Account Control (UAC) A feature within Windows Vista designed to prevent unauthorized changes to your computer. UAC behavior can be manipulated through local policy or Group Policy and will typically prompt a standard user to provide administrative credentials, and prompt an administrative user to continue.

User State Migration Tool (USMT) A tool used to migrate user files and settings during an upgrade. USMT version 3.0 is used to migrate from Windows XP to Windows Vista. USMT is used within larger enterprises. It includes both ScanState and LoadState.

Volume Shadow Copy service A service accessible via the Services applet. It is used for backups and, if stopped, backups may fail.

WDDM Windows Display Driver Model is a graphic driver model created specifically for Windows Vista. Vista Aero requires a driver that supports WDDM to function properly.

WiFi Protected Access (WPA) WPA provides security for wireless networks and comes in two versions: WPA and WPA2. Due to security weaknesses discovered in WEP, WPA was released as an interim fix, with WPA2 later released as a permanent fix.

WiFi Protected Access—Enterprise (WPA-Enterprise) This is used in larger networks to provide security for wireless networks and comes in two versions: WPA-Enterprise and WPA2-Enterprise. It requires an authorization server where credentials are validated before access to the network is authorized.

WiFi Protected Access—Personal This is used in homes and small offices to provide security for wireless networks and comes in two versions: WPA-Personal and WPA2-Personal. This is also referred to as preshared key (PSK) mode.

Windows Aero A graphical interface in Windows Vista. It includes graphical features such as translucent glass and Windows Flip 3D. It requires at least 128MB of graphics RAM, and support for the Windows Display Driver Model (WDDM). A minimum of 512MB of system RAM is also required, though Aero won't start automatically unless you have more than 512MB of system RAM.

Windows Backup and Restore Center A tool used to perform backups and restores of data. You can pick what types of data you want to back up (such as documents, audio, and video). If data is lost, you can restore all data, or individual files.

Windows Calendar A built-in tool that can be used to keep track of appointments, remind you of appointments, and track tasks. Calendars can be published and shared between users.

Windows Complete PC Backup and Restore A tool used to create a complete image of your computer, including the system, applications, and all your data. If you have a catastrophic failure, you can restore the entire image. You can restore by booting into the installation DVD and selecting Repair to access the System Recovery Options menu.

Windows Defender An anti-spyware tool. Spyware is known as malicious software (malware) and can be damaging to your computer. Windows Defender can be run in Safe mode or when the system is booted normally.

Windows Deployment Services (WDS) A Windows Server 2008 server role that can be used to deploy images to multiple computers.

Windows Display Driver Model (WDDM) A graphic driver model created specifically for Windows Vista and required by Windows Aero. Windows Aero won't run without a graphics card that includes a WDDM-capable driver.

Windows DVD Maker An application within Windows Vista Home Premium and Windows Vista Ultimate you can use to create DVDs of movies, pictures, and slideshows.

Windows Easy Transfer Tool This tool will allow users to transfer files and settings from one computer to another. It is used as part of a migration from one computer running Windows XP to another computer running Windows Vista.

Windows Fax and Scan A replacement for the fax console in previous versions of Windows. It can be used to fax and scan documents and pictures.

Windows Firewall Software used to block traffic from accessing your system. When enabled, it only allows specifically allowed traffic and blocks all other traffic.

Windows Imaging format(WIM) A collection of image files. Each image within the Windows imaging file is a complete operating system installation. Custom images can be included that also include applications and settings.

Windows Internet Name System (WINS) A server used to resolve NetBIOS names to IP addresses. WINS is used in private networks (not on the Internet) as one of several name resolution methods.

Windows Mail A program within Windows Vista that allows you to access e-mail and newsgroups. It replaces Outlook Express, which was included in earlier versions of Windows.

Windows Media Center Windows Media Center is used for viewing photos, watching DVDs, and even watching and recording TV.

Windows Media Player An application within Windows Vista that allows you rip music, burn music to CDs, and sync files with a portable music player, along with playing audio and video files.

Windows Meeting Space A collaboration program that allows users to share the computer's desktop or a specific application with other users in the network. Windows Meeting Space is Vista's replacement for the Windows NetMeeting, which was used in previous editions of Windows.

Windows Mobile Device Center A free download that can be used to add improvements and features for Windows Mobile devices. It can be used to easily synchronize information such as e-mail, contacts, and calendar items.

Windows Mobility Device Center A built-in tool within Windows Vista that you can use to access mobile PC settings such as power plans, connectivity, and synchronization.

Windows Movie Maker A built-in application that can be used to import, edit, and arrange audio, video, and images to create movies.

Windows Photo Gallery A built-in application that can be used to view, manage, and edit digital pictures.

Windows Preinstallation Environment (WinPE) A minimal 32-bit operating system. The WinPE environment for Vista (and Windows Server 2008) was built on the Windows Vista kernel. WinPE is used during the preinstallation and deployment phases, and can also be used for system recovery.

Windows Resource Checker (SFC) A command-line tool that can be used to check and repair system files. For example, you can use the following command to verify and repair a system file named kernel32.dll: `sfc/VerifyFile=c:\Windows\System32\kernel32.dll`. Note that the name of the command is `sfc`, not wrc.

As with any command-line tool, enter the /? with the command (as in `sfc /?`) at the command line for additional help.

Windows Security Center   A Control Panel applet that monitors security essentials (the firewall, automatic updating, malware protection, and other security settings). It provides feedback to the user when security settings indicate the computer is vulnerable.

Windows Sidebar   A vertical bar displayed on side of your desktop. It includes gadgets (mini-programs) that provide information at a glance. You can add and remove gadgets, and many are created independently and uploaded to the Microsoft Web site.

Windows SideShow   A platform in Windows that uses add-in programs or gadgets to extend information from your computer onto a peripheral device.

Windows System Image Manager (Windows SIM).   A tool used to create answer files. Answer files can be created on a test computer and then transferred to a reference computer before the image is created.

Windows Update   A tool used to identify updates that need to be downloaded and installed to keep your computer up-to-date and safe from security vulnerabilities. Windows Update is included with Windows Vista, but Microsoft Update must be downloaded and installed.

Windows Vista Upgrade Advisor   A tool you can use to check hardware compatibility for systems you are considering upgrading to Windows Vista.

Wired Equivalent Privacy (WEP)   An older security method intended to provide security for wireless networks similar to what is found on a wired network. It has significant security weaknesses and should be replaced with WPA or WPA2.

Wireless access point (WAP)   A wireless access point is used by wireless clients to connect to a wireless network. WAPs typically also act as routers providing access to a wired network, including access to the Internet.

INDEX

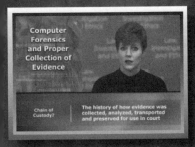

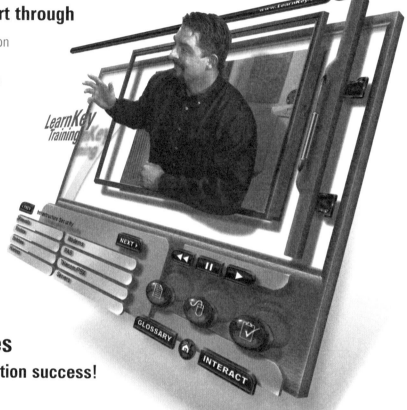